INFORMATION PRIVACY
STATUTES AND REGULATIONS
2010-2011

This compendium of information privacy statutes and regulations is designed for use both as a stand-alone resource as well as a statutory supplement to our casebooks:

INFORMATION PRIVACY LAW
(3rd edition, 2009)

PRIVACY, INFORMATION, AND TECHNOLOGY
(2nd edition, 2009)

PRIVACY AND THE MEDIA
(1st edition, 2009)

For more information about the casebooks as well as additional resources, visit:

http://informationprivacylaw.com

ASPEN PUBLISHERS

INFORMATION PRIVACY
STATUTES AND REGULATIONS
2010-2011

Paul M. Schwartz
Professor of Law
U.C. Berkeley School of Law

Daniel J. Solove
Professor of Law
George Washington University Law School

Wolters Kluwer
Law & Business

AUSTIN BOSTON CHICAGO NEW YORK THE NETHERLANDS

http://lawschool.aspenpublishers.com

To contact Customer Care, e-mail customer.care@aspenpublishers.com, call 1-800-234-1660, fax 1-800-901-9075, or mail correspondence to:

Aspen Publishers
Attn: Order Department
PO Box 990
Frederick, MD 21705

Printed in the United States of America.

1 2 3 4 5 6 7 8 9 0

ISBN 978-0-7355-9401-2

ISSN 1940-7017

About Wolters Kluwer Law & Business

Wolters Kluwer Law & Business is a leading provider of research information and workflow solutions in key specialty areas. The strengths of the individual brands of Aspen Publishers, CCH, Kluwer Law International and Loislaw are aligned within Wolters Kluwer Law & Business to provide comprehensive, in-depth solutions and expert-authored content for the legal, professional and education markets.

CCH was founded in 1913 and has served more than four generations of business professionals and their clients. The CCH products in the Wolters Kluwer Law & Business group are highly regarded electronic and print resources for legal, securities, antitrust and trade regulation, government contracting, banking, pension, payroll, employment and labor, and healthcare reimbursement and compliance professionals.

Aspen Publishers is a leading information provider for attorneys, business professionals and law students. Written by preeminent authorities, Aspen products offer analytical and practical information in a range of specialty practice areas from securities law and intellectual property to mergers and acquisitions and pension/benefits. Aspen's trusted legal education resources provide professors and students with high-quality, up-to-date and effective resources for successful instruction and study in all areas of the law.

Kluwer Law International supplies the global business community with comprehensive English-language international legal information. Legal practitioners, corporate counsel and business executives around the world rely on the Kluwer Law International journals, loose-leafs, books and electronic products for authoritative information in many areas of international legal practice.

Loislaw is a premier provider of digitized legal content to small law firm practitioners of various specializations. Loislaw provides attorneys with the ability to quickly and efficiently find the necessary legal information they need, when and where they need it, by facilitating access to primary law as well as state-specific law, records, forms and treatises.

Wolters Kluwer Law & Business, a unit of Wolters Kluwer, is headquartered in New York and Riverwoods, Illinois. Wolters Kluwer is a leading multinational publisher and information services company.

CONTENTS

PREFACE

The publication of this compilation of leading statutes and regulations of information privacy law provides an ideal perspective for a look back over the past decade of information privacy law, and a look forward to the next decade. Over the past ten years, two important developments have been the rise of information privacy professionals and an increase in statutory and other kinds of information privacy regulations.

Regarding the first development, the past decade has seen the emergence of the information privacy professional. Thus, a Fortune 500 company will not only have a Chief Executive Officer and a Chief Financial Officer, but also a Chief Privacy Officer (CPO). The federal government has also instituted such a job at agencies, including the Department of Justice, Central Intelligence Agency, Internal Revenue Service, and Department of Homeland Security. There is even now a membership organization for experts in this field, the International Association of Privacy Professionals, and a privacy conference likely underway somewhere in the United States every week in the year. In the law academy, this professionalization has encouraged more schools to offer courses in information privacy law. This subject is not merely a fascinating and rewarding area for study, but a growth area for employment.

Regarding the second development, the past decade has seen a dramatic increase in information privacy statutes and regulations. Previously, the most intensive period for statutory information privacy law in the United States was the decade from 1968 to 1978. That period is bookmarked at its start by the conclusion of President Johnson's Great Society and at its conclusion by the Watergate scandal and its aftermath. Between 1968 and 1978, Congress enacted many important privacy statutes: the Bank Secrecy Act, the Fair Credit Reporting Act, the Family Educational Rights and Privacy Act, the Foreign Intelligence Surveillance Act, the Privacy Act, the Right to Financial Privacy Act, and the Wiretap Act.

If we fast-forward to the present, we are now in another intensive period of privacy regulation. The last few years have seen new laws and regulations, including the USA-Patriot Act, the CAN-SPAM Act, the Real ID Act, and the Video Voyeurism Prevention Act. In addition, the past years have seen major amendments to the Electronics Communication Privacy Act, the Fair Credit Reporting Act, and the Foreign Intelligence Surveillance Act.

What then of the next ten years? Yogi Berra, philosopher and member of the Baseball Hall of Fame, once said, "It's tough to make predictions, especially about the future." Heeding this insight, we will cautiously return to the two trends already noted. It is likely that the growth of privacy as a legal field will continue—in particular, the availability of the CPO as an organizational model is likely to encourage even more companies to institute such figures. Moreover, we think that the regulatory web of privacy law will continue to increase in its density. It is our hope that this compilation will assist privacy professionals, lawyers, regulators, and privacy students alike in understanding and practicing information privacy law.

For more information about our casebook, INFORMATION PRIVACY LAW, as well as additional resources, visit http://informationprivacylaw.com.

Paul M. Schwartz
Berkeley, California

Daniel J. Solove
Washington, D.C.

September 2009

ACKNOWLEDGMENTS

The authors would like to acknowledge the helpful research assistance of Cesar Alvarez, Alpa Patel, Laura Sullivan, and Pamela Tsao, students at U.C. Berkeley School of Law.

We welcome any suggestions or comments for the next edition—please email any feedback to pschwartz@law.berkeley.edu.

I.
PRIVACY AND THE MEDIA

Restatement (Second) of Torts (1977)

Statutes in Context

The four privacy torts were inspired by Samuel Warren and Louis Brandeis's seminal article *The Right to Privacy*, 4 Harv. L. Rev. 193 (1890). In 1960, the renowned torts scholar William Prosser published an article, *Privacy*, 48 Cal. L. Rev. 383 (1960), in which he articulated the four torts as they are known today. The following are the elements of the torts from the Restatement (Second) of Torts, published in 1977. The Restatement has had tremendous influence, and most states that adopt the torts use the Restatement's formulations.

General Principle, § 652A

(1) One who invades the right of privacy of another is subject to liability for the resulting harm to the interests of the other.

(2) The right of privacy is invaded by
  (a) unreasonable intrusion upon the seclusion of another, as stated in § 652B; or
  (b) appropriation of the other's name or likeness, as stated in § 652C; or
  (c) unreasonable publicity given to the other's private life, as stated in § 652D; or
  (d) publicity that unreasonably places the other in a false light before the public, as stated in § 652E.

Intrusion Upon Seclusion, § 652B

One who intentionally intrudes, physically or otherwise, upon the solitude or seclusion of another or his private affairs or concerns, is subject to liability to the other for invasion of his privacy, if the intrusion would be highly offensive to a reasonable person.

Appropriation of Name or Likeness, § 652C

One who appropriates to his own use or benefit the name or likeness of another is subject to liability to the other for invasion of his privacy.

Publicity Given to Private Life, § 652D

One who gives publicity to a matter concerning the private life of another is subject to liability to the other for invasion of his privacy, if the matter publicized is of a kind that

(a) would be highly offensive to a reasonable person, and

(b) is not of legitimate concern to the public.

Publicity Placing Person in False Light, § 652C

One who gives publicity to a matter concerning another that places the other before the public in a false light is subject to liability to the other for invasion of his privacy, if

(a) the false light in which the other was placed would be highly offensive to a reasonable person, and

(b) the actor had knowledge of or acted in reckless disregard as to the falsity of the publicized matter and the false light in which the other would be placed.

New York Civil Rights Law §§ 50-51 (1903)

Statutes in Context

The New York Civil Rights Law §§ 50-51 was the first privacy statute passed in response to Samuel Warren and Louis Brandeis's *The Right to Privacy*, 4 Harv. L. Rev. 193 (1890). In *Roberson v. Rochester Folding Box Co.*, 64 N.E. 442 (N.Y. 1902), the New York Court of Appeals refused to recognize a common law tort action for privacy invasions. A year later, in 1903, the New York legislature responded to the explicit invitation in *Roberson* to legislate by creating Civil Rights Law §§ 50-51.

---

§ 50. Right of privacy

A person, firm or corporation that uses for advertising purposes, or for the purposes of trade, the name, portrait or picture of any living person without having first obtained the written consent of such person, or if a minor of his or her parent or guardian, is guilty of a misdemeanor.

§ 51. Action for injunction and for damages

Any person whose name, portrait, picture or voice is used within this state for advertising purposes or for the purposes of trade without the written consent first obtained as above provided[1] may maintain an equitable action in the supreme court of this state against the person, firm or

[1] See § 50.

corporation so using his name, portrait, picture or voice, to prevent and restrain the use thereof; and may also sue and recover damages for any injuries sustained by reason of such use and if the defendant shall have knowingly used such person's name, portrait, picture or voice in such manner as is forbidden or declared to be unlawful by section fifty of this article, the jury, in its discretion, may award exemplary damages. But nothing contained in this article shall be so construed as to prevent any person, firm or corporation from selling or otherwise transferring any material containing such name, portrait, picture or voice in whatever medium to any user of such name, portrait, picture or voice, or to any third party for sale or transfer directly or indirectly to such a user, for use in a manner lawful under this article; nothing contained in this article shall be so construed as to prevent any person, firm or corporation, practicing the profession of photography, from exhibiting in or about his or its establishment specimens of the work of such establishment, unless the same is continued by such person, firm or corporation after written notice objecting thereto has been given by the person portrayed; and nothing contained in this article shall be so construed as to prevent any person, firm or corporation from using the name, portrait, picture or voice of any manufacturer or dealer in connection with the goods, wares and merchandise manufactured, produced or dealt in by him which he has sold or disposed of with such name, portrait, picture or voice used in connection therewith; or from using the name, portrait, picture or voice of any author, composer or artist in connection with his literary, musical or artistic productions which he has sold or disposed of with such name, portrait, picture or voice used in connection therewith. Nothing contained in this section shall be construed to prohibit the copyright owner of a sound recording from disposing of, dealing in, licensing or selling that sound recording to any party, if the right to dispose of, deal in, license or sell such sound recording has been conferred by contract or other written document by such living person or the holder of such right. Nothing contained in the foregoing sentence shall be deemed to abrogate or otherwise limit any rights or remedies otherwise conferred by federal law or state law.

California Anti-Paparazzi Act (1998)

California Civil Code § 1708.8

Statutes in Context

Sparked by Princess Diana's death in 1997, California passed the first anti-paparazzi statute in the United States in 1998. The Act remedies two forms of privacy invasion: physical and constructive invasions of privacy.

Cal Civ. Code § 1708.8. Physical or constructive invasion of privacy; damages and equitable remedies; employee-employer relationships; defenses

(a) A person is liable for physical invasion of privacy when the defendant knowingly enters onto the land of another person without permission or otherwise committed a trespass in order to physically invade the privacy of the plaintiff with the intent to capture any type of visual image, sound recording, or other physical impression of the plaintiff engaging in a personal or familial activity and the physical invasion occurs in a manner that is offensive to a reasonable person.

(b) A person is liable for constructive invasion of privacy when the defendant attempts to capture, in a manner that is offensive to a reasonable person, any type of visual image, sound recording, or other physical impression of the plaintiff engaging in a personal or familial activity under circumstances in which the plaintiff had a reasonable expectation of privacy, through the use of a visual or auditory enhancing device, regardless of whether there is a physical trespass, if this image, sound recording, or other physical impression could not have been achieved without a trespass unless the visual or auditory enhancing device was used.

(c) An assault committed with the intent to capture any type of visual image, sound recording, or other physical impression of the plaintiff is subject to subdivisions (d), (e), and (h).

(d) A person who commits any act described in subdivision (a), (b), or (c) is liable for up to three times the amount of any general and special damages that are proximately caused by the violation of this section. This person may also be liable for punitive damages, subject to proof according to Section 3294. If the plaintiff proves that the invasion of privacy was committed for a commercial purpose, the defendant shall also be subject to disgorgement to the plaintiff of any proceeds or other consideration obtained as a result of the violation of this section.

(e) A person who directs, solicits, actually induces, or actually causes another person, regardless of whether there is an employer-employee relationship, to violate any provision of subdivision (a), (b), or (c) is liable for any general, special, and consequential damages resulting from each said violation. In addition, the person that directs, solicits, instigates, induces, or otherwise causes another person, regardless of whether there is an employer-employee relationship, to violate this section shall be liable for punitive damages to the extent that an employer would be subject to punitive damages pursuant to subdivision (b) of Section 3294.

(f) Sale, transmission, publication, broadcast, or use of any image or recording of the type, or under the circumstances, described in this section shall not itself constitute a violation of this section, nor shall this section be construed to limit all other rights or remedies of plaintiff in law or equity, including, but not limited to, the publication of private facts.

(g) This section shall not be construed to impair or limit any otherwise lawful activities of law enforcement personnel or employees of governmental agencies or other entities, either public or private who, in the course and scope of their employment, and supported by an articulable suspicion, attempt to capture any type of visual image, sound recording, or other physical impression of a person during an investigation, surveillance, or monitoring of any conduct to obtain evidence of suspected illegal activity, the suspected violation of any administrative rule or regulation, a suspected fraudulent insurance claim, or any other suspected fraudulent conduct or activity involving a violation of law or pattern of business practices adversely affecting the public health or safety.

(h) In any action pursuant to this section, the court may grant equitable relief, including, but not limited to, an injunction and restraining order against further violations of subdivision (a) or (b).

(i) The rights and remedies provided in this section are cumulative and in addition to any other rights and remedies provided by law.

(j) It is not a defense to a violation of this section that no image, recording, or physical impression was captured or sold.

(k) For the purposes of this section, "for a commercial purpose" means any act done with the expectation of a sale, financial gain, or other consideration. A visual image, sound recording, or other physical impression shall not be found to have been, or intended to have been captured for a commercial purpose unless it is intended to be, or was in fact, sold, published, or transmitted.

(l) For the purposes of this section, "personal and familial activity" includes, but is not limited to, intimate details of the plaintiff's personal life, interactions with the plaintiff's family or significant others, or other aspects of plaintiff's private affairs or concerns. Personal and familial activity does not include illegal or otherwise criminal activity as delineated in subdivision (f). However, "personal and familial activity" shall include the activities of victims of crime in circumstances where either subdivision (a) or (b), or both, would apply.

(m) The provisions of this section are severable. If any provision of this section or its application is held invalid, that invalidity shall not affect other provisions or applications that can be given effect without the invalid provision or application.

Video Voyeurism Prevention Act (2004)

18 U.S.C. § 1801

Statutes in Context

In 2004, Congress enacted the Video Voyeurism Prevention Act to respond to growing concerns about the taking and posting online of "upskirt" photos. The Act has a highly limited jurisdictional scope, however, as it is limited to "the special maritime and territorial jurisdiction of the United States."

§ 1801. Video voyeurism

(a) Whoever, in the special maritime and territorial jurisdiction of the United States, has the intent to capture an image of a private area of an individual without their consent, and knowingly does so under circumstances in which the individual has a reasonable expectation of privacy, shall be fined under this title or imprisoned not more than one year, or both.

(b) In this section—

(1) the term "capture", with respect to an image, means to videotape, photograph, film, record by any means, or broadcast;

(2) the term "broadcast" means to electronically transmit a visual image with the intent that it be viewed by a person or persons;

(3) the term "a private area of the individual" means the naked or undergarment clad genitals, pubic area, buttocks, or female breast of that individual;

(4) the term "female breast" means any portion of the female breast below the top of the areola; and

(5) the term "under circumstances in which that individual has a reasonable expectation of privacy" means—

(A) circumstances in which a reasonable person would believe that he or she could disrobe in privacy, without being concerned that an image of a private area of the individual was being captured; or

(B) circumstances in which a reasonable person would believe that a private area of the individual would not be visible to the public, regardless of whether that person is in a public or private place .

(c) This section does not prohibit any lawful law enforcement, correctional, or intelligence activity.

Communications Decency Act § 230 (1996)

47 U.S.C. § 230

Statutes in Context

In *Stratton Oakmont, Inc. v. Prodigy Services Co.*, 23 Media L. Rep. 1794 (N.Y. Sup. 1995), a court concluded that an ISP could be liable for defamatory statements posted by one of its users. In response to this case, Congress passed § 230 of the Communications Decency Act (CDA) of 1996 to provide protection to ISPs from liability. The scope of § 230's immunity, however, has been in dispute, with most courts following *Zeran v. America Online, Inc.*, 129 F.3d 327 (4th Cir. 1997) and concluding that § 230 provides immunity against both publisher and distributor liability.

(a) Findings

The Congress finds the following:

(1) The rapidly developing array of Internet and other interactive computer services available to individual Americans represent an extraordinary advance in the availability of educational and informational resources to our citizens.

(2) These services offer users a great degree of control over the information that they receive, as well as the potential for even greater control in the future as technology develops.

(3) The Internet and other interactive computer services offer a forum for a true diversity of political discourse, unique opportunities for cultural development, and myriad avenues for intellectual activity.

(4) The Internet and other interactive computer services have flourished, to the benefit of all Americans, with a minimum of government regulation.

(5) Increasingly Americans are relying on interactive media for a variety of political, educational, cultural, and entertainment services.

(b) Policy

It is the policy of the United States--

(1) to promote the continued development of the Internet and other interactive computer services and other interactive media;

(2) to preserve the vibrant and competitive free market that presently exists for the Internet and other interactive computer services, unfettered by Federal or State regulation;

(3) to encourage the development of technologies which maximize user control over what information is received by individuals, families, and schools who use the Internet and other interactive computer services;

(4) to remove disincentives for the development and utilization of blocking and filtering technologies that empower parents to restrict their children's access to objectionable or inappropriate online material; and

(5) to ensure vigorous enforcement of Federal criminal laws to deter and punish trafficking in obscenity, stalking, and harassment by means of computer.

(c) Protection for "good samaritan" blocking and screening of offensive material

(1) Treatment of publisher or speaker

No provider or user of an interactive computer service shall be treated as the publisher or speaker of any information provided by another information content provider.

(2) Civil liability

No provider or user of an interactive computer service shall be held liable on account of—

(A) any action voluntarily taken in good faith to restrict access to or availability of material that the provider or user considers to be obscene, lewd, lascivious, filthy, excessively violent, harassing, or otherwise objectionable, whether or not such material is constitutionally protected; or

(B) any action taken to enable or make available to information content providers or others the technical means to restrict access to material described in paragraph (1).

(d) Obligations of interactive computer service

A provider of interactive computer service shall, at the time of entering an agreement with a customer for the provision of interactive computer service and in a manner deemed appropriate by the provider, notify such customer that parental control protections (such as computer hardware, software, or filtering services) are commercially available that may assist the customer in limiting access to material that is harmful to minors. Such notice shall identify, or provide the customer with access to information identifying, current providers of such protections.

(e) Effect on other laws

(1) No effect on criminal law

Nothing in this section shall be construed to impair the enforcement of section 223 or 231 of this title, chapter 71 (relating to obscenity) or 110 (relating to sexual exploitation of children) of Title 18, or any other Federal criminal statute.

(2) No effect on intellectual property law

Nothing in this section shall be construed to limit or expand any law pertaining to intellectual property.

(3) State law

Nothing in this section shall be construed to prevent any State from enforcing any State law that is consistent with this section. No cause of action may be brought and no liability may be imposed under any State or local law that is inconsistent with this section.

(4) No effect on Communications Privacy law

Nothing in this section shall be construed to limit the application of the Electronic Communications Privacy Act of 1986 or any of the amendments made by such Act, or any similar State law.

(f) Definitions

As used in this section:

(1) Internet

The term "Internet" means the international computer network of both Federal and non-Federal interoperable packet switched data networks.

(2) Interactive computer service

The term "interactive computer service" means any information service, system, or access software provider that provides or enables computer access by multiple users to a computer server, including specifically a service or system that provides access to the Internet and such systems operated or services offered by libraries or educational institutions.

(3) Information content provider

The term "information content provider" means any person or entity that is responsible, in whole or in part, for the creation or development of information provided through the Internet or any other interactive computer service.

(4) Access software provider

The term "access software provider" means a provider of software (including client or server software), or enabling tools that do any one or more of the following:

(A) filter, screen, allow, or disallow content;

(B) pick, choose, analyze, or digest content; or

(C) transmit, receive, display, forward, cache, search, subset, organize, reorganize, or translate content.

II.
PRIVACY AND LAW ENFORCEMENT

Electronic Communications Privacy Act (1986)

Statutes in Context

In 1968, Congress enacted Title III of the Omnibus Crime Control and Safe Streets Act of 1968, Pub. L. No. 90-351, codified at 18 U.S.C. §§ 2510-20. This Act is commonly referred to as "Title III" or the "Wiretap Act." In 1986, Congress modernized federal wiretap law by passing the Electronic Communications Privacy Act (ECPA). ECPA includes three acts: (1) the Wiretap Act (the updated version of Title III); (2) the Stored Communications Act; and (3) the Pen Register Act.

In order to comprehend how each of the three acts comprising ECPA works, it is important to know that ECPA classifies all communications into three types: (1) "wire communications"; (2) "oral communications"; and (3) "electronic communications." Each type of communication is protected differently. As a general matter, wire communications receive the most protection, and electronic communications receive the least.

Wiretap Act (Title III)
18 U.S.C. §§ 2510-2522

§ 2510. Definitions

As used in this chapter—

(1) "wire communication" means any aural transfer made in whole or in part through the use of facilities for the transmission of communications by the aid of wire, cable, or other like connection between the point of origin and the point of reception (including the use of such connection in a switching station) furnished or operated by any person engaged in providing or operating such facilities for the transmission of interstate or foreign communications or communications affecting interstate or foreign commerce;

(2) "oral communication" means any oral communication uttered by a person exhibiting an expectation that such communication is not subject to interception under circumstances justifying such expectation, but such term does not include any electronic communication;

(3) "State" means any State of the United States, the District of Columbia, the Commonwealth of Puerto Rico, and any territory or possession of the United States;

(4) "intercept" means the aural or other acquisition of the contents of any wire, electronic, or oral communication through the use of any electronic, mechanical, or other device.

(5) "electronic, mechanical, or other device" means any device or apparatus which can be used to intercept a wire, oral, or electronic communication other than—

(a) any telephone or telegraph instrument, equipment or facility, or any component thereof, (i) furnished to the subscriber or user by a provider of wire or electronic communication service in the ordinary course of its business and being used by the subscriber or user in the ordinary course of its business or furnished by such subscriber or user for connection to the facilities of such service and used in the ordinary course of its business; or (ii) being used by a provider of wire or electronic communication service in the ordinary course of its business, or by an investigative or law enforcement officer in the ordinary course of his duties;

(b) a hearing aid or similar device being used to correct subnormal hearing to not better than normal;

(6) "person" means any employee, or agent of the United States or any State or political subdivision thereof, and any individual, partnership, association, joint stock company, trust, or corporation;

(7) "Investigative or law enforcement officer" means any officer of the United States or of a State or political subdivision thereof, who is empowered by law to conduct investigations of or to make arrests for offenses enumerated in this chapter, and any attorney authorized by law to prosecute or participate in the prosecution of such offenses;

(8) "contents", when used with respect to any wire, oral, or electronic communication, includes any information concerning the substance, purport, or meaning of that communication;

(9) "Judge of competent jurisdiction" means—

(a) a judge of a United States district court or a United States court of appeals; and

(b) a judge of any court of general criminal jurisdiction of a State who is authorized by a statute of that State to enter orders authorizing interceptions of wire, oral, or electronic communications;

(10) "communication common carrier" has the meaning given that term in section 3 of the Communications Act of 1934;

(11) "aggrieved person" means a person who was a party to any intercepted wire, oral, or electronic communication or a person against whom the interception was directed;

(12) "electronic communication" means any transfer of signs, signals, writing, images, sounds, data, or intelligence of any nature transmitted in whole or in part by a wire, radio, electromagnetic, photoelectronic or photooptical system that affects interstate or foreign commerce, but does not include—

(A) any wire or oral communication;

(B) any communication made through a tone-only paging device;

(C) any communication from a tracking device (as defined in section 3117 of this title); or

(D) electronic funds transfer information stored by a financial institution in a communications system used for the electronic storage and transfer of funds;

(13) "user" means any person or entity who—

(A) uses an electronic communication service; and

(B) is duly authorized by the provider of such service to engage in such use;

(14) "electronic communications system" means any wire, radio, electromagnetic, photooptical or photoelectronic facilities for the transmission of wire or electronic communications, and any computer facilities or related electronic equipment for the electronic storage of such communications;

(15) "electronic communication service" means any service which provides to users thereof the ability to send or receive wire or electronic communications;

(16) "readily accessible to the general public" means, with respect to a radio communication, that such communication is not—

(A) scrambled or encrypted;

(B) transmitted using modulation techniques whose essential parameters have been withheld from the public with the intention of preserving the privacy of such communication;

(C) carried on a subcarrier or other signal subsidiary to a radio transmission;

(D) transmitted over a communication system provided by a common carrier, unless the communication is a tone only paging system communication; or

(E) transmitted on frequencies allocated under part 25, subpart D, E, or F of part 74, or part 94 of the Rules of the Federal Communications Commission, unless, in the case of a communication transmitted on a frequency allocated under part 74 that is not exclusively allocated to broadcast auxiliary services, the communication is a two-way voice communication by radio;

(17) "electronic storage" means—

(A) any temporary, intermediate storage of a wire or electronic communication incidental to the electronic transmission thereof; and

(B) any storage of such communication by an electronic communication service for purposes of backup protection of such communication;

(18) "aural transfer" means a transfer containing the human voice at any point between and including the point of origin and the point of reception;

(19) "foreign intelligence information", for purposes of section 2517(6) of this title, means—

(A) information, whether or not concerning a United States person, that relates to the ability of the United States to protect against—

(i) actual or potential attack or other grave hostile acts of a foreign power or an agent of a foreign power;

(ii) sabotage or international terrorism by a foreign power or an agent of a foreign power; or

(iii) clandestine intelligence activities by an intelligence service or network of a foreign power or by an agent of a foreign power; or

(B) information, whether or not concerning a United States person, with respect to a foreign power or foreign territory that relates to—

(i) the national defense or the security of the United States; or

(ii) the conduct of the foreign affairs of the United States;

(20) "protected computer" has the meaning set forth in section 1030; and

(21) "computer trespasser"—

(A) means a person who accesses a protected computer without authorization and thus has no reasonable expectation of privacy in any communication transmitted to, through, or from the protected computer; and

(B) does not include a person known by the owner or operator of the protected computer to have an existing contractual relationship with the owner or operator of the protected computer for access to all or part of the protected computer.

§ 2511. Interception and disclosure of wire, oral, or electronic communications prohibited

(1) Except as otherwise specifically provided in this chapter any person who—

(a) intentionally intercepts, endeavors to intercept, or procures any other person to intercept or endeavor to intercept, any wire, oral, or electronic communication;

(b) intentionally uses, endeavors to use, or procures any other person to use or endeavor to use any electronic, mechanical, or other device to intercept any oral communication when—

(i) such device is affixed to, or otherwise transmits a signal through, a wire, cable, or other like connection used in wire communication; or

(ii) such device transmits communications by radio, or interferes with the transmission of such communication; or

(iii) such person knows, or has reason to know, that such device or any component thereof has been sent through the mail or transported in interstate or foreign commerce; or

(iv) such use or endeavor to use (A) takes place on the premises of any business or other commercial establishment the operations of which affect interstate or foreign commerce; or (B) obtains or is for the purpose of obtaining information relating to the operations of any business or other commercial establishment the operations of which affect interstate or foreign commerce; or

(v) such person acts in the District of Columbia, the Commonwealth of Puerto Rico, or any territory or possession of the United States;

(c) intentionally discloses, or endeavors to disclose, to any other person the contents of any wire, oral, or electronic communication, knowing or having reason to know that the information was obtained through the interception of a wire, oral, or electronic communication in violation of this subsection;

(d) intentionally uses, or endeavors to use, the contents of any wire, oral, or electronic communication, knowing or having reason to know that the information was obtained through the interception of a wire, oral, or electronic communication in violation of this subsection; or

(e) (i) intentionally discloses, or endeavors to disclose, to any other person the contents of any wire, oral, or electronic communication, intercepted by means authorized by sections 2511(2)(a)(ii), 2511(2)(b)-(c), 2511(2)(e), 2516, and 2518 of this chapter, (ii) knowing or having reason to know that the information was obtained through the interception of such a communication in connection with a criminal investigation, (iii) having obtained or received the information in connection with a criminal investigation, and (iv) with intent to improperly obstruct, impede, or interfere with a duly authorized criminal investigation,

shall be punished as provided in subsection (4) or shall be subject to suit as provided in subsection (5).

(2)(a)(i) It shall not be unlawful under this chapter for an operator of a switchboard, or an officer, employee, or agent of a provider of wire or electronic communication service, whose facilities are used in the transmission of a wire or electronic communication, to intercept, disclose, or use that communication in the normal course of his employment while engaged in any activity which is a necessary incident to the rendition of his service or to the protection of the rights or property of the provider of that service, except that a provider of wire communication service to the public shall not utilize service observing or random monitoring except for mechanical or service quality control checks.

(ii) Notwithstanding any other law, providers of wire or electronic communication service, their officers, employees, and agents, landlords, custodians, or other persons, are authorized to provide information, facilities, or technical assistance to persons authorized by law to intercept wire, oral, or electronic communications or to conduct electronic surveillance, as defined in section 101 of the Foreign Intelligence Surveillance Act of 1978, if such provider, its officers, employees, or agents, landlord, custodian, or other specified person, has been provided with—

(A) a court order directing such assistance signed by the authorizing judge, or

(B) a certification in writing by a person specified in section 2518(7) of this title or the Attorney General of the United States that no warrant or court order is required by law, that all statutory requirements have been met, and that the specified assistance is required,

setting forth the period of time during which the provision of the information, facilities, or technical assistance is authorized and specifying the information, facilities, or technical assistance required. No provider of wire or electronic communication service, officer, employee, or agent thereof, or landlord, custodian, or other specified person shall disclose the existence of any interception or surveillance or the device used to accomplish the interception or surveillance with respect to which the person has been furnished a court order or certification under this chapter, except as may otherwise be required by legal process and then only after prior notification to the Attorney General or to the principal prosecuting attorney of a State or any political subdivision of a State, as may be appropriate. Any such disclosure, shall render such person liable for the civil damages provided for in section 2520. No cause of action shall lie in any court against any provider of wire or electronic communication service, its officers, employees, or agents, landlord, custodian, or other specified person for providing information, facilities, or assistance in accordance with the terms of a court order, statutory authorization, or certification under this chapter.

(b) It shall not be unlawful under this chapter for an officer, employee, or agent of the Federal Communications Commission, in the normal course of his employment and in discharge of the monitoring responsibilities exercised by the Commission in the enforcement of chapter 5 of title 47 of the United States Code, to intercept a wire or electronic communication, or oral communication transmitted by radio, or to disclose or use the information thereby obtained.

(c) It shall not be unlawful under this chapter for a person acting under color of law to intercept a wire, oral, or electronic communication, where such person is a party to the communication or one of the parties to the communication has given prior consent to such interception.

(d) It shall not be unlawful under this chapter for a person not acting under color of law to intercept a wire, oral, or electronic communication where such person is a party to the communication or where one of the parties to the communication has given prior consent to such interception unless such communication is intercepted for the purpose of committing any criminal or tortious act in violation of the Constitution or laws of the United States or of any State.

(e) Notwithstanding any other provision of this title or section 705 or 706 of the Communications Act of 1934, it shall not be unlawful for an officer, employee, or agent of the United States in the normal course of his official duty to conduct electronic surveillance, as defined in section 101 of the Foreign Intelligence Surveillance Act of 1978, as authorized by that Act.

(f) Nothing contained in this chapter or chapter 121 or 206 of this title, or section 705 of the Communications Act of 1934, shall be deemed to affect the acquisition by the United States Government of foreign intelligence information from international or foreign communications, or foreign intelligence activities conducted in accordance with otherwise applicable Federal law involving a foreign electronic communications system, utilizing a means other than electronic surveillance as defined in section 101 of the Foreign Intelligence Surveillance Act of 1978, and procedures in this chapter or chapter 121 and the Foreign Intelligence Surveillance Act of 1978 shall be the exclusive means by which electronic surveillance, as defined in section 101 of such Act, and the interception of domestic wire, oral, and electronic communications may be conducted.

(g) It shall not be unlawful under this chapter or chapter 121 of this title for any person—

(i) to intercept or access an electronic communication made through an electronic communication system that is configured so that such electronic communication is readily accessible to the general public;

(ii) to intercept any radio communication which is transmitted—

(I) by any station for the use of the general public, or that relates to ships, aircraft, vehicles, or persons in distress;

(II) by any governmental, law enforcement, civil defense, private land mobile, or public safety communications system, including police and fire, readily accessible to the general public;

(III) by a station operating on an authorized frequency within the bands allocated to the amateur, citizens band, or general mobile radio services; or

(IV) by any marine or aeronautical communications system;

(iii) to engage in any conduct which—

(I) is prohibited by section 633 of the Communications Act of 1934; or

(II) is excepted from the application of section 705(a) of the Communications Act of 1934 by section 705(b) of that Act;

(iv) to intercept any wire or electronic communication the transmission of which is causing harmful interference to any lawfully operating station or consumer electronic equipment, to the extent necessary to identify the source of such interference; or

(v) for other users of the same frequency to intercept any radio communication made through a system that utilizes frequencies monitored by individuals engaged in the provision or the use of such system, if such communication is not scrambled or encrypted.

(h) It shall not be unlawful under this chapter—

(i) to use a pen register or a trap and trace device (as those terms are defined for the purposes of chapter 206 (relating to pen registers and trap and trace devices) of this title); or

(ii) for a provider of electronic communication service to record the fact that a wire or electronic communication was initiated or completed in order to protect such provider, another provider furnishing service toward the completion of the wire or electronic communication, or a user of that service, from fraudulent, unlawful or abusive use of such service.

(i) It shall not be unlawful under this chapter for a person acting under color of law to intercept the wire or electronic communications of a computer trespasser transmitted to, through, or from the protected computer, if—

(I) the owner or operator of the protected computer authorizes the interception of the computer trespasser's communications on the protected computer;

(II) the person acting under color of law is lawfully engaged in an investigation;

(III) the person acting under color of law has reasonable grounds to believe that the contents of the computer trespasser's communications will be relevant to the investigation; and

(IV) such interception does not acquire communications other than those transmitted to or from the computer trespasser.

(3)(a) Except as provided in paragraph (b) of this subsection, a person or entity providing an electronic communication service to the public shall not intentionally divulge the contents of any communication (other than one to such person or entity, or an agent thereof) while in transmission on that service to any person or entity other than an addressee or intended recipient of such communication or an agent of such addressee or intended recipient.

(b) A person or entity providing electronic communication service to the public may divulge the contents of any such communication—

(i) as otherwise authorized in section 2511(2)(a) or 2517 of this title;

(ii) with the lawful consent of the originator or any addressee or intended recipient of such communication;

(iii) to a person employed or authorized, or whose facilities are used, to forward such communication to its destination; or

(iv) which were inadvertently obtained by the service provider and which appear to pertain to the commission of a crime, if such divulgence is made to a law enforcement agency.

(4)(a) Except as provided in paragraph (b) of this subsection or in subsection (5), whoever violates subsection (1) of this section shall be fined under this title or imprisoned not more than five years, or both.

(b) Conduct otherwise an offense under this subsection that consists of or relates to the interception of a satellite transmission that is not encrypted or scrambled and that is transmitted—

(i) to a broadcasting station for purposes of retransmission to the general public; or

(ii) as an audio subcarrier intended for redistribution to facilities open to the public, but not including data transmissions or telephone calls,

is not an offense under this subsection unless the conduct is for the purposes of direct or indirect commercial advantage or private financial gain.

[**(c)** Redesignated (b)]

(5)(a)(i) If the communication is—

(A) a private satellite video communication that is not scrambled or encrypted and the conduct in violation of this chapter is the private viewing of that communication and is not for a tortious or illegal purpose or for purposes of direct or indirect commercial advantage or private commercial gain; or

(B) a radio communication that is transmitted on frequencies allocated under subpart D of part 74 of the rules of the Federal Communications Commission that is not scrambled or encrypted and the conduct in violation of this chapter is not for a tortious or illegal purpose or for purposes of direct or indirect commercial advantage or private commercial gain,

then the person who engages in such conduct shall be subject to suit by the Federal Government in a court of competent jurisdiction.

(ii) In an action under this subsection—

(A) if the violation of this chapter is a first offense for the person under paragraph (a) of subsection (4) and such person has not been found liable in a civil action under section 2520 of this title, the Federal Government shall be entitled to appropriate injunctive relief; and

(B) if the violation of this chapter is a second or subsequent offense under paragraph (a) of subsection (4) or such person has been found liable in any prior civil action under section 2520, the person shall be subject to a mandatory $500 civil fine.

(b) The court may use any means within its authority to enforce an injunction issued under paragraph (ii)(A), and shall impose a civil fine of not less than $500 for each violation of such an injunction.

§ 2512. Manufacture, distribution, possession, and advertising of wire, oral, or electronic communication intercepting devices prohibited

(1) Except as otherwise specifically provided in this chapter, any person who intentionally—

(a) sends through the mail, or sends or carries in interstate or foreign commerce, any electronic, mechanical, or other device, knowing or having reason to know that the design of such device renders it primarily useful for the purpose of the surreptitious interception of wire, oral, or electronic communications;

(b) manufactures, assembles, possesses, or sells any electronic, mechanical, or other device, knowing or having reason to know that the design of such device renders it primarily useful for the purpose of the surreptitious interception of wire, oral, or electronic communications, and that such device or any component thereof has been or will be sent through the mail or transported in interstate or foreign commerce; or

(c) places in any newspaper, magazine, handbill, or other publication or disseminates by electronic means any advertisement of—

(i) any electronic, mechanical, or other device knowing the content of the advertisement and knowing or having reason to know that the design of such device renders it primarily useful for the purpose of the surreptitious interception of wire, oral, or electronic communications; or

(ii) any other electronic, mechanical, or other device, where such advertisement promotes the use of such device for the purpose of the surreptitious interception of wire, oral, or electronic communications,

knowing the content of the advertisement and knowing or having reason to know that such advertisement will be sent through the mail or transported in interstate or foreign commerce,

shall be fined under this title or imprisoned not more than five years, or both.

(2) It shall not be unlawful under this section for—

(a) a provider of wire or electronic communication service or an officer, agent, or employee of, or a person under contract with, such a provider, in the normal course of the business of providing that wire or electronic communication service, or

(b) an officer, agent, or employee of, or a person under contract with, the United States, a State, or a political subdivision thereof, in the normal course of the activities of the United States, a State, or a political subdivision thereof,

to send through the mail, send or carry in interstate or foreign commerce, or manufacture, assemble, possess, or sell any electronic, mechanical, or other device knowing or having reason to know that the design of such device renders it primarily useful for the purpose of the surreptitious interception of wire, oral, or electronic communications.

(3) It shall not be unlawful under this section to advertise for sale a device described in subsection (1) of this section if the advertisement is mailed, sent, or carried in interstate or foreign commerce solely to a domestic provider of wire or electronic communication service or to an agency of the United States, a State, or a political subdivision thereof which is duly authorized to use such device.

§ 2513. Confiscation of wire, oral, or electronic communication intercepting devices

Any electronic, mechanical, or other device used, sent, carried, manufactured, assembled, possessed, sold, or advertised in violation of section 2511 or section 2512 of this chapter may be seized and forfeited to the United States. All provisions of law relating to (1) the seizure, summary and judicial forfeiture, and condemnation of vessels, vehicles, merchandise, and baggage for violations of the customs laws contained in title 19 of the United States Code, (2) the disposition of such vessels, vehicles, merchandise, and baggage or the proceeds from the sale thereof, (3) the remission or mitigation of such forfeiture, (4) the compromise of claims, and (5) the award of compensation to informers in respect of such forfeitures, shall apply to seizures and forfeitures incurred, or alleged to have been incurred, under the provisions of this section, insofar as applicable and not inconsistent with the provisions of this section; except that such duties as are imposed upon the collector of customs or any other person with respect to the seizure and forfeiture of vessels, vehicles, merchandise, and baggage under the provisions of the customs laws contained in title 19 of the United States Code shall be performed with respect to seizure and forfeiture of electronic, mechanical, or other intercepting devices under this section by such officers, agents, or other persons as may be authorized or designated for that purpose by the Attorney General.

[§ 2514. Repealed. Pub.L. 91-452, Title II, § 227(a), Oct. 15, 1970, 84 Stat. 930]

§ 2515. Prohibition of use as evidence of intercepted wire or oral communications

Whenever any wire or oral communication has been intercepted, no part of the contents of such communication and no evidence derived therefrom may be received in evidence in any trial, hearing, or other proceeding in or before any court, grand jury, department, officer, agency, regulatory body, legislative committee, or other authority of the United States, a State, or a political subdivision thereof if the disclosure of that information would be in violation of this chapter.

§ 2516. Authorization for interception of wire, oral, or electronic communications

(1) The Attorney General, Deputy Attorney General, Associate Attorney General [FN1], or any Assistant Attorney General, any acting Assistant Attorney General, or any Deputy Assistant Attorney General or acting Deputy Assistant Attorney General in the Criminal Division or National Security Division specially designated by the Attorney General, may authorize an application to a Federal judge of competent jurisdiction for, and such judge may grant in conformity with section 2518 of this chapter an order authorizing or approving the interception of wire or oral communications by the Federal Bureau of Investigation, or a Federal agency having responsibility for the investigation of the offense as to which the application is made, when such interception may provide or has provided evidence of—

(a) any offense punishable by death or by imprisonment for more than one year under sections 2122 and 2274 through 2277 of title 42 of the United States Code (relating to the enforcement of the Atomic Energy Act of 1954), section 2284 of title 42 of the United States Code (relating to sabotage of nuclear facilities or fuel), or under the following chapters of this title: chapter 10 (relating to biological weapons) [FN2] chapter 37 (relating to espionage), chapter 55 (relating to kidnapping), chapter 90 (relating to protection of trade secrets), chapter 105 (relating to sabotage), chapter 115 (relating to treason), chapter 102 (relating to riots), chapter 65 (relating to malicious mischief), chapter 111 (relating to destruction of vessels), or chapter 81 (relating to piracy);

(b) a violation of section 186 or section 501(c) of title 29, United States Code (dealing with restrictions on payments and loans to labor organizations), or any offense which involves murder, kidnapping, robbery, or extortion, and which is punishable under this title;

(c) any offense which is punishable under the following sections of this title: section 37 (relating to violence at international airports), section 43 (relating to animal enterprise terrorism), section 81 (arson within special maritime and territorial jurisdiction), section 201 (bribery of public officials and witnesses), section 215 (relating to bribery of bank officials), section 224 (bribery in sporting contests), subsection (d), (e), (f), (g), (h), or (i) of section 844 (unlawful use of explosives), section 1032 (relating to concealment of assets), section 1084 (transmission of wagering information), section 751 (relating to escape), section 832 (relating to nuclear and weapons of mass destruction threats), section 842 (relating to explosive materials), section 930 (relating to possession of weapons in Federal facilities), section 1014 (relating to loans and credit applications generally; renewals and discounts), section 1114 (relating to officers and employees of the United States), section 1116 (relating to protection of foreign officials), sections 1503, 1512, and 1513 (influencing or injuring an officer, juror, or witness generally), section 1510 (obstruction of criminal investigations), section 1511 (obstruction of State or local law enforcement), section 1591 (sex trafficking of children by force, fraud, or coercion), section 1751 (Presidential and Presidential staff assassination, kidnapping, and assault), section 1951 (interference with commerce by threats or violence), section 1952 (interstate and foreign travel or transportation in aid of racketeering enterprises), section 1958 (relating to use of interstate commerce facilities in the commission of murder for hire), section 1959 (relating to violent crimes in aid of racketeering activity), section 1954 (offer, acceptance, or solicitation to influence operations of employee benefit plan), section 1955 (prohibition of business enterprises of gambling), section 1956 (laundering of monetary instruments), section 1957 (relating to engaging in monetary transactions in property derived from specified unlawful activity), section 659 (theft from interstate shipment), section 664 (embezzlement from pension and welfare funds), section 1343 (fraud by wire, radio, or television), section 1344 (relating to bank fraud), section 1992 (relating to terrorist attacks against mass transportation), sections 2251 and 2252 (sexual exploitation of children), section 2251A (selling or buying of children), section 2252A (relating to material constituting or containing child pornography), section 1466A (relating to child obscenity), section 2260 (production of sexually explicit depictions of a minor for importation into the United States), sections 2421, 2422, 2423, and 2425 (relating to transportation for illegal sexual activity and related crimes), sections 2312, 2313, 2314, and 2315 (interstate transportation of stolen property), section 2321 (relating to trafficking in certain motor vehicles or motor vehicle parts), section 2340A (relating to torture), section 1203 (relating to hostage taking), section 1029 (relating to fraud and related activity in connection with access devices), section 3146 (relating to penalty for failure to appear), section 3521(b)(3) (relating to witness relocation and assistance), section 32 (relating to destruction of aircraft or aircraft facilities), section 38 (relating to aircraft parts fraud), section 1963 (violations with respect to racketeer influenced and corrupt organizations), section 115 (relating to threatening or retaliating against a Federal official), section 1341 (relating to mail fraud), a felony violation of section 1030 (relating to computer fraud and abuse), section 351 (violations with respect to congressional, Cabinet, or Supreme Court assassinations, kidnapping, and assault), section 831 (relating to prohibited transactions involving nuclear materials), section 33 (relating to destruction of motor vehicles or motor vehicle facilities), section 175 (relating to biological weapons), section 175c (relating to variola virus), section 956 (conspiracy to harm persons or property overseas), section [FN3] a felony violation of section 1028 (relating to production of false identification documentation), section 1425 (relating to the procurement of citizenship or nationalization unlawfully), section 1426 (relating to the reproduction of naturalization or citizenship papers), section 1427 (relating to the sale of naturalization or citizenship papers), section 1541 (relating to passport issuance without authority), section 1542 (relating to false statements in passport applications), section 1543 (relating to forgery or false use of passports), section 1544 (relating to misuse of passports), or section 1546 (relating to fraud and misuse of visas, permits, and other documents);

(d) any offense involving counterfeiting punishable under section 471, 472, or 473 of this title;

(e) any offense involving fraud connected with a case under title 11 or the manufacture, importation, receiving, concealment, buying, selling, or otherwise dealing in narcotic drugs, marihuana, or other dangerous drugs, punishable under any law of the United States;

(f) any offense including extortionate credit transactions under sections 892, 893, or 894 of this title;

(g) a violation of section 5322 of title 31, United States Code (dealing with the reporting of currency transactions), or section 5324 of title 31, United States Code (relating to structuring transactions to evade reporting requirement prohibited);

(h) any felony violation of sections 2511 and 2512 (relating to interception and disclosure of certain communications and to certain intercepting devices) of this title;

(i) any felony violation of chapter 71 (relating to obscenity) of this title;

(j) any violation of section 60123(b) (relating to destruction of a natural gas pipeline), section 46502 (relating to aircraft piracy), the second sentence of section 46504 (relating to assault on a flight crew with dangerous weapon), or section 46505(b)(3) or (c) (relating to explosive or incendiary devices, or endangerment of human life, by means of weapons on aircraft) of title 49;

(k) any criminal violation of section 2778 of title 22 (relating to the Arms Export Control Act);

(l) the location of any fugitive from justice from an offense described in this section;

(m) a violation of section 274, 277, or 278 of the Immigration and Nationality Act (8 U.S.C. 1324, 1327, or 1328) (relating to the smuggling of aliens);

(n) any felony violation of sections 922 and 924 of title 18, United States Code (relating to firearms);

(o) any violation of section 5861 of the Internal Revenue Code of 1986 (relating to firearms);

(p) a felony violation of section 1028 (relating to production of false identification documents), section 1542 (relating to false statements in passport applications), section 1546 (relating to fraud and misuse of visas, permits, and other documents, [FN4] section 1028A (relating to aggravated identity theft)) [FN5] of this title or a violation of section 274, 277, or 278 of the Immigration and Nationality Act (relating to the smuggling of aliens); or [FN6]

(q) any criminal violation of section 229 (relating to chemical weapons): or sections [FN7] 2332, 2332a, 2332b, 2332d, 2332f, 2332g, 2332h [FN8] 2339, 2339A, 2339B, 2339C, or 2339D of this title (relating to terrorism);

(r) any criminal violation of section 1 (relating to illegal restraints of trade or commerce), 2 (relating to illegal monopolizing of trade or commerce), or 3 (relating to illegal restraints of trade or commerce in territories or the District of Columbia) of the Sherman Act (15 U.S.C. 1, 2, 3); or

(s) any conspiracy to commit any offense described in any subparagraph of this paragraph.

(2) The principal prosecuting attorney of any State, or the principal prosecuting attorney of any political subdivision thereof, if such attorney is authorized by a statute of that State to make application to a State court judge of competent jurisdiction for an order authorizing or approving the interception of wire, oral, or electronic communications, may apply to such judge for, and such judge may grant in conformity with section 2518 of this chapter and with the applicable State statute an order authorizing, or approving the interception of wire, oral, or electronic communications by investigative or law enforcement officers having responsibility for the investigation of the offense as to which the application is made, when such interception may provide or has provided evidence of the commission of the offense of murder, kidnapping, gambling, robbery, bribery, extortion, or dealing in narcotic drugs, marihuana or other dangerous drugs, or other crime dangerous to life, limb, or property, and punishable by imprisonment for more than one year, designated in any applicable State statute authorizing such interception, or any conspiracy to commit any of the foregoing offenses.

(3) Any attorney for the Government (as such term is defined for the purposes of the Federal Rules of Criminal Procedure) may authorize an application to a Federal judge of competent jurisdiction for, and such judge may grant, in conformity with section 2518 of this title, an order authorizing or approving the interception of electronic communications by an investigative or law enforcement officer having responsibility for the investigation of the offense as to which the application is made, when such interception may provide or has provided evidence of any Federal felony.

§ 2517. Authorization for disclosure and use of intercepted wire, oral, or electronic communications

(1) Any investigative or law enforcement officer who, by any means authorized by this chapter, has obtained knowledge of the contents of any wire, oral, or electronic communication, or evidence derived therefrom, may disclose such contents to another investigative or law enforcement officer to the extent that such disclosure is appropriate to the proper performance of the official duties of the officer making or receiving the disclosure.

(2) Any investigative or law enforcement officer who, by any means authorized by this chapter, has obtained knowledge of the contents of any wire, oral, or electronic communication or evidence derived therefrom may use such contents to the extent such use is appropriate to the proper performance of his official duties.

(3) Any person who has received, by any means authorized by this chapter, any information concerning a wire, oral, or electronic communication, or evidence derived therefrom intercepted in accordance with the provisions of this chapter may disclose the contents of that communication or such derivative evidence while giving testimony under oath or affirmation in any proceeding held under the authority of the United States or of any State or political subdivision thereof.

(4) No otherwise privileged wire, oral, or electronic communication intercepted in accordance with, or in violation of, the provisions of this chapter shall lose its privileged character.

(5) When an investigative or law enforcement officer, while engaged in intercepting wire, oral, or electronic communications in the manner authorized herein, intercepts wire, oral, or electronic communications relating to offenses other than those specified in the order of authorization or approval, the contents thereof, and evidence derived therefrom, may be disclosed or used as provided in subsections (1) and (2) of this section. Such contents and any evidence derived therefrom may be used under subsection (3) of this section when authorized or approved by a judge of competent jurisdiction where such judge finds on subsequent application that the contents were otherwise intercepted in accordance with the provisions of this chapter. Such application shall be made as soon as practicable.

(6) Any investigative or law enforcement officer, or attorney for the Government, who by any means authorized by this chapter, has obtained knowledge of the contents of any wire, oral, or electronic communication, or evidence derived therefrom, may disclose such contents to any other Federal law enforcement, intelligence, protective, immigration, national defense, or national security official to the extent that such contents include foreign intelligence or counterintelligence (as defined in section 3 of the National Security Act of 1947 (50 U.S.C. 401a)), or foreign intelligence information (as defined in subsection (19) of section 2510 of this title), to assist the official who is to receive that information in the performance of his official duties. Any Federal official who receives information pursuant to this provision may use that information only as necessary in the conduct of that person's official duties subject to any limitations on the unauthorized disclosure of such information.

(7) Any investigative or law enforcement officer, or other Federal official in carrying out official duties as such Federal official, who by any means authorized by this chapter, has obtained knowledge of the contents of any wire, oral, or electronic communication, or evidence derived therefrom, may disclose such contents or derivative evidence to a foreign investigative or law enforcement officer to the extent that such disclosure is appropriate to the proper performance of the official duties of the officer making or receiving the disclosure, and foreign investigative or law enforcement officers may use or disclose such contents or derivative evidence to the extent such use or disclosure is appropriate to the proper performance of their official duties.

(8) Any investigative or law enforcement officer, or other Federal official in carrying out official duties as such Federal official, who by any means authorized by this chapter, has obtained knowledge of the contents of any wire, oral, or electronic communication, or evidence derived therefrom, may disclose such contents or derivative evidence to any appropriate Federal, State, local, or foreign government official to the extent that such contents or derivative evidence reveals a threat of actual or potential attack or other grave hostile acts of a foreign power or an agent of a foreign power, domestic or international sabotage, domestic or international terrorism, or clandestine intelligence gathering activities by an intelligence service or network of a foreign power or by an agent of a foreign power, within the United States or elsewhere, for the purpose of preventing or responding to such a threat. Any official who receives information pursuant to this provision may use that information only as necessary in the conduct of that person's official duties subject to any limitations on the unauthorized disclosure of such information, and any State, local, or foreign official who receives information pursuant to this provision may use that information only consistent with such guidelines as the Attorney General and Director of Central Intelligence shall jointly issue.

§ 2518. Procedure for interception of wire, oral, or electronic communications

(1) Each application for an order authorizing or approving the interception of a wire, oral, or electronic communication under this chapter shall be made in writing upon oath or affirmation to a judge of competent jurisdiction and shall state the applicant's authority to make such application. Each application shall include the following information:

(a) the identity of the investigative or law enforcement officer making the application, and the officer authorizing the application;

(b) a full and complete statement of the facts and circumstances relied upon by the applicant, to justify his belief that an order should be issued, including (i) details as to the particular offense that has been, is being, or is about to be committed, (ii) except as provided in subsection (11), a particular description of the nature and location of the facilities from which or the place where the communication is to be intercepted, (iii) a particular description of the type of communications sought to be intercepted, (iv) the identity of the person, if known, committing the offense and whose communications are to be intercepted;

(c) a full and complete statement as to whether or not other investigative procedures have been tried and failed or why they reasonably appear to be unlikely to succeed if tried or to be too dangerous;

(d) a statement of the period of time for which the interception is required to be maintained. If the nature of the investigation is such that the authorization for interception should not automatically terminate when the described type of communication has been first obtained, a particular description of facts establishing probable cause to believe that additional communications of the same type will occur thereafter;

(e) a full and complete statement of the facts concerning all previous applications known to the individual authorizing and making the application, made to any judge for authorization to intercept, or for approval of interceptions of, wire, oral, or electronic communications involving any of the same persons, facilities or places specified in the application, and the action taken by the judge on each such application; and

(f) where the application is for the extension of an order, a statement setting forth the results thus far obtained from the interception, or a reasonable explanation of the failure to obtain such results.

(2) The judge may require the applicant to furnish additional testimony or documentary evidence in support of the application.

(3) Upon such application the judge may enter an ex parte order, as requested or as modified, authorizing or approving interception of wire, oral, or electronic communications within the territorial jurisdiction of the court in which the judge is sitting (and outside that jurisdiction but within the United States in the case of a mobile interception device authorized by a Federal court within such jurisdiction), if the judge determines on the basis of the facts submitted by the applicant that—

(a) there is probable cause for belief that an individual is committing, has committed, or is about to commit a particular offense enumerated in section 2516 of this chapter;

(b) there is probable cause for belief that particular communications concerning that offense will be obtained through such interception;

(c) normal investigative procedures have been tried and have failed or reasonably appear to be unlikely to succeed if tried or to be too dangerous;

(d) except as provided in subsection (11), there is probable cause for belief that the facilities from which, or the place where, the wire, oral, or electronic communications are to be intercepted are being used, or are about to be used, in connection with the commission of such offense, or are leased to, listed in the name of, or commonly used by such person.

(4) Each order authorizing or approving the interception of any wire, oral, or electronic communication under this chapter shall specify—

(a) the identity of the person, if known, whose communications are to be intercepted;

(b) the nature and location of the communications facilities as to which, or the place where, authority to intercept is granted;

(c) a particular description of the type of communication sought to be intercepted, and a statement of the particular offense to which it relates;

(d) the identity of the agency authorized to intercept the communications, and of the person authorizing the application; and

(e) the period of time during which such interception is authorized, including a statement as to whether or not the interception shall automatically terminate when the described communication has been first obtained.

An order authorizing the interception of a wire, oral, or electronic communication under this chapter shall, upon request of the applicant, direct that a provider of wire or electronic communication service, landlord, custodian or other person shall furnish the applicant forthwith all information, facilities, and technical assistance necessary to accomplish the interception unobtrusively and with a minimum of interference with the services that such service provider, landlord, custodian, or person is according the person whose communications are to be intercepted. Any provider of wire or electronic communication service, landlord, custodian or other person furnishing such facilities or technical assistance shall be compensated therefor by the applicant for reasonable expenses incurred in providing such facilities or assistance. Pursuant to section 2522 of this chapter, an order may also be issued to enforce the assistance capability and capacity requirements under the Communications Assistance for Law Enforcement Act.

(5) No order entered under this section may authorize or approve the interception of any wire, oral, or electronic communication for any period longer than is necessary to achieve the objective of the authorization, nor in any event longer than thirty days. Such thirty-day period begins on the earlier of the day on which the investigative or law enforcement officer first begins to conduct an interception under the order or ten days after the order is entered. Extensions of an order may be granted, but only upon application for an extension made in accordance with subsection (1) of this section and the court making the findings required by subsection (3) of this section. The period of extension shall be no longer than the authorizing judge deems necessary to achieve the purposes for which it was granted and in no event for longer than thirty days. Every order and extension thereof shall contain a provision that the authorization to intercept shall be executed as soon as practicable, shall be conducted in such a way as to minimize the interception of communications not otherwise subject to interception under this chapter, and must terminate upon attainment of the authorized objective, or in any event in thirty days. In the event the intercepted communication is in a code or foreign language, and an expert in that foreign language or code is not reasonably available during the interception period, minimization may be accomplished as soon as practicable after such interception. An interception under this chapter may be conducted in whole or in part by Government personnel, or by an individual operating under a contract with the Government, acting under the supervision of an investigative or law enforcement officer authorized to conduct the interception.

(6) Whenever an order authorizing interception is entered pursuant to this chapter, the order may require reports to be made to the judge who issued the order showing what progress has been made toward achievement of the authorized objective and the need for continued interception. Such reports shall be made at such intervals as the judge may require.

(7) Notwithstanding any other provision of this chapter, any investigative or law enforcement officer, specially designated by the Attorney General, the Deputy Attorney General, the Associate Attorney General, or by the principal prosecuting attorney of any State or subdivision thereof acting pursuant to a statute of that State, who reasonably determines that—

(a) an emergency situation exists that involves—

(i) immediate danger of death or serious physical injury to any person,

(ii) conspiratorial activities threatening the national security interest, or

(iii) conspiratorial activities characteristic of organized crime,

that requires a wire, oral, or electronic communication to be intercepted before an order authorizing such interception can, with due diligence, be obtained, and

(b) there are grounds upon which an order could be entered under this chapter to authorize such interception,

may intercept such wire, oral, or electronic communication if an application for an order approving the interception is made in accordance with this section within forty-eight hours after the interception has occurred, or begins to occur. In the absence of an order, such interception shall immediately terminate when the communication sought is obtained or when the application for the order is denied, whichever is earlier. In the event such application for approval is denied, or in any other case where the interception is terminated without an order having been issued, the contents of any wire, oral, or electronic communication intercepted shall be treated as having been obtained in violation of this chapter, and an inventory shall be served as provided for in subsection (d) of this section on the person named in the application.

(8) (a) The contents of any wire, oral, or electronic communication intercepted by any means authorized by this chapter shall, if possible, be recorded on tape or wire or other comparable device. The recording of the contents of any wire, oral, or electronic communication under this subsection shall be done in such a way as will protect the recording from editing or other alterations. Immediately upon the expiration of the period of the order, or extensions thereof, such recordings shall be made available to the judge issuing such order and sealed under his directions. Custody of the recordings shall be wherever the judge orders. They shall not be destroyed except upon an order of the issuing or denying judge and in any event shall be kept for ten years. Duplicate recordings may be made for use or disclosure pursuant to the provisions of subsections (1) and (2) of section 2517 of this chapter for investigations. The presence of the seal provided for by this subsection, or a satisfactory explanation for the absence thereof, shall be a prerequisite for the use or disclosure of the contents of any wire, oral, or electronic communication or evidence derived therefrom under subsection (3) of section 2517.

(b) Applications made and orders granted under this chapter shall be sealed by the judge. Custody of the applications and orders shall be wherever the judge directs. Such applications and orders shall be disclosed only upon a showing of good cause before a judge of competent jurisdiction and shall not be destroyed except on order of the issuing or denying judge, and in any event shall be kept for ten years.

(c) Any violation of the provisions of this subsection may be punished as contempt of the issuing or denying judge.

(d) Within a reasonable time but not later than ninety days after the filing of an application for an order of approval under section 2518(7)(b) which is denied or the termination of the period of an order or extensions thereof, the issuing or denying judge shall cause to be served, on the persons named in the order or the application, and such other parties to intercepted communications as the judge may determine in his discretion that is in the interest of justice, an inventory which shall include notice of—

(1) the fact of the entry of the order or the application;

(2) the date of the entry and the period of authorized, approved or disapproved interception, or the denial of the application; and

(3) the fact that during the period wire, oral, or electronic communications were or were not intercepted.

The judge, upon the filing of a motion, may in his discretion make available to such person or his counsel for inspection such portions of the intercepted communications, applications and orders as the judge determines to be in the interest of justice. On an ex parte showing of good cause to a judge of competent jurisdiction the serving of the inventory required by this subsection may be postponed.

(9) The contents of any wire, oral, or electronic communication intercepted pursuant to this chapter or evidence derived therefrom shall not be received in evidence or otherwise disclosed in any trial, hearing, or other proceeding in a Federal or State court unless each party, not less than ten days before the trial, hearing, or proceeding, has been furnished with a copy of the court order, and accompanying application, under which the interception was authorized or approved. This ten-day period may be waived by the judge if he finds that it was not possible to furnish the party with the above information ten days before the trial, hearing, or proceeding and that the party will not be prejudiced by the delay in receiving such information.

(10)(a) Any aggrieved person in any trial, hearing, or proceeding in or before any court, department, officer, agency, regulatory body, or other authority of the United States, a State, or a political subdivision thereof, may move to suppress the contents of any wire or oral communication intercepted pursuant to this chapter, or evidence derived therefrom, on the grounds that—

(i) the communication was unlawfully intercepted;

(ii) the order of authorization or approval under which it was intercepted is insufficient on its face; or

(iii) the interception was not made in conformity with the order of authorization or approval.

Such motion shall be made before the trial, hearing, or proceeding unless there was no opportunity to make such motion or the person was not aware of the grounds of the motion. If the motion is granted, the contents of the intercepted wire or oral communication, or evidence derived therefrom, shall be treated as having been obtained in violation of this chapter. The judge, upon the filing of such motion by the aggrieved person, may in his discretion make available to the aggrieved person or his counsel for inspection such portions of the intercepted communication or evidence derived therefrom as the judge determines to be in the interests of justice.

(b) In addition to any other right to appeal, the United States shall have the right to appeal from an order granting a motion to suppress made under paragraph (a) of this subsection, or the denial of an application for an order of approval, if the United States attorney shall certify to the judge or other official granting such motion or denying such application that the appeal is not taken for purposes of delay. Such appeal shall be taken within thirty days after the date the order was entered and shall be diligently prosecuted.

(c) The remedies and sanctions described in this chapter with respect to the interception of electronic communications are the only judicial remedies and sanctions for nonconstitutional violations of this chapter involving such communications.

(11) The requirements of subsections (1)(b)(ii) and (3)(d) of this section relating to the specification of the facilities from which, or the place where, the communication is to be intercepted do not apply if—

(a) in the case of an application with respect to the interception of an oral communication—

(i) the application is by a Federal investigative or law enforcement officer and is approved by the Attorney General, the Deputy Attorney General, the Associate Attorney General, an Assistant Attorney General, or an acting Assistant Attorney General;

(ii) the application contains a full and complete statement as to why such specification is not practical and identifies the person committing the offense and whose communications are to be intercepted; and

(iii) the judge finds that such specification is not practical; and

(b) in the case of an application with respect to a wire or electronic communication—

(i) the application is by a Federal investigative or law enforcement officer and is approved by the Attorney General, the Deputy Attorney General, the Associate Attorney General, an Assistant Attorney General, or an acting Assistant Attorney General;

(ii) the application identifies the person believed to be committing the offense and whose communications are to be intercepted and the applicant makes a showing that there is probable cause to believe that the person's actions could have the effect of thwarting interception from a specified facility;

(iii) the judge finds that such showing has been adequately made; and

(iv) the order authorizing or approving the interception is limited to interception only for such time as it is reasonable to presume that the person identified in the application is or was reasonably proximate to the instrument through which such communication will be or was transmitted.

(12) An interception of a communication under an order with respect to which the requirements of subsections (1)(b)(ii) and (3)(d) of this section do not apply by reason of subsection (11)(a) shall not begin until the place where the communication is to be intercepted is ascertained by the person implementing the interception order. A provider of wire or electronic communications service that has received an order as provided for in subsection (11)(b) may move the court to modify or quash the order on the ground that its assistance with respect to the interception cannot be performed in a timely or reasonable fashion. The court, upon notice to the government, shall decide such a motion expeditiously.

§ 2519. Reports concerning intercepted wire, oral, or electronic communications

(1) Within thirty days after the expiration of an order (or each extension thereof) entered under section 2518, or the denial of an order approving an interception, the issuing or denying judge shall report to the Administrative Office of the United States Courts—

(a) the fact that an order or extension was applied for;

(b) the kind of order or extension applied for (including whether or not the order was an order with respect to which the requirements of sections 2518(1)(b)(ii) and 2518(3)(d) of this title did not apply by reason of section 2518(11) of this title);

(c) the fact that the order or extension was granted as applied for, was modified, or was denied;

(d) the period of interceptions authorized by the order, and the number and duration of any extensions of the order;

(e) the offense specified in the order or application, or extension of an order;

(f) the identity of the applying investigative or law enforcement officer and agency making the application and the person authorizing the application; and

(g) the nature of the facilities from which or the place where communications were to be intercepted.

(2) In January of each year the Attorney General, an Assistant Attorney General specially designated by the Attorney General, or the principal prosecuting attorney of a State, or the principal prosecuting attorney for any political subdivision of a State, shall report to the Administrative Office of the United States Courts—

(a) the information required by paragraphs (a) through (g) of subsection (1) of this section with respect to each application for an order or extension made during the preceding calendar year;

(b) a general description of the interceptions made under such order or extension, including (i) the approximate nature and frequency of incriminating communications intercepted, (ii) the approximate nature and frequency of other communications intercepted, (iii) the approximate number of persons whose communications were intercepted, (iv) the number of orders in which encryption was encountered and whether such encryption prevented law enforcement from obtaining the plain text of communications intercepted pursuant to such order, and (v) the approximate nature, amount, and cost of the manpower and other resources used in the interceptions;

(c) the number of arrests resulting from interceptions made under such order or extension, and the offenses for which arrests were made;

(d) the number of trials resulting from such interceptions;

(e) the number of motions to suppress made with respect to such interceptions, and the number granted or denied;

(f) the number of convictions resulting from such interceptions and the offenses for which the convictions were obtained and a general assessment of the importance of the interceptions; and

(g) the information required by paragraphs (b) through (f) of this subsection with respect to orders or extensions obtained in a preceding calendar year.

(3) In April of each year the Director of the Administrative Office of the United States Courts shall transmit to the Congress a full and complete report concerning the number of applications for orders authorizing or approving the interception of wire, oral, or electronic communications pursuant to this chapter and the number of orders and extensions granted or denied pursuant to this chapter during the preceding calendar year. Such report shall include a summary and analysis of the data required to be filed with the Administrative Office by subsections (1) and (2) of this section. The Director of the Administrative Office of the United States Courts is authorized to issue binding regulations dealing with the content and form of the reports required to be filed by subsections (1) and (2) of this section.

§ 2520. Recovery of civil damages authorized

(a) In general.—Except as provided in section 2511(2)(a)(ii), any person whose wire, oral, or electronic communication is intercepted, disclosed, or intentionally used in violation of this chapter may in a civil action recover from the person or entity, other than the United States, which engaged in that violation such relief as may be appropriate.

(b) Relief.—In an action under this section, appropriate relief includes—

(1) such preliminary and other equitable or declaratory relief as may be appropriate;

(2) damages under subsection (c) and punitive damages in appropriate cases; and

(3) a reasonable attorney's fee and other litigation costs reasonably incurred.

(c) Computation of damages.—(1) In an action under this section, if the conduct in violation of this chapter is the private viewing of a private satellite video communication that is not scrambled or encrypted or if the communication is a radio communication that is transmitted on frequencies allocated under subpart D of part 74 of the rules of the Federal Communications Commission that is not scrambled or encrypted and the conduct is not for a tortious or illegal purpose or for purposes of direct or indirect commercial advantage or private commercial gain, then the court shall assess damages as follows:

(A) If the person who engaged in that conduct has not previously been enjoined under section 2511(5) and has not been found liable in a prior civil action under this section, the court shall assess the greater of the sum of actual damages suffered by the plaintiff, or statutory damages of not less than $50 and not more than $500.

(B) If, on one prior occasion, the person who engaged in that conduct has been enjoined under section 2511(5) or has been found liable in a civil action under this section, the court shall assess the greater of the sum of actual damages suffered by the plaintiff, or statutory damages of not less than $100 and not more than $1000.

(2) In any other action under this section, the court may assess as damages whichever is the greater of—

(A) the sum of the actual damages suffered by the plaintiff and any profits made by the violator as a result of the violation; or

(B) statutory damages of whichever is the greater of $100 a day for each day of violation or $10,000.

(d) Defense.—A good faith reliance on—

(1) a court warrant or order, a grand jury subpoena, a legislative authorization, or a statutory authorization;

(2) a request of an investigative or law enforcement officer under section 2518(7) of this title; or

(3) a good faith determination that section 2511(3) or 2511(2)(i) of this title permitted the conduct complained of;

is a complete defense against any civil or criminal action brought under this chapter or any other law.

(e) Limitation.—A civil action under this section may not be commenced later than two years after the date upon which the claimant first has a reasonable opportunity to discover the violation.

(f) Administrative discipline.—If a court or appropriate department or agency determines that the United States or any of its departments or agencies has violated any provision of this chapter, and the court or appropriate department or agency finds that the circumstances surrounding the violation raise serious questions about whether or not an officer or employee of the United States acted willfully or intentionally with respect to the violation, the department or agency shall, upon receipt of a true and correct copy of the decision and findings of the court or appropriate department or agency promptly initiate a proceeding to determine whether disciplinary action against the officer or employee is warranted. If the head of the department or agency involved determines that disciplinary action is not warranted, he or she shall notify the Inspector General with jurisdiction over the department or agency concerned and shall provide the Inspector General with the reasons for such determination.

(g) Improper disclosure is violation.—Any willful disclosure or use by an investigative or law enforcement officer or governmental entity of information beyond the extent permitted by section 2517 is a violation of this chapter for purposes of section 2520(a).

§ 2521. Injunction against illegal interception

Whenever it shall appear that any person is engaged or is about to engage in any act which constitutes or will constitute a felony violation of this chapter, the Attorney General may initiate a civil action in a district court of the United States to enjoin such violation. The court shall proceed as soon as practicable to the hearing and determination of such an action, and may, at any time before final determination, enter such a restraining order or prohibition, or take such other action, as is warranted to prevent a continuing and substantial injury to the United States or to any person or class of persons for whose protection the action is brought. A proceeding under this section is governed by the Federal Rules of Civil Procedure, except that, if an indictment has been returned against the respondent, discovery is governed by the Federal Rules of Criminal Procedure.

§ 2522. Enforcement of the Communications Assistance for Law Enforcement Act

(a) Enforcement by court issuing surveillance order.—If a court authorizing an interception under this chapter, a State statute, or the Foreign Intelligence Surveillance Act of 1978 (50 U.S.C. 1801 et seq.) or authorizing use of a pen register or a trap and trace device under chapter 206 or a State statute finds that a telecommunications carrier has failed to comply with the requirements of the Communications Assistance for Law Enforcement Act, the court may, in accordance with section 108 of such Act, direct that the carrier comply forthwith and may direct that a provider of support services to the carrier or the manufacturer of the carrier's transmission or switching equipment furnish forthwith modifications necessary for the carrier to comply.

(b) Enforcement upon application by Attorney General.—The Attorney General may, in a civil action in the appropriate United States district court, obtain an order, in accordance with section 108 of the Communications Assistance for Law Enforcement Act, directing that a telecommunications carrier, a manufacturer of telecommunications transmission or switching equipment, or a provider of telecommunications support services comply with such Act.

(c) Civil penalty.—

(1) In general.—A court issuing an order under this section against a telecommunications carrier, a manufacturer of telecommunications transmission or switching equipment, or a provider of telecommunications support services may impose a civil penalty of up to $10,000 per day for each day in violation after the issuance of the order or after such future date as the court may specify.

(2) Considerations.—In determining whether to impose a civil penalty and in determining its amount, the court shall take into account—

(A) the nature, circumstances, and extent of the violation;

(B) the violator's ability to pay, the violator's good faith efforts to comply in a timely manner, any effect on the violator's ability to continue to do business, the degree of culpability, and the length of any delay in undertaking efforts to comply; and

(C) such other matters as justice may require.

(d) Definitions.—As used in this section, the terms defined in section 102 of the Communications Assistance for Law Enforcement Act have the meanings provided, respectively, in such section.

Stored Communications Act
18 U.S.C. §§ 2710-2712

§ 2701. Unlawful access to stored communications

(a) Offense.—Except as provided in subsection (c) of this section whoever—

(1) intentionally accesses without authorization a facility through which an electronic communication service is provided; or

(2) intentionally exceeds an authorization to access that facility;

and thereby obtains, alters, or prevents authorized access to a wire or electronic communication while it is in electronic storage in such system shall be punished as provided in subsection (b) of this section.

(b) Punishment.—The punishment for an offense under subsection (a) of this section is—

(1) if the offense is committed for purposes of commercial advantage, malicious destruction or damage, or private commercial gain, or in furtherance of any criminal or tortious act in violation of the Constitution or laws of the United States or any State—

(A) a fine under this title or imprisonment for not more than 5 years, or both, in the case of a first offense under this subparagraph; and

(B) a fine under this title or imprisonment for not more than 10 years, or both, for any subsequent offense under this subparagraph; and

(2) in any other case—

(A) a fine under this title or imprisonment for not more than 1 year or both, in the case of a first offense under this paragraph; and

(B) a fine under this title or imprisonment for not more than 5 years, or both, in the case of an offense under this subparagraph that occurs after a conviction of another offense under this section.

(c) Exceptions.—Subsection (a) of this section does not apply with respect to conduct authorized—

(1) by the person or entity providing a wire or electronic communications service;

(2) by a user of that service with respect to a communication of or intended for that user; or

(3) in section 2703, 2704 or 2518 of this title.

§ 2702. Voluntary disclosure of customer communications or records

(a) Prohibitions.—Except as provided in subsection (b) or (c)—

(1) a person or entity providing an electronic communication service to the public shall not knowingly divulge to any person or entity the contents of a communication while in electronic storage by that service; and

(2) a person or entity providing remote computing service to the public shall not knowingly divulge to any person or entity the contents of any communication which is carried or maintained on that service—

(A) on behalf of, and received by means of electronic transmission from (or created by means of computer processing of communications received by means of electronic transmission from), a subscriber or customer of such service;

(B) solely for the purpose of providing storage or computer processing services to such subscriber or customer, if the provider is not authorized to access the contents of any such communications for purposes of providing any services other than storage or computer processing; and

(3) a provider of remote computing service or electronic communication service to the public shall not knowingly divulge a record or other information pertaining to a subscriber to or customer of such service (not including the contents of communications covered by paragraph (1) or (2)) to any governmental entity.

(b) Exceptions for disclosure of communications.— A provider described in subsection (a) may divulge the contents of a communication—

(1) to an addressee or intended recipient of such communication or an agent of such addressee or intended recipient;

(2) as otherwise authorized in section 2517, 2511(2)(a), or 2703 of this title;

(3) with the lawful consent of the originator or an addressee or intended recipient of such communication, or the subscriber in the case of remote computing service;

(4) to a person employed or authorized or whose facilities are used to forward such communication to its destination;

(5) as may be necessarily incident to the rendition of the service or to the protection of the rights or property of the provider of that service;

(6) to the National Center for Missing and Exploited Children, in connection with a report submitted thereto under section 227 of the Victims of Child Abuse Act of 1990 (42 U.S.C. 13032);

(7) to a law enforcement agency—

(A) if the contents—

(i) were inadvertently obtained by the service provider; and

(ii) appear to pertain to the commission of a crime; or

[**(B)** Repealed. Pub.L. 108-21, Title V, § 508(b)(1)(A), Apr. 30, 2003, 117 Stat. 684]

[**(C)** Repealed. Pub.L. 107-296, Title II, § 225(d)(1)(C), Nov. 25, 2002, 116 Stat. 2157]

(8) to a governmental entity, if the provider, in good faith, believes that an emergency involving danger of death or serious physical injury to any person requires disclosure without delay of communications relating to the emergency.

(c) Exceptions for disclosure of customer records.—A provider described in subsection (a) may divulge a record or other information pertaining to a subscriber to or customer of such service (not including the contents of communications covered by subsection (a)(1) or (a)(2))—

(1) as otherwise authorized in section 2703;

(2) with the lawful consent of the customer or subscriber;

(3) as may be necessarily incident to the rendition of the service or to the protection of the rights or property of the provider of that service;

(4) to a governmental entity, if the provider, in good faith, believes that an emergency involving danger of death or serious physical injury to any person requires disclosure without delay of information relating to the emergency;

(5) to the National Center for Missing and Exploited Children, in connection with a report submitted thereto under section 227 of the Victims of Child Abuse Act of 1990 (42 U.S.C. 13032); or

(6) to any person other than a governmental entity.

(d) Reporting of emergency disclosures.—On an annual basis, the Attorney General shall submit to the Committee on the Judiciary of the House of Representatives and the Committee on the Judiciary of the Senate a report containing—

(1) the number of accounts from which the Department of Justice has received voluntary disclosures under subsection (b)(8); and

(2) a summary of the basis for disclosure in those instances where—

(A) voluntary disclosures under subsection (b)(8) were made to the Department of Justice; and

(B) the investigation pertaining to those disclosures was closed without the filing of criminal charges.

§ 2703. Required disclosure of customer communications or records

(a) Contents of wire or electronic communications in electronic storage.—A governmental entity may require the disclosure by a provider of electronic communication service of the contents of a wire or electronic communication, that is in electronic storage in an electronic communications system for one hundred and eighty days or less, only pursuant to a warrant issued using the procedures described in the Federal Rules of Criminal Procedure by a court with jurisdiction over the offense under investigation or equivalent State warrant. A governmental entity may require the disclosure by a provider of electronic communications services of the contents of a wire or electronic communication that has been in electronic storage in an electronic communications system for more than one hundred and eighty days by the means available under subsection (b) of this section.

(b) Contents of wire or electronic communications in a remote computing service.—(1) A governmental entity may require a provider of remote computing service to disclose the contents of any wire or electronic communication to which this paragraph is made applicable by paragraph (2) of this subsection—

(A) without required notice to the subscriber or customer, if the governmental entity obtains a warrant issued using the procedures described in the Federal Rules of Criminal Procedure by a court with jurisdiction over the offense under investigation or equivalent State warrant; or

(B) with prior notice from the governmental entity to the subscriber or customer if the governmental entity—

(i) uses an administrative subpoena authorized by a Federal or State statute or a Federal or State grand jury or trial subpoena; or

(ii) obtains a court order for such disclosure under subsection (d) of this section;

except that delayed notice may be given pursuant to section 2705 of this title.

(2) Paragraph (1) is applicable with respect to any wire or electronic communication that is held or maintained on that service—

(A) on behalf of, and received by means of electronic transmission from (or created by means of computer processing of communications received by means of electronic transmission from), a subscriber or customer of such remote computing service; and

(B) solely for the purpose of providing storage or computer processing services to such subscriber or customer, if the provider is not authorized to access the contents of any such communications for purposes of providing any services other than storage or computer processing.

(c) Records concerning electronic communication service or remote computing service.—(1) A governmental entity may require a provider of electronic communication service or remote computing service to disclose a record or other information pertaining to a subscriber to or customer of such service (not including the contents of communications) only when the governmental entity—

(A) obtains a warrant issued using the procedures described in the Federal Rules of Criminal Procedure by a court with jurisdiction over the offense under investigation or equivalent State warrant;

(B) obtains a court order for such disclosure under subsection (d) of this section;

(C) has the consent of the subscriber or customer to such disclosure;

(D) submits a formal written request relevant to a law enforcement investigation concerning telemarketing fraud for the name, address, and place of business of a subscriber or customer of such provider, which subscriber or customer is engaged in telemarketing (as such term is defined in section 2325 of this title); or

(E) seeks information under paragraph (2).

(2) A provider of electronic communication service or remote computing service shall disclose to a governmental entity the—

(A) name;

(B) address;

(C) local and long distance telephone connection records, or records of session times and durations;

(D) length of service (including start date) and types of service utilized;

(E) telephone or instrument number or other subscriber number or identity, including any temporarily assigned network address; and

(F) means and source of payment for such service (including any credit card or bank account number), of a subscriber to or customer of such service when the governmental entity uses an administrative subpoena authorized by a Federal or State statute or a Federal or State grand jury or trial subpoena or any means available under paragraph (1).

(3) A governmental entity receiving records or information under this subsection is not required to provide notice to a subscriber or customer.

(d) Requirements for court order.—A court order for disclosure under subsection (b) or (c) may be issued by any court that is a court of competent jurisdiction and shall issue only if the governmental entity offers specific and articulable facts showing that there are reasonable grounds to believe that the contents of a wire or electronic communication, or the records or other information sought, are relevant and material to an ongoing criminal investigation. In the case of a State governmental authority, such a court order shall not issue if prohibited by the law of such State. A court issuing an order pursuant to this section, on a motion made promptly by the service provider, may quash or modify such order, if the information or records requested are unusually voluminous in nature or compliance with such order otherwise would cause an undue burden on such provider.

(e) No cause of action against a provider disclosing information under this chapter.—No cause of action shall lie in any court against any provider of wire or electronic communication service, its officers, employees, agents, or other specified persons for providing information, facilities, or assistance in accordance with the terms of a court order, warrant, subpoena, statutory authorization, or certification under this chapter.

(f) Requirement to preserve evidence.—

(1) In general.—A provider of wire or electronic communication services or a remote computing service, upon the request of a governmental entity, shall take all necessary steps to preserve records and other evidence in its possession pending the issuance of a court order or other process.

(2) Period of retention.—Records referred to in paragraph (1) shall be retained for a period of 90 days, which shall be extended for an additional 90- day period upon a renewed request by the governmental entity.

(g) Presence of officer not required.—Notwithstanding section 3105 of this title, the presence of an officer shall not be required for service or execution of a search warrant issued in accordance with this chapter requiring disclosure by a provider of electronic communications service or remote computing service of the contents of communications or records or other information pertaining to a subscriber to or customer of such service.

§ 2704. Backup preservation

(a) Backup preservation.—(1) A governmental entity acting under section 2703(b)(2) may include in its subpoena or court order a requirement that the service provider to whom the request is directed create a backup copy of the contents of the electronic communications sought in order to preserve those communications. Without notifying the subscriber or customer of such subpoena or court order, such service provider shall create such backup copy as soon as practicable consistent with its regular business practices and shall confirm to the governmental entity that such backup copy has been made. Such backup copy shall be created within two business days after receipt by the service provider of the subpoena or court order.

(2) Notice to the subscriber or customer shall be made by the governmental entity within three days after receipt of such confirmation, unless such notice is delayed pursuant to section 2705(a).

(3) The service provider shall not destroy such backup copy until the later of—

(A) the delivery of the information; or

(B) the resolution of any proceedings (including appeals of any proceeding) concerning the government's subpoena or court order.

(4) The service provider shall release such backup copy to the requesting governmental entity no sooner than fourteen days after the governmental entity's notice to the subscriber or customer if such service provider—

(A) has not received notice from the subscriber or customer that the subscriber or customer has challenged the governmental entity's request; and

(B) has not initiated proceedings to challenge the request of the governmental entity.

(5) A governmental entity may seek to require the creation of a backup copy under subsection (a)(1) of this section if in its sole discretion such entity determines that there is reason to believe that notification under section 2703 of this title of the existence of the subpoena or court order may result in destruction of or tampering with evidence. This determination is not subject to challenge by the subscriber or customer or service provider.

(b) Customer challenges.—(1) Within fourteen days after notice by the governmental entity to the subscriber or customer under subsection (a)(2) of this section, such subscriber or customer may file a motion to quash such subpoena or vacate such court order, with copies served upon the governmental entity and with written notice of such challenge to the service provider. A motion to vacate a court order shall be filed in the court which issued such order. A motion to quash a subpoena shall be filed in the appropriate United States district court or State court. Such motion or application shall contain an affidavit or sworn statement—

(A) stating that the applicant is a customer or subscriber to the service from which the contents of electronic communications maintained for him have been sought; and

(B) stating the applicant's reasons for believing that the records sought are not relevant to a legitimate law enforcement inquiry or that there has not been substantial compliance with the provisions of this chapter in some other respect.

(2) Service shall be made under this section upon a governmental entity by delivering or mailing by registered or certified mail a copy of the papers to the person, office, or department specified in the notice which the customer has received pursuant to this chapter. For the purposes of this section, the term "delivery" has the meaning given that term in the Federal Rules of Civil Procedure.

(3) If the court finds that the customer has complied with paragraphs (1) and (2) of this subsection, the court shall order the governmental entity to file a sworn response, which may be filed in camera if the governmental entity includes in its response the reasons which make in camera review appropriate. If the court is unable to determine the motion or application on the basis of the parties' initial allegations and response, the court may conduct such additional proceedings as it deems appropriate. All such proceedings shall be completed and the motion or application decided as soon as practicable after the filing of the governmental entity's response.

(4) If the court finds that the applicant is not the subscriber or customer for whom the communications sought by the governmental entity are maintained, or that there is a reason to believe that the law enforcement inquiry is legitimate and that the communications sought are relevant to that inquiry, it shall deny the motion or application and order such process enforced. If the court finds that the applicant is the subscriber or customer for whom the communications sought by the governmental entity are maintained, and that there is not a reason to believe that the communications sought are relevant to a legitimate law enforcement inquiry, or that there has not been substantial compliance with the provisions of this chapter, it shall order the process quashed.

(5) A court order denying a motion or application under this section shall not be deemed a final order and no interlocutory appeal may be taken therefrom by the customer.

§ 2705. Delayed notice

(a) Delay of notification.—(1) A governmental entity acting under section 2703(b) of this title may—

(A) where a court order is sought, include in the application a request, which the court shall grant, for an order delaying the notification required under section 2703(b) of this title for a period not to exceed ninety days, if the court determines that there is reason to believe that notification of the existence of the court order may have an adverse result described in paragraph (2) of this subsection; or

(B) where an administrative subpoena authorized by a Federal or State statute or a Federal or State grand jury subpoena is obtained, delay the notification required under section 2703(b) of this title for a period not to exceed ninety days upon the execution of a written certification of a supervisory official that there is reason to believe that notification of the existence of the subpoena may have an adverse result described in paragraph (2) of this subsection.

(2) An adverse result for the purposes of paragraph (1) of this subsection is—

(A) endangering the life or physical safety of an individual;

(B) flight from prosecution;

(C) destruction of or tampering with evidence;

(D) intimidation of potential witnesses; or

(E) otherwise seriously jeopardizing an investigation or unduly delaying a trial.

(3) The governmental entity shall maintain a true copy of certification under paragraph (1)(B).

(4) Extensions of the delay of notification provided in section 2703 of up to ninety days each may be granted by the court upon application, or by certification by a governmental entity, but only in accordance with subsection (b) of this section.

(5) Upon expiration of the period of delay of notification under paragraph (1) or (4) of this subsection, the governmental entity shall serve upon, or deliver by registered or first-class mail to, the customer or subscriber a copy of the process or request together with notice that—

(A) states with reasonable specificity the nature of the law enforcement inquiry; and

(B) informs such customer or subscriber—

(i) that information maintained for such customer or subscriber by the service provider named in such process or request was supplied to or requested by that governmental authority and the date on which the supplying or request took place;

(ii) that notification of such customer or subscriber was delayed;

(iii) what governmental entity or court made the certification or determination pursuant to which that delay was made; and

(iv) which provision of this chapter allowed such delay.

(6) As used in this subsection, the term "supervisory official" means the investigative agent in charge or assistant investigative agent in charge or an equivalent of an investigating agency's headquarters or regional office, or the chief prosecuting attorney or the first assistant prosecuting attorney or an equivalent of a prosecuting attorney's headquarters or regional office.

(b) Preclusion of notice to subject of governmental access.—A governmental entity acting under section 2703, when it is not required to notify the subscriber or customer under section 2703(b)(1), or to the extent that it may delay such notice pursuant to subsection (a) of this section, may apply to a court for an order commanding a provider of electronic communications service or remote computing service to whom a warrant, subpoena, or court order is directed, for such period as the court deems appropriate, not to notify any other person of the existence of the warrant, subpoena, or court order. The court shall enter such an order if it determines that there is reason to believe that notification of the existence of the warrant, subpoena, or court order will result in—

(1) endangering the life or physical safety of an individual;

(2) flight from prosecution;

(3) destruction of or tampering with evidence;

(4) intimidation of potential witnesses; or

(5) otherwise seriously jeopardizing an investigation or unduly delaying a trial.

§ 2706. Cost reimbursement

(a) Payment.—Except as otherwise provided in subsection (c), a governmental entity obtaining the contents of communications, records, or other information under section 2702, 2703, or 2704 of this title shall pay to the person or entity assembling or providing such information a fee for reimbursement for such costs as are reasonably necessary and which have been directly incurred in searching for, assembling, reproducing, or otherwise providing such information. Such reimbursable costs shall include any costs due to necessary disruption of normal operations of any electronic communication service or remote computing service in which such information may be stored.

(b) Amount.—The amount of the fee provided by subsection (a) shall be as mutually agreed by the governmental entity and the person or entity providing the information, or, in the absence of agreement, shall be as determined by the court which issued the order for production of such information (or the court before which a criminal prosecution relating to such information would be brought, if no court order was issued for production of the information).

(c) Exception.— The requirement of subsection (a) of this section does not apply with respect to records or other information maintained by a communications common carrier that relate to telephone toll records and telephone listings obtained under section 2703 of this title. The court may, however, order a payment as described in subsection (a) if the court determines the information required is unusually voluminous in nature or otherwise caused an undue burden on the provider.

§ 2707. Civil action

(a) Cause of action.—Except as provided in section 2703(e), any provider of electronic communication service, subscriber, or other person aggrieved by any violation of this chapter in which the conduct constituting the violation is engaged in with a knowing or intentional state of mind may, in a civil action, recover from the person or entity, other than the United States, which engaged in that violation such relief as may be appropriate.

(b) Relief.—In a civil action under this section, appropriate relief includes—

(1) such preliminary and other equitable or declaratory relief as may be appropriate;

(2) damages under subsection (c); and

(3) a reasonable attorney's fee and other litigation costs reasonably incurred.

(c) Damages.—The court may assess as damages in a civil action under this section the sum of the actual damages suffered by the plaintiff and any profits made by the violator as a result of the violation, but in no case shall a person entitled to recover receive less than the sum of $1,000. If the violation is willful or intentional, the court may assess punitive damages. In the case of a successful action to enforce liability under this section, the court may assess the costs of the action, together with reasonable attorney fees determined by the court.

(d) Administrative discipline.—If a court or appropriate department or agency determines that the United States or any of its departments or agencies has violated any provision of this chapter, and the court or appropriate department or agency finds that the circumstances surrounding the violation raise serious questions about whether or not an officer or employee of the United States acted willfully or intentionally with respect to the violation, the department or agency shall, upon receipt of a true and correct copy of the decision and findings of the court or appropriate department or agency promptly initiate a proceeding to determine whether disciplinary action against the officer or employee is warranted. If the head of the department or agency involved determines that disciplinary action is not warranted, he or she shall notify the Inspector General with jurisdiction over the department or agency concerned and shall provide the Inspector General with the reasons for such determination.

(e) Defense.—A good faith reliance on—

(1) a court warrant or order, a grand jury subpoena, a legislative authorization, or a statutory authorization (including a request of a governmental entity under section 2703(f) of this title);

(2) a request of an investigative or law enforcement officer under section 2518(7) of this title; or

(3) a good faith determination that section 2511(3) of this title permitted the conduct complained of;

is a complete defense to any civil or criminal action brought under this chapter or any other law.

(f) Limitation.—A civil action under this section may not be commenced later than two years after the date upon which the claimant first discovered or had a reasonable opportunity to discover the violation.

(g) Improper disclosure.—Any willful disclosure of a 'record', as that term is defined in section 552a(a) of title 5, United States Code, obtained by an investigative or law enforcement officer, or a governmental entity, pursuant to section 2703 of this title, or from a device installed pursuant to section 3123 or 3125 of this title, that is not a disclosure made in the proper performance of the official functions of the officer or governmental entity making the disclosure, is a violation of this chapter. This provision shall not apply to information previously lawfully disclosed (prior to the commencement of any civil or administrative proceeding under this chapter) to the public by a Federal, State, or local governmental entity or by the plaintiff in a civil action under this chapter.

§ 2708. Exclusivity of remedies

The remedies and sanctions described in this chapter are the only judicial remedies and sanctions for nonconstitutional violations of this chapter.

§ 2709. Counterintelligence access to telephone toll and transactional records

(a) Duty to provide.—A wire or electronic communication service provider shall comply with a request for subscriber information and toll billing records information, or electronic communication transactional records in its custody or possession made by the Director of the Federal Bureau of Investigation under subsection (b) of this section.

(b) Required certification.—The Director of the Federal Bureau of Investigation, or his designee in a position not lower than Deputy Assistant Director at Bureau headquarters or a Special Agent in Charge in a Bureau field office designated by the Director, may—

(1) request the name, address, length of service, and local and long distance toll billing records of a person or entity if the Director (or his designee) certifies in writing to the wire or electronic communication service provider to which the request is made that the name, address, length of service, and toll billing records sought are relevant to an authorized investigation to protect against international terrorism or clandestine intelligence activities, provided that such an investigation of a United States person is not conducted solely on the basis of activities protected by the first amendment to the Constitution of the United States; and

(2) request the name, address, and length of service of a person or entity if the Director (or his designee) certifies in writing to the wire or electronic communication service provider to which the request is made that the information sought is relevant to an authorized investigation to protect against international terrorism or clandestine intelligence activities, provided that such an investigation of a United States person is not conducted solely upon the basis of activities protected by the first amendment to the Constitution of the United States.

(c) Prohibition of certain disclosure.—

(1) If the Director of the Federal Bureau of Investigation, or his designee in a position not lower than Deputy Assistant Director at Bureau headquarters or a Special Agent in Charge in a Bureau field office designated by the Director, certifies that otherwise there may result a danger to the national security of the United States, interference with a criminal, counterterrorism, or counterintelligence investigation, interference with diplomatic relations, or danger to the life or physical safety of any person, no wire or electronic communications service provider, or officer, employee, or agent thereof, shall disclose to any person (other than those to whom such disclosure is necessary to comply with the request or an attorney to obtain legal advice or legal assistance with respect to the request) that the Federal Bureau of Investigation has sought or obtained access to information or records under this section.

(2) The request shall notify the person or entity to whom the request is directed of the nondisclosure requirement under paragraph (1).

(3) Any recipient disclosing to those persons necessary to comply with the request or to an attorney to obtain legal advice or legal assistance with respect to the request shall inform such person of any applicable nondisclosure requirement. Any person who receives a disclosure under this subsection shall be subject to the same prohibitions on disclosure under paragraph (1).

(4) At the request of the Director of the Federal Bureau of Investigation or the designee of the Director, any person making or intending to make a disclosure under this section shall identify to the Director or such designee the person to whom such disclosure will be made or to whom such disclosure was made prior to the request, except that nothing in this section shall require a person to inform the Director or such designee of the identity of an attorney to whom disclosure was made or will be made to obtain legal advice or legal assistance with respect to the request under subsection (a).

(d) Dissemination by bureau.—The Federal Bureau of Investigation may disseminate information and records obtained under this section only as provided in guidelines approved by the Attorney General for foreign intelligence collection and foreign counterintelligence investigations conducted by the Federal Bureau of Investigation, and, with respect to dissemination to an agency of the United States, only if such information is clearly relevant to the authorized responsibilities of such agency.

(e) Requirement that certain congressional bodies be informed.—On a semiannual basis the Director of the Federal Bureau of Investigation shall fully inform the Permanent Select Committee on Intelligence of the House of Representatives and the Select Committee on Intelligence of the Senate, and the Committee on the Judiciary of the House of Representatives and the Committee on the Judiciary of the Senate, concerning all requests made under subsection (b) of this section.

(f) Libraries.—A library (as that term is defined in section 213(1) of the Library Services and Technology Act (20 U.S.C. 9122(1)), the services of which include access to the Internet, books, journals, magazines, newspapers, or other similar forms of communication in print or digitally by patrons for their use, review, examination, or circulation, is not a wire or electronic communication service provider for purposes of this section, unless the library is providing the services defined in section 2510(15) ("electronic communication service") of this title.

§ 2710 – [Editorial Note: This section is the Video Privacy Protection Act. See Chapter 7 in this compilation for the text of the Act.]

§ 2711. Definitions for chapter

As used in this chapter—

(1) the terms defined in section 2510 of this title have, respectively, the definitions given such terms in that section;

(2) the term "remote computing service" means the provision to the public of computer storage or processing services by means of an electronic communications system;

(3) the term "court of competent jurisdiction" has the meaning assigned by section 3127, and includes any Federal court within that definition, without geographic limitation; and

(4) the term "governmental entity" means a department or agency of the United States or any State or political subdivision thereof.

§ 2712. Civil actions against the United States

(a) In general.—Any person who is aggrieved by any willful violation of this chapter or of chapter 119 of this title or of sections 106(a), 305(a), or 405(a) of the Foreign Intelligence Surveillance Act of 1978 (50 U. S.C. 1801 et seq.) may commence an action in United States District Court against the United States to recover money damages. In any such action, if a person who is aggrieved successfully establishes such a violation of this chapter or of chapter 119 of this title or of the above specific provisions of title 50, the Court may assess as damages—

(1) actual damages, but not less than $10,000, whichever amount is greater; and

(2) litigation costs, reasonably incurred.

(b) Procedures.—(1) Any action against the United States under this section may be commenced only after a claim is presented to the appropriate department or agency under the procedures of the Federal Tort Claims Act, as set forth in title 28, United States Code.

(2) Any action against the United States under this section shall be forever barred unless it is presented in writing to the appropriate Federal agency within 2 years after such claim accrues or unless action is begun within 6 months after the date of mailing, by certified or registered mail, of notice of final denial of the claim by the agency to which it was presented. The claim shall accrue on the date upon which the claimant first has a reasonable opportunity to discover the violation.

(3) Any action under this section shall be tried to the court without a jury.

(4) Notwithstanding any other provision of law, the procedures set forth in section 106(f), 305(g), or 405(f) of the Foreign Intelligence Surveillance Act of 1978 (50 U.S.C. 1801 et seq.) shall be the exclusive means by which materials governed by those sections may be reviewed.

(5) An amount equal to any award against the United States under this section shall be reimbursed by the department or agency concerned to the fund described in section 1304 of title 31, United States Code, out of any appropriation, fund, or other account (excluding any part of such appropriation, fund, or account that is available for the enforcement of any Federal law) that is available for the operating expenses of the department or agency concerned.

(c) Administrative discipline.—If a court or appropriate department or agency determines that the United States or any of its departments or agencies has violated any provision of this chapter, and the court or appropriate department or agency finds that the circumstances surrounding the violation raise serious questions about whether or not an officer or employee of the United States acted willfully or intentionally with respect to the violation, the department or agency shall, upon receipt of a true and correct copy of the decision and findings of the court or appropriate department or agency promptly initiate a proceeding to determine whether disciplinary action against the officer or employee is warranted. If the head of the department or agency involved determines that disciplinary action is not warranted, he or she shall notify the Inspector General with jurisdiction over the department or agency concerned and shall provide the Inspector General with the reasons for such determination.

(d) Exclusive remedy.—Any action against the United States under this subsection shall be the exclusive remedy against the United States for any claims within the purview of this section.

(e) Stay of proceedings.—(1) Upon the motion of the United States, the court shall stay any action commenced under this section if the court determines that civil discovery will adversely affect the ability of the Government to conduct a related investigation or the prosecution of a related criminal case. Such a stay shall toll the limitations periods of paragraph (2) of subsection (b).

(2) In this subsection, the terms "related criminal case" and "related investigation" mean an actual prosecution or investigation in progress at the time at which the request for the stay or any subsequent motion to lift the stay is made. In determining whether an investigation or a criminal case is related to an action commenced under this section, the court shall consider the degree of similarity between the parties, witnesses, facts, and circumstances involved in the 2 proceedings, without requiring that any one or more factors be identical.

(3) In requesting a stay under paragraph (1), the Government may, in appropriate cases, submit evidence ex parte in order to avoid disclosing any matter that may adversely affect a related investigation or a related criminal case. If the Government makes such an ex parte submission, the plaintiff shall be given an opportunity to make a submission to the court, not ex parte, and the court may, in its discretion, request further information from either party.

Pen Register Act
18 U.S.C. § 3121-3123

§ 3121. General prohibition on pen register and trap and trace device use; exception

(a) In general.—Except as provided in this section, no person may install or use a pen register or a trap and trace device without first obtaining a court order under section 3123 of this title or under the Foreign Intelligence Surveillance Act of 1978 (50 U.S.C. 1801 et seq.).

(b) Exception.—The prohibition of subsection (a) does not apply with respect to the use of a pen register or a trap and trace device by a provider of electronic or wire communication service—

> **(1)** relating to the operation, maintenance, and testing of a wire or electronic communication service or to the protection of the rights or property of such provider, or to the protection of users of that service from abuse of service or unlawful use of service; or
>
> **(2)** to record the fact that a wire or electronic communication was initiated or completed in order to protect such provider, another provider furnishing service toward the completion of the wire communication, or a user of that service, from fraudulent, unlawful or abusive use of service; or (3) where the consent of the user of that service has been obtained.

(c) Limitation.—A government agency authorized to install and use a pen register or trap and trace device under this chapter or under State law shall use technology reasonably available to it that restricts the recording or decoding of electronic or other impulses to the dialing, routing, addressing, and signaling information utilized in the processing and transmitting of wire or electronic communications so as not to include the contents of any wire or electronic communications.

(d) Penalty.—Whoever knowingly violates subsection (a) shall be fined under this title or imprisoned not more than one year, or both.

§ 3122. Application for an order for a pen register or a trap and trace device

(a) Application.—(1) An attorney for the Government may make application for an order or an extension of an order under section 3123 of this title authorizing or approving the installation and use of a pen register or a trap and trace device under this chapter, in writing under oath or equivalent affirmation, to a court of competent jurisdiction.

(2) Unless prohibited by State law, a State investigative or law enforcement officer may make application for an order or an extension of an order under section 3123 of this title authorizing or approving the installation and use of a pen register or a trap and trace device under this chapter, in writing under oath or equivalent affirmation, to a court of competent jurisdiction of such State.

(b) Contents of application.—An application under subsection (a) of this section shall include—

(1) the identity of the attorney for the Government or the State law enforcement or investigative officer making the application and the identity of the law enforcement agency conducting the investigation; and

(2) a certification by the applicant that the information likely to be obtained is relevant to an ongoing criminal investigation being conducted by that agency.

§ 3123. Issuance of an order for a pen register or a trap and trace device

(a) In general.—

(1) Attorney for the Government.—Upon an application made under section 3122(a)(1), the court shall enter an ex parte order authorizing the installation and use of a pen register or trap and trace device anywhere within the United States, if the court finds that the attorney for the Government has certified to the court that the information likely to be obtained by such installation and use is relevant to an ongoing criminal investigation. The order, upon service of that order, shall apply to any person or entity providing wire or electronic communication service in the United States whose assistance may facilitate the execution of the order. Whenever such an order is served on any person or entity not specifically named in the order, upon request of such person or entity, the attorney for the Government or law enforcement or investigative officer that is serving the order shall provide written or electronic certification that the order applies to the person or entity being served.

(2) State investigative or law enforcement officer.—Upon an application made under section 3122(a)(2), the court shall enter an ex parte order authorizing the installation and use of a pen register or trap and trace device within the jurisdiction of the court, if the court finds that the State law enforcement or investigative officer has certified to the court that the information likely to be obtained by such installation and use is relevant to an ongoing criminal investigation.

(3)(A) Where the law enforcement agency implementing an ex parte order under this subsection seeks to do so by installing and using its own pen register or trap and trace device on a packet-switched data network of a provider of electronic communication service to the public, the agency shall ensure that a record will be maintained which will identify—

(i) any officer or officers who installed the device and any officer or officers who accessed the device to obtain information from the network;

(ii) the date and time the device was installed, the date and time the device was uninstalled, and the date, time, and duration of each time the device is accessed to obtain information;

(iii) the configuration of the device at the time of its installation and any subsequent modification thereof; and

(iv) any information which has been collected by the device.

To the extent that the pen register or trap and trace device can be set automatically to record this information electronically, the record shall be maintained electronically throughout the installation and use of such device.

(B) The record maintained under subparagraph (A) shall be provided ex parte and under seal to the court which entered the ex parte order authorizing the installation and use of the device within 30 days after termination of the order (including any extensions thereof).

(b) Contents of order.—An order issued under this section—

(1) shall specify—
(A) the identity, if known, of the person to whom is leased or in whose name is listed the telephone line or other facility to which the pen register or trap and trace device is to be attached or applied;

(B) the identity, if known, of the person who is the subject of the criminal investigation;

(C) the attributes of the communications to which the order applies, including the number or other identifier and, if known, the location of the telephone line or other facility to which the pen register or trap and trace device is to be attached or applied, and, in the case of an order authorizing installation and use of a trap and trace device under subsection (a)(2), the geographic limits of the order; and".

(D) a statement of the offense to which the information likely to be obtained by the pen register or trap and trace device relates; and

(2) shall direct, upon the request of the applicant, the furnishing of information, facilities, and technical assistance necessary to accomplish the installation of the pen register or trap and trace device under section 3124 of this title.

(c) Time period and extensions.—(1) An order issued under this section shall authorize the installation and use of a pen register or a trap and trace device for a period not to exceed sixty days.

(2) Extensions of such an order may be granted, but only upon an application for an order under section 3122 of this title and upon the judicial finding required by subsection (a) of this section. The period of extension shall be for a period not to exceed sixty days.

(d) Nondisclosure of existence of pen register or a trap and trace device.—An order authorizing or approving the installation and use of a pen register or a trap and trace device shall direct that—

(1) the order be sealed until otherwise ordered by the court; and

(2) the person owning or leasing the line or other facility to which the pen register or a trap and trace device is attached, or applied, or who is obligated by the order to provide assistance to the applicant, not disclose the existence of the pen register or trap and trace device or the existence of the investigation to the listed subscriber, or to any other person, unless or until otherwise ordered by the court.

Privacy Protection Act (1980)

42 U.S.C. § 2000aa

Statutes in Context

In *Zurcher v. The Stanford Daily*, 436 U.S. 547 (1978), the Supreme Court held that law enforcement officials could search a newspaper office for evidence pertaining to a crime. Nobody at the newspaper was a suspect; the officials wanted to obtain photos the newspaper had. The Court concluded that a search warrant was sufficient to protect the paper's First Amendment rights. In 1980, Congress responded to *Zurcher* by passing the Privacy Protection Act (PPA).

§ 2000aa. Searches and seizures by government officers and employees in connection with investigation or prosecution of criminal offenses

(a) Work product materials

Notwithstanding any other law, it shall be unlawful for a government officer or employee, in connection with the investigation or prosecution of a criminal offense, to search for or seize any work product materials possessed by a person reasonably believed to have a purpose to disseminate to the public a newspaper, book, broadcast, or other similar form of public communication, in or affecting interstate or foreign commerce; but this provision shall not impair or affect the ability of any government officer or employee, pursuant to otherwise applicable law, to search for or seize such materials, if—

(1) there is probable cause to believe that the person possessing such materials has committed or is committing the criminal offense to which the materials relate: *Provided, however*, That a government officer or employee may not search for or seize such materials under the provisions of this paragraph if the offense to which the materials relate consists of the receipt, possession, communication, or withholding of such materials or the information contained therein (but such a search or seizure may be conducted under the provisions of this paragraph if the offense consists of the receipt, possession, or communication of information relating to the national defense, classified information, or restricted data under the provisions of section 793, 794, 797, or 798 of Title 18, or section 2274, 2275 or 2277 of this title, or section 783 of Title 50, or if the offense involves the production, possession, receipt, mailing, sale, distribution, shipment, or transportation of child pornography, the sexual exploitation of children, or the sale or purchase of children under section 2251, 2251A, 2252, or 2252A of Title 18); or

(2) there is reason to believe that the immediate seizure of such materials is necessary to prevent the death of, or serious bodily injury to, a human being.

(b) Other documents

Notwithstanding any other law, it shall be unlawful for a government officer or employee, in connection with the investigation or prosecution of a criminal offense, to search for or seize documentary materials, other than work product materials, possessed by a person in connection with a purpose to disseminate to the public a newspaper, book, broadcast, or other similar form of public communication, in or affecting interstate or foreign commerce; but this provision shall not impair or affect the ability of any government officer or employee, pursuant to otherwise applicable law, to search for or seize such materials, if—

(1) there is probable cause to believe that the person possessing such materials has committed or is committing the criminal offense to which the materials relate: *Provided, however*, That a government officer or employee may not search for or seize such materials under the provisions of this paragraph if the offense to which the materials relate consists of the receipt, possession, communication, or withholding of such materials or the information contained therein (but such a search or seizure may be conducted under the provisions of this paragraph if the offense consists of the receipt, possession, or communication of information relating to the national defense, classified information, or restricted data under the provisions of section 793, 794, 797, or 798 of Title 18, or section 2274, 2275, or 2277 of this title, or section 783 of Title 50, or if the offense involves the production, possession, receipt, mailing, sale, distribution, shipment, or transportation of child pornography, the sexual exploitation of children, or the sale or purchase of children under section 2251, 2251A, 2252, or 2252A of Title 18);

(2) there is reason to believe that the immediate seizure of such materials is necessary to prevent the death of, or serious bodily injury to, a human being;

(3) there is reason to believe that the giving of notice pursuant to a subpoena duces tecum would result in the destruction, alteration, or concealment of such materials; or

(4) such materials have not been produced in response to a court order directing compliance with a subpoena duces tecum, and—

(A) all appellate remedies have been exhausted; or

(B) there is reason to believe that the delay in an investigation or trial occasioned by further proceedings relating to the subpoena would threaten the interests of justice.

(c) Objections to court ordered subpoenas; affidavits

In the event a search warrant is sought pursuant to paragraph (4)(B) of subsection (b) of this section, the person possessing the materials shall be afforded adequate opportunity to submit an affidavit setting forth the basis for any contention that the materials sought are not subject to seizure.

§ 2000aa-5. Border and customs searches

This chapter shall not impair or affect the ability of a government officer or employee, pursuant to otherwise applicable law, to conduct searches and seizures at the borders of, or at international points of, entry into the United States in order to enforce the customs laws of the United States.

§ 2000aa-6. Civil actions by aggrieved persons

(a) Right of action

A person aggrieved by a search for or seizure of materials in violation of this chapter shall have a civil cause of action for damages for such search or seizure—

(1) against the United States, against a State which has waived its sovereign immunity under the Constitution to a claim for damages resulting from a violation of this chapter, or against any other governmental unit, all of which shall be liable for violations of this chapter by their officers or employees while acting within the scope or under color of their office or employment; and
(2) against an officer or employee of a State who has violated this chapter while acting within the scope or under color of his office or employment, if such State has not waived its sovereign immunity as provided in paragraph (1).

(b) Good faith defense

It shall be a complete defense to a civil action brought under paragraph (2) of subsection (a) of this section that the officer or employee had a reasonable good faith belief in the lawfulness of his conduct.

(c) Official immunity

The United States, a State, or any other governmental unit liable for violations of this chapter under subsection (a)(1) of this section, may not assert as a defense to a claim arising under this chapter the immunity of the officer or employee whose violation is complained of or his reasonable good faith belief in the lawfulness of his conduct, except that such a defense may be asserted if the violation complained of is that of a judicial officer.

(d) Exclusive nature of remedy

The remedy provided by subsection (a)(1) of this section against the United States, a State, or any other governmental unit is exclusive of any other civil action or proceeding for conduct constituting a violation of this chapter, against the officer or employee whose violation gave rise to the claim, or against the estate of such officer or employee.

(e) Admissibility of evidence

Evidence otherwise admissible in a proceeding shall not be excluded on the basis of a violation of this chapter.

(f) Damages; costs and attorneys' fees

A person having a cause of action under this section shall be entitled to recover actual damages but not less than liquidated damages of $1,000, and such reasonable attorneys' fees and other litigation costs reasonably incurred as the court, in its discretion, may award: *Provided, however*, That the United States, a State, or any other governmental unit shall not be liable for interest prior to judgment.

(g) Attorney General; claims settlement; regulations

The Attorney General may settle a claim for damages brought against the United States under this section, and shall promulgate regulations to provide for the commencement of an administrative inquiry following a determination of a violation of this chapter by an officer or employee of the United States and for the imposition of administrative sanctions against such officer or employee, if warranted.

(h) Jurisdiction

The district courts shall have original jurisdiction of all civil actions arising under this section.

§ 2000aa-7. Definitions

(a) "Documentary materials", as used in this chapter, means materials upon which information is recorded, and includes, but is not limited to, written or printed materials, photographs, motion picture films, negatives, video tapes, audio tapes, and other mechanically, magentically or electronically recorded cards, tapes, or discs, but does not include contraband or the fruits of a crime or things otherwise criminally possessed, or property designed or intended for use, or which is or has been used as, the means of committing a criminal offense.

(b) "Work product materials", as used in this chapter, means materials, other than contraband or the fruits of a crime or things otherwise criminally possessed, or property designed or intended for use, or which is or has been used, as the means of committing a criminal offense, and—

> **(1)** in anticipation of communicating such materials to the public, are prepared, produced, authored, or created, whether by the person in possession of the materials or by any other person;
>
> **(2)** are possessed for the purposes of communicating such materials to the public; and
>
> **(3)** include mental impressions, conclusions, opinions, or theories of the person who prepared, produced, authored, or created such material.

(c) "Any other governmental unit", as used in this chapter, includes the District of Columbia, the Commonwealth of Puerto Rico, any territory or possession of the United States, and any local government, unit of local government, or any unit of State government.

§ 2000aa-11. Guidelines for Federal officers and employees

(a) Procedures to obtain documentary evidence; protection of certain privacy interests

The Attorney General shall, within six months of October 13, 1980, issue guidelines for the procedures to be employed by any Federal officer or employee, in connection with the investigation or prosecution of an offense, to obtain documentary materials in the private possession of a person when the person is not reasonably believed to be a suspect in such offense or related by blood or marriage to such a suspect, and when the materials sought are not contraband or the fruits or instrumentalities of an offense. The Attorney General shall incorporate in such guidelines—

> **(1)** a recognition of the personal privacy interests of the person in possession of such documentary materials;
>
> **(2)** a requirement that the least intrusive method or means of obtaining such materials be used which do not substantially jeopardize the availability or usefulness of the materials sought to be obtained;

(3) a recognition of special concern for privacy interests in cases in which a search or seizure for such documents would intrude upon a known confidential relationship such as that which may exist between clergyman and parishioner; lawyer and client; or doctor and patient; and

(4) a requirement that an application for a warrant to conduct a search governed by this subchapter be approved by an attorney for the government, except that in an emergency situation the application may be approved by another appropriate supervisory official if within 24 hours of such emergency the appropriate United States Attorney is notified.

(b) Use of search warrants; reports to Congress

The Attorney General shall collect and compile information on, and report annually to the Committees on the Judiciary of the Senate and the House of Representatives on the use of search warrants by Federal officers and employees for documentary materials described in subsection (a)(3) of this section.

§ 2000aa-12. Binding nature of guidelines; disciplinary actions for violations; legal proceedings for non-compliance prohibited

Guidelines issued by the Attorney General under this subchapter shall have the full force and effect of Department of Justice regulations and any violation of these guidelines shall make the employee or officer involved subject to appropriate administrative disciplinary action. However, an issue relating to the compliance, or the failure to comply, with guidelines issued pursuant to this subchapter may not be litigated, and a court may not entertain such an issue as the basis for the suppression or exclusion of evidence.

Computer Fraud and Abuse Act (1984)

18 U.S.C. § 1030

Statutes in Context

The Computer Fraud and Abuse Act (CFAA) provides criminal and civil penalties for unauthorized access to computers. Originally passed in 1984, the statute was amended updated throughout the 1990s. Several states have similar statutes regarding the misuse of computers.

§ 1030. Fraud and related activity in connection with computers

(a) Whoever—

(1) having knowingly accessed a computer without authorization or exceeding authorized access, and by means of such conduct having obtained information that has been determined by the United States Government pursuant to an Executive order or statute to require protection against unauthorized disclosure for reasons of national defense or foreign relations, or any restricted data, as defined in paragraph y. of section 11 of the Atomic Energy Act of 1954, with reason to believe that such information so obtained could be used to the injury of the United States, or to the advantage of any foreign nation willfully communicates, delivers, transmits, or causes to be communicated, delivered, or transmitted, or attempts to communicate, deliver, transmit or cause to be communicated, delivered, or transmitted the same to any person not entitled to receive it, or willfully retains the same and fails to deliver it to the officer or employee of the United States entitled to receive it;

(2) intentionally accesses a computer without authorization or exceeds authorized access, and thereby obtains—

(A) information contained in a financial record of a financial institution, or of a card issuer as defined in section 1602(n) of title 15, or contained in a file of a consumer reporting agency on a consumer, as such terms are defined in the Fair Credit Reporting Act (15 U.S.C. 1681 et seq.);

(B) information from any department or agency of the United States; or

(C) information from any protected computer if the conduct involved an interstate or foreign communication;

(3) intentionally, without authorization to access any nonpublic computer of a department or agency of the United States, accesses such a computer of that department or agency that is exclusively for the use of the Government of the United States or, in the case of a computer not exclusively for such use, is used by or for the Government of the United States and such conduct affects that use by or for the Government of the United States;

(4) knowingly and with intent to defraud, accesses a protected computer without authorization, or exceeds authorized access, and by means of such conduct furthers the intended fraud and obtains anything of value, unless the object of the fraud and the thing obtained consists only of the use of the computer and the value of such use is not more than $5,000 in any 1-year period;

(5)(A)(i) knowingly causes the transmission of a program, information, code, or command, and as a result of such conduct, intentionally causes damage without authorization, to a protected computer;

(ii) intentionally accesses a protected computer without authorization, and as a result of such conduct, recklessly causes damage; or

(iii) intentionally accesses a protected computer without authorization, and as a result of such conduct, causes damage; and

(B) by conduct described in clause (i), (ii), or (iii) of subparagraph (A), caused (or, in the case of an attempted offense, would, if completed, have caused)—

> **(i)** loss to 1 or more persons during any 1-year period (and, for purposes of an investigation, prosecution, or other proceeding brought by the United States only, loss resulting from a related course of conduct affecting 1 or more other protected computers) aggregating at least $5,000 in value;
>
> **(ii)** the modification or impairment, or potential modification or impairment, of the medical examination, diagnosis, treatment, or care of 1 or more individuals;
>
> **(iii)** physical injury to any person;
>
> **(iv)** a threat to public health or safety; or
>
> **(v)** damage affecting a computer system used by or for a government entity in furtherance of the administration of justice, national defense, or national security;

(6) knowingly and with intent to defraud traffics (as defined in section 1029) in any password or similar information through which a computer may be accessed without authorization, if—

> **(A)** such trafficking affects interstate or foreign commerce; or
>
> **(B)** such computer is used by or for the Government of the United States;

(7) with intent to extort from any person any money or other thing of value, transmits in interstate or foreign commerce any communication containing any threat to cause damage to a protected computer;

shall be punished as provided in subsection (c) of this section.

(b) Whoever attempts to commit an offense under subsection (a) of this section shall be punished as provided in subsection (c) of this section.

(c) The punishment for an offense under subsection (a) or (b) of this section is—

(1)(A) a fine under this title or imprisonment for not more than ten years, or both, in the case of an offense under subsection (a)(1) of this section which does not occur after a conviction for another offense under this section, or an attempt to commit an offense punishable under this subparagraph; and

(B) a fine under this title or imprisonment for not more than twenty years, or both, in the case of an offense under subsection (a)(1) of this section which occurs after a conviction for another offense under this section, or an attempt to commit an offense punishable under this subparagraph;

(2)(A) except as provided in subparagraph (B), a fine under this title or imprisonment for not more than one year, or both, in the case of an offense under subsection (a)(2), (a)(3), (a)(5)(A)(iii), or (a)(6) of this section which does not occur after a conviction for another offense under this section, or an attempt to commit an offense punishable under this subparagraph;

(B) a fine under this title or imprisonment for not more than 5 years, or both, in the case of an offense under subsection (a)(2), or an attempt to commit an offense punishable under this subparagraph, if—

(i) the offense was committed for purposes of commercial advantage or private financial gain;

(ii) the offense was committed in furtherance of any criminal or tortious act in violation of the Constitution or laws of the United States or of any State; or

(iii) the value of the information obtained exceeds $5,000; and

(C) a fine under this title or imprisonment for not more than ten years, or both, in the case of an offense under subsection (a)(2), (a)(3) or (a)(6) of this section which occurs after a conviction for another offense under this section, or an attempt to commit an offense punishable under this subparagraph;

(3)(A) a fine under this title or imprisonment for not more than five years, or both, in the case of an offense under subsection (a)(4) or (a)(7) of this section which does not occur after a conviction for another offense under this section, or an attempt to commit an offense punishable under this subparagraph; and

(B) a fine under this title or imprisonment for not more than ten years, or both, in the case of an offense under subsection (a)(4), (a)(5)(A)(iii), or (a)(7) of this section which occurs after a conviction for another offense under this section, or an attempt to commit an offense punishable under this subparagraph;

(4)(A) except as provided in paragraph (5), a fine under this title, imprisonment for not more than 10 years, or both, in the case of an offense under subsection (a)(5)(A)(i), or an attempt to commit an offense punishable under that subsection;

(B) a fine under this title, imprisonment for not more than 5 years, or both, in the case of an offense under subsection (a)(5)(A)(ii), or an attempt to commit an offense punishable under that subsection;

(C) except as provided in paragraph (5), a fine under this title, imprisonment for not more than 20 years, or both, in the case of an offense under subsection (a)(5)(A)(i) or (a)(5)(A)(ii), or an attempt to commit an offense punishable under either subsection, that occurs after a conviction for another offense under this section; and

(5)(A) if the offender knowingly or recklessly causes or attempts to cause serious bodily injury from conduct in violation of subsection (a)(5)(A)(i), a fine under this title or imprisonment for not more than 20 years, or both; and

(B) if the offender knowingly or recklessly causes or attempts to cause death from conduct in violation of subsection (a)(5)(A)(i), a fine under this title or imprisonment for any term of years or for life, or both.

(d)(1) The United States Secret Service shall, in addition to any other agency having such authority, have the authority to investigate offenses under this section.

(2) The Federal Bureau of Investigation shall have primary authority to investigate offenses under subsection (a)(1) for any cases involving espionage, foreign counterintelligence, information protected against unauthorized disclosure for reasons of national defense or foreign relations, or Restricted Data (as that term is defined in section 11y of the Atomic Energy Act of 1954 (42 U.S.C. 2014(y)), except for offenses affecting the duties of the United States Secret Service pursuant to section 3056(a) of this title.

(3) Such authority shall be exercised in accordance with an agreement which shall be entered into by the Secretary of the Treasury and the Attorney General.

(e) As used in this section—

(1) the term "computer" means an electronic, magnetic, optical, electrochemical, or other high speed data processing device performing logical, arithmetic, or storage functions, and includes any data storage facility or communications facility directly related to or operating in conjunction with such device, but such term does not include an automated typewriter or typesetter, a portable hand held calculator, or other similar device;

(2) the term "protected computer" means a computer—

(A) exclusively for the use of a financial institution or the United States Government, or, in the case of a computer not exclusively for such use, used by or for a financial institution or the United States Government and the conduct constituting the offense affects that use by or for the financial institution or the Government; or

(B) which is used in interstate or foreign commerce or communication, including a computer located outside the United States that is used in a manner that affects interstate or foreign commerce or communication of the United States;

(3) the term "State" includes the District of Columbia, the Commonwealth of Puerto Rico, and any other commonwealth, possession or territory of the United States;

(4) the term "financial institution" means—

(A) an institution, with deposits insured by the Federal Deposit Insurance Corporation;

(B) the Federal Reserve or a member of the Federal Reserve including any Federal Reserve Bank;

(C) a credit union with accounts insured by the National Credit Union Administration;

(D) a member of the Federal home loan bank system and any home loan bank;

(E) any institution of the Farm Credit System under the Farm Credit Act of 1971;

(F) a broker-dealer registered with the Securities and Exchange Commission pursuant to section 15 of the Securities Exchange Act of 1934;

(G) the Securities Investor Protection Corporation;

(H) a branch or agency of a foreign bank (as such terms are defined in paragraphs (1) and (3) of section 1(b) of the International Banking Act of 1978); and

(I) an organization operating under section 25 or section 25(a) of the Federal Reserve Act;

(5) the term "financial record" means information derived from any record held by a financial institution pertaining to a customer's relationship with the financial institution;

(6) the term "exceeds authorized access" means to access a computer with authorization and to use such access to obtain or alter information in the computer that the accesser is not entitled so to obtain or alter;

(7) the term "department of the United States" means the legislative or judicial branch of the Government or one of the executive departments enumerated in section 101 of title 5;

(8) the term "damage" means any impairment to the integrity or availability of data, a program, a system, or information;

(9) the term "government entity" includes the Government of the United States, any State or political subdivision of the United States, any foreign country, and any state, province, municipality, or other political subdivision of a foreign country;

(10) the term "conviction" shall include a conviction under the law of any State for a crime punishable by imprisonment for more than 1 year, an element of which is unauthorized access, or exceeding authorized access, to a computer;

(11) the term "loss" means any reasonable cost to any victim, including the cost of responding to an offense, conducting a damage assessment, and restoring the data, program, system, or information to its condition prior to the offense, and any revenue lost, cost incurred, or other consequential damages incurred because of interruption of service; and

(12) the term "person" means any individual, firm, corporation, educational institution, financial institution, governmental entity, or legal or other entity.

(f) This section does not prohibit any lawfully authorized investigative, protective, or intelligence activity of a law enforcement agency of the United States, a State, or a political subdivision of a State, or of an intelligence agency of the United States.

(g) Any person who suffers damage or loss by reason of a violation of this section may maintain a civil action against the violator to obtain compensatory damages and injunctive relief or other equitable relief. A civil action for a violation of this section may be brought only if the conduct involves 1 of the factors set forth in clause (i), (ii), (iii), (iv), or (v) of subsection (a)(5)(B).

Damages for a violation involving only conduct described in subsection (a)(5)(B)(i) are limited to economic damages. No action may be brought under this subsection unless such action is begun within 2 years of the date of the act complained of or the date of the discovery of the damage. No action may be brought under this subsection for the negligent design or manufacture of computer hardware, computer software, or firmware.

(h) The Attorney General and the Secretary of the Treasury shall report to the Congress annually, during the first 3 years following the date of the enactment of this subsection, concerning investigations and prosecutions under subsection (a)(5).

III.
NATIONAL SECURITY

Foreign Intelligence Surveillance Act (1978)

50 U.S.C. §§ 1801-1811, 1821-29, 1841-46, and 1861-62, as amended

---

Statutes in Context

The Foreign Intelligence Surveillance Act (FISA) establishes standards and procedures for the use of electronic surveillance to collect "foreign intelligence" within the United States. Its regime is designed to apply when the gathering of foreign intelligence is "a significant purpose" of the investigation. FISA provides procedures for electronic surveillance, covert searches, and the use of pen register and trap and trace devices. A special court, the Foreign Intelligence Surveillance Court, reviews requests for FISA orders. The proceedings are ex parte, with the Department of Justice making the applications to the court on behalf of the CIA and other agencies. In certain circumstances, FISA authorizes surveillance without first having to obtain a court order. The statute does not apply to surveillance outside the United States.

---

§ 1801. Definitions

As used in this subchapter:

(a) "Foreign power" means—

(1) a foreign government or any component thereof, whether or not recognized by the United States;

(2) a faction of a foreign nation or nations, not substantially composed of United States persons;

(3) an entity that is openly acknowledged by a foreign government or governments to be directed and controlled by such foreign government or governments;

(4) a group engaged in international terrorism or activities in preparation therefor;

(5) a foreign-based political organization, not substantially composed of United States persons;

(6) an entity that is directed and controlled by a foreign government or governments; or

(7) an entity not substantially composed of United States persons that is engaged in the international proliferation of weapons of mass destruction.

(b) "Agent of a foreign power" means—

(1) any person other than a United States person, who—

(A) acts in the United States as an officer or employee of a foreign power, or as a member of a foreign power as defined in subsection (a)(4) of this section;

(B) acts for or on behalf of a foreign power which engages in clandestine intelligence activities in the United States contrary to the interests of the United States, when the circumstances of such person's presence in the United States indicate that such person may engage in such activities in the United States, or when such person knowingly aids or abets any person in the conduct of such activities or knowingly conspires with any person to engage in such activities;

(C) engages in international terrorism or activities in preparation therefore;

(D) engages in the international proliferation of weapons of mass destruction, or activities in preparation therefor; or

(E) engages in the international proliferation of weapons of mass destruction, or activities in preparation therefor for or on behalf of a foreign power; or

(2) any person who—

(A) knowingly engages in clandestine intelligence gathering activities for or on behalf of a foreign power, which activities involve or may involve a violation of the criminal statutes of the United States;

(B) pursuant to the direction of an intelligence service or network of a foreign power, knowingly engages in any other clandestine intelligence activities for or on behalf of such foreign power, which activities involve or are about to involve a violation of the criminal statutes of the United States;

(C) knowingly engages in sabotage or international terrorism, or activities that are in preparation therefor, for or on behalf of a foreign power;

(D) knowingly enters the United States under a false or fraudulent identity for or on behalf of a foreign power or, while in the United States, knowingly assumes a false or fraudulent identity for or on behalf of a foreign power; or

(E) knowingly aids or abets any person in the conduct of activities described in subparagraph (A), (B), or (C) or knowingly conspires with any person to engage in activities described in subparagraph (A), (B), or (C).

(c) "International terrorism" means activities that—

(1) involve violent acts or acts dangerous to human life that are a violation of the criminal laws of the United States or of any State, or that would be a criminal violation if committed within the jurisdiction of the United States or any State;

(2) appear to be intended—

(A) to intimidate or coerce a civilian population;

(B) to influence the policy of a government by intimidation or coercion; or

(C) to affect the conduct of a government by assassination or kidnapping; and

(3) occur totally outside the United States, or transcend national boundaries in terms of the means by which they are accomplished, the persons they appear intended to coerce or intimidate, or the locale in which their perpetrators operate or seek asylum.

(d) "Sabotage" means activities that involve a violation of chapter 105 of Title 18, or that would involve such a violation if committed against the United States.

(e) "Foreign intelligence information" means—

(1) information that relates to, and if concerning a United States person is necessary to, the ability of the United States to protect against—

(A) actual or potential attack or other grave hostile acts of a foreign power or an agent of a foreign power;

(B) sabotage, international terrorism, or the international proliferation of weapons of mass destruction by a foreign power or an agent of a foreign power; or

(C) clandestine intelligence activities by an intelligence service or network of a foreign power or by an agent of a foreign power; or

(2) information with respect to a foreign power or foreign territory that relates to, and if concerning a United States person is necessary to—

(A) the national defense or the security of the United States; or

(B) the conduct of the foreign affairs of the United States.

(f) "Electronic surveillance" means—

(1) the acquisition by an electronic, mechanical, or other surveillance device of the contents of any wire or radio communication sent by or intended to be received by a particular, known United States person who is in the United States, if the contents are acquired by intentionally targeting that United States person, under circumstances in which a person has a reasonable expectation of privacy and a warrant would be required for law enforcement purposes;

(2) the acquisition by an electronic, mechanical, or other surveillance device of the contents of any wire communication to or from a person in the United States, without the consent of any party thereto, if such acquisition occurs in the United States, but does not include the acquisition of those communications of computer trespassers that would be permissible under section 2511(2)(i) of Title 18;

(3) the intentional acquisition by an electronic, mechanical, or other surveillance device of the contents of any radio communication, under circumstances in which a person has a reasonable expectation of privacy and a warrant would be required for law enforcement purposes, and if both the sender and all intended recipients are located within the United States; or

(4) the installation or use of an electronic, mechanical, or other surveillance device in the United States for monitoring to acquire information, other than from a wire or radio communication, under circumstances in which a person has a reasonable expectation of privacy and a warrant would be required for law enforcement purposes.

(g) "Attorney General" means the Attorney General of the United States (or Acting Attorney General), the Deputy Attorney General, or, upon the designation of the Attorney General, the Assistant Attorney General designated as the Assistant Attorney General for National Security under section 507A of title 28, United States Code.

(h) "Minimization procedures", with respect to electronic surveillance, means—

(1) specific procedures, which shall be adopted by the Attorney General, that are reasonably designed in light of the purpose and technique of the particular surveillance, to minimize the acquisition and retention, and prohibit the dissemination, of nonpublicly available information concerning unconsenting United States persons consistent with the need of the United States to obtain, produce, and disseminate foreign intelligence information;

(2) procedures that require that nonpublicly available information, which is not foreign intelligence information, as defined in subsection (e)(1) of this section, shall not be disseminated in a manner that identifies any United States person, without such person's consent, unless such person's identity is necessary to understand foreign intelligence information or assess its importance;

(3) notwithstanding paragraphs (1) and (2), procedures that allow for the retention and dissemination of information that is evidence of a crime which has been, is being, or is about to be committed and that is to be retained or disseminated for law enforcement purposes; and

(4) notwithstanding paragraphs (1), (2), and (3), with respect to any electronic surveillance approved pursuant to section 1802(a) of this title, procedures that require that no contents of any communication to which a United States person is a party shall be disclosed, disseminated, or used for any purpose or retained for longer than 72 hours unless a court order under section 1805 of this title is obtained or unless the Attorney General determines that the information indicates a threat of death or serious bodily harm to any person.

(i) "United States person" means a citizen of the United States, an alien lawfully admitted for permanent residence (as defined in section 1101(a)(20)of Title 8), an unincorporated association a substantial number of members of which are citizens of the United States or aliens lawfully admitted for permanent residence, or a corporation which is incorporated in the United States, but does not include a corporation or an association which is a foreign power, as defined in subsection (a)(1), (2), or (3) of this section.

(j) "United States", when used in a geographic sense, means all areas under the territorial sovereignty of the United States and the Trust Territory of the Pacific Islands.

(k) "Aggrieved person" means a person who is the target of an electronic surveillance or any other person whose communications or activities were subject to electronic surveillance.

(l) "Wire communication" means any communication while it is being carried by a wire, cable, or other like connection furnished or operated by any person engaged as a common carrier in providing or operating such facilities for the transmission of interstate or foreign communications.

(m) "Person" means any individual, including any officer or employee of the Federal Government, or any group, entity, association, corporation, or foreign power.

(n) "Contents", when used with respect to a communication, includes any information concerning the identity of the parties to such communication or the existence, substance, purport, or meaning of that communication.

(o) "State" means any State of the United States, the District of Columbia, the Commonwealth of Puerto Rico, the Trust Territory of the Pacific Islands, and any territory or possession of the United States.

(p) "Weapon of mass destruction" means—

> **(1)** any explosive, incendiary, or poison gas device that is designed, intended, or has the capability to cause a mass casualty incident;
>
> **(2)** any weapon that is designed, intended, or has the capability to cause death or serious bodily injury to a significant number of persons through the release, dissemination, or impact of toxic or poisonous chemicals or their precursors;
>
> **(3)** any weapon involving a biological agent, toxin, or vector (as such terms are defined in section 178 of Title 18) that is designed, intended, or has the capability to cause death, illness, or serious bodily injury to a significant number of persons; or
>
> **(4)** any weapon that is designed, intended, or has the capability to release radiation or radioactivity causing death, illness, or serious bodily injury to a significant number of persons.

§ 1802. Electronic surveillance authorization without court order; certification by Attorney General; reports to Congressional committees; transmittal under seal; duties and compensation of communication common carrier; applications; jurisdiction of court

(a)(1) Notwithstanding any other law, the President, through the Attorney General, may authorize electronic surveillance without a court order under this subchapter to acquire foreign intelligence information for periods of up to one year if the Attorney General certifies in writing under oath that—

> **(A)** the electronic surveillance is solely directed at—
>
> > **(i)** the acquisition of the contents of communications transmitted by means of communications used exclusively between or among foreign powers, as defined in section 1801(a)(1), (2), or (3) of this title; or
> >
> > **(ii)** the acquisition of technical intelligence, other than the spoken communications of individuals, from property or premises under the open and exclusive control of a foreign power, as defined in section 1801(a)(1), (2), or (3) of this title;
>
> **(B)** there is no substantial likelihood that the surveillance will acquire the contents of any communication to which a United States person is a party; and
>
> **(C)** the proposed minimization procedures with respect to such surveillance meet the definition of minimization procedures under section 1801(h) of this title; and

if the Attorney General reports such minimization procedures and any changes thereto to the House Permanent Select Committee on Intelligence and the Senate Select Committee on Intelligence at least thirty days prior to their effective date, unless the Attorney General determines immediate action is required and notifies the committees immediately of such minimization procedures and the reason for their becoming effective immediately.

(2) An electronic surveillance authorized by this subsection may be conducted only in accordance with the Attorney General's certification and the minimization procedures adopted by him. The Attorney General shall assess compliance with such procedures and shall report such assessments to the House Permanent Select Committee on Intelligence and the Senate Select Committee on Intelligence under the provisions of section 1808(a) of this title.

(3) The Attorney General shall immediately transmit under seal to the court established under section 1803(a) of this title a copy of his certification. Such certification shall be maintained under security measures established by the Chief Justice with the concurrence of the Attorney General, in consultation with the Director of National Intelligence, and shall remain sealed unless—

(A) an application for a court order with respect to the surveillance is made under sections 1801(h)(4) and 1804 of this title; or

(B) the certification is necessary to determine the legality of the surveillance under section 1806(f) of this title.

(4) With respect to electronic surveillance authorized by this subsection, the Attorney General may direct a specified communication common carrier to—

(A) furnish all information, facilities, or technical assistance necessary to accomplish the electronic surveillance in such a manner as will protect its secrecy and produce a minimum of interference with the services that such carrier is providing its customers; and

(B) maintain under security procedures approved by the Attorney General and the Director of National Intelligence any records concerning the surveillance or the aid furnished which such carrier wishes to retain.

The Government shall compensate, at the prevailing rate, such carrier for furnishing such aid.

(b) Applications for a court order under this subchapter are authorized if the President has, by written authorization, empowered the Attorney General to approve applications to the court having jurisdiction under section 1803 of this title, and a judge to whom an application is made may, notwithstanding any other law, grant an order, in conformity with section 1805 of this title, approving electronic surveillance of a foreign power or an agent of a foreign power for the purpose of obtaining foreign intelligence information, except that the court shall not have jurisdiction to grant any order approving electronic surveillance directed solely as described in paragraph (1)(A) of subsection (a) of this section unless such surveillance may involve the acquisition of communications of any United States person.

§ 1803. Designation of judges

(a) Court to hear applications and grant orders; record of denial; transmittal to court of review

(1) The Chief Justice of the United States shall publicly designate 11 district court judges from at least seven of the United States judicial circuits of whom no fewer than 3 shall reside within 20 miles of the District of Columbia who shall constitute a court which shall have jurisdiction to hear applications for and grant orders approving electronic surveillance anywhere within the United States under the procedures set forth in this chapter, except that no judge designated under this subsection (except when sitting en banc under paragraph (2)) shall hear the same application for electronic surveillance under this chapter which has been denied previously by another judge designated under this subsection. If any judge so designated denies an application for an order authorizing electronic surveillance under this chapter, such judge shall provide immediately for the record a written statement of each reason for his decision and, on motion of the United States, the record shall be transmitted, under seal, to the court of review established in subsection (b) of this section.

(2)(A) The court established under this subsection may, on its own initiative, or upon the request of the Government in any proceeding or a party under section 1861(f) of this title or paragraph (4) or (5) of section 1881a(h) of this title, hold a hearing or rehearing, en banc, when ordered by a majority of the judges that constitute such court upon a determination that—

(i) en banc consideration is necessary to secure or maintain uniformity of the court's decisions; or

(ii) the proceeding involves a question of exceptional importance.

(B) Any authority granted by this chapter to a judge of the court established under this subsection may be exercised by the court en banc. When exercising such authority, the court en banc shall comply with any requirements of this chapter on the exercise of such authority.

(C) For purposes of this paragraph, the court en banc shall consist of all judges who constitute the court established under this subsection.

(b) Court of review; record, transmittal to Supreme Court

The Chief Justice shall publicly designate three judges, one of whom shall be publicly designated as the presiding judge, from the United States district courts or courts of appeals who together shall comprise a court of review which shall have jurisdiction to review the denial of any application made under this chapter. If such court determines that the application was properly denied, the court shall immediately provide for the record a written statement of each reason for its decision and, on petition of the United States for a writ of certiorari, the record shall be transmitted under seal to the Supreme Court, which shall have jurisdiction to review such decision.

(c) Expeditious conduct of proceedings; security measures for maintenance of records

Proceedings under this chapter shall be conducted as expeditiously as possible. The record of proceedings under this chapter, including applications made and orders granted, shall be maintained under security measures established by the Chief Justice in consultation with the Attorney General and the Director of National Intelligence.

(d) Tenure

Each judge designated under this section shall so serve for a maximum of seven years and shall not be eligible for redesignation, except that the judges first designated under subsection (a) of this section shall be designated for terms of from one to seven years so that one term expires each year, and that judges first designated under subsection (b) of this section shall be designated for terms of three, five, and seven years.

(e)(1) Three judges designated under subsection (a) of this section who reside within 20 miles of the District of Columbia, or, if all of such judges are unavailable, other judges of the court established under subsection (a) of this section as may be designated by the presiding judge of such court, shall comprise a petition review pool which shall have jurisdiction to review petitions filed pursuant to section 1861(f)(1) or 1881a(h)(4) of this title.

(2) Not later than 60 days after March 9, 2006, the court established under subsection (a) of this section shall adopt and, consistent with the protection of national security, publish procedures for the review of petitions filed pursuant to section 1861(f)(1) or 1881a(h)(4) of this title by the panel established under paragraph (1). Such procedures shall provide that review of a petition shall be conducted in camera and shall also provide for the designation of an acting presiding judge.

(f)(1) A judge of the court established under subsection (a), the court established under subsection (b) or a judge of that court, or the Supreme Court of the United States or a justice of that court, may, in accordance with the rules of their respective courts, enter a stay of an order or an order modifying an order of the court established under subsection (a) or the court established under subsection (b) entered under any title of this chapter, while the court established under subsection (a) conducts a rehearing, while an appeal is pending to the court established under subsection (b), or while a petition of certiorari is pending in the Supreme Court of the United States, or during the pendency of any review by that court.

(2) The authority described in paragraph (1) shall apply to an order entered under any provision of this chapter.

(g)(1) The courts established pursuant to subsections (a) and (b) of this section may establish such rules and procedures, and take such actions, as are reasonably necessary to administer their responsibilities under this chapter.

(2) The rules and procedures established under paragraph (1), and any modifications of such rules and procedures, shall be recorded, and shall be transmitted to the following:

(A) All of the judges on the court established pursuant to subsection (a) of this section.

(B) All of the judges on the court of review established pursuant to subsection (b) of this section.

(C) The Chief Justice of the United States.

(D) The Committee on the Judiciary of the Senate.

(E) The Select Committee on Intelligence of the Senate.

(F) The Committee on the Judiciary of the House of Representatives.

(G) The Permanent Select Committee on Intelligence of the House of Representatives.

(3) The transmissions required by paragraph (2) shall be submitted in unclassified form, but may include a classified annex.

(i) Nothing in this chapter shall be construed to reduce or contravene the inherent authority of the court established under subsection (a) to determine or enforce compliance with an order or a rule of such court or with a procedure approved by such court.

§ 1804. Applications for court orders

(a) Submission by Federal officer; approval of Attorney General; contents

Each application for an order approving electronic surveillance under this subchapter shall be made by a Federal officer in writing upon oath or affirmation to a judge having jurisdiction under section 1803 of this title. Each application shall require the approval of the Attorney General based upon his finding that it satisfies the criteria and requirements of such application as set forth in this subchapter. It shall include—

(1) the identity of the Federal officer making the application;

(2) the identity, if known, or a description of the specific target of the electronic surveillance;

(3) a statement of the facts and circumstances relied upon by the applicant to justify his belief that—

(A) the target of the electronic surveillance is a foreign power or an agent of a foreign power; and

(B) each of the facilities or places at which the electronic surveillance is directed is being used, or is about to be used, by a foreign power or an agent of a foreign power;

(4) a statement of the proposed minimization procedures;

(5) a description of the nature of the information sought and the type of communications or activities to be subjected to the surveillance;

(6) a certification or certifications by the Assistant to the President for National Security Affairs, an executive branch official or officials designated by the President from among those executive officers employed in the area of national security or defense and appointed by the President with the advice and consent of the Senate, or the Deputy Director of the Federal Bureau of Investigation, if designated by the President as a certifying official—

(A) that the certifying official deems the information sought to be foreign intelligence information;

(B) that a significant purpose of the surveillance is to obtain foreign intelligence information;

(C) that such information cannot reasonably be obtained by normal investigative techniques;

(D) that designates the type of foreign intelligence information being sought according to the categories described in section 1801(e) of this title; and

(E) including a statement of the basis for the certification that—

(i) the information sought is the type of foreign intelligence information designated; and

(ii) such information cannot reasonably be obtained by normal investigative techniques;

(7) a summary statement of the means by which the surveillance will be effected and a statement whether physical entry is required to effect the surveillance;

(8) a statement of the facts concerning all previous applications that have been made to any judge under this subchapter involving any of the persons, facilities, or places specified in the application, and the action taken on each previous application; and

(9) a statement of the period of time for which the electronic surveillance is required to be maintained, and if the nature of the intelligence gathering is such that the approval of the use of electronic surveillance under this subchapter should not automatically terminate when the described type of information has first been obtained, a description of facts supporting the belief that additional information of the same type will be obtained thereafter.

(10) Redesignated (9)

(11) Repealed. Pub.L. 110-261, Title I, § 104(1)(A), July 10, 2008, 122 Stat. 2460

(b) Additional affidavits or certifications

The Attorney General may require any other affidavit or certification from any other officer in connection with the application.

(c) Additional information

The judge may require the applicant to furnish such other information as may be necessary to make the determinations required by section 1805 of this title.

(d) Personal review by Attorney General

(1)(A) Upon written request of the Director of the Federal Bureau of Investigation, the Secretary of Defense, the Secretary of State, the Director of National Intelligence, or the Director of the Central Intelligence Agency, the Attorney General shall personally review under subsection (a) of this section an application under that subsection for a target described in section 1801(b)(2) of this title.

(B) Except when disabled or otherwise unavailable to make a request referred to in subparagraph (A), an official referred to in that subparagraph may not delegate the authority to make a request referred to in that subparagraph.

(C) Each official referred to in subparagraph (A) with authority to make a request under that subparagraph shall take appropriate actions in advance to ensure that delegation of such authority is clearly established in the event such official is disabled or otherwise unavailable to make such request.

(2)(A) If as a result of a request under paragraph (1) the Attorney General determines not to approve an application under the second sentence of subsection (a) of this section for purposes of making the application under this section, the Attorney General shall provide written notice of the determination to the official making the request for the review of the application under that paragraph. Except when disabled or otherwise unavailable to make a determination under the preceding sentence, the Attorney General may not delegate the responsibility to make a determination under that sentence. The Attorney General shall take appropriate actions in advance to ensure that delegation of such responsibility is clearly established in the event the Attorney General is disabled or otherwise unavailable to make such determination.

(B) Notice with respect to an application under subparagraph (A) shall set forth the modifications, if any, of the application that are necessary in order for the Attorney General to approve the application under the second sentence of subsection (a) of this section for purposes of making the application under this section.

(C) Upon review of any modifications of an application set forth under subparagraph (B), the official notified of the modifications under this paragraph shall modify the application if such official determines that such modification is warranted. Such official shall supervise the making of any modification under this subparagraph. Except when disabled or otherwise unavailable to supervise the making of any modification under the preceding sentence, such official may not delegate the responsibility to supervise the making of any modification under that preceding sentence. Each such official shall take appropriate actions in advance to ensure that delegation of such responsibility is clearly established in the event such official is disabled or otherwise unavailable to supervise the making of such modification.

§ 1805. Issuance of order

(a) Necessary findings

Upon an application made pursuant to section 1804 of this title, the judge shall enter an ex parte order as requested or as modified approving the electronic surveillance if he finds that—

(1) the application has been made by a Federal officer and approved by the Attorney General;

(2) on the basis of the facts submitted by the applicant there is probable cause to believe that—

(A) the target of the electronic surveillance is a foreign power or an agent of a foreign power: Provided, That no United States person may be considered a foreign power or an agent of a foreign power solely upon the basis of activities protected by the first amendment to the Constitution of the United States; and

(B) each of the facilities or places at which the electronic surveillance is directed is being used, or is about to be used, by a foreign power or an agent of a foreign power;

(3) the proposed minimization procedures meet the definition of minimization procedures under section 1801(h) of this title; and

(4) the application which has been filed contains all statements and certifications required by section 1804 of this title and, if the target is a United States person, the certification or certifications are not clearly erroneous on the basis of the statement made under section 1804(a)(7)(E) of this title and any other information furnished under section 1804(d) of this title.

(5) Redesignated (4)

(b) Determination of probable cause

In determining whether or not probable cause exists for purposes of an order under subsection (a)(2) of this section, a judge may consider past activities of the target, as well as facts and circumstances relating to current or future activities of the target.

(c) Specifications and directions of orders

(1) Specifications

An order approving an electronic surveillance under this section shall specify—

(A) the identity, if known, or a description of the specific target of the electronic surveillance identified or described in the application pursuant to section 1804(a)(3) of this title;

(B) the nature and location of each of the facilities or places at which the electronic surveillance will be directed, if known;

(C) the type of information sought to be acquired and the type of communications or activities to be subjected to the surveillance;

(D) the means by which the electronic surveillance will be effected and whether physical entry will be used to effect the surveillance;

(E) the period of time during which the electronic surveillance is approved.

(F) Repealed. Pub.L. 110-261, Title I, § 105(a)(3)(C), July 10, 2008, 122 Stat. 2461

(2) Directions

An order approving an electronic surveillance under this section shall direct—

(A) that the minimization procedures be followed;

(B) that, upon the request of the applicant, a specified communication or other common carrier, landlord, custodian, or other specified person, or in circumstances where the Court finds, based upon specific facts provided in the application, that the actions of the target of the application may have the effect of thwarting the identification of a specified person, such other persons, furnish the applicant forthwith all information, facilities, or technical assistance necessary to accomplish the electronic surveillance in such a manner as will protect its secrecy and produce a minimum of interference with the services that such carrier, landlord, custodian, or other person is providing that target of electronic surveillance;

(C) that such carrier, landlord, custodian, or other person maintain under security procedures approved by the Attorney General and the Director of National Intelligence any records concerning the surveillance or the aid furnished that such person wishes to retain; and

(D) that the applicant compensate, at the prevailing rate, such carrier, landlord, custodian, or other person for furnishing such aid.

(3) Special directions for certain orders

An order approving an electronic surveillance under this section in circumstances where the nature and location of each of the facilities or places at which the surveillance will be directed is unknown shall direct the applicant to provide notice to the court within ten days after the date on which surveillance begins to be directed at any new facility or place, unless the court finds good cause to justify a longer period of up to 60 days, of—

(A) the nature and location of each new facility or place at which the electronic surveillance is directed;

(B) the facts and circumstances relied upon by the applicant to justify the applicant's belief that each new facility or place at which the electronic surveillance is directed is or was being used, or is about to be used, by the target of the surveillance;

(C) a statement of any proposed minimization procedures that differ from those contained in the original application or order, that may be necessitated by a change in the facility or place at which the electronic surveillance is directed; and

(D) the total number of electronic surveillances that have been or are being conducted under the authority of the order.

(d) Duration of order; extensions; review of circumstances under which information was acquired, retained or disseminated

(1) An order issued under this section may approve an electronic surveillance for the period necessary to achieve its purpose, or for ninety days, whichever is less, except that (A) an order under this section shall approve an electronic surveillance targeted against a foreign power, as defined in section 1801(a)(1), (2), or (3) of this title, for the period specified in the application or for one year, whichever is less, and (B) an order under this chapter for a surveillance targeted against an agent of a foreign power who is not a United States person may be for the period specified in the application or for 120 days, whichever is less.

(2) Extensions of an order issued under this subchapter may be granted on the same basis as an original order upon an application for an extension and new findings made in the same manner as required for an original order, except that (A) an extension of an order under this chapter for a surveillance targeted against a foreign power, as defined in paragraph (5), (6), or (7) of section 1801(a) of this title, or against a foreign power as defined in section 1801(a)(4) of this title that is not a United States person, may be for a period not to exceed one year if the judge finds probable cause to believe that no communication of any individual United States person will be acquired during the period, and (B) an extension of an order under this chapter for a surveillance targeted against an agent of a foreign power who is not a United States person may be for a period not to exceed 1 year.

(3) At or before the end of the period of time for which electronic surveillance is approved by an order or an extension, the judge may assess compliance with the minimization procedures by reviewing the circumstances under which information concerning United States persons was acquired, retained, or disseminated.

(e)(1) Notwithstanding any other provision of this subchapter, the Attorney General may authorize the emergency employment of electronic surveillance if the Attorney General—

(A) reasonably determines that an emergency situation exists with respect to the employment of electronic surveillance to obtain foreign intelligence information before an order authorizing such surveillance can with due diligence be obtained;

(B) reasonably determines that the factual basis for the issuance of an order under this subchapter to approve such electronic surveillance exists;

(C) informs, either personally or through a designee, a judge having jurisdiction under section 1803 of this title at the time of such authorization that the decision has been made to employ emergency electronic surveillance; and

(D) makes an application in accordance with this subchapter to a judge having jurisdiction under section 1803 of this title as soon as practicable, but not later than 7 days after the Attorney General authorizes such surveillance.

(2) If the Attorney General authorizes the emergency employment of electronic surveillance under paragraph (1), the Attorney General shall require that the minimization procedures required by this subchapter for the issuance of a judicial order be followed.

(3) In the absence of a judicial order approving such electronic surveillance, the surveillance shall terminate when the information sought is obtained, when the application for the order is denied, or after the expiration of 7 days from the time of authorization by the Attorney General, whichever is earliest.

(4) A denial of the application made under this subsection may be reviewed as provided in section 1803 of this title.

(5) In the event that such application for approval is denied, or in any other case where the electronic surveillance is terminated and no order is issued approving the surveillance, no information obtained or evidence derived from such surveillance shall be received in evidence or otherwise disclosed in any trial, hearing, or other proceeding in or before any court, grand jury, department, office, agency, regulatory body, legislative committee, or other authority of the United States, a State, or political subdivision thereof, and no information concerning any United States person acquired from such surveillance shall subsequently be used or disclosed in any other manner by Federal officers or employees without the consent of such person, except with the approval of the Attorney General if the information indicates a threat of death or serious bodily harm to any person.

(6) The Attorney General shall assess compliance with the requirements of paragraph (5).

(f) Testing of electronic equipment; discovering unauthorized electronic surveillance; training of intelligence personnel

Notwithstanding any other provision of this subchapter, officers, employees, or agents of the United States are authorized in the normal course of their official duties to conduct electronic surveillance not targeted against the communications of any particular person or persons, under procedures approved by the Attorney General, solely to--

(1) test the capability of electronic equipment, if–

(A) it is not reasonable to obtain the consent of the persons incidentally subjected to the surveillance;

(B) the test is limited in extent and duration to that necessary to determine the capability of the equipment;

(C) the contents of any communication acquired are retained and used only for the purpose of determining the capability of the equipment, are disclosed only to test personnel, and are destroyed before or immediately upon completion of the test; and:

(D) Provided, That the test may exceed ninety days only with the prior approval of the Attorney General;

(2) determine the existence and capability of electronic surveillance equipment being used by persons not authorized to conduct electronic surveillance, if—

(A) it is not reasonable to obtain the consent of persons incidentally subjected to the surveillance;

(B) such electronic surveillance is limited in extent and duration to that necessary to determine the existence and capability of such equipment; and

(C) any information acquired by such surveillance is used only to enforce chapter 119 of Title 18, or section 605 of Title 47, or to protect information from unauthorized surveillance; or

(3) train intelligence personnel in the use of electronic surveillance equipment, if—

(A) it is not reasonable to—

(i) obtain the consent of the persons incidentally subjected to the surveillance;

(ii) train persons in the course of surveillances otherwise authorized by this subchapter; or

(iii) train persons in the use of such equipment without engaging in electronic surveillance;

(B) such electronic surveillance is limited in extent and duration to that necessary to train the personnel in the use of the equipment; and

(C) no contents of any communication acquired are retained or disseminated for any purpose, but are destroyed as soon as reasonably possible.

(g) Retention of certifications, applications and orders

Certifications made by the Attorney General pursuant to section 1802(a) of this title and applications made and orders granted under this subchapter shall be retained for a period of at least ten years from the date of the certification or application.

(h) Release from liability

No cause of action shall lie in any court against any provider of a wire or electronic communication service, landlord, custodian, or other person (including any officer, employee, agent, or other specified person thereof) that furnishes any information, facilities, or technical assistance in accordance with a court order or request for emergency assistance under this chapter for electronic surveillance or physical search.

(i) In any case in which the Government makes an application to a judge under this subchapter to conduct electronic surveillance involving communications and the judge grants such application, upon the request of the applicant, the judge shall also authorize the installation and use of pen registers and trap and trace devices, and direct the disclosure of the information set forth in section 1842(d)(2) of this title.

§ 1806. Use of information

(a) Compliance with minimization procedures; privileged communications; lawful purposes

Information acquired from an electronic surveillance conducted pursuant to this subchapter concerning any United States person may be used and disclosed by Federal officers and employees without the consent of the United States person only in accordance with the minimization procedures required by this subchapter. No otherwise privileged communication obtained in accordance with, or in violation of, the provisions of this subchapter shall lose its privileged character. No information acquired from an electronic surveillance pursuant to this subchapter may be used or disclosed by Federal officers or employees except for lawful purposes.

(b) Statement for disclosure

No information acquired pursuant to this subchapter shall be disclosed for law enforcement purposes unless such disclosure is accompanied by a statement that such information, or any information derived therefrom, may only be used in a criminal proceeding with the advance authorization of the Attorney General.

(c) Notification by United States

Whenever the Government intends to enter into evidence or otherwise use or disclose in any trial, hearing, or other proceeding in or before any court, department, officer, agency, regulatory body, or other authority of the United States, against an aggrieved person, any information obtained or derived from an electronic surveillance of that aggrieved person pursuant to the authority of this subchapter, the Government shall, prior to the trial, hearing, or other proceeding or at a reasonable time prior to an effort to so disclose or so use that information or submit it in evidence, notify the aggrieved person and the court or other authority in which the information is to be disclosed or used that the Government intends to so disclose or so use such information.

(d) Notification by States or political subdivisions

Whenever any State or political subdivision thereof intends to enter into evidence or otherwise use or disclose in any trial, hearing, or other proceeding in or before any court, department, officer, agency, regulatory body, or other authority of a State or a political subdivision thereof, against an aggrieved person any information obtained or derived from an electronic surveillance of that aggrieved person pursuant to the authority of this subchapter, the State or political subdivision thereof shall notify the aggrieved person, the court or other authority in which the information is to be disclosed or used, and the Attorney General that the State or political subdivision thereof intends to so disclose or so use such information.

(e) Motion to suppress

Any person against whom evidence obtained or derived from an electronic surveillance to which he is an aggrieved person is to be, or has been, introduced or otherwise used or disclosed in any trial, hearing, or other proceeding in or before any court, department, officer, agency, regulatory body, or other authority of the United States, a State, or a political subdivision thereof, may move to suppress the evidence obtained or derived from such electronic surveillance on the grounds that—

(1) the information was unlawfully acquired; or

(2) the surveillance was not made in conformity with an order of authorization or approval.

Such a motion shall be made before the trial, hearing, or other proceeding unless there was no opportunity to make such a motion or the person was not aware of the grounds of the motion.

(f) In camera and ex parte review by district court

Whenever a court or other authority is notified pursuant to subsection (c) or (d) of this section, or whenever a motion is made pursuant to subsection (e) of this section, or whenever any motion or request is made by an aggrieved person pursuant to any other statute or rule of the United States or any State before any court or other authority of the United States or any State to discover or obtain applications or orders or other materials relating to electronic surveillance or to discover, obtain, or suppress evidence or information obtained or derived from electronic surveillance under this chapter, the United States district court or, where the motion is made before another authority, the United States district court in the same district as the authority, shall, notwithstanding any other law, if the Attorney General files an affidavit under oath that disclosure or an adversary hearing would harm the national security of the United States, review in camera and ex parte the application, order, and such other materials relating to the surveillance as may be necessary to determine whether the surveillance of the aggrieved person was lawfully authorized and conducted. In making this determination, the court may disclose to the aggrieved person, under appropriate security procedures and protective orders, portions of the application, order, or other materials relating to the surveillance only where such disclosure is necessary to make an accurate determination of the legality of the surveillance.

(g) Suppression of evidence; denial of motion

If the United States district court pursuant to subsection (f) of this section determines that the surveillance was not lawfully authorized or conducted, it shall, in accordance with the requirements of law, suppress the evidence which was unlawfully obtained or derived from electronic surveillance of the aggrieved person or otherwise grant the motion of the aggrieved person. If the court determines that the surveillance was lawfully authorized and conducted, it shall deny the motion of the aggrieved person except to the extent that due process requires discovery or disclosure.

(h) Finality of orders

Orders granting motions or requests under subsection (g) of this section, decisions under this section that electronic surveillance was not lawfully authorized or conducted, and orders of the United States district court requiring review or granting disclosure of applications, orders, or other materials relating to a surveillance shall be final orders and binding upon all courts of the United States and the several States except a United States court of appeals and the Supreme Court.

(i) Destruction of unintentionally acquired information

In circumstances involving the unintentional acquisition by an electronic, mechanical, or other surveillance device of the contents of any communication, under circumstances in which a person has a reasonable expectation of privacy and a warrant would be required for law enforcement purposes, and if both the sender and all intended recipients are located within the United States, such contents shall be destroyed upon recognition, unless the Attorney General determines that the contents indicate a threat of death or serious bodily harm to any person.

(j) Notification of emergency employment of electronic surveillance; contents; postponement, suspension or elimination

If an emergency employment of electronic surveillance is authorized under section 1805(e) of this title and a subsequent order approving the surveillance is not obtained, the judge shall cause to be served on any United States person named in the application and on such other United States persons subject to electronic surveillance as the judge may determine in his discretion it is in the interest of justice to serve, notice of—

> **(1)** the fact of the application;
>
> **(2)** the period of the surveillance; and
>
> **(3)** the fact that during the period information was or was not obtained.

On an ex parte showing of good cause to the judge the serving of the notice required by this subsection may be postponed or suspended for a period not to exceed ninety days. Thereafter, on a further ex parte showing of good cause, the court shall forego ordering the serving of the notice required under this subsection.

(k) Consultation with Federal law enforcement officer

> **(1)** Federal officers who conduct electronic surveillance to acquire foreign intelligence information under this title may consult with Federal law enforcement officers or law enforcement personnel of a State or political subdivision of a State (including the chief executive officer of that State or political subdivision who has the authority to appoint or direct the chief law enforcement officer of that State or political subdivision) to coordinate efforts to investigate or protect against
>
> > **(A)** actual or potential attack or other grave hostile acts of a foreign power or an agent of a foreign power;

(B) sabotage, international terrorism, or the international proliferation of weapons of mass destruction by a foreign power or an agent of a foreign power; or

(C) clandestine intelligence activities by an intelligence service or network of a foreign power or by an agent of a foreign power.

(2) Coordination authorized under paragraph (1) shall not preclude the certification required by section 1804(a)(7)(B) of this title or the entry of an order under section 1805 of this title.

§ 1807. Report to Administrative Office of the United States Court and to Congress

In April of each year, the Attorney General shall transmit to the Administrative Office of the United States Court and to Congress a report setting forth with respect to the preceding calendar year—

(a) the total number of applications made for orders and extensions of orders approving electronic surveillance under this subchapter; and

(b) the total number of such orders and extensions either granted, modified, or denied.

§ 1808. Report of Attorney General to Congressional committees; limitation on authority or responsibility of information gathering activities of Congressional committees; report of Congressional committees to Congress

(a)(1) On a semiannual basis the Attorney General shall fully inform the House Permanent Select Committee on Intelligence and the Senate Select Committee on Intelligence, and the Committee on the Judiciary of the Senate, concerning all electronic surveillance under this subchapter. Nothing in this subchapter shall be deemed to limit the authority and responsibility of the appropriate committees of each House of Congress to obtain such information as they may need to carry out their respective functions and duties.

(2) Each report under the first sentence of paragraph (1) shall include a description of—

(A) the total number of applications made for orders and extensions of orders approving electronic surveillance under this subchapter where the nature and location of each facility or place at which the electronic surveillance will be directed is unknown;

(B) each criminal case in which information acquired under this chapter has been authorized for use at trial during the period covered by such report; and

(C) the total number of emergency employments of electronic surveillance under section 1805(e) of this title and the total number of subsequent orders approving or denying such electronic surveillance.

(b) On or before one year after October 25, 1978, and on the same day each year for four years thereafter, the Permanent Select Committee on Intelligence and the Senate Select Committee on Intelligence shall report respectively to the House of Representatives and the Senate, concerning the implementation of this chapter. Said reports shall include but not be limited to an analysis and recommendations concerning whether this chapter should be (1) amended, (2) repealed, or (3) permitted to continue in effect without amendment.

§ 1809. Criminal sanctions

(a) Prohibited activities

A person is guilty of an offense if he intentionally—

> **(1)** engages in electronic surveillance under color of law except as authorized by this chapter, chapter 119, 121, or 206 of Title 18 or any express statutory authorization that is an additional exclusive means for conducting electronic surveillance under section 1812 of this title; or
>
> **(2)** discloses or uses information obtained under color of law by electronic surveillance, knowing or having reason to know that the information was obtained through electronic surveillance not authorized by this chapter, chapter 119, 121, or 206 of Title 18 or any express statutory authorization that is an additional exclusive means for conducting electronic surveillance under section 1812 of this title.

(b) Defense

It is a defense to a prosecution under subsection (a) of this section that the defendant was a law enforcement or investigative officer engaged in the course of his official duties and the electronic surveillance was authorized by and conducted pursuant to a search warrant or court order of a court of competent jurisdiction.

(c) Penalties

An offense described in this section is punishable by a fine of not more than $10,000 or imprisonment for not more than five years, or both.

(d) Federal jurisdiction

There is Federal jurisdiction over an offense under this section if the person committing the offense was an officer or employee of the United States at the time the offense was committed.

§ 1810. Civil liability

An aggrieved person, other than a foreign power or an agent of a foreign power, as defined in section 1801(a) or (b)(1)(A) of this title, respectively, who has been subjected to an electronic surveillance or about whom information obtained by electronic surveillance of such person has been disclosed or used in violation of section 1809 of this title shall have a cause of action against any person who committed such violation and shall be entitled to recover—

(a) actual damages, but not less than liquidated damages of $1,000 or $100 per day for each day of violation, whichever is greater;

(b) punitive damages; and

(c) reasonable attorney's fees and other investigation and litigation costs reasonably incurred.

§ 1811. Authorization during time of war

Notwithstanding any other law, the President, through the Attorney General, may authorize electronic surveillance without a court order under this subchapter to acquire foreign intelligence information for a period not to exceed fifteen calendar days following a declaration of war by the Congress.

§ 1821. Definitions

As used in this subchapter:

(1) The terms “foreign power”, “agent of a foreign power”, “‘international terrorism”, “sabotage”, “foreign intelligence information”, “Attorney General”, “United States person”, “United States”, “person”, “weapon of mass destruction,” and “State” shall have the same meanings as in section 1801 of this title, except as specifically provided by this subchapter.

(2) “Aggrieved person” means a person whose premises, property, information, or material is the target of physical search or any other person whose premises, property, information, or material was subject to physical search.

(3) “Foreign Intelligence Surveillance Court” means the court established by section 1803(a) of this title.

(4) “Minimization procedures” with respect to physical search, means—

> **(A)** specific procedures, which shall be adopted by the Attorney General, that are reasonably designed in light of the purposes and technique of the particular physical search, to minimize the acquisition and retention, and prohibit the dissemination, of nonpublicly available information concerning unconsenting United States persons consistent with the need of the United States to obtain, produce, and disseminate foreign intelligence information;
>
> **(B)** procedures that require that nonpublicly available information, which is not foreign intelligence information, as defined in section 1801(e)(1) of this title, shall not be disseminated in a manner that identifies any United States person, without such person’s consent, unless such person’s identity is necessary to understand such foreign intelligence information or assess its importance;
>
> **(C)** notwithstanding subparagraphs (A) and (B), procedures that allow for the retention and dissemination of information that is evidence of a crime which has been, is being, or is about to be committed and that is to be retained or disseminated for law enforcement purposes; and
>
> **(D)** notwithstanding subparagraphs (A), (B), and (C), with respect to any physical search approved pursuant to section 1822(a) of this title, procedures that require that no information, material, or property of a United States person shall be disclosed, disseminated, or used for any purpose or retained for longer than 72 hours unless a court order under section 1824 of this title is obtained or unless the Attorney General determines that the information indicates a threat of death or serious bodily harm to any person.

(5) “Physical search” means any physical intrusion within the United States into premises or property (including examination of the interior of property by technical means) that is intended to result in a seizure, reproduction, inspection, or alteration of information, material, or property, under circumstances in which a person has a reasonable expectation of privacy and a warrant would be required for law enforcement purposes, but does not include (A) “electronic surveillance”, as defined in section 1801(f) of this title, or (B) the acquisition by the United States Government of foreign intelligence information from international or foreign communications, or foreign intelligence activities conducted in accordance with otherwise applicable Federal law involving a foreign electronic communications system, utilizing a means other than electronic surveillance as defined in section 1801(f) of this title.

§ 1822. Authorization of physical searches for foreign intelligence purposes

(a) Presidential authorization

(1) Notwithstanding any other provision of law, the President, acting through the Attorney General, may authorize physical searches without a court order under this subchapter to acquire foreign intelligence information for periods of up to one year if—

(A) the Attorney General certifies in writing under oath that—

(i) the physical search is solely directed at premises, information, material, or property used exclusively by, or under the open and exclusive control of, a foreign power or powers (as defined in section 1801(a)(1), (2), or (3) of this title);

(ii) there is no substantial likelihood that the physical search will involve the premises, information, material, or property of a United States person; and

(iii) the proposed minimization procedures with respect to such physical search meet the definition of minimization procedures under paragraphs (1) through (4) of section 1821(4) of this title; and

(B) the Attorney General reports such minimization procedures and any changes thereto to the Permanent Select Committee on Intelligence of the House of Representatives and the Select Committee on Intelligence of the Senate at least 30 days before their effective date, unless the Attorney General determines that immediate action is required and notifies the committees immediately of such minimization procedures and the reason for their becoming effective immediately.

(2) A physical search authorized by this subsection may be conducted only in accordance with the certification and minimization procedures adopted by the Attorney General. The Attorney General shall assess compliance with such procedures and shall report such assessments to the Permanent Select Committee on Intelligence of the House of Representatives and the Select Committee on Intelligence of the Senate under the provisions of section 1826 of this title.

(3) The Attorney General shall immediately transmit under seal to the Foreign Intelligence Surveillance Court a copy of the certification. Such certification shall be maintained under security measures established by the Chief Justice of the United States with the concurrence of the Attorney General, in consultation with the Director of National Intelligence, and shall remain sealed unless—

(A) an application for a court order with respect to the physical search is made under section 1821(4) of this title and section 1823 of this title; or

(B) the certification is necessary to determine the legality of the physical search under section 1825(g) of this title.

(4)(A) With respect to physical searches authorized by this subsection, the Attorney General may direct a specified landlord, custodian, or other specified person to—

(i) furnish all information, facilities, or assistance necessary to accomplish the physical search in such a manner as will protect its secrecy and produce a minimum of interference with the services that such landlord, custodian, or other person is providing the target of the physical search; and

(ii) maintain under security procedures approved by the Attorney General and the Director of National Intelligence any records concerning the search or the aid furnished that such person wishes to retain.

(B) The Government shall compensate, at the prevailing rate, such landlord, custodian, or other person for furnishing such aid.

(b) Application for order; authorization

Applications for a court order under this subchapter are authorized if the President has, by written authorization, empowered the Attorney General to approve applications to the Foreign Intelligence Surveillance Court. Notwithstanding any other provision of law, a judge of the court to whom application is made may grant an order in accordance with section 1824 of this title approving a physical search in the United States of the premises, property, information, or material of a foreign power or an agent of a foreign power for the purpose of collecting foreign intelligence information.

(c) Jurisdiction of Foreign Intelligence Surveillance Court

The Foreign Intelligence Surveillance Court shall have jurisdiction to hear applications for and grant orders approving a physical search for the purpose of obtaining foreign intelligence information anywhere within the United States under the procedures set forth in this subchapter, except that no judge (except when sitting en banc) shall hear the same application which has been denied previously by another judge designated under section 1803(a) of this title. If any judge so designated denies an application for an order authorizing a physical search under this subchapter, such judge shall provide immediately for the record a written statement of each reason for such decision and, on motion of the United States, the record shall be transmitted, under seal, to the court of review established under section 1803(b) of this title.

(d) Court of review; record; transmittal to Supreme Court

The court of review established under section 1803(b) of this title shall have jurisdiction to review the denial of any application made under this subchapter. If such court determines that the application was properly denied, the court shall immediately provide for the record a written statement of each reason for its decision and, on petition of the United States for a writ of certiorari, the record shall be transmitted under seal to the Supreme Court, which shall have jurisdiction to review such decision.

(e) Expeditious conduct of proceedings; security measures for maintenance of records

Judicial proceedings under this subchapter shall be concluded as expeditiously as possible. The record of proceedings under this subchapter, including applications made and orders granted, shall be maintained under security measures established by the Chief Justice of the United States in consultation with the Attorney General and the Director of National Intelligence.

§ 1823. Application for order

(a) Submission by Federal officer; approval of Attorney General; contents

Each application for an order approving a physical search under this subchapter shall be made by a Federal officer in writing upon oath or affirmation to a judge of the Foreign Intelligence Surveillance Court. Each application shall require the approval of the Attorney General based upon the Attorney General's finding that it satisfies the criteria and requirements for such application as set forth in this subchapter. Each application shall include—

(1) the identity of the Federal officer making the application;

(2) the identity, if known, or a description of the target of the search, and a description of the premises or property to be searched and of the information, material, or property to be seized, reproduced, or altered;

(3) a statement of the facts and circumstances relied upon by the applicant to justify the applicant's belief that—

(A) the target of the physical search is a foreign power or an agent of a foreign power;

(B) the premises or property to be searched contains foreign intelligence information; and

(C) the premises or property to be searched is or is about to be owned, used, possessed by, or is in transit to or from a foreign power or an agent of a foreign power;

(4) a statement of the proposed minimization procedures;

(5) a statement of the nature of the foreign intelligence sought and the manner in which the physical search is to be conducted;

(6) a certification or certifications by the Assistant to the President for National Security Affairs an executive branch official or officials designated by the President from among those executive branch officers employed in the area of national security or defense and appointed by the President, by and with the advice and consent of the Senate, or the Deputy Director of the Federal Bureau of Investigation, if designated by the President as a certifying official—

(A) that the certifying official deems the information sought to be foreign intelligence information;

(B) that a significant purpose of the search is to obtain foreign intelligence information;

(C) that such information cannot reasonably be obtained by normal investigative techniques;

(D) that designates the type of foreign intelligence information being sought according to the categories described in section 1801(e) of this title; and

(E) includes a statement explaining the basis for the certifications required by subparagraphs (C) and (D);

(7) where the physical search involves a search of the residence of a United States person, the Attorney General shall state what investigative techniques have previously been utilized to obtain the foreign intelligence information concerned and the degree to which these techniques resulted in acquiring such information; and

(8) a statement of the facts concerning all previous applications that have been made to any judge under this subchapter involving any of the persons, premises, or property specified in the application, and the action taken on each previous application.

(b) Additional affidavits or certifications

The Attorney General may require any other affidavit or certification from any other officer in connection with the application.

(c) Additional information

The judge may require the applicant to furnish such other information as may be necessary to make the determinations required by section 1824 of this title.

(d) Personal review by Attorney General

(1)(A) Upon written request of the Director of the Federal Bureau of Investigation, the Secretary of Defense, the Secretary of State, the Director of National Intelligence, or the Director of the Central Intelligence Agency, the Attorney General shall personally review under subsection (a) of this section an application under that subsection for a target described in section 1801(b)(2) of this title.

(B) Except when disabled or otherwise unavailable to make a request referred to in subparagraph (A), an official referred to in that subparagraph may not delegate the authority to make a request referred to in that subparagraph.

(C) Each official referred to in subparagraph (A) with authority to make a request under that subparagraph shall take appropriate actions in advance to ensure that delegation of such authority is clearly established in the event such official is disabled or otherwise unavailable to make such request.

(2)(A) If as a result of a request under paragraph (1) the Attorney General determines not to approve an application under the second sentence of subsection (a) of this section for purposes of making the application under this section, the Attorney General shall provide written notice of the determination to the official making the request for the review of the application under that paragraph. Except when disabled or otherwise unavailable to make a determination under the preceding sentence, the Attorney General may not delegate the responsibility to make a determination under that sentence. The Attorney General shall take appropriate actions in advance to ensure that delegation of such responsibility is clearly established in the event the Attorney General is disabled or otherwise unavailable to make such determination.

(B) Notice with respect to an application under subparagraph (A) shall set forth the modifications, if any, of the application that are necessary in order for the Attorney General to approve the application under the second sentence of subsection (a) of this section for purposes of making the application under this section.

(C) Upon review of any modifications of an application set forth under subparagraph (B), the official notified of the modifications under this paragraph shall modify the application if such official determines that such modification is warranted. Such official shall supervise the making of any modification under this subparagraph. Except when disabled or otherwise unavailable to supervise the making of any modification under the preceding sentence, such official may not delegate the responsibility to supervise the making of any modification under that preceding sentence. Each such official shall take appropriate actions in advance to ensure that delegation of such responsibility is clearly established in the event such official is disabled or otherwise unavailable to supervise the making of such modification.

§ 1824. Issuance of order

(a) Necessary findings

Upon an application made pursuant to section 1823 of this title, the judge shall enter an ex parte order as requested or as modified approving the physical search if the judge finds that—

(1) the application has been made by a Federal officer and approved by the Attorney General;

(2) on the basis of the facts submitted by the applicant there is probable cause to believe that—

(A) the target of the physical search is a foreign power or an agent of a foreign power, except that no United States person may be considered an agent of a foreign power solely upon the basis of activities protected by the first amendment to the Constitution of the United States; and

(B) the premises or property to be searched is or is about to be owned, used, possessed by, or is in transit to or from an agent of a foreign power or a foreign power;

(3) the proposed minimization procedures meet the definition of minimization contained in this subchapter; and

(4) the application which has been filed contains all statements and certifications required by section 1823 of this title, and, if the target is a United States person, the certification or certifications are not clearly erroneous on the basis of the statement made under section 1823(a)(6)(E) of this title and any other information furnished under section 1823(c) of this title.

(b) Determination of probable cause

In determining whether or not probable cause exists for purposes of an order under subsection (a)(3) of this section, a judge may consider past activities of the target, as well as facts and circumstances relating to current or future activities of the target.

(c) Specifications and directions of orders

An order approving a physical search under this section shall—

(1) specify—

(A) the identity, if known, or a description of the target of the physical search;

(B) the nature and location of each of the premises or property to be searched;

(C) the type of information, material, or property to be seized, altered, or reproduced;

(D) a statement of the manner in which the physical search is to be conducted and, whenever more than one physical search is authorized under the order, the authorized scope of each search and what minimization procedures shall apply to the information acquired by each search; and

(E) the period of time during which physical searches are approved; and

(2) direct—

(A) that the minimization procedures be followed;

(B) that, upon the request of the applicant, a specified landlord, custodian, or other specified person furnish the applicant forthwith all information, facilities, or assistance necessary to accomplish the physical search in such a manner as will protect its secrecy and produce a minimum of interference with the services that such landlord, custodian, or other person is providing the target of the physical search;

(C) that such landlord, custodian, or other person maintain under security procedures approved by the Attorney General and the Director of National Intelligence any records concerning the search or the aid furnished that such person wishes to retain;

(D) that the applicant compensate, at the prevailing rate, such landlord, custodian, or other person for furnishing such aid; and

(E) that the Federal officer conducting the physical search promptly report to the court the circumstances and results of the physical search.

(d) Duration of order; extensions; assessment of compliance

(1) An order issued under this section may approve a physical search for the period necessary to achieve its purpose, or for 90 days, whichever is less, except that (A) an order under this section shall approve a physical search targeted against a foreign power, as defined in paragraph (1), (2), or (3) of section 1801(a) of this title, for the period specified in the application or for one year, whichever is less, and (B) an order under this section for a physical search targeted against an agent of a foreign power who is not a United States person may be for the period specified in the application or for 120 days, whichever is less.

(2) Extensions of an order issued under this subchapter may be granted on the same basis as the original order upon an application for an extension and new findings made in the same manner as required for the original order, except that an extension of an order under this chapter for a physical search targeted against a foreign power, as defined in paragraph (5), (6), or (7) of section 1801(a) of this title, or against a foreign power, as defined in section 1801(a)(4) of this title, that is not a United States person, or against an agent of a foreign power who is not a United States person, may be for a period not to exceed one year if the judge finds probable cause to believe that no property of any individual United States person will be acquired during the period.

(3) At or before the end of the period of time for which a physical search is approved by an order or an extension, or at any time after a physical search is carried out, the judge may assess compliance with the minimization procedures by reviewing the circumstances under which information concerning United States persons was acquired, retained, or disseminated.

(e)(1) Notwithstanding any other provision of this subchapter, the Attorney General may authorize the emergency employment of a physical search if the Attorney General—

(A) reasonably determines that an emergency situation exists with respect to the employment of a physical search to obtain foreign intelligence information before an order authorizing such physical search can with due diligence be obtained;

(B) reasonably determines that the factual basis for issuance of an order under this subchapter to approve such physical search exists;

(C) informs, either personally or through a designee, a judge of the Foreign Intelligence Surveillance Court at the time of such authorization that the decision has been made to employ an emergency physical search; and

(D) makes an application in accordance with this subchapter to a judge of the Foreign Intelligence Surveillance Court as soon as practicable, but not more than 7 days after the Attorney General authorizes such physical search.

(2) If the Attorney General authorizes the emergency employment of a physical search under paragraph (1), the Attorney General shall require that the minimization procedures required by this subchapter for the issuance of a judicial order be followed.

(3) In the absence of a judicial order approving such physical search, the physical search shall terminate when the information sought is obtained, when the application for the order is denied, or after the expiration of 7 days from the time of authorization by the Attorney General, whichever is earliest.

(4) A denial of the application made under this subsection may be reviewed as provided in section 1803 of this title.

(5) In the event that such application for approval is denied, or in any other case where the physical search is terminated and no order is issued approving the physical search, no information obtained or evidence derived from such physical search shall be received in evidence or otherwise disclosed in any trial, hearing, or other proceeding in or before any court, grand jury, department, office, agency, regulatory body, legislative committee, or other authority of the United States, a State, or political subdivision thereof, and no information concerning any United States person acquired from such physical search shall subsequently be used or disclosed in any other manner by Federal officers or employees without the consent of such person, except with the approval of the Attorney General if the information indicates a threat of death or serious bodily harm to any person.

(6) The Attorney General shall assess compliance with the requirements of paragraph (5).

(f) Retention of applications and orders

Applications made and orders granted under this subchapter shall be retained for a period of at least 10 years from the date of the application.

§ 1825. Use of information

(a) Compliance with minimization procedures; lawful purposes

Information acquired from a physical search conducted pursuant to this subchapter concerning any United States person may be used and disclosed by Federal officers and employees without the consent of the United States person only in accordance with the minimization procedures required by this subchapter. No information acquired from a physical search pursuant to this subchapter may be used or disclosed by Federal officers or employees except for lawful purposes.

(b) Notice of search and identification of property seized, altered, or reproduced

Where a physical search authorized and conducted pursuant to section 1824 of this title involves the residence of a United States person, and, at any time after the search the Attorney General determines there is no national security interest in continuing to maintain the secrecy of the search, the Attorney General shall provide notice to the United States person whose residence was searched of the fact of the search conducted pursuant to this chapter and shall identify any property of such person seized, altered, or reproduced during such search.

(c) Statement for disclosure

No information acquired pursuant to this subchapter shall be disclosed for law enforcement purposes unless such disclosure is accompanied by a statement that such information, or any information derived therefrom, may only be used in a criminal proceeding with the advance authorization of the Attorney General.

(d) Notification by United States

Whenever the United States intends to enter into evidence or otherwise use or disclose in any trial, hearing, or other proceeding in or before any court, department, officer, agency, regulatory body, or other authority of the United States, against an aggrieved person, any information obtained or derived from a physical search pursuant to the authority of this subchapter, the United States shall, prior to the trial, hearing, or the other proceeding or at a reasonable time prior to an effort to so disclose or so use that information or submit it in evidence, notify the aggrieved person and the court or other authority in which the information is to be disclosed or used that the United States intends to so disclose or so use such information.

(e) Notification by States or political subdivisions

Whenever any State or political subdivision thereof intends to enter into evidence or otherwise use or disclose in any trial, hearing, or other proceeding in or before any court, department, officer, agency, regulatory body, or other authority of a State or a political subdivision thereof against an aggrieved person any information obtained or derived from a physical search pursuant to the authority of this subchapter, the State or political subdivision thereof shall notify the aggrieved person, the court or other authority in which the information is to be disclosed or used, and the Attorney General that the State or political subdivision thereof intends to so disclose or so use such information.

(f) Motion to suppress

> **(1)** Any person against whom evidence obtained or derived from a physical search to which he is an aggrieved person is to be, or has been, introduced or otherwise used or disclosed in any trial, hearing, or other proceeding in or before any court, department, officer, agency,

regulatory body, or other authority of the United States, a State, or a political subdivision thereof, may move to suppress the evidence obtained or derived from such search on the grounds that—

(A) the information was unlawfully acquired; or

(B) the physical search was not made in conformity with an order of authorization or approval.

(2) Such a motion shall be made before the trial, hearing, or other proceeding unless there was no opportunity to make such a motion or the person was not aware of the grounds of the motion.

(g) In camera and ex parte review by district court

Whenever a court or other authority is notified pursuant to subsection (d) or (e) of this section, or whenever a motion is made pursuant to subsection (f) of this section, or whenever any motion or request is made by an aggrieved person pursuant to any other statute or rule of the United States or any State before any court or other authority of the United States or any State to discover or obtain applications or orders or other materials relating to a physical search authorized by this subchapter or to discover, obtain, or suppress evidence or information obtained or derived from a physical search authorized by this subchapter, the United States district court or, where the motion is made before another authority, the United States district court in the same district as the authority shall, notwithstanding any other provision of law, if the Attorney General files an affidavit under oath that disclosure or any adversary hearing would harm the national security of the United States, review in camera and ex parte the application, order, and such other materials relating to the physical search as may be necessary to determine whether the physical search of the aggrieved person was lawfully authorized and conducted. In making this determination, the court may disclose to the aggrieved person, under appropriate security procedures and protective orders, portions of the application, order, or other materials relating to the physical search, or may require the Attorney General to provide to the aggrieved person a summary of such materials, only where such disclosure is necessary to make an accurate determination of the legality of the physical search.

(h) Suppression of evidence; denial of motion

If the United States district court pursuant to subsection (g) of this section determines that the physical search was not lawfully authorized or conducted, it shall, in accordance with the requirements of law, suppress the evidence which was unlawfully obtained or derived from the physical search of the aggrieved person or otherwise grant the motion of the aggrieved person. If the court determines that the physical search was lawfully authorized or conducted, it shall deny the motion of the aggrieved person except to the extent that due process requires discovery or disclosure.

(i) Finality of orders

Orders granting motions or requests under subsection (h) of this section, decisions under this section that a physical search was not lawfully authorized or conducted, and orders of the United States district court requiring review or granting disclosure of applications, orders, or other materials relating to the physical search shall be final orders and binding upon all courts of the United States and the several States except a United States Court of Appeals or the Supreme Court.

(j) Notification of emergency execution of physical search; contents; postponement, suspension, or elimination

(1) If an emergency execution of a physical search is authorized under section 1824(d) of this title and a subsequent order approving the search is not obtained, the judge shall cause to be served on any United States person named in the application and on such other United States persons subject to the search as the judge may determine in his discretion it is in the interests of justice to serve, notice of—

(A) the fact of the application;

(B) the period of the search; and

(C) the fact that during the period information was or was not obtained.

(2) On an ex parte showing of good cause to the judge, the serving of the notice required by this subsection may be postponed or suspended for a period not to exceed 90 days. Thereafter, on a further ex parte showing of good cause, the court shall forego ordering the serving of the notice required under this subsection.

(k) Consultation with Federal law enforcement officers

(1) Federal officers who conduct physical searches to acquire foreign intelligence information under this subchapter may consult with Federal law enforcement officers or law enforcement personnel of a State or political subdivision of a State (including the chief executive officer of that State or political subdivision who has the authority to appoint or direct the chief law enforcement officer of that State or political subdivision) to coordinate efforts to investigate or protect against

(A) actual or potential attack or other grave hostile acts of a foreign power or an agent of a foreign power;

(B) sabotage, international terrorism, or the proliferation of weapons of mass destruction by a foreign power or an agent of a foreign power; or

(C) clandestine intelligence activities by an intelligence service or network of a foreign power or by an agent of a foreign power.

(2) Coordination authorized under paragraph (1) shall not preclude the certification required by section 1823(a)(6) of this title or the entry of an order under section 1824 of this title.

§ 1826. Congressional oversight

On a semiannual basis the Attorney General shall fully inform the Permanent Select Committee on Intelligence of the House of Representatives and the Select Committee on Intelligence of the Senate, and the Committee on the Judiciary of the Senate, concerning all physical searches conducted pursuant to this subchapter. On a semiannual basis the Attorney General shall also provide to those committees and the Committee on the Judiciary of the House of Representatives a report setting forth with respect to the preceding six-month period—

(1) the total number of applications made for orders approving physical searches under this subchapter;

(2) the total number of such orders either granted, modified, or denied;

(3) the number of physical searches which involved searches of the residences, offices, or personal property of United States persons, and the number of occasions, if any, where the Attorney General provided notice pursuant to section 1825(b) of this title; and

(4) the total number of emergency physical searches authorized by the Attorney General under section 1824(e) of this title and the total number of subsequent orders approving or denying such physical searches.

§ 1827. Penalties

(a) Prohibited activities

A person is guilty of an offense if he intentionally—

(1) under color of law for the purpose of obtaining foreign intelligence information, executes a physical search within the United States except as authorized by statute; or

(2) discloses or uses information obtained under color of law by physical search within the United States, knowing or having reason to know that the information was obtained through physical search not authorized by statute, for the purpose of obtaining intelligence information.

(b) Defense

It is a defense to a prosecution under subsection (a) of this section that the defendant was a law enforcement or investigative officer engaged in the course of his official duties and the physical search was authorized by and conducted pursuant to a search warrant or court order of a court of competent jurisdiction.

(c) Fine or imprisonment

An offense described in this section is punishable by a fine of not more than $10,000 or imprisonment for not more than five years, or both.

(d) Federal jurisdiction

There is Federal jurisdiction over an offense under this section if the person committing the offense was an officer or employee of the United States at the time the offense was committed.

§ 1828. Civil liability

An aggrieved person, other than a foreign power or an agent of a foreign power, as defined in section 1801(a) or (b)(1)(A), respectively, of this title, whose premises, property, information, or material has been subjected to a physical search within the United States or about whom information obtained by such a physical search has been disclosed or used in violation of section 1827 of this title shall have a cause of action against any person who committed such violation and shall be entitled to recover—

(1) actual damages, but not less than liquidated damages of $1,000 or $100 per day for each day of violation, whichever is greater;

(2) punitive damages; and

(3) reasonable attorney's fees and other investigative and litigation costs reasonably incurred.

§ 1829. Authorization during time of war

Notwithstanding any other provision of law, the President, through the Attorney General, may authorize physical searches without a court order under this subchapter to acquire foreign intelligence information for a period not to exceed 15 calendar days following a declaration of war by the Congress.

§ 1841. Definitions

As used in this subchapter:

(1) The terms "foreign power", "agent of a foreign power", "international terrorism", "foreign intelligence information", "Attorney General", "United States person", "United States", "person", and "State" shall have the same meanings as in section 1801 of this title.

(2) The terms "pen register" and "trap and trace device" have the meanings given such terms in section 3127 of Title 18.

(3) The term "aggrieved person" means any person—

> **(A)** whose telephone line was subject to the installation or use of a pen register or trap and trace device authorized by this subchapter; or
>
> **(B)** whose communication instrument or device was subject to the use of a pen register or trap and trace device authorized by this subchapter to capture incoming electronic or other communications impulses.

§ 1842. Pen registers and trap and trace devices for foreign intelligence and international terrorism investigations

(a) Application for authorization or approval

> **(1)** Notwithstanding any other provision of law, the Attorney General or a designated attorney for the Government may make an application for an order or an extension of an order authorizing or approving the installation and use of a pen register or trap and trace device for any investigation to obtain foreign intelligence information not concerning a United States person or to protect against international terrorism or clandestine intelligence activities, provided that such investigation of a United States person is not conducted solely upon the basis of activities protected by the first amendment to the Constitution which is being conducted by the Federal Bureau of Investigation under such guidelines as the Attorney General approves pursuant to Executive Order No. 12333, or a successor order.
>
> **(2)** The authority under paragraph (1) is in addition to the authority under subchapter I of this chapter to conduct the electronic surveillance referred to in that paragraph.

(b) Form of application; recipient

Each application under this section shall be in writing under oath or affirmation to—

(1) a judge of the court established by section 1803(a) of this title; or

(2) a United States Magistrate Judge under chapter 43 of Title 28, who is publicly designated by the Chief Justice of the United States to have the power to hear applications for and grant orders approving the installation and use of a pen register or trap and trace device on behalf of a judge of that court.

(c) Executive approval; contents of application

Each application under this section shall require the approval of the Attorney General, or a designated attorney for the Government, and shall include—

(1) the identity of the Federal officer seeking to use the pen register or trap and trace device covered by the application; and

(2) a certification by the applicant that the information likely to be obtained is foreign intelligence information not concerning a United States person or is relevant to an ongoing investigation to protect against international terrorism or clandestine intelligence activities, provided that such investigation of a United States person is not conducted solely upon the basis of activities protected by the first amendment to the Constitution.

(3) Repealed. Pub.L. 107-56, Title II, § 214(a)(3), Oct. 26, 2001, 115 Stat. 286

(d) Ex parte judicial order of approval

(1) Upon an application made pursuant to this section, the judge shall enter an ex parte order as requested, or as modified, approving the installation and use of a pen register or trap and trace device if the judge finds that the application satisfies the requirements of this section.

(2) An order issued under this section—

(A) shall specify—

(i) the identity, if known, of the person who is the subject of the investigation;

(ii) the identity, if known, of the person to whom is leased or in whose name is listed the telephone line or other facility to which the pen register or trap and trace device is to be attached or applied; and

(iii) the attributes of the communications to which the order applies, such as the number or other identifier, and, if known, the location of the telephone line or other facility to which the pen register or trap and trace device is to be attached or applied and, in the case of a trap and trace device, the geographic limits of the trap and trace order;

(B) shall direct that—

(i) upon request of the applicant, the provider of a wire or electronic communication service, landlord, custodian, or other person shall furnish any information, facilities, or technical assistance necessary to accomplish the installation and operation of the pen register or trap and trace device in such a manner as will protect its secrecy and produce a minimum amount of interference with the services that such provider, landlord, custodian, or other person is providing the person concerned;

(ii) such provider, landlord, custodian, or other person—

(I) shall not disclose the existence of the investigation or of the pen register or trap and trace device to any person unless or until ordered by the court; and

(II) shall maintain, under security procedures approved by the Attorney General and the Director of National Intelligence pursuant to section 1805(b)(2)(C) of this title, any records concerning the pen register or trap and trace device or the aid furnished; and

(iii) the applicant shall compensate such provider, landlord, custodian, or other person for reasonable expenses incurred by such provider, landlord, custodian, or other person in providing such information, facilities, or technical assistance; and

(C) shall direct that, upon the request of the applicant, the provider of a wire or electronic communication service shall disclose to the Federal officer using the pen register or trap and trace device covered by the order—

(i) in the case of the customer or subscriber using the service covered by the order (for the period specified by the order)—

(I) the name of the customer or subscriber;

(II) the address of the customer or subscriber;

(III) the telephone or instrument number, or other subscriber number or identifier, of the customer or subscriber, including any temporarily assigned network address or associated routing or transmission information;

(IV) the length of the provision of service by such provider to the customer or subscriber and the types of services utilized by the customer or subscriber;

(V) in the case of a provider of local or long distance telephone service, any local or long distance telephone records of the customer or subscriber;

(VI) if applicable, any records reflecting period of usage (or sessions) by the customer or subscriber; and

(VII) any mechanisms and sources of payment for such service, including the number of any credit card or bank account utilized for payment for such service; and

(ii) if available, with respect to any customer or subscriber of incoming or outgoing communications to or from the service covered by the order—

(I) the name of such customer or subscriber;

(II) the address of such customer or subscriber;

(III) the telephone or instrument number, or other subscriber number or identifier, of such customer or subscriber, including any temporarily assigned network address or associated routing or transmission information; and

(IV) the length of the provision of service by such provider to such customer or subscriber and the types of services utilized by such customer or subscriber.

(e) Time limitation

(1) Except as provided in paragraph (2), an order issued under this section shall authorize the installation and use of a pen register or trap and trace device for a period not to exceed 90 days. Extensions of such an order may be granted, but only upon an application for an order under this section and upon the judicial finding required by subsection (d) of this section. The period of extension shall be for a period not to exceed 90 days.

(2) In the case of an application under subsection (c) of this section where the applicant has certified that the information likely to be obtained is foreign intelligence information not concerning a United States person, an order, or an extension of an order, under this section may be for a period not to exceed one year.

(f) Cause of action barred

No cause of action shall lie in any court against any provider of a wire or electronic communication service, landlord, custodian, or other person (including any officer, employee, agent, or other specified person thereof) that furnishes any information, facilities, or technical assistance under subsection (d) of this section in accordance with the terms of an order issued under this section.

(g) Furnishing of results

Unless otherwise ordered by the judge, the results of a pen register or trap and trace device shall be furnished at reasonable intervals during regular business hours for the duration of the order to the authorized Government official or officials.

§ 1843. Authorization during emergencies

(a) Requirements for authorization

Notwithstanding any other provision of this subchapter, when the Attorney General makes a determination described in subsection (b) of this section, the Attorney General may authorize the installation and use of a pen register or trap and trace device on an emergency basis to gather foreign intelligence information not concerning a United States person or information to protect against international terrorism or clandestine intelligence activities, provided that such investigation of a United States person is not conducted solely upon the basis of activities protected by the first amendment to the Constitution if—

(1) a judge referred to in section 1842(b) of this title is informed by the Attorney General or his designee at the time of such authorization that the decision has been made to install and use the pen register or trap and trace device, as the case may be, on an emergency basis; and

(2) an application in accordance with section 1842 of this title is made to such judge as soon as practicable, but not more than 7 days, after the Attorney General authorizes the installation and use of the pen register or trap and trace device, as the case may be, under this section.

(b) Determination of emergency and factual basis

A determination under this subsection is a reasonable determination by the Attorney General that—

> **(1)** an emergency requires the installation and use of a pen register or trap and trace device to obtain foreign intelligence information not concerning a United States person or information to protect against international terrorism or clandestine intelligence activities, provided that such investigation of a United States person is not conducted solely upon the basis of activities protected by the first amendment to the Constitution before an order authorizing the installation and use of the pen register or trap and trace device, as the case may be, can with due diligence be obtained under section 1842 of this title; and
>
> **(2)** the factual basis for issuance of an order under such section 1842 of this title to approve the installation and use of the pen register or trap and trace device, as the case may be, exists.

(c) Effect of absence of order

> **(1)** In the absence of an order applied for under subsection (a)(2) of this section approving the installation and use of a pen register or trap and trace device authorized under this section, the installation and use of the pen register or trap and trace device, as the case may be, shall terminate at the earlier of—
>
> > **(A)** when the information sought is obtained;
> >
> > **(B)** when the application for the order is denied under section 1842 of this title; or
> >
> > **(C)** 7 days after the time of the authorization by the Attorney General.
>
> **(2)** In the event that an application for an order applied for under subsection (a)(2) of this section is denied, or in any other case where the installation and use of a pen register or trap and trace device under this section is terminated and no order under section 1842 of this title is issued approving the installation and use of the pen register or trap and trace device, as the case may be, no information obtained or evidence derived from the use of the pen register or trap and trace device, as the case may be, shall be received in evidence or otherwise disclosed in any trial, hearing, or other proceeding in or before any court, grand jury, department, office, agency, regulatory body, legislative committee, or other authority of the United States, a State, or political subdivision thereof, and no information concerning any United States person acquired from the use of the pen register or trap and trace device, as the case may be, shall subsequently be used or disclosed in any other manner by Federal officers or employees without the consent of such person, except with the approval of the Attorney General if the information indicates a threat of death or serious bodily harm to any person.

§ 1844. Authorization during time of war

Notwithstanding any other provision of law, the President, through the Attorney General, may authorize the use of a pen register or trap and trace device without a court order under this subchapter to acquire foreign intelligence information for a period not to exceed 15 calendar days following a declaration of war by Congress.

§ 1845. Use of information

(a) In general

(1) Information acquired from the use of a pen register or trap and trace device installed pursuant to this subchapter concerning any United States person may be used and disclosed by Federal officers and employees without the consent of the United States person only in accordance with the provisions of this section.

(2) No information acquired from a pen register or trap and trace device installed and used pursuant to this subchapter may be used or disclosed by Federal officers or employees except for lawful purposes.

(b) Disclosure for law enforcement purposes

No information acquired pursuant to this subchapter shall be disclosed for law enforcement purposes unless such disclosure is accompanied by a statement that such information, or any information derived therefrom, may only be used in a criminal proceeding with the advance authorization of the Attorney General.

(c) Notification of intended disclosure by United States

Whenever the United States intends to enter into evidence or otherwise use or disclose in any trial, hearing, or other proceeding in or before any court, department, officer, agency, regulatory body, or other authority of the United States against an aggrieved person any information obtained or derived from the use of a pen register or trap and trace device pursuant to this subchapter, the United States shall, before the trial, hearing, or the other proceeding or at a reasonable time before an effort to so disclose or so use that information or submit it in evidence, notify the aggrieved person and the court or other authority in which the information is to be disclosed or used that the United States intends to so disclose or so use such information.

(d) Notification of intended disclosure by State or political subdivision

Whenever any State or political subdivision thereof intends to enter into evidence or otherwise use or disclose in any trial, hearing, or other proceeding in or before any court, department, officer, agency, regulatory body, or other authority of the State or political subdivision thereof against an aggrieved person any information obtained or derived from the use of a pen register or trap and trace device pursuant to this subchapter, the State or political subdivision thereof shall notify the aggrieved person, the court or other authority in which the information is to be disclosed or used, and the Attorney General that the State or political subdivision thereof intends to so disclose or so use such information.

(e) Motion to suppress

(1) Any aggrieved person against whom evidence obtained or derived from the use of a pen register or trap and trace device is to be, or has been, introduced or otherwise used or disclosed in any trial, hearing, or other proceeding in or before any court, department, officer, agency, regulatory body, or other authority of the United States, or a State or political subdivision thereof, may move to suppress the evidence obtained or derived from the use of the pen register or trap and trace device, as the case may be, on the grounds that—

(A) the information was unlawfully acquired; or

(B) the use of the pen register or trap and trace device, as the case may be, was not made in conformity with an order of authorization or approval under this subchapter.

(2) A motion under paragraph (1) shall be made before the trial, hearing, or other proceeding unless there was no opportunity to make such a motion or the aggrieved person concerned was not aware of the grounds of the motion.

(f) In camera and ex parte review

(1) Whenever a court or other authority is notified pursuant to subsection (c) or (d) of this section, whenever a motion is made pursuant to subsection (e) of this section, or whenever any motion or request is made by an aggrieved person pursuant to any other statute or rule of the United States or any State before any court or other authority of the United States or any State to discover or obtain applications or orders or other materials relating to the use of a pen register or trap and trace device authorized by this subchapter or to discover, obtain, or suppress evidence or information obtained or derived from the use of a pen register or trap and trace device authorized by this subchapter, the United States district court or, where the motion is made before another authority, the United States district court in the same district as the authority shall, notwithstanding any other provision of law and if the Attorney General files an affidavit under oath that disclosure or any adversary hearing would harm the national security of the United States, review in camera and ex parte the application, order, and such other materials relating to the use of the pen register or trap and trace device, as the case may be, as may be necessary to determine whether the use of the pen register or trap and trace device, as the case may be, was lawfully authorized and conducted.

(2) In making a determination under paragraph (1), the court may disclose to the aggrieved person, under appropriate security procedures and protective orders, portions of the application, order, or other materials relating to the use of the pen register or trap and trace device, as the case may be, or may require the Attorney General to provide to the aggrieved person a summary of such materials, only where such disclosure is necessary to make an accurate determination of the legality of the use of the pen register or trap and trace device, as the case may be.

(g) Effect of determination of lawfulness

(1) If the United States district court determines pursuant to subsection (f) of this section that the use of a pen register or trap and trace device was not lawfully authorized or conducted, the court may, in accordance with the requirements of law, suppress the evidence which was unlawfully obtained or derived from the use of the pen register or trap and trace device, as the case may be, or otherwise grant the motion of the aggrieved person.

(2) If the court determines that the use of the pen register or trap and trace device, as the case may be, was lawfully authorized or conducted, it may deny the motion of the aggrieved person except to the extent that due process requires discovery or disclosure.

(h) Binding final orders

Orders granting motions or requests under subsection (g) of this section, decisions under this section that the use of a pen register or trap and trace device was not lawfully authorized or conducted, and orders of the United States district court requiring review or granting disclosure of applications, orders, or other materials relating to the installation and use of a pen register or trap and trace device shall be final orders and binding upon all courts of the United States and the several States except a United States Court of Appeals or the Supreme Court.

§ 1846. Congressional oversight

(a) On a semiannual basis, the Attorney General shall fully inform the Permanent Select Committee on Intelligence of the House of Representatives and the Select Committee on Intelligence of the Senate, and the Committee on the Judiciary of the House of Representatives and the Committee on the Judiciary of the Senate, concerning all uses of pen registers and trap and trace devices pursuant to this subchapter.

(b) On a semiannual basis, the Attorney General shall also provide to the committees referred to in subsection (a) of this section and to the Committees on the Judiciary of the House of Representatives and the Senate a report setting forth with respect to the preceding 6-month period—

(1) the total number of applications made for orders approving the use of pen registers or trap and trace devices under this subchapter;

(2) the total number of such orders either granted, modified, or denied; and

(3) the total number of pen registers and trap and trace devices whose installation and use was authorized by the Attorney General on an emergency basis under section 1843 of this title, and the total number of subsequent orders approving or denying the installation and use of such pen registers and trap and trace devices.

§ 1861. Access to certain business records for foreign intelligence and international terrorism investigations

(a)(1) Subject to paragraph (3), the Director of the Federal Bureau of Investigation or a designee of the Director (whose rank shall be no lower than Assistant Special Agent in Charge) may make an application for an order requiring the production of any tangible things (including books, records, papers, documents, and other items) for an investigation to obtain foreign intelligence information not concerning a United States person or to protect against international terrorism or clandestine intelligence activities, provided that such investigation of a United States person is not conducted solely upon the basis of activities protected by the first amendment to the Constitution.

(2) An investigation conducted under this section shall

(A) be conducted under guidelines approved by the Attorney General under Executive Order 12333 (or a successor order); and

(B) not be conducted of a United States person solely upon the basis of activities protected by the first amendment to the Constitution of the United States.

(3) In the case of an application for an order requiring the production of library circulation records, library patron lists, book sales records, book customer lists, firearms sales records, tax return records, educational records, or medical records containing information that would identify a person, the Director of the Federal Bureau of Investigation may delegate the authority to make such application to either the Deputy Director of the Federal Bureau of Investigation or the Executive Assistant Director for National Security (or any successor position). The Deputy Director or the Executive Assistant Director may not further delegate such authority.

(b) Each application under this section

(1) shall be made to—

(A) a judge of the court established by section 1803(a) of this title; or

(B) a United States Magistrate Judge under chapter 43 of Title 28, who is publicly designated by the Chief Justice of the United States to have the power to hear applications and grant orders for the production of tangible things under this section on behalf of a judge of that court; and

(2) shall include—

(A) a statement of facts showing that there are reasonable grounds to believe that the tangible things sought are relevant to an authorized investigation (other than a threat assessment) conducted in accordance with subsection (a)(2) of this section to obtain foreign intelligence information not concerning a United States person or to protect against international terrorism or clandestine intelligence activities, such things being presumptively relevant to an authorized investigation if the applicant shows in the statement of the facts that they pertain to—

(i) a foreign power or an agent of a foreign power;

(ii) the activities of a suspected agent of a foreign power who is the subject of such authorized investigation; or

(iii) an individual in contact with, or known to, a suspected agent of a foreign power who is the subject of such authorized investigation; and

(B) an enumeration of the minimization procedures adopted by the Attorney General under subsection (g) of this section that are applicable to the retention and dissemination by the Federal Bureau of Investigation of any tangible things to be made available to the Federal Bureau of Investigation based on the order requested in such application.

(c)(1) Upon an application made pursuant to this section, if the judge finds that the application meets the requirements of subsections (a) and (b) of this section, the judge shall enter an ex parte order as requested, or as modified, approving the release of tangible things. Such order shall direct that minimization procedures adopted pursuant to subsection (g) of this section be followed.

(2) An order under this subsection—

(A) shall describe the tangible things that are ordered to be produced with sufficient particularity to permit them to be fairly identified;

(B) shall include the date on which the tangible things must be provided, which shall allow a reasonable period of time within which the tangible things can be assembled and made available;

(C) shall provide clear and conspicuous notice of the principles and procedures described in subsection (d) of this section;

(D) may only require the production of a tangible thing if such thing can be obtained with a subpoena duces tecum issued by a court of the United States in aid of a grand jury investigation or with any other order issued by a court of the United States directing the production of records or tangible things; and

(E) shall not disclose that such order is issued for purposes of an investigation described in subsection (a) of this section.

(d)(1) No person shall disclose to any other person that the Federal bureau of investigation has sought or obtained tangible things pursuant to an order under this section, other than to

(A) those persons to whom disclosure is necessary to comply with such order;

(B) an attorney to obtain legal advice or assistance with respect to the production of things in response to the order; or

(C) other persons as permitted by the Director of the Federal Bureau of Investigation or the designee of the Director.

(2)(A) A person to whom disclosure is made pursuant to paragraph (1) shall be subject to the nondisclosure requirements applicable to a person to whom an order is directed under this section in the same manner as such person.

(B) Any person who discloses to a person described in subparagraph (A), (B), or (C) of paragraph (1) that the Federal Bureau of Investigation has sought or obtained tangible things pursuant to an order under this section shall notify such person of the nondisclosure requirements of this subsection.

(C) At the request of the Director of the Federal Bureau of Investigation or the designee of the Director, any person making or intending to make a disclosure under subparagraph (A) or (C) of paragraph (1) shall identify to the Director or such designee the person to whom such disclosure will be made or to whom such disclosure was made prior to the request.

(e) A person who, in good faith, produces tangible things under an order pursuant to this section shall not be liable to any other person for such production. Such production shall not be deemed to constitute a waiver of any privilege in any other proceeding or context.

(f)(1) In this subsection—

(A) the term "production order" means an order to produce any tangible thing under this section; and

(B) the term "nondisclosure order" means an order imposed under subsection (d) of this section.

(2)(A)(i) A person receiving a production order may challenge the legality of that order by filing a petition with the pool established by section 1803(e)(1) of this title. Not less than 1 year after the date of the issuance of the production order, the recipient of a production order may challenge the nondisclosure order imposed in connection with such production order by filing a petition to modify or set aside such nondisclosure order, consistent with the requirements of subparagraph (C), with the pool established by section 1803(e)(1) of this title.

(ii) The presiding judge shall immediately assign a petition under clause (i) to 1 of the judges serving in the pool established by section 1803(e)(1) of this title. Not later than 72 hours after the assignment of such petition, the assigned judge shall conduct an initial review of the petition. If the assigned judge determines that the petition is frivolous, the assigned judge shall immediately deny the petition and affirm the production order or nondisclosure order. If the assigned judge determines the petition is not frivolous, the assigned judge shall promptly consider the petition in accordance with the procedures established under section 1803(e)(2) of this title.

(iii) The assigned judge shall promptly provide a written statement for the record of the reasons for any determination under this subsection. Upon the request of the Government, any order setting aside a nondisclosure order shall be stayed pending review pursuant to paragraph (3).

(B) A judge considering a petition to modify or set aside a production order may grant such petition only if the judge finds that such order does not meet the requirements of this section or is otherwise unlawful. If the judge does not modify or set aside the production order, the judge shall immediately affirm such order, and order the recipient to comply therewith.

(C)(i) A judge considering a petition to modify or set aside a nondisclosure order may grant such petition only if the judge finds that there is no reason to believe that disclosure may endanger the national security of the United States, interfere with a criminal, counterterrorism, or counterintelligence investigation, interfere with diplomatic relations, or endanger the life or physical safety of any person.

(ii) If, upon filing of such a petition, the Attorney General, Deputy Attorney General, an Assistant Attorney General, or the Director of the Federal Bureau of Investigation certifies that disclosure may endanger the national security of the United States or interfere with diplomatic relations, such certification shall be treated as conclusive, unless the judge finds that the certification was made in bad faith.

(iii) If the judge denies a petition to modify or set aside a nondisclosure order, the recipient of such order shall be precluded for a period of 1 year from filing another such petition with respect to such nondisclosure order.

(D) Any production or nondisclosure order not explicitly modified or set aside consistent with this subsection shall remain in full effect.

(3) A petition for review of a decision under paragraph (2) to affirm, modify, or set aside an order by the Government or any person receiving such order shall be made to the court of review established under section 1803(b) of this title, which shall have jurisdiction to consider such petitions. The court of review shall provide for the record a written statement of the reasons for its decision and, on petition by the Government or any person receiving such order for writ of certiorari, the record shall be transmitted under seal to the Supreme Court of the United States, which shall have jurisdiction to review such decision.

(4) Judicial proceedings under this subsection shall be concluded as expeditiously as possible. The record of proceedings, including petitions filed, orders granted, and statements of reasons for decision, shall be maintained under security measures established by the Chief Justice of the United States, in consultation with the Attorney General and the Director of National Intelligence.

(5) All petitions under this subsection shall be filed under seal. In any proceedings under this subsection, the court shall, upon request of the Government, review ex parte and in camera any Government submission, or portions thereof, which may include classified information.

(g) Minimization procedures

(1) In general

Not later than 180 days after March 9, 2006, the Attorney General shall adopt specific minimization procedures governing the retention and dissemination by the Federal Bureau of Investigation of any tangible things, or information therein, received by the Federal Bureau of Investigation in response to an order under this subchapter.

(2) Defined

In this section, the term "minimization procedures" means—

(A) specific procedures that are reasonably designed in light of the purpose and technique of an order for the production of tangible things, to minimize the retention, and prohibit the dissemination, of nonpublicly available information concerning unconsenting United States persons consistent with the need of the United States to obtain, produce, and disseminate foreign intelligence information;

(B) procedures that require that nonpublicly available information, which is not foreign intelligence information, as defined in section 1801(e)(1) of this title, shall not be disseminated in a manner that identifies any United States person, without such person's consent, unless such person's identity is necessary to understand foreign intelligence information or assess its importance; and

(C) notwithstanding subparagraphs (A) and (B), procedures that allow for the retention and dissemination of information that is evidence of a crime which has been, is being, or is about to be committed and that is to be retained or disseminated for law enforcement purposes.

(h) Use of information

Information acquired from tangible things received by the Federal Bureau of Investigation in response to an order under this subchapter concerning any United States person may be used and disclosed by Federal officers and employees without the consent of the United States person only in accordance with the minimization procedures adopted pursuant to subsection (g) of this section. No otherwise privileged information acquired from tangible things received by the Federal Bureau of Investigation in accordance with the provisions of this subchapter shall lose its privileged character. No information acquired from tangible things received by the Federal Bureau of Investigation in response to an order under this subchapter may be used or disclosed by Federal officers or employees except for lawful purposes.

§ 1862. Congressional oversight

(a) On a annual basis, the Attorney General shall fully inform the Permanent Select Committee on Intelligence of the House of Representatives and the Select Committee on Intelligence and the Committee on the Judiciary of the Senate concerning all requests for the production of tangible things under section 1861 of this title.

(b) In April of each year, the Attorney General shall submit to the House and Senate Committees on the Judiciary and the House Permanent Select Committee on Intelligence and the Senate Select Committee on Intelligence a report setting forth with respect to the preceding calendar year—

(1) the total number of applications made for orders approving requests for the production of tangible things under section 1861 of this title;

(2) the total number of such orders either granted, modified, or denied; and

(3) the number of such orders either granted, modified, or denied for the production of each of the following:

(A) Library circulation records, library patron lists, book sales records, or book customer lists.

(B) Firearms sales records.

(C) Tax return records.

(D) Educational records.

(E) Medical records containing information that would identify a person.

(c)(1) In April of each year, the Attorney General shall submit to Congress a report setting forth with respect to the preceding year—

(A) the total number of applications made for orders approving requests for the production of tangible things under section 1861 of this title; and

(B) the total number of such orders either granted, modified, or denied.

(2) Each report under this subsection shall be submitted in unclassified form.

§ 1871. Semiannual report of the Attorney General

(a) Report

On a semiannual basis, the Attorney General shall submit to the Permanent Select Committee on Intelligence of the House of Representatives, the Select Committee on Intelligence of the Senate, and the Committees on the Judiciary of the House of Representatives and the Senate, in a manner consistent with the protection of the national security, a report setting forth with respect to the preceding 6-month period—

(1) the aggregate number of persons targeted for orders issued under this chapter, including a breakdown of those targeted for—

(A) electronic surveillance under section 1805 of this title;

(B) physical searches under section 1824 of this title;

(C) pen registers under section 1842 of this title;

(D) access to records under section 1861 of this title;

(E) acquisitions under section 1881b of this title; and

(F) acquisitions under section 1881c of this title;

(2) the number of individuals covered by an order issued pursuant to section 1801(b)(1)(C) of this title;

(3) the number of times that the Attorney General has authorized that information obtained under this chapter may be used in a criminal proceeding or any information derived therefrom may be used in a criminal proceeding;

(4) a summary of significant legal interpretations of this chapter involving matters before the Foreign Intelligence Surveillance Court or the Foreign Intelligence Surveillance Court of Review, including interpretations presented in applications or pleadings filed with the Foreign Intelligence Surveillance Court or the Foreign Intelligence Surveillance Court of Review by the Department of Justice; and

(5) copies of all decisions, orders, or opinions of the Foreign Intelligence Surveillance Court or Foreign Intelligence Surveillance Court of Review that include significant construction or interpretation of the provisions of this chapter.

(b) Frequency

The first report under this section shall be submitted not later than 6 months after December 17, 2004. Subsequent reports under this section shall be submitted semi-annually thereafter.

(c) Submissions to Congress

The Attorney General shall submit to the committees of Congress referred to in subsection (a)—

(1) a copy of any decision, order, or opinion issued by the Foreign Intelligence Surveillance Court or the Foreign Intelligence Surveillance Court of Review that includes significant construction or interpretation of any provision of this chapter, and any pleadings, applications, or memoranda of law associated with such decision, order, or opinion, not later than 45 days after such decision, order, or opinion is issued; and

(2) a copy of each such decision, order, or opinion, and any pleadings, applications, or memoranda of law associated with such decision, order, or opinion, that was issued during the 5-year period ending on July 10, 2008 and not previously submitted in a report under subsection (a).

(d) Protection of national security

The Attorney General, in consultation with the Director of National Intelligence, may authorize redactions of materials described in subsection (c) that are provided to the committees of Congress referred to in subsection (a), if such redactions are necessary to protect the national security of the United States and are limited to sensitive sources and methods information or the identities of targets.

(e) Definitions

In this section:

(1) Foreign Intelligence Surveillance Court

The term "Foreign Intelligence Surveillance Court" means the court established under section 1803(a) of this title.

(2) Foreign Intelligence Surveillance Court of Review

The term "Foreign Intelligence Surveillance Court of Review" means the court established under section 1803(b) of this title.

§ 1881. Definitions

(a) In general

The terms "agent of a foreign power", "Attorney General", "contents", "electronic surveillance", "foreign intelligence information", "foreign power", "person", "United States", and "United States person" have the meanings given such terms in section 1801 of this title, except as specifically provided in this subchapter.

(b) Additional definitions

(1) Congressional intelligence committees

The term "congressional intelligence committees" means—

(A) the Select Committee on Intelligence of the Senate; and

(B) the Permanent Select Committee on Intelligence of the House of Representatives.

(2) Foreign Intelligence Surveillance Court; Court

The terms "Foreign Intelligence Surveillance Court" and "Court" mean the court established under section 1803(a) of this title.

(3) Foreign Intelligence Surveillance Court of Review; Court of Review

The terms "Foreign Intelligence Surveillance Court of Review" and "Court of Review" mean the court established under section 1803(b) of this title.

(4) Electronic communication service provider

The term "electronic communication service provider" means—

(A) a telecommunications carrier, as that term is defined in section 153 of Title 47;

(B) a provider of electronic communication service, as that term is defined in section 2510 of Title 18;

(C) a provider of a remote computing service, as that term is defined in section 2711 of Title 18;

(D) any other communication service provider who has access to wire or electronic communications either as such communications are transmitted or as such communications are stored; or

(E) an officer, employee, or agent of an entity described in subparagraph (A), (B), (C), or (D).

(5) Intelligence community

The term “intelligence community” has the meaning given the term in section 401a(4) of this title.

§ 1885. Definitions

In this subchapter:

(1) Assistance

The term “assistance” means the provision of, or the provision of access to, information (including communication contents, communications records, or other information relating to a customer or communication), facilities, or another form of assistance.

(2) Civil action

The term “civil action” includes a covered civil action.

(3) Congressional intelligence committees

The term “congressional intelligence committees” means—

(A) the Select Committee on Intelligence of the Senate; and

(B) the Permanent Select Committee on Intelligence of the House of Representatives.

(4) Contents

The term “contents” has the meaning given that term in section 1801(n) of this title.

(5) Covered civil action

The term “covered civil action” means a civil action filed in a Federal or State court that—

(A) alleges that an electronic communication service provider furnished assistance to an element of the intelligence community; and

(B) seeks monetary or other relief from the electronic communication service provider related to the provision of such assistance.

(6) Electronic communication service provider

The term "electronic communication service provider" means—

(A) a telecommunications carrier, as that term is defined in section 153 of Title 47;

(B) a provider of electronic communication service, as that term is defined in section 2510 of Title 18;

(C) a provider of a remote computing service, as that term is defined in section 2711 of Title 18;

(D) any other communication service provider who has access to wire or electronic communications either as such communications are transmitted or as such communications are stored;

(E) a parent, subsidiary, affiliate, successor, or assignee of an entity described in subparagraph (A), (B), (C), or (D); or

(F) an officer, employee, or agent of an entity described in subparagraph (A), (B), (C), (D), or (E).

(7) Intelligence community

The term "intelligence community" has the meaning given the term in section 401a(4) of this title.

(8) Person

The term "person" means—

(A) an electronic communication service provider; or

(B) a landlord, custodian, or other person who may be authorized or required to furnish assistance pursuant to—

(i) an order of the court established under section 1803(a) of this title directing such assistance;

(ii) a certification in writing under section 2511(2)(a)(ii)(B) or 2709(b) of Title 18; or

(iii) a directive under section 1802(a)(4), 1805b(e), or 1881a(h) of this title.

(9) State

The term "State" means any State, political subdivision of a State, the Commonwealth of Puerto Rico, the District of Columbia, and any territory or possession of the United States, and includes any officer, public utility commission, or other body authorized to regulate an electronic communication service provider.

National Security Letter Provisions

18 U.S.C. § 2709, 12 U.S.C. § 3414 and 15 U.S.C. § 1681u, as amended

Statutes in Context

The FBI is granted the ability to seek different kinds of information pursuant to its National Security Letter authority. This authority does not require judicial approval, but certifications within the FBI itself. The relevant statutory provisions are codified in the Stored Communications Act, the Right to Financial Privacy Act, and the Fair Credit Reporting Act.

Stored Communications Act
18 U.S.C. § 2709

§ 2709. Counterintelligence access to telephone toll and transactional records

(a) Duty to provide.—A wire or electronic communication service provider shall comply with a request for subscriber information and toll billing records information, or electronic communication transactional records in its custody or possession made by the Director of the Federal Bureau of Investigation under subsection (b) of this section.

(b) Required certification.—The Director of the Federal Bureau of Investigation, or his designee in a position not lower than Deputy Assistant Director at Bureau headquarters or a Special Agent in Charge in a Bureau field office designated by the Director, may—

(1) request the name, address, length of service, and local and long distance toll billing records of a person or entity if the Director (or his designee) certifies in writing to the wire or electronic communication service provider to which the request is made that the name, address, length of service, and toll billing records sought are relevant to an authorized investigation to protect against international terrorism or clandestine intelligence activities, provided that such an investigation of a United States person is not conducted solely on the basis of activities protected by the first amendment to the Constitution of the United States; and

(2) request the name, address, and length of service of a person or entity if the Director (or his designee) certifies in writing to the wire or electronic communication service provider to which the request is made that the information sought is relevant to an authorized investigation to protect against international terrorism or clandestine intelligence activities, provided that such an investigation of a United States person is not conducted solely upon the basis of activities protected by the first amendment to the Constitution of the United States.

(c) Prohibition of certain disclosure.—

(1) If the Director of the Federal Bureau of Investigation, or his designee in a position not lower than Deputy Assistant Director at Bureau headquarters or a Special Agent in Charge in a Bureau field office designated by the Director, certifies that otherwise there may result a danger to the national security of the United States, interference with a criminal, counterterrorism, or counterintelligence investigation, interference with diplomatic relations, or danger to the life or physical safety of any person, no wire or electronic communications service provider, or officer, employee, or agent thereof, shall disclose to any person (other than those to whom such disclosure is necessary to comply with the request or an attorney to obtain legal advice or legal assistance with respect to the request) that the Federal Bureau of Investigation has sought or obtained access to information or records under this section.

(2) The request shall notify the person or entity to whom the request is directed of the nondisclosure requirement under paragraph (1).

(3) Any recipient disclosing to those persons necessary to comply with the request or to an attorney to obtain legal advice or legal assistance with respect to the request shall inform such person of any applicable nondisclosure requirement. Any person who receives a disclosure under this subsection shall be subject to the same prohibitions on disclosure under paragraph (1).

(4) At the request of the Director of the Federal Bureau of Investigation or the designee of the Director, any person making or intending to make a disclosure under this section shall identify to the Director or such designee the person to whom such disclosure will be made or to whom such disclosure was made prior to the request, except that nothing in this section shall require a person to inform the Director or such designee of the identity of an attorney to whom disclosure was made or will be made to obtain legal advice or legal assistance with respect to the request under subsection (a).

(d) Dissemination by bureau.—The Federal Bureau of Investigation may disseminate information and records obtained under this section only as provided in guidelines approved by the Attorney General for foreign intelligence collection and foreign counterintelligence investigations conducted by the Federal Bureau of Investigation, and, with respect to dissemination to an agency of the United States, only if such information is clearly relevant to the authorized responsibilities of such agency.

(e) Requirement that certain congressional bodies be informed.—On a semiannual basis the Director of the Federal Bureau of Investigation shall fully inform the Permanent Select Committee on Intelligence of the House of Representatives and the Select Committee on Intelligence of the Senate, and the Committee on the Judiciary of the House of Representatives and the Committee on the Judiciary of the Senate, concerning all requests made under subsection (b) of this section.

(f) Libraries.—A library (as that term is defined in section 213(1) of the Library Services and Technology Act (20 U.S.C. 9122(1)), the services of which include access to the Internet, books, journals, magazines, newspapers, or other similar forms of communication in print or digitally by patrons for their use, review, examination, or circulation, is not a wire or electronic communication service provider for purposes of this section, unless the library is providing the services defined in section 2510(15) ("electronic communication service") of this title.

Right to Financial Privacy Act
12 U.S.C. § 3414

§ 3414. Special procedures

(a)(1) Nothing in this chapter (except sections 3415, 3417, 3418, and 3421 of this title) shall apply to the production and disclosure of financial records pursuant to requests from—

> **(A)** a Government authority authorized to conduct foreign counter- or foreign positive-intelligence activities for purposes of conducting such activities;
>
> **(B)** the Secret Service for the purpose of conducting its protective functions (18 U.S.C. 3056; 18 U.S.C. 3056A, Public Law 90-331, as amended); or
>
> **(C)** a Government authority authorized to conduct investigations of, or intelligence or counterintelligence analyses related to, international terrorism for the purpose of conducting such investigations or analyses.

(2) In the instances specified in paragraph (1), the Government authority shall submit to the financial institution the certificate required in section 3403(b) of this title signed by a supervisory official of a rank designated by the head of the Government authority.

(3)(A) If the Government authority described in paragraph (1) or the Secret Service, as the case may be, certifies that otherwise there may result a danger to the national security of the United States, interference with a criminal, counterterrorism, or counterintelligence investigation, interference with diplomatic relations, or danger to the life or physical safety of any person, no financial institution, or officer, employee, or agent of such institution, shall disclose to any person (other than those to whom such disclosure is necessary to comply with the request or an attorney to obtain legal advice or legal assistance with respect to the request) that the Government authority or the Secret Service has sought or obtained access to a customer's financial records.

> **(B)** The request shall notify the person or entity to whom the request is directed of the nondisclosure requirement under subparagraph (A).
>
> **(C)** Any recipient disclosing to those persons necessary to comply with the request or to an attorney to obtain legal advice or legal assistance with respect to the request shall inform such persons of any applicable nondisclosure requirement. Any person who receives a disclosure under this subsection shall be subject to the same prohibitions on disclosure under subparagraph (A).
>
> **(D)** At the request of the authorized Government authority or the Secret Service, any person making or intending to make a disclosure under this section shall identify to the requesting official of the authorized Government authority or the Secret Service the person to whom such disclosure will be made or to whom such disclosure was made prior to the request, except that nothing in this section shall require a person to inform the requesting official of the authorized Government authority or the Secret Service of the identity of an attorney to whom disclosure was made or will be made to obtain legal

advice or legal assistance with respect to the request for financial records under this subsection.

(4) The Government authority specified in paragraph (1) shall compile an annual tabulation of the occasions in which this section was used.

(5)(A) Financial institutions, and officers, employees, and agents thereof, shall comply with a request for a customer's or entity's financial records made pursuant to this subsection by the Federal Bureau of Investigation when the Director of the Federal Bureau of Investigation (or the Director's designee in a position not lower than Deputy Assistant Director at Bureau headquarters or a Special Agent in Charge in a Bureau field office designated by the Director) certifies in writing to the financial institution that such records are sought for foreign counter intelligence purposes to protect against international terrorism or clandestine intelligence activities, provided that such an investigation of a United States person is not conducted solely upon the basis of activities protected by the first amendment to the Constitution of the United States.

(B) The Federal Bureau of Investigation may disseminate information obtained pursuant to this paragraph only as provided in guidelines approved by the Attorney General for foreign intelligence collection and foreign counterintelligence investigations conducted by the Federal Bureau of Investigation, and, with respect to dissemination to an agency of the United States, only if such information is clearly relevant to the authorized responsibilities of such agency.

(C) On the dates provided in section 415b of Title 50, the Attorney General shall fully inform the congressional intelligence committees (as defined in section 401a of Title 50) concerning all requests made pursuant to this paragraph.

(D) Prohibition of certain disclosure.—

(i) If the Director of the Federal Bureau of Investigation, or his designee in a position not lower than Deputy Assistant Director at Bureau headquarters or a Special Agent in Charge in a Bureau field office designated by the Director, certifies that otherwise there may result a danger to the national security of the United States, interference with a criminal, counterterrorism, or counterintelligence investigation, interference with diplomatic relations, or danger to the life or physical safety of any person, no financial institution, or officer, employee, or agent of such institution, shall disclose to any person (other than those to whom such disclosure is necessary to comply with the request or an attorney to obtain legal advice or legal assistance with respect to the request) that the Federal Bureau of Investigation has sought or obtained access to a customer's or entity's financial records under subparagraph (A).

(ii) The request shall notify the person or entity to whom the request is directed of the nondisclosure requirement under clause (i).

(iii) Any recipient disclosing to those persons necessary to comply with the request or to an attorney to obtain legal advice or legal assistance with respect to the request shall inform such persons of any applicable nondisclosure requirement. Any person who receives a disclosure under this subsection shall be subject to the same prohibitions on disclosure under clause (i).

(iv) At the request of the Director of the Federal Bureau of Investigation or the designee of the Director, any person making or intending to make a disclosure under this section shall identify to the Director or such designee the person to whom such disclosure will be made or to whom such disclosure was made prior to the request, except that nothing in this section shall require a person to inform the Director or such designee of the identity of an attorney to whom disclosure was made or will be made to obtain legal advice or legal assistance with respect to the request for financial records under subparagraph (A).

(b)(1) Nothing in this chapter shall prohibit a Government authority from obtaining financial records from a financial institution if the Government authority determines that delay in obtaining access to such records would create imminent danger of—

(A) physical injury to any person;

(B) serious property damage; or

(C) flight to avoid prosecution.

(2) In the instances specified in paragraph (1), the Government shall submit to the financial institution the certificate required in section 3403(b) of this title signed by a supervisory official of a rank designated by the head of the Government authority.

(3) Within five days of obtaining access to financial records under this subsection, the Government authority shall file with the appropriate court a signed, sworn statement of a supervisory official of a rank designated by the head of the Government authority setting forth the grounds for the emergency access. The Government authority shall thereafter comply with the notice provisions of section 3409(c) of this title.

(4) The Government authority specified in paragraph (1) shall compile an annual tabulation of the occasions in which this section was used.

(d) For purposes of this section, and sections 3415 and 3417 of this title insofar as they relate to the operation of this section, the term "financial institution" has the same meaning as in subsections (a)(2) and(c)(1) of section 5312 of Title 31, except that, for purposes of this section, such term shall include only such a financial institution any part of which is located inside any State or territory of the United States, the District of Columbia, Puerto Rico, Guam, American Samoa, the Commonwealth of the Northern Mariana Islands, or the United States Virgin Islands.

Fair Credit Reporting Act
15 U.S.C. § 1681u

§ 1681u. Disclosures to FBI for counterintelligence purposes

(a) Identity of financial institutions

Notwithstanding section 1681b of this title or any other provision of this subchapter, a consumer reporting agency shall furnish to the Federal Bureau of Investigation the names and addresses of all financial institutions (as that term is defined in section 3401 of Title 12) at which a consumer maintains or has maintained an account, to the extent that information is in the files of the agency, when presented with a written request for that information, signed by the Director of the Federal Bureau of Investigation, or the Director's designee in a position not lower than Deputy Assistant Director at Bureau headquarters or a Special Agent in Charge of a Bureau field office designated by the Director, which certifies compliance with this section. The Director or the Director's designee may make such a certification only if the Director or the Director's designee has determined in writing, that such information is sought for the conduct of an authorized investigation to protect against international terrorism or clandestine intelligence activities, provided that such an investigation of a United States person is not conducted solely upon the basis of activities protected by the first amendment to the Constitution of the United States.

(b) Identifying information

Notwithstanding the provisions of section 1681b of this title or any other provision of this subchapter, a consumer reporting agency shall furnish identifying information respecting a consumer, limited to name, address, former addresses, places of employment, or former places of employment, to the Federal Bureau of Investigation when presented with a written request, signed by the Director or the Director's designee in a position not lower than Deputy Assistant Director at Bureau headquarters or a Special Agent in Charge of a Bureau field office designated by the Director, which certifies compliance with this subsection. The Director or the Director's designee may make such a certification only if the Director or the Director's designee has determined in writing that such information is sought for the conduct of an authorized investigation to protect against international terrorism or clandestine intelligence activities, provided that such an investigation of a United States person is not conducted solely upon the basis of activities protected by the first amendment to the Constitution of the United States.

(c) Court order for disclosure of consumer reports

Notwithstanding section 1681b of this title or any other provision of this subchapter, if requested in writing by the Director of the Federal Bureau of Investigation, or a designee of the Director in a position not lower than Deputy Assistant Director at Bureau headquarters or a Special Agent in Charge in a Bureau field office designated by the Director, a court may issue an order ex parte directing a consumer reporting agency to furnish a consumer report to the Federal Bureau of Investigation, upon a showing in camera that the consumer report is sought for the conduct of an authorized investigation to protect against international terrorism or clandestine intelligence activities, provided that such an investigation of a United States person is not conducted solely upon the basis of activities protected by the first amendment to the Constitution of the United States.

The terms of an order issued under this subsection shall not disclose that the order is issued for purposes of a counterintelligence investigation.

(d) Confidentiality

> **(1)** If the Director of the Federal Bureau of Investigation, or his designee in a position not lower than Deputy Assistant Director at Bureau headquarters or a Special Agent in Charge in a Bureau field office designated by the Director, certifies that otherwise there may result a danger to the national security of the United States, interference with a criminal, counterterrorism, or counterintelligence investigation, interference with diplomatic relations, or danger to the life or physical safety of any person, no consumer reporting agency or officer, employee, or agent of a consumer reporting agency shall disclose to any person (other than those to whom such disclosure is necessary to comply with the request or an attorney to obtain legal advice or legal assistance with respect to the request) that the Federal Bureau of Investigation has sought or obtained the identity of financial institutions or a consumer report

respecting any consumer under subsection (a), (b), or (c) of this section, and no consumer reporting agency or officer, employee, or agent of a consumer reporting agency shall include in any consumer report any information that would indicate that the Federal Bureau of Investigation has sought or obtained such information on a consumer report.

(2) The request shall notify the person or entity to whom the request is directed of the nondisclosure requirement under paragraph (1).

(3) Any recipient disclosing to those persons necessary to comply with the request or to an attorney to obtain legal advice or legal assistance with respect to the request shall inform such persons of any applicable nondisclosure requirement. Any person who receives a disclosure under this subsection shall be subject to the same prohibitions on disclosure under paragraph (1).

(4) At the request of the Director of the Federal Bureau of Investigation or the designee of the Director, any person making or intending to make a disclosure under this section shall identify to the Director or such designee the person to whom such disclosure will be made or to whom such disclosure was made prior to the request, except that nothing in this section shall require a person to inform the Director or such designee of the identity of an attorney to whom disclosure was made or will be made to obtain legal advice or legal assistance with respect to the request for the identity of financial institutions or a consumer report respecting any consumer under this section.

(e) Payment of fees

The Federal Bureau of Investigation shall, subject to the availability of appropriations, pay to the consumer reporting agency assembling or providing report or information in accordance with procedures established under this section a fee for reimbursement for such costs as are reasonably necessary and which have been directly incurred in searching, reproducing, or transporting books, papers, records, or other data required or requested to be produced under this section.

(f) Limit on dissemination

The Federal Bureau of Investigation may not disseminate information obtained pursuant to this section outside of the Federal Bureau of Investigation, except to other Federal agencies as may be necessary for the approval or conduct of a foreign counterintelligence investigation, or, where the information concerns a person subject to the Uniform Code of Military Justice, to appropriate investigative authorities within the military department concerned as may be necessary for the conduct of a joint foreign counterintelligence investigation.

(g) Rules of construction

Nothing in this section shall be construed to prohibit information from being furnished by the Federal Bureau of Investigation pursuant to a subpoena or court order, in connection with a judicial or administrative proceeding to enforce the provisions of this subchapter. Nothing in this section shall be construed to authorize or permit the withholding of information from the Congress.

(h) Reports to Congress

(1) On a semiannual basis, the Attorney General shall fully inform the Permanent Select Committee on Intelligence and the Committee on Banking, Finance and Urban Affairs of the House of Representatives, and the Select Committee on Intelligence and the Committee on

Banking, Housing, and Urban Affairs of the Senate concerning all requests made pursuant to subsections (a), (b), and (c) of this section.

(2) In the case of the semiannual reports required to be submitted under paragraph (1) to the Permanent Select Committee on Intelligence of the House of Representatives and the Select Committee on Intelligence of the Senate, the submittal dates for such reports shall be as provided in section 415b of Title 50.

(i) Damages

Any agency or department of the United States obtaining or disclosing any consumer reports, records, or information contained therein in violation of this section is liable to the consumer to whom such consumer reports, records, or information relate in an amount equal to the sum of—

(1) $100, without regard to the volume of consumer reports, records, or information involved;

(2) any actual damages sustained by the consumer as a result of the disclosure;

(3) if the violation is found to have been willful or intentional, such punitive damages as a court may allow; and

(4) in the case of any successful action to enforce liability under this subsection, the costs of the action, together with reasonable attorney fees, as determined by the court.

(j) Disciplinary actions for violations

If a court determines that any agency or department of the United States has violated any provision of this section and the court finds that the circumstances surrounding the violation raise questions of whether or not an officer or employee of the agency or department acted willfully or intentionally with respect to the violation, the agency or department shall promptly initiate a proceeding to determine whether or not disciplinary action is warranted against the officer or employee who was responsible for the violation.

(k) Good-faith exception

Notwithstanding any other provision of this subchapter, any consumer reporting agency or agent or employee thereof making disclosure of consumer reports or identifying information pursuant to this subsection in good-faith reliance upon a certification of the Federal Bureau of Investigation pursuant to provisions of this section shall not be liable to any person for such disclosure under this subchapter, the constitution of any State, or any law or regulation of any State or any political subdivision of any State.

(l) Limitation of remedies

Notwithstanding any other provision of this subchapter, the remedies and sanctions set forth in this section shall be the only judicial remedies and sanctions for violation of this section.

(m) Injunctive relief

In addition to any other remedy contained in this section, injunctive relief shall be available to require compliance with the procedures of this section. In the event of any successful action under this subsection, costs together with reasonable attorney fees, as determined by the court, may be recovered.

IV.
GOVERNMENT RECORDS

Freedom of Information Act (1966)

5 U.S.C. § 552, as amended

Statutes in Context

The Freedom of Information Act (FOIA) grants all persons the right to inspect and copy records and documents maintained by any federal agency, federal corporation, or federal department. FOIA contains nine enumerated exemptions to its disclosure requirements. These include two privacy exemptions. One privacy exemption is for "personnel and medical files and similar files the disclosure of which would constitute a clearly unwarranted invasion of personal privacy." 5 USC § 552(b)(6). The second privacy exemption concerns "law enforcement records" to the extent to which the disclosure "could reasonably be expected to constitute an unwarranted invasion of privacy." 5 USC § 552(b)(7).

---

§ 552. Public information; agency rules, opinions, orders, records, and proceedings

(a) Each agency shall make available to the public information as follows:

(1) Each agency shall separately state and currently publish in the Federal Register for the guidance of the public—

(A) descriptions of its central and field organization and the established places at which, the employees (and in the case of a uniformed service, the members) from whom, and the methods whereby, the public may obtain information, make submittals or requests, or obtain decisions;

(B) statements of the general course and method by which its functions are channeled and determined, including the nature and requirements of all formal and informal procedures available;

(C) rules of procedure, descriptions of forms available or the places at which forms may be obtained, and instructions as to the scope and contents of all papers, reports, or examinations;

(D) substantive rules of general applicability adopted as authorized by law, and statements of general policy or interpretations of general applicability formulated and adopted by the agency; and

(E) each amendment, revision, or repeal of the foregoing.

Except to the extent that a person has actual and timely notice of the terms thereof, a person may not in any manner be required to resort to, or be adversely affected by, a matter required to be published in the Federal Register and not so published. For the purpose of this paragraph, matter reasonably available to the class of persons affected thereby is deemed published in the Federal Register when incorporated by reference therein with the approval of the Director of the Federal Register.

(2) Each agency, in accordance with published rules, shall make available for public inspection and copying—

(A) final opinions, including concurring and dissenting opinions, as well as orders, made in the adjudication of cases;

(B) those statements of policy and interpretations which have been adopted by the agency and are not published in the Federal Register;

(C) administrative staff manuals and instructions to staff that affect a member of the public;

(D) copies of all records, regardless of form or format, which have been released to any person under paragraph (3) and which, because of the nature of their subject matter, the agency determines have become or are likely to become the subject of subsequent requests for substantially the same records; and

(E) a general index of the records referred to under subparagraph (D);

unless the materials are promptly published and copies offered for sale. For records created on or after November 1, 1996, within one year after such date, each agency shall make such records available, including by computer telecommunications or, if computer telecommunications means have not been established by the agency, by other electronic means. To the extent required to prevent a clearly unwarranted invasion of personal privacy, an agency may delete identifying details when it makes available or publishes an opinion, statement of policy, interpretation, staff manual, instruction, or copies of records referred to in subparagraph (D). However, in each case the justification for the deletion shall be explained fully in writing, and the extent of such deletion shall be indicated on the portion of the record which is made available or published, unless including that indication would harm an interest protected by the exemption in subsection (b) under which the deletion is made. If technically feasible, the extent of the deletion shall be indicated at the place in the record where the deletion was made. Each agency shall also maintain and make available for public inspection and copying current indexes providing identifying information for the public as to any matter issued, adopted, or promulgated after July 4, 1967, and required by this paragraph to be made available or published. Each agency shall promptly publish, quarterly or more frequently, and distribute (by sale or otherwise) copies of each index or supplements thereto unless it determines by order published in the Federal Register that the publication would be unnecessary and impracticable, in which case the agency shall nonetheless provide copies of such index on request at a cost not to exceed the direct cost of duplication. Each agency shall make the index referred to in subparagraph (E) available by computer telecommunications by December 31, 1999. A final order, opinion, statement of policy, interpretation, or staff manual or instruction that affects a member of the public may be relied on, used, or cited as precedent by an agency against a party other than an agency only if—

(i) it has been indexed and either made available or published as provided by this paragraph; or

(ii) the party has actual and timely notice of the terms thereof.

(3)(A) Except with respect to the records made available under paragraphs (1) and (2) of this subsection, and except as provided in subparagraph (E), each agency, upon any request for records which (i) reasonably describes such records and (ii) is made in accordance with published rules stating the time, place, fees (if any), and procedures to be followed, shall make the records promptly available to any person.

(B) In making any record available to a person under this paragraph, an agency shall provide the record in any form or format requested by the person if the record is readily reproducible by the agency in that form or format. Each agency shall make reasonable efforts to maintain its records in forms or formats that are reproducible for purposes of this section.

(C) In responding under this paragraph to a request for records, an agency shall make reasonable efforts to search for the records in electronic form or format, except when such efforts would significantly interfere with the operation of the agency's automated information system.

(D) For purposes of this paragraph, the term "search" means to review, manually or by automated means, agency records for the purpose of locating those records which are responsive to a request.

(E) An agency, or part of an agency, that is an element of the intelligence community (as that term is defined in section 3(4) of the National Security Act of 1947 (50 U.S.C. 401a(4))) shall not make any record available under this paragraph to—

(i) any government entity, other than a State, territory, commonwealth, or district of the United States, or any subdivision thereof; or

(ii) a representative of a government entity described in clause (i).

(4)(A)(i) In order to carry out the provisions of this section, each agency shall promulgate regulations, pursuant to notice and receipt of public comment, specifying the schedule of fees applicable to the processing of requests under this section and establishing procedures and guidelines for determining when such fees should be waived or reduced. Such schedule shall conform to the guidelines which shall be promulgated, pursuant to notice and receipt of public comment, by the Director of the Office of Management and Budget and which shall provide for a uniform schedule of fees for all agencies.

(ii) Such agency regulations shall provide that—

(I) fees shall be limited to reasonable standard charges for document search, duplication, and review, when records are requested for commercial use;

(II) fees shall be limited to reasonable standard charges for document duplication when records are not sought for commercial use and the request is made by an educational or noncommercial scientific institution, whose purpose is scholarly or scientific research; or a representative of the news media; and

(III) for any request not described in (I) or (II), fees shall be limited to reasonable standard charges for document search and duplication.

(iii) Documents shall be furnished without any charge or at a charge reduced below the fees established under clause (ii) if disclosure of the information is in the public interest because it is likely to contribute significantly to public understanding of the operations or activities of the government and is not primarily in the commercial interest of the requester.

(iv) Fee schedules shall provide for the recovery of only the direct costs of search, duplication, or review. Review costs shall include only the direct costs incurred during the initial examination of a document for the purposes of determining whether the documents must be disclosed under this section and for the purposes of withholding any portions exempt from disclosure under this section. Review costs may not include any costs incurred in resolving issues of law or policy that may be raised in the course of processing a request under this section. No fee may be charged by any agency under this section—

> **(I)** if the costs of routine collection and processing of the fee are likely to equal or exceed the amount of the fee; or
>
> **(II)** for any request described in clause (ii)(II) or (III) of this subparagraph for the first two hours of search time or for the first one hundred pages of duplication.

(v) No agency may require advance payment of any fee unless the requester has previously failed to pay fees in a timely fashion, or the agency has determined that the fee will exceed $250.

(vi) Nothing in this subparagraph shall supersede fees chargeable under a statute specifically providing for setting the level of fees for particular types of records.

(vii) In any action by a requester regarding the waiver of fees under this section, the court shall determine the matter de novo: *Provided*, That the court's review of the matter shall be limited to the record before the agency.

(B) On complaint, the district court of the United States in the district in which the complainant resides, or has his principal place of business, or in which the agency records are situated, or in the District of Columbia, has jurisdiction to enjoin the agency from withholding agency records and to order the production of any agency records improperly withheld from the complainant. In such a case the court shall determine the matter de novo, and may examine the contents of such agency records in camera to determine whether such records or any part thereof shall be withheld under any of the exemptions set forth in subsection (b) of this section, and the burden is on the agency to sustain its action. In addition to any other matters to which a court accords substantial weight, a court shall accord substantial weight to an affidavit of an agency concerning the agency's determination as to technical feasibility under paragraph (2)(C) and subsection (b) and reproducibility under paragraph (3)(B).

(C) Notwithstanding any other provision of law, the defendant shall serve an answer or otherwise plead to any complaint made under this subsection within thirty days after service upon the defendant of the pleading in which such complaint is made, unless the court otherwise directs for good cause shown.

[**(D)** Repealed. Pub.L. 98-620, Title IV, § 402(2), Nov. 8, 1984, 98 Stat. 3357]

(E) The court may assess against the United States reasonable attorney fees and other litigation costs reasonably incurred in any case under this section in which the complainant has substantially prevailed.

(F) Whenever the court orders the production of any agency records improperly withheld from the complainant and assesses against the United States reasonable attorney fees and other litigation costs, and the court additionally issues a written finding that the circumstances surrounding the withholding raise questions whether agency personnel acted arbitrarily or capriciously with respect to the withholding, the Special Counsel shall promptly initiate a proceeding to determine whether disciplinary action is warranted against the officer or employee who was primarily responsible for the withholding. The Special Counsel, after investigation and consideration of the evidence submitted, shall submit his findings and recommendations to the administrative authority of the agency concerned and shall send copies of the findings and recommendations to the officer or employee or his representative. The administrative authority shall take the corrective action that the Special Counsel recommends.

(G) In the event of noncompliance with the order of the court, the district court may punish for contempt the responsible employee, and in the case of a uniformed service, the responsible member.

(5) Each agency having more than one member shall maintain and make available for public inspection a record of the final votes of each member in every agency proceeding.

(6)(A) Each agency, upon any request for records made under paragraph (1), (2), or (3) of this subsection, shall—

(i) determine within 20 days (excepting Saturdays, Sundays, and legal public holidays) after the receipt of any such request whether to comply with such request and shall immediately notify the person making such request of such determination and the reasons therefor, and of the right of such person to appeal to the head of the agency any adverse determination; and

(ii) make a determination with respect to any appeal within twenty days (excepting Saturdays, Sundays, and legal public holidays) after the receipt of such appeal. If on appeal the denial of the request for records is in whole or in part upheld, the agency shall notify the person making such request of the provisions for judicial review of that determination under paragraph (4) of this subsection.

(B)(i) In unusual circumstances as specified in this subparagraph, the time limits prescribed in either clause (i) or clause (ii) of subparagraph (A) may be extended by written notice to the person making such request setting forth the unusual circumstances for such extension and the date on which a determination is expected to be dispatched. No such notice shall specify a date that would result in an extension for more than ten working days, except as provided in clause (ii) of this subparagraph.

(ii) With respect to a request for which a written notice under clause (i) extends the time limits prescribed under clause (i) of subparagraph (A), the agency shall notify the person making the request if the request cannot be processed within the time limit specified in that clause and shall provide the person an opportunity to limit the scope of the request so that it may be processed within that time limit or an opportunity to arrange with the agency an alternative time frame for processing the request or a modified request. Refusal by the person to reasonably modify the request or arrange such an alternative time frame shall be considered as a factor in determining whether exceptional circumstances exist for purposes of subparagraph (C).

(iii) As used in this subparagraph, "unusual circumstances" means, but only to the extent reasonably necessary to the proper processing of the particular requests—

(I) the need to search for and collect the requested records from field facilities or other establishments that are separate from the office processing the request;

(II) the need to search for, collect, and appropriately examine a voluminous amount of separate and distinct records which are demanded in a single request; or

(III) the need for consultation, which shall be conducted with all practicable speed, with another agency having a substantial interest in the determination of the request or among two or more components of the agency having substantial subject-matter interest therein.

(iv) Each agency may promulgate regulations, pursuant to notice and receipt of public comment, providing for the aggregation of certain requests by the same requestor, or by a group of requestors acting in concert, if the agency reasonably believes that such requests actually constitute a single request, which would otherwise satisfy the unusual circumstances specified in this subparagraph, and the requests involve clearly related matters. Multiple requests involving unrelated matters shall not be aggregated.

(C)(i) Any person making a request to any agency for records under paragraph (1), (2), or (3) of this subsection shall be deemed to have exhausted his administrative remedies with respect to such request if the agency fails to comply with the applicable time limit provisions of this paragraph. If the Government can show exceptional circumstances exist and that the agency is exercising due diligence in responding to the request, the court may retain jurisdiction and allow the agency additional time to complete its review of the records. Upon any determination by an agency to comply with a request for records, the records shall be made promptly available to such person making such request. Any notification of denial of any request for records under this subsection shall set forth the names and titles or positions of each person responsible for the denial of such request.

(ii) For purposes of this subparagraph, the term "exceptional circumstances" does not include a delay that results from a predictable agency workload of requests under this section, unless the agency demonstrates reasonable progress in reducing its backlog of pending requests.

(iii) Refusal by a person to reasonably modify the scope of a request or arrange an alternative time frame for processing a request (or a modified request) under clause (ii) after being given an opportunity to do so by the agency to whom the person made the request shall be considered as a factor in determining whether exceptional circumstances exist for purposes of this subparagraph.

(D)(i) Each agency may promulgate regulations, pursuant to notice and receipt of public comment, providing for multitrack processing of requests for records based on the amount of work or time (or both) involved in processing requests.

(ii) Regulations under this subparagraph may provide a person making a request that does not qualify for the fastest multitrack processing an opportunity to limit the scope of the request in order to qualify for faster processing.

(iii) This subparagraph shall not be considered to affect the requirement under subparagraph (C) to exercise due diligence.

(E)(i) Each agency shall promulgate regulations, pursuant to notice and receipt of public comment, providing for expedited processing of requests for records—

(I) in cases in which the person requesting the records demonstrates a compelling need; and

(II) in other cases determined by the agency.

(ii) Notwithstanding clause (i), regulations under this subparagraph must ensure—

(I) that a determination of whether to provide expedited processing shall be made, and notice of the determination shall be provided to the person making the request, within 10 days after the date of the request; and

(II) expeditious consideration of administrative appeals of such determinations of whether to provide expedited processing.

(iii) An agency shall process as soon as practicable any request for records to which the agency has granted expedited processing under this subparagraph. Agency action to deny or affirm denial of a request for expedited processing pursuant to this subparagraph, and failure by an agency to respond in a timely manner to such a request shall be subject to judicial review under paragraph (4), except that the judicial review shall be based on the record before the agency at the time of the determination.

(iv) A district court of the United States shall not have jurisdiction to review an agency denial of expedited processing of a request for records after the agency has provided a complete response to the request.

(v) For purposes of this subparagraph, the term "compelling need" means—

(I) that a failure to obtain requested records on an expedited basis under this paragraph could reasonably be expected to pose an imminent threat to the life or physical safety of an individual; or

(II) with respect to a request made by a person primarily engaged in disseminating information, urgency to inform the public concerning actual or alleged Federal Government activity.

(vi) A demonstration of a compelling need by a person making a request for expedited processing shall be made by a statement certified by such person to be true and correct to the best of such person's knowledge and belief.

(F) In denying a request for records, in whole or in part, an agency shall make a reasonable effort to estimate the volume of any requested matter the provision of which is denied, and shall provide any such estimate to the person making the request, unless providing such estimate would harm an interest protected by the exemption in subsection (b) pursuant to which the denial is made.

(b) This section does not apply to matters that are—

(1) (A) specifically authorized under criteria established by an Executive order to be kept secret in the interest of national defense or foreign policy and (B) are in fact properly classified pursuant to such Executive order;

(2) related solely to the internal personnel rules and practices of an agency;

(3) specifically exempted from disclosure by statute (other than section 552b of this title), provided that such statute (A) requires that the matters be withheld from the public in such a manner as to leave no discretion on the issue, or (B) establishes particular criteria for withholding or refers to particular types of matters to be withheld;

(4) trade secrets and commercial or financial information obtained from a person and privileged or confidential;

(5) inter-agency or intra-agency memorandums or letters which would not be available by law to a party other than an agency in litigation with the agency;

(6) personnel and medical files and similar files the disclosure of which would constitute a clearly unwarranted invasion of personal privacy;

(7) records or information compiled for law enforcement purposes, but only to the extent that the production of such law enforcement records or information (A) could reasonably be expected to interfere with enforcement proceedings, (B) would deprive a person of a right to a fair trial or an impartial adjudication, (C) could reasonably be expected to constitute an unwarranted invasion of personal privacy, (D) could reasonably be expected to disclose the identity of a confidential source, including a State, local, or foreign agency or authority or any private institution which furnished information on a confidential basis, and, in the case of a record or information compiled by criminal law enforcement authority in the course of a criminal investigation or by an agency conducting a lawful national security intelligence investigation, information furnished by a confidential source, (E) would disclose techniques and procedures for law enforcement investigations or prosecutions, or would disclose guidelines for law enforcement investigations or prosecutions if such disclosure could reasonably be expected to risk circumvention of the law, or (F) could reasonably be expected to endanger the life or physical safety of any individual;

(8) contained in or related to examination, operating, or condition reports prepared by, on behalf of, or for the use of an agency responsible for the regulation or supervision of financial institutions; or

(9) geological and geophysical information and data, including maps, concerning wells.

Any reasonably segregable portion of a record shall be provided to any person requesting such record after deletion of the portions which are exempt under this subsection. The amount of information deleted shall be indicated on the released portion of the record, unless including that indication would harm an interest protected by the exemption in this subsection under which the deletion is made. If technically feasible, the amount of the information deleted shall be indicated at the place in the record where such deletion is made.

(c)(1) Whenever a request is made which involves access to records described in subsection (b)(7)(A) and—

(A) the investigation or proceeding involves a possible violation of criminal law; and

(B) there is reason to believe that (i) the subject of the investigation or proceeding is not aware of its pendency, and (ii) disclosure of the existence of the records could reasonably be expected to interfere with enforcement proceedings,

the agency may, during only such time as that circumstance continues, treat the records as not subject to the requirements of this section.

(2) Whenever informant records maintained by a criminal law enforcement agency under an informant's name or personal identifier are requested by a third party according to the informant's name or personal identifier, the agency may treat the records as not subject to the requirements of this section unless the informant's status as an informant has been officially confirmed.

(3) Whenever a request is made which involves access to records maintained by the Federal Bureau of Investigation pertaining to foreign intelligence or counterintelligence, or international terrorism, and the existence of the records is classified information as provided in subsection (b)(1), the Bureau may, as long as the existence of the records remains classified information, treat the records as not subject to the requirements of this section.

(d) This section does not authorize withholding of information or limit the availability of records to the public, except as specifically stated in this section. This section is not authority to withhold information from Congress.

(e)(1) On or before February 1 of each year, each agency shall submit to the Attorney General of the United States a report which shall cover the preceding fiscal year and which shall include—

> **(A)** the number of determinations made by the agency not to comply with requests for records made to such agency under subsection (a) and the reasons for each such determination;
>
> **(B)(i)** the number of appeals made by persons under subsection (a)(6), the result of such appeals, and the reason for the action upon each appeal that results in a denial of information; and
>
> **(ii)** a complete list of all statutes that the agency relies upon to authorize the agency to withhold information under subsection (b)(3), a description of whether a court has upheld the decision of the agency to withhold information under each such statute, and a concise description of the scope of any information withheld;
>
> **(C)** the number of requests for records pending before the agency as of September 30 of the preceding year, and the median number of days that such requests had been pending before the agency as of that date;
>
> **(D)** the number of requests for records received by the agency and the number of requests which the agency processed;
>
> **(E)** the median number of days taken by the agency to process different types of requests;
>
> **(F)** the total amount of fees collected by the agency for processing requests; and
>
> **(G)** the number of full-time staff of the agency devoted to processing requests for records under this section, and the total amount expended by the agency for processing such requests.

(2) Each agency shall make each such report available to the public including by computer telecommunications, or if computer telecommunications means have not been established by the agency, by other electronic means.

(3) The Attorney General of the United States shall make each report which has been made available by electronic means available at a single electronic access point. The Attorney General of the United States shall notify the Chairman and ranking minority member of the Committee on Government Reform and Oversight of the House of Representatives and the Chairman and ranking minority member of the Committees on Governmental Affairs and the Judiciary of the Senate, no later than April 1 of the year in which each such report is issued, that such reports are available by electronic means.

(4) The Attorney General of the United States, in consultation with the Director of the Office of Management and Budget, shall develop reporting and performance guidelines in connection with reports required by this subsection by October 1, 1997, and may establish additional requirements for such reports as the Attorney General determines may be useful.

(5) The Attorney General of the United States shall submit an annual report on or before April 1 of each calendar year which shall include for the prior calendar year a listing of the number of cases arising under this section, the exemption involved in each case, the disposition of such case, and the cost, fees, and penalties assessed under subparagraphs (E), (F), and (G) of subsection (a)(4). Such report shall also include a description of the efforts undertaken by the Department of Justice to encourage agency compliance with this section.

(f) For purposes of this section, the term—

> **(1)** "agency" as defined in section 551(1) of this title includes any executive department, military department, Government corporation, Government controlled corporation, or other establishment in the executive branch of the Government (including the Executive Office of the President), or any independent regulatory agency; and
>
> **(2)** "record" and any other term used in this section in reference to information includes any information that would be an agency record subject to the requirements of this section when maintained by an agency in any format, including an electronic format.

(g) The head of each agency shall prepare and make publicly available upon request, reference material or a guide for requesting records or information from the agency, subject to the exemptions in subsection (b), including—

> **(1)** an index of all major information systems of the agency;
>
> **(2)** a description of major information and record locator systems maintained by the agency; and
>
> **(3)** a handbook for obtaining various types and categories of public information from the agency pursuant to chapter 35 of title 44, and under this section.

Critical Infrastructure Information Act (2002)

6 U.S.C. §§ 131-134, as amended

Statutes in Context

The Critical Infrastructure Information Act creates a new FOIA exemption for critical infrastructure information. Such information, when voluntarily submitted to a covered federal agency, is exempt from release under FOIA.

§ 131. Definitions

In this part:

(1) Agency

The term "agency" has the meaning given it in section 551 of Title 5.

(2) Covered Federal agency

The term "covered Federal agency" means the Department of Homeland Security.

(3) Critical infrastructure information

The term "critical infrastructure information" means information not customarily in the public domain and related to the security of critical infrastructure or protected systems—

> **(A)** actual, potential, or threatened interference with, attack on, compromise of, or incapacitation of critical infrastructure or protected systems by either physical or computer-based attack or other similar conduct (including the misuse of or unauthorized access to all types of communications and data transmission systems) that violates Federal, State, or local law, harms interstate commerce of the United States, or threatens public health or safety;
>
> **(B)** the ability of any critical infrastructure or protected system to resist such interference, compromise, or incapacitation, including any planned or past assessment, projection, or estimate of the vulnerability of critical infrastructure or a protected system, including security testing, risk evaluation thereto, risk management planning, or risk audit; or
>
> **(C)** any planned or past operational problem or solution regarding critical infrastructure or protected systems, including repair, recovery, reconstruction, insurance, or continuity, to the extent it is related to such interference, compromise, or incapacitation.

(4) Critical infrastructure protection program

The term "critical infrastructure protection program" means any component or bureau of a covered Federal agency that has been designated by the President or any agency head to receive critical infrastructure information.

(5) Information Sharing and Analysis Organization

The term "Information Sharing and Analysis Organization" means any formal or informal entity or collaboration created or employed by public or private sector organizations, for purposes of—

(A) gathering and analyzing critical infrastructure information in order to better understand security problems and interdependencies related to critical infrastructure and protected systems, so as to ensure the availability, integrity, and reliability thereof;

(B) communicating or disclosing critical infrastructure information to help prevent, detect, mitigate, or recover from the effects of a interference, compromise, or a incapacitation problem related to critical infrastructure or protected systems; and

(C) voluntarily disseminating critical infrastructure information to its members, State, local, and Federal Governments, or any other entities that may be of assistance in carrying out the purposes specified in subparagraphs (A) and (B).

(6) Protected system

The term "protected system"—

(A) means any service, physical or computer-based system, process, or procedure that directly or indirectly affects the viability of a facility of critical infrastructure; and

(B) includes any physical or computer-based system, including a computer, computer system, computer or communications network, or any component hardware or element thereof, software program, processing instructions, or information or data in transmission or storage therein, irrespective of the medium of transmission or storage.

(7) Voluntary

(A) In general

The term "voluntary", in the case of any submittal of critical infrastructure information to a covered Federal agency, means the submittal thereof in the absence of such agency's exercise of legal authority to compel access to or submission of such information and may be accomplished by a single entity or an Information Sharing and Analysis Organization on behalf of itself or its members.

(B) Exclusions

The term "voluntary"—

(i) in the case of any action brought under the securities laws as is defined in section 78c(a)(47) of Title 15—

(I) does not include information or statements contained in any documents or materials filed with the Securities and Exchange Commission, or with Federal banking regulators, pursuant to section 78l(i) of Title 15; and

(II) with respect to the submittal of critical infrastructure information, does not include any disclosure or writing that when made accompanied the solicitation of an offer or a sale of securities; and

(ii) does not include information or statements submitted or relied upon as a basis for making licensing or permitting determinations, or during regulatory proceedings.

§ 132. Designation of critical infrastructure protection program

A critical infrastructure protection program may be designated as such by one of the following:

(1) The President.

(2) The Secretary of Homeland Security.

§ 133. Protection of voluntarily shared critical infrastructure information

(a) Protection

(1) In general

Notwithstanding any other provision of law, critical infrastructure information (including the identity of the submitting person or entity) that is voluntarily submitted to a covered Federal agency for use by that agency regarding the security of critical infrastructure and protected systems, analysis, warning, interdependency study, recovery, reconstitution, or other informational purpose, when accompanied by an express statement specified in paragraph (2)—

(A) shall be exempt from disclosure under section 552 of Title 5 (commonly referred to as the Freedom of Information Act);

(B) shall not be subject to any agency rules or judicial doctrine regarding ex parte communications with a decision making official;

(C) shall not, without the written consent of the person or entity submitting such information, be used directly by such agency, any other Federal, State, or local authority, or any third party, in any civil action arising under Federal or State law if such information is submitted in good faith;

(D) shall not, without the written consent of the person or entity submitting such information, be used or disclosed by any officer or employee of the United States for purposes other than the purposes of this part, except—

(i) in furtherance of an investigation or the prosecution of a criminal act; or

(ii) when disclosure of the information would be—

(I) to either House of Congress, or to the extent of matter within its jurisdiction, any committee or subcommittee thereof, any joint committee thereof or subcommittee of any such joint committee; or

(II) to the Comptroller General, or any authorized representative of the Comptroller General, in the course of the performance of the duties of the Government Accountability Office.

(E) shall not, if provided to a State or local government or government agency—

(i) be made available pursuant to any State or local law requiring disclosure of information or records;

(ii) otherwise be disclosed or distributed to any party by said State or local government or government agency without the written consent of the person or entity submitting such information; or

(iii) be used other than for the purpose of protecting critical infrastructure or protected systems, or in furtherance of an investigation or the prosecution of a criminal act; and

(F) does not constitute a waiver of any applicable privilege or protection provided under law, such as trade secret protection.

(2) Express statement

For purposes of paragraph (1), the term "express statement", with respect to information or records, means—

(A) in the case of written information or records, a written marking on the information or records substantially similar to the following: "This information is voluntarily submitted to the Federal Government in expectation of protection from disclosure as provided by the provisions of the Critical Infrastructure Information Act of 2002."; or

(B) in the case of oral information, a similar written statement submitted within a reasonable period following the oral communication.

(b) Limitation

No communication of critical infrastructure information to a covered Federal agency made pursuant to this subtitle shall be considered to be an action subject to the requirements of the Federal Advisory Committee Act (5 U.S.C. App. 2).

(c) Independently obtained information

Nothing in this section shall be construed to limit or otherwise affect the ability of a State, local, or Federal Government entity, agency, or authority, or any third party, under applicable law, to obtain critical infrastructure information in a manner not covered by subsection (a) of this section, including any information lawfully and properly disclosed generally or broadly to the public and to use such information in any manner permitted by law.

(d) Treatment of voluntary submittal of information

The voluntary submittal to the Government of information or records that are protected from disclosure by this subtitle shall not be construed to constitute compliance with any requirement to submit such information to a Federal agency under any other provision of law.

(e) Procedures

(1) In general

The Secretary of the Department of Homeland Security shall, in consultation with appropriate representatives of the National Security Council and the Office of Science and Technology Policy, establish uniform procedures for the receipt, care, and storage by Federal agencies of critical infrastructure information that is voluntarily submitted to the Government. The procedures shall be established not later than 90 days after November 25, 2002.

(2) Elements

The procedures established under paragraph (1) shall include mechanisms regarding—

(A) the acknowledgement of receipt by Federal agencies of critical infrastructure information that is voluntarily submitted to the Government;

(B) the maintenance of the identification of such information as voluntarily submitted to the Government for purposes of and subject to the provisions of this subtitle;

(C) the care and storage of such information; and

(D) the protection and maintenance of the confidentiality of such information so as to permit the sharing of such information within the Federal Government and with State and local governments, and the issuance of notices and warnings related to the protection of critical infrastructure and protected systems, in such manner as to protect from public disclosure the identity of the submitting person or entity, or information that is proprietary, business sensitive, relates specifically to the submitting person or entity, and is otherwise not appropriately in the public domain.

(f) Penalties

Whoever, being an officer or employee of the United States or of any department or agency thereof, knowingly publishes, divulges, discloses, or makes known in any manner or to any extent not authorized by law, any critical infrastructure information protected from disclosure by this subtitle coming to him in the course of this employment or official duties or by reason of any examination or investigation made by, or return, report, or record made to or filed with, such department or agency or officer or employee thereof, shall be fined under Title 18, imprisoned not more than 1 year, or both, and shall be removed from office or employment.

(g) Authority to issue warnings

The Federal Government may provide advisories, alerts, and warnings to relevant companies, targeted sectors, other governmental entities, or the general public regarding potential threats to critical infrastructure as appropriate. In issuing a warning, the Federal Government shall take appropriate actions to protect from disclosure—

(1) the source of any voluntarily submitted critical infrastructure information that forms the basis for the warning; or

(2) information that is proprietary, business sensitive, relates specifically to the submitting person or entity, or is otherwise not appropriately in the public domain.

(h) Authority to delegate

The President may delegate authority to a critical infrastructure protection program, designated under section 132 of this title, to enter into a voluntary agreement to promote critical infrastructure security, including with any Information Sharing and Analysis Organization, or a plan of action as otherwise defined in section 2158 of the Appendix to Title 50.

§ 134. No private right of action

Nothing in this part may be construed to create a private right of action for enforcement of any provision of this chapter.

Privacy Act (1974)

5 U.S.C. § 552a, as amended

Statutes in Context

Despite its sweeping name, the Privacy Act regulates the information use only of federal agencies. It does not apply to businesses or private sector organizations, or state or local governmental entities. The Privacy Act establishes restrictions and responsibilities for federal agencies maintaining records about individuals. It also provides a right of individuals to review records about themselves and to ask that the agency holding the information correct any inaccuracies in the information.

§ 552a. Records maintained on individuals

(a) Definitions.—For purposes of this section—

(1) the term "agency" means agency as defined in section 552(e) of this title;

(2) the term "individual" means a citizen of the United States or an alien lawfully admitted for permanent residence;

(3) the term "maintain" includes maintain, collect, use, or disseminate;

(4) the term "record" means any item, collection, or grouping of information about an individual that is maintained by an agency, including, but not limited to, his education, financial transactions, medical history, and criminal or employment history and that contains his name, or the identifying number, symbol, or other identifying particular assigned to the individual, such as a finger or voice print or a photograph;

(5) the term "system of records" means a group of any records under the control of any agency from which information is retrieved by the name of the individual or by some identifying number, symbol, or other identifying particular assigned to the individual;

(6) the term "statistical record" means a record in a system of records maintained for statistical research or reporting purposes only and not used in whole or in part in making any determination about an identifiable individual, except as provided by section 8 of title 13;

(7) the term "routine use" means, with respect to the disclosure of a record, the use of such record for a purpose which is compatible with the purpose for which it was collected;

(8) the term "matching program"—

(A) means any computerized comparison of—

(i) two or more automated systems of records or a system of records with non-Federal records for the purpose of—

(I) establishing or verifying the eligibility of, or continuing compliance with statutory and regulatory requirements by, applicants for, recipients or beneficiaries of, participants in, or providers of services with respect to, cash or in-kind assistance or payments under Federal benefit programs, or

(II) recouping payments or delinquent debts under such Federal benefit programs, or

(ii) two or more automated Federal personnel or payroll systems of records or a system of Federal personnel or payroll records with non-Federal records,

(B) but does not include—

(i) matches performed to produce aggregate statistical data without any personal identifiers;

(ii) matches performed to support any research or statistical project, the specific data of which may not be used to make decisions concerning the rights, benefits, or privileges of specific individuals;

(iii) matches performed, by an agency (or component thereof) which performs as its principal function any activity pertaining to the enforcement of criminal laws, subsequent to the initiation of a specific criminal or civil law enforcement investigation of a named person or persons for the purpose of gathering evidence against such person or persons;

(iv) matches of tax information (I) pursuant to section 6103(d) of the Internal Revenue Code of 1986, (II) for purposes of tax administration as defined in section 6103(b)(4) of such Code, (III) for the purpose of intercepting a tax refund due an individual under authority granted by section 404(e), 464, or 1137 of the Social Security Act; or (IV) for the purpose of intercepting a tax refund due an individual under any other tax refund intercept program authorized by statute which has been determined by the Director of the Office of Management and Budget to contain verification, notice, and hearing requirements that are substantially similar to the procedures in section 1137 of the Social Security Act;

(v) matches—

(I) using records predominantly relating to Federal personnel, that are performed for routine administrative purposes (subject to guidance provided by the Director of the Office of Management and Budget pursuant to subsection (v)); or

(II) conducted by an agency using only records from systems of records maintained by that agency;

if the purpose of the match is not to take any adverse financial, personnel, disciplinary, or other adverse action against Federal personnel [FN1]

(vi) matches performed for foreign counterintelligence purposes or to produce background checks for security clearances of Federal personnel or Federal contractor personnel;

(vii) matches performed incident to a levy described in section 6103(k)(8) of the Internal Revenue Code of 1986; or

(viii) matches performed pursuant to section 202(x)(3) or 1611(e)(1) of the Social Security Act (42 U.S.C. 402(x)(3), 1382(e)(1));

(9) the term "recipient agency" means any agency, or contractor thereof, receiving records contained in a system of records from a source agency for use in a matching program;

(10) the term "non-Federal agency" means any State or local government, or agency thereof, which receives records contained in a system of records from a source agency for use in a matching program;

(11) the term "source agency" means any agency which discloses records contained in a system of records to be used in a matching program, or any State or local government, or agency thereof, which discloses records to be used in a matching program;

(12) the term "Federal benefit program" means any program administered or funded by the Federal Government, or by any agent or State on behalf of the Federal Government, providing cash or in-kind assistance in the form of payments, grants, loans, or loan guarantees to individuals; and

(13) the term "Federal personnel" means officers and employees of the Government of the United States, members of the uniformed services (including members of the Reserve Components), individuals [FN2] entitled to receive immediate or deferred retirement benefits under any retirement program of the Government of the United States (including survivor benefits).

(b) Conditions of disclosure.—No agency shall disclose any record which is contained in a system of records by any means of communication to any person, or to another agency, except pursuant to a written request by, or with the prior written consent of, the individual to whom the record pertains, unless disclosure of the record would be—

(1) to those officers and employees of the agency which maintains the record who have a need for the record in the performance of their duties;

(2) required under section 552 of this title;

(3) for a routine use as defined in subsection (a)(7) of this section and described under subsection (e)(4)(D) of this section;

(4) to the Bureau of the Census for purposes of planning or carrying out a census or survey or related activity pursuant to the provisions of title 13;

(5) to a recipient who has provided the agency with advance adequate written assurance that the record will be used solely as a statistical research or reporting record, and the record is to be transferred in a form that is not individually identifiable;

(6) to the National Archives and Records Administration as a record which has sufficient historical or other value to warrant its continued preservation by the United States Government, or for evaluation by the Archivist of the United States or the designee of the Archivist to determine whether the record has such value;

(7) to another agency or to an instrumentality of any governmental jurisdiction within or under the control of the United States for a civil or criminal law enforcement activity if the activity is authorized by law, and if the head of the agency or instrumentality has made a written request to the agency which maintains the record specifying the particular portion desired and the law enforcement activity for which the record is sought;

(8) to a person pursuant to a showing of compelling circumstances affecting the health or safety of an individual if upon such disclosure notification is transmitted to the last known address of such individual;

(9) to either House of Congress, or, to the extent of matter within its jurisdiction, any committee or subcommittee thereof, any joint committee of Congress or subcommittee of any such joint committee;

(10) to the Comptroller General, or any of his authorized representatives, in the course of the performance of the duties of the Government Accountability Office;

(11) pursuant to the order of a court of competent jurisdiction; or

(12) to a consumer reporting agency in accordance with section 3711(e) of title 31.

(c) Accounting of certain disclosures.—Each agency, with respect to each system of records under its control, shall—

(1) except for disclosures made under subsections (b)(1) or (b)(2) of this section, keep an accurate accounting of—

(A) the date, nature, and purpose of each disclosure of a record to any person or to another agency made under subsection (b) of this section; and

(B) the name and address of the person or agency to whom the disclosure is made;

(2) retain the accounting made under paragraph (1) of this subsection for at least five years or the life of the record, whichever is longer, after the disclosure for which the accounting is made;

(3) except for disclosures made under subsection (b)(7) of this section, make the accounting made under paragraph (1) of this subsection available to the individual named in the record at his request; and

(4) inform any person or other agency about any correction or notation of dispute made by the agency in accordance with subsection (d) of this section of any record that has been disclosed to the person or agency if an accounting of the disclosure was made.

(d) Access to records.—Each agency that maintains a system of records shall—

(1) upon request by any individual to gain access to his record or to any information pertaining to him which is contained in the system, permit him and upon his request, a person of his own choosing to accompany him, to review the record and have a copy made of all or any portion thereof in a form comprehensible to him, except that the agency may require the individual to furnish a written statement authorizing discussion of that individual's record in the accompanying person's presence;

(2) permit the individual to request amendment of a record pertaining to him and—

(A) not later than 10 days (excluding Saturdays, Sundays, and legal public holidays) after the date of receipt of such request, acknowledge in writing such receipt; and

(B) promptly, either—

(i) make any correction of any portion thereof which the individual believes is not accurate, relevant, timely, or complete; or

(ii) inform the individual of its refusal to amend the record in accordance with his request, the reason for the refusal, the procedures established by the agency for the individual to request a review of that refusal by the head of the agency or an officer designated by the head of the agency, and the name and business address of that official;

(3) permit the individual who disagrees with the refusal of the agency to amend his record to request a review of such refusal, and not later than 30 days (excluding Saturdays, Sundays, and legal public holidays) from the date on which the individual requests such review, complete such review and make a final determination unless, for good cause shown, the head of the agency extends such 30-day period; and if, after his review, the reviewing official also refuses to amend the record in accordance with the request, permit the individual to file with the agency a concise statement setting forth the reasons for his disagreement with the refusal of the agency, and notify the individual of the provisions for judicial review of the reviewing official's determination under subsection (g)(1)(A) of this section;

(4) in any disclosure, containing information about which the individual has filed a statement of disagreement, occurring after the filing of the statement under paragraph (3) of this subsection, clearly note any portion of the record which is disputed and provide copies of the statement and, if the agency deems it appropriate, copies of a concise statement of the reasons of the agency for not making the amendments requested, to persons or other agencies to whom the disputed record has been disclosed; and

(5) nothing in this section shall allow an individual access to any information compiled in reasonable anticipation of a civil action or proceeding.

(e) Agency requirements.—Each agency that maintains a system of records shall—

(1) maintain in its records only such information about an individual as is relevant and necessary to accomplish a purpose of the agency required to be accomplished by statute or by executive order of the President;

(2) collect information to the greatest extent practicable directly from the subject individual when the information may result in adverse determinations about an individual's rights, benefits, and privileges under Federal programs;

(3) inform each individual whom it asks to supply information, on the form which it uses to collect the information or on a separate form that can be retained by the individual—

(A) the authority (whether granted by statute, or by executive order of the President) which authorizes the solicitation of the information and whether disclosure of such information is mandatory or voluntary;

(B) the principal purpose or purposes for which the information is intended to be used;

(C) the routine uses which may be made of the information, as published pursuant to paragraph (4)(D) of this subsection; and

(D) the effects on him, if any, of not providing all or any part of the requested information;

(4) subject to the provisions of paragraph (11) of this subsection, publish in the Federal Register upon establishment or revision a notice of the existence and character of the system of records, which notice shall include—

(A) the name and location of the system;

(B) the categories of individuals on whom records are maintained in the system;

(C) the categories of records maintained in the system;

(D) each routine use of the records contained in the system, including the categories of users and the purpose of such use;

(E) the policies and practices of the agency regarding storage, retrievability, access controls, retention, and disposal of the records;

(F) the title and business address of the agency official who is responsible for the system of records;

(G) the agency procedures whereby an individual can be notified at his request if the system of records contains a record pertaining to him;

(H) the agency procedures whereby an individual can be notified at his request how he can gain access to any record pertaining to him contained in the system of records, and how he can contest its content; and

(I) the categories of sources of records in the system;

(5) maintain all records which are used by the agency in making any determination about any individual with such accuracy, relevance, timeliness, and completeness as is reasonably necessary to assure fairness to the individual in the determination;

(6) prior to disseminating any record about an individual to any person other than an agency, unless the dissemination is made pursuant to subsection (b)(2) of this section, make reasonable efforts to assure that such records are accurate, complete, timely, and relevant for agency purposes;

(7) maintain no record describing how any individual exercises rights guaranteed by the First Amendment unless expressly authorized by statute or by the individual about whom the record is maintained or unless pertinent to and within the scope of an authorized law enforcement activity;

(8) make reasonable efforts to serve notice on an individual when any record on such individual is made available to any person under compulsory legal process when such process becomes a matter of public record;

(9) establish rules of conduct for persons involved in the design, development, operation, or maintenance of any system of records, or in maintaining any record, and instruct each such person with respect to such rules and the requirements of this section, including any other rules and procedures adopted pursuant to this section and the penalties for noncompliance;

(10) establish appropriate administrative, technical, and physical safeguards to insure the security and confidentiality of records and to protect against any anticipated threats or hazards to their security or integrity which could result in substantial harm, embarrassment, inconvenience, or unfairness to any individual on whom information is maintained;

(11) at least 30 days prior to publication of information under paragraph (4)(D) of this subsection, publish in the Federal Register notice of any new use or intended use of the information in the system, and provide an opportunity for interested persons to submit written data, views, or arguments to the agency; and

(12) if such agency is a recipient agency or a source agency in a matching program with a non-Federal agency, with respect to any establishment or revision of a matching program, at least 30 days prior to conducting such program, publish in the Federal Register notice of such establishment or revision.

(f) Agency rules.—In order to carry out the provisions of this section, each agency that maintains a system of records shall promulgate rules, in accordance with the requirements (including general notice) of section 553 of this title, which shall—

(1) establish procedures whereby an individual can be notified in response to his request if any system of records named by the individual contains a record pertaining to him;

(2) define reasonable times, places, and requirements for identifying an individual who requests his record or information pertaining to him before the agency shall make the record or information available to the individual;

(3) establish procedures for the disclosure to an individual upon his request of his record or information pertaining to him, including special procedure, if deemed necessary, for the disclosure to an individual of medical records, including psychological records, pertaining to him;

(4) establish procedures for reviewing a request from an individual concerning the amendment of any record or information pertaining to the individual, for making a determination on the request, for an appeal within the agency of an initial adverse agency determination, and for whatever additional means may be necessary for each individual to be able to exercise fully his rights under this section; and

(5) establish fees to be charged, if any, to any individual for making copies of his record, excluding the cost of any search for and review of the record.

The Office of the Federal Register shall biennially compile and publish the rules promulgated under this subsection and agency notices published under subsection (e)(4) of this section in a form available to the public at low cost.

(g)(1) Civil remedies.—Whenever any agency

(A) makes a determination under subsection (d)(3) of this section not to amend an individual's record in accordance with his request, or fails to make such review in conformity with that subsection;

(B) refuses to comply with an individual request under subsection (d)(1) of this section;

(C) fails to maintain any record concerning any individual with such accuracy, relevance, timeliness, and completeness as is necessary to assure fairness in any determination relating to the qualifications, character, rights, or opportunities of, or benefits to the individual that may be made on the basis of such record, and consequently a determination is made which is adverse to the individual; or

(D) fails to comply with any other provision of this section, or any rule promulgated thereunder, in such a way as to have an adverse effect on an individual,

the individual may bring a civil action against the agency, and the district courts of the United States shall have jurisdiction in the matters under the provisions of this subsection.

(2)(A) In any suit brought under the provisions of subsection (g)(1)(A) of this section, the court may order the agency to amend the individual's record in accordance with his request or in such other way as the court may direct. In such a case the court shall determine the matter de novo.

(B) The court may assess against the United States reasonable attorney fees and other litigation costs reasonably incurred in any case under this paragraph in which the complainant has substantially prevailed.

(3)(A) In any suit brought under the provisions of subsection (g)(1)(B) of this section, the court may enjoin the agency from withholding the records and order the production to the complainant of any agency records improperly withheld from him. In such a case the court shall determine the matter de novo, and may examine the contents of any agency records in camera to determine whether the records or any portion thereof may be withheld under any of the exemptions set forth in subsection (k) of this section, and the burden is on the agency to sustain its action.

(B) The court may assess against the United States reasonable attorney fees and other litigation costs reasonably incurred in any case under this paragraph in which the complainant has substantially prevailed.

(4) In any suit brought under the provisions of subsection (g)(1)(C) or (D) of this section in which the court determines that the agency acted in a manner which was intentional or willful, the United States shall be liable to the individual in an amount equal to the sum of—

(A) actual damages sustained by the individual as a result of the refusal or failure, but in no case shall a person entitled to recovery receive less than the sum of $1,000; and

(B) the costs of the action together with reasonable attorney fees as determined by the court.

(5) An action to enforce any liability created under this section may be brought in the district court of the United States in the district in which the complainant resides, or has his principal place of business, or in which the agency records are situated, or in the District of Columbia, without regard to the amount in controversy, within two years from the date on which the cause of action arises, except that where an agency has materially and willfully misrepresented any information required under this section to be disclosed to an individual and the information so misrepresented is material to establishment of the liability of the agency to the individual under this section, the action may be brought at any time within two years after discovery by the individual of the misrepresentation. Nothing in this section shall be construed to authorize any civil action by reason of any injury sustained as the result of a disclosure of a record prior to September 27, 1975.

(h) Rights of legal guardians.—For the purposes of this section, the parent of any minor, or the legal guardian of any individual who has been declared to be incompetent due to physical or mental incapacity or age by a court of competent jurisdiction, may act on behalf of the individual.

(i)(1) Criminal penalties.—Any officer or employee of an agency, who by virtue of his employment or official position, has possession of, or access to, agency records which contain individually identifiable information the disclosure of which is prohibited by this section or by rules or regulations established thereunder, and who knowing that disclosure of the specific material is so prohibited, willfully discloses the material in any manner to any person or agency not entitled to receive it, shall be guilty of a misdemeanor and fined not more than $5,000.

(2) Any officer or employee of any agency who willfully maintains a system of records without meeting the notice requirements of subsection (e)(4) of this section shall be guilty of a misdemeanor and fined not more than $5,000.

(3) Any person who knowingly and willfully requests or obtains any record concerning an individual from an agency under false pretenses shall be guilty of a misdemeanor and fined not more than $5,000.

(j) General exemptions.—The head of any agency may promulgate rules, in accordance with the requirements (including general notice) of sections 553(b)(1), (2), and (3), (c), and (e) of this title, to exempt any system of records within the agency from any part of this section except subsections (b), (c)(1) and (2), (e)(4)(A) through (F), (e)(6), (7), (9), (10), and (11), and (i) if the system of records is—

> **(1)** maintained by the Central Intelligence Agency; or
>
> **(2)** maintained by an agency or component thereof which performs as its principal function any activity pertaining to the enforcement of criminal laws, including police efforts to prevent, control, or reduce crime or to apprehend criminals, and the activities of prosecutors, courts, correctional, probation, pardon, or parole authorities, and which consists of (A) information compiled for the purpose of identifying individual criminal offenders and alleged offenders and consisting only of identifying data and notations of arrests, the nature and disposition of criminal charges, sentencing, confinement, release, and parole and probation status; (B) information compiled for the purpose of a criminal investigation, including reports of informants and investigators, and associated with an identifiable individual; or (C) reports identifiable to an individual compiled at any stage of the process of enforcement of the criminal laws from arrest or indictment through release from supervision.

At the time rules are adopted under this subsection, the agency shall include in the statement required under section 553(c) of this title, the reasons why the system of records is to be exempted from a provision of this section.

(k) Specific exemptions.—The head of any agency may promulgate rules, in accordance with the requirements (including general notice) of sections 553(b)(1), (2), and (3), (c), and (e) of this title, to exempt any system of records within the agency from subsections (c)(3), (d), (e)(1), (e)(4)(G), (H), and (I) and (f) of this section if the system of records is—

(1) subject to the provisions of section 552(b)(1) of this title;

(2) investigatory material compiled for law enforcement purposes, other than material within the scope of subsection (j)(2) of this section: *Provided, however*, That if any individual is denied any right, privilege, or benefit that he would otherwise be entitled by Federal law, or for which he would otherwise be eligible, as a result of the maintenance of such material, such material shall be provided to such individual, except to the extent that the disclosure of such material would reveal the identity of a source who furnished information to the Government under an express promise that the identity of the source would be held in confidence, or, prior to the effective date of this section, under an implied promise that the identity of the source would be held in confidence;

(3) maintained in connection with providing protective services to the President of the United States or other individuals pursuant to section 3056 of title 18;

(4) required by statute to be maintained and used solely as statistical records;

(5) investigatory material compiled solely for the purpose of determining suitability, eligibility, or qualifications for Federal civilian employment, military service, Federal contracts, or access to classified information, but only to the extent that the disclosure of such material would reveal the identity of a source who furnished information to the Government under an express promise that the identity of the source would be held in confidence, or, prior to the effective date of this section, under an implied promise that the identity of the source would be held in confidence;

(6) testing or examination material used solely to determine individual qualifications for appointment or promotion in the Federal service the disclosure of which would compromise the objectivity or fairness of the testing or examination process; or

(7) evaluation material used to determine potential for promotion in the armed services, but only to the extent that the disclosure of such material would reveal the identity of a source who furnished information to the Government under an express promise that the identity of the source would be held in confidence, or, prior to the effective date of this section, under an implied promise that the identity of the source would be held in confidence.

At the time rules are adopted under this subsection, the agency shall include in the statement required under section 553(c) of this title, the reasons why the system of records is to be exempted from a provision of this section.

(*l*)(1) Archival records.—Each agency record which is accepted by the Archivist of the United States for storage, processing, and servicing in accordance with section 3103 of title 44 shall, for the purposes of this section, be considered to be maintained by the agency which deposited the record and shall be subject to the provisions of this section. The Archivist of the United States shall not disclose the record except to the agency which maintains the record, or under rules established by that agency which are not inconsistent with the provisions of this section.

(2) Each agency record pertaining to an identifiable individual which was transferred to the National Archives of the United States as a record which has sufficient historical or other value to warrant its continued preservation by the United States Government, prior to the effective date of this section, shall, for the purposes of this section, be considered to be maintained by the National Archives and shall not be subject to the provisions of this section, except that a statement generally describing such records (modeled after the requirements relating to records subject to subsections (e)(4)(A) through (G) of this section) shall be published in the Federal Register.

(3) Each agency record pertaining to an identifiable individual which is transferred to the National Archives of the United States as a record which has sufficient historical or other value to warrant its continued preservation by the United States Government, on or after the effective date of this section, shall, for the purposes of this section, be considered to be maintained by the National Archives and shall be exempt from the requirements of this section except subsections (e)(4)(A) through (G) and (e)(9) of this section.

(m)(1) Government contractors.—When an agency provides by a contract for the operation by or on behalf of the agency of a system of records to accomplish an agency function, the agency shall, consistent with its authority, cause the requirements of this section to be applied to such system. For purposes of subsection (i) of this section any such contractor and any employee of such contractor, if such contract is agreed to on or after the effective date of this section, shall be considered to be an employee of an agency.

(2) A consumer reporting agency to which a record is disclosed under section 3711(e) of title 31 shall not be considered a contractor for the purposes of this section.

(n) Mailing lists.—An individual's name and address may not be sold or rented by an agency unless such action is specifically authorized by law. This provision shall not be construed to require the withholding of names and addresses otherwise permitted to be made public.

(o) Matching agreements.—(1) No record which is contained in a system of records may be disclosed to a recipient agency or non-Federal agency for use in a computer matching program except pursuant to a written agreement between the source agency and the recipient agency or non-Federal agency specifying—

(A) the purpose and legal authority for conducting the program;

(B) the justification for the program and the anticipated results, including a specific estimate of any savings;

(C) a description of the records that will be matched, including each data element that will be used, the approximate number of records that will be matched, and the projected starting and completion dates of the matching program;

(D) procedures for providing individualized notice at the time of application, and notice periodically thereafter as directed by the Data Integrity Board of such agency (subject to guidance provided by the Director of the Office of Management and Budget pursuant to subsection (v)), to—

(i) applicants for and recipients of financial assistance or payments under Federal benefit programs, and

(ii) applicants for and holders of positions as Federal personnel,

that any information provided by such applicants, recipients, holders, and individuals may be subject to verification through matching programs;

(E) procedures for verifying information produced in such matching program as required by subsection (p);

(F) procedures for the retention and timely destruction of identifiable records created by a recipient agency or non-Federal agency in such matching program;

(G) procedures for ensuring the administrative, technical, and physical security of the records matched and the results of such programs;

(H) prohibitions on duplication and redisclosure of records provided by the source agency within or outside the recipient agency or the non-Federal agency, except where required by law or essential to the conduct of the matching program;

(I) procedures governing the use by a recipient agency or non-Federal agency of records provided in a matching program by a source agency, including procedures governing return of the records to the source agency or destruction of records used in such program;

(J) information on assessments that have been made on the accuracy of the records that will be used in such matching program; and

(K) that the Comptroller General may have access to all records of a recipient agency or a non-Federal agency that the Comptroller General deems necessary in order to monitor or verify compliance with the agreement.

(2)(A) A copy of each agreement entered into pursuant to paragraph (1) shall—

(i) be transmitted to the Committee on Governmental Affairs of the Senate and the Committee on Government Operations of the House of Representatives; and

(ii) be available upon request to the public.

(B) No such agreement shall be effective until 30 days after the date on which such a copy is transmitted pursuant to subparagraph (A)(i).

(C) Such an agreement shall remain in effect only for such period, not to exceed 18 months, as the Data Integrity Board of the agency determines is appropriate in light of the purposes, and length of time necessary for the conduct, of the matching program.

(D) Within 3 months prior to the expiration of such an agreement pursuant to subparagraph (C), the Data Integrity Board of the agency may, without additional review, renew the matching agreement for a current, ongoing matching program for not more than one additional year if—

(i) such program will be conducted without any change; and

(ii) each party to the agreement certifies to the Board in writing that the program has been conducted in compliance with the agreement.

(p) Verification and opportunity to contest findings.—(1) In order to protect any individual whose records are used in a matching program, no recipient agency, non-Federal agency, or source agency may suspend, terminate, reduce, or make a final denial of any financial assistance or payment under a Federal benefit program to such individual, or take other adverse action against such individual, as a result of information produced by such matching program, until—

(A)(i) the agency has independently verified the information; or

(ii) the Data Integrity Board of the agency, or in the case of a non-Federal agency the Data Integrity Board of the source agency, determines in accordance with guidance issued by the Director of the Office of Management and Budget that—

(I) the information is limited to identification and amount of benefits paid by the source agency under a Federal benefit program; and

(II) there is a high degree of confidence that the information provided to the recipient agency is accurate;

(B) the individual receives a notice from the agency containing a statement of its findings and informing the individual of the opportunity to contest such findings; and

(C)(i) the expiration of any time period established for the program by statute or regulation for the individual to respond to that notice; or

(ii) in the case of a program for which no such period is established, the end of the 30-day period beginning on the date on which notice under subparagraph (B) is mailed or otherwise provided to the individual.

(2) Independent verification referred to in paragraph (1) requires investigation and confirmation of specific information relating to an individual that is used as a basis for an adverse action against the individual, including where applicable investigation and confirmation of—

(A) the amount of any asset or income involved;

(B) whether such individual actually has or had access to such asset or income for such individual's own use; and

(C) the period or periods when the individual actually had such asset or income.

(3) Notwithstanding paragraph (1), an agency may take any appropriate action otherwise prohibited by such paragraph if the agency determines that the public health or public safety may be adversely affected or significantly threatened during any notice period required by such paragraph.

(q) Sanctions.—(1) Notwithstanding any other provision of law, no source agency may disclose any record which is contained in a system of records to a recipient agency or non-Federal agency for a matching program if such source agency has reason to believe that the requirements of subsection (p), or any matching agreement entered into pursuant to subsection (o), or both, are not being met by such recipient agency.

(2) No source agency may renew a matching agreement unless—

(A) the recipient agency or non-Federal agency has certified that it has complied with the provisions of that agreement; and

(B) the source agency has no reason to believe that the certification is inaccurate.

(r) Report on new systems and matching programs.—Each agency that proposes to establish or make a significant change in a system of records or a matching program shall provide adequate advance notice of any such proposal (in duplicate) to the Committee on Government Operations of the House of Representatives, the Committee on Governmental Affairs of the Senate, and the Office of Management and Budget in order to permit an evaluation of the probable or potential effect of such proposal on the privacy or other rights of individuals.

(s) Biennial report.—The President shall biennially submit to the Speaker of the House of Representatives and the President pro tempore of the Senate a report—

(1) describing the actions of the Director of the Office of Management and Budget pursuant to section 6 of the Privacy Act of 1974 during the preceding 2 years;

(2) describing the exercise of individual rights of access and amendment under this section during such years;

(3) identifying changes in or additions to systems of records;

(4) containing such other information concerning administration of this section as may be necessary or useful to the Congress in reviewing the effectiveness of this section in carrying out the purposes of the Privacy Act of 1974.

(t)(1) Effect of other laws.—No agency shall rely on any exemption contained in section 552 of this title to withhold from an individual any record which is otherwise accessible to such individual under the provisions of this section.

(2) No agency shall rely on any exemption in this section to withhold from an individual any record which is otherwise accessible to such individual under the provisions of section 552 of this title.

(u) Data Integrity Boards.—(1) Every agency conducting or participating in a matching program shall establish a Data Integrity Board to oversee and coordinate among the various components of such agency the agency's implementation of this section.

(2) Each Data Integrity Board shall consist of senior officials designated by the head of the agency, and shall include any senior official designated by the head of the agency as responsible for implementation of this section, and the inspector general of the agency, if any. The inspector general shall not serve as chairman of the Data Integrity Board.

(3) Each Data Integrity Board—

(A) shall review, approve, and maintain all written agreements for receipt or disclosure of agency records for matching programs to ensure compliance with subsection (o), and all relevant statutes, regulations, and guidelines;

(B) shall review all matching programs in which the agency has participated during the year, either as a source agency or recipient agency, determine compliance with applicable laws, regulations, guidelines, and agency agreements, and assess the costs and benefits of such programs;

(C) shall review all recurring matching programs in which the agency has participated during the year, either as a source agency or recipient agency, for continued justification for such disclosures;

(D) shall compile an annual report, which shall be submitted to the head of the agency and the Office of Management and Budget and made available to the public on request, describing the matching activities of the agency, including—

(i) matching programs in which the agency has participated as a source agency or recipient agency;

(ii) matching agreements proposed under subsection (o) that were disapproved by the Board;

(iii) any changes in membership or structure of the Board in the preceding year;

(iv) the reasons for any waiver of the requirement in paragraph (4) of this section for completion and submission of a cost-benefit analysis prior to the approval of a matching program;

(v) any violations of matching agreements that have been alleged or identified and any corrective action taken; and

(vi) any other information required by the Director of the Office of Management and Budget to be included in such report;

(E) shall serve as a clearinghouse for receiving and providing information on the accuracy, completeness, and reliability of records used in matching programs;

(F) shall provide interpretation and guidance to agency components and personnel on the requirements of this section for matching programs;

(G) shall review agency recordkeeping and disposal policies and practices for matching programs to assure compliance with this section; and

(H) may review and report on any agency matching activities that are not matching programs.

(4)(A) Except as provided in subparagraphs (B) and (C), a Data Integrity Board shall not approve any written agreement for a matching program unless the agency has completed and submitted to such Board a cost-benefit analysis of the proposed program and such analysis demonstrates that the program is likely to be cost effective. [FN3]

(B) The Board may waive the requirements of subparagraph (A) of this paragraph if it determines in writing, in accordance with guidelines prescribed by the Director of the Office of Management and Budget, that a cost-benefit analysis is not required.

(C) A cost-benefit analysis shall not be required under subparagraph (A) prior to the initial approval of a written agreement for a matching program that is specifically required by statute. Any subsequent written agreement for such a program shall not be approved by the Data Integrity

Board unless the agency has submitted a cost-benefit analysis of the program as conducted under the preceding approval of such agreement.

(5)(A) If a matching agreement is disapproved by a Data Integrity Board, any party to such agreement may appeal the disapproval to the Director of the Office of Management and Budget. Timely notice of the filing of such an appeal shall be provided by the Director of the Office of Management and Budget to the Committee on Governmental Affairs of the Senate and the Committee on Government Operations of the House of Representatives.

(B) The Director of the Office of Management and Budget may approve a matching agreement notwithstanding the disapproval of a Data Integrity Board if the Director determines that—

> **(i)** the matching program will be consistent with all applicable legal, regulatory, and policy requirements;
>
> **(ii)** there is adequate evidence that the matching agreement will be cost-effective; and
>
> **(iii)** the matching program is in the public interest.

(C) The decision of the Director to approve a matching agreement shall not take effect until 30 days after it is reported to committees described in subparagraph (A).

(D) If the Data Integrity Board and the Director of the Office of Management and Budget disapprove a matching program proposed by the inspector general of an agency, the inspector general may report the disapproval to the head of the agency and to the Congress.

(6) In the reports required by paragraph (3)(D), agency matching activities that are not matching programs may be reported on an aggregate basis, if and to the extent necessary to protect ongoing law enforcement or counterintelligence investigations.

(v) Office of Management and Budget responsibilities.—The Director of the Office of Management and Budget shall—

> **(1)** develop and, after notice and opportunity for public comment, prescribe guidelines and regulations for the use of agencies in implementing the provisions of this section; and
>
> **(2)** provide continuing assistance to and oversight of the implementation of this section by agencies.

Drivers Privacy Protection Act (1994)

18 U.S.C. §§ 2721-2725, as amended

Statutes in Context

The Drivers Privacy Protection Act (DPPA) prohibits a state department of motor vehicles (DMV) from disclosing any personal information about any individual obtained by the department in connection with a motor vehicle record. A state DMV can disclose personal information only if the individual driver affirmatively consents (opts in). The DPPA contains a number of exceptions to this rule of non-disclosure. As examples, a state DMV can disclose information for purposes of law enforcement, motor vehicle product recalls, legal proceedings, and insurance claims investigations. It also permits disclosures to licensed private investigative agencies or security services.

§ 2721. Prohibition on release and use of certain personal information from State motor vehicle records

(a) In general.—A State department of motor vehicles, and any officer, employee, or contractor thereof, shall not knowingly disclose or otherwise make available to any person or entity:

> **(1)** personal information, as defined in 18 U.S.C. 2725(3), about any individual obtained by the department in connection with a motor vehicle record, except as provided in subsection (b) of this section; or
>
> **(2)** highly restricted personal information, as defined in 18 U.S.C. 2725(4), about any individual obtained by the department in connection with a motor vehicle record, without the express consent of the person to whom such information applies, except uses permitted in subsections (b)(1), (b)(4), (b)(6), and (b)(9): *Provided,* That subsection (a)(2) shall not in any way affect the use of organ donation information on an individual's driver's license or affect the administration of organ donation initiatives in the States.

(b) Permissible uses.—Personal information referred to in subsection (a) shall be disclosed for use in connection with matters of motor vehicle or driver safety and theft, motor vehicle emissions, motor vehicle product alterations, recalls, or advisories, performance monitoring of motor vehicles and dealers by motor vehicle manufacturers, and removal of non-owner records from the original owner records of motor vehicle manufacturers to carry out the purposes of titles I and IV of the Anti Car Theft Act of 1992, the Automobile Information Disclosure Act (15 U.S.C. 1231 et seq.), the Clean Air Act (42 U.S.C. 7401 et seq.), and chapters 301, 305, and 321-331 of title 49, and, subject to subsection (a)(2), may be disclosed as follows:

> **(1)** For use by any government agency, including any court or law enforcement agency, in carrying out its functions, or any private person or entity acting on behalf of a Federal, State, or local agency in carrying out its functions.

(2) For use in connection with matters of motor vehicle or driver safety and theft; motor vehicle emissions; motor vehicle product alterations, recalls, or advisories; performance monitoring of motor vehicles, motor vehicle parts and dealers; motor vehicle market research activities, including survey research; and removal of non-owner records from the original owner records of motor vehicle manufacturers.

(3) For use in the normal course of business by a legitimate business or its agents, employees, or contractors, but only—

(A) to verify the accuracy of personal information submitted by the individual to the business or its agents, employees, or contractors; and

(B) if such information as so submitted is not correct or is no longer correct, to obtain the correct information, but only for the purposes of preventing fraud by, pursuing legal remedies against, or recovering on a debt or security interest against, the individual.

(4) For use in connection with any civil, criminal, administrative, or arbitral proceeding in any Federal, State, or local court or agency or before any self-regulatory body, including the service of process, investigation in anticipation of litigation, and the execution or enforcement of judgments and orders, or pursuant to an order of a Federal, State, or local court.

(5) For use in research activities, and for use in producing statistical reports, so long as the personal information is not published, redisclosed, or used to contact individuals.

(6) For use by any insurer or insurance support organization, or by a self-insured entity, or its agents, employees, or contractors, in connection with claims investigation activities, antifraud activities, rating or underwriting.

(7) For use in providing notice to the owners of towed or impounded vehicles.

(8) For use by any licensed private investigative agency or licensed security service for any purpose permitted under this subsection.

(9) For use by an employer or its agent or insurer to obtain or verify information relating to a holder of a commercial driver's license that is required under chapter 313 of title 49.

(10) For use in connection with the operation of private toll transportation facilities.

(11) For any other use in response to requests for individual motor vehicle records if the State has obtained the express consent of the person to whom such personal information pertains.

(12) For bulk distribution for surveys, marketing or solicitations if the State has obtained the express consent of the person to whom such personal information pertains.

(13) For use by any requester, if the requester demonstrates it has obtained the written consent of the individual to whom the information pertains.

(14) For any other use specifically authorized under the law of the State that holds the record, if such use is related to the operation of a motor vehicle or public safety.

(c) Resale or redisclosure.—An authorized recipient of personal information (except a recipient under subsection (b)(11) or (12)) may resell or redisclose the information only for a use permitted under subsection (b) (but not for uses under subsection (b) (11) or (12)). An authorized recipient under subsection (b)(11) may resell or redisclose personal information for any purpose. An authorized recipient under subsection (b)(12) may resell or redisclose personal information pursuant to subsection (b)(12). Any authorized recipient (except a recipient under subsection (b) (11)) that resells or rediscloses personal information covered by this chapter must keep for a period of 5 years records identifying each person or entity that receives information and the permitted purpose for which the information will be used and must make such records available to the motor vehicle department upon request.

(d) Waiver procedures.—A State motor vehicle department may establish and carry out procedures under which the department or its agents, upon receiving a request for personal information that does not fall within one of the exceptions in subsection (b), may mail a copy of the request to the individual about whom the information was requested, informing such individual of the request, together with a statement to the effect that the information will not be released unless the individual waives such individual's right to privacy under this section.

(e) Prohibition on conditions.—No State may condition or burden in any way the issuance of an individual's motor vehicle record as defined in 18 U.S.C. 2725(1) to obtain express consent. Nothing in this paragraph shall be construed to prohibit a State from charging an administrative fee for issuance of a motor vehicle record.

§ 2722. Additional unlawful acts

(a) Procurement for unlawful purpose.—It shall be unlawful for any person knowingly to obtain or disclose personal information, from a motor vehicle record, for any use not permitted under section 2721(b) of this title.

(b) False representation.—It shall be unlawful for any person to make false representation to obtain any personal information from an individual's motor vehicle record.

§ 2723. Penalties

(a) Criminal fine.—A person who knowingly violates this chapter shall be fined under this title.

(b) Violations by State department of motor vehicles.—Any State department of motor vehicles that has a policy or practice of substantial noncompliance with this chapter shall be subject to a civil penalty imposed by the Attorney General of not more than $5,000 a day for each day of substantial noncompliance.

§ 2724. Civil action

(a) Cause of action.—A person who knowingly obtains, discloses or uses personal information, from a motor vehicle record, for a purpose not permitted under this chapter shall be liable to the individual to whom the information pertains, who may bring a civil action in a United States district court.

(b) Remedies.—The court may award—

(1) actual damages, but not less than liquidated damages in the amount of $2,500;

(2) punitive damages upon proof of willful or reckless disregard of the law;

(3) reasonable attorneys' fees and other litigation costs reasonably incurred; and

(4) such other preliminary and equitable relief as the court determines to be appropriate.

§ 2725. Definitions

In this chapter—

(1) "motor vehicle record" means any record that pertains to a motor vehicle operator's permit, motor vehicle title, motor vehicle registration, or identification card issued by a department of motor vehicles;

(2) "person" means an individual, organization or entity, but does not include a State or agency thereof;

(3) "personal information" means information that identifies an individual, including an individual's photograph, social security number, driver identification number, name, address (but not the 5-digit zip code), telephone number, and medical or disability information, but does not include information on vehicular accidents, driving violations, and driver's status.

(4) "highly restricted personal information" means an individual's photograph or image, social security number, medical or disability information; and

(5) "express consent" means consent in writing, including consent conveyed electronically that bears an electronic signature as defined in section 106(5) of Public Law 106-229.

Real ID Act (2005)

18 U.S.C.A. § 1028 and note to 49 U.S.C.A. § 30301, as amended

Statutes in Context

The Real ID Act sets minimum document requirements for state driver's licenses or identification cards before a federal agency may accept them for any official purpose.

§ 1028. Fraud and related activity in connection with identification documents, authentication features, and information

(a) Whoever, in a circumstance described in subsection (c) of this section—

(1) knowingly and without lawful authority produces an identification document, authentication feature, or a false identification document;

(2) knowingly transfers an identification document, authentication feature, or a false identification document knowing that such document or feature was stolen or produced without lawful authority;

(3) knowingly possesses with intent to use unlawfully or transfer unlawfully five or more identification documents (other than those issued lawfully for the use of the possessor), authentication features, or false identification documents;

(4) knowingly possesses an identification document (other than one issued lawfully for the use of the possessor), authentication feature, or a false identification document, with the intent such document or feature be used to defraud the United States;

(5) knowingly produces, transfers, or possesses a document-making implement or authentication feature with the intent such document-making implement or authentication feature will be used in the production of a false identification document or another document-making implement or authentication feature which will be so used;

(6) knowingly possesses an identification document or authentication feature that is or appears to be an identification document or authentication feature of the United States or a sponsoring entity of an event designated as a special event of national significance which is stolen or produced without lawful authority knowing that such document or feature was stolen or produced without such authority;

(7) knowingly transfers, possesses, or uses, without lawful authority, a means of identification of another person with the intent to commit, or to aid or abet, or in connection with, any unlawful activity that constitutes a violation of Federal law, or that constitutes a felony under any applicable State or local law; or

(8) knowingly traffics in false or actual authentication features for use in false identification documents, document-making implements, or means of identification;

shall be punished as provided in subsection (b) of this section.

(b) The punishment for an offense under subsection (a) of this section is—

(1) except as provided in paragraphs (3) and (4), a fine under this title or imprisonment for not more than 15 years, or both, if the offense is—

(A) the production or transfer of an identification document, authentication feature, or false identification document that is or appears to be—

(i) an identification document or authentication feature issued by or under the authority of the United States; or

(ii) a birth certificate, or a driver's license or personal identification card;

(B) the production or transfer of more than five identification documents, authentication features, or false identification documents;

(C) an offense under paragraph (5) of such subsection; or

(D) an offense under paragraph (7) of such subsection that involves the transfer, possession, or use of 1 or more means of identification if, as a result of the offense, any individual committing the offense obtains anything of value aggregating $1,000 or more during any 1-year period;

(2) except as provided in paragraphs (3) and (4), a fine under this title or imprisonment for not more than 5 years, or both, if the offense is—

(A) any other production, transfer, or use of a means of identification, an identification document, authentication feature, or a false identification document; or

(B) an offense under paragraph (3) or (7) of such subsection;

(3) a fine under this title or imprisonment for not more than 20 years, or both, if the offense is committed—

(A) to facilitate a drug trafficking crime (as defined in section 929(a)(2));

(B) in connection with a crime of violence (as defined in section 924(c)(3)); or

(C) after a prior conviction under this section becomes final;

(4) a fine under this title or imprisonment for not more than 30 years, or both, if the offense is committed to facilitate an act of domestic terrorism (as defined under section 2331(5) of this title) or an act of international terrorism (as defined in section 2331(1) of this title);

(5) in the case of any offense under subsection (a), forfeiture to the United States of any personal property used or intended to be used to commit the offense; and

(6) a fine under this title or imprisonment for not more than one year, or both, in any other case.

(c) The circumstance referred to in subsection (a) of this section is that—

(1) the identification document, authentication feature, or false identification document is or appears to be issued by or under the authority of the United States or a sponsoring entity of an event designated as a special event of national significance or the document-making implement is designed or suited for making such an identification document, authentication feature, or false identification document;

(2) the offense is an offense under subsection (a) (4) of this section; or

(3) either—

(A) the production, transfer, possession, or use prohibited by this section is in or affects interstate or foreign commerce, including the transfer of a document by electronic means; or

(B) the means of identification, identification document, false identification document, or document-making implement is transported in the mail in the course of the production, transfer, possession, or use prohibited by this section.

(d) In this section and section 1028A—

(1) the term "authentication feature" means any hologram, watermark, certification, symbol, code, image, sequence of numbers or letters, or other feature that either individually or in combination with another feature is used by the issuing authority on an identification document, document-making implement, or means of identification to determine if the document is counterfeit, altered, or otherwise falsified;

(2) the term "document-making implement" means any implement, impression, template, computer file, computer disc, electronic device, or computer hardware or software, that is specifically configured or primarily used for making an identification document, a false identification document, or another document-making implement;

(3) the term "identification document" means a document made or issued by or under the authority of the United States Government, a State, political subdivision of a State, a sponsoring entity of an event designated as a special event of national significance, a foreign government, political subdivision of a foreign government, an international governmental or an international quasi-governmental organization which, when completed with information concerning a particular individual, is of a type intended or commonly accepted for the purpose of identification of individuals;

(4) the term "false identification document" means a document of a type intended or commonly accepted for the purposes of identification of individuals that—

(A) is not issued by or under the authority of a governmental entity or was issued under the authority of a governmental entity but was subsequently altered for purposes of deceit; and

(B) appears to be issued by or under the authority of the United States Government, a State, a political subdivision of a State, a sponsoring entity of an event designated by the

President as a special event of national significance, a foreign government, a political subdivision of a foreign government, or an international governmental or quasi-governmental organization;

(5) the term "false authentication feature" means an authentication feature that—

(A) is genuine in origin, but, without the authorization of the issuing authority, has been tampered with or altered for purposes of deceit;

(B) is genuine, but has been distributed, or is intended for distribution, without the authorization of the issuing authority and not in connection with a lawfully made identification document, document-making implement, or means of identification to which such authentication feature is intended to be affixed or embedded by the respective issuing authority; or

(C) appears to be genuine, but is not;

(6) the term "issuing authority"—

(A) means any governmental entity or agency that is authorized to issue identification documents, means of identification, or authentication features; and

(B) includes the United States Government, a State, a political subdivision of a State, a sponsoring entity of an event designated by the President as a special event of national significance, a foreign government, a political subdivision of a foreign government, or an international government or quasi-governmental organization;

(7) the term "means of identification" means any name or number that may be used, alone or in conjunction with any other information, to identify a specific individual, including any—

(A) name, social security number, date of birth, official State or government issued driver's license or identification number, alien registration number, government passport number, employer or taxpayer identification number;

(B) unique biometric data, such as fingerprint, voice print, retina or iris image, or other unique physical representation;

(C) unique electronic identification number, address, or routing code; or

(D) telecommunication identifying information or access device (as defined in section 1029(e));

(8) the term "personal identification card" means an identification document issued by a State or local government solely for the purpose of identification;

(9) the term "produce" includes alter, authenticate, or assemble;

(10) the term "transfer" includes selecting an identification document, false identification document, or document-making implement and placing or directing the placement of such identification document, false identification document, or document-making implement on an online location where it is available to others;

(11) the term "State" includes any State of the United States, the District of Columbia, the Commonwealth of Puerto Rico, and any other commonwealth, possession, or territory of the United States; and

(12) the term "traffic" means—

(A) to transport, transfer, or otherwise dispose of, to another, as consideration for anything of value; or

(B) to make or obtain control of with intent to so transport, transfer, or otherwise dispose of.

(e) This section does not prohibit any lawfully authorized investigative, protective, or intelligence activity of a law enforcement agency of the United States, a State, or a political subdivision of a State, or of an intelligence agency of the United States, or any activity authorized under chapter 224 of this title.

(f) Attempt and conspiracy.—Any person who attempts or conspires to commit any offense under this section shall be subject to the same penalties as those prescribed for the offense, the commission of which was the object of the attempt or conspiracy.

(g) Forfeiture procedures.—The forfeiture of property under this section, including any seizure and disposition of the property and any related judicial or administrative proceeding, shall be governed by the provisions of section 413 (other than subsection (d) of that section) of the Comprehensive Drug Abuse Prevention and Control Act of 1970 (21 U.S.C. 853).

(h) Forfeiture; disposition.—In the circumstance in which any person is convicted of a violation of subsection (a), the court shall order, in addition to the penalty prescribed, the forfeiture and destruction or other disposition of all illicit authentication features, identification documents, document-making implements, or means of identification.

(i) Rule of construction.—For purpose of subsection (a)(7), a single identification document or false identification document that contains 1 or more means of identification shall be construed to be 1 means of identification.

§ 30301, Note

SEC. 201. DEFINITIONS.

In this title, the following definitions apply:

(1) DRIVER'S LICENSE.—The term "driver's license" means a motor vehicle operator's license, as defined in section 30301 of title 49, United States Code.

(2) IDENTIFICATION CARD.—The term "identification card" means a personal identification card, as defined in section 1028(d) of title 18, United States Code, issued by a State.

(3) OFFICIAL PURPOSE.—The term "official purpose" includes but is not limited to accessing Federal facilities, boarding federally regulated commercial aircraft, entering nuclear power plants, and any other purposes that the Secretary shall determine.

(4) SECRETARY.—The term "Secretary" means the Secretary of Homeland Security.

(5) STATE.—The term "State" means a State of the United States, the District of Columbia, Puerto Rico, the Virgin Islands, Guam, American Samoa, the Northern Mariana Islands, the Trust Territory of the Pacific Islands, and any other territory or possession of the United States.

SEC. 202. MINIMUM DOCUMENT REQUIREMENTS AND ISSUANCE STANDARDS FOR FEDERAL RECOGNITION.

(a) MINIMUM STANDARDS FOR FEDERAL USE.—

(1) IN GENERAL.—Beginning 3 years after the date of the enactment of this division, a Federal agency may not accept, for any official purpose, a driver's license or identification card issued by a State to any person unless the State is meeting the requirements of this section.

(2) STATE CERTIFICATIONS.—The Secretary shall determine whether a State is meeting the requirements of this section based on certifications made by the State to the Secretary. Such certifications shall be made at such times and in such manner as the Secretary, in consultation with the Secretary of Transportation, may prescribe by regulation.

(b) MINIMUM DOCUMENT REQUIREMENTS.—To meet the requirements of this section, a State shall include, at a minimum, the following information and features on each driver's license and identification card issued to a person by the State:

(1) The person's full legal name.

(2) The person's date of birth.

(3) The person's gender.

(4) The person's driver's license or identification card number.

(5) A digital photograph of the person.

(6) The person's address of principle residence.

(7) The person's signature.

(8) Physical security features designed to prevent tampering, counterfeiting, or duplication of the document for fraudulent purposes.

(9) A common machine-readable technology, with defined minimum data elements.

(c) MINIMUM ISSUANCE STANDARDS.—

(1) IN GENERAL.—To meet the requirements of this section, a State shall require, at a minimum, presentation and verification of the following information before issuing a driver's license or identification card to a person:

(A) A photo identity document, except that a non-photo identity document is acceptable if it includes both the person's full legal name and date of birth.

(B) Documentation showing the person's date of birth.

(C) Proof of the person's social security account number or verification that the person is not eligible for a social security account number.

(D) Documentation showing the person's name and address of principal residence.

(2) SPECIAL REQUIREMENTS.—

(A) IN GENERAL.—To meet the requirements of this section, a State shall comply with the minimum standards of this paragraph.

(B) EVIDENCE OF LAWFUL STATUS.—A State shall require, before issuing a driver's license or identification card to a person, valid documentary evidence that the person—

(i) is a citizen or national of the United States;

(ii) is an alien lawfully admitted for permanent or temporary residence in the United States;

(iii) has conditional permanent resident status in the United States;

(iv) has an approved application for asylum in the United States or has entered into the United States in refugee status;

(v) has a valid, unexpired nonimmigrant visa or nonimmigrant visa status for entry into the United States;

(vi) has a pending application for asylum in the United States;

(vii) has a pending or approved application for temporary protected status in the United States;

(viii) has approved deferred action status; or

(ix) has a pending application for adjustment of status to that of an alien lawfully admitted for permanent residence in the United States or conditional permanent resident status in the United States.

(C) TEMPORARY DRIVERS' LICENSES AND IDENTIFICATION CARDS.—

(i) IN GENERAL.—If a person presents evidence under any of clauses (v) through (ix) of subparagraph (B), the State may only issue a temporary driver's license or temporary identification card to the person.

(ii) EXPIRATION DATE.—A temporary driver's license or temporary identification card issued pursuant to this subparagraph shall be valid only during the period of time of the applicant's authorized stay in the United States or, if there is no definite end to the period of authorized stay, a period of one year.

(iii) DISPLAY OF EXPIRATION DATE.—A temporary driver's license or temporary identification card issued pursuant to this subparagraph shall clearly indicate that it is temporary and shall state the date on which it expires.

(iv) RENEWAL.—A temporary driver's license or temporary identification card issued pursuant to this subparagraph may be renewed only upon presentation of valid documentary evidence that the status by which the applicant qualified for the temporary driver's license or temporary identification card has been extended by the Secretary of Homeland Security.

(3) VERIFICATION OF DOCUMENTS.—To meet the requirements of this section, a State shall implement the following procedures:

(A) Before issuing a driver's license or identification card to a person, the State shall verify, with the issuing agency, the issuance, validity, and completeness of each document required to be presented by the person under paragraph (1) or (2).

(B) The State shall not accept any foreign document, other than an official passport, to satisfy a requirement of paragraph (1) or (2).

(C) Not later than September 11, 2005, the State shall enter into a memorandum of understanding with the Secretary of Homeland Security to routinely utilize the automated system known as Systematic Alien Verification for Entitlements, as provided for by section 404 of the Illegal Immigration Reform and Immigrant Responsibility Act of 1996 (110 Stat. 3009-664), to verify the legal presence status of a person, other than a United States citizen, applying for a driver's license or identification card.

(d) OTHER REQUIREMENTS.—To meet the requirements of this section, a State shall adopt the following practices in the issuance of drivers' licenses and identification cards:

(1) Employ technology to capture digital images of identity source documents so that the images can be retained in electronic storage in a transferable format.

(2) Retain paper copies of source documents for a minimum of 7 years or images of source documents presented for a minimum of 10 years.

(3) Subject each person applying for a driver's license or identification card to mandatory facial image capture.

(4) Establish an effective procedure to confirm or verify a renewing applicant's information.

(5) Confirm with the Social Security Administration a social security account number presented by a person using the full social security account number. In the event that a social security account number is already registered to or associated with another person to which any State has issued a driver's license or identification card, the State shall resolve the discrepancy and take appropriate action.

(6) Refuse to issue a driver's license or identification card to a person holding a driver's license issued by another State without confirmation that the person is terminating or has terminated the driver's license.

(7) Ensure the physical security of locations where drivers' licenses and identification cards are produced and the security of document materials and papers from which drivers' licenses and identification cards are produced.

(8) Subject all persons authorized to manufacture or produce drivers' licenses and identification cards to appropriate security clearance requirements.

(9) Establish fraudulent document recognition training programs for appropriate employees engaged in the issuance of drivers' licenses and identification cards.

(10) Limit the period of validity of all driver's licenses and identification cards that are not temporary to a period that does not exceed 8 years.

(11) In any case in which the State issues a driver's license or identification card that does not satisfy the requirements of this section, ensure that such license or identification card—

(A) clearly states on its face that it may not be accepted by any Federal agency for federal identification or any other official purpose; and

(B) uses a unique design or color indicator to alert Federal agency and other law enforcement personnel that it may not be accepted for any such purpose.

(12) Provide electronic access to all other States to information contained in the motor vehicle database of the State.

(13) Maintain a State motor vehicle database that contains, at a minimum—

(A) all data fields printed on drivers' licenses and identification cards issued by the State; and

(B) motor vehicle drivers' histories, including motor vehicle violations, suspensions, and points on licenses.

SEC. 203. TRAFFICKING IN AUTHENTICATION FEATURES FOR USE IN FALSE IDENTIFICATION DOCUMENTS.

(a) CRIMINAL PENALTY.—Section 1028(a)(8) of title 18, United States Code, is amended by striking "false authentication features" and inserting "false or actual authentication features".

(b) USE OF FALSE DRIVER'S LICENSE AT AIRPORTS.—

(1) IN GENERAL.—The Secretary shall enter, into the appropriate aviation security screening database, appropriate information regarding any person convicted of using a false driver's license at an airport (as such term is defined in section 40102 of title 49, United States Code).

(2) FALSE DEFINED.—In this subsection, the term "false" has the same meaning such term has under section 1028(d) of title 18, United States Code.

SEC. 204. GRANTS TO STATES.

(a) IN GENERAL.—The Secretary may make grants to a State to assist the State in conforming to the minimum standards set forth in this title.

(b) AUTHORIZATION OF APPROPRIATIONS.—There are authorized to be appropriated to the Secretary for each of the fiscal years 2005 through 2009 such sums as may be necessary to carry out this title.

SEC. 205. AUTHORITY.

(a) PARTICIPATION OF SECRETARY OF TRANSPORTATION AND STATES.—All authority to issue regulations, set standards, and issue grants under this title shall be carried out by the Secretary, in consultation with the Secretary of Transportation and the States.

(b) EXTENSIONS OF DEADLINES.—The Secretary may grant to a State an extension of time to meet the requirements of section 202(a)(1) if the State provides adequate justification for noncompliance.**SEC. 206. REPEAL.**

[Omitted. Repealed Pub.L. 108-458, Title VII, § 7212, Dec. 17, 2004, 118 Stat. 3827, set out as a note under this section.]

SEC. 207. LIMITATION ON STATUTORY CONSTRUCTION.

Nothing in this title shall be construed to affect the authorities or responsibilities of the Secretary of Transportation or the States under chapter 303 of title 49, United States Code.

Communications Assistance for Law Enforcement Act (1994)

47 U.S.C. §§ 1001-1010, § 1021, as amended

Statutes in Context

The Communications Assistance for Law Enforcement Act (CALEA) requires telecommunications providers to create facilities that will be able to isolate and intercept electronic communications and deliver them to law enforcement personnel.

§ 1001. Definitions

For purposes of this subchapter—

(1) The terms defined in section 2510 of Title 18 have, respectively, the meanings stated in that section.

(2) The term "call-identifying information" means dialing or signaling information that identifies the origin, direction, destination, or termination of each communication generated or received by a subscriber by means of any equipment, facility, or service of a telecommunications carrier.

(3) The term "Commission" means the Federal Communications Commission.

(4) The term "electronic messaging services" means software-based services that enable the sharing of data, images, sound, writing, or other information among computing devices controlled by the senders or recipients of the messages.

(5) The term "government" means the government of the United States and any agency or instrumentality thereof, the District of Columbia, any commonwealth, territory, or possession of the United States, and any State or political subdivision thereof authorized by law to conduct electronic surveillance.

(6) The term "information services"—

(A) means the offering of a capability for generating, acquiring, storing, transforming, processing, retrieving, utilizing, or making available information via telecommunications; and

(B) includes—

(i) a service that permits a customer to retrieve stored information from, or file information for storage in, information storage facilities;

(ii) electronic publishing; and

(iii) electronic messaging services; but

(C) does not include any capability for a telecommunications carrier's internal management, control, or operation of its telecommunications network.

(7) The term "telecommunications support services" means a product, software, or service used by a telecommunications carrier for the internal signaling or switching functions of its telecommunications network.

(8) The term "telecommunications carrier"—

(A) means a person or entity engaged in the transmission or switching of wire or electronic communications as a common carrier for hire; and

(B) includes—

(i) a person or entity engaged in providing commercial mobile service (as defined in section 332(d) of this title); or

(ii) a person or entity engaged in providing wire or electronic communication switching or transmission service to the extent that the Commission finds that such service is a replacement for a substantial portion of the local telephone exchange service and that it is in the public interest to deem such a person or entity to be a telecommunications carrier for purposes of this subchapter; but

(C) does not include—

(i) persons or entities insofar as they are engaged in providing information services; and

(ii) any class or category of telecommunications carriers that the Commission exempts by rule after consultation with the Attorney General.

§ 1002. Assistance capability requirements

(a) Capability requirements

Except as provided in subsections (b), (c), and (d) of this section and sections 1007(a) and 1008(b) and (d) of this title, a telecommunications carrier shall ensure that its equipment, facilities, or services that provide a customer or subscriber with the ability to originate, terminate, or direct communications are capable of—

(1) expeditiously isolating and enabling the government, pursuant to a court order or other lawful authorization, to intercept, to the exclusion of any other communications, all wire and electronic communications carried by the carrier within a service area to or from equipment, facilities, or services of a subscriber of such carrier concurrently with their transmission to or from the subscriber's equipment, facility, or service, or at such later time as may be acceptable to the government;

(2) expeditiously isolating and enabling the government, pursuant to a court order or other lawful authorization, to access call-identifying information that is reasonably available to the carrier—

(A) before, during, or immediately after the transmission of a wire or electronic communication (or at such later time as may be acceptable to the government); and

(B) in a manner that allows it to be associated with the communication to which it pertains,

except that, with regard to information acquired solely pursuant to the authority for pen registers and trap and trace devices (as defined in section 3127 of Title 18), such call-identifying information shall not include any information that may disclose the physical location of the subscriber (except to the extent that the location may be determined from the telephone number);

(3) delivering intercepted communications and call-identifying information to the government, pursuant to a court order or other lawful authorization, in a format such that they may be transmitted by means of equipment, facilities, or services procured by the government to a location other than the premises of the carrier; and

(4) facilitating authorized communications interceptions and access to call-identifying information unobtrusively and with a minimum of interference with any subscriber's telecommunications service and in a manner that protects—

(A) the privacy and security of communications and call-identifying information not authorized to be intercepted; and

(B) information regarding the government's interception of communications and access to call-identifying information.

(b) Limitations

(1) Design of features and systems configurations

This subchapter does not authorize any law enforcement agency or officer—

(A) to require any specific design of equipment, facilities, services, features, or system configurations to be adopted by any provider of a wire or electronic communication service, any manufacturer of telecommunications equipment, or any provider of telecommunications support services; or

(B) to prohibit the adoption of any equipment, facility, service, or feature by any provider of a wire or electronic communication service, any manufacturer of telecommunications equipment, or any provider of telecommunications support services.

(2) Information services; private networks and interconnection services and facilities

The requirements of subsection (a) of this section do not apply to—

(A) information services; or

(B) equipment, facilities, or services that support the transport or switching of communications for private networks or for the sole purpose of interconnecting telecommunications carriers.

(3) Encryption

A telecommunications carrier shall not be responsible for decrypting, or ensuring the government's ability to decrypt, any communication encrypted by a subscriber or customer, unless the encryption was provided by the carrier and the carrier possesses the information necessary to decrypt the communication.

(c) Emergency or exigent circumstances

In emergency or exigent circumstances (including those described in sections 2518(7) or (11)(b) and 3125 of Title 18 and section 1805(e) of Title 50), a carrier at its discretion may comply with subsection (a)(3) of this section by allowing monitoring at its premises if that is the only means of accomplishing the interception or access.

(d) Mobile service assistance requirements

A telecommunications carrier that is a provider of commercial mobile service (as defined in section 332(d) of this title) offering a feature or service that allows subscribers to redirect, hand off, or assign their wire or electronic communications to another service area or another service provider or to utilize facilities in another service area or of another service provider shall ensure that, when the carrier that had been providing assistance for the interception of wire or electronic communications or access to call-identifying information pursuant to a court order or lawful authorization no longer has access to the content of such communications or call-identifying information within the service area in which interception has been occurring as a result of the subscriber's use of such a feature or service, information is made available to the government (before, during, or immediately after the transfer of such communications) identifying the provider of a wire or electronic communication service that has acquired access to the communications.

§ 1003. Notices of capacity requirements

(a) Notices of maximum and actual capacity requirements

(1) In general

Not later than 1 year after October 25, 1994, after consulting with State and local law enforcement agencies, telecommunications carriers, providers of telecommunications support services, and manufacturers of telecommunications equipment, and after notice and comment, the Attorney General shall publish in the Federal Register and provide to appropriate telecommunications industry associations and standard-setting organizations—

(A) notice of the actual number of communication interceptions, pen registers, and trap and trace devices, representing a portion of the maximum capacity set forth under subparagraph (B), that the Attorney General estimates that government agencies authorized to conduct electronic surveillance may conduct and use simultaneously by the date that is 4 years after October 25, 1994; and

(B) notice of the maximum capacity required to accommodate all of the communication interceptions, pen registers, and trap and trace devices that the Attorney General estimates that government agencies authorized to conduct electronic surveillance may conduct and use simultaneously after the date that is 4 years after October 25, 1994.

(2) Basis of notices

The notices issued under paragraph (1)—

(A) may be based upon the type of equipment, type of service, number of subscribers, type or size or carrier, nature of service area, or any other measure; and

(B) shall identify, to the maximum extent practicable, the capacity required at specific geographic locations.

(b) Compliance with capacity notices

(1) Initial capacity

Within 3 years after the publication by the Attorney General of a notice of capacity requirements or within 4 years after October 25, 1994, whichever is longer, a telecommunications carrier shall, subject to subsection (e) of this section, ensure that its systems are capable of—

(A) accommodating simultaneously the number of interceptions, pen registers, and trap and trace devices set forth in the notice under subsection (a)(1)(A) of this section; and

(B) expanding to the maximum capacity set forth in the notice under subsection (a)(1)(B) of this section.

(2) Expansion to maximum capacity

After the date described in paragraph (1), a telecommunications carrier shall, subject to subsection (e) of this section, ensure that it can accommodate expeditiously any increase in the actual number of communication interceptions, pen registers, and trap and trace devices that authorized agencies may seek to conduct and use, up to the maximum capacity requirement set forth in the notice under subsection (a)(1)(B) of this section.

(c) Notices of increased maximum capacity requirements

(1) Notice

The Attorney General shall periodically publish in the Federal Register, after notice and comment, notice of any necessary increases in the maximum capacity requirement set forth in the notice under subsection (a)(1)(B) of this section.

(2) Compliance

Within 3 years after notice of increased maximum capacity requirements is published under paragraph (1), or within such longer time period as the Attorney General may specify, a telecommunications carrier shall, subject to subsection (e) of this section, ensure that its systems are capable of expanding to the increased maximum capacity set forth in the notice.

(d) Carrier statement

Within 180 days after the publication by the Attorney General of a notice of capacity requirements pursuant to subsection (a) or (c) of this section, a telecommunications carrier shall submit to the Attorney General a statement identifying any of its systems or services that do not have the capacity to accommodate simultaneously the number of interceptions, pen registers, and trap and trace devices set forth in the notice under such subsection.

(e) Reimbursement required for compliance

The Attorney General shall review the statements submitted under subsection (d) of this section and may, subject to the availability of appropriations, agree to reimburse a telecommunications carrier for costs directly associated with modifications to attain such capacity requirement that are determined to be reasonable in accordance with section 1008(e) of this title. Until the Attorney General agrees to reimburse such carrier for such modification, such carrier shall be considered to be in compliance with the capacity notices under subsection (a) or (c) of this section.

§ 1004. Systems security and integrity

A telecommunications carrier shall ensure that any interception of communications or access to call-identifying information effected within its switching premises can be activated only in accordance with a court order or other lawful authorization and with the affirmative intervention of an individual officer or employee of the carrier acting in accordance with regulations prescribed by the Commission.

§ 1005. Cooperation of equipment manufacturers and providers of telecommunications support services

(a) Consultation

A telecommunications carrier shall consult, as necessary, in a timely fashion with manufacturers of its telecommunications transmission and switching equipment and its providers of telecommunications support services for the purpose of ensuring that current and planned equipment, facilities, and services comply with the capability requirements of section 1002 of this title and the capacity requirements identified by the Attorney General under section 1003 of this title.

(b) Cooperation

Subject to sections 1003(e), 1007(a), and 1008(b) and (d) of this title, a manufacturer of telecommunications transmission or switching equipment and a provider of telecommunications support services shall, on a reasonably timely basis and at a reasonable charge, make available to the telecommunications carriers using its equipment, facilities, or services such features or modifications as are necessary to permit such carriers to comply with the capability requirements of section 1002 of this title and the capacity requirements identified by the Attorney General under section 1003 of this title.

§ 1006. Technical requirements and standards; extension of compliance date

(a) Safe harbor

(1) Consultation

To ensure the efficient and industry-wide implementation of the assistance capability requirements under section 1002 of this title, the Attorney General, in coordination with other Federal, State, and local law enforcement agencies, shall consult with appropriate associations and standard-setting organizations of the telecommunications industry, with representatives of users of telecommunications equipment, facilities, and services, and with State utility commissions.

(2) Compliance under accepted standards

A telecommunications carrier shall be found to be in compliance with the assistance capability requirements under section 1002 of this title, and a manufacturer of telecommunications transmission or switching equipment or a provider of telecommunications support services shall be found to be in compliance with section 1005 of this title, if the carrier, manufacturer, or support service provider is in compliance with publicly available technical requirements or standards adopted by an industry association or standard-setting organization, or by the Commission under subsection (b) of this section, to meet the requirements of section 1002 of this title.

(3) Absence of standards

The absence of technical requirements or standards for implementing the assistance capability requirements of section 1002 of this title shall not—

(A) preclude a telecommunications carrier, manufacturer, or telecommunications support services provider from deploying a technology or service; or

(B) relieve a carrier, manufacturer, or telecommunications support services provider of the obligations imposed by section 1002 or 1005 of this title, as applicable.

(b) Commission authority

If industry associations or standard-setting organizations fail to issue technical requirements or standards or if a Government agency or any other person believes that such requirements or standards are deficient, the agency or person may petition the Commission to establish, by rule, technical requirements or standards that—

(1) meet the assistance capability requirements of section 1002 of this title by cost-effective methods;

(2) protect the privacy and security of communications not authorized to be intercepted;

(3) minimize the cost of such compliance on residential ratepayers;

(4) serve the policy of the United States to encourage the provision of new technologies and services to the public; and

(5) provide a reasonable time and conditions for compliance with and the transition to any new standard, including defining the obligations of telecommunications carriers under section 1002 of this title during any transition period.

(c) Extension of compliance date for equipment, facilities, and services

(1) Petition

A telecommunications carrier proposing to install or deploy, or having installed or deployed, any equipment, facility, or service prior to the effective date of section 1002 of this title may petition the Commission for 1 or more extensions of the deadline for complying with the assistance capability requirements under section 1002 of this title.

(2) Grounds for extension

The Commission may, after consultation with the Attorney General, grant an extension under this subsection, if the Commission determines that compliance with the assistance capability requirements under section 1002 of this title is not reasonably achievable through application of technology available within the compliance period.

(3) Length of extension

An extension under this subsection shall extend for no longer than the earlier of—

(A) the date determined by the Commission as necessary for the carrier to comply with the assistance capability requirements under section 1002 of this title; or

(B) the date that is 2 years after the date on which the extension is granted.

(4) Applicability of extension

An extension under this subsection shall apply to only that part of the carrier's business on which the new equipment, facility, or service is used.

§ 1007. Enforcement orders

(a) Grounds for issuance

A court shall issue an order enforcing this subchapter under section 2522 of Title 18 only if the court finds that—

(1) alternative technologies or capabilities or the facilities of another carrier are not reasonably available to law enforcement for implementing the interception of communications or access to call-identifying information; and

(2) compliance with the requirements of this subchapter is reasonably achievable through the application of available technology to the equipment, facility, or service at issue or would have been reasonably achievable if timely action had been taken.

(b) Time for compliance

Upon issuing an order enforcing this subchapter, the court shall specify a reasonable time and conditions for complying with its order, considering the good faith efforts to comply in a timely manner, any effect on the carrier's, manufacturer's, or service provider's ability to continue to do business, the degree of culpability or delay in undertaking efforts to comply, and such other matters as justice may require.

(c) Limitations

An order enforcing this subchapter may not—

(1) require a telecommunications carrier to meet the Government's demand for interception of communications and acquisition of call-identifying information to any extent in excess of the capacity for which the Attorney General has agreed to reimburse such carrier;

(2) require any telecommunications carrier to comply with assistance capability requirement of section 1002 of this title if the Commission has determined (pursuant to section 1008(b)(1) of this title) that compliance is not reasonably achievable, unless the Attorney General has agreed (pursuant to section 1008(b)(2) of this title) to pay the costs described in section 1008(b)(2)(A) of this title; or

(3) require a telecommunications carrier to modify, for the purpose of complying with the assistance capability requirements of section 1002 of this title, any equipment, facility, or service deployed on or before January 1, 1995, unless—

(A) the Attorney General has agreed to pay the telecommunications carrier for all reasonable costs directly associated with modifications necessary to bring the equipment, facility, or service into compliance with those requirements; or

(B) the equipment, facility, or service has been replaced or significantly upgraded or otherwise undergoes major modification.

§ 1008. Payment of costs of telecommunications carriers to comply with capability requirements

(a) Equipment, facilities, and services deployed on or before January 1, 1995

The Attorney General may, subject to the availability of appropriations, agree to pay telecommunications carriers for all reasonable costs directly associated with the modifications performed by carriers in connection with equipment, facilities, and services installed or deployed on or before January 1, 1995, to establish the capabilities necessary to comply with section 1002 of this title.

(b) Equipment, facilities, and services deployed after January 1, 1995

(1) Determinations of reasonably achievable

The Commission, on petition from a telecommunications carrier or any other interested person, and after notice to the Attorney General, shall determine whether compliance with the assistance capability requirements of section 1002 of this title is reasonably achievable with respect to any equipment, facility, or service installed or deployed after January 1, 1995. The Commission shall make such determination within 1 year after the date such petition is filed. In making such determination, the Commission shall determine whether compliance would impose significant difficulty or expense on the carrier or on the users of the carrier's systems and shall consider the following factors:

(A) The effect on public safety and national security.

(B) The effect on rates for basic residential telephone service.

(C) The need to protect the privacy and security of communications not authorized to be intercepted.

(D) The need to achieve the capability assistance requirements of section 1002 of this title by cost-effective methods.

(E) The effect on the nature and cost of the equipment, facility, or service at issue.

(F) The effect on the operation of the equipment, facility, or service at issue.

(G) The policy of the United States to encourage the provision of new technologies and services to the public.

(H) The financial resources of the telecommunications carrier.

(I) The effect on competition in the provision of telecommunications services.

(J) The extent to which the design and development of the equipment, facility, or service was initiated before January 1, 1995.

(K) Such other factors as the Commission determines are appropriate.

(2) Compensation

If compliance with the assistance capability requirements of section 1002 of this title is not reasonably achievable with respect to equipment, facilities, or services deployed after January 1, 1995—

(A) the Attorney General, on application of a telecommunications carrier, may agree, subject to the availability of appropriations, to pay the telecommunications carrier for the additional reasonable costs of making compliance with such assistance capability requirements reasonably achievable; and

(B) if the Attorney General does not agree to pay such costs, the telecommunications carrier shall be deemed to be in compliance with such capability requirements.

(c) Allocation of funds for payment

The Attorney General shall allocate funds appropriated to carry out this subchapter in accordance with law enforcement priorities determined by the Attorney General.

(d) Failure to make payment with respect to equipment, facilities, and services deployed on or before January 1, 1995

If a carrier has requested payment in accordance with procedures promulgated pursuant to subsection (e) of this section, and the Attorney General has not agreed to pay the telecommunications carrier for all reasonable costs directly associated with modifications necessary to bring any equipment, facility, or service deployed on or before January 1, 1995, into compliance with the assistance capability requirements of section 1002 of this title, such equipment, facility, or service shall be considered to be in compliance with the assistance capability requirements of section 1002 of this title until the equipment, facility, or service is replaced or significantly upgraded or otherwise undergoes major modification.

(e) Cost control regulations

(1) In general

The Attorney General shall, after notice and comment, establish regulations necessary to effectuate timely and cost-efficient payment to telecommunications carriers under this subchapter, under chapters 119 and 121 of Title 18, and under the Foreign Intelligence Surveillance Act of 1978 (50 U.S.C. 1801 et seq.).

(2) Contents of regulations

The Attorney General, after consultation with the Commission, shall prescribe regulations for purposes of determining reasonable costs under this subchapter. Such regulations shall seek to minimize the cost to the Federal Government and shall—

(A) permit recovery from the Federal Government of—

(i) the direct costs of developing the modifications described in subsection (a) of this section, of providing the capabilities requested under subsection (b)(2) of this section, or of providing the capacities requested under section 1003(e) of this title, but only to the extent that such costs have not been recovered from any other governmental or nongovernmental entity;

(ii) the costs of training personnel in the use of such capabilities or capacities; and

(iii) the direct costs of deploying or installing such capabilities or capacities;

(B) in the case of any modification that may be used for any purpose other than lawfully authorized electronic surveillance by a law enforcement agency of a government, permit recovery of only the incremental cost of making the modification suitable for such law enforcement purposes; and

(C) maintain the confidentiality of trade secrets.

(3) Submission of claims

Such regulations shall require any telecommunications carrier that the Attorney General has agreed to pay for modifications pursuant to this section and that has installed or deployed such modification to submit to the Attorney General a claim for payment that contains or is accompanied by such information as the Attorney General may require.

§ 1009. Authorization of appropriations

There are authorized to be appropriated to carry out this subchapter a total of $500,000,000 for fiscal years 1995, 1996, 1997, and 1998. Such sums are authorized to remain available until expended.

§ 1010. Reports

(a) Reports by Attorney General

(1) In general

On or before November 30, 1995, and on or before November 30 of each year thereafter, the Attorney General shall submit to Congress and make available to the public a report on the amounts paid during the preceding fiscal year to telecommunications carriers under sections 1003(e) and 1008 of this title.

(2) Contents

A report under paragraph (1) shall include—

(A) a detailed accounting of the amounts paid to each carrier and the equipment, facility, or service for which the amounts were paid; and

(B) projections of the amounts expected to be paid in the current fiscal year, the carriers to which payment is expected to be made, and the equipment, facilities, or services for which payment is expected to be made.

(b) Reports by Comptroller General and Inspector General

(1) On or before April 1, 1996, the Comptroller General of the United States, and every two years thereafter, the Inspector General of the Department of Justice, shall submit to the Congress a report, after consultation with the Attorney General and the telecommunications industry—

(A) describing the type of equipment, facilities, and services that have been brought into compliance under this subchapter; and

(B) reflecting its analysis of the reasonableness and cost-effectiveness of the payments made by the Attorney General to telecommunications carriers for modifications necessary to ensure compliance with this subchapter.

(2) Compliance cost estimates

A report under paragraph (1) shall include findings and conclusions on the costs to be incurred by telecommunications carriers to comply with the assistance capability requirements of section 1002 of this title after the effective date of such section 1002 of this title, including projections of the amounts expected to be incurred and a description of the equipment, facilities, or services for which they are expected to be incurred.

§ 1021. Department of Justice Telecommunications Carrier Compliance Fund

(a) Establishment of Fund

There is hereby established in the United States Treasury a fund to be known as the Department of Justice Telecommunications Carrier Compliance Fund (hereafter referred to as "the Fund"), which shall be available without fiscal year limitation to the Attorney General for making payments to telecommunications carriers, equipment manufacturers, and providers of telecommunications support services pursuant to section 1008 of this title.

(b) Deposits to Fund

Notwithstanding any other provision of law, any agency of the United States with law enforcement or intelligence responsibilities may deposit as offsetting collections to the Fund any unobligated balances that are available until expended, upon compliance with any Congressional notification requirements for reprogrammings of funds applicable to the appropriation from which the deposit is to be made.

(c) Termination

(1) The Attorney General may terminate the Fund at such time as the Attorney General determines that the Fund is no longer necessary.

(2) Any balance in the Fund at the time of its termination shall be deposited in the General Fund of the Treasury.

(3) A decision of the Attorney General to terminate the Fund shall not be subject to judicial review.

(d) Availability of funds for expenditure

Funds shall not be available for obligation unless an implementation plan as set forth in subsection (e) of this section is submitted to each member of the Committees on the Judiciary and Appropriations of both the House of Representatives and the Senate and the Congress does not by law block or prevent the obligation of such funds. Such funds shall be treated as a reprogramming of funds under section 605 of the Department of Commerce, Justice, and State, the Judiciary, and Related Agencies Appropriations Act, 1997, and shall not be available for obligation or expenditure except in compliance with the procedures set forth in that section and this section.

(e) Implementation plan

The implementation plan shall include:

> **(1)** the law enforcement assistance capability requirements and an explanation of law enforcement's recommended interface;
>
> **(2)** the proposed actual and maximum capacity requirements for the number of simultaneous law enforcement communications intercepts, pen registers, and trap and trace devices that authorized law enforcement agencies may seek to conduct, set forth on a county-by-county basis for wireline services and on a market service area basis for wireless services, and the historical baseline of electronic surveillance activity upon which such capacity requirements are based;
>
> **(3)** a prioritized list of carrier equipment, facilities, and services deployed on or before January 1, 1995, to be modified by carriers at the request of law enforcement based on its investigative needs;
>
> **(4)** a projected reimbursement plan that estimates the cost for the coming fiscal year and for each fiscal year thereafter, based on the prioritization of law enforcement needs as outlined in (3), of modification by carriers of equipment, facilities and services, installed on or before January 1, 1995.

(f) Annual report to Congress

The Attorney General shall submit to the Congress each year a report specifically detailing all deposits and expenditures made pursuant to subchapter I of this chapter in each fiscal year. This report shall be submitted to each member of the Committees on the Judiciary and Appropriations of both the House of Representatives and the Senate, and to the Speaker and minority leader of the House of Representatives and to the majority and minority leaders of the Senate, no later than 60 days after the end of each fiscal year.

V.
HEALTH AND GENETIC PRIVACY

Health Insurance Portability and Accountability Act Regulations (2002)

45 C.F.R. 164

Statutes in Context

The Health Insurance Portability and Accountability Act (HIPAA) Regulations establish requirements for privacy and security for all health care entities that fall under the Act's jurisdiction.

§ 164.102 Statutory basis.

The provisions of this part are adopted pursuant to the Secretary's authority to prescribe standards, requirements, and implementation specifications under part C of title XI of the Act and section 264 of Public Law 104-191.

§ 164.103 Definitions.

As used in this part, the following terms have the following meanings:

Common control exists if an entity has the power, directly or indirectly, significantly to influence or direct the actions or policies of another entity.

Common ownership exists if an entity or entities possess an ownership or equity interest of 5 percent or more in another entity.

Covered functions means those functions of a covered entity the performance of which makes the entity a health plan, health care provider, or health care clearinghouse.

Health care component means a component or combination of components of a hybrid entity designated by the hybrid entity in accordance with § 164.105(a)(2)(iii)(C).

Hybrid entity means a single legal entity:

(1) That is a covered entity;

(2) Whose business activities include both covered and non-covered functions; and

(3) That designates health care components in accordance with paragraph § 164.105(a)(2)(iii)(C).

Plan sponsor is defined as defined at section 3(16)(B) of ERISA, 29 U.S.C. 1002(16)(B).

Required by law means a mandate contained in law that compels an entity to make a use or disclosure of protected health information and that is enforceable in a court of law. Required by law includes, but is not limited to, court orders and court-ordered warrants; subpoenas or summons issued by a court, grand jury, a governmental or tribal inspector general, or an administrative body authorized to require the production of information; a civil or an authorized investigative demand; Medicare conditions of participation with respect to health care providers participating in the program; and statutes or regulations that require the production of information, including statutes or regulations that require such information if payment is sought under a government program providing public benefits.

§ 164.104 Applicability.

(a) Except as otherwise provided, the standards, requirements, and implementation specifications adopted under this part apply to the following entities:

> **(1)** A health plan.
>
> **(2)** A health care clearinghouse.
>
> **(3)** A health care provider who transmits any health information in electronic form in connection with a transaction covered by this subchapter.

(b) When a health care clearinghouse creates or receives protected health information as a business associate of another covered entity, or other than as a business associate of a covered entity, the clearinghouse must comply with § 164.105 relating to organizational requirements for covered entities, including the designation of health care components of a covered entity.

§ 164.105 Organizational requirements.

(a)(1) Standard: Health care component. If a covered entity is a hybrid entity, the requirements of subparts C and E of this part, other than the requirements of this section, § 164.314, and § 164.504, apply only to the health care component(s) of the entity, as specified in this section.

> **(2) Implementation specifications:**
>
> > **(i) Application of other provisions.** In applying a provision of subparts C and E of this part, other than the requirements of this section, § 164.314, and § 164.504, to a hybrid entity:
> >
> > > **(A)** A reference in such provision to a "covered entity" refers to a health care component of the covered entity;
> > >
> > > **(B)** A reference in such provision to a "health plan," "covered health care provider," or "health care clearinghouse," refers to a health care component of the covered entity if such health care component performs the functions of a health plan, health care provider, or health care clearinghouse, as applicable;
> > >
> > > **(C)** A reference in such provision to "protected health information" refers to protected health information that is created or received by or on behalf of the health care component of the covered entity; and

(D) A reference in such provision to "electronic protected health information" refers to electronic protected health information that is created, received, maintained, or transmitted by or on behalf of the health care component of the covered entity.

(ii) Safeguard requirements. The covered entity that is a hybrid entity must ensure that a health care component of the entity complies with the applicable requirements of this section and subparts C and E of this part. In particular, and without limiting this requirement, such covered entity must ensure that:

(A) Its health care component does not disclose protected health information to another component of the covered entity in circumstances in which subpart E of this part would prohibit such disclosure if the health care component and the other component were separate and distinct legal entities;

(B) Its health care component protects electronic protected health information with respect to another component of the covered entity to the same extent that it would be required under subpart C of this part to protect such information if the health care component and the other component were separate and distinct legal entities;

(C) A component that is described by paragraph (a)(2)(iii)(C)(2) of this section does not use or disclose protected health information that it creates or receives from or on behalf of the health care component in a way prohibited by subpart E of this part;

(D) A component that is described by paragraph (a)(2)(iii)(C)(2) of this section that creates, receives, maintains, or transmits electronic protected health information on behalf of the health care component is in compliance with subpart C of this part; and

(E) If a person performs duties for both the health care component in the capacity of a member of the workforce of such component and for another component of the entity in the same capacity with respect to that component, such workforce member must not use or disclose protected health information created or received in the course of or incident to the member's work for the health care component in a way prohibited by subpart E of this part.

(iii) Responsibilities of the covered entity. A covered entity that is a hybrid entity has the following responsibilities:

(A) For purposes of subpart C of part 160 of this subchapter, pertaining to compliance and enforcement, the covered entity has the responsibility of complying with subpart E of this part.

(B) The covered entity is responsible for complying with § 164.316(a) and § 164.530(i), pertaining to the implementation of policies and procedures to ensure compliance with applicable requirements of this section and subparts C and E of this part, including the safeguard requirements in paragraph (a)(2)(ii) of this section.

(C) The covered entity is responsible for designating the components that are part of one or more health care components of the covered entity and documenting the designation in accordance with paragraph (c) of this section, provided that, if the covered entity designates a health care component or components, it must include any component that would meet the definition of covered entity if it were a separate legal entity. Health care component(s) also may include a component only to the extent that it performs:

(1) Covered functions; or

(2) Activities that would make such component a business associate of a component that performs covered functions if the two components were separate legal entities.

(b)(1) Standard: Affiliated covered entities. Legally separate covered entities that are affiliated may designate themselves as a single covered entity for purposes of subparts C and E of this part.

(1) Implementation specifications:

(i) Requirements for designation of an affiliated covered entity.

(A) Legally separate covered entities may designate themselves (including any health care component of such covered entity) as a single affiliated covered entity, for purposes of subparts C and E of this part, if all of the covered entities designated are under common ownership or control.

(B) The designation of an affiliated covered entity must be documented and the documentation maintained as required by paragraph (c) of this section.

(ii) Safeguard requirements. An affiliated covered entity must ensure that:

(A) The affiliated covered entity's creation, receipt, maintenance, or transmission of electronic protected health information complies with the applicable requirements of subpart C of this part;

(B) The affiliated covered entity's use and disclosure of protected health information comply with the applicable requirements of subpart E of this part; and

(C) If the affiliated covered entity combines the functions of a health plan, health care provider, or health care clearinghouse, the affiliated covered entity complies with § 164.308(a)(4)(ii)(A) and § 164.504(g), as applicable.

(c)(1) Standard: Documentation. A covered entity must maintain a written or electronic record of a designation as required by paragraphs (a) or (b) of this section.

(2) Implementation specification: Retention period. A covered entity must retain the documentation as required by paragraph (c)(1) of this section for 6 years from the date of its creation or the date when it last was in effect, whichever is later.

§ 164.106 Relationship to other parts.

In complying with the requirements of this part, covered entities are required to comply with the applicable provisions of parts 160 and 162 of this subchapter.

§ 164.302 Applicability.

A covered entity must comply with the applicable standards, implementation specifications, and requirements of this subpart with respect to electronic protected health information.

§ 164.304 Definitions.

As used in this subpart, the following terms have the following meanings:

Access means the ability or the means necessary to read, write, modify, or communicate data/information or otherwise use any system resource. (This definition applies to "access" as used in this subpart, not as used in subpart E of this part.)

Administrative safeguards are administrative actions, and policies and procedures, to manage the selection, development, implementation, and maintenance of security measures to protect electronic protected health information and to manage the conduct of the covered entity's workforce in relation to the protection of that information.

Authentication means the corroboration that a person is the one claimed.

Availability means the property that data or information is accessible and useable upon demand by an authorized person.

Confidentiality means the property that data or information is not made available or disclosed to unauthorized persons or processes.

Encryption means the use of an algorithmic process to transform data into a form in which there is a low probability of assigning meaning without use of a confidential process or key.

Facility means the physical premises and the interior and exterior of a building(s).

Information system means an interconnected set of information resources under the same direct management control that shares common functionality. A system normally includes hardware, software, information, data, applications, communications, and people.

Integrity means the property that data or information have not been altered or destroyed in an unauthorized manner.

Malicious software means software, for example, a virus, designed to damage or disrupt a system.

Password means confidential authentication information composed of a string of characters.

Physical safeguards are physical measures, policies, and procedures to protect a covered entity's electronic information systems and related buildings and equipment, from natural and environmental hazards, and unauthorized intrusion.

Security or Security measures encompass all of the administrative, physical, and technical safeguards in an information system.

Security incident means the attempted or successful unauthorized access, use, disclosure, modification, or destruction of information or interference with system operations in an information system.

Technical safeguards means the technology and the policy and procedures for its use that protect electronic protected health information and control access to it.

User means a person or entity with authorized access.

Workstation means an electronic computing device, for example, a laptop or desktop computer, or any other device that performs similar functions, and electronic media stored in its immediate environment.

§ 164.306 Security standards: General rules.

(a) General requirements. Covered entities must do the following:

(1) Ensure the confidentiality, integrity, and availability of all electronic protected health information the covered entity creates, receives, maintains, or transmits.

(2) Protect against any reasonably anticipated threats or hazards to the security or integrity of such information.

(3) Protect against any reasonably anticipated uses or disclosures of such information that are not permitted or required under subpart E of this part.

(4) Ensure compliance with this subpart by its workforce.

(b) Flexibility of approach.

(1) Covered entities may use any security measures that allow the covered entity to reasonably and appropriately implement the standards and implementation specifications as specified in this subpart.

(2) In deciding which security measures to use, a covered entity must take into account the following factors:

(i) The size, complexity, and capabilities of the covered entity.

(ii) The covered entity's technical infrastructure, hardware, and software security capabilities.

(iii) The costs of security measures.

(iv) The probability and criticality of potential risks to electronic protected health information.

(c) Standards. A covered entity must comply with the standards as provided in this section and in § 164.308, § 164.310, § 164.312, § 164.314, and § 164.316 with respect to all electronic protected health information.

(d) Implementation specifications.

In this subpart:

(1) Implementation specifications are required or addressable. If an implementation specification is required, the word "Required" appears in parentheses after the title of the implementation specification. If an implementation specification is addressable, the word "Addressable" appears in parentheses after the title of the implementation specification.

(2) When a standard adopted in § 164.308, § 164.310, § 164.312, § 164.314, or § 164.316 includes required implementation specifications, a covered entity must implement the implementation specifications.

(3) When a standard adopted in § 164.308, § 164.310, § 164.312, § 164.314, or § 164.316 includes addressable implementation specifications, a covered entity must—

(i) Assess whether each implementation specification is a reasonable and appropriate safeguard in its environment, when analyzed with reference to the likely contribution to protecting the entity's electronic protected health information; and

(ii) As applicable to the entity—

(A) Implement the implementation specification if reasonable and appropriate; or

(B) If implementing the implementation specification is not reasonable and appropriate—

(1) Document why it would not be reasonable and appropriate to implement the implementation specification; and

(2) Implement an equivalent alternative measure if reasonable and appropriate.

(e) Maintenance. Security measures implemented to comply with standards and implementation specifications adopted under § 164.105 and this subpart must be reviewed and modified as needed to continue provision of reasonable and appropriate protection of electronic protected health information as described at § 164.316.

§ 164.308 Administrative safeguards.

(a) A covered entity must, in accordance with § 164.306:

(1)(i) Standard: Security management process. Implement policies and procedures to prevent, detect, contain, and correct security violations.

(ii) Implementation specifications:

(A) Risk analysis (Required). Conduct an accurate and thorough assessment of the potential risks and vulnerabilities to the confidentiality, integrity, and availability of electronic protected health information held by the covered entity.

(B) Risk management (Required). Implement security measures sufficient to reduce risks and vulnerabilities to a reasonable and appropriate level to comply with § 164.306(a).

(C) Sanction policy (Required). Apply appropriate sanctions against workforce members who fail to comply with the security policies and procedures of the covered entity.

(D) Information system activity review (Required). Implement procedures to regularly review records of information system activity, such as audit logs, access reports, and security incident tracking reports.

(2) Standard: Assigned security responsibility. Identify the security official who is responsible for the development and implementation of the policies and procedures required by this subpart for the entity.

(3)(i) Standard: Workforce security. Implement policies and procedures to ensure that all members of its workforce have appropriate access to electronic protected health information, as provided under paragraph (a)(4) of this section, and to prevent those workforce members who do not have access under paragraph (a)(4) of this section from obtaining access to electronic protected health information.

(ii) Implementation specifications:

> **(A)** Authorization and/or supervision (Addressable). Implement procedures for the authorization and/or supervision of workforce members who work with electronic protected health information or in locations where it might be accessed.
>
> **(B)** Workforce clearance procedure (Addressable). Implement procedures to determine that the access of a workforce member to electronic protected health information is appropriate.
>
> **(C)** Termination procedures (Addressable). Implement procedures for terminating access to electronic protected health information when the employment of a workforce member ends or as required by determinations made as specified in paragraph (a)(3)(ii)(B) of this section.

(4)(i) Standard: Information access management. Implement policies and procedures for authorizing access to electronic protected health information that are consistent with the applicable requirements of subpart E of this part.

(ii) Implementation specifications:

> **(A)** Isolating health care clearinghouse functions (Required). If a health care clearinghouse is part of a larger organization, the clearinghouse must implement policies and procedures that protect the electronic protected health information of the clearinghouse from unauthorized access by the larger organization.
>
> **(B)** Access authorization (Addressable). Implement policies and procedures for granting access to electronic protected health information, for example, through access to a workstation, transaction, program, process, or other mechanism.
>
> **(C)** Access establishment and modification (Addressable). Implement policies and procedures that, based upon the entity's access authorization policies, establish, document, review, and modify a user's right of access to a workstation, transaction, program, or process.

(5)(i) Standard: Security awareness and training. Implement a security awareness and training program for all members of its workforce (including management).

(ii) Implementation specifications. Implement:

> **(A)** Security reminders (Addressable). Periodic security updates.

(B) Protection from malicious software (Addressable). Procedures for guarding against, detecting, and reporting malicious software.

(C) Log-in monitoring (Addressable). Procedures for monitoring log-in attempts and reporting discrepancies.

(D) Password management (Addressable). Procedures for creating, changing, and safeguarding passwords.

(6)(i) Standard: Security incident procedures. Implement policies and procedures to address security incidents.

(ii) Implementation specification: Response and Reporting (Required). Identify and respond to suspected or known security incidents; mitigate, to the extent practicable, harmful effects of security incidents that are known to the covered entity; and document security incidents and their outcomes.

(7)(i) Standard: Contingency plan. Establish (and implement as needed) policies and procedures for responding to an emergency or other occurrence (for example, fire, vandalism, system failure, and natural disaster) that damages systems that contain electronic protected health information.

(ii) Implementation specifications:

(A) Data backup plan (Required). Establish and implement procedures to create and maintain retrievable exact copies of electronic protected health information.

(B) Disaster recovery plan (Required). Establish (and implement as needed) procedures to restore any loss of data.

(C) Emergency mode operation plan (Required). Establish (and implement as needed) procedures to enable continuation of critical business processes for protection of the security of electronic protected health information while operating in emergency mode.

(D) Testing and revision procedures (Addressable). Implement procedures for periodic testing and revision of contingency plans.

(E) Applications and data criticality analysis (Addressable). Assess the relative criticality of specific applications and data in support of other contingency plan components.

(8) Standard: Evaluation. Perform a periodic technical and nontechnical evaluation, based initially upon the standards implemented under this rule and subsequently, in response to environmental or operational changes affecting the security of electronic protected health information, that establishes the extent to which an entity's security policies and procedures meet the requirements of this subpart.

(b)(1) Standard: Business associate contracts and other arrangements. A covered entity, in accordance with § 164.306, may permit a business associate to create, receive, maintain, or transmit electronic protected health information on the covered entity's behalf only if the covered entity obtains satisfactory assurances, in accordance with § 164.314(a) that the business associate will appropriately safeguard the information.

(2) This standard does not apply with respect to—

(i) The transmission by a covered entity of electronic protected health information to a health care provider concerning the treatment of an individual.

(ii) The transmission of electronic protected health information by a group health plan or an HMO or health insurance issuer on behalf of a group health plan to a plan sponsor, to the extent that the requirements of § 164.314(b)and § 164.504(f) apply and are met; or

(iii) The transmission of electronic protected health information from or to other agencies providing the services at § 164.502(e)(1)(ii)(C), when the covered entity is a health plan that is a government program providing public benefits, if the requirements of § 164.502(e)(1)(ii)(C) are met.

(3) A covered entity that violates the satisfactory assurances it provided as a business associate of another covered entity will be in noncompliance with the standards, implementation specifications, and requirements of this paragraph and § 164.314(a).

(4) Implementation specifications: Written contract or other arrangement (Required). Document the satisfactory assurances required by paragraph (b)(1) of this section through a written contract or other arrangement with the business associate that meets the applicable requirements of § 164.314(a).

§ 164.310 Physical safeguards.

A covered entity must, in accordance with § 164.306:

(a)(1) Standard: Facility access controls. Implement policies and procedures to limit physical access to its electronic information systems and the facility or facilities in which they are housed, while ensuring that properly authorized access is allowed.

(2) Implementation specifications:

(i) Contingency operations (Addressable). Establish (and implement as needed) procedures that allow facility access in support of restoration of lost data under the disaster recovery plan and emergency mode operations plan in the event of an emergency.

(ii) Facility security plan (Addressable). Implement policies and procedures to safeguard the facility and the equipment therein from unauthorized physical access, tampering, and theft.

(iii) Access control and validation procedures (Addressable). Implement procedures to control and validate a person's access to facilities based on their role or function, including visitor control, and control of access to software programs for testing and revision.

(iv) Maintenance records (Addressable). Implement policies and procedures to document repairs and modifications to the physical components of a facility which are related to security (for example, hardware, walls, doors, and locks).

(b) Standard: Workstation use. Implement policies and procedures that specify the proper functions to be performed, the manner in which those functions are to be performed, and the physical attributes of the surroundings of a specific workstation or class of workstation that can access electronic protected health information.

(c) Standard: Workstation security. Implement physical safeguards for all workstations that access electronic protected health information, to restrict access to authorized users.

(d)(1) Standard: Device and media controls. Implement policies and procedures that govern the receipt and removal of hardware and electronic media that contain electronic protected health information into and out of a facility, and the movement of these items within the facility.

(2) Implementation specifications:

(i) Disposal (Required). Implement policies and procedures to address the final disposition of electronic protected health information, and/or the hardware or electronic media on which it is stored.

(ii) Media re-use (Required). Implement procedures for removal of electronic protected health information from electronic media before the media are made available for re-use.

(iii) Accountability (Addressable). Maintain a record of the movements of hardware and electronic media and any person responsible therefore.

(iv) Data backup and storage (Addressable). Create a retrievable, exact copy of electronic protected health information, when needed, before movement of equipment.

§ 164.312 Technical safeguards.

A covered entity must, in accordance with § 164.306:

(a)(1) Standard: Access control. Implement technical policies and procedures for electronic information systems that maintain electronic protected health information to allow access only to those persons or software programs that have been granted access rights as specified in § 164.308(a)(4).

(2) Implementation specifications:

(i) Unique user identification (Required). Assign a unique name and/or number for identifying and tracking user identity.

(ii) Emergency access procedure (Required). Establish (and implement as needed) procedures for obtaining necessary electronic protected health information during an emergency.

(iii) Automatic logoff (Addressable). Implement electronic procedures that terminate an electronic session after a predetermined time of inactivity.

(iv) Encryption and decryption (Addressable). Implement a mechanism to encrypt and decrypt electronic protected health information.

(b) Standard: Audit controls. Implement hardware, software, and/or procedural mechanisms that record and examine activity in information systems that contain or use electronic protected health information.

(c)(1) Standard: Integrity. Implement policies and procedures to protect electronic protected health information from improper alteration or destruction.

(2) Implementation specification: Mechanism to authenticate electronic protected health information (Addressable). Implement electronic mechanisms to corroborate that electronic protected health information has not been altered or destroyed in an unauthorized manner.

(d) Standard: Person or entity authentication. Implement procedures to verify that a person or entity seeking access to electronic protected health information is the one claimed.

(e)(1) Standard: Transmission security. Implement technical security measures to guard against unauthorized access to electronic protected health information that is being transmitted over an electronic communications network.

(2) Implementation specifications:

(i) Integrity controls (Addressable). Implement security measures to ensure that electronically transmitted electronic protected health information is not improperly modified without detection until disposed of.

(ii) Encryption (Addressable). Implement a mechanism to encrypt electronic protected health information whenever deemed appropriate.

§ 164.314 Organizational requirements.

(a)(1) Standard: Business associate contracts or other arrangements.

(i) The contract or other arrangement between the covered entity and its business associate required by § 164.308(b) must meet the requirements of paragraph (a)(2)(i) or (a)(2)(ii) of this section, as applicable.

(ii) A covered entity is not in compliance with the standards in §164.502(e) and paragraph (a) of this section if the covered entity knew of a pattern of an activity or practice of the business associate that constituted a material breach or violation of the business associate's obligation under the contract or other arrangement, unless the covered entity took reasonable steps to cure the breach or end the violation, as applicable, and, if such steps were unsuccessful—

(A) Terminated the contract or arrangement, if feasible; or

(B) If termination is not feasible, reported the problem to the Secretary.

(2) Implementation specifications (Required).

(i) Business associate contracts. The contract between a covered entity and a business associate must provide that the business associate will—

(A) Implement administrative, physical, and technical safeguards that reasonably and appropriately protect the confidentiality, integrity, and availability of the electronic protected health information that it creates, receives, maintains, or transmits on behalf of the covered entity as required by this subpart;

(B) Ensure that any agent, including a subcontractor, to whom it provides such information agrees to implement reasonable and appropriate safeguards to protect it;

(C) Report to the covered entity any security incident of which it becomes aware;

(D) Authorize termination of the contract by the covered entity, if the covered entity determines that the business associate has violated a material term of the contract.

(ii) Other arrangements.

(A) When a covered entity and its business associate are both governmental entities, the covered entity is in compliance with paragraph (a)(1) of this section, if—

(1) It enters into a memorandum of understanding with the business associate that contains terms that accomplish the objectives of paragraph (a)(2)(i) of this section; or

(2) Other law (including regulations adopted by the covered entity or its business associate) contains requirements applicable to the business associate that accomplish the objectives of paragraph (a)(2)(i) of this section.

(B) If a business associate is required by law to perform a function or activity on behalf of a covered entity or to provide a service described in the definition of business associate as specified in § 160.103 of this subchapter to a covered entity, the covered entity may permit the business associate to create, receive, maintain, or transmit electronic protected health information on its behalf to the extent necessary to comply with the legal mandate without meeting the requirements of paragraph (a)(2)(i) of this section, provided that the covered entity attempts in good faith to obtain satisfactory assurances as required by paragraph (a)(2)(ii)(A) of this section, and documents the attempt and the reasons that these assurances cannot be obtained.

(C) The covered entity may omit from its other arrangements authorization of the termination of the contract by the covered entity, as required by paragraph (a)(2)(i)(D) of this section if such authorization is inconsistent with the statutory obligations of the covered entity or its business associate.

(b)(1) Standard: Requirements for group health plans. Except when the only electronic protected health information disclosed to a plan sponsor is disclosed pursuant to § 164.504(f)(1)(ii) or (iii), or as authorized under § 164.508, a group health plan must ensure that its plan documents provide that the plan sponsor will reasonably and appropriately safeguard electronic protected health information created, received, maintained, or transmitted to or by the plan sponsor on behalf of the group health plan.

(2) Implementation specifications (Required). The plan documents of the group health plan must be amended to incorporate provisions to require the plan sponsor to—

(i) Implement administrative, physical, and technical safeguards that reasonably and appropriately protect the confidentiality, integrity, and availability of the electronic protected health information that it creates, receives, maintains, or transmits on behalf of the group health plan;

(ii) Ensure that the adequate separation required by § 164.504(f)(2)(iii) is supported by reasonable and appropriate security measures;

(iii) Ensure that any agent, including a subcontractor, to whom it provides this information agrees to implement reasonable and appropriate security measures to protect the information; and

(iv) Report to the group health plan any security incident of which it becomes aware.

§ 164.316 Policies and procedures and documentation requirements.

A covered entity must, in accordance with § 164.306:

(a) Standard: Policies and procedures. Implement reasonable and appropriate policies and procedures to comply with the standards, implementation specifications, or other requirements of this subpart, taking into account those factors specified in § 164.306(b)(2)(i), (ii), (iii), and (iv). This standard is not to be construed to permit or excuse an action that violates any other standard, implementation specification, or other requirements of this subpart. A covered entity may change its policies and procedures at any time, provided that the changes are documented and are implemented in accordance with this subpart.

(b)(1) Standard: Documentation.

(i) Maintain the policies and procedures implemented to comply with this subpart in written (which may be electronic) form; and

(ii) If an action, activity or assessment is required by this subpart to be documented, maintain a written (which may be electronic) record of the action, activity, or assessment.

(2) Implementation specifications:

(i) Time limit (Required). Retain the documentation required by paragraph (b)(1) of this section for 6 years from the date of its creation or the date when it last was in effect, whichever is later.

(ii) Availability (Required). Make documentation available to those persons responsible for implementing the procedures to which the documentation pertains.

(iii) Updates (Required). Review documentation periodically, and update as needed, in response to environmental or operational changes affecting the security of the electronic protected health information.

§ 164.318 Compliance dates for the initial implementation of the security standards.

(a) Health plan.

(1) A health plan that is not a small health plan must comply with the applicable requirements of this subpart no later than April 20, 2005.

(2) A small health plan must comply with the applicable requirements of this subpart no later than April 20, 2006.

(b) Health care clearinghouse. A health care clearinghouse must comply with the applicable requirements of this subpart no later than April 20, 2005.

(c) Health care provider. A covered health care provider must comply with the applicable requirements of this subpart no later than April 20, 2005.

§ 164.500 Applicability.

(a) Except as otherwise provided herein, the standards, requirements, and implementation specifications of this subpart apply to covered entities with respect to protected health information.

(b) Health care clearinghouses must comply with the standards, requirements, and implementation specifications as follows:

(1) When a health care clearinghouse creates or receives protected health information as a business associate of another covered entity, the clearinghouse must comply with:

(i) Section 164.500 relating to applicability;

(ii) Section 164.501 relating to definitions;

(iii) Section 164.502 relating to uses and disclosures of protected health information, except that a clearinghouse is prohibited from using or disclosing protected health information other than as permitted in the business associate contract under which it created or received the protected health information;

(iv) Section 164.504 relating to the organizational requirements for covered entities;

(v) Section 164.512 relating to uses and disclosures for which individual authorization or an opportunity to agree or object is not required, except that a clearinghouse is prohibited from using or disclosing protected health information other than as permitted in the business associate contract under which it created or received the protected health information;

(vi) Section 164.532 relating to transition requirements; and

(vii) Section 164.534 relating to compliance dates for initial implementation of the privacy standards.

(2) When a health care clearinghouse creates or receives protected health information other than as a business associate of a covered entity, the clearinghouse must comply with all of the standards, requirements, and implementation specifications of this subpart.

(c) The standards, requirements, and implementation specifications of this subpart do not apply to the Department of Defense or to any other federal agency, or non-governmental organization acting on its behalf, when providing health care to overseas foreign national beneficiaries.

§ 164.501 Definitions.

As used in this subpart, the following terms have the following meanings:

Correctional institution means any penal or correctional facility, jail, reformatory, detention center, work farm, halfway house, or residential community program center operated by, or under contract to, the United States, a State, a territory, a political subdivision of a State or territory, or an Indian tribe, for the confinement or rehabilitation of persons charged with or convicted of a criminal offense or other persons held in lawful custody. Other persons held in lawful custody includes juvenile offenders adjudicated delinquent, aliens detained awaiting deportation, persons committed to mental institutions through the criminal justice system, witnesses, or others awaiting charges or trial.

Data aggregation means, with respect to protected health information created or received by a business associate in its capacity as the business associate of a covered entity, the combining of such protected health information by the business associate with the protected health information received by the business associate in its capacity as a business associate of another covered entity, to permit data analyses that relate to the health care operations of the respective covered entities.

Designated record set means:

(1) A group of records maintained by or for a covered entity that is:

> **(i)** The medical records and billing records about individuals maintained by or for a covered health care provider;
>
> **(ii)** The enrollment, payment, claims adjudication, and case or medical management record systems maintained by or for a health plan; or
>
> **(iii)** Used, in whole or in part, by or for the covered entity to make decisions about individuals.

(2) For purposes of this paragraph, the term record means any item, collection, or grouping of information that includes protected health information and is maintained, collected, used, or disseminated by or for a covered entity.

Direct treatment relationship means a treatment relationship between an individual and a health care provider that is not an indirect treatment relationship.

Health care operations means any of the following activities of the covered entity to the extent that the activities are related to covered functions:

> **(1)** Conducting quality assessment and improvement activities, including outcomes evaluation and development of clinical guidelines, provided that the obtaining of generalizable knowledge is not the primary purpose of any studies resulting from such activities; population-based activities relating to improving health or reducing health care costs, protocol development, case management and care coordination, contacting of health care providers and patients with information about treatment alternatives; and related functions that do not include treatment;
>
> **(2)** Reviewing the competence or qualifications of health care professionals, evaluating practitioner and provider performance, health plan performance, conducting training programs in which students, trainees, or practitioners in areas of health care learn under supervision to practice or improve their skills as health care providers, training of non-health care professionals, accreditation, certification, licensing, or credentialing activities;
>
> **(3)** Underwriting, premium rating, and other activities relating to the creation, renewal or replacement of a contract of health insurance or health benefits, and ceding, securing, or placing a contract for reinsurance of risk relating to claims for health care (including stop-loss insurance and excess of loss insurance), provided that the requirements of § 164.514(g) are met, if applicable;
>
> **(4)** Conducting or arranging for medical review, legal services, and auditing functions, including fraud and abuse detection and compliance programs;
>
> **(5)** Business planning and development, such as conducting cost-management and planning-related analyses related to managing and operating the entity, including formulary development and administration, development or improvement of methods of payment or coverage policies; and
>
> **(6)** Business management and general administrative activities of the entity, including, but not limited to:

(i) Management activities relating to implementation of and compliance with the requirements of this subchapter;

(ii) Customer service, including the provision of data analyses for policy holders, plan sponsors, or other customers, provided that protected health information is not disclosed to such policy holder, plan sponsor, or customer.

(iii) Resolution of internal grievances;

(iv) The sale, transfer, merger, or consolidation of all or part of the covered entity with another covered entity, or an entity that following such activity will become a covered entity and due diligence related to such activity; and

(v) Consistent with the applicable requirements of § 164.514, creating de-identified health information or a limited data set, and fundraising for the benefit of the covered entity.

Health oversight agency means an agency or authority of the United States, a State, a territory, a political subdivision of a State or territory, or an Indian tribe, or a person or entity acting under a grant of authority from or contract with such public agency, including the employees or agents of such public agency or its contractors or persons or entities to whom it has granted authority, that is authorized by law to oversee the health care system (whether public or private) or government programs in which health information is necessary to determine eligibility or compliance, or to enforce civil rights laws for which health information is relevant.

Indirect treatment relationship means a relationship between an individual and a health care provider in which:

(1) The health care provider delivers health care to the individual based on the orders of another health care provider; and

(2) The health care provider typically provides services or products, or reports the diagnosis or results associated with the health care, directly to another health care provider, who provides the services or products or reports to the individual.

Inmate means a person incarcerated in or otherwise confined to a correctional institution.

Law enforcement official means an officer or employee of any agency or authority of the United States, a State, a territory, a political subdivision of a State or territory, or an Indian tribe, who is empowered by law to:

(1) Investigate or conduct an official inquiry into a potential violation of law; or

(2) Prosecute or otherwise conduct a criminal, civil, or administrative proceeding arising from an alleged violation of law.

Marketing means:

(1) To make a communication about a product or service that encourages recipients of the communication to purchase or use the product or service, unless the communication is made:

(i) To describe a health-related product or service (or payment for such product or service) that is provided by, or included in a plan of benefits of, the covered entity making the communication, including communications about: the entities participating in a health care provider network or health plan network; replacement of, or enhancements to, a health plan; and health-related products or services available only to a health plan enrollee that add value to, but are not part of, a plan of benefits.

(ii) For treatment of the individual; or

(iii) For case management or care coordination for the individual, or to direct or recommend alternative treatments, therapies, health care providers, or settings of care to the individual.

(2) An arrangement between a covered entity and any other entity whereby the covered entity discloses protected health information to the other entity, in exchange for direct or indirect remuneration, for the other entity or its affiliate to make a communication about its own product or service that encourages recipients of the communication to purchase or use that product or service.

Payment means:

(1) The activities undertaken by:

(i) A health plan to obtain premiums or to determine or fulfill its responsibility for coverage and provision of benefits under the health plan; or

(ii) A health care provider or health plan to obtain or provide reimbursement for the provision of health care; and

(2) The activities in paragraph (1) of this definition relate to the individual to whom health care is provided and include, but are not limited to:

(i) Determinations of eligibility or coverage (including coordination of benefits or the determination of cost sharing amounts), and adjudication or subrogation of health benefit claims;

(ii) Risk adjusting amounts due based on enrollee health status and demographic characteristics;

(iii) Billing, claims management, collection activities, obtaining payment under a contract for reinsurance (including stop-loss insurance and excess of loss insurance), and related health care data processing;

(iv) Review of health care services with respect to medical necessity, coverage under a health plan, appropriateness of care, or justification of charges;

(v) Utilization review activities, including precertification and preauthorization of services, concurrent and retrospective review of services; and

(vi) Disclosure to consumer reporting agencies of any of the following protected health information relating to collection of premiums or reimbursement:

(A) Name and address;

(B) Date of birth;

(C) Social security number;

(D) Payment history;

(E) Account number; and

(F) Name and address of the health care provider and/or health plan.

Psychotherapy notes means notes recorded (in any medium) by a health care provider who is a mental health professional documenting or analyzing the contents of conversation during a private counseling session or a group, joint, or family counseling session and that are separated from the rest of the individual's medical record. Psychotherapy notes excludes medication prescription and monitoring, counseling session start and stop times, the modalities and frequencies of treatment furnished, results of clinical tests, and any summary of the following items: Diagnosis, functional status, the treatment plan, symptoms, prognosis, and progress to date.

Public health authority means an agency or authority of the United States, a State, a territory, a political subdivision of a State or territory, or an Indian tribe, or a person or entity acting under a grant of authority from or contract with such public agency, including the employees or agents of such public agency or its contractors or persons or entities to whom it has granted authority, that is responsible for public health matters as part of its official mandate.

Research means a systematic investigation, including research development, testing, and evaluation, designed to develop or contribute to generalizable knowledge.

Treatment means the provision, coordination, or management of health care and related services by one or more health care providers, including the coordination or management of health care by a health care provider with a third party; consultation between health care providers relating to a patient; or the referral of a patient for health care from one health care provider to another.

§ 164.502 Uses and disclosures of protected health information: general rules.

(a) Standard. A covered entity may not use or disclose protected health information, except as permitted or required by this subpart or by subpart C of part 160 of this subchapter.

(1) Permitted uses and disclosures. A covered entity is permitted to use or disclose protected health information as follows:

(i) To the individual;

(ii) For treatment, payment, or health care operations, as permitted by and in compliance with § 164.506;

(iii) Incident to a use or disclosure otherwise permitted or required by this subpart, provided that the covered entity has complied with the applicable requirements of § 164.502(b), §

164.514(d), and § 164.530(c) with respect to such otherwise permitted or required use or disclosure;

(iv) Pursuant to and in compliance with a valid authorization under § 164.508;

(v) Pursuant to an agreement under, or as otherwise permitted by, § 164.510; and

(vi) As permitted by and in compliance with this section, § 164.512, or § 164.514(e), (f), or (g).

(2) Required disclosures. A covered entity is required to disclose protected health information:

(i) To an individual, when requested under, and required by § 164.524 or § 164.528; and

(ii) When required by the Secretary under subpart C of part 160 of this subchapter to investigate or determine the covered entity's compliance with this subpart.

(b) Standard: Minimum necessary.

(1) Minimum necessary applies. When using or disclosing protected health information or when requesting protected health information from another covered entity, a covered entity must make reasonable efforts to limit protected health information to the minimum necessary to accomplish the intended purpose of the use, disclosure, or request.

(2) Minimum necessary does not apply. This requirement does not apply to:

(i) Disclosures to or requests by a health care provider for treatment;

(ii) Uses or disclosures made to the individual, as permitted under paragraph (a)(1)(i) of this section or as required by paragraph (a)(2)(i) of this section;

(iii) Uses or disclosures made pursuant to an authorization under § 164.508;

(iv) Disclosures made to the Secretary in accordance with subpart C of part 160 of this subchapter;

(v) Uses or disclosures that are required by law, as described by § 164.512(a); and

(vi) Uses or disclosures that are required for compliance with applicable requirements of this subchapter.

(c) Standard: Uses and disclosures of protected health information subject to an agreed upon restriction. A covered entity that has agreed to a restriction pursuant to § 164.522(a)(1) may not use or disclose the protected health information covered by the restriction in violation of such restriction, except as otherwise provided in § 164.522(a).

(d) Standard: Uses and disclosures of de-identified protected health information.

(1) Uses and disclosures to create de-identified information. A covered entity may use protected health information to create information that is not individually identifiable health information or disclose protected health information only to a business associate for such purpose, whether or not the de-identified information is to be used by the covered entity.

(2) Uses and disclosures of de-identified information. Health information that meets the standard and implementation specifications for de-identification under § 164.514(a) and (b) is considered not to be individually identifiable health information, i.e., de-identified. The requirements of this subpart do not apply to information that has been de-identified in accordance with the applicable requirements of § 164.514, provided that:

(i) Disclosure of a code or other means of record identification designed to enable coded or otherwise de-identified information to be re-identified constitutes disclosure of protected health information; and

(ii) If de-identified information is re-identified, a covered entity may use or disclose such re-identified information only as permitted or required by this subpart.

(e)(1) Standard: Disclosures to business associates.

(i) A covered entity may disclose protected health information to a business associate and may allow a business associate to create or receive protected health information on its behalf, if the covered entity obtains satisfactory assurance that the business associate will appropriately safeguard the information.

(ii) This standard does not apply:

(A) With respect to disclosures by a covered entity to a health care provider concerning the treatment of the individual;

(B) With respect to disclosures by a group health plan or a health insurance issuer or HMO with respect to a group health plan to the plan sponsor, to the extent that the requirements of § 164.504(f) apply and are met; or

(C) With respect to uses or disclosures by a health plan that is a government program providing public benefits, if eligibility for, or enrollment in, the health plan is determined by an agency other than the agency administering the health plan, or if the protected health information used to determine enrollment or eligibility in the health plan is collected by an agency other than the agency administering the health plan, and such activity is authorized by law, with respect to the collection and sharing of individually identifiable health information for the performance of such functions by the health plan and the agency other than the agency administering the health plan.

(iii) A covered entity that violates the satisfactory assurances it provided as a business associate of another covered entity will be in noncompliance with the standards, implementation specifications, and requirements of this paragraph and § 164.504(e).

(2) Implementation specification: documentation. A covered entity must document the satisfactory assurances required by paragraph (e)(1) of this section through a written contract or other written agreement or arrangement with the business associate that meets the applicable requirements of § 164.504(e).

(f) Standard: Deceased individuals. A covered entity must comply with the requirements of this subpart with respect to the protected health information of a deceased individual.

(g)(1) Standard: Personal representatives. As specified in this paragraph, a covered entity must, except as provided in paragraphs (g)(3) and (g)(5) of this section, treat a personal representative as the individual for purposes of this subchapter.

(2) Implementation specification: adults and emancipated minors. If under applicable law a person has authority to act on behalf of an individual who is an adult or an emancipated minor in making decisions related to health care, a covered entity must treat such person as a personal representative under this subchapter, with respect to protected health information relevant to such personal representation.

(3)(i) Implementation specification: unemancipated minors. If under applicable law a parent, guardian, or other person acting in loco parentis has authority to act on behalf of an individual who is an unemancipated minor in making decisions related to health care, a covered entity must treat such person as a personal representative under this subchapter, with respect to protected health information relevant to such personal representation, except that such person may not be a personal representative of an unemancipated minor, and the minor has the authority to act as an individual, with respect to protected health information pertaining to a health care service, if:

> **(A)** The minor consents to such health care service; no other consent to such health care service is required by law, regardless of whether the consent of another person has also been obtained; and the minor has not requested that such person be treated as the personal representative;
>
> **(B)** The minor may lawfully obtain such health care service without the consent of a parent, guardian, or other person acting in loco parentis, and the minor, a court, or another person authorized by law consents to such health care service; or
>
> **(C)** A parent, guardian, or other person acting in loco parentis assents to an agreement of confidentiality between a covered health care provider and the minor with respect to such health care service.

(ii) Notwithstanding the provisions of paragraph (g)(3)(i) of this section:

> **(A)** If, and to the extent, permitted or required by an applicable provision of State or other law, including applicable case law, a covered entity may disclose, or provide access in accordance with § 164.524 to, protected health information about an unemancipated minor to a parent, guardian, or other person acting in loco parentis;
>
> **(B)** If, and to the extent, prohibited by an applicable provision of State or other law, including applicable case law, a covered entity may not disclose, or provide access in accordance with § 164.524 to, protected health information about an unemancipated minor to a parent, guardian, or other person acting in loco parentis; and
>
> **(C)** Where the parent, guardian, or other person acting in loco parentis, is not the personal representative under paragraphs (g)(3)(i)(A), (B), or (C) of this section and where there is no applicable access provision under State or other law, including case law, a covered entity may provide or deny access under § 164.524 to a parent, guardian, or other person acting in loco parentis, if such action is consistent with State or other applicable law, provided that such decision must be made by a licensed health care professional, in the exercise of professional judgment.

(4) Implementation specification: Deceased individuals. If under applicable law an executor, administrator, or other person has authority to act on behalf of a deceased individual or of the individual's estate, a covered entity must treat such person as a personal representative under this subchapter, with respect to protected health information relevant to such personal representation.

(5) Implementation specification: Abuse, neglect, endangerment situations. Notwithstanding a State law or any requirement of this paragraph to the contrary, a covered entity may elect not to treat a person as the personal representative of an individual if:

(i) The covered entity has a reasonable belief that:

(A) The individual has been or may be subjected to domestic violence, abuse, or neglect by such person; or

(B) Treating such person as the personal representative could endanger the individual; and

(ii) The covered entity, in the exercise of professional judgment, decides that it is not in the best interest of the individual to treat the person as the individual's personal representative.

(h) Standard: Confidential communications. A covered health care provider or health plan must comply with the applicable requirements of § 164.522(b) in communicating protected health information.

(i) Standard: Uses and disclosures consistent with notice. A covered entity that is required by § 164.520 to have a notice may not use or disclose protected health information in a manner inconsistent with such notice. A covered entity that is required by § 164.520(b)(1)(iii) to include a specific statement in its notice if it intends to engage in an activity listed in § 164.520(b)(1)(iii)(A)-(C), may not use or disclose protected health information for such activities, unless the required statement is included in the notice.

(j) Standard: Disclosures by whistleblowers and workforce member crime victims.

(1) Disclosures by whistleblowers. A covered entity is not considered to have violated the requirements of this subpart if a member of its workforce or a business associate discloses protected health information, provided that:

(i) The workforce member or business associate believes in good faith that the covered entity has engaged in conduct that is unlawful or otherwise violates professional or clinical standards, or that the care, services, or conditions provided by the covered entity potentially endangers one or more patients, workers, or the public; and

(ii) The disclosure is to:

(A) A health oversight agency or public health authority authorized by law to investigate or otherwise oversee the relevant conduct or conditions of the covered entity or to an appropriate health care accreditation organization for the purpose of reporting the allegation of failure to meet professional standards or misconduct by the covered entity; or

(B) An attorney retained by or on behalf of the workforce member or business associate for the purpose of determining the legal options of the workforce member or business associate with regard to the conduct described in paragraph (j)(1)(i) of this section.

(2) Disclosures by workforce members who are victims of a crime. A covered entity is not considered to have violated the requirements of this subpart if a member of its workforce who is the victim of a criminal act discloses protected health information to a law enforcement official, provided that:

(i) The protected health information disclosed is about the suspected perpetrator of the criminal act; and

(ii) The protected health information disclosed is limited to the information listed in § 164.512(f)(2)(i).

§ 164.504 Uses and disclosures: Organizational requirements.

(a) Definitions. As used in this section:

Plan administration functions means administration functions performed by the plan sponsor of a group health plan on behalf of the group health plan and excludes functions performed by the plan sponsor in connection with any other benefit or benefit plan of the plan sponsor.

Summary health information means information, that may be individually identifiable health information, and:

(1) That summarizes the claims history, claims expenses, or type of claims experienced by individuals for whom a plan sponsor has provided health benefits under a group health plan; and

(2) From which the information described at § 164.514(b)(2)(i) has been deleted, except that the geographic information described in § 164.514(b)(2)(i)(B) need only be aggregated to the level of a five digit zip code.

(b) to (d) [Reserved]

(e)(1) Standard: Business associate contracts.

(i) The contract or other arrangement between the covered entity and the business associate required by § 164.502(e)(2) must meet the requirements of paragraph (e)(2) or (e)(3) of this section, as applicable.

(ii) A covered entity is not in compliance with the standards in § 164.502(e) and paragraph (e) of this section, if the covered entity knew of a pattern of activity or practice of the business associate that constituted a material breach or violation of the business associate's obligation under the contract or other arrangement, unless the covered entity took reasonable steps to cure the breach or end the violation, as applicable, and, if such steps were unsuccessful:

(A) Terminated the contract or arrangement, if feasible; or

(B) If termination is not feasible, reported the problem to the Secretary.

(2) Implementation specifications: Business associate contracts. A contract between the covered entity and a business associate must:

(i) Establish the permitted and required uses and disclosures of such information by the business associate. The contract may not authorize the business associate to use or further disclose the information in a manner that would violate the requirements of this subpart, if done by the covered entity, except that:

(A) The contract may permit the business associate to use and disclose protected health information for the proper management and administration of the business associate, as provided in paragraph (e)(4) of this section; and

(B) The contract may permit the business associate to provide data aggregation services relating to the health care operations of the covered entity.

(ii) Provide that the business associate will:

(A) Not use or further disclose the information other than as permitted or required by the contract or as required by law;

(B) Use appropriate safeguards to prevent use or disclosure of the information other than as provided for by its contract;

(C) Report to the covered entity any use or disclosure of the information not provided for by its contract of which it becomes aware;

(D) Ensure that any agents, including a subcontractor, to whom it provides protected health information received from, or created or received by the business associate on behalf of, the covered entity agrees to the same restrictions and conditions that apply to the business associate with respect to such information;

(E) Make available protected health information in accordance with § 164.524;

(F) Make available protected health information for amendment and incorporate any amendments to protected health information in accordance with § 164.526;

(G) Make available the information required to provide an accounting of disclosures in accordance with § 164.528;

(H) Make its internal practices, books, and records relating to the use and disclosure of protected health information received from, or created or received by the business associate on behalf of, the covered entity available to the Secretary for purposes of determining the covered entity's compliance with this subpart; and

(I) At termination of the contract, if feasible, return or destroy all protected health information received from, or created or received by the business associate on behalf of, the covered entity that the business associate still maintains in any form and retain no copies of such information or, if such return or destruction is not feasible, extend the protections of the contract to the information and limit further uses and disclosures to those purposes that make the return or destruction of the information infeasible.

(iii) Authorize termination of the contract by the covered entity, if the covered entity determines that the business associate has violated a material term of the contract.

(3) Implementation specifications: Other arrangements.

(i) If a covered entity and its business associate are both governmental entities:

(A) The covered entity may comply with paragraph (e) of this section by entering into a memorandum of understanding with the business associate that contains terms that accomplish the objectives of paragraph (e)(2) of this section.

(B) The covered entity may comply with paragraph (e) of this section, if other law (including regulations adopted by the covered entity or its business associate) contains requirements applicable to the business associate that accomplish the objectives of paragraph (e)(2) of this section.

(ii) If a business associate is required by law to perform a function or activity on behalf of a covered entity or to provide a service described in the definition of business associate in § 160.103 of this subchapter to a covered entity, such covered entity may disclose protected health information to the business associate to the extent necessary to comply with the legal mandate without meeting the requirements of this paragraph (e), provided that the covered entity attempts in good faith to obtain satisfactory assurances as required by paragraph (e)(3)(i) of this section, and, if such attempt fails, documents the attempt and the reasons that such assurances cannot be obtained.

(iii) The covered entity may omit from its other arrangements the termination authorization required by paragraph (e)(2)(iii) of this section, if such authorization is inconsistent with the statutory obligations of the covered entity or its business associate.

(4) Implementation specifications: Other requirements for contracts and other arrangements.

(i) The contract or other arrangement between the covered entity and the business associate may permit the business associate to use the information received by the business associate in its capacity as a business associate to the covered entity, if necessary:

(A) For the proper management and administration of the business associate; or

(B) To carry out the legal responsibilities of the business associate.

(ii) The contract or other arrangement between the covered entity and the business associate may permit the business associate to disclose the information received by the business associate in its capacity as a business associate for the purposes described in paragraph (e)(4)(i) of this section, if:

(A) The disclosure is required by law; or

(B)(1) The business associate obtains reasonable assurances from the person to whom the information is disclosed that it will be held confidentially and used or further disclosed only as required by law or for the purpose for which it was disclosed to the person; and

(2) The person notifies the business associate of any instances of which it is aware in which the confidentiality of the information has been breached.

(f)(1) Standard: Requirements for group health plans.

(i) Except as provided under paragraph (f)(1)(ii) or (iii) of this section or as otherwise authorized under § 164.508, a group health plan, in order to disclose protected health information to the plan sponsor or to provide for or permit the disclosure of protected health information to the plan sponsor by a health insurance issuer or HMO with respect to the group health plan, must ensure that the plan documents restrict uses and disclosures of such information by the plan sponsor consistent with the requirements of this subpart.

(ii) The group health plan, or a health insurance issuer or HMO with respect to the group health plan, may disclose summary health information to the plan sponsor, if the plan sponsor requests the summary health information for the purpose of:

(A) Obtaining premium bids from health plans for providing health insurance coverage under the group health plan; or

(B) Modifying, amending, or terminating the group health plan.

(iii) The group health plan, or a health insurance issuer or HMO with respect to the group health plan, may disclose to the plan sponsor information on whether the individual is participating in the group health plan, or is enrolled in or has disenrolled from a health insurance issuer or HMO offered by the plan.

(2) Implementation specifications: Requirements for plan documents. The plan documents of the group health plan must be amended to incorporate provisions to:

(i) Establish the permitted and required uses and disclosures of such information by the plan sponsor, provided that such permitted and required uses and disclosures may not be inconsistent with this subpart.

(ii) Provide that the group health plan will disclose protected health information to the plan sponsor only upon receipt of a certification by the plan sponsor that the plan documents have been amended to incorporate the following provisions and that the plan sponsor agrees to:

(A) Not use or further disclose the information other than as permitted or required by the plan documents or as required by law;

(B) Ensure that any agents, including a subcontractor, to whom it provides protected health information received from the group health plan agree to the same restrictions and conditions that apply to the plan sponsor with respect to such information;

(C) Not use or disclose the information for employment-related actions and decisions or in connection with any other benefit or employee benefit plan of the plan sponsor;

(D) Report to the group health plan any use or disclosure of the information that is inconsistent with the uses or disclosures provided for of which it becomes aware;

(E) Make available protected health information in accordance with § 164.524;

(F) Make available protected health information for amendment and incorporate any amendments to protected health information in accordance with § 164.526;

(G) Make available the information required to provide an accounting of disclosures in accordance with § 164.528;

(H) Make its internal practices, books, and records relating to the use and disclosure of protected health information received from the group health plan available to the Secretary for purposes of determining compliance by the group health plan with this subpart;

(I) If feasible, return or destroy all protected health information received from the group health plan that the sponsor still maintains in any form and retain no copies of such information when no longer needed for the purpose for which disclosure was made, except that, if such return or destruction is not feasible, limit further uses and disclosures to those purposes that make the return or destruction of the information infeasible; and

(J) Ensure that the adequate separation required in paragraph (f)(2)(iii) of this section is established.

(iii) Provide for adequate separation between the group health plan and the plan sponsor. The plan documents must:

(A) Describe those employees or classes of employees or other persons under the control of the plan sponsor to be given access to the protected health information to be disclosed, provided that any employee or person who receives protected health information relating to payment under, health care operations of, or other matters pertaining to the group health plan in the ordinary course of business must be included in such description;

(B) Restrict the access to and use by such employees and other persons described in paragraph (f)(2)(iii)(A) of this section to the plan administration functions that the plan sponsor performs for the group health plan; and

(C) Provide an effective mechanism for resolving any issues of noncompliance by persons described in paragraph (f)(2)(iii)(A) of this section with the plan document provisions required by this paragraph.

(3) Implementation specifications: Uses and disclosures. A group health plan may:

(i) Disclose protected health information to a plan sponsor to carry out plan administration functions that the plan sponsor performs only consistent with the provisions of paragraph (f)(2) of this section;

(ii) Not permit a health insurance issuer or HMO with respect to the group health plan to disclose protected health information to the plan sponsor except as permitted by this paragraph;

(iii) Not disclose and may not permit a health insurance issuer or HMO to disclose protected health information to a plan sponsor as otherwise permitted by this paragraph unless a statement required by § 164.520(b)(1)(iii)(C) is included in the appropriate notice; and

(iv) Not disclose protected health information to the plan sponsor for the purpose of employment-related actions or decisions or in connection with any other benefit or employee benefit plan of the plan sponsor.

(g) Standard: Requirements for a covered entity with multiple covered functions.

(1) A covered entity that performs multiple covered functions that would make the entity any combination of a health plan, a covered health care provider, and a health care clearinghouse, must comply with the standards, requirements, and implementation specifications of this subpart, as applicable to the health plan, health care provider, or health care clearinghouse covered functions performed.

(2) A covered entity that performs multiple covered functions may use or disclose the protected health information of individuals who receive the covered entity's health plan or health care provider services, but not both, only for purposes related to the appropriate function being performed.

§ 164.506 Uses and disclosures to carry out treatment, payment, or health care operations.

(a) Standard: Permitted uses and disclosures. Except with respect to uses or disclosures that require an authorization under § 164.508(a)(2) and (3), a covered entity may use or disclose protected health information for treatment, payment, or health care operations as set forth in paragraph (c) of this section, provided that such use or disclosure is consistent with other applicable requirements of this subpart.

(b) Standard: Consent for uses and disclosures permitted.

(1) A covered entity may obtain consent of the individual to use or disclose protected health information to carry out treatment, payment, or health care operations.

(2) Consent, under paragraph (b) of this section, shall not be effective to permit a use or disclosure of protected health information when an authorization, under § 164.508, is required or when another condition must be met for such use or disclosure to be permissible under this subpart.

(c) Implementation specifications: Treatment, payment, or health care operations.

(1) A covered entity may use or disclose protected health information for its own treatment, payment, or health care operations.

(2) A covered entity may disclose protected health information for treatment activities of a health care provider.

(3) A covered entity may disclose protected health information to another covered entity or a health care provider for the payment activities of the entity that receives the information.

(4) A covered entity may disclose protected health information to another covered entity for health care operations activities of the entity that receives the information, if each entity either has or had a relationship with the individual who is the subject of the protected health information being requested, the protected health information pertains to such relationship, and the disclosure is:

(i) For a purpose listed in paragraph (1) or (2) of the definition of health care operations; or

(ii) For the purpose of health care fraud and abuse detection or compliance.

(5) A covered entity that participates in an organized health care arrangement may disclose protected health information about an individual to another covered entity that participates in the organized health care arrangement for any health care operations activities of the organized health care arrangement.

§ 164.508 Uses and disclosures for which an authorization is required.

(a) Standard: authorizations for uses and disclosures—

(1) Authorization required: general rule. Except as otherwise permitted or required by this subchapter, a covered entity may not use or disclose protected health information without an authorization that is valid under this section. When a covered entity obtains or receives a valid authorization for its use or disclosure of protected health information, such use or disclosure must be consistent with such authorization.

(2) Authorization required: psychotherapy notes. Notwithstanding any provision of this subpart, other than the transition provisions in § 164.532, a covered entity must obtain an authorization for any use or disclosure of psychotherapy notes, except:

(i) To carry out the following treatment, payment, or health care operations:

(A) Use by the originator of the psychotherapy notes for treatment;

(B) Use or disclosure by the covered entity for its own training programs in which students, trainees, or practitioners in mental health learn under supervision to practice or improve their skills in group, joint, family, or individual counseling; or

(C) Use or disclosure by the covered entity to defend itself in a legal action or other proceeding brought by the individual; and

(ii) A use or disclosure that is required by § 164.502(a)(2)(ii) or permitted by § 164.512(a); § 164.512(d) with respect to the oversight of the originator of the psychotherapy notes; § 164.512(g)(1); or § 164.512(j)(1)(i).

(3) Authorization required: Marketing.

(i) Notwithstanding any provision of this subpart, other than the transition provisions in § 164.532, a covered entity must obtain an authorization for any use or disclosure of protected health information for marketing, except if the communication is in the form of:

(A) A face-to-face communication made by a covered entity to an individual; or

(B) A promotional gift of nominal value provided by the covered entity.

(ii) If the marketing involves direct or indirect remuneration to the covered entity from a third party, the authorization must state that such remuneration is involved.

(b) Implementation specifications: general requirements—

(1) Valid authorizations.

(i) A valid authorization is a document that meets the requirements in paragraphs (a)(3)(ii), (c)(1), and (c)(2) of this section, as applicable.

(ii) A valid authorization may contain elements or information in addition to the elements required by this section, provided that such additional elements or information are not inconsistent with the elements required by this section.

(2) Defective authorizations. An authorization is not valid, if the document submitted has any of the following defects:

(i) The expiration date has passed or the expiration event is known by the covered entity to have occurred;

(ii) The authorization has not been filled out completely, with respect to an element described by paragraph (c) of this section, if applicable;

(iii) The authorization is known by the covered entity to have been revoked;

(iv) The authorization violates paragraph (b)(3) or (4) of this section, if applicable;

(v) Any material information in the authorization is known by the covered entity to be false.

(3) Compound authorizations. An authorization for use or disclosure of protected health information may not be combined with any other document to create a compound authorization, except as follows:

(i) An authorization for the use or disclosure of protected health information for a research study may be combined with any other type of written permission for the same research study, including another authorization for the use or disclosure of protected health information for such research or a consent to participate in such research;

(ii) An authorization for a use or disclosure of psychotherapy notes may only be combined with another authorization for a use or disclosure of psychotherapy notes;

(iii) An authorization under this section, other than an authorization for a use or disclosure of psychotherapy notes, may be combined with any other such authorization under this section, except when a covered entity has conditioned the provision of treatment, payment, enrollment in the health plan, or eligibility for benefits under paragraph (b)(4) of this section on the provision of one of the authorizations.

(4) Prohibition on conditioning of authorizations. A covered entity may not condition the provision to an individual of treatment, payment, enrollment in the health plan, or eligibility for benefits on the provision of an authorization, except:

(i) A covered health care provider may condition the provision of research-related treatment on provision of an authorization for the use or disclosure of protected health information for such research under this section;

(ii) A health plan may condition enrollment in the health plan or eligibility for benefits on provision of an authorization requested by the health plan prior to an individual's enrollment in the health plan, if:

> **(A)** The authorization sought is for the health plan's eligibility or enrollment determinations relating to the individual or for its underwriting or risk rating determinations; and
>
> **(B)** The authorization is not for a use or disclosure of psychotherapy notes under paragraph (a)(2) of this section; and

(iii) A covered entity may condition the provision of health care that is solely for the purpose of creating protected health information for disclosure to a third party on provision of an authorization for the disclosure of the protected health information to such third party.

(5) Revocation of authorizations. An individual may revoke an authorization provided under this section at any time, provided that the revocation is in writing, except to the extent that:

(i) The covered entity has taken action in reliance thereon; or

(ii) If the authorization was obtained as a condition of obtaining insurance coverage, other law provides the insurer with the right to contest a claim under the policy or the policy itself.

(6) Documentation. A covered entity must document and retain any signed authorization under this section as required by § 164.530(j).

(c) Implementation specifications: Core elements and requirements—

(1) Core elements. A valid authorization under this section must contain at least the following elements:

(i) A description of the information to be used or disclosed that identifies the information in a specific and meaningful fashion.

(ii) The name or other specific identification of the person(s), or class of persons, authorized to make the requested use or disclosure.

(iii) The name or other specific identification of the person(s), or class of persons, to whom the covered entity may make the requested use or disclosure.

(iv) A description of each purpose of the requested use or disclosure. The statement "at the request of the individual" is a sufficient description of the purpose when an individual initiates the authorization and does not, or elects not to, provide a statement of the purpose.

(v) An expiration date or an expiration event that relates to the individual or the purpose of the use or disclosure. The statement "end of the research study," "none," or similar language is sufficient if the authorization is for a use or disclosure of protected health information for research, including for the creation and maintenance of a research database or research repository.

(vi) Signature of the individual and date. If the authorization is signed by a personal representative of the individual, a description of such representative's authority to act for the individual must also be provided.

(2) Required statements. In addition to the core elements, the authorization must contain statements adequate to place the individual on notice of all of the following:

(i) The individual's right to revoke the authorization in writing, and either:

(A) The exceptions to the right to revoke and a description of how the individual may revoke the authorization; or

(B) To the extent that the information in paragraph (c)(2)(i)(A) of this section is included in the notice required by § 164.520, a reference to the covered entity's notice.

(ii) The ability or inability to condition treatment, payment, enrollment or eligibility for benefits on the authorization, by stating either:

(A) The covered entity may not condition treatment, payment, enrollment or eligibility for benefits on whether the individual signs the authorization when the prohibition on conditioning of authorizations in paragraph (b)(4) of this section applies; or

(B) The consequences to the individual of a refusal to sign the authorization when, in accordance with paragraph (b)(4) of this section, the covered entity can condition treatment, enrollment in the health plan, or eligibility for benefits on failure to obtain such authorization.

(iii) The potential for information disclosed pursuant to the authorization to be subject to redisclosure by the recipient and no longer be protected by this subpart.

(3) Plain language requirement. The authorization must be written in plain language.

(4) Copy to the individual. If a covered entity seeks an authorization from an individual for a use or disclosure of protected health information, the covered entity must provide the individual with a copy of the signed authorization.

§ 164.510 Uses and disclosures requiring an opportunity for the individual to agree or to object.

A covered entity may use or disclose protected health information, provided that the individual is informed in advance of the use or disclosure and has the opportunity to agree to or prohibit or restrict the use or disclosure, in accordance with the applicable requirements of this section. The covered entity may orally inform the individual of and obtain the individual's oral agreement or objection to a use or disclosure permitted by this section.

(a) Standard: use and disclosure for facility directories.

(1) Permitted uses and disclosure. Except when an objection is expressed in accordance with paragraphs (a)(2) or (3) of this section, a covered health care provider may:

(i) Use the following protected health information to maintain a directory of individuals in its facility:

(A) The individual's name;

(B) The individual's location in the covered health care provider's facility;

(C) The individual's condition described in general terms that does not communicate specific medical information about the individual; and

(D) The individual's religious affiliation; and

(ii) Disclose for directory purposes such information:

(A) To members of the clergy; or

(B) Except for religious affiliation, to other persons who ask for the individual by name.

(2) Opportunity to object. A covered health care provider must inform an individual of the protected health information that it may include in a directory and the persons to whom it may disclose such information (including disclosures to clergy of information regarding religious affiliation) and provide the individual with the opportunity to restrict or prohibit some or all of the uses or disclosures permitted by paragraph (a)(1) of this section.

(3) Emergency circumstances.

(i) If the opportunity to object to uses or disclosures required by paragraph (a)(2) of this section cannot practicably be provided because of the individual's incapacity or an emergency treatment circumstance, a covered health care provider may use or disclose some or all of the protected health information permitted by paragraph (a)(1) of this section for the facility's directory, if such disclosure is:

(A) Consistent with a prior expressed preference of the individual, if any, that is known to the covered health care provider; and

(B) In the individual's best interest as determined by the covered health care provider, in the exercise of professional judgment.

(ii) The covered health care provider must inform the individual and provide an opportunity to object to uses or disclosures for directory purposes as required by paragraph (a)(2) of this section when it becomes practicable to do so.

(b) Standard: uses and disclosures for involvement in the individual's care and notification purposes.

(1) Permitted uses and disclosures.

(i) A covered entity may, in accordance with paragraphs (b)(2) or (3) of this section, disclose to a family member, other relative, or a close personal friend of the individual, or any other person identified by the individual, the protected health information directly relevant to such person's involvement with the individual's care or payment related to the individual's health care.

(ii) A covered entity may use or disclose protected health information to notify, or assist in the notification of (including identifying or locating), a family member, a personal representative of the individual, or another person responsible for the care of the individual of the individual's location, general condition, or death. Any such use or disclosure of protected health information for such notification purposes must be in accordance with paragraphs (b)(2), (3), or (4) of this section, as applicable.

(2) Uses and disclosures with the individual present. If the individual is present for, or otherwise available prior to, a use or disclosure permitted by paragraph (b)(1) of this section and has the capacity to make health care decisions, the covered entity may use or disclose the protected health information if it:

(i) Obtains the individual's agreement;

(ii) Provides the individual with the opportunity to object to the disclosure, and the individual does not express an objection; or

(iii) Reasonably infers from the circumstances, based the exercise of professional judgment, that the individual does not object to the disclosure.

(3) Limited uses and disclosures when the individual is not present. If the individual is not present, or the opportunity to agree or object to the use or disclosure cannot practicably be provided because of the individual's incapacity or an emergency circumstance, the covered entity may, in the exercise of professional judgment, determine whether the disclosure is in the best interests of the individual and, if so, disclose only the protected health information that is directly relevant to the person's involvement with the individual's health care. A covered entity may use professional judgment and its experience with common practice to make reasonable inferences of the individual's best interest in allowing a person to act on behalf of the individual to pick up filled prescriptions, medical supplies, X-rays, or other similar forms of protected health information.

(4) Use and disclosures for disaster relief purposes. A covered entity may use or disclose protected health information to a public or private entity authorized by law or by its charter to assist in disaster relief efforts, for the purpose of coordinating with such entities the uses or disclosures permitted by paragraph (b)(1)(ii) of this section. The requirements in paragraphs (b)(2) and (3) of this section apply to such uses and disclosure to the extent that the covered entity, in the exercise of professional judgment, determines that the requirements do not interfere with the ability to respond to the emergency circumstances.

§ 164.512 Uses and disclosures for which an authorization or opportunity to agree or object is not required.

A covered entity may use or disclose protected health information without the written authorization of the individual, as described in § 164.508, or the opportunity for the individual to agree or object as described in § 164.510, in the situations covered by this section, subject to the applicable requirements of this section. When the covered entity is required by this section to inform the individual of, or when the individual may agree to, a use or disclosure permitted by this section, the covered entity's information and the individual's agreement may be given orally.

(a) Standard: Uses and disclosures required by law.

(1) A covered entity may use or disclose protected health information to the extent that such use or disclosure is required by law and the use or disclosure complies with and is limited to the relevant requirements of such law.

(2) A covered entity must meet the requirements described in paragraph (c), (e), or (f) of this section for uses or disclosures required by law.

(b) Standard: uses and disclosures for public health activities.

(1) Permitted disclosures. A covered entity may disclose protected health information for the public health activities and purposes described in this paragraph to:

(i) A public health authority that is authorized by law to collect or receive such information for the purpose of preventing or controlling disease, injury, or disability, including, but not limited to, the reporting of disease, injury, vital events such as birth or death, and the conduct of public health surveillance, public health investigations, and public health interventions; or, at the direction of a public health authority, to an official of a foreign government agency that is acting in collaboration with a public health authority;

(ii) A public health authority or other appropriate government authority authorized by law to receive reports of child abuse or neglect;

(iii) A person subject to the jurisdiction of the Food and Drug Administration (FDA) with respect to an FDA-regulated product or activity for which that person has responsibility, for the purpose of activities related to the quality, safety or effectiveness of such FDA-regulated product or activity. Such purposes include:

(A) To collect or report adverse events (or similar activities with respect to food or dietary supplements), product defects or problems (including problems with the use or labeling of a product), or biological product deviations;

(B) To track FDA-regulated products;

(C) To enable product recalls, repairs, or replacement, or lookback (including locating and notifying individuals who have received products that have been recalled, withdrawn, or are the subject of lookback); or

(D) To conduct post marketing surveillance;

(iv) A person who may have been exposed to a communicable disease or may otherwise be at risk of contracting or spreading a disease or condition, if the covered entity or public health authority is authorized by law to notify such person as necessary in the conduct of a public health intervention or investigation; or

(v) An employer, about an individual who is a member of the workforce of the employer, if:

(A) The covered entity is a covered health care provider who is a member of the workforce of such employer or who provides health care to the individual at the request of the employer:

(1) To conduct an evaluation relating to medical surveillance of the workplace; or

(2) To evaluate whether the individual has a work-related illness or injury;

(B) The protected health information that is disclosed consists of findings concerning a work-related illness or injury or a workplace-related medical surveillance;

(C) The employer needs such findings in order to comply with its obligations, under 29 CFR parts 1904 through 1928, 30 CFR parts 50 through 90, or under state law having a similar purpose, to record such illness or injury or to carry out responsibilities for workplace medical surveillance; and

(D) The covered health care provider provides written notice to the individual that protected health information relating to the medical surveillance of the workplace and work-related illnesses and injuries is disclosed to the employer:

(1) By giving a copy of the notice to the individual at the time the health care is provided; or

(2) If the health care is provided on the work site of the employer, by posting the notice in a prominent place at the location where the health care is provided.

(2) Permitted uses. If the covered entity also is a public health authority, the covered entity is permitted to use protected health information in all cases in which it is permitted to disclose such information for public health activities under paragraph (b)(1) of this section.

(c) Standard: Disclosures about victims of abuse, neglect or domestic violence.

(1) Permitted disclosures. Except for reports of child abuse or neglect permitted by paragraph (b)(1)(ii) of this section, a covered entity may disclose protected health information about an individual whom the covered entity reasonably believes to be a victim of abuse, neglect, or domestic violence to a government authority, including a social service or protective services agency, authorized by law to receive reports of such abuse, neglect, or domestic violence:

(i) To the extent the disclosure is required by law and the disclosure complies with and is limited to the relevant requirements of such law;

(ii) If the individual agrees to the disclosure; or

(iii) To the extent the disclosure is expressly authorized by statute or regulation and:

(A) The covered entity, in the exercise of professional judgment, believes the disclosure is necessary to prevent serious harm to the individual or other potential victims; or

(B) If the individual is unable to agree because of incapacity, a law enforcement or other public official authorized to receive the report represents that the protected health information for which disclosure is sought is not intended to be used against the individual and that an immediate enforcement activity that depends upon the disclosure would be materially and adversely affected by waiting until the individual is able to agree to the disclosure.

(2) Informing the individual. A covered entity that makes a disclosure permitted by paragraph (c)(1) of this section must promptly inform the individual that such a report has been or will be made, except if:

(i) The covered entity, in the exercise of professional judgment, believes informing the individual would place the individual at risk of serious harm; or

(ii) The covered entity would be informing a personal representative, and the covered entity reasonably believes the personal representative is responsible for the abuse, neglect, or other injury, and that informing such person would not be in the best interests of the individual as determined by the covered entity, in the exercise of professional judgment.

(d) Standard: Uses and disclosures for health oversight activities.

(1) Permitted disclosures. A covered entity may disclose protected health information to a health oversight agency for oversight activities authorized by law, including audits; civil, administrative, or criminal investigations; inspections; licensure or disciplinary actions; civil, administrative, or criminal proceedings or actions; or other activities necessary for appropriate oversight of:

(i) The health care system;

(ii) Government benefit programs for which health information is relevant to beneficiary eligibility;

(iii) Entities subject to government regulatory programs for which health information is necessary for determining compliance with program standards; or

(iv) Entities subject to civil rights laws for which health information is necessary for determining compliance.

(2) Exception to health oversight activities. For the purpose of the disclosures permitted by paragraph (d)(1) of this section, a health oversight activity does not include an investigation or other activity in which the individual is the subject of the investigation or activity and such investigation or other activity does not arise out of and is not directly related to:

(i) The receipt of health care;

(ii) A claim for public benefits related to health; or

(iii) Qualification for, or receipt of, public benefits or services when a patient's health is integral to the claim for public benefits or services.

(3) Joint activities or investigations. Nothwithstanding paragraph (d)(2) of this section, if a health oversight activity or investigation is conducted in conjunction with an oversight activity or investigation relating to a claim for public benefits not related to health, the joint activity or investigation is considered a health oversight activity for purposes of paragraph (d) of this section.

(4) Permitted uses. If a covered entity also is a health oversight agency, the covered entity may use protected health information for health oversight activities as permitted by paragraph (d) of this section.

(e) Standard: Disclosures for judicial and administrative proceedings.

(1) Permitted disclosures. A covered entity may disclose protected health information in the course of any judicial or administrative proceeding:

(i) In response to an order of a court or administrative tribunal, provided that the covered entity discloses only the protected health information expressly authorized by such order; or

(ii) In response to a subpoena, discovery request, or other lawful process, that is not accompanied by an order of a court or administrative tribunal, if:

(A) The covered entity receives satisfactory assurance, as described in paragraph (e)(1)(iii) of this section, from the party seeking the information that reasonable efforts have been made by such party to ensure that the individual who is the subject of the protected health information that has been requested has been given notice of the request; or

(B) The covered entity receives satisfactory assurance, as described in paragraph (e)(1)(iv) of this section, from the party seeking the information that reasonable efforts have been made by such party to secure a qualified protective order that meets the requirements of paragraph (e)(1)(v) of this section.

(iii) For the purposes of paragraph (e)(1)(ii)(A) of this section, a covered entity receives satisfactory assurances from a party seeking protecting health information if the covered entity receives from such party a written statement and accompanying documentation demonstrating that:

(A) The party requesting such information has made a good faith attempt to provide written notice to the individual (or, if the individual's location is unknown, to mail a notice to the individual's last known address);

(B) The notice included sufficient information about the litigation or proceeding in which the protected health information is requested to permit the individual to raise an objection to the court or administrative tribunal; and

(C) The time for the individual to raise objections to the court or administrative tribunal has elapsed, and:

(1) No objections were filed; or

(2) All objections filed by the individual have been resolved by the court or the administrative tribunal and the disclosures being sought are consistent with such resolution.

(iv) For the purposes of paragraph (e)(1)(ii)(B) of this section, a covered entity receives satisfactory assurances from a party seeking protected health information, if the covered entity receives from such party a written statement and accompanying documentation demonstrating that:

(A) The parties to the dispute giving rise to the request for information have agreed to a qualified protective order and have presented it to the court or administrative tribunal with jurisdiction over the dispute; or

(B) The party seeking the protected health information has requested a qualified protective order from such court or administrative tribunal.

(v) For purposes of paragraph (e)(1) of this section, a qualified protective order means, with respect to protected health information requested under paragraph (e)(1)(ii) of this section, an order of a court or of an administrative tribunal or a stipulation by the parties to the litigation or administrative proceeding that:

(A) Prohibits the parties from using or disclosing the protected health information for any purpose other than the litigation or proceeding for which such information was requested; and

(B) Requires the return to the covered entity or destruction of the protected health information (including all copies made) at the end of the litigation or proceeding.

(vi) Nothwithstanding paragraph (e)(1)(ii) of this section, a covered entity may disclose protected health information in response to lawful process described in paragraph (e)(1)(ii) of this section without receiving satisfactory assurance under paragraph (e)(1)(ii)(A) or (B) of this section, if the covered entity makes reasonable efforts to provide notice to the individual sufficient to meet the requirements of paragraph (e)(1)(iii) of this section or to seek a qualified protective order sufficient to meet the requirements of paragraph (e)(1)(iv) of this section.

(2) Other uses and disclosures under this section. The provisions of this paragraph do not supersede other provisions of this section that otherwise permit or restrict uses or disclosures of protected health information.

(f) Standard: Disclosures for law enforcement purposes. A covered entity may disclose protected health information for a law enforcement purpose to a law enforcement official if the conditions in paragraphs (f)(1) through (f)(6) of this section are met, as applicable.

(1) Permitted disclosures: Pursuant to process and as otherwise required by law. A covered entity may disclose protected health information:

(i) As required by law including laws that require the reporting of certain types of wounds or other physical injuries, except for laws subject to paragraph (b)(1)(ii) or (c)(1)(i) of this section; or

(ii) In compliance with and as limited by the relevant requirements of:

(A) A court order or court-ordered warrant, or a subpoena or summons issued by a judicial officer;

(B) A grand jury subpoena; or

(C) An administrative request, including an administrative subpoena or summons, a civil or an authorized investigative demand, or similar process authorized under law, provided that:

(1) The information sought is relevant and material to a legitimate law enforcement inquiry;

(2) The request is specific and limited in scope to the extent reasonably practicable in light of the purpose for which the information is sought; and

(3) De-identified information could not reasonably be used.

(2) Permitted disclosures: Limited information for identification and location purposes. Except for disclosures required by law as permitted by paragraph (f)(1) of this section, a covered entity may disclose protected health information in response to a law enforcement official's request for such information for the purpose of identifying or locating a suspect, fugitive, material witness, or missing person, provided that:

(i) The covered entity may disclose only the following information:

(A) Name and address;

(B) Date and place of birth;

(C) Social security number;

(D) ABO blood type and rh factor;

(E) Type of injury;

(F) Date and time of treatment;

(G) Date and time of death, if applicable; and

(H) A description of distinguishing physical characteristics, including height, weight, gender, race, hair and eye color, presence or absence of facial hair (beard or moustache), scars, and tattoos.

(ii) Except as permitted by paragraph (f)(2)(i) of this section, the covered entity may not disclose for the purposes of identification or location under paragraph (f)(2) of this section any protected health information related to the individual's DNA or DNA analysis, dental records, or typing, samples or analysis of body fluids or tissue.

(3) Permitted disclosure: Victims of a crime. Except for disclosures required by law as permitted by paragraph (f)(1) of this section, a covered entity may disclose protected health information in response to a law enforcement official's request for such information about an individual who is or is suspected to be a victim of a crime, other than disclosures that are subject to paragraph (b) or (c) of this section, if:

(i) The individual agrees to the disclosure; or

(ii) The covered entity is unable to obtain the individual's agreement because of incapacity or other emergency circumstance, provided that:

> **(A)** The law enforcement official represents that such information is needed to determine whether a violation of law by a person other than the victim has occurred, and such information is not intended to be used against the victim;
>
> **(B)** The law enforcement official represents that immediate law enforcement activity that depends upon the disclosure would be materially and adversely affected by waiting until the individual is able to agree to the disclosure; and
>
> **(C)** The disclosure is in the best interests of the individual as determined by the covered entity, in the exercise of professional judgment.

(4) Permitted disclosure: Decedents. A covered entity may disclose protected health information about an individual who has died to a law enforcement official for the purpose of alerting law enforcement of the death of the individual if the covered entity has a suspicion that such death may have resulted from criminal conduct.

(5) Permitted disclosure: Crime on premises. A covered entity may disclose to a law enforcement official protected health information that the covered entity believes in good faith constitutes evidence of criminal conduct that occurred on the premises of the covered entity.

(6) Permitted disclosure: Reporting crime in emergencies.

(i) A covered health care provider providing emergency health care in response to a medical emergency, other than such emergency on the premises of the covered health care provider, may disclose protected health information to a law enforcement official if such disclosure appears necessary to alert law enforcement to:

> **(A)** The commission and nature of a crime;
>
> **(B)** The location of such crime or of the victim(s) of such crime; and
>
> **(C)** The identity, description, and location of the perpetrator of such crime.

(ii) If a covered health care provider believes that the medical emergency described in paragraph (f)(6)(i) of this section is the result of abuse, neglect, or domestic violence of the individual in need of emergency health care, paragraph (f)(6)(i) of this section does not apply and any disclosure to a law enforcement official for law enforcement purposes is subject to paragraph (c) of this section.

(g) Standard: Uses and disclosures about decedents.

(1) Coroners and medical examiners. A covered entity may disclose protected health information to a coroner or medical examiner for the purpose of identifying a deceased person, determining a cause of death, or other duties as authorized by law. A covered entity that also performs the duties of a coroner or medical examiner may use protected health information for the purposes described in this paragraph.

(2) Funeral directors. A covered entity may disclose protected health information to funeral directors, consistent with applicable law, as necessary to carry out their duties with respect to the decedent. If necessary for funeral directors to carry out their duties, the covered entity may disclose the protected health information prior to, and in reasonable anticipation of, the individual's death.

(h) Standard: Uses and disclosures for cadaveric organ, eye or tissue donation purposes. A covered entity may use or disclose protected health information to organ procurement organizations or other entities engaged in the procurement, banking, or transplantation of cadaveric organs, eyes, or tissue for the purpose of facilitating organ, eye or tissue donation and transplantation.

(i) Standard: Uses and disclosures for research purposes.

(1) Permitted uses and disclosures. A covered entity may use or disclose protected health information for research, regardless of the source of funding of the research, provided that:

(i) Board approval of a waiver of authorization. The covered entity obtains documentation that an alteration to or waiver, in whole or in part, of the individual authorization required by § 164.508 for use or disclosure of protected health information has been approved by either:

(A) An Institutional Review Board (IRB), established in accordance with 7 CFR lc.107, 10 CFR 745.107, 14 CFR 1230.107, 15 CFR 27.107, 16 CFR1028.107, 21 CFR 56.107, 22 CFR 225.107, 24 CFR 60.107, 28 CFR 46.107, 32 CFR 219.107, 34 CFR 97.107, 38 CFR 16.107, 40 CFR 26.107, 45 CFR 46.107, 45 CFR 690.107, or 49 CFR 11.107; or

(B) A privacy board that:

(1) Has members with varying backgrounds and appropriate professional competency as necessary to review the effect of the research protocol on the individual's privacy rights and related interests;

(2) Includes at least one member who is not affiliated with the covered entity, not affiliated with any entity conducting or sponsoring the research, and not related to any person who is affiliated with any of such entities; and

(3) Does not have any member participating in a review of any project in which the member has a conflict of interest.

(ii) Reviews preparatory to research. The covered entity obtains from the researcher representations that:

(A) Use or disclosure is sought solely to review protected health information as necessary to prepare a research protocol or for similar purposes preparatory to research;

(B) No protected health information is to be removed from the covered entity by the researcher in the course of the review; and

(C) The protected health information for which use or access is sought is necessary for the research purposes.

(iii) Research on decedent's information. The covered entity obtains from the researcher:

(A) Representation that the use or disclosure sought is solely for research on the protected health information of decedents;

(B) Documentation, at the request of the covered entity, of the death of such individuals; and

(C) Representation that the protected health information for which use or disclosure is sought is necessary for the research purposes.

(2) Documentation of waiver approval. For a use or disclosure to be permitted based on documentation of approval of an alteration or waiver, under paragraph (i)(1)(i) of this section, the documentation must include all of the following:

(i) Identification and date of action. A statement identifying the IRB or privacy board and the date on which the alteration or waiver of authorization was approved;

(ii) Waiver criteria. A statement that the IRB or privacy board has determined that the alteration or waiver, in whole or in part, of authorization satisfies the following criteria:

(A) The use or disclosure of protected health information involves no more than a minimal risk to the privacy of individuals, based on, at least, the presence of the following elements;

(1) An adequate plan to protect the identifiers from improper use and disclosure;

(2) An adequate plan to destroy the identifiers at the earliest opportunity consistent with conduct of the research, unless there is a health or research justification for retaining the identifiers or such retention is otherwise required by law; and

(3) Adequate written assurances that the protected health information will not be reused or disclosed to any other person or entity, except as required by law, for authorized oversight of the research study, or for other research for which the use or disclosure of protected health information would be permitted by this subpart;

(B) The research could not practicably be conducted without the waiver or alteration; and

(C) The research could not practicably be conducted without access to and use of the protected health information.

(iii) Protected health information needed. A brief description of the protected health information for which use or access has been determined to be necessary by the IRB or privacy board has determined, pursuant to paragraph (i)(2)(ii)(C) of this section;

(iv) Review and approval procedures. A statement that the alteration or waiver of authorization has been reviewed and approved under either normal or expedited review procedures, as follows:

(A) An IRB must follow the requirements of the Common Rule, including the normal review procedures (7 CFR 1c.108(b), 10 CFR 745.108(b), 14 CFR 1230.108(b), 15 CFR 27.108(b), 16 CFR 1028.108(b), 21 CFR 56.108(b), 22 CFR 225.108(b), 24 CFR 60.108(b), 28 CFR 46.108(b), 32 CFR 219.108(b), 34 CFR 97.108(b), 38 CFR 16.108(b), 40 CFR 26.108(b), 45 CFR 46.108(b), 45 CFR 690.108(b), or 49 CFR 11.108(b)) or the expedited review procedures (7 CFR 1c.110, 10 CFR 745.110, 14 CFR 1230.110, 15 CFR 27.110, 16 CFR 1028.110, 21 CFR 56.110, 22 CFR 225.110, 24 CFR 60.110, 28 CFR 46.110, 32 CFR 219.110, 34 CFR 97.110, 38 CFR 16.110, 40 CFR 26.110, 45 CFR 46.110, 45 CFR 690.110, or 49 CFR 11.110);

(B) A privacy board must review the proposed research at convened meetings at which a majority of the privacy board members are present, including at least one member who satisfies the criterion stated in paragraph (i)(1)(i)(B)(2) of this section, and the alteration or waiver of authorization must be approved by the majority of the privacy board members present at the meeting, unless the privacy board elects to use an expedited review procedure in accordance with paragraph (i)(2)(iv)(C) of this section;

(C) A privacy board may use an expedited review procedure if the research involves no more than minimal risk to the privacy of the individuals who are the subject of the protected health information for which use or disclosure is being sought. If the privacy board elects to use an expedited review procedure, the review and approval of the alteration or waiver of authorization may be carried out by the chair of the privacy board, or by one or more members of the privacy board as designated by the chair; and

(v) Required signature. The documentation of the alteration or waiver of authorization must be signed by the chair or other member, as designated by the chair, of the IRB or the privacy board, as applicable.

(j) Standard: Uses and disclosures to avert a serious threat to health or safety.

(1) Permitted disclosures. A covered entity may, consistent with applicable law and standards of ethical conduct, use or disclose protected health information, if the covered entity, in good faith, believes the use or disclosure:

(i)(A) Is necessary to prevent or lessen a serious and imminent threat to the health or safety of a person or the public; and

(B) Is to a person or persons reasonably able to prevent or lessen the threat, including the target of the threat; or

(ii) Is necessary for law enforcement authorities to identify or apprehend an individual:

(A) Because of a statement by an individual admitting participation in a violent crime that the covered entity reasonably believes may have caused serious physical harm to the victim; or

(B) Where it appears from all the circumstances that the individual has escaped from a correctional institution or from lawful custody, as those terms are defined in § 164.501.

(2) Use or disclosure not permitted. A use or disclosure pursuant to paragraph (j)(1)(ii)(A) of this section may not be made if the information described in paragraph (j)(1)(ii)(A) of this section is learned by the covered entity:

(i) In the course of treatment to affect the propensity to commit the criminal conduct that is the basis for the disclosure under paragraph (j)(1)(ii)(A) of this section, or counseling or therapy; or

(ii) Through a request by the individual to initiate or to be referred for the treatment, counseling, or therapy described in paragraph (j)(2)(i) of this section.

(3) Limit on information that may be disclosed. A disclosure made pursuant to paragraph (j)(1)(ii)(A) of this section shall contain only the statement described in paragraph (j)(1)(ii)(A) of this section and the protected health information described in paragraph (f)(2)(i) of this section.

(4) Presumption of good faith belief. A covered entity that uses or discloses protected health information pursuant to paragraph (j)(1) of this section is presumed to have acted in good faith with regard to a belief described in paragraph (j)(1)(i) or (ii) of this section, if the belief is based upon the covered entity's actual knowledge or in reliance on a credible representation by a person with apparent knowledge or authority.

(k) Standard: Uses and disclosures for specialized government functions.

(1) Military and veterans activities.

(i) Armed Forces personnel. A covered entity may use and disclose the protected health information of individuals who are Armed Forces personnel for activities deemed necessary by appropriate military command authorities to assure the proper execution of the military mission, if the appropriate military authority has published by notice in the Federal Register the following information:

(A) Appropriate military command authorities; and

(B) The purposes for which the protected health information may be used or disclosed.

(ii) Separation or discharge from military service. A covered entity that is a component of the Departments of Defense or Transportation may disclose to the Department of Veterans Affairs (DVA) the protected health information of an individual who is a member of the Armed Forces upon the separation or discharge of the individual from military service for the purpose of a determination by DVA of the individual's eligibility for or entitlement to benefits under laws administered by the Secretary of Veterans Affairs.

(iii) Veterans. A covered entity that is a component of the Department of Veterans Affairs may use and disclose protected health information to components of the Department that determine eligibility for or entitlement to, or that provide, benefits under the laws administered by the Secretary of Veterans Affairs.

(iv) Foreign military personnel. A covered entity may use and disclose the protected health information of individuals who are foreign military personnel to their appropriate foreign military authority for the same purposes for which uses and disclosures are permitted for Armed Forces personnel under the notice published in the Federal Register pursuant to paragraph (k)(1)(i) of this section.

(2) National security and intelligence activities. A covered entity may disclose protected health information to authorized federal officials for the conduct of lawful intelligence, counter-intelligence, and other national security activities authorized by the National Security Act (50 U.S.C. 401, et seq.) and implementing authority (e.g., Executive Order 12333).

(3) Protective services for the President and others. A covered entity may disclose protected health information to authorized federal officials for the provision of protective services to the President or other persons authorized by 18 U.S.C. 3056, or to foreign heads of state or other persons authorized by 22 U.S.C. 2709(a)(3), or to for the conduct of investigations authorized by 18 U.S.C. 871 and 879.

(4) Medical suitability determinations. A covered entity that is a component of the Department of State may use protected health information to make medical suitability determinations and may disclose whether or not the individual was determined to be medically suitable to the officials in the Department of State who need access to such information for the following purposes:

(i) For the purpose of a required security clearance conducted pursuant to Executive Orders 10450 and 12698;

(ii) As necessary to determine worldwide availability or availability for mandatory service abroad under sections 101(a)(4) and 504 of the Foreign Service Act; or

(iii) For a family to accompany a Foreign Service member abroad, consistent with section 101(b)(5) and 904 of the Foreign Service Act.

(5) Correctional institutions and other law enforcement custodial situations.

(i) Permitted disclosures. A covered entity may disclose to a correctional institution or a law enforcement official having lawful custody of an inmate or other individual protected health information about such inmate or individual, if the correctional institution or such law enforcement official represents that such protected health information is necessary for:

(A) The provision of health care to such individuals;

(B) The health and safety of such individual or other inmates;

(C) The health and safety of the officers or employees of or others at the correctional institution;

(D) The health and safety of such individuals and officers or other persons responsible for the transporting of inmates or their transfer from one institution, facility, or setting to another;

(E) Law enforcement on the premises of the correctional institution; and

(F) The administration and maintenance of the safety, security, and good order of the correctional institution.

(ii) Permitted uses. A covered entity that is a correctional institution may use protected health information of individuals who are inmates for any purpose for which such protected health information may be disclosed.

(iii) No application after release. For the purposes of this provision, an individual is no longer an inmate when released on parole, probation, supervised release, or otherwise is no longer in lawful custody.

(6) Covered entities that are government programs providing public benefits.

(i) A health plan that is a government program providing public benefits may disclose protected health information relating to eligibility for or enrollment in the health plan to another agency administering a government program providing public benefits if the sharing of eligibility or enrollment information among such government agencies or the maintenance of such information in a single or combined data system accessible to all such government agencies is required or expressly authorized by statute or regulation.

(ii) A covered entity that is a government agency administering a government program providing public benefits may disclose protected health information relating to the program to another covered entity that is a government agency administering a government program providing public benefits if the programs serve the same or similar populations and the disclosure of protected health information is necessary to coordinate the covered functions of such programs or to improve administration and management relating to the covered functions of such programs.

(l) Standard: Disclosures for workers' compensation. A covered entity may disclose protected health information as authorized by and to the extent necessary to comply with laws relating to workers' compensation or other similar programs, established by law, that provide benefits for work-related injuries or illness without regard to fault.

§ 164.514 Other requirements relating to uses and disclosures of protected health information.

(a) Standard: de-identification of protected health information. Health information that does not identify an individual and with respect to which there is no reasonable basis to believe that the information can be used to identify an individual is not individually identifiable health information.

(b) Implementation specifications: requirements for de-identification of protected health information. A covered entity may determine that health information is not individually identifiable health information only if:

(1) A person with appropriate knowledge of and experience with generally accepted statistical and scientific principles and methods for rendering information not individually identifiable:

(i) Applying such principles and methods, determines that the risk is very small that the information could be used, alone or in combination with other reasonably available information, by an anticipated recipient to identify an individual who is a subject of the information; and

(ii) Documents the methods and results of the analysis that justify such determination; or

(2)(i) The following identifiers of the individual or of relatives, employers, or household members of the individual, are removed:

(A) Names;

(B) All geographic subdivisions smaller than a State, including street address, city, county, precinct, zip code, and their equivalent geocodes, except for the initial three digits of a zip code if, according to the current publicly available data from the Bureau of the Census:

(1) The geographic unit formed by combining all zip codes with the same three initial digits contains more than 20,000 people; and

(2) The initial three digits of a zip code for all such geographic units containing 20,000 or fewer people is changed to 000.

(C) All elements of dates (except year) for dates directly related to an individual, including birth date, admission date, discharge date, date of death; and all ages over 89 and all elements of dates (including year) indicative of such age, except that such ages and elements may be aggregated into a single category of age 90 or older;

(D) Telephone numbers;

(E) Fax numbers;

(F) Electronic mail addresses;

(G) Social security numbers;

(H) Medical record numbers;

(I) Health plan beneficiary numbers;

(J) Account numbers;

(K) Certificate/license numbers;

(L) Vehicle identifiers and serial numbers, including license plate numbers;

(M) Device identifiers and serial numbers;

(N) Web Universal Resource Locators (URLs);

(O) Internet Protocol (IP) address numbers;

(P) Biometric identifiers, including finger and voice prints;

(Q) Full face photographic images and any comparable images; and

(R) Any other unique identifying number, characteristic, or code, except as permitted by paragraph (c) of this section; and

(ii) The covered entity does not have actual knowledge that the information could be used alone or in combination with other information to identify an individual who is a subject of the information.

(c) Implementation specifications: re-identification. A covered entity may assign a code or other means of record identification to allow information de-identified under this section to be re-identified by the covered entity, provided that:

(1) Derivation. The code or other means of record identification is not derived from or related to information about the individual and is not otherwise capable of being translated so as to identify the individual; and

(2) Security. The covered entity does not use or disclose the code or other means of record identification for any other purpose, and does not disclose the mechanism for re-identification.

(d)(1) Standard: minimum necessary requirements. In order to comply with § 164.502(b) and this section, a covered entity must meet the requirements of paragraphs (d)(2) through (d)(5) of this section with respect to a request for, or the use and disclosure of, protected health information.

(2) Implementation specifications: minimum necessary uses of protected health information.

(i) A covered entity must identify:

(A) Those persons or classes of persons, as appropriate, in its workforce who need access to protected health information to carry out their duties; and

(B) For each such person or class of persons, the category or categories of protected health information to which access is needed and any conditions appropriate to such access.

(ii) A covered entity must make reasonable efforts to limit the access of such persons or classes identified in paragraph (d)(2)(i)(A) of this section to protected health information consistent with paragraph (d)(2)(i)(B) of this section.

(3) Implementation specification: Minimum necessary disclosures of protected health information.

(i) For any type of disclosure that it makes on a routine and recurring basis, a covered entity must implement policies and procedures (which may be standard protocols) that limit the protected health information disclosed to the amount reasonably necessary to achieve the purpose of the disclosure.

(ii) For all other disclosures, a covered entity must:

(A) Develop criteria designed to limit the protected health information disclosed to the information reasonably necessary to accomplish the purpose for which disclosure is sought; and

(B) Review requests for disclosure on an individual basis in accordance with such criteria.

(iii) A covered entity may rely, if such reliance is reasonable under the circumstances, on a requested disclosure as the minimum necessary for the stated purpose when:

(A) Making disclosures to public officials that are permitted under § 164.512, if the public official represents that the information requested is the minimum necessary for the stated purpose(s);

(B) The information is requested by another covered entity;

(C) The information is requested by a professional who is a member of its workforce or is a business associate of the covered entity for the purpose of providing professional services to the covered entity, if the professional represents that the information requested is the minimum necessary for the stated purpose(s); or

(D) Documentation or representations that comply with the applicable requirements of § 164.512(i) have been provided by a person requesting the information for research purposes.

(4) Implementation specifications: Minimum necessary requests for protected health information.

(i) A covered entity must limit any request for protected health information to that which is reasonably necessary to accomplish the purpose for which the request is made, when requesting such information from other covered entities.

(ii) For a request that is made on a routine and recurring basis, a covered entity must implement policies and procedures (which may be standard protocols) that limit the protected health information requested to the amount reasonably necessary to accomplish the purpose for which the request is made.

(iii) For all other requests, a covered entity must:

(A) Develop criteria designed to limit the request for protected health information to the information reasonably necessary to accomplish the purpose for which the request is made; and

(B) Review requests for disclosure on an individual basis in accordance with such criteria.

(5) Implementation specification: Other content requirement. For all uses, disclosures, or requests to which the requirements in paragraph (d) of this section apply, a covered entity may not use, disclose or request an entire medical record, except when the entire medical record is specifically justified as the amount that is reasonably necessary to accomplish the purpose of the use, disclosure, or request.

(e)(1) Standard: Limited data set. A covered entity may use or disclose a limited data set that meets the requirements of paragraphs (e)(2) and (e)(3) of this section, if the covered entity enters into a data use agreement with the limited data set recipient, in accordance with paragraph (e)(4) of this section.

(2) Implementation specification: Limited data set: A limited data set is protected health information that excludes the following direct identifiers of the individual or of relatives, employers, or household members of the individual:

(i) Names;

(ii) Postal address information, other than town or city, State, and zip code;

(iii) Telephone numbers;

(iv) Fax numbers;

(v) Electronic mail addresses;

(vi) Social security numbers;

(vii) Medical record numbers;

(viii) Health plan beneficiary numbers;

(ix) Account numbers;

(x) Certificate/license numbers;

(xi) Vehicle identifiers and serial numbers, including license plate numbers;

(xii) Device identifiers and serial numbers;

(xiii) Web Universal Resource Locators (URLs);

(xiv) Internet Protocol (IP) address numbers;

(xv) Biometric identifiers, including finger and voice prints; and

(xvi) Full face photographic images and any comparable images.

(3) Implementation specification: Permitted purposes for uses and disclosures.

(i) A covered entity may use or disclose a limited data set under paragraph (e)(1) of this section only for the purposes of research, public health, or health care operations.

(ii) A covered entity may use protected health information to create a limited data set that meets the requirements of paragraph (e)(2) of this section, or disclose protected health information only to a business associate for such purpose, whether or not the limited data set is to be used by the covered entity.

(4) Implementation specifications: Data use agreement.—

(i) Agreement required. A covered entity may use or disclose a limited data set under paragraph (e)(1) of this section only if the covered entity obtains satisfactory assurance, in the form of a data use agreement that meets the requirements of this section, that the limited data set recipient will only use or disclose the protected health information for limited purposes.

(ii) Contents. A data use agreement between the covered entity and the limited data set recipient must:

(A) Establish the permitted uses and disclosures of such information by the limited data set recipient, consistent with paragraph (e)(3) of this section. The data use agreement may not authorize the limited data set recipient to use or further disclose the information in a manner that would violate the requirements of this subpart, if done by the covered entity;

(B) Establish who is permitted to use or receive the limited data set; and

(C) Provide that the limited data set recipient will:

(1) Not use or further disclose the information other than as permitted by the data use agreement or as otherwise required by law;

(2) Use appropriate safeguards to prevent use or disclosure of the information other than as provided for by the data use agreement;

(3) Report to the covered entity any use or disclosure of the information not provided for by its data use agreement of which it becomes aware;

(4) Ensure that any agents, including a subcontractor, to whom it provides the limited data set agrees to the same restrictions and conditions that apply to the limited data set recipient with respect to such information; and

(5) Not identify the information or contact the individuals.

(iii) Compliance.

(A) A covered entity is not in compliance with the standards in paragraph (e) of this section if the covered entity knew of a pattern of activity or practice of the limited data set recipient that constituted a material breach or violation of the data use agreement, unless the covered entity took reasonable steps to cure the breach or end the violation, as applicable, and, if such steps were unsuccessful:

(1) Discontinued disclosure of protected health information to the recipient; and

(2) Reported the problem to the Secretary.

(B) A covered entity that is a limited data set recipient and violates a data use agreement will be in noncompliance with the standards, implementation specifications, and requirements of paragraph (e) of this section.

(f)(1) Standard: Uses and disclosures for fundraising. A covered entity may use, or disclose to a business associate or to an institutionally related foundation, the following protected health information for the purpose of raising funds for its own benefit, without an authorization meeting the requirements of § 164.508:

(i) Demographic information relating to an individual; and

(ii) Dates of health care provided to an individual.

(2) Implementation specifications: Fundraising requirements.

(i) The covered entity may not use or disclose protected health information for fundraising purposes as otherwise permitted by paragraph (f)(1) of this section unless a statement required by § 164.520(b)(1)(iii)(B) is included in the covered entity's notice;

(ii) The covered entity must include in any fundraising materials it sends to an individual under this paragraph a description of how the individual may opt out of receiving any further fundraising communications.

(iii) The covered entity must make reasonable efforts to ensure that individuals who decide to opt out of receiving future fundraising communications are not sent such communications.

(g) Standard: Uses and disclosures for underwriting and related purposes. If a health plan receives protected health information for the purpose of underwriting, premium rating, or other activities relating to the creation, renewal, or replacement of a contract of health insurance or health benefits, and if such health insurance or health benefits are not placed with the health plan, such health plan may not use or disclose such protected health information for any other purpose, except as may be required by law.

(h)(1) Standard: Verification requirements. Prior to any disclosure permitted by this subpart, a covered entity must:

(i) Except with respect to disclosures under § 164.510, verify the identity of a person requesting protected health information and the authority of any such person to have access to protected health information under this subpart, if the identity or any such authority of such person is not known to the covered entity; and

(ii) Obtain any documentation, statements, or representations, whether oral or written, from the person requesting the protected health information when such documentation, statement, or representation is a condition of the disclosure under this subpart.

(2) Implementation specifications: Verification.

(i) Conditions on disclosures. If a disclosure is conditioned by this subpart on particular documentation, statements, or representations from the person requesting the protected health information, a covered entity may rely, if such reliance is reasonable under the circumstances, on documentation, statements, or representations that, on their face, meet the applicable requirements.

(A) The conditions in § 164.512(f)(1)(ii)(C) may be satisfied by the administrative subpoena or similar process or by a separate written statement that, on its face, demonstrates that the applicable requirements have been met.

(B) The documentation required by § 164.512(i)(2) may be satisfied by one or more written statements, provided that each is appropriately dated and signed in accordance with § 164.512(i)(2)(i) and (v).

(ii) Identity of public officials. A covered entity may rely, if such reliance is reasonable under the circumstances, on any of the following to verify identity when the disclosure of protected health information is to a public official or a person acting on behalf of the public official:

(A) If the request is made in person, presentation of an agency identification badge, other official credentials, or other proof of government status;

(B) If the request is in writing, the request is on the appropriate government letterhead; or

(C) If the disclosure is to a person acting on behalf of a public official, a written statement on appropriate government letterhead that the person is acting under the government's authority or other evidence or documentation of agency, such as a contract for services, memorandum of understanding, or purchase order, that establishes that the person is acting on behalf of the public official.

(iii) Authority of public officials. A covered entity may rely, if such reliance is reasonable under the circumstances, on any of the following to verify authority when the disclosure of protected health information is to a public official or a person acting on behalf of the public official:

(A) A written statement of the legal authority under which the information is requested, or, if a written statement would be impracticable, an oral statement of such legal authority;

(B) If a request is made pursuant to legal process, warrant, subpoena, order, or other legal process issued by a grand jury or a judicial or administrative tribunal is presumed to constitute legal authority.

(iv) Exercise of professional judgment. The verification requirements of this paragraph are met if the covered entity relies on the exercise of professional judgment in making a use or disclosure in accordance with § 164.510 or acts on a good faith belief in making a disclosure in accordance with § 164.512(j).

§ 164.520 Notice of privacy practices for protected health information.

(a) Standard: notice of privacy practices—

(1) Right to notice. Except as provided by paragraph (a)(2) or (3) of this section, an individual has a right to adequate notice of the uses and disclosures of protected health information that may be made by the covered entity, and of the individual's rights and the covered entity's legal duties with respect to protected health information.

(2) Exception for group health plans.

(i) An individual enrolled in a group health plan has a right to notice:

(A) From the group health plan, if, and to the extent that, such an individual does not receive health benefits under the group health plan through an insurance contract with a health insurance issuer or HMO; or

(B) From the health insurance issuer or HMO with respect to the group health plan through which such individuals receive their health benefits under the group health plan.

(ii) A group health plan that provides health benefits solely through an insurance contract with a health insurance issuer or HMO, and that creates or receives protected health information in addition to summary health information as defined in § 164.504(a) or information on whether the individual is participating in the group health plan, or is enrolled in or has disenrolled from a health insurance issuer or HMO offered by the plan, must:

(A) Maintain a notice under this section; and

(B) Provide such notice upon request to any person. The provisions of paragraph (c)(1) of this section do not apply to such group health plan.

(iii) A group health plan that provides health benefits solely through an insurance contract with a health insurance issuer or HMO, and does not create or receive protected health information other than summary health information as defined in § 164.504(a) or information on whether an individual is participating in the group health plan, or is enrolled in or has disenrolled from a health insurance issuer or HMO offered by the plan, is not required to maintain or provide a notice under this section.

(3) Exception for inmates. An inmate does not have a right to notice under this section, and the requirements of this section do not apply to a correctional institution that is a covered entity.

(b) Implementation specifications: content of notice—

(1) Required elements. The covered entity must provide a notice that is written in plain language and that contains the elements required by this paragraph.

(i) Header. The notice must contain the following statement as a header or otherwise prominently displayed: "THIS NOTICE DESCRIBES HOW MEDICAL INFORMATION ABOUT YOU MAY BE USED AND DISCLOSED AND HOW YOU CAN GET ACCESS TO THIS INFORMATION. PLEASE REVIEW IT CAREFULLY."

(ii) Uses and disclosures. The notice must contain:

(A) A description, including at least one example, of the types of uses and disclosures that the covered entity is permitted by this subpart to make for each of the following purposes: treatment, payment, and health care operations.

(B) A description of each of the other purposes for which the covered entity is permitted or required by this subpart to use or disclose protected health information without the individual's written authorization.

(C) If a use or disclosure for any purpose described in paragraphs (b)(1)(ii)(A) or (B) of this section is prohibited or materially limited by other applicable law, the description of such use or disclosure must reflect the more stringent law as defined in § 160.202 of this subchapter.

(D) For each purpose described in paragraph (b)(1)(ii)(A) or (B) of this section, the description must include sufficient detail to place the individual on notice of the uses and disclosures that are permitted or required by this subpart and other applicable law.

(E) A statement that other uses and disclosures will be made only with the individual's written authorization and that the individual may revoke such authorization as provided by § 164.508(b)(5).

(iii) Separate statements for certain uses or disclosures. If the covered entity intends to engage in any of the following activities, the description required by paragraph (b)(1)(ii)(A) of this section must include a separate statement, as applicable, that:

(A) The covered entity may contact the individual to provide appointment reminders or information about treatment alternatives or other health-related benefits and services that may be of interest to the individual;

(B) The covered entity may contact the individual to raise funds for the covered entity; or

(C) A group health plan, or a health insurance issuer or HMO with respect to a group health plan, may disclose protected health information to the sponsor of the plan.

(iv) Individual rights. The notice must contain a statement of the individual's rights with respect to protected health information and a brief description of how the individual may exercise these rights, as follows:

(A) The right to request restrictions on certain uses and disclosures of protected health information as provided by § 164.522(a), including a statement that the covered entity is not required to agree to a requested restriction;

(B) The right to receive confidential communications of protected health information as provided by § 164.522(b), as applicable;

(C) The right to inspect and copy protected health information as provided by § 164.524;

(D) The right to amend protected health information as provided by § 164.526;

(E) The right to receive an accounting of disclosures of protected health information as provided by § 164.528; and

(F) The right of an individual, including an individual who has agreed to receive the notice electronically in accordance with paragraph (c)(3) of this section, to obtain a paper copy of the notice from the covered entity upon request.

(v) Covered entity's duties. The notice must contain:

(A) A statement that the covered entity is required by law to maintain the privacy of protected health information and to provide individuals with notice of its legal duties and privacy practices with respect to protected health information;

(B) A statement that the covered entity is required to abide by the terms of the notice currently in effect; and

(C) For the covered entity to apply a change in a privacy practice that is described in the notice to protected health information that the covered entity created or received prior to issuing a revised notice, in accordance with § 164.530(i)(2)(ii), a statement that it reserves the right to change the terms of its notice and to make the new notice provisions effective for all protected health information that it maintains. The statement must also describe how it will provide individuals with a revised notice.

(vi) Complaints. The notice must contain a statement that individuals may complain to the covered entity and to the Secretary if they believe their privacy rights have been violated, a brief description of how the individual may file a complaint with the covered entity, and a statement that the individual will not be retaliated against for filing a complaint.

(vii) Contact. The notice must contain the name, or title, and telephone number of a person or office to contact for further information as required by § 164.530(a)(1)(ii).

(viii) Effective date. The notice must contain the date on which the notice is first in effect, which may not be earlier than the date on which the notice is printed or otherwise published.

(2) Optional elements.

(i) In addition to the information required by paragraph (b)(1) of this section, if a covered entity elects to limit the uses or disclosures that it is permitted to make under this subpart, the covered entity may describe its more limited uses or disclosures in its notice, provided that the covered entity may not include in its notice a limitation affecting its right to make a use or disclosure that is required by law or permitted by § 164.512(j)(1)(i).

(ii) For the covered entity to apply a change in its more limited uses and disclosures to protected health information created or received prior to issuing a revised notice, in accordance with § 164.530(i)(2)(ii), the notice must include the statements required by paragraph (b)(1)(v)(C) of this section.

(3) Revisions to the notice. The covered entity must promptly revise and distribute its notice whenever there is a material change to the uses or disclosures, the individual's rights, the covered entity's legal duties, or other privacy practices stated in the notice. Except when required by law, a material change to any term of the notice may not be implemented prior to the effective date of the notice in which such material change is reflected.

(c) Implementation specifications: Provision of notice. A covered entity must make the notice required by this section available on request to any person and to individuals as specified in paragraphs (c)(1) through (c)(3) of this section, as applicable.

(1) Specific requirements for health plans.

(i) A health plan must provide notice:

(A) No later than the compliance date for the health plan, to individuals then covered by the plan;

(B) Thereafter, at the time of enrollment, to individuals who are new enrollees; and

(C) Within 60 days of a material revision to the notice, to individuals then covered by the plan.

(ii) No less frequently than once every three years, the health plan must notify individuals then covered by the plan of the availability of the notice and how to obtain the notice.

(iii) The health plan satisfies the requirements of paragraph (c)(1) of this section if notice is provided to the named insured of a policy under which coverage is provided to the named insured and one or more dependents.

(iv) If a health plan has more than one notice, it satisfies the requirements of paragraph (c)(1) of this section by providing the notice that is relevant to the individual or other person requesting the notice.

(2) Specific requirements for certain covered health care providers. A covered health care provider that has a direct treatment relationship with an individual must:

(i) Provide the notice:

(A) No later than the date of the first service delivery, including service delivered electronically, to such individual after the compliance date for the covered health care provider; or

(B) In an emergency treatment situation, as soon as reasonably practicable after the emergency treatment situation.

(ii) Except in an emergency treatment situation, make a good faith effort to obtain a written acknowledgment of receipt of the notice provided in accordance with paragraph (c)(2)(i) of this section, and if not obtained, document its good faith efforts to obtain such acknowledgment and the reason why the acknowledgment was not obtained;

(iii) If the covered health care provider maintains a physical service delivery site:

(A) Have the notice available at the service delivery site for individuals to request to take with them; and

(B) Post the notice in a clear and prominent location where it is reasonable to expect individuals seeking service from the covered health care provider to be able to read the notice; and

(iv) Whenever the notice is revised, make the notice available upon request on or after the effective date of the revision and promptly comply with the requirements of paragraph (c)(2)(iii) of this section, if applicable.

(3) Specific requirements for electronic notice.

(i) A covered entity that maintains a web site that provides information about the covered entity's customer services or benefits must prominently post its notice on the web site and make the notice available electronically through the web site.

(ii) A covered entity may provide the notice required by this section to an individual by e-mail, if the individual agrees to electronic notice and such agreement has not been withdrawn. If the covered entity knows that the e-mail transmission has failed, a paper copy of the notice must be provided to the individual. Provision of electronic notice by the covered entity will satisfy the provision requirements of paragraph (c) of this section when timely made in accordance with paragraph (c)(1) or (2) of this section.

(iii) For purposes of paragraph (c)(2)(i) of this section, if the first service delivery to an individual is delivered electronically, the covered health care provider must provide electronic notice automatically and contemporaneously in response to the individual's first request for service. The requirements in paragraph (c)(2)(ii) of this section apply to electronic notice.

(iv) The individual who is the recipient of electronic notice retains the right to obtain a paper copy of the notice from a covered entity upon request.

(d) Implementation specifications: Joint notice by separate covered entities. Covered entities that participate in organized health care arrangements may comply with this section by a joint notice, provided that:

(1) The covered entities participating in the organized health care arrangement agree to abide by the terms of the notice with respect to protected health information created or received by the covered entity as part of its participation in the organized health care arrangement;

(2) The joint notice meets the implementation specifications in paragraph (b) of this section, except that the statements required by this section may be altered to reflect the fact that the notice covers more than one covered entity; and

(i) Describes with reasonable specificity the covered entities, or class of entities, to which the joint notice applies;

(ii) Describes with reasonable specificity the service delivery sites, or classes of service delivery sites, to which the joint notice applies; and

(iii) If applicable, states that the covered entities participating in the organized health care arrangement will share protected health information with each other, as necessary to carry out treatment, payment, or health care operations relating to the organized health care arrangement.

(3) The covered entities included in the joint notice must provide the notice to individuals in accordance with the applicable implementation specifications of paragraph (c) of this section. Provision of the joint notice to an individual by any one of the covered entities included in the joint notice will satisfy the provision requirement of paragraph (c) of this section with respect to all others covered by the joint notice.

(e) Implementation specifications: Documentation. A covered entity must document compliance with the notice requirements, as required by § 164.530(j), by retaining copies of the notices issued by the covered entity and, if applicable, any written acknowledgments of receipt of the notice or documentation of good faith efforts to obtain such written acknowledgment, in accordance with paragraph (c)(2)(ii) of this section.

§ 164.522 Rights to request privacy protection for protected health information.

(a)(1) Standard: Right of an individual to request restriction of uses and disclosures.

(i) A covered entity must permit an individual to request that the covered entity restrict:

(A) Uses or disclosures of protected health information about the individual to carry out treatment, payment, or health care operations; and

(B) Disclosures permitted under § 164.510(b).

(ii) A covered entity is not required to agree to a restriction.

(iii) A covered entity that agrees to a restriction under paragraph (a)(1)(i) of this section may not use or disclose protected health information in violation of such restriction, except that, if the individual who requested the restriction is in need of emergency treatment and the restricted protected health information is needed to provide the emergency treatment, the covered entity may use the restricted protected health information, or may disclose such information to a health care provider, to provide such treatment to the individual.

(iv) If restricted protected health information is disclosed to a health care provider for emergency treatment under paragraph (a)(1)(iii) of this section, the covered entity must request that such health care provider not further use or disclose the information.

(v) A restriction agreed to by a covered entity under paragraph (a) of this section, is not effective under this subpart to prevent uses or disclosures permitted or required under §§ 164.502(a)(2)(ii), 164.510(a) or 164.512.

(2) Implementation specifications: Terminating a restriction. A covered entity may terminate its agreement to a restriction, if :

(i) The individual agrees to or requests the termination in writing;

(ii) The individual orally agrees to the termination and the oral agreement is documented; or

(iii) The covered entity informs the individual that it is terminating its agreement to a restriction, except that such termination is only effective with respect to protected health information created or received after it has so informed the individual.

(3) Implementation specification: Documentation. A covered entity that agrees to a restriction must document the restriction in accordance with § 164.530(j).

(b)(1) Standard: Confidential communications requirements.

(i) A covered health care provider must permit individuals to request and must accommodate reasonable requests by individuals to receive communications of protected health information from the covered health care provider by alternative means or at alternative locations.

(ii) A health plan must permit individuals to request and must accommodate reasonable requests by individuals to receive communications of protected health information from the health plan by alternative means or at alternative locations, if the individual clearly states that the disclosure of all or part of that information could endanger the individual.

(2) Implementation specifications: Conditions on providing confidential communications.

(i) A covered entity may require the individual to make a request for a confidential communication described in paragraph (b)(1) of this section in writing.

(ii) A covered entity may condition the provision of a reasonable accommodation on:

(A) When appropriate, information as to how payment, if any, will be handled; and

(B) Specification of an alternative address or other method of contact.

(iii) A covered health care provider may not require an explanation from the individual as to the basis for the request as a condition of providing communications on a confidential basis.

(iv) A health plan may require that a request contain a statement that disclosure of all or part of the information to which the request pertains could endanger the individual.

§ 164.524 Access of individuals to protected health information.

(a) Standard: Access to protected health information.

(1) Right of access. Except as otherwise provided in paragraph (a)(2) or (a)(3) of this section, an individual has a right of access to inspect and obtain a copy of protected health information about the individual in a designated record set, for as long as the protected health information is maintained in the designated record set, except for:

(i) Psychotherapy notes;

(ii) Information compiled in reasonable anticipation of, or for use in, a civil, criminal, or administrative action or proceeding; and

(iii) Protected health information maintained by a covered entity that is:

(A) Subject to the Clinical Laboratory Improvements Amendments of 1988, 42 U.S.C. 263a, to the extent the provision of access to the individual would be prohibited by law; or

(B) Exempt from the Clinical Laboratory Improvements Amendments of 1988, pursuant to 42 CFR 493.3(a)(2).

(2) Unreviewable grounds for denial. A covered entity may deny an individual access without providing the individual an opportunity for review, in the following circumstances.

(i) The protected health information is excepted from the right of access by paragraph (a)(1) of this section.

(ii) A covered entity that is a correctional institution or a covered health care provider acting under the direction of the correctional institution may deny, in whole or in part, an inmate's request to obtain a copy of protected health information, if obtaining such copy would jeopardize the health, safety, security, custody, or rehabilitation of the individual or of other inmates, or the safety of any officer, employee, or other person at the correctional institution or responsible for the transporting of the inmate.

(iii) An individual's access to protected health information created or obtained by a covered health care provider in the course of research that includes treatment may be temporarily suspended for as long as the research is in progress, provided that the individual has agreed to the denial of access when consenting to participate in the research that includes treatment, and the covered health care provider has informed the individual that the right of access will be reinstated upon completion of the research.

(iv) An individual's access to protected health information that is contained in records that are subject to the Privacy Act, 5 U.S.C. 552a, may be denied, if the denial of access under the Privacy Act would meet the requirements of that law.

(v) An individual's access may be denied if the protected health information was obtained from someone other than a health care provider under a promise of confidentiality and the access requested would be reasonably likely to reveal the source of the information.

(3) Reviewable grounds for denial. A covered entity may deny an individual access, provided that the individual is given a right to have such denials reviewed, as required by paragraph (a)(4) of this section, in the following circumstances:

(i) A licensed health care professional has determined, in the exercise of professional judgment, that the access requested is reasonably likely to endanger the life or physical safety of the individual or another person;

(ii) The protected health information makes reference to another person (unless such other person is a health care provider) and a licensed health care professional has determined, in the exercise of professional judgment, that the access requested is reasonably likely to cause substantial harm to such other person; or

(iii) The request for access is made by the individual's personal representative and a licensed health care professional has determined, in the exercise of professional judgment, that the provision of access to such personal representative is reasonably likely to cause substantial harm to the individual or another person.

(4) Review of a denial of access. If access is denied on a ground permitted under paragraph (a)(3) of this section, the individual has the right to have the denial reviewed by a licensed health care professional who is designated by the covered entity to act as a reviewing official and who did not participate in the original decision to deny. The covered entity must provide or deny access in accordance with the determination of the reviewing official under paragraph (d)(4) of this section.

(b) Implementation specifications: requests for access and timely action.

(1) Individual's request for access. The covered entity must permit an individual to request access to inspect or to obtain a copy of the protected health information about the individual that is maintained in a designated record set. The covered entity may require individuals to make requests for access in writing, provided that it informs individuals of such a requirement.

(2) Timely action by the covered entity.

(i) Except as provided in paragraph (b)(2)(ii) of this section, the covered entity must act on a request for access no later than 30 days after receipt of the request as follows.

(A) If the covered entity grants the request, in whole or in part, it must inform the individual of the acceptance of the request and provide the access requested, in accordance with paragraph (c) of this section.

(B) If the covered entity denies the request, in whole or in part, it must provide the individual with a written denial, in accordance with paragraph (d) of this section.

(ii) If the request for access is for protected health information that is not maintained or accessible to the covered entity on-site, the covered entity must take an action required by paragraph (b)(2)(i) of this section by no later than 60 days from the receipt of such a request.

(iii) If the covered entity is unable to take an action required by paragraph (b)(2)(i)(A) or (B) of this section within the time required by paragraph (b)(2)(i) or (ii) of this section, as applicable, the covered entity may extend the time for such actions by no more than 30 days, provided that:

(A) The covered entity, within the time limit set by paragraph (b)(2)(i) or (ii) of this section, as applicable, provides the individual with a written statement of the reasons for the delay and the date by which the covered entity will complete its action on the request; and

(B) The covered entity may have only one such extension of time for action on a request for access.

(c) Implementation specifications: Provision of access. If the covered entity provides an individual with access, in whole or in part, to protected health information, the covered entity must comply with the following requirements.

(1) Providing the access requested. The covered entity must provide the access requested by individuals, including inspection or obtaining a copy, or both, of the protected health information about them in designated record sets. If the same protected health information that is the subject of a request for access is maintained in more than one designated record set or at more than one location, the covered entity need only produce the protected health information once in response to a request for access.

(2) Form of access requested.

(i) The covered entity must provide the individual with access to the protected health information in the form or format requested by the individual, if it is readily producible in such form or format; or, if not, in a readable hard copy form or such other form or format as agreed to by the covered entity and the individual.

(ii) The covered entity may provide the individual with a summary of the protected health information requested, in lieu of providing access to the protected health information or may provide an explanation of the protected health information to which access has been provided, if:

(A) The individual agrees in advance to such a summary or explanation; and

(B) The individual agrees in advance to the fees imposed, if any, by the covered entity for such summary or explanation.

(3) Time and manner of access. The covered entity must provide the access as requested by the individual in a timely manner as required by paragraph (b)(2) of this section, including arranging with the individual for a convenient time and place to inspect or obtain a copy of the protected health information, or mailing the copy of the protected health information at the individual's request. The covered entity may discuss the scope, format, and other aspects of the request for access with the individual as necessary to facilitate the timely provision of access.

(4) Fees. If the individual requests a copy of the protected health information or agrees to a summary or explanation of such information, the covered entity may impose a reasonable, cost-based fee, provided that the fee includes only the cost of:

(i) Copying, including the cost of supplies for and labor of copying, the protected health information requested by the individual;

(ii) Postage, when the individual has requested the copy, or the summary or explanation, be mailed; and

(iii) Preparing an explanation or summary of the protected health information, if agreed to by the individual as required by paragraph (c)(2)(ii) of this section.

(d) Implementation specifications: Denial of access. If the covered entity denies access, in whole or in part, to protected health information, the covered entity must comply with the following requirements.

(1) Making other information accessible. The covered entity must, to the extent possible, give the individual access to any other protected health information requested, after excluding the protected health information as to which the covered entity has a ground to deny access.

(2) Denial. The covered entity must provide a timely, written denial to the individual, in accordance with paragraph (b)(2) of this section. The denial must be in plain language and contain:

(i) The basis for the denial;

(ii) If applicable, a statement of the individual's review rights under paragraph (a)(4) of this section, including a description of how the individual may exercise such review rights; and

(iii) A description of how the individual may complain to the covered entity pursuant to the complaint procedures in § 164.530(d) or to the Secretary pursuant to the procedures in § 160.306. The description must include the name, or title, and telephone number of the contact person or office designated in § 164.530(a)(1)(ii).

(3) Other responsibility. If the covered entity does not maintain the protected health information that is the subject of the individual's request for access, and the covered entity knows where the requested information is maintained, the covered entity must inform the individual where to direct the request for access.

(4) Review of denial requested. If the individual has requested a review of a denial under paragraph (a)(4) of this section, the covered entity must designate a licensed health care professional, who was not directly involved in the denial to review the decision to deny access. The covered entity must promptly refer a request for review to such designated reviewing official. The designated reviewing official must determine, within a reasonable period of time, whether or not to deny the access requested based on the standards in paragraph (a)(3) of this section. The covered entity must promptly provide written notice to the individual of the determination of the designated reviewing official and take other action as required by this section to carry out the designated reviewing official's determination.

(e) Implementation specification: Documentation. A covered entity must document the following and retain the documentation as required by § 164.530(j):

(1) The designated record sets that are subject to access by individuals; and

(2) The titles of the persons or offices responsible for receiving and processing requests for access by individuals.

§ 164.526 Amendment of protected health information.

(a) Standard: Right to amend.

(1) Right to amend. An individual has the right to have a covered entity amend protected health information or a record about the individual in a designated record set for as long as the protected health information is maintained in the designated record set.

(2) Denial of amendment. A covered entity may deny an individual's request for amendment, if it determines that the protected health information or record that is the subject of the request:

(i) Was not created by the covered entity, unless the individual provides a reasonable basis to believe that the originator of protected health information is no longer available to act on the requested amendment;

(ii) Is not part of the designated record set;

(iii) Would not be available for inspection under § 164.524; or

(iv) Is accurate and complete.

(b) Implementation specifications: requests for amendment and timely action.

(1) Individual's request for amendment. The covered entity must permit an individual to request that the covered entity amend the protected health information maintained in the designated record set. The covered entity may require individuals to make requests for amendment in writing and to provide a reason to support a requested amendment, provided that it informs individuals in advance of such requirements.

(2) Timely action by the covered entity.

(i) The covered entity must act on the individual's request for an amendment no later than 60 days after receipt of such a request, as follows.

(A) If the covered entity grants the requested amendment, in whole or in part, it must take the actions required by paragraphs (c)(1) and (2) of this section.

(B) If the covered entity denies the requested amendment, in whole or in part, it must provide the individual with a written denial, in accordance with paragraph (d)(1) of this section.

(ii) If the covered entity is unable to act on the amendment within the time required by paragraph (b)(2)(i) of this section, the covered entity may extend the time for such action by no more than 30 days, provided that:

(A) The covered entity, within the time limit set by paragraph (b)(2)(i) of this section, provides the individual with a written statement of the reasons for the delay and the date by which the covered entity will complete its action on the request; and

(B) The covered entity may have only one such extension of time for action on a request for an amendment.

(c) Implementation specifications: Accepting the amendment. If the covered entity accepts the requested amendment, in whole or in part, the covered entity must comply with the following requirements.

(1) Making the amendment. The covered entity must make the appropriate amendment to the protected health information or record that is the subject of the request for amendment by, at a minimum, identifying the records in the designated record set that are affected by the amendment and appending or otherwise providing a link to the location of the amendment.

(2) Informing the individual. In accordance with paragraph (b) of this section, the covered entity must timely inform the individual that the amendment is accepted and obtain the individual's identification of and agreement to have the covered entity notify the relevant persons with which the amendment needs to be shared in accordance with paragraph (c)(3) of this section.

(3) Informing others. The covered entity must make reasonable efforts to inform and provide the amendment within a reasonable time to:

(i) Persons identified by the individual as having received protected health information about the individual and needing the amendment; and

(ii) Persons, including business associates, that the covered entity knows have the protected health information that is the subject of the amendment and that may have relied, or could foreseeably rely, on such information to the detriment of the individual.

(d) Implementation specifications: Denying the amendment. If the covered entity denies the requested amendment, in whole or in part, the covered entity must comply with the following requirements.

(1) Denial. The covered entity must provide the individual with a timely, written denial, in accordance with paragraph (b)(2) of this section. The denial must use plain language and contain:

(i) The basis for the denial, in accordance with paragraph (a)(2) of this section;

(ii) The individual's right to submit a written statement disagreeing with the denial and how the individual may file such a statement;

(iii) A statement that, if the individual does not submit a statement of disagreement, the individual may request that the covered entity provide the individual's request for amendment and the denial with any future disclosures of the protected health information that is the subject of the amendment; and

(iv) A description of how the individual may complain to the covered entity pursuant to the complaint procedures established in § 164.530(d) or to the Secretary pursuant to the procedures established in § 160.306. The description must include the name, or title, and telephone number of the contact person or office designated in § 164.530(a)(1)(ii).

(2) Statement of disagreement. The covered entity must permit the individual to submit to the covered entity a written statement disagreeing with the denial of all or part of a requested amendment and the basis of such disagreement. The covered entity may reasonably limit the length of a statement of disagreement.

(3) Rebuttal statement. The covered entity may prepare a written rebuttal to the individual's statement of disagreement. Whenever such a rebuttal is prepared, the covered entity must provide a copy to the individual who submitted the statement of disagreement.

(4) Recordkeeping. The covered entity must, as appropriate, identify the record or protected health information in the designated record set that is the subject of the disputed amendment and append or otherwise link the individual's request for an amendment, the covered entity's denial of the request, the individual's statement of disagreement, if any, and the covered entity's rebuttal, if any, to the designated record set.

(5) Future disclosures.

(i) If a statement of disagreement has been submitted by the individual, the covered entity must include the material appended in accordance with paragraph (d)(4) of this section, or, at the election of the covered entity, an accurate summary of any such information, with any subsequent disclosure of the protected health information to which the disagreement relates.

(ii) If the individual has not submitted a written statement of disagreement, the covered entity must include the individual's request for amendment and its denial, or an accurate summary of such information, with any subsequent disclosure of the protected health information only if the individual has requested such action in accordance with paragraph (d)(1)(iii) of this section.

(iii) When a subsequent disclosure described in paragraph (d)(5)(i) or (ii) of this section is made using a standard transaction under part 162 of this subchapter that does not permit the additional material to be included with the disclosure, the covered entity may separately transmit the material required by paragraph (d)(5)(i) or (ii) of this section, as applicable, to the recipient of the standard transaction.

(e) Implementation specification: Actions on notices of amendment. A covered entity that is informed by another covered entity of an amendment to an individual's protected health information, in accordance with paragraph (c)(3) of this section, must amend the protected health information in designated record sets as provided by paragraph (c)(1) of this section.

(f) Implementation specification: Documentation. A covered entity must document the titles of the persons or offices responsible for receiving and processing requests for amendments by individuals and retain the documentation as required by § 164.530(j).

§ 164.528 Accounting of disclosures of protected health information.

(a) Standard: Right to an accounting of disclosures of protected health information.

(1) An individual has a right to receive an accounting of disclosures of protected health information made by a covered entity in the six years prior to the date on which the accounting is requested, except for disclosures:

(i) To carry out treatment, payment and health care operations as provided in § 164.506;

(ii) To individuals of protected health information about them as provided in § 164.502;

(iii) Incident to a use or disclosure otherwise permitted or required by this subpart, as provided in § 164.502;

(iv) Pursuant to an authorization as provided in § 164.508;

(v) For the facility's directory or to persons involved in the individual's care or other notification purposes as provided in § 164.510;

(vi) For national security or intelligence purposes as provided in § 164.512(k)(2);

(vii) To correctional institutions or law enforcement officials as provided in § 164.512(k)(5);

(viii) As part of a limited data set in accordance with § 164.514(e); or

(ix) That occurred prior to the compliance date for the covered entity.

(2)(i) The covered entity must temporarily suspend an individual's right to receive an accounting of disclosures to a health oversight agency or law enforcement official, as provided in § 164.512(d) or (f), respectively, for the time specified by such agency or official, if such agency or official provides the covered entity with a written statement that such an accounting to the individual would be reasonably likely to impede the agency's activities and specifying the time for which such a suspension is required.

(ii) If the agency or official statement in paragraph (a)(2)(i) of this section is made orally, the covered entity must:

(A) Document the statement, including the identity of the agency or official making the statement;

(B) Temporarily suspend the individual's right to an accounting of disclosures subject to the statement; and

(C) Limit the temporary suspension to no longer than 30 days from the date of the oral statement, unless a written statement pursuant to paragraph (a)(2)(i) of this section is submitted during that time.

(3) An individual may request an accounting of disclosures for a period of time less than six years from the date of the request.

(b) Implementation specifications: Content of the accounting. The covered entity must provide the individual with a written accounting that meets the following requirements.

(1) Except as otherwise provided by paragraph (a) of this section, the accounting must include disclosures of protected health information that occurred during the six years (or such shorter time period at the request of the individual as provided in paragraph (a)(3) of this section) prior to the date of the request for an accounting, including disclosures to or by business associates of the covered entity.

(2) Except as otherwise provided by paragraphs (b)(3) or (b)(4) of this section, the accounting must include for each disclosure:

(i) The date of the disclosure;

(ii) The name of the entity or person who received the protected health information and, if known, the address of such entity or person;

(iii) A brief description of the protected health information disclosed; and

(iv) A brief statement of the purpose of the disclosure that reasonably informs the individual of the basis for the disclosure or, in lieu of such statement, a copy of a written request for a disclosure under §§ 164.502(a)(2)(ii) or 164.512, if any.

(3) If, during the period covered by the accounting, the covered entity has made multiple disclosures of protected health information to the same person or entity for a single purpose under §§ 164.502(a)(2)(ii) or 164.512, the accounting may, with respect to such multiple disclosures, provide:

(i) The information required by paragraph (b)(2) of this section for the first disclosure during the accounting period;

(ii) The frequency, periodicity, or number of the disclosures made during the accounting period; and

(iii) The date of the last such disclosure during the accounting period.

(4)(i) If, during the period covered by the accounting, the covered entity has made disclosures of protected health information for a particular research purpose in accordance with § 164.512(i) for 50 or more individuals, the accounting may, with respect to such disclosures for which the protected health information about the individual may have been included, provide:

(A) The name of the protocol or other research activity;

(B) A description, in plain language, of the research protocol or other research activity, including the purpose of the research and the criteria for selecting particular records;

(C) A brief description of the type of protected health information that was disclosed;

(D) The date or period of time during which such disclosures occurred, or may have occurred, including the date of the last such disclosure during the accounting period;

(E) The name, address, and telephone number of the entity that sponsored the research and of the researcher to whom the information was disclosed; and

(F) A statement that the protected health information of the individual may or may not have been disclosed for a particular protocol or other research activity.

(ii) If the covered entity provides an accounting for research disclosures, in accordance with paragraph (b)(4) of this section, and if it is reasonably likely that the protected health information of the individual was disclosed for such research protocol or activity, the covered entity shall, at the request of the individual, assist in contacting the entity that sponsored the research and the researcher.

(c) Implementation specifications: Provision of the accounting.

(1) The covered entity must act on the individual's request for an accounting, no later than 60 days after receipt of such a request, as follows.

(i) The covered entity must provide the individual with the accounting requested; or

(ii) If the covered entity is unable to provide the accounting within the time required by paragraph (c)(1) of this section, the covered entity may extend the time to provide the accounting by no more than 30 days, provided that:

(A) The covered entity, within the time limit set by paragraph (c)(1) of this section, provides the individual with a written statement of the reasons for the delay and the date by which the covered entity will provide the accounting; and

(B) The covered entity may have only one such extension of time for action on a request for an accounting.

(2) The covered entity must provide the first accounting to an individual in any 12 month period without charge. The covered entity may impose a reasonable, cost-based fee for each subsequent request for an accounting by the same individual within the 12 month period, provided that the covered entity informs the individual in advance of the fee and provides the individual with an opportunity to withdraw or modify the request for a subsequent accounting in order to avoid or reduce the fee.

(d) Implementation specification: Documentation. A covered entity must document the following and retain the documentation as required by § 164.530(j):

(1) The information required to be included in an accounting under paragraph (b) of this section for disclosures of protected health information that are subject to an accounting under paragraph (a) of this section;

(2) The written accounting that is provided to the individual under this section; and

(3) The titles of the persons or offices responsible for receiving and processing requests for an accounting by individuals.

§ 164.530 Administrative requirements.

(a)(1) Standard: Personnel designations.

(i) A covered entity must designate a privacy official who is responsible for the development and implementation of the policies and procedures of the entity.

(ii) A covered entity must designate a contact person or office who is responsible for receiving complaints under this section and who is able to provide further information about matters covered by the notice required by § 164.520.

(2) Implementation specification: Personnel designations. A covered entity must document the personnel designations in paragraph (a)(1) of this section as required by paragraph (j) of this section.

(b)(1) Standard: Training. A covered entity must train all members of its workforce on the policies and procedures with respect to protected health information required by this subpart, as necessary and appropriate for the members of the workforce to carry out their function within the covered entity.

(2) Implementation specifications: Training.

(i) A covered entity must provide training that meets the requirements of paragraph (b)(1) of this section, as follows:

(A) To each member of the covered entity's workforce by no later than the compliance date for the covered entity;

(B) Thereafter, to each new member of the workforce within a reasonable period of time after the person joins the covered entity's workforce; and

(C) To each member of the covered entity's workforce whose functions are affected by a material change in the policies or procedures required by this subpart, within a reasonable period of time after the material change becomes effective in accordance with paragraph (i) of this section.

(ii) A covered entity must document that the training as described in paragraph (b)(2)(i) of this section has been provided, as required by paragraph (j) of this section.

(c)(1) Standard: Safeguards. A covered entity must have in place appropriate administrative, technical, and physical safeguards to protect the privacy of protected health information.

(2)(i) Implementation specification: Safeguards. A covered entity must reasonably safeguard protected health information from any intentional or unintentional use or disclosure that is in violation of the standards, implementation specifications or other requirements of this subpart.

(ii) A covered entity must reasonably safeguard protected health information to limit incidental uses or disclosures made pursuant to an otherwise permitted or required use or disclosure.

(d)(1) Standard: Complaints to the covered entity. A covered entity must provide a process for individuals to make complaints concerning the covered entity's policies and procedures required by this subpart or its compliance with such policies and procedures or the requirements of this subpart.

(2) Implementation specification: Documentation of complaints. As required by paragraph (j) of this section, a covered entity must document all complaints received, and their disposition, if any.

(e)(1) Standard: Sanctions. A covered entity must have and apply appropriate sanctions against members of its workforce who fail to comply with the privacy policies and procedures of the covered entity or the requirements of this subpart. This standard does not apply to a member of the covered entity's workforce with respect to actions that are covered by and that meet the conditions of § 164.502(j) or paragraph (g)(2) of this section.

(2) Implementation specification: Documentation. As required by paragraph (j) of this section, a covered entity must document the sanctions that are applied, if any.

(f) Standard: Mitigation. A covered entity must mitigate, to the extent practicable, any harmful effect that is known to the covered entity of a use or disclosure of protected health information in violation of its policies and procedures or the requirements of this subpart by the covered entity or its business associate.

(g) Standard: refraining from intimidating or retaliatory acts. A covered entity—

(1) May not intimidate, threaten, coerce, discriminate against, or take other retaliatory action against any individual for the exercise by the individual of any right established, or for participation in any process provided for by this subpart, including the filing of a complaint under this section; and

(2) Must refrain from intimidation and retaliation as provided in § 160.316 of this subchapter.

(h) Standard: Waiver of rights. A covered entity may not require individuals to waive their rights under § 160.306 of this subchapter or this subpart as a condition of the provision of treatment, payment, enrollment in a health plan, or eligibility for benefits.

(i)(1) Standard: Policies and procedures. A covered entity must implement policies and procedures with respect to protected health information that are designed to comply with the standards, implementation specifications, or other requirements of this subpart. The policies and procedures must be reasonably designed, taking into account the size of and the type of activities that relate to protected health information undertaken by the covered entity, to ensure such compliance. This standard is not to be construed to permit or excuse an action that violates any other standard, implementation specification, or other requirement of this subpart.

(2) Standard: Changes to policies or procedures.

(i) A covered entity must change its policies and procedures as necessary and appropriate to comply with changes in the law, including the standards, requirements, and implementation specifications of this subpart;

(ii) When a covered entity changes a privacy practice that is stated in the notice described in § 164.520, and makes corresponding changes to its policies and procedures, it may make the changes effective for protected health information that it created or received prior to the effective date of the notice revision, if the covered entity has, in accordance with § 164.520(b)(1)(v)(C), included in the notice a statement reserving its right to make such a change in its privacy practices; or

(iii) A covered entity may make any other changes to policies and procedures at any time, provided that the changes are documented and implemented in accordance with paragraph (i)(5) of this section.

(3) Implementation specification: Changes in law. Whenever there is a change in law that necessitates a change to the covered entity's policies or procedures, the covered entity must promptly document and implement the revised policy or procedure. If the change in law materially affects the content of the notice required by § 164.520, the covered entity must promptly make the appropriate revisions to the notice in accordance with § 164.520(b)(3). Nothing in this paragraph may be used by a covered entity to excuse a failure to comply with the law.

(4) Implementation specifications: Changes to privacy practices stated in the notice.

(i) To implement a change as provided by paragraph (i)(2)(ii) of this section, a covered entity must:

(A) Ensure that the policy or procedure, as revised to reflect a change in the covered entity's privacy practice as stated in its notice, complies with the standards, requirements, and implementation specifications of this subpart;

(B) Document the policy or procedure, as revised, as required by paragraph (j) of this section; and

(C) Revise the notice as required by § 164.520(b)(3) to state the changed practice and make the revised notice available as required by § 164.520(c). The covered entity may not implement a change to a policy or procedure prior to the effective date of the revised notice.

(ii) If a covered entity has not reserved its right under § 164.520(b)(1)(v)(C) to change a privacy practice that is stated in the notice, the covered entity is bound by the privacy practices as stated in the notice with respect to protected health information created or received while such notice is in effect. A covered entity may change a privacy practice that is stated in the notice, and the related policies and procedures, without having reserved the right to do so, provided that:

(A) Such change meets the implementation specifications in paragraphs (i)(4)(i)(A)-(C) of this section; and

(B) Such change is effective only with respect to protected health information created or received after the effective date of the notice.

(5) Implementation specification: Changes to other policies or procedures. A covered entity may change, at any time, a policy or procedure that does not materially affect the content of the notice required by § 164.520, provided that:

(i) The policy or procedure, as revised, complies with the standards, requirements, and implementation specifications of this subpart; and

(ii) Prior to the effective date of the change, the policy or procedure, as revised, is documented as required by paragraph (j) of this section.

(j)(1) Standard: Documentation. A covered entity must:

(i) Maintain the policies and procedures provided for in paragraph (i) of this section in written or electronic form;

(ii) If a communication is required by this subpart to be in writing, maintain such writing, or an electronic copy, as documentation; and

(iii) If an action, activity, or designation is required by this subpart to be documented, maintain a written or electronic record of such action, activity, or designation.

(2) Implementation specification: Retention period. A covered entity must retain the documentation required by paragraph (j)(1) of this section for six years from the date of its creation or the date when it last was in effect, whichever is later.

(k) Standard: Group health plans.

(1) A group health plan is not subject to the standards or implementation specifications in paragraphs (a) through (f) and (i) of this section, to the extent that:

(i) The group health plan provides health benefits solely through an insurance contract with a health insurance issuer or an HMO; and

(ii) The group health plan does not create or receive protected health information, except for:

(A) Summary health information as defined in § 164.504(a); or

(B) Information on whether the individual is participating in the group health plan, or is enrolled in or has disenrolled from a health insurance issuer or HMO offered by the plan.

(2) A group health plan described in paragraph (k)(1) of this section is subject to the standard and implementation specification in paragraph (j) of this section only with respect to plan documents amended in accordance with § 164.504(f).

§ 164.532 Transition provisions.

(a) Standard: Effect of prior authorizations. Notwithstanding §§ 164.508 and 164.512(i), a covered entity may use or disclose protected health information, consistent with paragraphs (b) and (c) of this section, pursuant to an authorization or other express legal permission obtained from an individual permitting the use or disclosure of protected health information, informed consent of the individual to participate in research, or a waiver of informed consent by an IRB.

(b) Implementation specification: Effect of prior authorization for purposes other than research. Notwithstanding any provisions in § 164.508, a covered entity may use or disclose protected health information that it created or received prior to the applicable compliance date of this subpart pursuant to an authorization or other express legal permission obtained from an individual prior to the applicable compliance date of this subpart, provided that the authorization or other express legal permission specifically permits such use or disclosure and there is no agreed-to restriction in accordance with § 164.522(a).

(c) Implementation specification: Effect of prior permission for research. Notwithstanding any provisions in §§ 164.508 and 164.512(i), a covered entity may, to the extent allowed by one of the following permissions, use or disclose, for research, protected health information that it created or received either before or after the applicable compliance date of this subpart, provided that there is no agreed-to restriction in accordance with § 164.522(a), and the covered entity has obtained, prior to the applicable compliance date, either:

> **(1)** An authorization or other express legal permission from an individual to use or disclose protected health information for the research;
>
> **(2)** The informed consent of the individual to participate in the research; or
>
> **(3)** A waiver, by an IRB, of informed consent for the research, in accordance with 7 CFR 1c.116(d), 10 CFR 745.116(d), 14 CFR 1230.116(d), 15 CFR 27.116(d), 16 CFR 1028.116(d), 21 CFR 50.24, 22 CFR 225.116(d), 24 CFR 60.116(d), 28 CFR 46.116(d), 32 CFR 219.116(d), 34 CFR 97.116(d), 38 CFR 16.116(d), 40 CFR 26.116(d), 45 CFR 46.116(d), 45 CFR 690.116(d), or 49 CFR 11.116(d), provided that a covered entity must obtain authorization in accordance with § 164.508 if, after the compliance date, informed consent is sought from an individual participating in the research.

(d) Standard: Effect of prior contracts or other arrangements with business associates. Notwithstanding any other provisions of this subpart, a covered entity, other than a small health plan, may disclose protected health information to a business associate and may allow a business associate to create, receive, or use protected health information on its behalf pursuant to a written contract or other written arrangement with such business associate that does not comply with §§ 164.502(e) and 164.504(e) consistent with the requirements, and only for such time, set forth in paragraph (e) of this section.

(e) Implementation specification: Deemed compliance—

> **(1) Qualification.** Notwithstanding other sections of this subpart, a covered entity, other than a small health plan, is deemed to be in compliance with the documentation and contract requirements of §§ 164.502(e) and 164.504(e), with respect to a particular business associate relationship, for the time period set forth in paragraph (e)(2) of this section, if:
>
> **(i)** Prior to October 15, 2002, such covered entity has entered into and is operating pursuant to a written contract or other written arrangement with a business associate for such business

associate to perform functions or activities or provide services that make the entity a business associate; and

(ii) The contract or other arrangement is not renewed or modified from October 15, 2002, until the compliance date set forth in § 164.534.

(2) Limited deemed compliance period. A prior contract or other arrangement that meets the qualification requirements in paragraph (e) of this section, shall be deemed compliant until the earlier of:

(i) The date such contract or other arrangement is renewed or modified on or after the compliance date set forth in § 164.534; or

(ii) April 14, 2004.

(3) Covered entity responsibilities. Nothing in this section shall alter the requirements of a covered entity to comply with part 160, subpart C of this subchapter and §§ 164.524, 164.526, 164.528, and 164.530(f) with respect to protected health information held by a business associate.

§ 164.534 Compliance dates for initial implementation of the privacy standards.

(a) Health care providers. A covered health care provider must comply with the applicable requirements of this subpart no later than April 14, 2003.

(b) Health plans. A health plan must comply with the applicable requirements of this subpart no later than the following as applicable:

(1) Health plans other than small health plans. April 14, 2003.

(2) Small health plans. April 14, 2004.

(c) Health clearinghouses. A health care clearinghouse must comply with the applicable requirements of this subpart no later than April 14, 2003.

DNA Identification Act (1994)

42 U.S.C.A. §§ 14131 – 14134, as amended

Statutes in Context

The DNA Identification Act establishes rules under which the FBI is to create an index of DNA identification records. The statute also sets out the information to be contained in this index and the circumstances under which these data are to be disclosed to other agencies and individuals.

§ 14131. Quality assurance and proficiency testing standards

(a) Publication of quality assurance and proficiency testing standards

(1)(A) Not later than 180 days after September 13, 1994, the Director of the Federal Bureau of Investigation shall appoint an advisory board on DNA quality assurance methods from among nominations proposed by the head of the National Academy of Sciences and professional societies of crime laboratory officials.

(B) The advisory board shall include as members scientists from State, local, and private forensic laboratories, molecular geneticists and population geneticists not affiliated with a forensic laboratory, and a representative from the National Institute of Standards and Technology.

(C) The advisory board shall develop, and if appropriate, periodically revise, recommended standards for quality assurance, including standards for testing the proficiency of forensic laboratories, and forensic analysts, in conducting analyses of DNA.

(2) The Director of the Federal Bureau of Investigation, after taking into consideration such recommended standards, shall issue (and revise from time to time) standards for quality assurance, including standards for testing the proficiency of forensic laboratories, and forensic analysts, in conducting analyses of DNA.

(3) The standards described in paragraphs (1) and (2) shall specify criteria for quality assurance and proficiency tests to be applied to the various types of DNA analyses used by forensic laboratories. The standards shall also include a system for grading proficiency testing performance to determine whether a laboratory is performing acceptably.

(4) Until such time as the advisory board has made recommendations to the Director of the Federal Bureau of Investigation and the Director has acted upon those recommendations, the quality assurance guidelines adopted by the technical working group on DNA analysis methods shall be deemed the Director's standards for purposes of this section.

(b) Administration of advisory board

(1) For administrative purposes, the advisory board appointed under subsection (a) of this section shall be considered an advisory board to the Director of the Federal Bureau of Investigation.

(2) Section 14 of the Federal Advisory Committee Act (5 U.S.C. App.) shall not apply with respect to the advisory board appointed under subsection (a) of this section.

(3) The DNA advisory board established under this section shall be separate and distinct from any other advisory board administered by the FBI, and is to be administered separately.

(4) The board shall cease to exist on the date 5 years after the initial appointments are made to the board, unless the existence of the board is extended by the Director of the Federal Bureau of Investigation.

(c) Proficiency testing program

(1) Not later than 1 year after the effective date of this Act, the Director of the National Institute of Justice shall certify to the Committees on the Judiciary of the House and Senate that—

(A) the Institute has entered into a contract with, or made a grant to, an appropriate entity for establishing, or has taken other appropriate action to ensure that there is established, not later than 2 years after September 13, 1994, a blind external proficiency testing program for DNA analyses, which shall be available to public and private laboratories performing forensic DNA analyses;

(B) a blind external proficiency testing program for DNA analyses is already readily available to public and private laboratories performing forensic DNA analyses; or

(C) it is not feasible to have blind external testing for DNA forensic analyses.

(2) As used in this subsection, the term "blind external proficiency test" means a test that is presented to a forensic laboratory through a second agency and appears to the analysts to involve routine evidence.

(3) Notwithstanding any other provision of law, the Attorney General shall make available to the Director of the National Institute of Justice during the first fiscal year in which funds are distributed under this subtitle up to $250,000 from the funds available under part X of Title I of the Omnibus Crime Control and Safe Streets Act of 1968 to carry out this subsection.

§ 14132. Index to facilitate law enforcement exchange of DNA identification information

(a) Establishment of index

The Director of the Federal Bureau of Investigation may establish an index of—

(1) DNA identification records of—

(A) persons convicted of crimes;

(B) persons who have been charged in an indictment or information with a crime; and

(C) other persons whose DNA samples are collected under applicable legal authorities, provided that DNA samples that are voluntarily submitted solely for elimination purposes shall not be included in the National DNA Index System;

(2) analyses of DNA samples recovered from crime scenes;

(3) analyses of DNA samples recovered from unidentified human remains; and

(4) analyses of DNA samples voluntarily contributed from relatives of missing persons.

(b) Information

The index described in subsection (a) of this section shall include only information on DNA identification records and DNA analyses that are—

(1) based on analyses performed by or on behalf of a criminal justice agency (or the Secretary of Defense in accordance with section 1565 of Title 10) in accordance with publicly available standards that satisfy or exceed the guidelines for a quality assurance program for DNA analysis, issued by the Director of the Federal Bureau of Investigation under section 14131 of this title;

(2) prepared by laboratories that—

(A) not later than 2 years after October 30, 2004, have been accredited by a nonprofit professional association of persons actively involved in forensic science that is nationally recognized within the forensic science community; and

(B) undergo external audits, not less than once every 2 years, that demonstrate compliance with standards established by the Director of the Federal Bureau of Investigation; and

(3) maintained by Federal, State, and local criminal justice agencies (or the Secretary of Defense in accordance with section 1565 of Title 10) pursuant to rules that allow disclosure of stored DNA samples and DNA analyses only—

(A) to criminal justice agencies for law enforcement identification purposes;

(B) in judicial proceedings, if otherwise admissible pursuant to applicable statutes or rules;

(C) for criminal defense purposes, to a defendant, who shall have access to samples and analyses performed in connection with the case in which such defendant is charged; or

(D) if personally identifiable information is removed, for a population statistics database, for identification research and protocol development purposes, or for quality control purposes.

(c) Failure to comply

Access to the index established by this section is subject to cancellation if the quality control and privacy requirements described in subsection (b) of this section are not met.

(d) Expungement of records

(1) By director

(A) The Director of the Federal Bureau of Investigation shall promptly expunge from the index described in subsection (a) of this section the DNA analysis of a person included in the index—

(i) on the basis of conviction for a qualifying Federal offense or a qualifying District of Columbia offense (as determined under sections 14135a, 14135b of this title, respectively), if the Director receives, for each conviction of the person of a qualifying offense, a certified copy of a final court order establishing that such conviction has been overturned; or

(ii) on the basis of an arrest under the authority of the United States, if the Attorney General receives, for each charge against the person on the basis of which the analysis was or could have been included in the index, a certified copy of a final court order establishing that such charge has been dismissed or has resulted in an acquittal or that no charge was filed within the applicable time period.

(B) For purposes of subparagraph (A), the term "qualifying offense" means any of the following offenses:

(i) A qualifying Federal offense, as determined under section 14135a of this title.

(ii) A qualifying District of Columbia offense, as determined under section 14135b of this title.

(iii) A qualifying military offense, as determined under section 1565 of Title 10.

(C) For purposes of subparagraph (A), a court order is not "final" if time remains for an appeal or application for discretionary review with respect to the order.

(2) By States

(A) As a condition of access to the index described in subsection (a) of this section, a State shall promptly expunge from that index the DNA analysis of a person included in the index by that State if—

(i) the responsible agency or official of that State receives, for each conviction of the person of an offense on the basis of which that analysis was or could have been included in the index, a certified copy of a final court order establishing that such conviction has been overturned; or

(ii) the person has not been convicted of an offense on the basis of which that analysis was or could have been included in the index, and the responsible agency or official of that State receives, for each charge against the person on the basis of which the analysis was or could have been included in the index, a certified copy of a final court order establishing that such charge has been dismissed or has resulted in an acquittal or that no charge was filed within the applicable time period.

(B) For purposes of subparagraph (A), a court order is not "final" if time remains for an appeal or application for discretionary review with respect to the order.

(e) Repealed. Pub.L. 109-162, Title X, § 1002(4), Jan. 5, 2006, 119 Stat. 3085

§ 14133. Federal Bureau of Investigation

(a) Proficiency testing requirements

(1) Generally

(A) Personnel at the Federal Bureau of Investigation who perform DNA analyses shall undergo semiannual external proficiency testing by a DNA proficiency testing program meeting the standards issued under section 14131 of this title.

(B) Within 1 year after September 13, 1994, the Director of the Federal Bureau of Investigation shall arrange for periodic blind external tests to determine the proficiency of DNA analysis performed at the Federal Bureau of Investigation laboratory.

(C) In this paragraph, "blind external test" means a test that is presented to the laboratory through a second agency and appears to the analysts to involve routine evidence.

(2) Report

For 5 years after September 13, 1994, the Director of the Federal Bureau of Investigation shall submit to the Committees on the Judiciary of the House and Senate an annual report on the results of each of the tests described in paragraph (1).

(b) Privacy protection standards

(1) Generally

Except as provided in paragraph (2), the results of DNA tests performed for a Federal law enforcement agency for law enforcement purposes may be disclosed only—

(A) to criminal justice agencies for law enforcement identification purposes;

(B) in judicial proceedings, if otherwise admissible pursuant to applicable statues or rules; and

(C) for criminal defense purposes, to a defendant, who shall have access to samples and analyses performed in connection with the case in which such defendant is charged.

(2) Exception

If personally identifiable information is removed, test results may be disclosed for a population statistics database, for identification research and protocol development purposes, or for quality control purposes.

(c) Criminal penalty

(1) A person who—

(A) by virtue of employment or official position, has possession of, or access to, individually identifiable DNA information indexed in a database created or maintained by any Federal law enforcement agency; and

(B) knowingly discloses such information in any manner to any person or agency not authorized to receive it,

shall be fined not more than $100,000.

(2) A person who, without authorization, knowingly obtains DNA samples or individually identifiable DNA information indexed in a database created or maintained by any Federal law enforcement agency shall be fined not more than $250,000, or imprisoned for a period of not more than one year, or both.

§ 14134. Authorization of appropriations

There are authorized to be appropriated to the Federal Bureau of Investigation to carry out sections 14131, 14132, and 14133 of this title—

(1) $5,500,000 for fiscal year 1996;

(2) $8,000,000 for fiscal year 1997;

(3) $8,000,000 for fiscal year 1998;

(4) $2,500,000 for fiscal year 1999; and

(5) $1,000,000 for fiscal year 2000.

VI.
FINANCIAL PRIVACY

Fair Credit Reporting Act (1970)

15 U.S.C. § 1681, as amended

Statutes in Context

The Fair Credit Reporting Act (FCRA) applies to any "consumer reporting agency" that furnishes a "consumer report." A consumer report is any communication by a consumer reporting agency bearing on a consumer's credit worthiness, or personal characteristics used for the purpose of serving to establish the consumer's eligibility for credit, insurance, employment or other purposes. 15 U.S.C. § 1681b(d). Under the Act, a consumer reporting agency can furnish a consumer report only under certain circumstances or certain uses. FCRA also regulates the use of consumer reports for purposes such as law enforcement and employment. FCRA does permit credit reports to be used, without consumer authorization, for transactions that consist of a firm offer of credit.

In 2003, Congress amended FCRA with the Fair and Accurate Credit Transactions Act (FACTA). FACTA provides that consumers may alert one credit reporting agency of potential fraud, and that the credit reporting agency must notify the other credit reporting agencies. FACTA also provides that a credit reporting agency must block the reporting of information after an alleged identity theft and provide a free credit report to consumers once a year.

---

§ 1681. Congressional findings and statement of purpose

(a) Accuracy and fairness of credit reporting

The Congress makes the following findings:

(1) The banking system is dependent upon fair and accurate credit reporting. Inaccurate credit reports directly impair the efficiency of the banking system, and unfair credit reporting methods undermine the public confidence which is essential to the continued functioning of the banking system.

(2) An elaborate mechanism has been developed for investigating and evaluating the credit worthiness, credit standing, credit capacity, character, and general reputation of consumers.

(3) Consumer reporting agencies have assumed a vital role in assembling and evaluating consumer credit and other information on consumers.

(4) There is a need to insure that consumer reporting agencies exercise their grave responsibilities with fairness, impartiality, and a respect for the consumer's right to privacy.

(b) Reasonable procedures

It is the purpose of this subchapter to require that consumer reporting agencies adopt reasonable procedures for meeting the needs of commerce for consumer credit, personnel, insurance, and other information in a manner which is fair and equitable to the consumer, with regard to the confidentiality, accuracy, relevancy, and proper utilization of such information in accordance with the requirements of this subchapter.

§ 1681a. Definitions; rules of construction

(a) Definitions and rules of construction set forth in this section are applicable for the purposes of this subchapter.**(b)** The term "person" means any individual, partnership, corporation, trust, estate, cooperative, association, government or governmental subdivision or agency, or other entity.

(c) The term "consumer" means an individual.

(d) Consumer report.

(1) In general.

The term "consumer report" means any written, oral, or other communication of any information by a consumer reporting agency bearing on a consumer's credit worthiness, credit standing, credit capacity, character, general reputation, personal characteristics, or mode of living which is used or expected to be used or collected in whole or in part for the purpose of serving as a factor in establishing the consumer's eligibility for—

(A) credit or insurance to be used primarily for personal, family, or household purposes;

(B) employment purposes; or

(C) any other purpose authorized under section 1681b of this title.

(2) Exclusions.

Except as provided in paragraph (3), the term "consumer report" does not include—

(A) subject to section 1681s-3 of this title, any—

(i) report containing information solely as to transactions or experiences between the consumer and the person making the report;

(ii) communication of that information among persons related by common ownership or affiliated by corporate control; or

(iii) communication of other information among persons related by common ownership or affiliated by corporate control, if it is clearly and conspicuously disclosed to the consumer that the information may be communicated among such persons and the consumer is given the opportunity, before the time that the information is initially communicated, to direct that such information not be communicated among such persons;

(B) any authorization or approval of a specific extension of credit directly or indirectly by the issuer of a credit card or similar device;

(C) any report in which a person who has been requested by a third party to make a specific extension of credit directly or indirectly to a consumer conveys his or her decision with respect to such request, if the third party advises the consumer of the name and address of the person to whom the request was made, and such person makes the disclosures to the consumer required under section 1681m of this title; or

(D) a communication described in subsection (o) or (x) of this section.

(3) Restriction on sharing of medical information

Except for information or any communication of information disclosed as provided in section 1681b(g)(3) of this title, the exclusions in paragraph (2) shall not apply with respect to information disclosed to any person related by common ownership or affiliated by corporate control, if the information is—

(A) medical information;

(B) an individualized list or description based on the payment transactions of the consumer for medical products or services; or

(C) an aggregate list of identified consumers based on payment transactions for medical products or services.

(e) The term "investigative consumer report" means a consumer report or portion thereof in which information on a consumer's character, general reputation, personal characteristics, or mode of living is obtained through personal interviews with neighbors, friends, or associates of the consumer reported on or with others with whom he is acquainted or who may have knowledge concerning any such items of information. However, such information shall not include specific factual information on a consumer's credit record obtained directly from a creditor of the consumer or from a consumer reporting agency when such information was obtained directly from a creditor of the consumer or from the consumer.

(f) The term "consumer reporting agency" means any person which, for monetary fees, dues, or on a cooperative nonprofit basis, regularly engages in whole or in part in the practice of assembling or evaluating consumer credit information or other information on consumers for the purpose of furnishing consumer reports to third parties, and which uses any means or facility of interstate commerce for the purpose of preparing or furnishing consumer reports.

(g) The term "file", when used in connection with information on any consumer, means all of the information on that consumer recorded and retained by a consumer reporting agency regardless of how the information is stored.

(h) The term "employment purposes" when used in connection with a consumer report means a report used for the purpose of evaluating a consumer for employment, promotion, reassignment or retention as an employee.

(i) Medical information

The term "medical information"—

(1) means information or data, whether oral or recorded, in any form or medium, created by or derived from a health care provider or the consumer, that relates to—

(A) the past, present, or future physical, mental, or behavioral health or condition of an individual;

(B) the provision of health care to an individual; or

(C) the payment for the provision of health care to an individual.

(2) does not include the age or gender of a consumer, demographic information about the consumer, including a consumer's residence address or e-mail address, or any other information about a consumer that does not relate to the physical, mental, or behavioral health or condition of a consumer, including the existence or value of any insurance policy.

(j) Definitions relating to child support obligations

(1) Overdue support

The term "overdue support" has the meaning given to such term in section 666(e) of Title 42.

(2) State or local child support enforcement agency

The term "State or local child support enforcement agency" means a State or local agency which administers a State or local program for establishing and enforcing child support obligations.

(k) Adverse action.

(1) Actions included.

The term "adverse action"—

(A) has the same meaning as in section 1691(d)(6) of this title; and

(B) means—

(i) a denial or cancellation of, an increase in any charge for, or a reduction or other adverse or unfavorable change in the terms of coverage or amount of, any insurance, existing or applied for, in connection with the underwriting of insurance;

(ii) a denial of employment or any other decision for employment purposes that adversely affects any current or prospective employee;

(iii) a denial or cancellation of, an increase in any charge for, or any other adverse or unfavorable change in the terms of, any license or benefit described in section 1681b(a)(3)(D) of this title; and

(iv) an action taken or determination that is—

(I) made in connection with an application that was made by, or a transaction that was initiated by, any consumer, or in connection with a review of an account under section 1681b(a)(3)(F)(ii) of this title; and

(II) adverse to the interests of the consumer.

(2) Applicable findings, decisions, commentary, and orders.

For purposes of any determination of whether an action is an adverse action under paragraph (1)(A), all appropriate final findings, decisions, commentary, and orders issued under section 1691(d)(6) of this title by the Board of Governors of the Federal Reserve System or any court shall apply.

(l) Firm offer of credit or insurance.

The term "firm offer of credit or insurance" means any offer of credit or insurance to a consumer that will be honored if the consumer is determined, based on information in a consumer report on the consumer, to meet the specific criteria used to select the consumer for the offer, except that the offer may be further conditioned on one or more of the following:

(1) The consumer being determined, based on information in the consumer's application for the credit or insurance, to meet specific criteria bearing on credit worthiness or insurability, as applicable, that are established—

(A) before selection of the consumer for the offer; and

(B) for the purpose of determining whether to extend credit or insurance pursuant to the offer.

(2) Verification

(A) that the consumer continues to meet the specific criteria used to select the consumer for the offer, by using information in a consumer report on the consumer, information in the consumer's application for the credit or insurance, or other information bearing on the credit worthiness or insurability of the consumer; or

(B) of the information in the consumer's application for the credit or insurance, to determine that the consumer meets the specific criteria bearing on credit worthiness or insurability.

(3) The consumer furnishing any collateral that is a requirement for the extension of the credit or insurance that was—

(A) established before selection of the consumer for the offer of credit or insurance; and

(B) disclosed to the consumer in the offer of credit or insurance.

(m) Credit or insurance transaction that is not initiated by the consumer.

The term "credit or insurance transaction that is not initiated by the consumer" does not include the use of a consumer report by a person with which the consumer has an account or insurance policy, for purposes of—

(1) reviewing the account or insurance policy; or

(2) collecting the account.

(n) State.

The term "State" means any State, the Commonwealth of Puerto Rico, the District of Columbia, and any territory or possession of the United States.

(o) Excluded communications.

A communication is described in this subsection if it is a communication—

(1) that, but for subsection (d)(2)(D) of this section, would be an investigative consumer report;

(2) that is made to a prospective employer for the purpose of—

(A) procuring an employee for the employer; or

(B) procuring an opportunity for a natural person to work for the employer;

(3) that is made by a person who regularly performs such procurement;

(4) that is not used by any person for any purpose other than a purpose described in subparagraph (A) or (B) of paragraph (2); and

(5) with respect to which—

(A) the consumer who is the subject of the communication—

(i) consents orally or in writing to the nature and scope of the communication, before the collection of any information for the purpose of making the communication;

(ii) consents orally or in writing to the making of the communication to a prospective employer, before the making of the communication; and

(iii) in the case of consent under clause (i) or (ii) given orally, is provided written confirmation of that consent by the person making the communication, not later than 3 business days after the receipt of the consent by that person;

(B) the person who makes the communication does not, for the purpose of making the communication, make any inquiry that if made by a prospective employer of the consumer who is the subject of the communication would violate any applicable Federal or State equal employment opportunity law or regulation; and

(C) the person who makes the communication—

(i) discloses in writing to the consumer who is the subject of the communication, not later than 5 business days after receiving any request from the consumer for such disclosure, the nature and substance of all information in the consumer's file at the time of the request, except that the sources of any information that is acquired solely for use in making the communication and is actually used for no other purpose, need not be disclosed other than under appropriate discovery procedures in any court of competent jurisdiction in which an action is brought; and

(ii) notifies the consumer who is the subject of the communication, in writing, of the consumer's right to request the information described in clause (i).

(p) Consumer reporting agency that compiles and maintains files on consumers on a nationwide basis.

The term "consumer reporting agency that compiles and maintains files on consumers on a nationwide basis" means a consumer reporting agency that regularly engages in the practice of assembling or evaluating, and maintaining, for the purpose of furnishing consumer reports to third parties bearing on a consumer's credit worthiness, credit standing, or credit capacity, each of the following regarding consumers residing nationwide:

(1) Public record information.

(2) Credit account information from persons who furnish that information regularly and in the ordinary course of business.

(q) Definitions relating to fraud alerts

(1) Active duty military consumer

The term "active duty military consumer" means a consumer in military service who—

(A) is on active duty (as defined in section 101(d)(1) of Title 10) or is a reservist performing duty under a call or order to active duty under a provision of law referred to in section 101(a)(13) of Title 10; and

(B) is assigned to service away from the usual duty station of the consumer.

(2) Fraud alert; active duty alert

The terms "fraud alert" and "active duty alert" mean a statement in the file of a consumer that—

(A) notifies all prospective users of a consumer report relating to the consumer that the consumer may be a victim of fraud, including identity theft, or is an active duty military consumer, as applicable; and

(B) is presented in a manner that facilitates a clear and conspicuous view of the statement described in subparagraph (A) by any person requesting such consumer report.

(3) Identity theft

The term "identity theft" means a fraud committed using the identifying information of another person, subject to such further definition as the Commission may prescribe, by regulation.

(4) Identity theft report

The term "identity theft report" has the meaning given that term by rule of the Commission, and means, at a minimum, a report—

(A) that alleges an identity theft;

(B) that is a copy of an official, valid report filed by a consumer with an appropriate Federal, State, or local law enforcement agency, including the United States Postal Inspection Service, or such other government agency deemed appropriate by the Commission; and

(C) the filing of which subjects the person filing the report to criminal penalties relating to the filing of false information if, in fact, the information in the report is false.

(5) New credit plan

The term "new credit plan" means a new account under an open end credit plan (as defined in section 1602(i) of this title) or a new credit transaction not under an open end credit plan.

(r) Credit and debit related terms

(1) Card issuer

The term "card issuer" means—

(A) a credit card issuer, in the case of a credit card; and

(B) a debit card issuer, in the case of a debit card.

(2) Credit card

The term "credit card" has the same meaning as in section 1602 of this title.

(3) Debit card

The term "debit card" means any card issued by a financial institution to a consumer for use in initiating an electronic fund transfer from the account of the consumer at such financial institution, for the purpose of transferring money between accounts or obtaining money, property, labor, or services.

(4) Account and electronic fund transfer

The terms "account" and "electronic fund transfer" have the same meanings as in section 1693a of this title.

(5) Credit and creditor

The terms "credit" and "creditor" have the same meanings as in section 1691a of this title.

(s) Federal banking agency

The term "Federal banking agency" has the same meaning as in section 1813 of Title 12.

(t) Financial institution

The term "financial institution" means a State or National bank, a State or Federal savings and loan association, a mutual savings bank, a State or Federal credit union, or any other person that, directly or indirectly, holds a transaction account (as defined in section 461(b) of Title 12) belonging to a consumer.

(u) Reseller

The term "reseller" means a consumer reporting agency that—

(1) assembles and merges information contained in the database of another consumer reporting agency or multiple consumer reporting agencies concerning any consumer for purposes of furnishing such information to any third party, to the extent of such activities; and

(2) does not maintain a database of the assembled or merged information from which new consumer reports are produced.

(v) Commission

The term "Commission" means the Federal Trade Commission.

(w) Nationwide specialty consumer reporting agency

The term "nationwide specialty consumer reporting agency" means a consumer reporting agency that compiles and maintains files on consumers on a nationwide basis relating to—

(1) medical records or payments;

(2) residential or tenant history;

(3) check writing history;

(4) employment history; or

(5) insurance claims.

(x) Exclusion of certain communications for employee investigations

(1) Communications described in this subsection

A communication is described in this subsection if—

(A) but for subsection (d)(2)(D) of this section, the communication would be a consumer report;

(B) the communication is made to an employer in connection with an investigation of—

(i) suspected misconduct relating to employment; or

(ii) compliance with Federal, State, or local laws and regulations, the rules of a self-regulatory organization, or any preexisting written policies of the employer;

(C) the communication is not made for the purpose of investigating a consumer's credit worthiness, credit standing, or credit capacity; and

(D) the communication is not provided to any person except—

(i) to the employer or an agent of the employer;

(ii) to any Federal or State officer, agency, or department, or any officer, agency, or department of a unit of general local government;

(iii) to any self-regulatory organization with regulatory authority over the activities of the employer or employee;

(iv) as otherwise required by law; or

(v) pursuant to section 1681f of this title.

(2) Subsequent disclosure

After taking any adverse action based in whole or in part on a communication described in paragraph (1), the employer shall disclose to the consumer a summary containing the nature and substance of the communication upon which the adverse action is based, except that the sources of information acquired solely for use in preparing what would be but for subsection (d)(2)(D) of this section an investigative consumer report need not be disclosed.

(3) Self-regulatory organization defined

For purposes of this subsection, the term "self-regulatory organization" includes any self-regulatory organization (as defined in section 78c(a)(26) of this title), any entity established under title I of the Sarbanes-Oxley Act of 2002, any board of trade designated by the Commodity Futures Trading Commission, and any futures association registered with such Commission.

§ 1681b. Permissible purposes of consumer reports

(a) In general

Subject to subsection (c) of this section, any consumer reporting agency may furnish a consumer report under the following circumstances and no other:

(1) In response to the order of a court having jurisdiction to issue such an order, or a subpoena issued in connection with proceedings before a Federal grand jury.

(2) In accordance with the written instructions of the consumer to whom it relates.

(3) To a person which it has reason to believe—

(A) intends to use the information in connection with a credit transaction involving the consumer on whom the information is to be furnished and involving the extension of credit to, or review or collection of an account of, the consumer; or

(B) intends to use the information for employment purposes; or

(C) intends to use the information in connection with the underwriting of insurance involving the consumer; or

(D) intends to use the information in connection with a determination of the consumer's eligibility for a license or other benefit granted by a governmental instrumentality required by law to consider an applicant's financial responsibility or status; or

(E) intends to use the information, as a potential investor or servicer, or current insurer, in connection with a valuation of, or an assessment of the credit or prepayment risks associated with, an existing credit obligation; or

(F) otherwise has a legitimate business need for the information—

(i) in connection with a business transaction that is initiated by the consumer; or

(ii) to review an account to determine whether the consumer continues to meet the terms of the account.

(4) In response to a request by the head of a State or local child support enforcement agency (or a State or local government official authorized by the head of such an agency), if the person making the request certifies to the consumer reporting agency that—

(A) the consumer report is needed for the purpose of establishing an individual's capacity to make child support payments or determining the appropriate level of such payments;

(B) the paternity of the consumer for the child to which the obligation relates has been established or acknowledged by the consumer in accordance with State laws under which the obligation arises (if required by those laws);

(C) the person has provided at least 10 days' prior notice to the consumer whose report is requested, by certified or registered mail to the last known address of the consumer, that the report will be requested; and

(D) the consumer report will be kept confidential, will be used solely for a purpose described in subparagraph (A), and will not be used in connection with any other civil, administrative, or criminal proceeding, or for any other purpose.

(5) To an agency administering a State plan under section 654 of Title 42 for use to set an initial or modified child support award.

(6) To the Federal Deposit Insurance Corporation or the National Credit Union Administration as part of its preparation for its appointment or as part of its exercise of powers, as conservator, receiver, or liquidating agent for an insured depository institution or insured credit union under the Federal Deposit Insurance Act or the Federal Credit Union Act, or other applicable Federal or State law, or in connection with the resolution or liquidation of a failed or failing insured depository institution or insured credit union, as applicable.

(b) Conditions for furnishing and using consumer reports for employment purposes

(1) Certification from user

A consumer reporting agency may furnish a consumer report for employment purposes only if—

(A) the person who obtains such report from the agency certifies to the agency that—

(i) the person has complied with paragraph (2) with respect to the consumer report, and the person will comply with paragraph (3) with respect to the consumer report if paragraph (3) becomes applicable; and

(ii) information from the consumer report will not be used in violation of any applicable Federal or State equal employment opportunity law or regulation; and

(B) the consumer reporting agency provides with the report, or has previously provided, a summary of the consumer's rights under this subchapter, as prescribed by the Federal Trade Commission under section 1681g(c)(3) of this title.

(2) Disclosure to consumer

(A) In general

Except as provided in subparagraph (B), a person may not procure a consumer report, or cause a consumer report to be procured, for employment purposes with respect to any consumer, unless—

(i) a clear and conspicuous disclosure has been made in writing to the consumer at any time before the report is procured or caused to be procured, in a document that consists solely of the disclosure, that a consumer report may be obtained for employment purposes; and

(ii) the consumer has authorized in writing (which authorization may be made on the document referred to in clause (i)) the procurement of the report by that person.

(B) Application by mail, telephone, computer, or other similar means

If a consumer described in subparagraph (C) applies for employment by mail, telephone, computer, or other similar means, at any time before a consumer report is procured or caused to be procured in connection with that application—

(i) the person who procures the consumer report on the consumer for employment purposes shall provide to the consumer, by oral, written, or electronic means, notice that a consumer report may be obtained for employment purposes, and a summary of the consumer's rights under section 1681m(a)(3) of this title; and

(ii) the consumer shall have consented, orally, in writing, or electronically to the procurement of the report by that person.

(C) Scope

Subparagraph (B) shall apply to a person procuring a consumer report on a consumer in connection with the consumer's application for employment only if—

(i) the consumer is applying for a position over which the Secretary of Transportation has the power to establish qualifications and maximum hours of service pursuant to the provisions of section 31502 of Title 49, or a position subject to safety regulation by a State transportation agency; and

(ii) as of the time at which the person procures the report or causes the report to be procured the only interaction between the consumer and the person in connection with that employment application has been by mail, telephone, computer, or other similar means.

(3) Conditions on use for adverse actions

(A) In general

Except as provided in subparagraph (B), in using a consumer report for employment purposes, before taking any adverse action based in whole or in part on the report, the person intending to take such adverse action shall provide to the consumer to whom the report relates—

(i) a copy of the report; and

(ii) a description in writing of the rights of the consumer under this subchapter, as prescribed by the Federal Trade Commission under section 1681g(c)(3) of this title.

(B) Application by mail, telephone, computer, or other similar means

(i) If a consumer described in subparagraph (C) applies for employment by mail, telephone, computer, or other similar means, and if a person who has procured a consumer report on the consumer for employment purposes takes adverse action on the employment application based in whole or in part on the report, then the person must provide to the consumer to whom the report relates, in lieu of the notices required under subparagraph (A) of this section and under section 1681m(a) of this title, within 3 business days of taking such action, an oral, written or electronic notification—

(I) that adverse action has been taken based in whole or in part on a consumer report received from a consumer reporting agency;

(II) of the name, address and telephone number of the consumer reporting agency that furnished the consumer report (including a toll-free telephone number established by the agency if the agency compiles and maintains files on consumers on a nationwide basis);

(III) that the consumer reporting agency did not make the decision to take the adverse action and is unable to provide to the consumer the specific reasons why the adverse action was taken; and

(IV) that the consumer may, upon providing proper identification, request a free copy of a report and may dispute with the consumer reporting agency the accuracy or completeness of any information in a report.

(ii) If, under clause (B)(i)(IV), the consumer requests a copy of a consumer report from the person who procured the report, then, within 3 business days of receiving the consumer's request, together with proper identification, the person must send or provide to the consumer a copy of a report and a copy of the consumer's rights as prescribed by the Federal Trade Commission under section 1681g(c)(3) of this title.

(C) Scope

Subparagraph (B) shall apply to a person procuring a consumer report on a consumer in connection with the consumer's application for employment only if—

(i) the consumer is applying for a position over which the Secretary of Transportation has the power to establish qualifications and maximum hours of service pursuant to the provisions of section 31502 of Title 49, or a position subject to safety regulation by a State transportation agency; and

(ii) as of the time at which the person procures the report or causes the report to be procured the only interaction between the consumer and the person in connection with that employment application has been by mail, telephone, computer, or other similar means.

(4) Exception for national security investigations

(A) In general

In the case of an agency or department of the United States Government which seeks to obtain and use a consumer report for employment purposes, paragraph (3) shall not apply to any adverse action by such agency or department which is based in part on such consumer report, if the head of such agency or department makes a written finding that—

(i) the consumer report is relevant to a national security investigation of such agency or department;

(ii) the investigation is within the jurisdiction of such agency or department;

(iii) there is reason to believe that compliance with paragraph (3) will—

(I) endanger the life or physical safety of any person;

(II) result in flight from prosecution;

(III) result in the destruction of, or tampering with, evidence relevant to the investigation;

(IV) result in the intimidation of a potential witness relevant to the investigation;

(V) result in the compromise of classified information; or

(VI) otherwise seriously jeopardize or unduly delay the investigation or another official proceeding.

(B) Notification of consumer upon conclusion of investigation

Upon the conclusion of a national security investigation described in subparagraph (A), or upon the determination that the exception under subparagraph (A) is no longer required for the reasons set forth in such subparagraph, the official exercising the authority in such subparagraph shall provide to the consumer who is the subject of the consumer report with regard to which such finding was made—

(i) a copy of such consumer report with any classified information redacted as necessary;

(ii) notice of any adverse action which is based, in part, on the consumer report; and

(iii) the identification with reasonable specificity of the nature of the investigation for which the consumer report was sought.

(C) Delegation by head of agency or department

For purposes of subparagraphs (A) and (B), the head of any agency or department of the United States Government may delegate his or her authorities under this paragraph to an official of such agency or department who has personnel security responsibilities and is a member of the Senior Executive Service or equivalent civilian or military rank.

(D) Definitions

For purposes of this paragraph, the following definitions shall apply:

(i) Classified information.—The term "classified information" means information that is protected from unauthorized disclosure under Executive Order No. 12958 or successor orders.

(ii) National security investigation.—The term "national security investigation" means any official inquiry by an agency or department of the United States Government to determine the eligibility of a consumer to receive access or continued access to classified information or to determine whether classified information has been lost or compromised.

(E) Repealed. Pub.L. 108-177, Title III, § 361(j), Dec. 13, 2003, 117 Stat. 2625

(F) Redesignated (D)

(c) Furnishing reports in connection with credit or insurance transactions that are not initiated by the consumer

(1) In general

A consumer reporting agency may furnish a consumer report relating to any consumer pursuant to subparagraph (A) or (C) of subsection (a)(3) of this section in connection with any credit or insurance transaction that is not initiated by the consumer only if—

(A) the consumer authorizes the agency to provide such report to such person; or

(B)(i) the transaction consists of a firm offer of credit or insurance;

(ii) the consumer reporting agency has complied with subsection (e) of this section; and

(iii) there is not in effect an election by the consumer, made in accordance with subsection (e) of this section, to have the consumer's name and address excluded from lists of names provided by the agency pursuant to this paragraph.

(2) Limits on information received under paragraph (1)(B)

A person may receive pursuant to paragraph (1)(B) only—

(A) the name and address of a consumer;

(B) an identifier that is not unique to the consumer and that is used by the person solely for the purpose of verifying the identity of the consumer; and

(C) other information pertaining to a consumer that does not identify the relationship or experience of the consumer with respect to a particular creditor or other entity.

(3) Information regarding inquiries

Except as provided in section 1681g(a)(5) of this title, a consumer reporting agency shall not furnish to any person a record of inquiries in connection with a credit or insurance transaction that is not initiated by a consumer.

(d) Reserved

(e) Election of consumer to be excluded from lists

(1) In general

A consumer may elect to have the consumer's name and address excluded from any list provided by a consumer reporting agency under subsection (c)(1)(B) of this section in connection with a credit or insurance transaction that is not initiated by the consumer, by notifying the agency in accordance with paragraph (2) that the consumer does not consent to any use of a consumer report relating to the consumer in connection with any credit or insurance transaction that is not initiated by the consumer.

(2) Manner of notification

A consumer shall notify a consumer reporting agency under paragraph (1)—

(A) through the notification system maintained by the agency under paragraph (5); or

(B) by submitting to the agency a signed notice of election form issued by the agency for purposes of this subparagraph.

(3) Response of agency after notification through system

Upon receipt of notification of the election of a consumer under paragraph (1) through the notification system maintained by the agency under paragraph (5), a consumer reporting agency shall—

(A) inform the consumer that the election is effective only for the 5-year period following the election if the consumer does not submit to the agency a signed notice of election form issued by the agency for purposes of paragraph (2)(B); and

(B) provide to the consumer a notice of election form, if requested by the consumer, not later than 5 business days after receipt of the notification of the election through the system established under paragraph (5), in the case of a request made at the time the consumer provides notification through the system.

(4) Effectiveness of election

An election of a consumer under paragraph (1)—

(A) shall be effective with respect to a consumer reporting agency beginning 5 business days after the date on which the consumer notifies the agency in accordance with paragraph (2);

(B) shall be effective with respect to a consumer reporting agency—

(i) subject to subparagraph (C), during the 5-year period beginning 5 business days after the date on which the consumer notifies the agency of the election, in the case of an election for which a consumer notifies the agency only in accordance with paragraph (2)(A); or

(ii) until the consumer notifies the agency under subparagraph (C), in the case of an election for which a consumer notifies the agency in accordance with paragraph (2)(B);

(C) shall not be effective after the date on which the consumer notifies the agency, through the notification system established by the agency under paragraph (5), that the election is no longer effective; and

(D) shall be effective with respect to each affiliate of the agency.

(5) Notification system

(A) In general

Each consumer reporting agency that, under subsection (c)(1)(B) of this section, furnishes a consumer report in connection with a credit or insurance transaction that is not initiated by a consumer, shall—

(i) establish and maintain a notification system, including a toll-free telephone number, which permits any consumer whose consumer report is maintained by the agency to notify the agency, with appropriate identification, of the consumer's election to have the consumer's name and address excluded from any such list of names and addresses provided by the agency for such a transaction; and

(ii) publish by not later than 365 days after September 30, 1996, and not less than annually thereafter, in a publication of general circulation in the area served by the agency—

(I) a notification that information in consumer files maintained by the agency may be used in connection with such transactions; and

(II) the address and toll-free telephone number for consumers to use to notify the agency of the consumer's election under clause (i).

(B) Establishment and maintenance as compliance

Establishment and maintenance of a notification system (including a toll-free telephone number) and publication by a consumer reporting agency on the agency's own behalf and on behalf of any of its affiliates in accordance with this paragraph is deemed to be compliance with this paragraph by each of those affiliates.

(6) Notification system by agencies that operate nationwide

Each consumer reporting agency that compiles and maintains files on consumers on a nationwide basis shall establish and maintain a notification system for purposes of paragraph (5) jointly with other such consumer reporting agencies.

(f) Certain use or obtaining of information prohibited

A person shall not use or obtain a consumer report for any purpose unless—

(1) the consumer report is obtained for a purpose for which the consumer report is authorized to be furnished under this section; and

(2) the purpose is certified in accordance with section 1681e of this title by a prospective user of the report through a general or specific certification.

(g) Protection of medical information

(1) Limitation on consumer reporting agencies

A consumer reporting agency shall not furnish for employment purposes, or in connection with a credit or insurance transaction, a consumer report that contains medical information (other than medical contact information treated in the manner required under section 605(a)(6) of this title) about a consumer, unless—

(A) if furnished in connection with an insurance transaction, the consumer affirmatively consents to the furnishing of the report;

(B) if furnished for employment purposes or in connection with a credit transaction—

(i) the information to be furnished is relevant to process or effect the employment or credit transaction; and

(ii) the consumer provides specific written consent for the furnishing of the report that describes in clear and conspicuous language the use for which the information will be furnished; or

(C) the information to be furnished pertains solely to transactions, accounts, or balances relating to debts arising from the receipt of medical services, products, or devises, where such information, other than account status or amounts, is restricted or reported using codes that do not identify, or do not provide information sufficient to infer, the specific provider or the nature of such services, products, or devices, as provided in section 1681c(a)(6) of this title.

(2) Limitation on creditors

Except as permitted pursuant to paragraph (3)(C) or regulations prescribed under paragraph (5)(A), a creditor shall not obtain or use medical information (other than medical information treated in the manner required under section 605(a)(6) of this title) pertaining to a consumer in connection with any determination of the consumer's eligibility, or continued eligibility, for credit.

(3) Actions authorized by Federal law, insurance activities and regulatory determinations

Section 1681a(d)(3) of this title shall not be construed so as to treat information or any communication of information as a consumer report if the information or communication is disclosed—

(A) in connection with the business of insurance or annuities, including the activities described in section 18B of the model Privacy of Consumer Financial and Health Information Regulation issued by the National Association of Insurance Commissioners (as in effect on January 1, 2003);

(B) for any purpose permitted without authorization under the Standards for Individually Identifiable Health Information promulgated by the Department of Health and Human Services pursuant to the Health Insurance Portability and Accountability Act of 1996, or referred to under section 1179 of such Act, or described in section 6802(e) of this title; or

(C) as otherwise determined to be necessary and appropriate, by regulation or order and subject to paragraph (6), by the Commission, any Federal banking agency or the National Credit Union Administration (with respect to any financial institution subject to the jurisdiction of such agency or Administration under paragraph (1), (2), or (3) of section 1681s(b) of this title, or the applicable State insurance authority (with respect to any person engaged in providing insurance or annuities).

(4) Limitation on redisclosure of medical information

Any person that receives medical information pursuant to paragraph (1) or (3) shall not disclose such information to any other person, except as necessary to carry out the purpose for which the information was initially disclosed, or as otherwise permitted by statute, regulation, or order.

(5) Regulations and effective date for paragraph (2)

(A) Regulations required

Each Federal banking agency and the National Credit Union Administration shall, subject to paragraph (6) and after notice and opportunity for comment, prescribe regulations that permit transactions under paragraph (2) that are determined to be necessary and appropriate to protect legitimate operational, transactional, risk, consumer, and other needs (and which shall include permitting actions necessary for administrative verification purposes), consistent with the intent of paragraph (2) to restrict the use of medical information for inappropriate purposes.

(B) Final regulations required

The Federal banking agencies and the National Credit Union Administration shall issue the regulations required under subparagraph (A) in final form before the end of the 6-month period beginning on the December 4, 2003.

(6) Coordination with other laws

No provision of this subsection shall be construed as altering, affecting, or superseding the applicability of any other provision of Federal law relating to medical confidentiality.

§ 1681c. Requirements relating to information contained in consumer reports

(a) Information excluded from consumer reports

Except as authorized under subsection (b) of this section, no consumer reporting agency may make any consumer report containing any of the following items of information:

(1) Cases under Title 11 or under the Bankruptcy Act that, from the date of entry of the order for relief or the date of adjudication, as the case may be, antedate the report by more than 10 years.

(2) Civil suits, civil judgments, and records of arrest that, from date of entry, antedate the report by more than seven years or until the governing statute of limitations has expired, whichever is the longer period.

(3) Paid tax liens which, from date of payment, antedate the report by more than seven years.

(4) Accounts placed for collection or charged to profit and loss which antedate the report by more than seven years.

(5) Any other adverse item of information, other than records of convictions of crimes which antedates the report by more than seven years.

(6) The name, address, and telephone number of any medical information furnisher that has notified the agency of its status, unless—

(A) such name, address, and telephone number are restricted or reported using codes that do not identify, or provide information sufficient to infer, the specific provider or the nature of such services, products, or devices to a person other than the consumer; or

(B) the report is being provided to an insurance company for a purpose relating to engaging in the business of insurance other than property and casualty insurance.

(b) Exempted cases

The provisions of paragraphs (1) through (5) of subsection (a) of this section are not applicable in the case of any consumer credit report to be used in connection with—

(1) a credit transaction involving, or which may reasonably be expected to involve, a principal amount of $150,000 or more;

(2) the underwriting of life insurance involving, or which may reasonably be expected to involve, a face amount of $150,000 or more; or

(3) the employment of any individual at an annual salary which equals, or which may reasonably be expected to equal $75,000, or more.

(c) Running of reporting period

(1) In general.—The 7-year period referred to in paragraphs (4) and (6) of subsection (a) of this section shall begin, with respect to any delinquent account that is placed for collection (internally or by referral to a third party, whichever is earlier), charged to profit and loss, or subjected to any similar action, upon the expiration of the 180-day period beginning on the date of the commencement of the delinquency which immediately preceded the collection activity, charge to profit and loss, or similar action.

(2) Effective date.—Paragraph (1) shall apply only to items of information added to the file of a consumer on or after the date that is 455 days after September 30, 1996.

(d) Information required to be disclosed

(1) Title 11 information

Any consumer reporting agency that furnishes a consumer report that contains information regarding any case involving the consumer that arises under Title 11 shall include in the report an identification of the chapter of such Title 11 under which such case arises if provided by the source of the information. If any case arising or filed under Title 11 is withdrawn by the consumer before a final judgment, the consumer reporting agency shall include in the report that such case or filing was withdrawn upon receipt of documentation certifying such withdrawal.

(2) Key factor in credit score information

Any consumer reporting agency that furnishes a consumer report that contains any credit score or any other risk score or predictor on any consumer shall include in the report a clear and conspicuous statement that a key factor (as defined in section 1681g(f)(2)(B) of this title) that adversely affected such score or predictor was the number of enquiries, if such a predictor was in fact a key factor that adversely affected such score. This paragraph shall not apply to a check services company, acting as such, which issues authorizations for the purpose of approving or processing negotiable instruments, electronic fund transfers, or similar methods of payments, but only to the extent that such company is engaged in such activities.

(e) Indication of closure of account by consumer

If a consumer reporting agency is notified pursuant to section 1681s-2(a)(4) of this title that a credit account of a consumer was voluntarily closed by the consumer, the agency shall indicate that fact in any consumer report that includes information related to the account.

(f) Indication of dispute by consumer

If a consumer reporting agency is notified pursuant to section 1681s-2(a)(3) of this title that information regarding a consumer who was furnished to the agency is disputed by the consumer, the agency shall indicate that fact in each consumer report that includes the disputed information.

(g) Truncation of credit card and debit card numbers

(1) In general

Except as otherwise provided in this subsection, no person that accepts credit cards or debit cards for the transaction of business shall print more than the last 5 digits of the card number or the expiration date upon any receipt provided to the cardholder at the point of the sale or transaction.

(2) Limitation

This subsection shall apply only to receipts that are electronically printed, and shall not apply to transactions in which the sole means of recording a credit card or debit card account number is by handwriting or by an imprint or copy of the card.

(3) Effective date

This subsection shall become effective—

(A) 3 years after December 4, 2003, with respect to any cash register or other machine or device that electronically prints receipts for credit card or debit card transactions that is in use before January 1, 2005; and

(B) 1 year after December 4, 2003, with respect to any cash register or other machine or device that electronically prints receipts for credit card or debit card transactions that is first put into use on or after January 1, 2005.

(h) Notice of discrepancy in address

(1) In general

If a person has requested a consumer report relating to a consumer from a consumer reporting agency described in section 1681a(p) of this title, the request includes an address for the consumer that substantially differs from the addresses in the file of the consumer, and the agency provides a consumer report in response to the request, the consumer reporting agency shall notify the requester of the existence of the discrepancy.

(2) Regulations

(A) Regulations required

The Federal banking agencies, the National Credit Union Administration, and the Commission shall jointly, with respect to the entities that are subject to their respective enforcement authority under section 1681s of this title, prescribe regulations providing guidance regarding reasonable policies and procedures that a user of a consumer report should employ when such user has received a notice of discrepancy under paragraph (1).

(B) Policies and procedures to be included

The regulations prescribed under subparagraph (A) shall describe reasonable policies and procedures for use by a user of a consumer report—

(i) to form a reasonable belief that the user knows the identity of the person to whom the consumer report pertains; and

(ii) if the user establishes a continuing relationship with the consumer, and the user regularly and in the ordinary course of business furnishes information to the consumer reporting agency from which the notice of discrepancy pertaining to the consumer was obtained, to reconcile the address of the consumer with the consumer reporting agency by furnishing such address to such consumer reporting agency as part of information regularly furnished by the user for the period in which the relationship is established.

§ 1681c-1. Identity theft prevention; fraud alerts and active duty alerts

(a) One-call fraud alerts

(1) Initial alerts

Upon the direct request of a consumer, or an individual acting on behalf of or as a personal representative of a consumer, who asserts in good faith a suspicion that the consumer has been or is about to become a victim of fraud or related crime, including identity theft, a consumer reporting agency described in section 1681a(p) of this title that maintains a file on the consumer and has received appropriate proof of the identity of the requester shall—

(A) include a fraud alert in the file of that consumer, and also provide that alert along with any credit score generated in using that file, for a period of not less than 90 days, beginning on the date of such request, unless the consumer or such representative requests that such fraud alert be removed before the end of such period, and the agency has received appropriate proof of the identity of the requester for such purpose; and

(B) refer the information regarding the fraud alert under this paragraph to each of the other consumer reporting agencies described in section 1681a(p) of this title, in accordance with procedures developed under section 1681s(f) of this title.

(2) Access to free reports

In any case in which a consumer reporting agency includes a fraud alert in the file of a consumer pursuant to this subsection, the consumer reporting agency shall—

(A) disclose to the consumer that the consumer may request a free copy of the file of the consumer pursuant to section 1681j(d) of this title; and

(B) provide to the consumer all disclosures required to be made under section 1681a of this title, without charge to the consumer, not later than 3 business days after any request described in subparagraph (A).

(b) Extended alerts

(1) In general

Upon the direct request of a consumer, or an individual acting on behalf of or as a personal representative of a consumer, who submits an identity theft report to a consumer reporting agency described in section 1681a(p) of this title that maintains a file on the consumer, if the agency has received appropriate proof of the identity of the requester, the agency shall—

(A) include a fraud alert in the file of that consumer, and also provide that alert along with any credit score generated in using that file, during the 7-year period beginning on the date of such request, unless the consumer or such representative requests that such fraud alert be removed before the end of such period and the agency has received appropriate proof of the identity of the requester for such purpose;

(B) during the 5-year period beginning on the date of such request, exclude the consumer from any list of consumers prepared by the consumer reporting agency and provided to any third party to offer credit or insurance to the consumer as part of a transaction that was not initiated by the consumer, unless the consumer or such representative requests that such exclusion be rescinded before the end of such period; and

(C) refer the information regarding the extended fraud alert under this paragraph to each of the other consumer reporting agencies described in section 1681a(p) of this title, in accordance with procedures developed under section 1681s(f) of this title.

(2) Access to free reports

In any case in which a consumer reporting agency includes a fraud alert in the file of a consumer pursuant to this subsection, the consumer reporting agency shall—

(A) disclose to the consumer that the consumer may request 2 free copies of the file of the consumer pursuant to section 1681j(d) of this title during the 12-month period beginning on the date on which the fraud alert was included in the file; and

(B) provide to the consumer all disclosures required to be made under section 1681g of this title, without charge to the consumer, not later than 3 business days after any request described in subparagraph (A).

(c) Active duty alerts

Upon the direct request of an active duty military consumer, or an individual acting on behalf of or as a personal representative of an active duty military consumer, a consumer reporting agency described in section 1681a(p) of this title that maintains a file on the active duty military consumer and has received appropriate proof of the identity of the requester shall—

(1) include an active duty alert in the file of that active duty military consumer, and also provide that alert along with any credit score generated in using that file, during a period of not less than 12 months, or such longer period as the Commission shall determine, by regulation, beginning on the date of the request, unless the active duty military consumer or such representative requests that such fraud alert be removed before the end of such period, and the agency has received appropriate proof of the identity of the requester for such purpose;

(2) during the 2-year period beginning on the date of such request, exclude the active duty military consumer from any list of consumers prepared by the consumer reporting agency and provided to any third party to offer credit or insurance to the consumer as part of a transaction that was not initiated by the consumer, unless the consumer requests that such exclusion be rescinded before the end of such period; and

(3) refer the information regarding the active duty alert to each of the other consumer reporting agencies described in section 1681a(p) of this title, in accordance with procedures developed under section 1681s(f) of this title.

(d) Procedures

Each consumer reporting agency described in section 1681a(p) of this title shall establish policies and procedures to comply with this section, including procedures that inform consumers of the availability of initial, extended, and active duty alerts and procedures that allow consumers and active duty military consumers to request initial, extended, or active duty alerts (as applicable) in a simple and easy manner, including by telephone.

(e) Referrals of alerts

Each consumer reporting agency described in section 1681a(p) of this title that receives a referral of a fraud alert or active duty alert from another consumer reporting agency pursuant to this section shall, as though the agency received the request from the consumer directly, follow the procedures required under—

(1) paragraphs (1)(A) and (2) of subsection (a) of this section, in the case of a referral under subsection (a)(1)(B) of this section;

(2) paragraphs (1)(A), (1)(B), and (2) of subsection (b) of this section, in the case of a referral under subsection (b)(1)(C) of this section; and

(3) paragraphs (1) and (2) of subsection (c) of this section, in the case of a referral under subsection (c)(3) of this section.

(f) Duty of reseller to reconvey alert
A reseller shall include in its report any fraud alert or active duty alert placed in the file of a consumer pursuant to this section by another consumer reporting agency.

(g) Duty of other consumer reporting agencies to provide contact information

If a consumer contacts any consumer reporting agency that is not described in section 1681a(p) of this title to communicate a suspicion that the consumer has been or is about to become a victim of fraud or related crime, including identity theft, the agency shall provide information to the consumer on how to contact the Commission and the consumer reporting agencies described in section 1681a(p) of this title to obtain more detailed information and request alerts under this section.

(h) Limitations on use of information for credit extensions

(1) Requirements for initial and active duty alerts

(A) Notification

Each initial fraud alert and active duty alert under this section shall include information that notifies all prospective users of a consumer report on the consumer to which the alert relates that the consumer does not authorize the establishment of any new credit plan or extension of credit, other than under an open-end credit plan (as defined in section 1602(i) of this title), in the name of the consumer, or issuance of an additional card on an existing credit account requested by a consumer, or any increase in credit limit on an existing credit account requested by a consumer, except in accordance with subparagraph (B).

(B) Limitation on users

(i) In general

No prospective user of a consumer report that includes an initial fraud alert or an active duty alert in accordance with this section may establish a new credit plan or extension of credit, other than under an open-end credit plan (as defined in section 1602(i) of this title), in the name of the consumer, or issue an additional card on an existing credit account requested by a consumer, or grant any increase in credit limit on an existing credit account requested by a consumer, unless the user utilizes reasonable policies and procedures to form a reasonable belief that the user knows the identity of the person making the request.

(ii) Verification

If a consumer requesting the alert has specified a telephone number to be used for identity verification purposes, before authorizing any new credit plan or extension described in clause (i) in the name of such consumer, a user of such consumer report shall contact the consumer using that telephone number or take reasonable steps to verify the consumer's identity and confirm that the application for a new credit plan is not the result of identity theft.

(2) Requirements for extended alerts

(A) Notification

Each extended alert under this section shall include information that provides all prospective users of a consumer report relating to a consumer with—

(i) notification that the consumer does not authorize the establishment of any new credit plan or extension of credit described in clause (i), other than under an open-end credit plan (as defined in section 1602(i) of this title), in the name of the consumer, or issuance of an additional card on an existing credit account requested by a consumer, or any increase in credit limit on an existing credit account requested by a consumer, except in accordance with subparagraph (B); and

(ii) a telephone number or other reasonable contact method designated by the consumer.

(B) Limitation on users

No prospective user of a consumer report or of a credit score generated using the information in the file of a consumer that includes an extended fraud alert in accordance with this section may establish a new credit plan or extension of credit, other than under an open-end credit plan (as defined in section 1602(i) of this title), in the name of the consumer, or issue an additional card on an existing credit account requested by a consumer, or any increase in credit limit on an existing credit account requested by a consumer, unless the user contacts the consumer in person or using the contact method described in subparagraph (A)(ii) to confirm that the application for a new credit plan or increase in credit limit, or request for an additional card is not the result of identity theft.

§ 1681c-2. Block of information resulting from identity theft

(a) Block

Except as otherwise provided in this section, a consumer reporting agency shall block the reporting of any information in the file of a consumer that the consumer identifies as information that resulted from an alleged identity theft, not later than 4 business days after the date of receipt by such agency of—

(1) appropriate proof of the identity of the consumer;

(2) a copy of an identity theft report;

(3) the identification of such information by the consumer; and

(4) a statement by the consumer that the information is not information relating to any transaction by the consumer.

(b) Notification

A consumer reporting agency shall promptly notify the furnisher of information identified by the consumer under subsection (a) of this section—

(1) that the information may be a result of identity theft;

(2) that an identity theft report has been filed;

(3) that a block has been requested under this section; and

(4) of the effective dates of the block.

(c) Authority to decline or rescind

(1) In general

A consumer reporting agency may decline to block, or may rescind any block, of information relating to a consumer under this section, if the consumer reporting agency reasonably determines that—

(A) the information was blocked in error or a block was requested by the consumer in error;

(B) the information was blocked, or a block was requested by the consumer, on the basis of a material misrepresentation of fact by the consumer relevant to the request to block; or

(C) the consumer obtained possession of goods, services, or money as a result of the blocked transaction or transactions.

(2) Notification to consumer

If a block of information is declined or rescinded under this subsection, the affected consumer shall be notified promptly, in the same manner as consumers are notified of the reinsertion of information under section 1681i(a)(5)(B) of this title.

(3) Significance of block

For purposes of this subsection, if a consumer reporting agency rescinds a block, the presence of information in the file of a consumer prior to the blocking of such information is not evidence of whether the consumer knew or should have known that the consumer obtained possession of any goods, services, or money as a result of the block.

(d) Exception for resellers

(1) No reseller file

This section shall not apply to a consumer reporting agency, if the consumer reporting agency—

(A) is a reseller;

(B) is not, at the time of the request of the consumer under subsection (a) of this section, otherwise furnishing or reselling a consumer report concerning the information identified by the consumer; and

(C) informs the consumer, by any means, that the consumer may report the identity theft to the Commission to obtain consumer information regarding identity theft.

(2) Reseller with file

The sole obligation of the consumer reporting agency under this section, with regard to any request of a consumer under this section, shall be to block the consumer report maintained by the consumer reporting agency from any subsequent use, if—

(A) the consumer, in accordance with the provisions of subsection (a) of this section, identifies, to a consumer reporting agency, information in the file of the consumer that resulted from identity theft; and

(B) the consumer reporting agency is a reseller of the identified information.

(3) Notice

In carrying out its obligation under paragraph (2), the reseller shall promptly provide a notice to the consumer of the decision to block the file. Such notice shall contain the name, address, and telephone number of each consumer reporting agency from which the consumer information was obtained for resale.

(e) Exception for verification companies

The provisions of this section do not apply to a check services company, acting as such, which issues authorizations for the purpose of approving or processing negotiable instruments, electronic fund transfers, or similar methods of payments, except that, beginning 4 business days after receipt of information described in paragraphs (1) through (3) of subsection (a) of this section, a check services company shall not report to a national consumer reporting agency described in section 1681a(p) of this title, any information identified in the subject identity theft report as resulting from identity theft.

(f) Access to blocked information by law enforcement agencies

No provision of this section shall be construed as requiring a consumer reporting agency to prevent a Federal, State, or local law enforcement agency from accessing blocked information in a consumer file to which the agency could otherwise obtain access under this title.

§ 1681d. Disclosure of investigative consumer reports

(a) Disclosure of fact of preparation

A person may not procure or cause to be prepared an investigative consumer report on any consumer unless—

(1) it is clearly and accurately disclosed to the consumer that an investigative consumer report including information as to his character, general reputation, personal characteristics, and mode of living, whichever are applicable, may be made, and such disclosure (A) is made in a writing mailed, or otherwise delivered, to the consumer, not later than three days after the date on which the report was first requested, and (B) includes a statement informing the consumer of his right to request the additional disclosures provided for under subsection (b) of this section and the written summary of the rights of the consumer prepared pursuant to section 1681g(c) of this title; and

(2) the person certifies or has certified to the consumer reporting agency that—

(A) the person has made the disclosures to the consumer required by paragraph (1); and

(B) the person will comply with subsection (b) of this section.

(b) Disclosure on request of nature and scope of investigation

Any person who procures or causes to be prepared an investigative consumer report on any consumer shall, upon written request made by the consumer within a reasonable period of time after the receipt by him of the disclosure required by subsection (a)(1) of this section, make a complete and accurate disclosure of the nature and scope of the investigation requested. This disclosure shall be made in a writing mailed, or otherwise delivered, to the consumer not later than five days after the date on which the request for such disclosure was received from the consumer or such report was first requested, whichever is the later.

(c) Limitation on liability upon showing of reasonable procedures for compliance with provisions

No person may be held liable for any violation of subsection (a) or (b) of this section if he shows by a preponderance of the evidence that at the time of the violation he maintained reasonable procedures to assure compliance with subsection (a) or (b) of this section.

(d) Prohibitions

(1) Certification.—A consumer reporting agency shall not prepare or furnish an investigative consumer report unless the agency has received a certification under subsection (a)(2) of this section from the person who requested the report.

(2) Inquiries.—A consumer reporting agency shall not make an inquiry for the purpose of preparing an investigative consumer report on a consumer for employment purposes if the making of the inquiry by an employer or prospective employer of the consumer would violate any applicable Federal or State equal employment opportunity law or regulation.

(3) Certain public record information.—Except as otherwise provided in section 1681k of this title, a consumer reporting agency shall not furnish an investigative consumer report that includes information that is a matter of public record and that relates to an arrest, indictment, conviction, civil judicial action, tax lien, or outstanding judgment, unless the agency has verified the accuracy of the information during the 30-day period ending on the date on which the report is furnished.

(4) Certain adverse information.—A consumer reporting agency shall not prepare or furnish an investigative consumer report on a consumer that contains information that is adverse to the interest of the consumer and that is obtained through a personal interview with a neighbor, friend, or associate of the consumer or with another person with whom the consumer is acquainted or who has knowledge of such item of information, unless—

(A) the agency has followed reasonable procedures to obtain confirmation of the information, from an additional source that has independent and direct knowledge of the information; or

(B) the person interviewed is the best possible source of the information.

§ 1681e. Compliance procedures

(a) Identity and purposes of credit users

Every consumer reporting agency shall maintain reasonable procedures designed to avoid violations of section 1681c of this title and to limit the furnishing of consumer reports to the purposes listed under section 1681b of this title. These procedures shall require that prospective users of the information identify themselves, certify the purposes for which the information is sought, and certify that the information will be used for no other purpose. Every consumer reporting agency shall make a reasonable effort to verify the identity of a new prospective user and the uses certified by such prospective user prior to furnishing such user a consumer report. No consumer reporting agency may furnish a consumer report to any person if it has reasonable grounds for believing that the consumer report will not be used for a purpose listed in section 1681b of this title.

(b) Accuracy of report

Whenever a consumer reporting agency prepares a consumer report it shall follow reasonable procedures to assure maximum possible accuracy of the information concerning the individual about whom the report relates.

(c) Disclosure of consumer reports by users allowed

A consumer reporting agency may not prohibit a user of a consumer report furnished by the agency on a consumer from disclosing the contents of the report to the consumer, if adverse action against the consumer has been taken by the user based in whole or in part on the report.

(d) Notice to users and furnishers of information

(1) Notice requirement.—A consumer reporting agency shall provide to any person—

> **(A)** who regularly and in the ordinary course of business furnishes information to the agency with respect to any consumer; or
>
> **(B)** to whom a consumer report is provided by the agency;

a notice of such person's responsibilities under this subchapter.

(2) Content of notice.—The Federal Trade Commission shall prescribe the content of notices under paragraph (1), and a consumer reporting agency shall be in compliance with this subsection if it provides a notice under paragraph (1) that is substantially similar to the Federal Trade Commission prescription under this paragraph.

(e) Procurement of consumer report for resale

(1) Disclosure.—A person may not procure a consumer report for purposes of reselling the report (or any information in the report) unless the person discloses to the consumer reporting agency that originally furnishes the report—

> **(A)** the identity of the end-user of the report (or information); and
>
> **(B)** each permissible purpose under section 1681b of this title for which the report is furnished to the end-user of the report (or information).

(2) Responsibilities of procurers for resale.—A person who procures a consumer report for purposes of reselling the report (or any information in the report) shall—

(A) establish and comply with reasonable procedures designed to ensure that the report (or information) is resold by the person only for a purpose for which the report may be furnished under section 1681b of this title, including by requiring that each person to which the report (or information) is resold and that resells or provides the report (or information) to any other person—

(i) identifies each end user of the resold report (or information);

(ii) certifies each purpose for which the report (or information) will be used; and

(iii) certifies that the report (or information) will be used for no other purpose; and

(B) before reselling the report, make reasonable efforts to verify the identifications and certifications made under subparagraph (A).

(3) Resale of consumer report to a federal agency or department.— Notwithstanding paragraph (1) or (2), a person who procures a consumer report for purposes of reselling the report (or any information in the report) shall not disclose the identity of the end-user of the report under paragraph (1) or (2) if—

(A) the end user is an agency or department of the United States Government which procures the report from the person for purposes of determining the eligibility of the consumer concerned to receive access or continued access to classified information (as defined in section 1681b(b)(4)(E)(i) of this title); and

(B) the agency or department certifies in writing to the person reselling the report that nondisclosure is necessary to protect classified information or the safety of persons employed by or contracting with, or undergoing investigation for work or contracting with the agency or department.

§ 1681f. Disclosures to governmental agencies

Notwithstanding the provisions of section 1681b of this title, a consumer reporting agency may furnish identifying information respecting any consumer, limited to his name, address, former addresses, places of employment, or former places of employment, to a governmental agency.

§ 1681g. Disclosures to consumers

(a) Information on file; sources; report recipients

Every consumer reporting agency shall, upon request, and subject to section 1681h(a)(1) of this title, clearly and accurately disclose to the consumer:

(1) All information in the consumer's file at the time of the request, except that—

(A) if the consumer to whom the file relates requests that the first 5 digits of the social security number (or similar identification number) of the consumer not be included in the disclosure and the consumer reporting agency has received appropriate proof of the identity of the requester, the consumer reporting agency shall so truncate such number in such disclosure; and

(B) nothing in this paragraph shall be construed to require a consumer reporting agency to disclose to a consumer any information concerning credit scores or any other risk scores or predictors relating to the consumer.

(2) The sources of the information; except that the sources of information acquired solely for use in preparing an investigative consumer report and actually used for no other purpose need not be disclosed: *Provided*, That in the event an action is brought under this subchapter, such sources shall be available to the plaintiff under appropriate discovery procedures in the court in which the action is brought.

(3)(A) Identification of each person (including each end-user identified under section 1681e(e)(1) of this title) that procured a consumer report—

(i) for employment purposes, during the 2-year period preceding the date on which the request is made; or

(ii) for any other purpose, during the 1-year period preceding the date on which the request is made.

(B) An identification of a person under subparagraph (A) shall include—

(i) the name of the person or, if applicable, the trade name (written in full) under which such person conducts business; and

(ii) upon request of the consumer, the address and telephone number of the person.

(C) Subparagraph (A) does not apply if—

(i) the end user is an agency or department of the United States Government that procures the report from the person for purposes of determining the eligibility of the consumer to whom the report relates to receive access or continued access to classified information (as defined in section 1681b(b)(4)(E)(i) of this title); and

(ii) the head of the agency or department makes a written finding as prescribed under section 1681b(b)(4)(A) of this title.

(4) The dates, original payees, and amounts of any checks upon which is based any adverse characterization of the consumer, included in the file at the time of the disclosure.

(5) A record of all inquiries received by the agency during the 1-year period preceding the request that identified the consumer in connection with a credit or insurance transaction that was not initiated by the consumer.

(6) If the consumer requests the credit file and not the credit score, a statement that the consumer may request and obtain a credit score.

(b) Exempt information

The requirements of subsection (a) of this section respecting the disclosure of sources of information and the recipients of consumer reports do not apply to information received or consumer reports furnished prior to the effective date of this subchapter except to the extent that the matter involved is contained in the files of the consumer reporting agency on that date.

(c) Summary of rights to obtain and dispute information in consumer reports and to obtain credit scores

(1) Commission summary of rights required

(A) In general

The Commission shall prepare a model summary of the rights of consumers under this subchapter.

(B) Content of summary

The summary of rights prepared under subparagraph (A) shall include a description of—

(i) the right of a consumer to obtain a copy of a consumer report under subsection (a) of this section from each consumer reporting agency;

(ii) the frequency and circumstances under which a consumer is entitled to receive a consumer report without charge under section 1681j of this title;

(iii) the right of a consumer to dispute information in the file of the consumer under section 1681i of this title;

(iv) the right of a consumer to obtain a credit score from a consumer reporting agency, and a description of how to obtain a credit score;

(v) the method by which a consumer can contact, and obtain a consumer report from, a consumer reporting agency without charge, as provided in the regulations of the Commission prescribed under section 211(c) of the Fair and Accurate Credit Transactions Act of 2003; and

(vi) the method by which a consumer can contact, and obtain a consumer report from, a consumer reporting agency described in section 1681a(w) of this title, as provided in the regulations of the Commission prescribed under section 1681j(a)(1)(C) of this title.

(C) Availability of summary of rights

The Commission shall—

(i) actively publicize the availability of the summary of rights prepared under this paragraph;

(ii) conspicuously post on its Internet website the availability of such summary of rights; and

(iii) promptly make such summary of rights available to consumers, on request.

(2) Summary of rights required to be included with agency disclosures

A consumer reporting agency shall provide to a consumer, with each written disclosure by the agency to the consumer under this section—

(A) the summary of rights prepared by the Commission under paragraph (1);

(B) in the case of a consumer reporting agency described in section 1681a(p) of this title, a toll-free telephone number established by the agency, at which personnel are accessible to consumers during normal business hours;

(C) a list of all Federal agencies responsible for enforcing any provision of this subchapter, and the address and any appropriate phone number of each such agency, in a form that will assist the consumer in selecting the appropriate agency;

(D) a statement that the consumer may have additional rights under State law, and that the consumer may wish to contact a State or local consumer protection agency or a State attorney general (or the equivalent thereof) to learn of those rights; and

(E) a statement that a consumer reporting agency is not required to remove accurate derogatory information from the file of a consumer, unless the information is outdated under section 1681c of this title or cannot be verified.

(d) Summary of rights of identity theft victims

(1) In general

The Commission, in consultation with the Federal banking agencies and the National Credit Union Administration, shall prepare a model summary of the rights of consumers under this subchapter with respect to the procedures for remedying the effects of fraud or identity theft involving credit, an electronic fund transfer, or an account or transaction at or with a financial institution or other creditor.

(2) Summary of rights and contact information

Beginning 60 days after the date on which the model summary of rights is prescribed in final form by the Commission pursuant to paragraph (1), if any consumer contacts a consumer reporting agency and expresses a belief that the consumer is a victim of fraud or identity theft involving credit, an electronic fund transfer, or an account or transaction at or with a financial institution or other creditor, the consumer reporting agency shall, in addition to any other action that the agency may take, provide the consumer with a summary of rights that contains all of the information required by the Commission under paragraph (1), and information on how to contact the Commission to obtain more detailed information.

(e) Information available to victims

(1) In general

For the purpose of documenting fraudulent transactions resulting from identity theft, not later than 30 days after the date of receipt of a request from a victim in accordance with paragraph (3), and subject to verification of the identity of the victim and the claim of identity theft in accordance with paragraph (2), a business entity that has provided credit to, provided for consideration products, goods, or services to, accepted payment from, or otherwise entered into a commercial transaction for consideration with, a person who has allegedly made unauthorized use of the means of identification of the victim, shall provide a copy of application and business transaction records in the control of the business entity, whether maintained by the business entity or by another person on behalf of the business entity, evidencing any transaction alleged to be a result of identity theft to—

(A) the victim;

(B) any Federal, State, or local government law enforcement agency or officer specified by the victim in such a request; or

(C) any law enforcement agency investigating the identity theft and authorized by the victim to take receipt of records provided under this subsection.

(2) Verification of identity and claim

Before a business entity provides any information under paragraph (1), unless the business entity, at its discretion, otherwise has a high degree of confidence that it knows the identity of the victim making a request under paragraph (1), the victim shall provide to the business entity—

(A) as proof of positive identification of the victim, at the election of the business entity—

(i) the presentation of a government-issued identification card;

(ii) personally identifying information of the same type as was provided to the business entity by the unauthorized person; or

(iii) personally identifying information that the business entity typically requests from new applicants or for new transactions, at the time of the victim's request for information, including any documentation described in clauses (i) and (ii); and

(B) as proof of a claim of identity theft, at the election of the business entity—

(i) a copy of a police report evidencing the claim of the victim of identity theft; and

(ii) a properly completed—

(I) copy of a standardized affidavit of identity theft developed and made available by the Commission; or

(II) an affidavit of fact that is acceptable to the business entity for that purpose.

(3) Procedures

The request of a victim under paragraph (1) shall—

(A) be in writing;

(B) be mailed to an address specified by the business entity, if any; and

(C) if asked by the business entity, include relevant information about any transaction alleged to be a result of identity theft to facilitate compliance with this section including—

(i) if known by the victim (or if readily obtainable by the victim), the date of the application or transaction; and

(ii) if known by the victim (or if readily obtainable by the victim), any other identifying information such as an account or transaction number.

(4) No charge to victim

Information required to be provided under paragraph (1) shall be so provided without charge.

(5) Authority to decline to provide information

A business entity may decline to provide information under paragraph (1) if, in the exercise of good faith, the business entity determines that—

(A) this subsection does not require disclosure of the information;

(B) after reviewing the information provided pursuant to paragraph (2), the business entity does not have a high degree of confidence in knowing the true identity of the individual requesting the information;

(C) the request for the information is based on a misrepresentation of fact by the individual requesting the information relevant to the request for information; or

(D) the information requested is Internet navigational data or similar information about a person's visit to a website or online service.

(6) Limitation on liability

Except as provided in section 1681s of this title, sections 1681n and 1681o of this title do not apply to any violation of this subsection.

(7) Limitation on civil liability

No business entity may be held civilly liable under any provision of Federal, State, or other law for disclosure, made in good faith pursuant to this subsection.

(8) No new recordkeeping obligation

Nothing in this subsection creates an obligation on the part of a business entity to obtain, retain, or maintain information or records that are not otherwise required to be obtained, retained, or maintained in the ordinary course of its business or under other applicable law.

(9) Rule of construction

(A) In general

No provision of subtitle A of title V of Public Law 106-102, prohibiting the disclosure of financial information by a business entity to third parties shall be used to deny disclosure of information to the victim under this subsection.

(B) Limitation

Except as provided in subparagraph (A), nothing in this subsection permits a business entity to disclose information, including information to law enforcement under subparagraphs (B) and (C) of paragraph (1), that the business entity is otherwise prohibited from disclosing under any other applicable provision of Federal or State law.

(10) Affirmative defense

In any civil action brought to enforce this subsection, it is an affirmative defense (which the defendant must establish by a preponderance of the evidence) for a business entity to file an affidavit or answer stating that—

(A) the business entity has made a reasonably diligent search of its available business records; and

(B) the records requested under this subsection do not exist or are not reasonably available.

(11) Definition of victim

For purposes of this subsection, the term "victim" means a consumer whose means of identification or financial information has been used or transferred (or has been alleged to have been used or transferred) without the authority of that consumer, with the intent to commit, or to aid or abet, an identity theft or a similar crime.

(12) Effective date

This subsection shall become effective 180 days after December 4, 2003.

(13) Effectiveness study

Not later than 18 months after December 4, 2003, the Comptroller General of the United States shall submit a report to Congress assessing the effectiveness of this provision.

(f) Disclosure of credit scores

(1) In general

Upon the request of a consumer for a credit score, a consumer reporting agency shall supply to the consumer a statement indicating that the information and credit scoring model may be different than the credit score that may be used by the lender, and a notice which shall include—

(A) the current credit score of the consumer or the most recent credit score of the consumer that was previously calculated by the credit reporting agency for a purpose related to the extension of credit;

(B) the range of possible credit scores under the model used;

(C) all of the key factors that adversely affected the credit score of the consumer in the model used, the total number of which shall not exceed 4, subject to paragraph (9);

(D) the date on which the credit score was created; and

(E) the name of the person or entity that provided the credit score or credit file upon which the credit score was created.

(2) Definitions

For purposes of this subsection, the following definitions shall apply:

(A) Credit score

The term “credit score”—

(i) means a numerical value or a categorization derived from a statistical tool or modeling system used by a person who makes or arranges a loan to predict the likelihood of certain credit behaviors, including default (and the numerical value or the categorization derived from such analysis may also be referred to as a “risk predictor” or “risk score”); and

(ii) does not include—

(I) any mortgage score or rating of an automated underwriting system that considers one or more factors in addition to credit information, including the loan to value ratio, the amount of down payment, or the financial assets of a consumer; or

(II) any other elements of the underwriting process or underwriting decision.

(B) Key factors

The term “key factors” means all relevant elements or reasons adversely affecting the credit score for the particular individual, listed in the order of their importance based on their effect on the credit score.

(3) Timeframe and manner of disclosure

The information required by this subsection shall be provided in the same timeframe and manner as the information described in subsection (a) of this section.

(4) Applicability to certain uses

This subsection shall not be construed so as to compel a consumer reporting agency to develop or disclose a score if the agency does not—

(A) distribute scores that are used in connection with residential real property loans; or

(B) develop scores that assist credit providers in understanding the general credit behavior of a consumer and predicting the future credit behavior of the consumer.

(5) Applicability to credit scores developed by another person

(A) In general

This subsection shall not be construed to require a consumer reporting agency that distributes credit scores developed by another person or entity to provide a further explanation of them, or to process a dispute arising pursuant to section 1681i of this title, except that the consumer reporting agency shall provide the consumer with the name and address and website for contacting the person or entity who developed the score or developed the methodology of the score.

(B) Exception

This paragraph shall not apply to a consumer reporting agency that develops or modifies scores that are developed by another person or entity.

(6) Maintenance of credit scores not required

This subsection shall not be construed to require a consumer reporting agency to maintain credit scores in its files.

(7) Compliance in certain cases

In complying with this subsection, a consumer reporting agency shall—

(A) supply the consumer with a credit score that is derived from a credit scoring model that is widely distributed to users by that consumer reporting agency in connection with residential real property loans or with a credit score that assists the consumer in understanding the credit scoring assessment of the credit behavior of the consumer and predictions about the future credit behavior of the consumer; and

(B) a statement indicating that the information and credit scoring model may be different than that used by the lender.

(8) Fair and reasonable fee

A consumer reporting agency may charge a fair and reasonable fee, as determined by the Commission, for providing the information required under this subsection.

(9) Use of enquiries as a key factor

If a key factor that adversely affects the credit score of a consumer consists of the number of enquiries made with respect to a consumer report, that factor shall be included in the disclosure pursuant to paragraph (1)(C) without regard to the numerical limitation in such paragraph.

(g) Disclosure of credit scores by certain mortgage lenders

(1) In general

Any person who makes or arranges loans and who uses a consumer credit score, as defined in subsection (f) of this section, in connection with an application initiated or sought by a consumer for a closed end loan or the establishment of an open end loan for a consumer purpose that is secured by 1 to 4 units of residential real property (hereafter in this subsection referred to as the "lender") shall provide the following to the consumer as soon as reasonably practicable:

(A) Information required under subsection (f)—

(i) In general

A copy of the information identified in subsection (f) of this section that was obtained from a consumer reporting agency or was developed and used by the user of the information.

(ii) Notice under subparagraph (D)

In addition to the information provided to it by a third party that provided the credit score or scores, a lender is only required to provide the notice contained in subparagraph (D).

(B) Disclosures in case of automated underwriting system

(i) In general

If a person that is subject to this subsection uses an automated underwriting system to underwrite a loan, that person may satisfy the obligation to provide a credit score by disclosing a credit score and associated key factors supplied by a consumer reporting agency.

(ii) Numerical credit score

However, if a numerical credit score is generated by an automated underwriting system used by an enterprise, and that score is disclosed to the person, the score shall be disclosed to the consumer consistent with subparagraph (C).

(iii) Enterprise defined

For purposes of this subparagraph, the term "enterprise" has the same meaning as in paragraph (6) of section 4502 of Title 12.

(C) Disclosures of credit scores not obtained from a consumer reporting agency

A person that is subject to the provisions of this subsection and that uses a credit score, other than a credit score provided by a consumer reporting agency, may satisfy the obligation to provide a credit score by disclosing a credit score and associated key factors supplied by a consumer reporting agency.

(D) Notice to home loan applicants

A copy of the following notice, which shall include the name, address, and telephone number of each consumer reporting agency providing a credit score that was used:

NOTICE TO THE HOME LOAN APPLICANT

In connection with your application for a home loan, the lender must disclose to you the score that a consumer reporting agency distributed to users and the lender used in connection with your home loan, and the key factors affecting your credit scores.

The credit score is a computer generated summary calculated at the time of the request and based on information that a consumer reporting agency or lender has on file. The scores are based on data about your credit history and payment patterns. Credit scores are important because they are used to assist the lender in determining whether you will obtain a loan. They may also be used to determine what interest rate you may be offered on the mortgage. Credit scores can change over time, depending on your conduct, how your credit history and payment patterns change, and how credit scoring technologies change.

Because the score is based on information in your credit history, it is very important that you review the credit-related information that is being furnished to make sure it is accurate. Credit records may vary from one company to another.

If you have questions about your credit score or the credit information that is furnished to you, contact the consumer reporting agency at the address and telephone number provided with this notice, or contact the lender, if the lender developed or generated the credit score. The consumer reporting agency plays no part in the decision to take any action on the loan application and is unable to provide you with specific reasons for the decision on a loan application.

If you have questions concerning the terms of the loan, contact the lender.

(E) Actions not required under this subsection

This subsection shall not require any person to—

(i) explain the information provided pursuant to subsection (f) of this section;

(ii) disclose any information other than a credit score or key factors, as defined in subsection (f) of this section;

(iii) disclose any credit score or related information obtained by the user after a loan has closed;

(iv) provide more than 1 disclosure per loan transaction; or

(v) provide the disclosure required by this subsection when another person has made the disclosure to the consumer for that loan transaction.

(F) No obligation for content

(i) In general

The obligation of any person pursuant to this subsection shall be limited solely to providing a copy of the information that was received from the consumer reporting agency.

(ii) Limit on liability

No person has liability under this subsection for the content of that information or for the omission of any information within the report provided by the consumer reporting agency.

(G) Person defined as excluding enterprise

As used in this subsection, the term “person” does not include an enterprise (as defined in paragraph (6) of section 4502 of Title 12).

(2) Prohibition on disclosure clauses null and void

(A) In general

Any provision in a contract that prohibits the disclosure of a credit score by a person who makes or arranges loans or a consumer reporting agency is void.

(B) No liability for disclosure under this subsection

A lender shall not have liability under any contractual provision for disclosure of a credit score pursuant to this subsection.

§ 1681h. Conditions and form of disclosure to consumers

(a) In general

(1) Proper identification.—A consumer reporting agency shall require, as a condition of making the disclosures required under section 1681g of this title, that the consumer furnish proper identification.

(2) Disclosure in writing.—Except as provided in subsection (b) of this section, the disclosures required to be made under section 1681(g) of this title shall be provided under that section in writing.

(b) Other forms of disclosure

(1) In general.—If authorized by a consumer, a consumer reporting agency may make the disclosures required under 1681g of this title—

(A) other than in writing; and

(B) in such form as may be—

(i) specified by the consumer in accordance with paragraph (2); and

(ii) available from the agency.

(2) Form.—A consumer may specify pursuant to paragraph (1) that disclosures under section 1681g of this title shall be made—

(A) in person, upon the appearance of the consumer at the place of business of the consumer reporting agency where disclosures are regularly provided, during normal business hours, and on reasonable notice;

(B) by telephone, if the consumer has made a written request for disclosure by telephone;

(C) by electronic means, if available from the agency; or

(D) by any other reasonable means that is available from the agency.

(c) Trained personnel

Any consumer reporting agency shall provide trained personnel to explain to the consumer any information furnished to him pursuant to section 1681g of this title.

(d) Persons accompanying consumer

The consumer shall be permitted to be accompanied by one other person of his choosing, who shall furnish reasonable identification. A consumer reporting agency may require the consumer to furnish a written statement granting permission to the consumer reporting agency to discuss the consumer's file in such person's presence.

(e) Limitation of liability

Except as provided in sections 1681n and 1681o of this title, no consumer may bring any action or proceeding in the nature of defamation, invasion of privacy, or negligence with respect to the reporting of information against any consumer reporting agency, any user of information, or any person who furnishes information to a consumer reporting agency, based on information disclosed pursuant to section 1681g, 1681h, or 1681m of this title, or based on information disclosed by a user of a consumer report to or for a consumer against whom the user has taken adverse action, based in whole or in part on the report except as to false information furnished with malice or willful intent to injure such consumer.

§ 1681i. Procedure in case of disputed accuracy

(a) Reinvestigations of disputed information

(1) Reinvestigation required.—

(A) In general.—Subject to subsection (f) of this section, if the completeness or accuracy of any item of information contained in a consumer's file at a consumer reporting agency is disputed by the consumer and the consumer notifies the agency directly, or indirectly through a reseller, of such dispute, the agency shall, free of charge, conduct a reasonable reinvestigation to determine whether the disputed information is inaccurate and record the current status of the disputed information, or delete the item from the file in accordance with paragraph (5), before the end of the 30-day period beginning on the date on which the agency receives the notice of the dispute from the consumer or reseller.

(B) Extension of period to reinvestigate.—Except as provided in subparagraph (C), the 30-day period described in subparagraph (A) may be extended for not more than 15 additional days if the consumer reporting agency receives information from the consumer during that 30-day period that is relevant to the reinvestigation.

(C) Limitations on extension of period to reinvestigate.—Subparagraph (B) shall not apply to any reinvestigation in which, during the 30-day period described in subparagraph (A), the information that is the subject of the reinvestigation is found to be inaccurate or incomplete or the consumer reporting agency determines that the information cannot be verified.

(2) Prompt notice of dispute to furnisher of information.—

(A) In general.—Before the expiration of the 5-business-day period beginning on the date on which a consumer reporting agency receives notice of a dispute from any consumer or a reseller in accordance with paragraph (1), the agency shall provide notification of the dispute to any person who provided any item of information in dispute, at the address and in the manner established with the person. The notice shall include all relevant information regarding the dispute that the agency has received from the consumer or reseller.

(B) Provision of other information.—The consumer reporting agency shall promptly provide to the person who provided the information in dispute all relevant information regarding the dispute that is received by the agency from the consumer or the reseller after the period referred to in subparagraph (A) and before the end of the period referred to in paragraph (1)(A).

(3) Determination that dispute is frivolous or irrelevant.—

(A) In general.—Notwithstanding paragraph (1), a consumer reporting agency may terminate a reinvestigation of information disputed by a consumer under that paragraph if the agency reasonably determines that the dispute by the consumer is frivolous or irrelevant, including by reason of a failure by a consumer to provide sufficient information to investigate the disputed information.

(B) Notice of determination.—Upon making any determination in accordance with subparagraph (A) that a dispute is frivolous or irrelevant, a consumer reporting agency shall notify the consumer of such determination not later than 5 business days after making such determination, by mail or, if authorized by the consumer for that purpose, by any other means available to the agency.

(C) Contents of notice.—A notice under subparagraph (B) shall include—

(i) the reasons for the determination under subparagraph (A); and

(ii) identification of any information required to investigate the disputed information, which may consist of a standardized form describing the general nature of such information.

(4) Consideration of consumer information.—In conducting any reinvestigation under paragraph (1) with respect to disputed information in the file of any consumer, the consumer reporting agency shall review and consider all relevant information submitted by the consumer in the period described in paragraph (1)(A) with respect to such disputed information.

(5) Treatment of inaccurate or unverifiable information.—

(A) In general.—If, after any reinvestigation under paragraph (1) of any information disputed by a consumer, an item of the information is found to be inaccurate or incomplete or cannot be verified, the consumer reporting agency shall—

(i) promptly delete that item of information from the file of the consumer, or modify that item of information, as appropriate, based on the results of the reinvestigation; and

(ii) promptly notify the furnisher of that information that the information has been modified or deleted from the file of the consumer.

(B) Requirements relating to reinsertion of previously deleted material.—

(i) Certification of accuracy of information.—If any information is deleted from a consumer's file pursuant to subparagraph (A), the information may not be reinserted in the file by the consumer reporting agency unless the person who furnishes the information certifies that the information is complete and accurate.

(ii) Notice to consumer.—If any information that has been deleted from a consumer's file pursuant to subparagraph (A) is reinserted in the file, the consumer reporting agency shall notify the consumer of the reinsertion in writing not later than 5 business days after the reinsertion or, if authorized by the consumer for that purpose, by any other means available to the agency.

(iii) Additional information.—As part of, or in addition to, the notice under clause (ii), a consumer reporting agency shall provide to a consumer in writing not later than 5 business days after the date of the reinsertion—

(I) a statement that the disputed information has been reinserted;

(II) the business name and address of any furnisher of information contacted and the telephone number of such furnisher, if reasonably available, or of any furnisher of information that contacted the consumer reporting agency, in connection with the reinsertion of such information; and

(III) a notice that the consumer has the right to add a statement to the consumer's file disputing the accuracy or completeness of the disputed information.

(C) Procedures to prevent reappearance.—A consumer reporting agency shall maintain reasonable procedures designed to prevent the reappearance in a consumer's file, and in consumer reports on the consumer, of information that is deleted pursuant to this paragraph (other than information that is reinserted in accordance with subparagraph (B)(i)).

(D) Automated reinvestigation system.—Any consumer reporting agency that compiles and maintains files on consumers on a nationwide basis shall implement an automated system through which furnishers of information to that consumer reporting agency may report the results of a reinvestigation that finds incomplete or inaccurate information in a consumer's file to other such consumer reporting agencies.

(6) Notice of results of reinvestigation.—

(A) In general.—A consumer reporting agency shall provide written notice to a consumer of the results of a reinvestigation under this subsection not later than 5 business days after the completion of the reinvestigation, by mail or, if authorized by the consumer for that purpose, by other means available to the agency.

(B) Contents.—As part of, or in addition to, the notice under subparagraph (A), a consumer reporting agency shall provide to a consumer in writing before the expiration of the 5-day period referred to in subparagraph (A)—

(i) a statement that the reinvestigation is completed;

(ii) a consumer report that is based upon the consumer's file as that file is revised as a result of the reinvestigation;

(iii) a notice that, if requested by the consumer, a description of the procedure used to determine the accuracy and completeness of the information shall be provided to the consumer by the agency, including the business name and address of any furnisher of information contacted in connection with such information and the telephone number of such furnisher, if reasonably available;

(iv) a notice that the consumer has the right to add a statement to the consumer's file disputing the accuracy or completeness of the information; and

(v) a notice that the consumer has the right to request under subsection (d) of this section that the consumer reporting agency furnish notifications under that subsection.

(7) Description of reinvestigation procedure.—A consumer reporting agency shall provide to a consumer a description referred to in paragraph (6)(B)(iii) by not later than 15 days after receiving a request from the consumer for that description.

(8) Expedited dispute resolution.—If a dispute regarding an item of information in a consumer's file at a consumer reporting agency is resolved in accordance with paragraph (5)(A) by the deletion of the disputed information by not later than 3 business days after the date on which the agency receives notice of the dispute from the consumer in accordance with paragraph (1)(A), then the agency shall not be required to comply with paragraphs (2), (6), and (7) with respect to that dispute if the agency—

(A) provides prompt notice of the deletion to the consumer by telephone;

(B) includes in that notice, or in a written notice that accompanies a confirmation and consumer report provided in accordance with subparagraph (C), a statement of the consumer's right to request under subsection (d) of this section that the agency furnish notifications under that subsection; and

(C) provides written confirmation of the deletion and a copy of a consumer report on the consumer that is based on the consumer's file after the deletion, not later than 5 business days after making the deletion.

(b) Statement of dispute

If the reinvestigation does not resolve the dispute, the consumer may file a brief statement setting forth the nature of the dispute. The consumer reporting agency may limit such statements to not more than one hundred words if it provides the consumer with assistance in writing a clear summary of the dispute.

(c) Notification of consumer dispute in subsequent consumer reports

Whenever a statement of a dispute is filed, unless there is reasonable grounds to believe that it is frivolous or irrelevant, the consumer reporting agency shall, in any subsequent consumer report containing the information in question, clearly note that it is disputed by the consumer and provide either the consumer's statement or a clear and accurate codification or summary thereof.

(d) Notification of deletion of disputed information

Following any deletion of information which is found to be inaccurate or whose accuracy can no longer be verified or any notation as to disputed information, the consumer reporting agency shall, at the request of the consumer, furnish notification that the item has been deleted or the statement, codification or summary pursuant to subsection (b) or (c) of this section to any person specifically designated by the consumer who has within two years prior thereto received a consumer report for employment purposes, or within six months prior thereto received a consumer report for any other purpose, which contained the deleted or disputed information.

(e) Treatment of complaints and report to Congress

(1) In general

The Commission shall—

(A) compile all complaints that it receives that a file of a consumer that is maintained by a consumer reporting agency described in section 1681a(p) of this title contains incomplete or inaccurate information, with respect to which, the consumer appears to have disputed the completeness or accuracy with the consumer reporting agency or otherwise utilized the procedures provided by subsection (a) of this section; and

(B) transmit each such complaint to each consumer reporting agency involved.

(2) Exclusion

Complaints received or obtained by the Commission pursuant to its investigative authority under the Federal Trade Commission Act shall not be subject to paragraph (1).

(3) Agency responsibilities

Each consumer reporting agency described in section 1681a(p) of this title that receives a complaint transmitted by the Commission pursuant to paragraph (1) shall—

(A) review each such complaint to determine whether all legal obligations imposed on the consumer reporting agency under this subchapter (including any obligation imposed by an applicable court or administrative order) have been met with respect to the subject matter of the complaint;

(B) provide reports on a regular basis to the Commission regarding the determinations of and actions taken by the consumer reporting agency, if any, in connection with its review of such complaints; and

(C) maintain, for a reasonable time period, records regarding the disposition of each such complaint that is sufficient to demonstrate compliance with this subsection.

(4) Rulemaking authority

The Commission may prescribe regulations, as appropriate to implement this subsection.

(5) Annual report

The Commission shall submit to the Committee on Banking, Housing, and Urban Affairs of the Senate and the Committee on Financial Services of the House of Representatives an annual report regarding information gathered by the Commission under this subsection.

(f) Reinvestigation requirement applicable to resellers

(1) Exemption from general reinvestigation requirement

Except as provided in paragraph (2), a reseller shall be exempt from the requirements of this section.

(2) Action required upon receiving notice of a dispute

If a reseller receives a notice from a consumer of a dispute concerning the completeness or accuracy of any item of information contained in a consumer report on such consumer produced by the reseller, the reseller shall, within 5 business days of receiving the notice, and free of charge—

(A) determine whether the item of information is incomplete or inaccurate as a result of an act or omission of the reseller; and

(B) if—

(i) the reseller determines that the item of information is incomplete or inaccurate as a result of an act or omission of the reseller, not later than 20 days after receiving the notice, correct the information in the consumer report or delete it; or

(ii) if the reseller determines that the item of information is not incomplete or inaccurate as a result of an act or omission of the reseller, convey the notice of the dispute, together with all relevant information provided by the consumer, to each consumer reporting agency that provided the reseller with the information that is the subject of the dispute, using an address or a notification mechanism specified by the consumer reporting agency for such notices.

(3) Responsibility of consumer reporting agency to notify consumer through reseller

Upon the completion of a reinvestigation under this section of a dispute concerning the completeness or accuracy of any information in the file of a consumer by a consumer reporting agency that received notice of the dispute from a reseller under paragraph (2)—

(A) the notice by the consumer reporting agency under paragraph (6), (7), or (8) of subsection (a) of this section shall be provided to the reseller in lieu of the consumer; and

(B) the reseller shall immediately reconvey such notice to the consumer, including any notice of a deletion by telephone in the manner required under paragraph (8)(A).

(4) Reseller reinvestigations

No provision of this subsection shall be construed as prohibiting a reseller from conducting a reinvestigation of a consumer dispute directly.

§ 1681j. Charges for certain disclosures

(a) Free annual disclosure

(1) Nationwide consumer reporting agencies

(A) In general

All consumer reporting agencies described in subsections (p) and (w) of section 1681a of this title shall make all disclosures pursuant to section 1681g of this title once during any 12-month period upon request of the consumer and without charge to the consumer.

(B) Centralized source

Subparagraph (A) shall apply with respect to a consumer reporting agency described in section 1681a(p) of this title only if the request from the consumer is made using the centralized source established for such purpose in accordance with section 211(c) of the Fair and Accurate Credit Transactions Act of 2003.

(C) Nationwide specialty consumer reporting agency

(i) In general

The Commission shall prescribe regulations applicable to each consumer reporting agency described in section 1681a of this title to require the establishment of a streamlined process for consumers to request consumer reports under subparagraph (A), which shall include, at a minimum, the establishment by each such agency of a toll-free telephone number for such requests.

(ii) Considerations

In prescribing regulations under clause (i), the Commission shall consider—

(I) the significant demands that may be placed on consumer reporting agencies in providing such consumer reports;

(II) appropriate means to ensure that consumer reporting agencies can satisfactorily meet those demands, including the efficacy of a system of staggering the availability to consumers of such consumer reports; and

(III) the ease by which consumers should be able to contact consumer reporting agencies with respect to access to such consumer reports.

(iii) Date of issuance

The Commission shall issue the regulations required by this subparagraph in final form not later than 6 months after December 4, 2003.

(iv) Consideration of ability to comply

The regulations of the Commission under this subparagraph shall establish an effective date by which each nationwide specialty consumer reporting agency (as defined in section 1681a of this title) shall be required to comply with subsection (a) of this section, which effective date—

(I) shall be established after consideration of the ability of each nationwide specialty consumer reporting agency to comply with subsection (a) of this section; and

(II) shall be not later than 6 months after the date on which such regulations are issued in final form (or such additional period not to exceed 3 months, as the Commission determines appropriate).

(2) Timing

A consumer reporting agency shall provide a consumer report under paragraph (1) not later than 15 days after the date on which the request is received under paragraph (1).

(3) Reinvestigations

Notwithstanding the time periods specified in section 1681i(a)(1) of this title, a reinvestigation under that section by a consumer reporting agency upon a request of a consumer that is made after receiving a consumer report under this subsection shall be completed not later than 45 days after the date on which the request is received.

(4) Exception for first 12 months of operation

This subsection shall not apply to a consumer reporting agency that has not been furnishing consumer reports to third parties on a continuing basis during the 12-month period preceding a request under paragraph (1), with respect to consumers residing nationwide.

(b) Free disclosure after adverse notice to consumer

Each consumer reporting agency that maintains a file on a consumer shall make all disclosures pursuant to section 1681g of this title without charge to the consumer if, not later than 60 days after receipt by such consumer of a notification pursuant to section 1681m of this title, or of a notification from a debt collection agency affiliated with that consumer reporting agency stating that the consumer's credit rating may be or has been adversely affected, the consumer makes a request under section 1681g of this title.

(c) Free disclosure under certain other circumstances

Upon the request of the consumer, a consumer reporting agency shall make all disclosures pursuant to section 1681g of this title once during any 12-month period without charge to that consumer if the consumer certifies in writing that the consumer—

(1) is unemployed and intends to apply for employment in the 60-day period beginning on the date on which the certification is made;

(2) is a recipient of public welfare assistance; or

(3) has reason to believe that the file on the consumer at the agency contains inaccurate information due to fraud.

(d) Free disclosures in connection with fraud alerts

Upon the request of a consumer, a consumer reporting agency described in section 1681a(p) of this title shall make all disclosures pursuant to section 1681g of this title without charge to the consumer, as provided in subsections (a)(2) and (b)(2) of section 1681c-1 of this title, as applicable.

(e) Other charges prohibited

A consumer reporting agency shall not impose any charge on a consumer for providing any notification required by this subchapter or making any disclosure required by this subchapter, except as authorized by subsection (f) of this section.

(f) Reasonable charges allowed for certain disclosures

(1) In general.—In the case of a request from a consumer other than a request that is covered by any of subsections (a) through (d) of this section, a consumer reporting agency may impose a reasonable charge on a consumer—

(A) for making a disclosure to the consumer pursuant to section 1681g of this title, which charge—

(i) shall not exceed $8; and

(ii) shall be indicated to the consumer before making the disclosure; and

(B) for furnishing, pursuant to section 1681i(d) of this title, following a reinvestigation under section 1681i(a) of this title, a statement, codification, or summary to a person designated by the consumer under that section after the 30-day period beginning on the date of notification of the consumer under paragraph (6) or (8) of section 1681i(a) of this title with respect to the reinvestigation, which charge—

(i) shall not exceed the charge that the agency would impose on each designated recipient for a consumer report; and

(ii) shall be indicated to the consumer before furnishing such information.

(2) Modification of amount.—The Federal Trade Commission shall increase the amount referred to in paragraph (1)(A)(i) on January 1 of each year, based proportionally on changes in the Consumer Price Index, with fractional changes rounded to the nearest fifty cents.

§ 1681k. Public record information for employment purposes

(a) In general

A consumer reporting agency which furnishes a consumer report for employment purposes and which for that purpose compiles and reports items of information on consumers which are matters of public record and are likely to have an adverse effect upon a consumer's ability to obtain employment shall—

(1) at the time such public record information is reported to the user of such consumer report, notify the consumer of the fact that public record information is being reported by the consumer reporting agency, together with the name and address of the person to whom such information is being reported; or

(2) maintain strict procedures designed to insure that whenever public record information which is likely to have an adverse effect on a consumer's ability to obtain employment is reported it is complete and up to date. For purposes of this paragraph, items of public record relating to arrests, indictments, convictions, suits, tax liens, and outstanding judgments shall be considered up to date if the current public record status of the item at the time of the report is reported.

(b) Exemption for National security investigations

Subsection (a) of this section does not apply in the case of an agency or department of the United States Government that seeks to obtain and use a consumer report for employment purposes, if the head of the agency or department makes a written finding as prescribed under section 1681b(b)(4)(A) of this title.

§ 1681l. Restrictions on investigative consumer reports

Whenever a consumer reporting agency prepares an investigative consumer report, no adverse information in the consumer report (other than information which is a matter of public record) may be included in a subsequent consumer report unless such adverse information has been verified in the process of making such subsequent consumer report, or the adverse information was received within the three-month period preceding the date the subsequent report is furnished.

§ 1681m. Requirements on users of consumer reports

(a) Duties of users taking adverse actions on basis of information contained in consumer reports

If any person takes any adverse action with respect to any consumer that is based in whole or in part on any information contained in a consumer report, the person shall—

(1) provide oral, written, or electronic notice of the adverse action to the consumer;

(2) provide to the consumer orally, in writing, or electronically—

(A) the name, address, and telephone number of the consumer reporting agency (including a toll-free telephone number established by the agency if the agency compiles and maintains files on consumers on a nationwide basis) that furnished the report to the person; and

(B) a statement that the consumer reporting agency did not make the decision to take the adverse action and is unable to provide the consumer the specific reasons why the adverse action was taken; and

(3) provide to the consumer an oral, written, or electronic notice of the consumer's right—

(A) to obtain, under section 1681j of this title, a free copy of a consumer report on the consumer from the consumer reporting agency referred to in paragraph (2), which notice shall include an indication of the 60-day period under that section for obtaining such a copy; and

(B) to dispute, under section 1681i of this title, with a consumer reporting agency the accuracy or completeness of any information in a consumer report furnished by the agency.

(b) Adverse action based on information obtained from third parties other than consumer reporting agencies

(1) In general.—Whenever credit for personal, family, or household purposes involving a consumer is denied or the charge for such credit is increased either wholly or partly because of information obtained from a person other than a consumer reporting agency bearing upon the consumer's credit worthiness, credit standing, credit capacity, character, general reputation, personal characteristics, or mode of living, the user of such information shall, within a reasonable period of time, upon the consumer's written request for the reasons for such adverse action received within sixty days after learning of such adverse action, disclose the nature of the information to the consumer. The user of such information shall clearly and accurately disclose to the consumer his right to make such written request at the time such adverse action is communicated to the consumer.

(2) Duties of person taking certain actions based on information provided by affiliate.—

(A) Duties, generally.—If a person takes an action described in subparagraph (B) with respect to a consumer, based in whole or in part on information described in subparagraph (C), the person shall—

(i) notify the consumer of the action, including a statement that the consumer may obtain the information in accordance with clause (ii); and

(ii) upon a written request from the consumer received within 60 days after transmittal of the notice required by clause (i), disclose to the consumer the nature of the information upon which the action is based by not later than 30 days after receipt of the request.

(B) Action described.—An action referred to in subparagraph (A) is an adverse action described in section 1681a(k)(1)(A) of this title, taken in connection with a transaction initiated by the consumer, or any adverse action described in clause (i) or (ii) of section 1681a(k)(1)(B) of this title.

(C) Information described.—Information referred to in subparagraph (A)—

(i) except as provided in clause (ii), is information that—

(I) is furnished to the person taking the action by a person related by common ownership or affiliated by common corporate control to the person taking the action; and

(II) bears on the credit worthiness, credit standing, credit capacity, character, general reputation, personal characteristics, or mode of living of the consumer; and

(ii) does not include—

(I) information solely as to transactions or experiences between the consumer and the person furnishing the information; or

(II) information in a consumer report.

(c) Reasonable procedures to assure compliance

No person shall be held liable for any violation of this section if he shows by a preponderance of the evidence that at the time of the alleged violation he maintained reasonable procedures to assure compliance with the provisions of this section.

(d) Duties of users making written credit or insurance solicitations on the basis of information contained in consumer files

(1) In general.—Any person who uses a consumer report on any consumer in connection with any credit or insurance transaction that is not initiated by the consumer, that is provided to that person under section 1681b(c)(1)(B) of this title, shall provide with each written solicitation made to the consumer regarding the transaction a clear and conspicuous statement that—

(A) information contained in the consumer's consumer report was used in connection with the transaction;

(B) the consumer received the offer of credit or insurance because the consumer satisfied the criteria for credit worthiness or insurability under which the consumer was selected for the offer;

(C) if applicable, the credit or insurance may not be extended if, after the consumer responds to the offer, the consumer does not meet the criteria used to select the consumer for the offer or any applicable criteria bearing on credit worthiness or insurability or does not furnish any required collateral;

(D) the consumer has a right to prohibit information contained in the consumer's file with any consumer reporting agency from being used in connection with any credit or insurance transaction that is not initiated by the consumer; and

(E) the consumer may exercise the right referred to in subparagraph (D) by notifying a notification system established under section 1681b(e) of this title.

(2) Disclosure of address and telephone number; format

A statement under paragraph (1) shall—

(A) include the address and toll-free telephone number of the appropriate notification system established under section 1681b(e) of this title; and

(B) be presented in such format and in such type size and manner as to be simple and easy to understand, as established by the Commission, by rule, in consultation with the Federal banking agencies and the National Credit Union Administration.

(3) Maintaining criteria on file.—A person who makes an offer of credit or insurance to a consumer under a credit or insurance transaction described in paragraph (1) shall maintain on file the criteria used to select the consumer to receive the offer, all criteria bearing on credit worthiness or insurability, as applicable, that are the basis for determining whether or not to extend credit or insurance pursuant to the offer, and any requirement for the furnishing of collateral as a condition of the extension of credit or insurance, until the expiration of the 3-year period beginning on the date on which the offer is made to the consumer.

(4) Authority of Federal agencies regarding unfair or deceptive acts or practices not affected.—This section is not intended to affect the authority of any Federal or State agency to enforce a prohibition against unfair or deceptive acts or practices, including the making of false or misleading statements in connection with a credit or insurance transaction that is not initiated by the consumer.

(e) Red flag guidelines and regulations required

(1) Guidelines

The Federal banking agencies, the National Credit Union Administration, and the Commission shall jointly, with respect to the entities that are subject to their respective enforcement authority under section 1681s of this title—

(A) establish and maintain guidelines for use by each financial institution and each creditor regarding identity theft with respect to account holders at, or customers of, such entities, and update such guidelines as often as necessary;

(B) prescribe regulations requiring each financial institution and each creditor to establish reasonable policies and procedures for implementing the guidelines established pursuant to subparagraph (A), to identify possible risks to account holders or customers or to the safety and soundness of the institution or customers; and

(C) prescribe regulations applicable to card issuers to ensure that, if a card issuer receives notification of a change of address for an existing account, and within a short period of time (during at least the first 30 days after such notification is received) receives a request for an additional or replacement card for the same account, the card issuer may not issue the additional or replacement card, unless the card issuer, in accordance with reasonable policies and procedures—

(i) notifies the cardholder of the request at the former address of the cardholder and provides to the cardholder
a means of promptly reporting incorrect address changes;

(ii) notifies the cardholder of the request by such other means of communication as the cardholder and the card issuer previously agreed to; or

(iii) uses other means of assessing the validity of the change of address, in accordance with reasonable policies and procedures established by the card issuer in accordance with the regulations prescribed under subparagraph (B).

(2) Criteria

(A) In general

In developing the guidelines required by paragraph (1)(A), the agencies described in paragraph (1) shall identify patterns, practices, and specific forms of activity that indicate the possible existence of identity theft.

(B) Inactive accounts

In developing the guidelines required by paragraph (1)(A), the agencies described in paragraph (1) shall consider including reasonable guidelines providing that when a transaction occurs with respect to a credit or deposit account that has been inactive for more than 2 years, the creditor or financial institution shall follow reasonable policies and procedures that provide for notice to be given to a consumer in a manner reasonably designed to reduce the likelihood of identity theft with respect to such account.

(3) Consistency with verification requirements

Guidelines established pursuant to paragraph (1) shall not be inconsistent with the policies and procedures required under section 5318(l) of Title 31.

(f) Prohibition on sale or transfer of debt caused by identity theft

(1) In general

No person shall sell, transfer for consideration, or place for collection a debt that such person has been notified under section 1681c-2 of this title has resulted from identity theft.

(2) Applicability

The prohibitions of this subsection shall apply to all persons collecting a debt described in paragraph (1) after the date of a notification under paragraph (1).

(3) Rule of construction

Nothing in this subsection shall be construed to prohibit—

(A) the repurchase of a debt in any case in which the assignee of the debt requires such repurchase because the debt has resulted from identity theft;

(B) the securitization of a debt or the pledging of a portfolio of debt as collateral in connection with a borrowing; or

(C) the transfer of debt as a result of a merger, acquisition, purchase and assumption transaction, or transfer of substantially all of the assets of an entity.

(g) Debt collector communications concerning identity theft

If a person acting as a debt collector (as that term is defined in subchapter V of this chapter) on behalf of a third party that is a creditor or other user of a consumer report is notified that any information relating to a debt that the person is attempting to collect may be fraudulent or may be the result of identity theft, that person shall—

(1) notify the third party that the information may be fraudulent or may be the result of identity theft; and

(2) upon request of the consumer to whom the debt purportedly relates, provide to the consumer all information to which the consumer would otherwise be entitled if the consumer were not a victim of identity theft, but wished to dispute the debt under provisions of law applicable to that person.

(h) Duties of users in certain credit transactions

(1) In general

Subject to rules prescribed as provided in paragraph (6), if any person uses a consumer report in connection with an application for, or a grant, extension, or other provision of, credit on material terms that are materially less favorable than the most favorable terms available to a substantial proportion of consumers from or through that person, based in whole or in part on a consumer report, the person shall provide an oral, written, or electronic notice to the consumer in the form and manner required by regulations prescribed in accordance with this subsection.

(2) Timing

The notice required under paragraph (1) may be provided at the time of an application for, or a grant, extension, or other provision of, credit or the time of communication of an approval of an application for, or grant, extension, or other provision of, credit, except as provided in the regulations prescribed under paragraph (6).

(3) Exceptions

No notice shall be required from a person under this subsection if—

(A) the consumer applied for specific material terms and was granted those terms, unless those terms were initially specified by the person after the transaction was initiated by the consumer and after the person obtained a consumer report; or

(B) the person has provided or will provide a notice to the consumer under subsection (a) of this section in connection with the transaction.

(4) Other notice not sufficient

A person that is required to provide a notice under subsection (a) of this section cannot meet that requirement by providing a notice under this subsection.

(5) Content and delivery of notice

A notice under this subsection shall, at a minimum—

(A) include a statement informing the consumer that the terms offered to the consumer are set based on information from a consumer report;

(B) identify the consumer reporting agency furnishing the report;

(C) include a statement informing the consumer that the consumer may obtain a copy of a consumer report from that consumer reporting agency without charge; and

(D) include the contact information specified by that consumer reporting agency for obtaining such consumer reports (including a toll-free telephone number established by the agency in the case of a consumer reporting agency described in section 1681a(p) of this title).

(6) Rulemaking

(A) Rules required

The Commission and the Board shall jointly prescribe rules.

(B) Content

Rules required by subparagraph (A) shall address, but are not limited to—

(i) the form, content, time, and manner of delivery of any notice under this subsection;

(ii) clarification of the meaning of terms used in this subsection, including what credit terms are material, and when credit terms are materially less favorable;

(iii) exceptions to the notice requirement under this subsection for classes of persons or transactions regarding which the agencies determine that notice would not significantly benefit consumers;

(iv) a model notice that may be used to comply with this subsection; and

(v) the timing of the notice required under paragraph (1), including the circumstances under which the notice must be provided after the terms offered to the consumer were set based on information from a consumer report.

(7) Compliance

A person shall not be liable for failure to perform the duties required by this section if, at the time of the failure, the person maintained reasonable policies and procedures to comply with this section.

(8) Enforcement

(A) No civil actions

Sections 1681n and 1681o of this title shall not apply to any failure by any person to comply with this section.

(B) Administrative enforcement

This section shall be enforced exclusively under section 1681s of this title by the Federal agencies and officials identified in that section.

§ 1681n. Civil liability for willful noncompliance

(a) In general

Any person who willfully fails to comply with any requirement imposed under this subchapter with respect to any consumer is liable to that consumer in an amount equal to the sum of—

(1)(A) any actual damages sustained by the consumer as a result of the failure or damages of not less than $100 and not more than $1,000; or

(B) in the case of liability of a natural person for obtaining a consumer report under false pretenses or knowingly without a permissible purpose, actual damages sustained by the consumer as a result of the failure or $1,000, whichever is greater;

(2) such amount of punitive damages as the court may allow; and

(3) in the case of any successful action to enforce any liability under this section, the costs of the action together with reasonable attorney's fees as determined by the court.

(b) Civil liability for knowing noncompliance

Any person who obtains a consumer report from a consumer reporting agency under false pretenses or knowingly without a permissible purpose shall be liable to the consumer reporting agency for actual damages sustained by the consumer reporting agency or $1,000, whichever is greater.

(c) Attorney's fees

Upon a finding by the court that an unsuccessful pleading, motion, or other paper filed in connection with an action under this section was filed in bad faith or for purposes of harassment, the court shall award to the prevailing party attorney's fees reasonable in relation to the work expended in responding to the pleading, motion, or other paper.

§ 1681o. Civil liability for negligent noncompliance

(a) In general

Any person who is negligent in failing to comply with any requirement imposed under this subchapter with respect to any consumer is liable to that consumer in an amount equal to the sum of—

(1) any actual damages sustained by the consumer as a result of the failure; and

(2) in the case of any successful action to enforce any liability under this section, the costs of the action together with reasonable attorney's fees as determined by the court.

(b) Attorney's fees

On a finding by the court that an unsuccessful pleading, motion, or other paper filed in connection with an action under this section was filed in bad faith or for purposes of harassment, the court shall award to the prevailing party attorney's fees reasonable in relation to the work expended in responding to the pleading, motion, or other paper.

§ 1681p. Jurisdiction of courts; limitation of actions

An action to enforce any liability created under this subchapter may be brought in any appropriate United States district court, without regard to the amount in controversy, or in any other court of competent jurisdiction, not later than the earlier of—

(1) 2 years after the date of discovery by the plaintiff of the violation that is the basis for such liability; or

(2) 5 years after the date on which the violation that is the basis for such liability occurs.

§ 1681q. Obtaining information under false pretenses

Any person who knowingly and willfully obtains information on a consumer from a consumer reporting agency under false pretenses shall be fined under Title 18, imprisoned for not more than 2 years, or both.

§ 1681r. Unauthorized disclosures by officers or employees

Any officer or employee of a consumer reporting agency who knowingly and willfully provides information concerning an individual from the agency's files to a person not authorized to receive that information shall be fined under Title 18, imprisoned for not more than 2 years, or both.

§ 1681s. Administrative enforcement

(a) Enforcement by Federal Trade Commission

(1) Enforcement by Federal Trade Commission. Compliance with the requirements imposed under this subchapter shall be enforced under the Federal Trade Commission Act [15 U.S.C.A. § 41 et seq.] by the Federal Trade Commission with respect to consumer reporting agencies and all other persons subject thereto, except to the extent that enforcement of the requirements imposed under this subchapter is specifically committed to some other government agency under subsection (b) hereof. For the purpose of the exercise by the Federal Trade Commission of its functions and powers under the Federal Trade Commission Act, a violation of any requirement or prohibition imposed under this subchapter shall constitute an unfair or deceptive act or practice in commerce in violation of section 5(a) of the Federal Trade Commission Act [15 U.S.C.A. § 45(a)] and shall be subject to enforcement by the Federal Trade Commission under section 5(b) thereof [15 U.S.C.A. § 45(b)] with respect to any consumer reporting agency or person subject to enforcement by the Federal Trade Commission pursuant to this subsection, irrespective of whether that person is engaged in commerce or meets any other jurisdictional tests in the Federal Trade Commission Act. The Federal Trade Commission shall have such procedural, investigative, and enforcement powers, including the power to issue procedural rules in enforcing compliance with the requirements imposed under this subchapter and to require the filing of reports, the production of documents, and the appearance of witnesses as though the applicable terms and conditions of the Federal Trade Commission Act were part of this subchapter. Any person violating any of the provisions of this subchapter shall be subject to the penalties and entitled to the privileges and immunities provided in the Federal Trade Commission Act as though the applicable terms and provisions thereof were part of this subchapter.

(2)(A) In the event of a knowing violation, which constitutes a pattern or practice of violations of this subchapter, the Commission may commence a civil action to recover a civil penalty in a district court of the United States against any person that violates this subchapter. In such action, such person shall be liable for a civil penalty of not more than $2,500 per violation.

(B) In determining the amount of a civil penalty under subparagraph (A), the court shall take into account the degree of culpability, any history of prior such conduct, ability to pay, effect on ability to continue to do business, and such other matters as justice may require.

(3) Notwithstanding paragraph (2), a court may not impose any civil penalty on a person for a violation of section 1681s-2(a)(1) of this title unless the person has been enjoined from committing the violation, or ordered not to commit the violation, in an action or proceeding brought by or on behalf of the Federal Trade Commission, and has violated the injunction or order, and the court may not impose any civil penalty for any violation occurring before the date of the violation of the injunction or order.

(b) Enforcement by other agencies

Compliance with the requirements imposed under this subchapter with respect to consumer reporting agencies, persons who use consumer reports from such agencies, persons who furnish information to such agencies, and users of information that are subject to subsection (d) of section 1681m of this title shall be enforced under—

(1) section 8 of the Federal Deposit Insurance Act [12 U.S.C.A. § 1818], in the case of—

(A) national banks, and Federal branches and Federal agencies of foreign banks, by the Office of the Comptroller of the Currency;

(B) member banks of the Federal Reserve System (other than national banks), branches and agencies of foreign banks (other than Federal branches, Federal agencies, and insured State branches of foreign banks), commercial lending companies owned or controlled by foreign banks, and organizations operating under section 25 or 25A of the Federal Reserve Act [12 U.S.C.A. § 601 et seq. or § 611 et seq.], by the Board of Governors of the Federal Reserve System; and

(C) banks insured by the Federal Deposit Insurance Corporation (other than members of the Federal Reserve System) and insured State branches of foreign banks, by the Board of Directors of the Federal Deposit Insurance Corporation;

(2) section 8 of the Federal Deposit Insurance Act [12 U.S.C.A. § 1818], by the Director of the Office of Thrift Supervision, in the case of a savings association the deposits of which are insured by the Federal Deposit Insurance Corporation.

(3) the Federal Credit Union Act [12 U.S.C.A. § 1751 et seq.], by the Administrator of the National Credit Union Administration with respect to any Federal credit union;

(4) subtitle IV of Title 49, by the Secretary of Transportation, with respect to all carriers subject to the jurisdiction of the Surface Transportation Board;

(5) part A of subtitle VII of Title 49, by the Secretary of Transportation with respect to any air carrier or foreign air carrier subject to that part; and

(6) the Packers and Stockyards Act, 1921 [7 U.S.C.A. § 181 et seq.] (except as provided in section 406 of that Act [7 U.S.C.A. § § 226, 227]), by the Secretary of Agriculture with respect to any activities subject to that Act.

The terms used in paragraph (1) that are not defined in this subchapter or otherwise defined in section 3(s) of the Federal Deposit Insurance Act (12 U.S.C. 1813(s)) shall have the meaning given to them in section 1(b) of the International Banking Act of 1978 (12 U.S.C. 3101).

(c) State action for violations

(1) Authority of States.—In addition to such other remedies as are provided under State law, if the chief law enforcement officer of a State, or an official or agency designated by a State, has reason to believe that any person has violated or is violating this subchapter, the State—

(A) may bring an action to enjoin such violation in any appropriate United States district court or in any other court of competent jurisdiction;

(B) subject to paragraph (5), may bring an action on behalf of the residents of the State to recover—

(i) damages for which the person is liable to such residents under sections 1681n and 1681o of this title as a result of the violation;

(ii) in the case of a violation described in any of paragraphs (1) through (3) of section 1681s-2(c) of this title, damages for which the person would, but for section 1681s-2(c) of this title, be liable to such residents as a result of the violation; or

(iii) damages of not more than $1,000 for each willful or negligent violation; and

(C) in the case of any successful action under subparagraph (A) or (B), shall be awarded the costs of the action and reasonable attorney fees as determined by the court.

(2) Rights of Federal regulators.—The State shall serve prior written notice of any action under paragraph (1) upon the Federal Trade Commission or the appropriate Federal regulator determined under subsection (b) of this section and provide the Commission or appropriate Federal regulator with a copy of its complaint, except in any case in which such prior notice is not feasible, in which case the State shall serve such notice immediately upon instituting such action. The Federal Trade Commission or appropriate Federal regulator shall have the right—

(A) to intervene in the action;

(B) upon so intervening, to be heard on all matters arising therein;

(C) to remove the action to the appropriate United States district court; and

(D) to file petitions for appeal.

(3) Investigatory powers.—For purposes of bringing any action under this subsection, nothing in this subsection shall prevent the chief law enforcement officer, or an official or agency designated by a State, from exercising the powers conferred on the chief law enforcement officer or such official by the laws of such State to conduct investigations or to administer oaths or affirmations or to compel the attendance of witnesses or the production of documentary and other evidence.

(4) Limitation on State action while Federal action pending.—If the Federal Trade Commission or the appropriate Federal regulator has instituted a civil action or an administrative action under section 8 of the Federal Deposit Insurance Act [12 U.S.C.A. § 1818] for a violation of this subchapter, no State may, during the pendency of such action, bring an action under this section against any defendant named in the complaint of the Commission or the appropriate Federal regulator for any violation of this subchapter that is alleged in that complaint.

(5) Limitations on State actions for certain violations

(A) Violation of injunction required.—A State may not bring an action against a person under paragraph (1)(B) for a violation described in any of paragraphs (1) through (3) of section 1681s-2(c) of this title, unless—

(i) the person has been enjoined from committing the violation, in an action brought by the State under paragraph (1)(A); and

(ii) the person has violated the injunction.

(B) Limitation on damages recoverable.—In an action against a person under paragraph (1)(B) for a violation described in any of paragraphs (1) through (3) of section 1681s-2(c) of this title, a State may not recover any damages incurred before the date of the violation of an injunction on which the action is based.

(d) Enforcement under other authority

For the purpose of the exercise by any agency referred to in subsection (b) of this section of its powers under any Act referred to in that subsection, a violation of any requirement imposed under this subchapter shall be deemed to be a violation of a requirement imposed under that Act. In addition to its powers under any provision of law specifically referred to in subsection (b) of this section, each of the agencies referred to in that subsection may exercise, for the purpose of enforcing compliance with any requirement imposed under this subchapter any other authority conferred on it by law.

(e) Regulatory authority

(1) The Federal banking agencies referred to in paragraphs (1) and (2) of subsection (b) shall jointly prescribe such regulations as necessary to carry out the purposes of this subchapter with respect to any persons identified under paragraphs (1) and (2) of subsection (b) of this section, and the Board of Governors of the Federal Reserve System shall have authority to prescribe regulations consistent with such joint regulations with respect to bank holding companies and affiliates (other than depository institutions and consumer reporting agencies) of such holding companies.

(2) The Board of the National Credit Union Administration shall prescribe such regulations as necessary to carry out the purposes of this subchapter with respect to any persons identified under paragraph (3) of subsection (b) of this section.

(f) Coordination of consumer complaint investigations

(1) In general

Each consumer reporting agency described in section 1681a(p) of this title shall develop and maintain procedures for the referral to each other such agency of any consumer complaint received by the agency alleging identity theft, or requesting a fraud alert under section 1681c-1 of this title or a block under section 1681c-2 of this title.

(2) Model form and procedure for reporting identity theft

The Commission, in consultation with the Federal banking agencies and the National Credit Union Administration, shall develop a model form and model procedures to be used by consumers who are victims of identity theft for contacting and informing creditors and consumer reporting agencies of the fraud.

(3) Annual summary reports

Each consumer reporting agency described in section 1681a(p) of this title shall submit an annual summary report to the Commission on consumer complaints received by the agency on identity theft or fraud alerts.

(g) FTC regulation of coding of trade names

If the Commission determines that a person described in paragraph (9) of section 1681s-c(a) of this title has not met the requirements of such paragraph, the Commission shall take action to ensure the person's compliance with such paragraph, which may include issuing model guidance or prescribing reasonable policies and procedures, as necessary to ensure that such person complies with such paragraph.

§ 1681s-1. Information on overdue child support obligations

Notwithstanding any other provision of this subchapter, a consumer reporting agency shall include in any consumer report furnished by the agency in accordance with section 1681b of this title, any information on the failure of the consumer to pay overdue support which—

(1) is provided—

(A) to the consumer reporting agency by a State or local child support enforcement agency; or

(B) to the consumer reporting agency and verified by any local, State, or Federal Government agency; and

(2) antedates the report by 7 years or less.

§ 1681s-2. Responsibilities of furnishers of information to consumer reporting agencies

(a) Duty of furnishers of information to provide accurate information

(1) Prohibition

(A) Reporting information with actual knowledge of errors

A person shall not furnish any information relating to a consumer to any consumer reporting agency if the person knows or has reasonable cause to believe that the information is inaccurate.

(B) Reporting information after notice and confirmation of errors

A person shall not furnish information relating to a consumer to any consumer reporting agency if—

(i) the person has been notified by the consumer, at the address specified by the person for such notices, that specific information is inaccurate; and

(ii) the information is, in fact, inaccurate.

(C) No address requirement

A person who clearly and conspicuously specifies to the consumer an address for notices referred to in subparagraph (B) shall not be subject to subparagraph (A); however, nothing in subparagraph (B) shall require a person to specify such an address.

(D) Definition

For purposes of subparagraph (A), the term "reasonable cause to believe that the information is inaccurate" means having specific knowledge, other than solely allegations by the consumer, that would cause a reasonable person to have substantial doubts about the accuracy of the information.

(2) Duty to correct and update information

A person who—

(A) regularly and in the ordinary course of business furnishes information to one or more consumer reporting agencies about the person's transactions or experiences with any consumer; and

(B) has furnished to a consumer reporting agency information that the person determines is not complete or accurate,

shall promptly notify the consumer reporting agency of that determination and provide to the agency any corrections to that information, or any additional information, that is necessary to make the information provided by the person to the agency complete and accurate, and shall not thereafter furnish to the agency any of the information that remains not complete or accurate.

(3) Duty to provide notice of dispute

If the completeness or accuracy of any information furnished by any person to any consumer reporting agency is disputed to such person by a consumer, the person may not furnish the information to any consumer reporting agency without notice that such information is disputed by the consumer.

(4) Duty to provide notice of closed accounts

A person who regularly and in the ordinary course of business furnishes information to a consumer reporting agency regarding a consumer who has a credit account with that person shall notify the agency of the voluntary closure of the account by the consumer, in information regularly furnished for the period in which the account is closed.

(5) Duty to provide notice of delinquency of accounts

(A) In general

A person who furnishes information to a consumer reporting agency regarding a delinquent account being placed for collection, charged to profit or loss, or subjected to any similar action shall, not later than 90 days after furnishing the information, notify the agency of the date of delinquency on the account, which shall be the month and year of the commencement of the delinquency on the account that immediately preceded the action.

(B) Rule of construction

For purposes of this paragraph only, and provided that the consumer does not dispute the information, a person that furnishes information on a delinquent account that is placed for collection, charged for profit or loss, or subjected to any similar action, complies with this paragraph, if—

(i) the person reports the same date of delinquency as that provided by the creditor to which the account was owed at the time at which the commencement of the delinquency occurred, if the creditor previously reported that date of delinquency to a consumer reporting agency;

(ii) the creditor did not previously report the date of delinquency to a consumer reporting agency, and the person establishes and follows reasonable procedures to obtain the date of delinquency from the creditor or another reliable source and reports that date to a consumer reporting agency as the date of delinquency; or

(iii) the creditor did not previously report the date of delinquency to a consumer reporting agency and the date of delinquency cannot be reasonably obtained as provided in clause (ii), the person establishes and follows reasonable procedures to ensure the date reported as the date of delinquency precedes the date on which the account is placed for collection, charged to profit or loss, or subjected to any similar action, and reports such date to the credit reporting agency.

(6) Duties of furnishers upon notice of identity theft-related information

(A) Reasonable procedures

A person that furnishes information to any consumer reporting agency shall have in place reasonable procedures to respond to any notification that it receives from a consumer reporting agency under section 1681c-2 of this title relating to information resulting from identity theft, to prevent that person from refurnishing such blocked information.

(B) Information alleged to result from identity theft

If a consumer submits an identity theft report to a person who furnishes information to a consumer reporting agency at the address specified by that person for receiving such reports stating that information maintained by such person that purports to relate to the consumer resulted from identity theft, the person may not furnish such information that purports to relate to the consumer to any consumer reporting agency, unless the person subsequently knows or is informed by the consumer that the information is correct.

(7) Negative information

(A) Notice to consumer required

(i) In general

If any financial institution that extends credit and regularly and in the ordinary course of business furnishes information to a consumer reporting agency described in section 1681a(p) of this title furnishes negative information to such an agency regarding credit extended to a customer, the financial institution shall provide a notice of such furnishing of negative information, in writing, to the customer.

(ii) Notice effective for subsequent submissions

After providing such notice, the financial institution may submit additional negative information to a consumer reporting agency described in section 1681a(p) of this title with respect to the same transaction, extension of credit, account, or customer without providing additional notice to the customer.

(B) Time of notice

(i) In general

The notice required under subparagraph (A) shall be provided to the customer prior to, or no later than 30 days after, furnishing the negative information to a consumer reporting agency described in section 1681a(p) of this title.

(ii) Coordination with new account disclosures

If the notice is provided to the customer prior to furnishing the negative information to a consumer reporting agency, the notice may not be included in the initial disclosures provided under section 1637(a) of this title.

(C) Coordination with other disclosures

The notice required under subparagraph (A)—

(i) may be included on or with any notice of default, any billing statement, or any other materials provided to the customer; and

(ii) must be clear and conspicuous.

(D) Model disclosure

(i) Duty of board to prepare

The Board shall prescribe a brief model disclosure a financial institution may use to comply with subparagraph (A), which shall not exceed 30 words.

(ii) Use of model not required

No provision of this paragraph shall be construed as requiring a financial institution to use any such model form prescribed by the Board.

(iii) Compliance using model

A financial institution shall be deemed to be in compliance with subparagraph (A) if the financial institution uses any such model form prescribed by the Board, or the financial institution uses any such model form and rearranges its format.

(E) Use of notice without submitting negative information

No provision of this paragraph shall be construed as requiring a financial institution that has provided a customer with a notice described in subparagraph (A) to furnish negative information about the customer to a consumer reporting agency.

(F) Safe harbor

A financial institution shall not be liable for failure to perform the duties required by this paragraph if, at the time of the failure, the financial institution maintained reasonable policies and procedures to comply with this paragraph or the financial institution reasonably believed that the institution is prohibited, by law, from contacting the consumer.

(G) Definitions

For purposes of this paragraph, the following definitions shall apply:

(i) Negative information

The term "negative information" means information concerning a customer's delinquencies, late payments, insolvency, or any form of default.

(ii) Customer; financial institution

The terms "customer" and "financial institution" have the same meanings as in section 6809 of this title.

(8) Ability of consumer to dispute information directly with furnisher

(A) In general

The Federal banking agencies, the National Credit Union Administration, and the Commission shall jointly prescribe regulations that shall identify the circumstances under which a furnisher shall be required to reinvestigate a dispute concerning the accuracy of information contained in a consumer report on the consumer, based on a direct request of a consumer.

(B) Considerations

In prescribing regulations under subparagraph (A), the agencies shall weigh—

(i) the benefits to consumers with the costs on furnishers and the credit reporting system;

(ii) the impact on the overall accuracy and integrity of consumer reports of any such requirements;

(iii) whether direct contact by the consumer with the furnisher would likely result in the most expeditious resolution of any such dispute; and

(iv) the potential impact on the credit reporting process if credit repair organizations, as defined in section 1679a(3) of this title, including entities that would be a credit repair organization, but for section 1679a(3)(B)(i) of this title, are able to circumvent the prohibition in subparagraph (G).

(C) Applicability

Subparagraphs (D) through (G) shall apply in any circumstance identified under the regulations promulgated under subparagraph (A).

(D) Submitting a notice of dispute

A consumer who seeks to dispute the accuracy of information shall provide a dispute notice directly to such person at the address specified by the person for such notices that—

(i) identifies the specific information that is being disputed;

(ii) explains the basis for the dispute; and

(iii) includes all supporting documentation required by the furnisher to substantiate the basis of the dispute.

(E) Duty of person after receiving notice of dispute

After receiving a notice of dispute from a consumer pursuant to subparagraph (D), the person that provided the information in dispute to a consumer reporting agency shall—

(i) conduct an investigation with respect to the disputed information;

(ii) review all relevant information provided by the consumer with the notice;

(iii) complete such person's investigation of the dispute and report the results of the investigation to the consumer before the expiration of the period under section 1681i(a)(1) of this title within which a consumer reporting agency would be required to complete its action if the consumer had elected to dispute the information under that section; and

(iv) if the investigation finds that the information reported was inaccurate, promptly notify each consumer reporting agency to which the person furnished the inaccurate information of that determination and provide to the agency any correction to that information that is necessary to make the information provided by the person accurate.

(F) Frivolous or irrelevant dispute

(i) In general

This paragraph shall not apply if the person receiving a notice of a dispute from a consumer reasonably determines that the dispute is frivolous or irrelevant, including—

(I) by reason of the failure of a consumer to provide sufficient information to investigate the disputed information; or

(II) the submission by a consumer of a dispute that is substantially the same as a dispute previously submitted by or for the consumer, either directly to the person or through a consumer reporting agency under subsection (b) of this section, with respect to which the person has already performed the person's duties under this paragraph or subsection (b), as applicable.

(ii) Notice of determination

Upon making any determination under clause (i) that a dispute is frivolous or irrelevant, the person shall notify the consumer of such determination not later than 5 business days after making such determination, by mail or, if authorized by the consumer for that purpose, by any other means available to the person.

(iii) Contents of notice

A notice under clause (ii) shall include—

(I) the reasons for the determination under clause (i); and

(II) identification of any information required to investigate the disputed information, which may consist of a standardized form describing the general nature of such information.

(G) Exclusion of credit repair organizations

This paragraph shall not apply if the notice of the dispute is submitted by, is prepared on behalf of the consumer by, or is submitted on a form supplied to the consumer by, a credit repair organization, as defined in section 1679a(3) of this title, or an entity that would be a credit repair organization, but for section 1679a(3)(B)(i) of this title.

(9) Duty to provide notice of status as medical information furnisher

A person whose primary business is providing medical services, products, or devices, or the person's agent or assignee, who furnishes information to a consumer reporting agency on a consumer shall be considered a medical information furnisher for purposes of this subchapter, and shall notify the agency of such status.

(b) Duties of furnishers of information upon notice of dispute

(1) In general

After receiving notice pursuant to section 1681i(a)(2) of this title of a dispute with regard to the completeness or accuracy of any information provided by a person to a consumer reporting agency, the person shall—

(A) conduct an investigation with respect to the disputed information;

(B) review all relevant information provided by the consumer reporting agency pursuant to section 1681i(a)(2) of this title;

(C) report the results of the investigation to the consumer reporting agency;

(D) if the investigation finds that the information is incomplete or inaccurate, report those results to all other consumer reporting agencies to which the person furnished the information and that compile and maintain files on consumers on a nationwide basis; and

(E) if an item of information disputed by a consumer is found to be inaccurate or incomplete or cannot be verified after any reinvestigation under paragraph (1), for purposes of reporting to a consumer reporting agency only, as appropriate, based on the results of the reinvestigation promptly—

(i) modify that item of information;

(ii) delete that item of information; or

(iii) permanently block the reporting of that item of information.

(2) Deadline

A person shall complete all investigations, reviews, and reports required under paragraph (1) regarding information provided by the person to a consumer reporting agency, before the expiration of the period under section 1681i(a)(1) of this title within which the consumer reporting agency is required to complete actions required by that section regarding that information.

(c) Limitation on liability

Except as provided in section 1681s(c)(1)(B) of this title, sections 1681n and 1681o of this title do not apply to any violation of—

(1) subsection (a) of this section, including any regulations issued thereunder;

(2) subsection (e) of this section, except that nothing in this paragraph shall limit, expand, or otherwise affect liability under section 1681n or 16810 of this title, as applicable, for violations of subsection (b) of this section; or

(3) subsection (e) of section 1681m of this title.

(d) Limitation on enforcement

The provisions of law described in paragraphs (1) through (3) of subsection (c) of this section (other than with respect to the exception described in paragraph (2) of subsection (c) of this section) shall be enforced exclusively as provided under section 1681s of this title by the Federal agencies and officials and the State officials identified in section 1681s of this title.

(e) Accuracy guidelines and regulations required

(1) Guidelines

The Federal banking agencies, the National Credit Union Administration, and the Commission shall, with respect to the entities that are subject to their respective enforcement authority under section 1681m of this title, and in coordination as described in paragraph (2)—

(A) establish and maintain guidelines for use by each person that furnishes information to a consumer reporting agency regarding the accuracy and integrity of the information relating to consumers that such entities furnish to consumer reporting agencies, and update such guidelines as often as necessary; and

(B) prescribe regulations requiring each person that furnishes information to a consumer reporting agency to establish reasonable policies and procedures for implementing the guidelines established pursuant to subparagraph (A).

(2) Coordination

Each agency required to prescribe regulations under paragraph (1) shall consult and coordinate with each other such agency so that, to the extent possible, the regulations prescribed by each such entity are consistent and comparable with the regulations prescribed by each other such agency.

(3) Criteria

In developing the guidelines required by paragraph (1)(A), the agencies described in paragraph (1) shall—

(A) identify patterns, practices, and specific forms of activity that can compromise the accuracy and integrity of information furnished to consumer reporting agencies;

(B) review the methods (including technological means) used to furnish information relating to consumers to consumer reporting agencies;

(C) determine whether persons that furnish information to consumer reporting agencies maintain and enforce policies to assure the accuracy and integrity of information furnished to consumer reporting agencies; and

(D) examine the policies and processes that persons that furnish information to consumer reporting agencies employ to conduct reinvestigations and correct inaccurate information relating to consumers that has been furnished to consumer reporting agencies.

§ 1681s-3. Affiliate sharing

(a) Special rule for solicitation for purposes of marketing

(1) Notice

Any person that receives from another person related to it by common ownership or affiliated by corporate control a communication of information that would be a consumer report, but for clauses (i), (ii), and (iii) of section 1681a(d)(2)(A) of this title, may not use the information to make a solicitation for marketing purposes to a consumer about its products or services, unless—

(A) it is clearly and conspicuously disclosed to the consumer that the information may be communicated among such persons for purposes of making such solicitations to the consumer; and

(B) the consumer is provided an opportunity and a simple method to prohibit the making of such solicitations to the consumer by such person.

(2) Consumer choice

(A) In general

The notice required under paragraph (1) shall allow the consumer the opportunity to prohibit all solicitations referred to in such paragraph, and may allow the consumer to choose from different options when electing to prohibit the sending of such solicitations, including options regarding the types of entities and information covered, and which methods of delivering solicitations the consumer elects to prohibit.

(B) Format

Notwithstanding subparagraph (A), the notice required under paragraph (1) shall be clear, conspicuous, and concise, and any method provided under paragraph (1)(B) shall be simple. The regulations prescribed to implement this section shall provide specific guidance regarding how to comply with such standards.

(3) Duration

(A) In general

The election of a consumer pursuant to paragraph (1)(B) to prohibit the making of solicitations shall be effective for at least 5 years, beginning on the date on which the person receives the election of the consumer, unless the consumer requests that such election be revoked.

(B) Notice upon expiration of effective period

At such time as the election of a consumer pursuant to paragraph (1)(B) is no longer effective, a person may not use information that the person receives in the manner described in paragraph (1) to make any solicitation for marketing purposes to the consumer, unless the consumer receives a notice and an opportunity, using a simple method, to extend the opt-out for another period of at least 5 years, pursuant to the procedures described in paragraph (1).

(4) Scope

This section shall not apply to a person—

(A) using information to make a solicitation for marketing purposes to a consumer with whom the person has a pre-existing business relationship;

(B) using information to facilitate communications to an individual for whose benefit the person provides employee benefit or other services pursuant to a contract with an employer related to and arising out of the current employment relationship or status of the individual as a participant or beneficiary of an employee benefit plan;

(C) using information to perform services on behalf of another person related by common ownership or affiliated by corporate control, except that this subparagraph shall not be construed as permitting a person to send solicitations on behalf of another person, if such other person would not be permitted to send the solicitation on its own behalf as a result of the election of the consumer to prohibit solicitations under paragraph (1)(B);

(D) using information in response to a communication initiated by the consumer;

(E) using information in response to solicitations authorized or requested by the consumer; or

(F) if compliance with this section by that person would prevent compliance by that person with any provision of State insurance laws pertaining to unfair discrimination in any State in which the person is lawfully doing business.

(5) No retroactivity

This subsection shall not prohibit the use of information to send a solicitation to a consumer if such information was received prior to the date on which persons are required to comply with regulations implementing this subsection.

(b) Notice for other purposes permissible

A notice or other disclosure under this section may be coordinated and consolidated with any other notice required to be issued under any other provision of law by a person that is subject to this section, and a notice or other disclosure that is equivalent to the notice required by subsection (a) of this section, and that is provided by a person described in subsection (a) of this section to a consumer together with disclosures required by any other provision of law, shall satisfy the requirements of subsection (a) of this section.

(c) User requirements

Requirements with respect to the use by a person of information received from another person related to it by common ownership or affiliated by corporate control, such as the requirements of this section, constitute requirements with respect to the exchange of information among persons affiliated by common ownership or common corporate control, within the meaning of section 1681t(b)(2) of this title.

(d) Definitions

For purposes of this section, the following definitions shall apply:

(1) Pre-existing business relationship

The term "pre-existing business relationship" means a relationship between a person, or a person's licensed agent, and a consumer, based on—

(A) a financial contract between a person and a consumer which is in force;

(B) the purchase, rental, or lease by the consumer of that person's goods or services, or a financial transaction (including holding an active account or a policy in force or having another continuing relationship) between the consumer and that person during the 18-month period immediately preceding the date on which the consumer is sent a solicitation covered by this section;

(C) an inquiry or application by the consumer regarding a product or service offered by that person, during the 3-month period immediately preceding the date on which the consumer is sent a solicitation covered by this section; or

(D) any other pre-existing customer relationship defined in the regulations implementing this section.

(2) Solicitation

The term "solicitation" means the marketing of a product or service initiated by a person to a particular consumer that is based on an exchange of information described in subsection (a) of this section, and is intended to encourage the consumer to purchase such product or service, but does not include communications that are directed at the general public or determined not to be a solicitation by the regulations prescribed under this section.

§ 1681t. Relation to State laws

(a) In general

Except as provided in subsections (b) and (c) of this section, this subchapter does not annul, alter, affect, or exempt any person subject to the provisions of this subchapter from complying with the laws of any State with respect to the collection, distribution, or use of any information on consumers, or for the prevention or mitigation of identity theft, except to the extent that those laws are inconsistent with any provision of this subchapter, and then only to the extent of the inconsistency.

(b) General exceptions

No requirement or prohibition may be imposed under the laws of any State—

(1) with respect to any subject matter regulated under—

(A) subsection (c) or (e) of section 1681b of this title, relating to the prescreening of consumer reports;

(B) section 1681i of this title, relating to the time by which a consumer reporting agency must take any action, including the provision of notification to a consumer or other person, in any procedure related to the disputed accuracy of information in a consumer's file, except that this subparagraph shall not apply to any State law in effect on September 30, 1996;

(C) subsections (a) and (b) of section 1681m of this title, relating to the duties of a person who takes any adverse action with respect to a consumer;

(D) section 1681m(d) of this title, relating to the duties of persons who use a consumer report of a consumer in connection with any credit or insurance transaction that is not initiated by the consumer and that consists of a firm offer of credit or insurance;

(E) section 1681c of this title, relating to information contained in consumer reports, except that this subparagraph shall not apply to any State law in effect on September 30, 1996;

(F) section 1681s-2 of this title, relating to the responsibilities of persons who furnish information to consumer reporting agencies, except that this paragraph shall not apply—

(i) with respect to section 54A(a) of chapter 93 of the Massachusetts Annotated Laws (as in effect on September 30, 1996); or

(ii) with respect to section 1785.25(a) of the California Civil Code (as in effect on September 30, 1996);

(G) section 1681g(e) of this title, relating to information available to victims under section 1681g(e) of this title;

(H) section 1681s-3 of this title, relating to the exchange and use of information to make a solicitation for marketing purposes; or

(I) section 1681m(h) of this title, relating to the duties of users of consumer reports to provide notice with respect to terms in certain credit transactions;

(2) with respect to the exchange of information among persons affiliated by common ownership or common corporate control, except that this paragraph shall not apply with respect to subsection (a) or (c)(1) of section 2480e of title 9, Vermont Statutes Annotated (as in effect on September 30, 1996);

(3) with respect to the disclosures required to be made under subsection (c), (d), (e), or (g) of section 1681g of this title, or subsection (f) of section 1681g of this title relating to the disclosure of credit scores for credit granting purposes, except that this paragraph—

(A) shall not apply with respect to sections 1785.10, 1785.16, and 1785.20.2 of the California Civil Code (as in effect on December 4, 2003) and section 1785.15 through section 1785.15.2 of such Code (as in effect on such date);

(B) shall not apply with respect to sections 5-3-106(2) and 212-14.3- 104.3 of the Colorado Revised Statutes (as in effect on December 4, 2003); and

(C) shall not be construed as limiting, annulling, affecting, or superseding any provision of the laws of any State regulating the use in an insurance activity, or regulating disclosures concerning such use, of a credit-based insurance score of a consumer by any person engaged in the business of insurance;

(4) with respect to the frequency of any disclosure under section 1681j(a) of this title, except that this paragraph shall not apply—

(A) with respect to section 12-14.3-105(1)(d) of the Colorado Revised Statutes (as in effect on December 4, 2003);

(B) with respect to section 10-1-393(29)(C) of the Georgia Code (as in effect on December 4, 2003);

(C) with respect to section 1316.2 of title 10 of the Maine Revised Statutes (as in effect on December 4, 2003);

(D) with respect to sections 14-1209(a)(1) and 14-1209(b)(1)(i) of the Commercial Law Article of the Code of Maryland (as in effect on December 4, 2003);

(E) with respect to section 59(d) and section 59(e) of chapter 93 of the General Laws of Massachusetts (as in effect December 4, 2003);

(F) with respect to section 56:11-37.10(a)(1) of the New Jersey Revised Statutes (as in effect on December 4, 2003); or

(G) with respect to section 2480c(a)(1) of title 9 of the Vermont Statutes Annotated (as in effect on December 4, 2003); or

(5) with respect to the conduct required by the specific provisions of—

(A) section 1681c(g) of this title;

(B) section 1681c-1 of this title;

(C) section 1681c-2 of this title;

(D) section 1681g(a)(1)(A) of this title;

(E) section 1681j(a) of this title;

(F) subsections (e), (f), and (g) of section 1681m of this title;

(G) section 1681s(f) of this title;

(H) section 1681s-2(a)(6) of this title; or

(I) section 1681w of this title.

(c) "Firm offer of credit or insurance" defined

Notwithstanding any definition of the term "firm offer of credit or insurance" (or any equivalent term) under the laws of any State, the definition of that term contained in section 1681a(l) of this title shall be construed to apply in the enforcement and interpretation of the laws of any State governing consumer reports.

(d) Limitations

Subsections (b) and (c) of this section do not affect any settlement, agreement, or consent judgment between any State Attorney General and any consumer reporting agency in effect on September 30, 1996.

§ 1681u. Disclosures to FBI for counterintelligence purposes

(a) Identity of financial institutions

Notwithstanding section 1681b of this title or any other provision of this subchapter, a consumer reporting agency shall furnish to the Federal Bureau of Investigation the names and addresses of all financial institutions (as that term is defined in section 3401 of Title 12) at which a consumer maintains or has maintained an account, to the extent that information is in the files of the agency, when presented with a written request for that information, signed by the Director of the Federal Bureau of Investigation, or the Director's designee in a position not lower than Deputy Assistant Director at Bureau headquarters or a Special Agent in Charge of a Bureau field office designated by the Director, which certifies compliance with this section. The Director or the Director's designee may make such a certification only if the Director or the Director's designee has determined in writing, that such information is sought for the conduct of an authorized investigation to protect against international terrorism or clandestine intelligence activities, provided that such an investigation of a United States person is not conducted solely upon the basis of activities protected by the first amendment to the Constitution of the United States.

(b) Identifying information

Notwithstanding the provisions of section 1681b of this title or any other provision of this subchapter, a consumer reporting agency shall furnish identifying information respecting a consumer, limited to name, address, former addresses, places of employment, or former places of employment, to the Federal Bureau of Investigation when presented with a written request, signed by the Director or the Director's designee in a position not lower than Deputy Assistant Director at Bureau headquarters or a Special Agent in Charge of a Bureau field office designated by the Director, which certifies compliance with this subsection. The Director or the Director's designee may make such a certification only if the Director or the Director's designee has determined in writing that such information is sought for the conduct of an authorized investigation to protect against international terrorism or clandestine intelligence activities, provided that such an investigation of a United States person is not conducted solely upon the basis of activities protected by the first amendment to the Constitution of the United States.

(c) Court order for disclosure of consumer reports

Notwithstanding section 1681b of this title or any other provision of this subchapter, if requested in writing by the Director of the Federal Bureau of Investigation, or a designee of the Director in a position not lower than Deputy Assistant Director at Bureau headquarters or a Special Agent in Charge in a Bureau field office designated by the Director, a court may issue an order ex parte directing a consumer reporting agency to furnish a consumer report to the Federal Bureau of Investigation, upon a showing in camera that the consumer report is sought for the conduct of an authorized investigation to protect against international terrorism or clandestine intelligence activities, provided that such an investigation of a United States person is not conducted solely upon the basis of activities protected by the first amendment to the Constitution of the United States.

The terms of an order issued under this subsection shall not disclose that the order is issued for purposes of a counterintelligence investigation.

(d) Confidentiality

(1) If the Director of the Federal Bureau of Investigation, or his designee in a position not lower than Deputy Assistant Director at Bureau headquarters or a Special Agent in Charge in a Bureau field office designated by the Director, certifies that otherwise there may result a danger to the national security of the United States, interference with a criminal, counterterrorism, or counterintelligence investigation, interference with diplomatic relations, or danger to the life or physical safety of any person, no consumer reporting agency or officer, employee, or agent of a consumer reporting agency shall disclose to any person (other than those to whom such disclosure is necessary to comply with the request or an attorney to obtain legal advice or legal assistance with respect to the request) that the Federal Bureau of Investigation has sought or obtained the identity of financial institutions or a consumer report respecting any consumer under subsection (a), (b), or (c) of this section, and no consumer reporting agency or officer, employee, or agent of a consumer reporting agency shall include in any consumer report any information that would indicate that the Federal Bureau of Investigation has sought or obtained such information on a consumer report.

(2) The request shall notify the person or entity to whom the request is directed of the nondisclosure requirement under paragraph (1).

(3) Any recipient disclosing to those persons necessary to comply with the request or to an attorney to obtain legal advice or legal assistance with respect to the request shall inform such persons of any applicable nondisclosure requirement. Any person who receives a disclosure under this subsection shall be subject to the same prohibitions on disclosure under paragraph (1).

(4) At the request of the Director of the Federal Bureau of Investigation or the designee of the Director, any person making or intending to make a disclosure under this section shall identify to the Director or such designee the person to whom such disclosure will be made or to whom such disclosure was made prior to the request, except that nothing in this section shall require a person to inform the Director or such designee of the identity of an attorney to whom disclosure was made or will be made to obtain legal advice or legal assistance with respect to the request for the identity of financial institutions or a consumer report respecting any consumer under this section.

(e) Payment of fees

The Federal Bureau of Investigation shall, subject to the availability of appropriations, pay to the consumer reporting agency assembling or providing report or information in accordance with procedures established under this section a fee for reimbursement for such costs as are reasonably necessary and which have been directly incurred in searching, reproducing, or transporting books, papers, records, or other data required or requested to be produced under this section.

(f) Limit on dissemination

The Federal Bureau of Investigation may not disseminate information obtained pursuant to this section outside of the Federal Bureau of Investigation, except to other Federal agencies as may be necessary for the approval or conduct of a foreign counterintelligence investigation, or, where the information concerns a person subject to the Uniform Code of Military Justice, to appropriate investigative authorities within the military department concerned as may be necessary for the conduct of a joint foreign counterintelligence investigation.

(g) Rules of construction

Nothing in this section shall be construed to prohibit information from being furnished by the Federal Bureau of Investigation pursuant to a subpoena or court order, in connection with a judicial or administrative proceeding to enforce the provisions of this subchapter. Nothing in this section shall be construed to authorize or permit the withholding of information from the Congress.

(h) Reports to Congress

(1) On a semiannual basis, the Attorney General shall fully inform the Permanent Select Committee on Intelligence and the Committee on Banking, Finance and Urban Affairs of the House of Representatives, and the Select Committee on Intelligence and the Committee on Banking, Housing, and Urban Affairs of the Senate concerning all requests made pursuant to subsections (a), (b), and (c) of this section.

(2) In the case of the semiannual reports required to be submitted under paragraph (1) to the Permanent Select Committee on Intelligence of the House of Representatives and the Select Committee on Intelligence of the Senate, the submittal dates for such reports shall be as provided in section 415b of Title 50.

(i) Damages

Any agency or department of the United States obtaining or disclosing any consumer reports, records, or information contained therein in violation of this section is liable to the consumer to whom such consumer reports, records, or information relate in an amount equal to the sum of—

(1) $100, without regard to the volume of consumer reports, records, or information involved;

(2) any actual damages sustained by the consumer as a result of the disclosure;

(3) if the violation is found to have been willful or intentional, such punitive damages as a court may allow; and

(4) in the case of any successful action to enforce liability under this subsection, the costs of the action, together with reasonable attorney fees, as determined by the court.

(j) Disciplinary actions for violations

If a court determines that any agency or department of the United States has violated any provision of this section and the court finds that the circumstances surrounding the violation raise questions of whether or not an officer or employee of the agency or department acted willfully or intentionally with respect to the violation, the agency or department shall promptly initiate a proceeding to determine whether or not disciplinary action is warranted against the officer or employee who was responsible for the violation.

(k) Good-faith exception

Notwithstanding any other provision of this subchapter, any consumer reporting agency or agent or employee thereof making disclosure of consumer reports or identifying information pursuant to this subsection in good-faith reliance upon a certification of the Federal Bureau of Investigation pursuant to provisions of this section shall not be liable to any person for such disclosure under this subchapter, the constitution of any State, or any law or regulation of any State or any political subdivision of any State.

(l) Limitation of remedies

Notwithstanding any other provision of this subchapter, the remedies and sanctions set forth in this section shall be the only judicial remedies and sanctions for violation of this section.

(m) Injunctive relief

In addition to any other remedy contained in this section, injunctive relief shall be available to require compliance with the procedures of this section. In the event of any successful action under this subsection, costs together with reasonable attorney fees, as determined by the court, may be recovered.

§ 1681v. Disclosures to governmental agencies for counterterrorism purposes

(a) Disclosure

Notwithstanding section 1681b of this title or any other provision of this subchapter, a consumer reporting agency shall furnish a consumer report of a consumer and all other information in a consumer's file to a government agency authorized to conduct investigations of, or intelligence or counterintelligence activities or analysis related to, international terrorism when presented with a written certification by such government agency that such information is necessary for the agency's conduct or such investigation, activity or analysis.

(b) Form of certification

The certification described in subsection (a) of this section shall be signed by a supervisory official designated by the head of a Federal agency or an officer of a Federal agency whose appointment to office is required to be made by the President, by and with the advice and consent of the Senate.

(c) Confidentiality

(1) If the head of a government agency authorized to conduct investigations of intelligence or counterintelligence activities or analysis related to international terrorism, or his designee, certifies that otherwise there may result a danger to the national security of the United States, interference with a criminal, counterterrorism, or counterintelligence investigation, interference with diplomatic relations, or danger to the life or physical safety of any person, no consumer reporting agency or officer, employee, or agent of such consumer reporting agency, shall disclose to any person (other than those to whom such disclosure is necessary to comply with the request or an attorney to obtain legal advice or legal assistance with respect to the request), or specify in any consumer report, that a government agency has sought or obtained access to information under subsection (a) of this section.

(2) The request shall notify the person or entity to whom the request is directed of the nondisclosure requirement under paragraph (1).

(3) Any recipient disclosing to those persons necessary to comply with the request or to any attorney to obtain legal advice or legal assistance with respect to the request shall inform such persons of any applicable nondisclosure requirement. Any person who receives a disclosure under this subsection shall be subject to the same prohibitions on disclosure under paragraph (1).

(4) At the request of the authorized government agency, any person making or intending to make a disclosure under this section shall identify to the requesting official of the authorized government agency the person to whom such disclosure will be made or to whom such disclosure was made prior to the request, except that nothing in this section shall require a person to inform the requesting official of the identity of an attorney to whom disclosure was made or will be made to obtain legal advice or legal assistance with respect to the request for information under subsection (a) of this section.

(d) Rule of construction

Nothing in section 1681u of this title shall be construed to limit the authority of the Director of the Federal Bureau of Investigation under this section.

(e) Safe harbor

Notwithstanding any other provision of this subchapter, any consumer reporting agency or agent or employee thereof making disclosure of consumer reports or other information pursuant to this section in good-faith reliance upon a certification of a government agency pursuant to the provisions of this section shall not be liable to any person for such disclosure under this subchapter, the constitution of any State, or any law or regulation of any State or any political subdivision of any State.

(f) Reports to Congress

(1) On a semi-annual basis, the Attorney General shall fully inform the Committee on the Judiciary, the Committee on Financial Services, and the Permanent Select Committee on Intelligence of the House of Representatives and the Committee on the Judiciary, the Committee on Banking, Housing, and Urban Affairs, and the Select Committee on Intelligence of the Senate concerning all requests made pursuant to subsection (a) of this section.

(2) In the case of the semiannual reports required to be submitted under paragraph (1) to the Permanent Select Committee on Intelligence of the House of Representatives and the Select Committee on Intelligence of the Senate, the submittal dates for such reports shall be as provided in section 415b of Title 50.

§ 1681w. Disposal of records

(a) Regulations

(1) In general

Not later than 1 year after December 4, 2003, the Federal banking agencies, the National Credit Union Administration, and the Commission with respect to the entities that are subject to their respective enforcement authority under section 1681s of this title, and the Securities and Exchange Commission, and in coordination as described in paragraph (2), shall issue final regulations requiring any person that maintains or otherwise possesses consumer information, or any compilation of consumer information, derived from consumer reports for a business purpose to properly dispose of any such information or compilation.

(2) Coordination

Each agency required to prescribe regulations under paragraph (1) shall—

(A) consult and coordinate with each other such agency so that, to the extent possible, the regulations prescribed by each such agency are consistent and comparable with the regulations by each such other agency; and

(B) ensure that such regulations are consistent with the requirements and regulations issued pursuant to Public Law 106-102 and other provisions of Federal law.

(3) Exemption authority

In issuing regulations under this section, the Federal banking agencies, the National Credit Union Administration, the Commission, and the Securities and Exchange Commission may exempt any person or class of persons from application of those regulations, as such agency deems appropriate to carry out the purpose of this section.

(b) Rule of construction

Nothing in this section shall be construed—

(1) to require a person to maintain or destroy any record pertaining to a consumer that is not imposed under other law; or

(2) to alter or affect any requirement imposed under any other provision of law to maintain or destroy such a record.

§ 1681x. Corporate and technological circumvention prohibited

The Commission shall prescribe regulations, to become effective not later than 90 days after December 4, 2003, to prevent a consumer reporting agency from circumventing or evading treatment as a consumer reporting agency described in section 1681a(p) of this title for purposes of this subchapter, including—

(1) by means of a corporate reorganization or restructuring, including a merger, acquisition, dissolution, divestiture, or asset sale of a consumer reporting agency; or

(2) by maintaining or merging public record and credit account information in a manner that is substantially equivalent to that described in paragraphs (1) and (2) of section 1681a(p) of this title, in the manner described in section 1681a(p) of this title.

Bank Secrecy Act (1970)

12 U.S.C. §§ 1951-1959, as amended

Statutes in Context

The Bank Secrecy Act requires that federally insured banks record the identities of account holders as well as copies of each check, draft, or other financial instrument. Further, the Act authorizes the Secretary of the Treasury to promulgate regulations for the reporting of domestic financial transactions. The enactment of the Act reflected a policy concern that a shift from paper to computer records would increase the difficulty of white-collar law enforcement.

§ 1951. Congressional findings and declaration of purpose

(a) The Congress finds that certain records maintained by businesses engaged in the functions described in section 1953(b) of this title have a high degree of usefulness in criminal, tax, and regulatory investigations and proceedings. The Congress further finds that the power to require reports of changes in the ownership, control, and managements of types of financial institutions referred to in section 1952 of this title may be necessary for the same purpose.

(b) It is the purpose of this chapter to require the maintenance of appropriate types of records and the making of appropriate reports by such businesses in the United States where such records or reports have a high degree of usefulness in criminal, tax, or regulatory investigations or proceedings.

§ 1952. Reports on ownership and control

Where the Secretary determines that the making of appropriate reports by uninsured banks or uninsured institutions of any type with respect to their ownership, control, and managements and any changes therein has a high degree of usefulness in criminal, tax, or regulatory investigations or proceedings, he may by regulation require such banks or institutions to make such reports as he determines in respect of such ownership, control, and managements and changes therein.

§ 1953. Recordkeeping and procedures

(a) Regulations

If the Secretary determines that the maintenance of appropriate records and procedures by any uninsured bank or uninsured institution, or any person engaging in the business of carrying on in the United States any of the functions referred to in subsection (b) of this section, has a high degree of usefulness in criminal, tax, or regulatory investigations or proceedings, and that, given the threat posed to the security of the Nation on and after the terrorist attacks against the United States on September 11, 2001, such records may also have a high degree of usefulness in the conduct of intelligence or counterintelligence activities, including analysis, to protect against international terrorism, he may by regulation require such bank, institution, or person—

(1) to require, retain, or maintain, with respect to its functions as an uninsured bank or uninsured institution or its functions referred to in subsection (b) of this section, any records or evidence of any type which the Secretary is authorized under section 1829b of this title to require insured banks to require, retain, or maintain; and

(2) to maintain procedures to assure compliance with requirements imposed under this chapter. For the purposes of any civil or criminal penalty, a separate violation of any requirement under this paragraph occurs with respect to each day and each separate office, branch, or place of business in which the violation occurs or continues.

(b) Institutions subject to recordkeeping requirements

The authority of the Secretary of the Treasury under subsection (a) of this section extends to any financial institution (as defined in section 5312(a)(2) of Title 31), other than any insured bank (as defined in section 1813(h) of this title) and any insured institution (as defined in section 1724(a) of this title), and any partner, officer, director, or employee of any such financial institution.

(c) Acceptance of automated records

The Secretary shall permit an uninsured bank or financial institution to retain or maintain records referred to in subsection (a) of this section in electronic or automated form, subject to terms and conditions established by the Secretary.

§ 1954. Injunctions

Whenever it appears to the Secretary that any person has engaged, is engaged, or is about to engage in any acts or practices constituting a violation of any regulation under this chapter, he may in his discretion bring an action, in the proper district court of the United States or the proper United States court of any territory or other place subject to the jurisdiction of the United States, to enjoin such acts or practices, and upon a proper showing a permanent or temporary injunction or restraining order shall be granted without bond. Upon application of the Secretary, any such court may also issue mandatory injunctions commanding any person to comply with any regulation of the Secretary under this chapter.

§ 1955. Civil penalties

(a) For each willful or grossly negligent violation of any regulation under this chapter, the Secretary may assess upon any person to which the regulation applies, or any person willfully causing a violation of the regulation, and, if such person is a partnership, corporation, or other entity, upon any partner, director, officer, or employee thereof who willfully or through gross negligence participates in the violation, a civil penalty not exceeding $10,000.

(b) In the event of the failure of any person to pay any penalty assessed under this section, a civil action for the recovery thereof may, in the discretion of the Secretary, be brought in the name of the United States.

§ 1956. Criminal penalty

Whoever willfully violates any regulation under this chapter shall be fined not more than $1,000 or imprisoned not more than one year, or both.

§ 1957. Additional criminal penalty in certain cases

Whoever willfully violates, or willfully causes a violation of any regulation under this chapter, section 1829b of this title, or section 1730d of this title, where the violation is committed in furtherance of the commission of any violation of Federal law punishable by imprisonment for more than one year, shall be fined not more than $10,000 or imprisoned not more than five years, or both.

§ 1958. Compliance

The Secretary shall have the responsibility to assure compliance with the requirements of this chapter and sections 1730d and 1829b of this title and may delegate such responsibility to the appropriate bank supervisory agency, or other supervisory agency.

§ 1959. Administrative procedure

The administrative procedure and judicial review provisions of subchapter II of chapter 5 and chapter 7 of Title 5 shall apply to all proceedings under this chapter, section 1829b of this title, and section 1730d of this title.

Right to Financial Privacy Act (1978)

12 U.S.C. §§ 3401-3422, as amended

Statutes in Context

In *United States v. Miller*, 425 U.S. 435 (1976), the Supreme Court found that there was no Fourth Amendment "reasonable expectation of privacy" in a person's financial information held by a bank. Accordingly, the Fourth Amendment did not regulate government access to checks, deposit slips, and other financial data. Two years after this decision, the Right to Financial Privacy Act partially filled this legal void. It prevents banks and other financial institutions from disclosing a person's financial information to the government unless the records are disclosed pursuant to a subpoena or a search warrant.

§ 3401. Definitions

For the purpose of this chapter, the term—

(1) "financial institution", except as provided in section 3414 of this title, means any office of a bank, savings bank, card issuer as defined in section 1602(n) of Title 15, industrial loan company, trust company, savings association, building and loan, or homestead association (including cooperative banks), credit union, or consumer finance institution, located in any State or territory of the United States, the District of Columbia, Puerto Rico, Guam, American Samoa, or the Virgin Islands;

(2) "financial record" means an original of, a copy of, or information known to have been derived from, any record held by a financial institution pertaining to a customer's relationship with the financial institution;

(3) "Government authority" means any agency or department of the United States, or any officer, employee, or agent thereof;

(4) "person" means an individual or a partnership of five or fewer individuals;

(5) "customer" means any person or authorized representative of that person who utilized or is utilizing any service of a financial institution, or for whom a financial institution is acting or has acted as a fiduciary, in relation to an account maintained in the person's name;

(6) "holding company" means—

(A) any bank holding company (as defined in section 1841 of this title);

(B) any company described in section 1843(f)(1) of this title; and

(C) any savings and loan holding company (as defined in the Home Owners' Loan Act [12 U.S.C.A. § 1461 et seq.]);

(7) "supervisory agency" means with respect to any particular financial institution, holding company, or any subsidiary of a financial institution or holding company, any of the following which has statutory authority to examine the financial condition, business operations, or records or transactions of that institution, holding company, or subsidiary—

(A) the Federal Deposit Insurance Corporation;

(B) Director, Office of Thrift Supervision;

(C) the National Credit Union Administration;

(D) the Board of Governors of the Federal Reserve System;

(E) the Comptroller of the Currency;

(F) the Securities and Exchange Commission;

(G) the Commodity Futures Trading Commission;

(H) the Secretary of the Treasury, with respect to the Bank Secrecy Act (Public Law 91-508, Title I [12 U.S.C.A. § 1951 et seq.]) and subchapter II of chapter 53 of Title 31; or

(I) any State banking or securities department or agency; and

(8) "law enforcement inquiry" means a lawful investigation or official proceeding inquiring into a violation of, or failure to comply with, any criminal or civil statute or any regulation, rule, or order issued pursuant thereto.

§ 3402. Access to financial records by Government authorities prohibited; exceptions

Except as provided by section 3403(c) or (d), 3413, or 3414 of this title, no Government authority may have access to or obtain copies of, or the information contained in the financial records of any customer from a financial institution unless the financial records are reasonably described and—

(1) such customer has authorized such disclosure in accordance with section 3404 of this title;

(2) such financial records are disclosed in response to an administrative subpoena or summons which meets the requirements of section 3405 of this title;

(3) such financial records are disclosed in response to a search warrant which meets the requirements of section 3406 of this title;

(4) such financial records are disclosed in response to a judicial subpoena which meets the requirements of section 3407 of this title; or

(5) such financial records are disclosed in response to a formal written request which meets the requirements of section 3408 of this title.

§ 3403. Confidentiality of financial records

(a) Release of records by financial institutions prohibited

No financial institution, or officer, employees, or agent of a financial institution, may provide to any Government authority access to or copies of, or the information contained in, the financial records of any customer except in accordance with the provisions of this chapter.

(b) Release of records upon certification of compliance with chapter

A financial institution shall not release the financial records of a customer until the Government authority seeking such records certifies in writing to the financial institution that it has complied with the applicable provisions of this chapter.

(c) Notification to Government authority of existence of relevant information in records

Nothing in this chapter shall preclude any financial institution, or any officer, employee, or agent of a financial institution, from notifying a Government authority that such institution, or officer, employee, or agent has information which may be relevant to a possible violation of any statute or regulation. Such information may include only the name or other identifying information concerning any individual, corporation, or account involved in and the nature of any suspected illegal activity. Such information may be disclosed notwithstanding any constitution, law, or regulation of any State or political subdivision thereof to the contrary. Any financial institution, or officer, employee, or agent thereof, making a disclosure of information pursuant to this subsection, shall not be liable to the customer under any law or regulation of the United States or any constitution, law, or regulation of any State or political subdivision thereof, for such disclosure or for any failure to notify the customer of such disclosure.

(d) Release of records as incident to perfection of security interest, proving a claim in bankruptcy, collecting a debt, or processing an application with regard to a Government loan, loan guarantee, etc.

(1) Nothing in this chapter shall preclude a financial institution, as an incident to perfecting a security interest, proving a claim in bankruptcy, or otherwise collecting on a debt owing either to the financial institution itself or in its role as a fiduciary, from providing copies of any financial record to any court or Government authority.

(2) Nothing in this chapter shall preclude a financial institution, as an incident to processing an application for assistance to a customer in the form of a Government loan, loan guaranty, or loan insurance agreement, or as an incident to processing a default on, or administering, a Government guaranteed or insured loan, from initiating contact with an appropriate Government authority for the purpose of providing any financial record necessary to permit such authority to carry out its responsibilities under a loan, loan guaranty, or loan insurance agreement.

§ 3404. Customer authorizations

(a) Statement furnished by customer to financial institution and Government authority; contents

A customer may authorize disclosure under section 3402(1) of this title if he furnishes to the financial institution and to the Government authority seeking to obtain such disclosure a signed and dated statement which—

(1) authorizes such disclosure for a period not in excess of three months;

(2) states that the customer may revoke such authorization at any time before the financial records are disclosed;

(3) identifies the financial records which are authorized to be disclosed;

(4) specifies the purposes for which, and the Government authority to which, such records may be disclosed; and

(5) states the customer's rights under this chapter.

(b) Authorization as condition of doing business prohibited

No such authorization shall be required as a condition of doing business with any financial institution.

(c) Right of customer to access to financial institution's record of disclosures

The customer has the right, unless the Government authority obtains a court order as provided in section 3409 of this title, to obtain a copy of the record which the financial institution shall keep of all instances in which the customer's record is disclosed to a Government authority pursuant to this section, including the identity of the Government authority to which such disclosure is made.

§ 3405. Administrative subpoena and summons

A Government authority may obtain financial records under section 3402(2) of this title pursuant to an administrative subpoena or summons otherwise authorized by law only if—

(1) there is reason to believe that the records sought are relevant to a legitimate law enforcement inquiry;

(2) a copy of the subpoena or summons has been served upon the customer or mailed to his last known address on or before the date on which the subpoena or summons was served on the financial institution together with the following notice which shall state with reasonable specificity the nature of the law enforcement inquiry:

"Records or information concerning your transactions held by the financial institution named in the attached subpoena or summons are being sought by this (agency or department) in accordance with the Right to Financial Privacy Act of 1978 [12 U.S.C.A. § 3401 et seq.] for the following purpose: If you desire that such records or information not be made available, you must:

"**1.** Fill out the accompanying motion paper and sworn statement or write one of your own, stating that you are the customer whose records are being requested by the Government and either giving the reasons you believe that the records are not relevant to the legitimate law enforcement inquiry stated in this notice or any other legal basis for objecting to the release of the records.

"**2.** File the motion and statement by mailing or delivering them to the clerk of any one of the following United States district courts:

"**3.** Serve the Government authority requesting the records by mailing or delivering a copy of your motion and statement to .

"**4.** Be prepared to come to court and present your position in further detail.

"**5.** You do not need to have a lawyer, although you may wish to employ one to represent you and protect your rights.

If you do not follow the above procedures, upon the expiration of ten days from the date of service or fourteen days from the date of mailing of this notice, the records or information requested therein will be made available. These records may be transferred to other Government authorities for legitimate law enforcement inquiries, in which event you will be notified after the transfer."; and

(3) ten days have expired from the date of service of the notice or fourteen days have expired from the date of mailing the notice to the customer and within such time period the customer has not filed a sworn statement and motion to quash in an appropriate court, or the customer challenge provisions of section 3410 of this title have been complied with.

§ 3406. Search warrants

(a) Applicability of Federal Rules of Criminal Procedure

A Government authority may obtain financial records under section 3402(3) of this title only if it obtains a search warrant pursuant to the Federal Rules of Criminal Procedure.

(b) Mailing of copy and notice to customer

No later than ninety days after the Government authority serves the search warrant, it shall mail to the customer's last known address a copy of the search warrant together with the following notice:

"Records or information concerning your transactions held by the financial institution named in the attached search warrant were obtained by this (agency or department) on (date) for the following purpose: . You may have rights under the Right to Financial Privacy Act of 1978 [12 U.S.C.A. § 3401 et seq.].".

(c) Court-ordered delays in mailing

Upon application of the Government authority, a court may grant a delay in the mailing of the notice required in subsection (b) of this section, which delay shall not exceed one hundred and eighty days following the service of the warrant, if the court makes the findings required in section 3409(a) of this title. If the court so finds, it shall enter an ex parte order granting the requested delay and an order prohibiting the financial institution from disclosing that records have been obtained or that a search warrant for such records has been executed. Additional delays of up to ninety days may be granted by the court upon application, but only in accordance with this subsection. Upon expiration of the period of delay of notification of the customer, the following notice shall be mailed to the customer along with a copy of the search warrant:

"Records or information concerning your transactions held by the financial institution named in the attached search warrant were obtained by this (agency or department) on (date). Notification was delayed beyond the statutory ninety-day delay period pursuant to a determination by the court that such notice would seriously jeopardize an investigation concerning. You may have rights under the Right to Financial Privacy Act of 1978 [12 U.S.C.A. § 3401 et seq.].".

§ 3407. Judicial subpoena

A Government authority may obtain financial records under section 3402(4) of this title pursuant to judicial subpoena only if—

(1) such subpoena is authorized by law and there is reason to believe that the records sought are relevant to a legitimate law enforcement inquiry;

(2) a copy of the subpoena has been served upon the customer or mailed to his last known address on or before the date on which the subpoena was served on the financial institution together with the following notice which shall state with reasonable specificity the nature of the law enforcement inquiry:

"Records or information concerning your transactions which are held by the financial institution named in the attached subpoena are being sought by this (agency or department or authority) in accordance with the Right to Financial Privacy Act of 1978 [12 U.S.C.A. § 3401 et seq.] for the following purpose: If you desire that such records or information not be made available, you must:

"**1.** Fill out the accompanying motion paper and sworn statement or write one of your own, stating that you are the customer whose records are being requested by the Government and either giving the reasons you believe that the records are not relevant to the legitimate law enforcement inquiry stated in this notice or any other legal basis for objecting to the release of the records.

"**2.** File the motion and statement by mailing or delivering them to the clerk of the Court.

"**3.** Serve the Government authority requesting the records by mailing or delivering a copy of your motion and statement to .

"**4.** Be prepared to come to court and present your position in further detail.

"**5.** You do not need to have a lawyer, although you may wish to employ one to represent you and protect your rights.

If you do not follow the above procedures, upon the expiration of ten days from the date of service or fourteen days from the date of mailing of this notice, the records or information requested therein will be made available. These records may be transferred to other government authorities for legitimate law enforcement inquiries, in which event you will be notified after the transfer;" and

(3) ten days have expired from the date of service or fourteen days from the date of mailing of the notice to the customer and within such time period the customer has not filed a sworn statement and motion to quash in an appropriate court, or the customer challenge provisions of section 3410 of this title have been complied with.

§ 3408. Formal written request

A Government authority may request financial records under section 3402(5) of this title pursuant to a formal written request only if—

(1) no administrative summons or subpoena authority reasonably appears to be available to that Government authority to obtain financial records for the purpose for which such records are sought;

(2) the request is authorized by regulations promulgated by the head of the agency or department;

(3) there is reason to believe that the records sought are relevant to a legitimate law enforcement inquiry; and

(4)(A) a copy of the request has been served upon the customer or mailed to his last known address on or before the date on which the request was made to the financial institution together with the following notice which shall state with reasonable specificity the nature of the law enforcement inquiry:

"Records or information concerning your transactions held by the financial institution named in the attached request are being sought by this (agency or department) in accordance with the Right to Financial Privacy Act of 1978 [12 U.S.C.A. § 3401 et seq.] for the following purpose:

"If you desire that such records or information not be made available, you must:

> "**1.** Fill out the accompanying motion paper and sworn statement or write one of your own, stating that you are the customer whose records are being requested by the Government and either giving the reasons you believe that the records are not relevant to the legitimate law enforcement inquiry stated in this notice or any other legal basis for objecting to the release of the records.
>
> "**2.** File the motion and statement by mailing or delivering them to the clerk of any one of the following United States District Courts:
>
> "**3.** Serve the Government authority requesting the records by mailing or delivering a copy of your motion and statement to .
>
> "**4.** Be prepared to come to court and present your position in further detail.
>
> "**5.** You do not need to have a lawyer, although you may wish to employ one to represent you and protect your rights.
>
> If you do not follow the above procedures, upon the expiration of ten days from the date of service or fourteen days from the date of mailing of this notice, the records or information requested therein may be made available. These records may be transferred to other Government authorities for legitimate law enforcement inquiries, in which event you will be notified after the transfer;" and

(B) ten days have expired from the date of service or fourteen days from the date of mailing of the notice by the customer and within such time period the customer has not filed a sworn statement and an application to enjoin the Government authority in an appropriate court, or the customer challenge provisions of section 3410 of this title have been complied with.

§ 3409. Delayed notice

(a) Application by Government authority; findings

Upon application of the Government authority, the customer notice required under section 3404(c), 3405(2), 3406(c), 3407(2), 3408(4), or 3412(b) of this title may be delayed by order of an appropriate court if the presiding judge or magistrate judge finds that—

(1) the investigation being conducted is within the lawful jurisdiction of the Government authority seeking the financial records;

(2) there is reason to believe that the records being sought are relevant to a legitimate law enforcement inquiry; and

(3) there is reason to believe that such notice will result in—

(A) endangering life or physical safety of any person;

(B) flight from prosecution;

(C) destruction of or tampering with evidence;

(D) intimidation of potential witnesses; or

(E) otherwise seriously jeopardizing an investigation or official proceeding or unduly delaying a trial or ongoing official proceeding to the same extent as the circumstances in the preceding subparagraphs.

An application for delay must be made with reasonable specificity.

(b) Grant of delay order; duration and specifications; extensions; copy of request and notice to customer

(1) If the court makes the findings required in paragraphs (1), (2), and (3) of subsection (a) of this section, it shall enter an ex parte order granting the requested delay for a period not to exceed ninety days and an order prohibiting the financial institution from disclosing that records have been obtained or that a request for records has been made, except that, if the records have been sought by a Government authority exercising financial controls over foreign accounts in the United States under section 5(b) of the Trading With the Enemy Act [12 U.S.C.A. § 95a, 50 App. U.S.C.A. § 5(b)], the International Emergency Economic Powers Act (title II, Public Law 95-223) [50 U.S.C.A. § 1701 et seq.], or section 287c of Title 22, and the court finds that there is reason to believe that such notice may endanger the lives or physical safety of a customer or group of customers, or any person or group of persons associated with a customer, the court may specify that the delay be indefinite.

(2) Extensions of the delay of notice provided in paragraph (1) of up to ninety days each may be granted by the court upon application, but only in accordance with this subsection.

(3) Upon expiration of the period of delay of notification under paragraph (1) or (2), the customer shall be served with or mailed a copy of the process or request together with the following notice which shall state with reasonable specificity the nature of the law enforcement inquiry:

"Records or information concerning your transactions which are held by the financial institution named in the attached process or request were supplied to or requested by the Government authority named in the process or request on (date). Notification was withheld pursuant to a determination by the (title of court so ordering) under the Right to Financial Privacy Act of 1978 [12 U.S.C.A. § 3401 et seq.] that such notice might (state reason). The purpose of the investigation or official proceeding was.".

(c) Notice requirement respecting emergency access to financial records

When access to financial records is obtained pursuant to section 3414(b) of this title (emergency access), the Government authority shall, unless a court has authorized delay of notice pursuant to subsections (a) and (b) of this section, as soon as practicable after such records are obtained serve upon the customer, or mail by registered or certified mail to his last known address, a copy of the request to the financial institution together with the following notice which shall state with reasonable specificity the nature of the law enforcement inquiry:

"Records concerning your transactions held by the financial institution named in the attached request were obtained by (agency or department) under the Right to Financial Privacy Act of 1978 [12 U.S.C.A. § 3401 et seq.] on (date) for the following purpose: Emergency access to such records was obtained on the grounds that (state grounds).".

(d) Preservation of memorandums, affidavits, or other papers

Any memorandum, affidavit, or other paper filed in connection with a request for delay in notification shall be preserved by the court. Upon petition by the customer to whom such records pertain, the court may order disclosure of such papers to the petitioner unless the court makes the findings required in subsection (a) of this section.

§ 3410. Customer challenges

(a) Filing of motion to quash or application to enjoin; proper court; contents

Within ten days of service or within fourteen days of mailing of a subpoena, summons, or formal written request, a customer may file a motion to quash an administrative summons or judicial subpoena, or an application to enjoin a Government authority from obtaining financial records pursuant to a formal written request, with copies served upon the Government authority. A motion to quash a judicial subpoena shall be filed in the court which issued the subpoena. A motion to quash an administrative summons or an application to enjoin a Government authority from obtaining records pursuant to a formal written request shall be filed in the appropriate United States district court. Such motion or application shall contain an affidavit or sworn statement-

(1) stating that the applicant is a customer of the financial institution from which financial records pertaining to him have been sought; and

(2) stating the applicant's reasons for believing that the financial records sought are not relevant to the legitimate law enforcement inquiry stated by the Government authority in its notice, or that there has not been substantial compliance with the provisions of this chapter.

Service shall be made under this section upon a Government authority by delivering or mailing by registered or certified mail a copy of the papers to the person, office, or department specified in the notice which the customer has received pursuant to this chapter. For the purposes of this section, "delivery" has the meaning stated in rule 5(b) of the Federal Rules of Civil Procedure.

(b) Filing of response; additional proceedings

If the court finds that the customer has complied with subsection (a) of this section, it shall order the Government authority to file a sworn response, which may be filed in camera if the Government includes in its response the reasons which make in camera review appropriate. If the court is unable to determine the motion or application on the basis of the parties' initial allegations and response, the court may conduct such additional proceedings as it deems appropriate. All such proceedings shall be completed and the motion or application decided within seven calendar days of the filing of the Government's response.

(c) Decision of court

If the court finds that the applicant is not the customer to whom the financial records sought by the Government authority pertain, or that there is a demonstrable reason to believe that the law enforcement inquiry is legitimate and a reasonable belief that the records sought are relevant to that inquiry, it shall deny the motion or application, and, in the case of an administrative summons or court order other than a search warrant, order such process enforced. If the court finds that the applicant is the customer to whom the records sought by the Government authority pertain, and that there is not a demonstrable reason to believe that the law enforcement inquiry is legitimate and a reasonable belief that the records sought are relevant to that inquiry, or that there has not been substantial compliance with the provisions of this chapter, it shall order the process quashed or shall enjoin the Government authority's formal written request.

§ 3411. Duty of financial institutions

Upon receipt of a request for financial records made by a Government authority under section 3405 or 3407 of this title, the financial institution shall, unless otherwise provided by law, proceed to assemble the records requested and must be prepared to deliver the records to the Government authority upon receipt of the certificate required under section 3403(b) of this title.

§ 3412. Use of information

(a) Transfer of financial records to other agencies or departments; certification

Financial records originally obtained pursuant to this chapter shall not be transferred to another agency or department unless the transferring agency or department certifies in writing that there is reason to believe that the records are relevant to a legitimate law enforcement inquiry, or intelligence or counterintelligence activity, investigation or analysis related to international terrorism within the jurisdiction of the receiving agency or department.

(b) Mailing of copy of certification and notice to customer

When financial records subject to this chapter are transferred pursuant to subsection (a) of this section, the transferring agency or department shall, within fourteen days, send to the customer a copy of the certification made pursuant to subsection (a) of this section and the following notice, which shall state the nature of the law enforcement inquiry with reasonable specificity: "Copies of, or information contained in, your financial records lawfully in possession of have been furnished to pursuant to the Right of Financial Privacy Act of 1978 [12 U.S.C.A. § 3401 et seq.] for the following purpose: If you believe that this transfer has not been made to further a legitimate law enforcement inquiry, you may have legal rights under the Financial Privacy Act of 1978 or the Privacy Act of 1974 [5 U.S.C.A. § 552a]."

(c) Court-ordered delays in mailing

Notwithstanding subsection (b) of this section, notice to the customer may be delayed if the transferring agency or department has obtained a court order delaying notice pursuant to section 3409(a) and (b) of this title and that order is still in effect, or if the receiving agency or department obtains a court order authorizing a delay in notice pursuant to section 3409(a) and (b) of this title. Upon the expiration of any such period of delay, the transferring agency or department shall serve to the customer the notice specified in subsection (b) of this section and the agency or department that obtained the court order authorizing a delay in notice pursuant to section 3409(a) and (b) of this title shall serve to the customer the notice specified in section 3409(b) of this title.

(d) Exchanges of examination reports by supervisory agencies; transfer of financial records to defend customer action; withholding of information

Nothing in this chapter prohibits any supervisory agency from exchanging examination reports or other information with another supervisory agency. Nothing in this chapter prohibits the transfer of a customer's financial records needed by counsel for a Government authority to defend an action brought by the customer. Nothing in this chapter shall authorize the withholding of information by any officer or employee of a supervisory agency from a duly authorized committee or subcommittee of the Congress.

(e) Exchange of records, reports, or other information

Notwithstanding section 3401(6) of this title or any other provision of law, the exchange of financial records, examination reports or other information with respect to a financial institution, holding company, or any subsidiary of a depository institution or holding company, among and between the five member supervisory agencies of the Federal Financial Institutions Examination Council, the Securities and Exchange Commission, the Federal Trade Commission, and the Commodity Futures Trading Commission is permitted.

(f) Transfer to Attorney General or Secretary of the Treasury

(1) In general

Nothing in this chapter shall apply when financial records obtained by an agency or department of the United States are disclosed or transferred to the Attorney General or the Secretary of the Treasury upon the certification by a supervisory level official of the transferring agency or department that—

(A) there is reason to believe that the records may be relevant to a violation of Federal criminal law; and

(B) the records were obtained in the exercise of the agency's or department's supervisory or regulatory functions.

(2) Limitation on use

Records so transferred shall be used only for criminal investigative or prosecutive purposes, for civil actions under section 1833a of this title, or for forfeiture under sections 981 or 982 of Title 18 by the Department of Justice and only for criminal investigative purposes relating to money laundering and other financial crimes by the Department of the Treasury and shall, upon completion of the investigation or prosecution (including any appeal), be returned only to the transferring agency or department. No agency or department so transferring such records shall be deemed to have waived any privilege applicable to those records under law.

§ 3413. Exceptions

(a) Disclosure of financial records not identified with particular customers

Nothing in this chapter prohibits the disclosure of any financial records or information which is not identified with or identifiable as being derived from the financial records of a particular customer.

(b) Disclosure to, or examination by, supervisory agency pursuant to exercise of supervisory, regulatory, or monetary functions with respect to financial institutions, holding companies, subsidiaries, institution-affiliated parties, or other persons

This chapter shall not apply to the examination by or disclosure to any supervisory agency of financial records or information in the exercise of its supervisory, regulatory, or monetary functions, including conservatorship or receivership functions, with respect to any financial institution, holding company, subsidiary of a financial institution or holding company, institution-affiliated party (within the meaning of section 1813(u) of this title) with respect to a financial institution, holding company, or subsidiary, or other person participating in the conduct of the affairs thereof.

(c) Disclosure pursuant to Title 26

Nothing in this chapter prohibits the disclosure of financial records in accordance with procedures authorized by Title 26.

(d) Disclosure pursuant to Federal statute or rule promulgated thereunder

Nothing in this chapter shall authorize the withholding of financial records or information required to be reported in accordance with any Federal statute or rule promulgated thereunder.

(e) Disclosure pursuant to Federal Rules of Criminal Procedure or comparable rules of other courts

Nothing in this chapter shall apply when financial records are sought by a Government authority under the Federal Rules of Civil or Criminal Procedure or comparable rules of other courts in connection with litigation to which the Government authority and the customer are parties.

(f) Disclosure pursuant to administrative subpoena issued by administrative law judge

Nothing in this chapter shall apply when financial records are sought by a Government authority pursuant to an administrative subpoena issued by an administrative law judge in an adjudicatory proceeding subject to section 554 of Title 5 and to which the Government authority and the customer are parties.

(g) Disclosure pursuant to legitimate law enforcement inquiry respecting name, address, account number, and type of account of particular customers

The notice requirements of this chapter and sections 3410 and 3412 of this title shall not apply when a Government authority by a means described in section 3402 of this title and for a legitimate law enforcement inquiry is seeking only the name, address, account number, and type of account of any customer or ascertainable group of customers associated (1) with a financial transaction or class of financial transactions, or (2) with a foreign country or subdivision thereof in the case of a Government authority exercising financial controls over foreign accounts in the United States under section 5(b) of the Trading With the Enemy Act [12 U.S.C.A. § 95a, 50 App. U.S.C.A. § 5(b)]; the International Emergency Economic Powers Act (Title II, Public Law 95-223) [50 U.S.C.A. § 1701 et seq.]; or section 287c of Title 22.

(h) Disclosure pursuant to lawful proceeding, investigation, etc., directed at financial institution or legal entity or consideration or administration respecting Government loans, loan guarantees, etc.

(1) Nothing in this chapter (except sections 3403, 3417 and 3418 of this title) shall apply when financial records are sought by a Government authority-

> **(A)** in connection with a lawful proceeding, investigation, examination, or inspection directed at a financial institution (whether or not such proceeding, investigation, examination, or inspection is also directed at a customer) or at a legal entity which is not a customer; or
>
> **(B)** in connection with the authority's consideration or administration of assistance to the customer in the form of a Government loan, loan guaranty, or loan insurance program.

(2) When financial records are sought pursuant to this subsection, the Government authority shall submit to the financial institution the certificate required by section 3403(b) of this title. For access pursuant to paragraph (1)(B), no further certification shall be required for subsequent access by the certifying Government authority during the term of the loan, loan guaranty, or loan insurance agreement.

(3) After the effective date of this chapter, whenever a customer applies for participation in a Government loan, loan guaranty, or loan insurance program, the Government authority administering such program shall give the customer written notice of the authority's access rights under this subsection. No further notification shall be required for subsequent access by that authority during the term of the loan, loan guaranty, or loan insurance agreement.

(4) Financial records obtained pursuant to this subsection may be used only for the purpose for which they were originally obtained, and may be transferred to another agency or department only when the transfer is to facilitate a lawful proceeding, investigation, examination, or inspection directed at a financial institution (whether or not such proceeding, investigation, examination, or inspection is also directed at a customer), or at a legal entity which is not a customer, except that-

> **(A)** nothing in this paragraph prohibits the use or transfer of a customer's financial records needed by counsel representing a Government authority in a civil action arising from a Government loan, loan guaranty, or loan insurance agreement; and
>
> **(B)** nothing in this paragraph prohibits a Government authority providing assistance to a customer in the form of a loan, loan guaranty, or loan insurance agreement from using or transferring financial records necessary to process, service or foreclose a loan, or to collect on an indebtedness to the Government resulting from a customer's default.

(5) Notification that financial records obtained pursuant to this subsection may relate to a potential civil, criminal, or regulatory violation by a customer may be given to an agency or department with jurisdiction over that violation, and such agency or department may then seek access to the records pursuant to the provisions of this chapter.

(6) Each financial institution shall keep a notation of each disclosure made pursuant to paragraph (1)(B) of this subsection, including the date of such disclosure and the Government authority to which it was made. The customer shall be entitled to inspect this information.

(i) Disclosure pursuant to issuance of subpoena or court order respecting grand jury proceeding

Nothing in this chapter (except sections 3415 and 3420 of this title) shall apply to any subpoena or court order issued in connection with proceedings before a grand jury, except that a court shall have authority to order a financial institution, on which a grand jury subpoena for customer records has been served, not to notify the customer of the existence of the subpoena or information that has been furnished to the grand jury, under the circumstances and for the period specified and pursuant to the procedures established in section 3409 of this title.

(j) Disclosure pursuant to proceeding, investigation, etc., instituted by Government Accountability Office and directed at a government authority

This chapter shall not apply when financial records are sought by the Government Accountability Office pursuant to an authorized proceeding, investigation, examination or audit directed at a government authority.

(k) Disclosure necessary for proper administration of programs of withholding taxes on nonresident aliens, Federal Old-Age, Survivors, and Disability Insurance Benefits, and Railroad Retirement Act Benefits

(1) Nothing in this chapter shall apply to the disclosure by the financial institution of the name and address of any customer to the Department of the Treasury, the Social Security Administration, or the Railroad Retirement Board, where the disclosure of such information is necessary to, and such information is used solely for the purpose of, the proper administration of section 1441 of Title 26, title II of the Social Security Act [42 U.S.C.A. § 401 et seq.], or the Railroad Retirement Act of 1974 [45 U.S.C.A. § 231 et seq.].

(2) Notwithstanding any other provision of law, any request authorized by paragraph (1) (and the information contained therein) may be used by the financial institution or its agents solely for the purpose of providing the customer's name and address to the Department of the Treasury, the Social Security Administration, or the Railroad Retirement Board and shall be barred from redisclosure by the financial institution or its agents.

(l) Crimes against financial institutions by insiders

Nothing in this chapter shall apply when any financial institution or supervisory agency provides any financial record of any officer, director, employee, or controlling shareholder (within the meaning of subparagraph (A) or (B) of section 1841(a)(2) of this title or subparagraph (A) or (B) of section 1730a(a)(2) of this title) of such institution, or of any major borrower from such institution who there is reason to believe may be acting in concert with any such officer, director, employee, or controlling shareholder, to the Attorney General of the United States, to a State law enforcement agency, or, in the case of a possible violation of subchapter II of chapter 53 of Title 31, to the Secretary of the Treasury if there is reason to believe that such record is relevant to a possible violation by such person of—

> **(1)** any law relating to crimes against financial institutions or supervisory agencies by directors, officers, employees, or controlling shareholders of, or by borrowers from, financial institutions; or

(2) any provision of subchapter II of chapter 53 of Title 31 or of section 1956 or 1957 of Title 18.

No supervisory agency which transfers any such record under this subsection shall be deemed to have waived any privilege applicable to that record under law.

(m) Disclosure to, or examination by, employees or agents of Board of Governors of Federal Reserve System or Federal Reserve Bank

This chapter shall not apply to the examination by or disclosure to employees or agents of the Board of Governors of the Federal Reserve System or any Federal Reserve Bank of financial records or information in the exercise of the Federal Reserve System's authority to extend credit to the financial institutions or others.

(n) Disclosure to, or examination by, Resolution Trust Corporation or its employees or agents

This chapter shall not apply to the examination by or disclosure to the Resolution Trust Corporation or its employees or agents of financial records or information in the exercise of its conservatorship, receivership, or liquidation functions with respect to a financial institution.

(o) Disclosure to, or examination by, Federal Housing Finance Board or Federal home loan banks

This chapter shall not apply to the examination by or disclosure to the Federal Housing Finance Board or any of the Federal home loan banks of financial records or information in the exercise of the Federal Housing Finance Board's authority to extend credit (either directly or through a Federal home loan bank) to financial institutions or others.

(p) Access to information necessary for administration of certain veteran benefits laws

(1) Nothing in this chapter shall apply to the disclosure by the financial institution of the name and address of any customer to the Department of Veterans Affairs where the disclosure of such information is necessary to, and such information is used solely for the purposes of, the proper administration of benefits programs under laws administered by the Secretary.

(2) Notwithstanding any other provision of law, any request authorized by paragraph (1) (and the information contained therein) may be used by the financial institution or its agents solely for the purpose of providing the customer's name and address to the Department of Veterans Affairs and shall be barred from redisclosure by the financial institution or its agents.

(q) Disclosure pursuant to Federal contractor-issued travel charge card

Nothing in this chapter shall apply to the disclosure of any financial record or information to a Government authority in conjunction with a Federal contractor-issued travel charge card issued for official Government travel.

§ 3414. Special procedures

(a)(1) Nothing in this chapter (except sections 3415, 3417, 3418, and 3421 of this title) shall apply to the production and disclosure of financial records pursuant to requests from—

(A) a Government authority authorized to conduct foreign counter- or foreign positive-intelligence activities for purposes of conducting such activities;

(B) the Secret Service for the purpose of conducting its protective functions (18 U.S.C. 3056; 18 U.S.C. 3056A, Public Law 90-331, as amended); or

(C) a Government authority authorized to conduct investigations of, or intelligence or counterintelligence analyses related to, international terrorism for the purpose of conducting such investigations or analyses.

(2) In the instances specified in paragraph (1), the Government authority shall submit to the financial institution the certificate required in section 3403(b) of this title signed by a supervisory official of a rank designated by the head of the Government authority.

(3)(A) If the Government authority described in paragraph (1) or the Secret Service, as the case may be, certifies that otherwise there may result a danger to the national security of the United States, interference with a criminal, counterterrorism, or counterintelligence investigation, interference with diplomatic relations, or danger to the life or physical safety of any person, no financial institution, or officer, employee, or agent of such institution, shall disclose to any person (other than those to whom such disclosure is necessary to comply with the request or an attorney to obtain legal advice or legal assistance with respect to the request) that the Government authority or the Secret Service has sought or obtained access to a customer's financial records.

(B) The request shall notify the person or entity to whom the request is directed of the nondisclosure requirement under subparagraph (A).

(C) Any recipient disclosing to those persons necessary to comply with the request or to an attorney to obtain legal advice or legal assistance with respect to the request shall inform such persons of any applicable nondisclosure requirement. Any person who receives a disclosure under this subsection shall be subject to the same prohibitions on disclosure under subparagraph (A).

(D) At the request of the authorized Government authority or the Secret Service, any person making or intending to make a disclosure under this section shall identify to the requesting official of the authorized Government authority or the Secret Service the person to whom such disclosure will be made or to whom such disclosure was made prior to the request, except that nothing in this section shall require a person to inform the requesting official of the authorized Government authority or the Secret Service of the identity of an attorney to whom disclosure was made or will be made to obtain legal advice or legal assistance with respect to the request for financial records under this subsection.

(4) The Government authority specified in paragraph (1) shall compile an annual tabulation of the occasions in which this section was used.

(5)(A) Financial institutions, and officers, employees, and agents thereof, shall comply with a request for a customer's or entity's financial records made pursuant to this subsection by the Federal Bureau of Investigation when the Director of the Federal Bureau of Investigation (or the Director's designee in a position not lower than Deputy Assistant Director at Bureau headquarters or a Special Agent in Charge in a Bureau field office designated by the Director) certifies in writing to the financial institution that such records are sought for foreign counter intelligence purposes to protect against international terrorism or clandestine intelligence activities, provided that such an investigation of a United States person is not conducted solely upon the basis of activities protected by the first amendment to the Constitution of the United States.

(B) The Federal Bureau of Investigation may disseminate information obtained pursuant to this paragraph only as provided in guidelines approved by the Attorney General for foreign intelligence collection and foreign counterintelligence investigations conducted by the Federal

Bureau of Investigation, and, with respect to dissemination to an agency of the United States, only if such information is clearly relevant to the authorized responsibilities of such agency.

(C) On the dates provided in section 415b of Title 50, the Attorney General shall fully inform the congressional intelligence committees (as defined in section 401a of Title 50) concerning all requests made pursuant to this paragraph.

(D) Prohibition of certain disclosure.—

(i) If the Director of the Federal Bureau of Investigation, or his designee in a position not lower than Deputy Assistant Director at Bureau headquarters or a Special Agent in Charge in a Bureau field office designated by the Director, certifies that otherwise there may result a danger to the national security of the United States, interference with a criminal, counterterrorism, or counterintelligence investigation, interference with diplomatic relations, or danger to the life or physical safety of any person, no financial institution, or officer, employee, or agent of such institution, shall disclose to any person (other than those to whom such disclosure is necessary to comply with the request or an attorney to obtain legal advice or legal assistance with respect to the request) that the Federal Bureau of Investigation has sought or obtained access to a customer's or entity's financial records under subparagraph (A).

(ii) The request shall notify the person or entity to whom the request is directed of the nondisclosure requirement under clause (i).

(iii) Any recipient disclosing to those persons necessary to comply with the request or to an attorney to obtain legal advice or legal assistance with respect to the request shall inform such persons of any applicable nondisclosure requirement. Any person who receives a disclosure under this subsection shall be subject to the same prohibitions on disclosure under clause (i).

(iv) At the request of the Director of the Federal Bureau of Investigation or the designee of the Director, any person making or intending to make a disclosure under this section shall identify to the Director or such designee the person to whom such disclosure will be made or to whom such disclosure was made prior to the request, except that nothing in this section shall require a person to inform the Director or such designee of the identity of an attorney to whom disclosure was made or will be made to obtain legal advice or legal assistance with respect to the request for financial records under subparagraph (A).

(b)(1) Nothing in this chapter shall prohibit a Government authority from obtaining financial records from a financial institution if the Government authority determines that delay in obtaining access to such records would create imminent danger of—

(A) physical injury to any person;

(B) serious property damage; or

(C) flight to avoid prosecution.

(2) In the instances specified in paragraph (1), the Government shall submit to the financial institution the certificate required in section 3403(b) of this title signed by a supervisory official of a rank designated by the head of the Government authority.

(3) Within five days of obtaining access to financial records under this subsection, the Government authority shall file with the appropriate court a signed, sworn statement of a supervisory official of a rank designated by the head of the Government authority setting forth the grounds for the emergency access. The Government authority shall thereafter comply with the notice provisions of section 3409(c) of this title.

(4) The Government authority specified in paragraph (1) shall compile an annual tabulation of the occasions in which this section was used.

(d) For purposes of this section, and sections 3415 and 3417 of this title insofar as they relate to the operation of this section, the term "financial institution" has the same meaning as in subsections (a)(2) and (c)(1) of section 5312 of Title 31, except that, for purposes of this section, such term shall include only such a financial institution any part of which is located inside any State or territory of the United States, the District of Columbia, Puerto Rico, Guam, American Samoa, the Commonwealth of the Northern Mariana Islands, or the United States Virgin Islands.

§ 3415. Cost reimbursement

Except for records obtained pursuant to section 3403(d) or 3413(a) through (h) of this title, or as otherwise provided by law, a Government authority shall pay to the financial institution assembling or providing financial records pertaining to a customer and in accordance with procedures established by this chapter a fee for reimbursement for such costs as are reasonably necessary and which have been directly incurred in searching for, reproducing, or transporting books, papers, records, or other data required or requested to be produced. The Board of Governors of the Federal Reserve System shall, by regulation, establish the rates and conditions under which such payment may be made.

§ 3416. Jurisdiction

An action to enforce any provision of this chapter may be brought in any appropriate United States district court without regard to the amount in controversy within three years from the date on which the violation occurs or the date of discovery of such violation, whichever is later.

§ 3417. Civil penalties

(a) Liability of agencies or departments of United States or financial institutions

Any agency or department of the United States or financial institution obtaining or disclosing financial records or information contained therein in violation of this chapter is liable to the customer to whom such records relate in an amount equal to the sum of—

(1) $100 without regard to the volume of records involved;

(2) any actual damages sustained by the customer as a result of the disclosure;

(3) such punitive damages as the court may allow, where the violation is found to have been willful or intentional; and

(4) in the case of any successful action to enforce liability under this section, the costs of the action together with reasonable attorney's fees as determined by the court.

(b) Disciplinary action for willful or intentional violation of chapter by agents or employees of department or agency

Whenever the court determines that any agency or department of the United States has violated any provision of this chapter and the court finds that the circumstances surrounding the violation raise questions of whether an officer or employee of the department or agency acted willfully or intentionally with respect to the violation, the Director of the Office of Personnel Management shall promptly initiate a proceeding to determine whether disciplinary action is warranted against the agent or employee who was primarily responsible for the violation. The Director after investigation and consideration of the evidence submitted, shall submit his findings and recommendations to the administrative authority of the agency concerned and shall send copies of the findings and recommendations to the officer or employee or his representative. The administrative authority shall take the corrective action that the Director recommends.

(c) Good faith defense

Any financial institution or agent or employee thereof making a disclosure of financial records pursuant to this chapter in good-faith reliance upon a certificate by any Government authority or pursuant to the provisions of section 3413(*l*) of this title shall not be liable to the customer for such disclosure under this chapter, the constitution of any State, or any law or regulation of any State or any political subdivision of any State.

(d) Exclusive judicial remedies and sanctions

The remedies and sanctions described in this chapter shall be the only authorized judicial remedies and sanctions for violations of this chapter.

§ 3418. Injunctive relief

In addition to any other remedy contained in this chapter, injunctive relief shall be available to require that the procedures of this chapter are complied with. In the event of any successful action, costs together with reasonable attorney's fees as determined by the court may be recovered.

§ 3419. Suspension of limitations

If any individual files a motion or application under this chapter which has the effect of delaying the access of a Government authority to financial records pertaining to such individual, any applicable statute of limitations shall be deemed to be tolled for the period extending from the date such motion or application was filed until the date upon which the motion or application is decided.

§ 3420. Grand jury information; notification of certain persons prohibited

(a) Financial records about a customer obtained from a financial institution pursuant to a subpoena issued under the authority of a Federal grand jury—

(1) shall be returned and actually presented to the grand jury unless the volume of such records makes such return and actual presentation impractical in which case the grand jury shall be provided with a description of the contents of the records.;

(2) shall be used only for the purpose of considering whether to issue an indictment or presentment by that grand jury, or of prosecuting a crime for which that indictment or presentment is issued, or for a purpose authorized by rule 6(e) of the Federal Rules of Criminal Procedure, or for a purpose authorized by section 1112(a);

(3) shall be destroyed or returned to the financial institution if not used for one of the purposes specified in paragraph (2); and

(4) shall not be maintained, or a description of the contents of such records shall not be maintained by any Government authority other than in the sealed records of the grand jury, unless such record has been used in the prosecution of a crime for which the grand jury issued an indictment or presentment or for a purpose authorized by rule 6(e) of the Federal Rules of Criminal Procedure.

(b)(1) No officer, director, partner, employee, or shareholder of, or agent or attorney for, a financial institution shall, directly or indirectly, notify any person named in a grand jury subpoena served on such institution in connection with an investigation relating to a possible—

(A) crime against any financial institution or supervisory agency or crime involving a violation of the Controlled Substance Act [21 U.S.C.A. § 801 et seq.], the Controlled Substances Import and Export Act [21 U.S.C.A. § 951 et seq.], section 1956 or 1957 of Title 18, sections 5313, 5316 and 5324 of Title 31, or section 6050I of Title 26; or

(B) conspiracy to commit such a crime,

about the existence or contents of such subpoena, or information that has been furnished to the grand jury in response to such subpoena.

(2) Section 1818 of this title and section 1786(k)(2) of this title shall apply to any violation of this subsection.

[§ 3421. Repealed. Pub.L. 104-66, Title III, § 3001(d), Dec. 21, 1995, 109 Stat. 734]

§ 3422. Applicability to Securities and Exchange Commission

Except as provided in the Securities Exchange Act of 1934 [15 U.S.C.A. § 78a et seq.], this chapter shall apply with respect to the Securities and Exchange Commission.

Internal Revenue Code § 6103 (1986)

26 U.S.C. § 6103, as amended

Statutes in Context

Prior to the enactment of Internal Revenue Code § 6103, applicable statutory law made tax return information a public record subject to disclosure restrictions. These restrictions were established by the President and expressed in Treasury Department regulations. The applicable regulations before enactment of Internal Revenue Code § 6103 restricted public access to tax return information but allowed tax data to be widely shared within the government. Internal Revenue Code § 6103 ended such executive discretion—tax return information can no longer be shared between government agencies unless a statute permits the disclosure. The law also enumerates a series of statutory provisions under which disclosure are permitted.

§ 6103. Confidentiality and disclosure of returns and return information

(a) General rule.—Returns and return information shall be confidential, and except as authorized by this title—

(1) no officer or employee of the United States,

(2) no officer or employee of any State, any local law enforcement agency receiving information under subsection (i)(7)(A), any local child support enforcement agency, or any local agency administering a program listed in subsection (l)(7)(D) who has or had access to returns or return information under this section or section 6104(c), and

(3) no other person (or officer or employee thereof) who has or had access to returns or return information under subsection (e)(1)(D)(iii), paragraph (6), (12), (16), (19), or (20) of subsection (l), paragraph (2) or (4)(B) of subsection (m), or subsection (n),

shall disclose any return or return information obtained by him in any manner in connection with his service as such an officer or an employee or otherwise or under the provisions of this section. For purposes of this subsection, the term "officer or employee" includes a former officer or employee.

(b) Definitions.—For purposes of this section—

(1) Return.—The term "return" means any tax or information return, declaration of estimated tax, or claim for refund required by, or provided for or permitted under, the provisions of this title which is filed with the Secretary by, on behalf of, or with respect to any person, and any amendment or supplement thereto, including supporting schedules, attachments, or lists which are supplemental to, or part of, the return so filed.

(2) Return information.—The term "return information" means—

(A) a taxpayer's identity, the nature, source, or amount of his income, payments, receipts, deductions, exemptions, credits, assets, liabilities, net worth, tax liability, tax withheld, deficiencies, overassessments, or tax payments, whether the taxpayer's return was, is being, or will be examined or subject to other investigation or processing, or any other data, received by, recorded by, prepared by, furnished to, or collected by the Secretary with respect to a return or with respect to the determination of the existence, or possible existence, of liability (or the amount thereof) of any person under this title for any tax, penalty, interest, fine, forfeiture, or other imposition, or offense,

(B) any part of any written determination or any background file document relating to such written determination (as such terms are defined in section 6110(b)) which is not open to public inspection under section 6110,

(C) any advance pricing agreement entered into by a taxpayer and the Secretary and any background information related to such agreement or any application for an advance pricing agreement, and

(D) any agreement under section 7121, and any similar agreement, and any background information related to such an agreement or request for such an agreement,

but such term does not include data in a form which cannot be associated with, or otherwise identify, directly or indirectly, a particular taxpayer. Nothing in the preceding sentence, or in any other provision of law, shall be construed to require the disclosure of standards used or to be used for the selection of returns for examination, or data used or to be used for determining such standards, if the Secretary determines that such disclosure will seriously impair assessment, collection, or enforcement under the internal revenue laws.

(3) Taxpayer return information.—The term "taxpayer return information" means return information as defined in paragraph (2) which is filed with, or furnished to, the Secretary by or on behalf of the taxpayer to whom such return information relates.

(4) Tax administration.—The term "tax administration"—

(A) means—

(i) the administration, management, conduct, direction, and supervision of the execution and application of the internal revenue laws or related statutes (or equivalent laws and statutes of a State) and tax conventions to which the United States is a party, and

(ii) the development and formulation of Federal tax policy relating to existing or proposed internal revenue laws, related statutes, and tax conventions, and

(B) includes assessment, collection, enforcement, litigation, publication, and statistical gathering functions under such laws, statutes, or conventions.

(5) State.—

(A) In general.—The term "State" means—

(i) any of the 50 States, the District of Columbia, the Commonwealth of Puerto Rico, the Virgin Islands, the Canal Zone, Guam, American Samoa, and the Commonwealth of the Northern Mariana Islands,

(ii) for purposes of subsections (a)(2), (b)(4), (d)(1), (h)(4), and (p), any municipality—

(I) with a population in excess of 250,000 (as determined under the most recent decennial United States census data available),

(II) which imposes a tax on income or wages, and

(III) with which the Secretary (in his sole discretion) has entered into an agreement regarding disclosure, and

(iii) for purposes of subsections (a)(2), (b)(4), (d)(1), (h)(4), and (p), any governmental entity—

(I) which is formed and operated by a qualified group of municipalities, and

(II) with which the Secretary (in his sole discretion) has entered into an agreement regarding disclosure.

(B) Regional income tax agencies.—For purposes of subparagraph (A)(iii)—

(i) Qualified group of municipalities.—The term "qualified group of municipalities" means, with respect to any governmental entity, 2 or more municipalities—

(I) each of which imposes a tax on income or wages,

(II) each of which, under the authority of a State statute, administers the laws relating to the imposition of such taxes through such entity, and

(III) which collectively have a population in excess of 250,000 (as determined under the most recent decennial United States census data available).

(ii) References to State law, etc.—For purposes of applying subparagraph (A)(iii) to the subsections referred to in such subparagraph, any reference in such subsections to State law, proceedings, or tax returns shall be treated as references to the law, proceedings, or tax returns, as the case may be, of the municipalities which form and operate the governmental entity referred to in such subparagraph.

(iii) Disclosure to contractors and other agents.—Notwithstanding any other provision of this section, no return or return information shall be disclosed to any contractor or other agent of a governmental entity referred to in subparagraph (A)(iii) unless such entity, to the satisfaction of the Secretary—

(I) has requirements in effect which require each such contractor or other agent which would have access to returns or return information to provide safeguards (within the meaning of subsection (p)(4)) to protect the confidentiality of such returns or return information,

(II) agrees to conduct an on-site review every 3 years (or a mid-point review in the case of contracts or agreements of less than 3 years in duration) of each contractor or other agent to determine compliance with such requirements,

(III) submits the findings of the most recent review conducted under subclause (II) to the Secretary as part of the report required by subsection (p)(4)(E), and

(IV) certifies to the Secretary for the most recent annual period that such contractor or other agent is in compliance with all such requirements.

The certification required by subclause (IV) shall include the name and address of each contractor and other agent, a description of the contract or agreement with such contractor or other agent, and the duration of such contract or agreement. The requirements of this clause shall not apply to disclosures pursuant to subsection (n) for purposes of Federal tax administration and a rule similar to the rule of subsection (p)(8)(B) shall apply for purposes of this clause.

(6) Taxpayer identity.—The term "taxpayer identity" means the name of a person with respect to whom a return is filed, his mailing address, his taxpayer identifying number (as described in section 6109), or a combination thereof.

(7) Inspection.—The terms "inspected" and "inspection" mean any examination of a return or return information.

(8) Disclosure.—The term "disclosure" means the making known to any person in any manner whatever a return or return information.

(9) Federal agency.—The term "Federal agency" means an agency within the meaning of section 551(1) of title 5, United States Code.

(10) Chief executive officer.—The term "chief executive officer" means, with respect to any municipality, any elected official and the chief official (even if not elected) of such municipality.

(11) Terrorist incident, threat, or activity.—The term "terrorist incident, threat, or activity" means an incident, threat, or activity involving an act of domestic terrorism (as defined in section 2331(5) of title 18, United States Code) or international terrorism (as defined in section 2331(1) of such title).

(c) Disclosure of returns and return information to designee of taxpayer.—The Secretary may, subject to such requirements and conditions as he may prescribe by regulations, disclose the return of any taxpayer, or return information with respect to such taxpayer, to such person or persons as the taxpayer may designate in a request for or consent to such disclosure, or to any other person at the taxpayer's request to the extent necessary to comply with a request for information or assistance made by the taxpayer to such other person. However, return information shall not be disclosed to such person or persons if the Secretary determines that such disclosure would seriously impair Federal tax administration.

(d) Disclosure to State tax officials and State and local law enforcement agencies.—

(1) In general.—Returns and return information with respect to taxes imposed by chapters 1, 2, 6, 11, 12, 21, 23, 24, 31, 32, 44, 51, and 52 and subchapter D of chapter 36 shall be open to inspection by, or disclosure to, any State agency, body, or commission, or its legal representative, which is charged under the laws of such State with responsibility for the administration of State tax laws for the purpose of, and only to the extent necessary in, the administration of such laws, including any procedures with respect to locating any person who may be entitled to a refund. Such inspection shall be permitted, or such disclosure made, only upon written request by the head of such agency, body, or commission, and only to the representatives of such agency, body, or commission designated in such written request as the individuals who are to inspect or to receive the returns or return information on behalf of such agency, body, or commission. Such representatives shall not include any individual who is the chief executive officer of such State or who is neither an employee or legal representative of such agency, body, or commission nor a person described in subsection (n). However, such return information shall not be disclosed to the extent that the Secretary determines that such disclosure would identify a confidential informant or seriously impair any civil or criminal tax investigation.

(2) Disclosure to State audit agencies.—

(A) In general.—Any returns or return information obtained under paragraph (1) by any State agency, body, or commission may be open to inspection by, or disclosure to, officers and employees of the State audit agency for the purpose of, and only to the extent necessary in, making an audit of the State agency, body, or commission referred to in paragraph (1).

(B) State audit agency.—For purposes of subparagraph (A), the term "State audit agency" means any State agency, body, or commission which is charged under the laws of the State with the responsibility of auditing State revenues and programs.

(3) Exception for reimbursement under section 7624.—Nothing in this section shall be construed to prevent the Secretary from disclosing to any State or local law enforcement agency which may receive a payment under section 7624 the amount of the recovered taxes with respect to which such a payment may be made.

(4) Availability and use of death information.—

(A) In general.—No returns or return information may be disclosed under paragraph (1) to any agency, body, or commission of any State (or any legal representative thereof) during any period during which a contract meeting the requirements of subparagraph (B) is not in effect between such State and the Secretary of Health and Human Services.

(B) Contractual requirements.—A contract meets the requirements of this subparagraph if—

(i) such contract requires the State to furnish the Secretary of Health and Human Services information concerning individuals with respect to whom death certificates (or equivalent documents maintained by the State or any subdivision thereof) have been officially filed with it, and

(ii) such contract does not include any restriction on the use of information obtained by such Secretary pursuant to such contract, except that such contract may provide that such information is only to be used by the Secretary (or any other Federal agency) for purposes of ensuring that Federal benefits or other payments are not erroneously paid to deceased individuals.

Any information obtained by the Secretary of Health and Human Services under such a contract shall be exempt from disclosure under section 552 of title 5, United States Code, and from the requirements of section 552a of such title 5.

(C) Special exception.—The provisions of subparagraph (A) shall not apply to any State which on July 1, 1993, was not, pursuant to a contract, furnishing the Secretary of Health and Human Services information concerning individuals with respect to whom death certificates (or equivalent documents maintained by the State or any subdivision thereof) have been officially filed with it.

(5) Disclosure for combined employment tax reporting.—

(A) In general.—The Secretary may disclose taxpayer identity information and signatures to any agency, body, or commission of any State for the purpose of carrying out with such agency, body, or commission a combined Federal and State employment tax reporting program approved by the Secretary. Subsections (a)(2) and (p)(4) and sections 7213 and 7213A shall not apply with respect to disclosures or inspections made pursuant to this paragraph.

(B) Termination.—The Secretary may not make any disclosure under this paragraph after December 31, 2007.

(6) Limitation on disclosure regarding regional income tax agencies treated as States.—For purposes of paragraph (1), inspection by or disclosure to an entity described in subsection (b)(5)(A)(iii) shall be for the purpose of, and only to the extent necessary in, the administration of the laws of the member municipalities in such entity relating to the imposition of a tax on income or wages. Such entity may not redisclose any return or return information received pursuant to paragraph (1) to any such member municipality.

(e) Disclosure to persons having material interest.—

(1) In general.—The return of a person shall, upon written request, be open to inspection by or disclosure to—

(A) in the case of the return of an individual—

(i) that individual,

(ii) the spouse of that individual if the individual and such spouse have signified their consent to consider a gift reported on such return as made one-half by him and one-half by the spouse pursuant to the provisions of section 2513; or

(iii) the child of that individual (or such child's legal representative) to the extent necessary to comply with the provisions of section 1(g);

(B) in the case of an income tax return filed jointly, either of the individuals with respect to whom the return is filed;

(C) in the case of the return of a partnership, any person who was a member of such partnership during any part of the period covered by the return;

(D) in the case of the return of a corporation or a subsidiary thereof—

(i) any person designated by resolution of its board of directors or other similar governing body,

(ii) any officer or employee of such corporation upon written request signed by any principal officer and attested to by the secretary or other officer,

(iii) any bona fide shareholder of record owning 1 percent or more of the outstanding stock of such corporation,

(iv) if the corporation was an S corporation, any person who was a shareholder during any part of the period covered by such return during which an election under section 1362(a) was in effect, or

(v) if the corporation has been dissolved, any person authorized by applicable State law to act for the corporation or any person who the Secretary finds to have a material interest which will be affected by information contained therein;

[**(vi)** Redesignated (v)]

(E) in the case of the return of an estate—

(i) the administrator, executor, or trustee of such estate, and

(ii) any heir at law, next of kin, or beneficiary under the will, of the decedent, but only if the Secretary finds that such heir at law, next of kin, or beneficiary has a material interest which will be affected by information contained therein; and

(F) in the case of the return of a trust—

(i) the trustee or trustees, jointly or separately, and

(ii) any beneficiary of such trust, but only if the Secretary finds that such beneficiary has a material interest which will be affected by information contained therein.

(2) Incompetency.—If an individual described in paragraph (1) is legally incompetent, the applicable return shall, upon written request, be open to inspection by or disclosure to the committee, trustee, or guardian of his estate.

(3) Deceased individuals.—The return of a decedent shall, upon written request, be open to inspection by or disclosure to—

(A) the administrator, executor, or trustee of his estate, and

(B) any heir at law, next of kin, or beneficiary under the will, of such decedent, or a donee of property, but only if the Secretary finds that such heir at law, next of kin, beneficiary, or donee has a material interest which will be affected by information contained therein.

(4) Title 11 cases and receivership proceedings.—If—

(A) there is a trustee in a title 11 case in which the debtor is the person with respect to whom the return is filed, or

(B) substantially all of the property of the person with respect to whom the return is filed is in the hands of a receiver,

such return or returns for prior years of such person shall, upon written request, be open to inspection by or disclosure to such trustee or receiver, but only if the Secretary finds that such trustee or receiver, in his fiduciary capacity, has a material interest which will be affected by information contained therein.

(5) Individual's title 11 case.—

(A) In general.—In any case to which section 1398 applies (determined without regard to section 1398(b)(1)), any return of the debtor for the taxable year in which the case commenced or any preceding taxable year shall, upon written request, be open to inspection by or disclosure to the trustee in such case.

(B) Return of estate available to debtor.—Any return of an estate in a case to which section 1398 applies shall, upon written request, be open to inspection by or disclosure to the debtor in such case.

(C) Special rule for involuntary cases.—In an involuntary case, no disclosure shall be made under subparagraph (A) until the order for relief has been entered by the court having jurisdiction of such case unless such court finds that such disclosure is appropriate for purposes of determining whether an order for relief should be entered.

(6) Attorney in fact.—Any return to which this subsection applies shall, upon written request, also be open to inspection by or disclosure to the attorney in fact duly authorized in writing by any of the persons described in paragraph (1), (2), (3), (4), (5), (8), or (9) to inspect the return or receive the information on his behalf, subject to the conditions provided in such paragraphs.

(7) Return information.—Return information with respect to any taxpayer may be open to inspection by or disclosure to any person authorized by this subsection to inspect any return of such taxpayer if the Secretary determines that such disclosure would not seriously impair Federal tax administration.

(8) Disclosure of collection activities with respect to joint return.—If any deficiency of tax with respect to a joint return is assessed and the individuals filing such return are no longer married or no longer reside in the same household, upon request in writing by either of such individuals, the Secretary shall disclose in writing to the individual making the request whether the Secretary has attempted to collect such deficiency from such other individual, the general nature of such collection activities, and the amount collected. The preceding sentence shall not apply to any deficiency which may not be collected by reason of section 6502.

(9) Disclosure of certain information where more than 1 person subject to penalty under section 6672.—If the Secretary determines that a person is liable for a penalty under section 6672(a) with respect to any failure, upon request in writing of such person, the Secretary shall disclose in writing to such person—

(A) the name of any other person whom the Secretary has determined to be liable for such penalty with respect to such failure, and

(B) whether the Secretary has attempted to collect such penalty from such other person, the general nature of such collection activities, and the amount collected.

(f) Disclosure to Committees of Congress.—

(1) Committee on Ways and Means, Committee on Finance, and Joint Committee on Taxation.—Upon written request from the chairman of the Committee on Ways and Means of the House of Representatives, the chairman of the Committee on Finance of the Senate, or the chairman of the Joint Committee on Taxation, the Secretary shall furnish such committee with any return or return information specified in such request, except that any return or return information which can be associated with, or otherwise identify, directly or indirectly, a particular taxpayer shall be furnished to such committee only when sitting in closed executive session unless such taxpayer otherwise consents in writing to such disclosure.

(2) Chief of Staff of Joint Committee on Taxation.—Upon written request by the Chief of Staff of the Joint Committee on Taxation, the Secretary shall furnish him with any return or return information specified in such request. Such Chief of Staff may submit such return or return information to any committee described in paragraph (1), except that any return or return information which can be associated with, or otherwise identify, directly or indirectly, a particular taxpayer shall be furnished to such committee only when sitting in closed executive session unless such taxpayer otherwise consents in writing to such disclosure.

(3) Other committees.—Pursuant to an action by, and upon written request by the chairman of, a committee of the Senate or the House of Representatives (other than a committee specified in paragraph (1)) specially authorized to inspect any return or return information by a resolution of the Senate or the House of Representatives or, in the case of a joint committee (other than the joint committee specified in paragraph (1)) by concurrent resolution, the Secretary shall furnish such committee, or a duly authorized and designated subcommittee thereof, sitting in closed executive session, with any return or return information which such resolution authorizes the committee or subcommittee to inspect. Any resolution described in this paragraph shall specify the purpose for which the return or return information is to be furnished and that such information cannot reasonably be obtained from any other source.

(4) Agents of committees and submission of information to Senate or House of Representatives.—

(A) Committees described in paragraph (1).—Any committee described in paragraph (1) or the Chief of Staff of the Joint Committee on Taxation shall have the authority, acting directly, or by or through such examiners or agents as the chairman of such committee or such chief of staff may designate or appoint, to inspect returns and return information at such time and in such manner as may be determined by such chairman or chief of staff. Any return or return information obtained by or on behalf of such committee pursuant to the provisions of this subsection may be submitted by the committee to the Senate or the House of Representatives, or to both. The Joint Committee on Taxation may also submit such return or return information to any other committee described in paragraph (1), except that any return or return information which can be associated with, or otherwise identify, directly or indirectly, a particular taxpayer shall be furnished to such committee only when sitting in closed executive session unless such taxpayer otherwise consents in writing to such disclosure.

(B) Other committees.—Any committee or subcommittee described in paragraph (3) shall have the right, acting directly, or by or through no more than four examiners or agents, designated or appointed in writing in equal numbers by the chairman and ranking minority member of such committee or subcommittee, to inspect returns and return information at such time and in such manner as may be determined by such chairman and ranking minority member. Any return or return information obtained by or on behalf of such committee or subcommittee pursuant to the provisions of this subsection may be submitted by the committee to the Senate or the House of Representatives, or to both, except that any return or return information which can be associated with, or otherwise identify, directly or indirectly, a particular taxpayer, shall be furnished to the Senate or the House of Representatives only when sitting in closed executive session unless such taxpayer otherwise consents in writing to such disclosure.

(5) Disclosure by whistleblower.—Any person who otherwise has or had access to any return or return information under this section may disclose such return or return information to a committee referred to in paragraph (1) or any individual authorized to receive or inspect information under paragraph (4)(A) if such person believes such return or return information may relate to possible misconduct, maladministration, or taxpayer abuse.

(g) Disclosure to President and certain other persons.—

(1) In general.—Upon written request by the President, signed by him personally, the Secretary shall furnish to the President, or to such employee or employees of the White House Office as the President may designate by name in such request, a return or return information with respect to any taxpayer named in such request. Any such request shall state—

(A) the name and address of the taxpayer whose return or return information is to be disclosed,

(B) the kind of return or return information which is to be disclosed,

(C) the taxable period or periods covered by such return or return information, and

(D) the specific reason why the inspection or disclosure is requested.

(2) Disclosure of return information as to Presidential appointees and certain other Federal Government appointees.—The Secretary may disclose to a duly authorized representative of the Executive Office of the President or to the head of any Federal agency, upon written request by the President or head of such agency, or to the Federal Bureau of Investigation on behalf of and upon written request by the President or such head, return information with respect to an individual who is designated as being under consideration for appointment to a position in the executive or judicial branch of the Federal Government. Such return information shall be limited to whether such individual—

(A) has filed returns with respect to the taxes imposed under chapter 1 for not more than the immediately preceding 3 years;

(B) has failed to pay any tax within 10 days after notice and demand, or has been assessed any penalty under this title for negligence, in the current year or immediately preceding 3 years;

(C) has been or is under investigation for possible criminal offenses under the internal revenue laws and the results of any such investigation; or

(D) has been assessed any civil penalty under this title for fraud.

Within 3 days of the receipt of any request for any return information with respect to any individual under this paragraph, the Secretary shall notify such individual in writing that such information has been requested under the provisions of this paragraph.

(3) Restriction on disclosure.—The employees to whom returns and return information are disclosed under this subsection shall not disclose such returns and return information to any other person except the President or the head of such agency without the personal written direction of the President or the head of such agency.

(4) Restriction on disclosure to certain employees.—Disclosure of returns and return information under this subsection shall not be made to any employee whose annual rate of basic pay is less than the annual rate of basic pay specified for positions subject to section 5316 of title 5, United States Code.

(5) Reporting requirements.—Within 30 days after the close of each calendar quarter, the President and the head of any agency requesting returns and return information under this subsection shall each file a report with the Joint Committee on Taxation setting forth the taxpayers with respect to whom such requests were made during such quarter under this subsection, the returns or return information involved, and the reasons for such requests. The President shall not be required to report on any request for returns and return information pertaining to an individual who was an officer or employee of the executive branch of the Federal Government at the time such request was made. Reports filed pursuant to this paragraph shall not be disclosed unless the Joint Committee on Taxation determines that disclosure thereof (including identifying details) would be in the national interest. Such reports shall be maintained by the Joint Committee on Taxation for a period not exceeding 2 years unless, within such period, the Joint Committee on Taxation determines that a disclosure to the Congress is necessary.

(h) Disclosure to certain Federal officers and employees for purposes of tax administration, etc.—

(1) Department of the Treasury.—Returns and return information shall, without written request, be open to inspection by or disclosure to officers and employees of the Department of the Treasury whose official duties require such inspection or disclosure for tax administration purposes.

(2) Department of Justice.—In a matter involving tax administration, a return or return information shall be open to inspection by or disclosure to officers and employees of the Department of Justice (including United States attorneys) personally and directly engaged in, and solely for their use in, any proceeding before a Federal grand jury or preparation for any proceeding (or investigation which may result in such a proceeding) before a Federal grand jury or any Federal or State court, but only if—

(A) the taxpayer is or may be a party to the proceeding, or the proceeding arose out of, or in connection with, determining the taxpayer's civil or criminal liability, or the collection of such civil liability in respect of any tax imposed under this title;

(B) the treatment of an item reflected on such return is or may be related to the resolution of an issue in the proceeding or investigation; or

(C) such return or return information relates or may relate to a transactional relationship between a person who is or may be a party to the proceeding and the taxpayer which affects, or may affect, the resolution of an issue in such proceeding or investigation.

(3) Form of request.—In any case in which the Secretary is authorized to disclose a return or return information to the Department of Justice pursuant to the provisions of this subsection—

(A) if the Secretary has referred the case to the Department of Justice, or if the proceeding is authorized by subchapter B of chapter 76, the Secretary may make such disclosure on his own motion, or

(B) if the Secretary receives a written request from the Attorney General, the Deputy Attorney General, or an Assistant Attorney General for a return of, or return information relating to, a person named in such request and setting forth the need for the disclosure, the Secretary shall disclose return or return the information so requested.

(4) Disclosure in judicial and administrative tax proceedings.—A return or return information may be disclosed in a Federal or State judicial or administrative proceeding pertaining to tax administration, but only—

(A) if the taxpayer is a party to the proceeding, or the proceeding arose out of, or in connection with, determining the taxpayer's civil or criminal liability, or the collection of such civil liability, in respect of any tax imposed under this title;

(B) if the treatment of an item reflected on such return is directly related to the resolution of an issue in the proceeding;

(C) if such return or return information directly relates to a transactional relationship between a person who is a party to the proceeding and the taxpayer which directly affects the resolution of an issue in the proceeding; or

(D) to the extent required by order of a court pursuant to section 3500 of title 18, United States Code, or rule 16 of the Federal Rules of Criminal Procedure, such court being authorized in the issuance of such order to give due consideration to congressional policy favoring the confidentiality of returns and return information as set forth in this title.

However, such return or return information shall not be disclosed as provided in subparagraph (A), (B), or (C) if the Secretary determines that such disclosure would identify a confidential informant or seriously impair a civil or criminal tax investigation.

(5) Withholding of tax from social security benefits.—Upon written request of the payor agency, the Secretary may disclose available return information from the master files of the Internal Revenue Service with respect to the address and status of an individual as a nonresident alien or as a citizen or resident of the United States to the Social Security Administration or the Railroad Retirement Board (whichever is appropriate) for purposes of carrying out its responsibilities for withholding tax under section 1441 from social security benefits (as defined in section 86(d)).

(6) Internal Revenue Service Oversight Board.—

(A) In general.—Notwithstanding paragraph (1), and except as provided in subparagraph (B), no return or return information may be disclosed to any member of the Oversight Board described in subparagraph (A) or (D) of section 7802(b)(1) or to any employee or detailee of such Board by reason of their service with the Board. Any request for information not permitted to be disclosed under the preceding sentence, and any contact relating to a specific taxpayer, made by any such individual to an officer or employee of the Internal Revenue Service shall be reported by such officer or employee to the Secretary, the Treasury Inspector General for Tax Administration, and the Joint Committee on Taxation.

(B) Exception for reports to the Board.—If—

(i) the Commissioner or the Treasury Inspector General for Tax Administration prepares any report or other matter for the Oversight Board in order to assist the Board in carrying out its duties; and

(ii) the Commissioner or such Inspector General determines it is necessary to include any return or return information in such report or other matter to enable the Board to carry out such duties,

such return or return information (other than information regarding taxpayer identity) may be disclosed to members, employees, or detailees of the Board solely for the purpose of carrying out such duties.

(i) Disclosure to Federal officers or employees for administration of Federal laws not relating to tax administration.—

(1) Disclosure of returns and return information for use in criminal investigations.—

(A) In general.—Except as provided in paragraph (6), any return or return information with respect to any specified taxable period or periods shall, pursuant to and upon the grant of an ex parte order by a Federal district court judge or magistrate under subparagraph (B), be open (but only to the extent necessary as provided in such order) to inspection by, or disclosure to, officers and employees of any Federal agency who are personally and directly engaged in—

(i) preparation for any judicial or administrative proceeding pertaining to the enforcement of a specifically designated Federal criminal statute (not involving tax administration) to which the United States or such agency is or may be a party,

(ii) any investigation which may result in such a proceeding, or

(iii) any Federal grand jury proceeding pertaining to enforcement of such a criminal statute to which the United States or such agency is or may be a party,

solely for the use of such officers and employees in such preparation, investigation, or grand jury proceeding.

(B) Application for order.—The Attorney General, the Deputy Attorney General, the Associate Attorney General, any Assistant Attorney General, any United States attorney, any special prosecutor appointed under section 593 of title 28, United States Code, or any attorney in charge of a criminal division organized crime strike force established pursuant to section 510 of title 28, United States Code, may authorize an application to a Federal district court judge or magistrate for the order referred to in subparagraph (A). Upon such application, such judge or magistrate may grant such order if he determines on the basis of the facts submitted by the applicant that—

(i) there is reasonable cause to believe, based upon information believed to be reliable, that a specific criminal act has been committed,

(ii) there is reasonable cause to believe that the return or return information is or may be relevant to a matter relating to the commission of such act, and

(iii) the return or return information is sought exclusively for use in a Federal criminal investigation or proceeding concerning such act, and the information sought to be disclosed cannot reasonably be obtained, under the circumstances, from another source.

(2) Disclosure of return information other than taxpayer return information for use in criminal investigations.—

(A) In general.—Except as provided in paragraph (6), upon receipt by the Secretary of a request which meets the requirements of subparagraph (B) from the head of any Federal agency or the Inspector General thereof, or, in the case of the Department of Justice, the Attorney General, the Deputy Attorney General, the Associate Attorney General, any Assistant Attorney General, the Director of the Federal Bureau of Investigation, the Administrator of the Drug Enforcement Administration, any United States attorney, any special prosecutor appointed under section 593 of title 28, United States Code, or any attorney in charge of a criminal division organized crime strike force established pursuant to section 510 of title 28, United States Code, the Secretary shall disclose return information (other than taxpayer return information) to officers and employees of such agency who are personally and directly engaged in—

(i) preparation for any judicial or administrative proceeding described in paragraph (1)(A)(i),

(ii) any investigation which may result in such a proceeding, or

(iii) any grand jury proceeding described in paragraph (1)(A)(iii),

solely for the use of such officers and employees in such preparation, investigation, or grand jury proceeding.

(B) Requirements.—A request meets the requirements of this subparagraph if the request is in writing and sets forth—

(i) the name and address of the taxpayer with respect to whom the requested return information relates;

(ii) the taxable period or periods to which such return information relates;

(iii) the statutory authority under which the proceeding or investigation described in subparagraph (A) is being conducted; and

(iv) the specific reason or reasons why such disclosure is, or may be, relevant to such proceeding or investigation.

(C) Taxpayer identity.—For purposes of this paragraph, a taxpayer's identity shall not be treated as taxpayer return information.

(3) Disclosure of return information to apprise appropriate officials of criminal or terrorist activities or emergency circumstances.—

(A) Possible violations of Federal criminal law.—

(i) In general.—Except as provided in paragraph (6), the Secretary may disclose in writing return information (other than taxpayer return information) which may constitute evidence of a violation of any Federal criminal law (not involving tax administration) to the extent necessary to apprise the head of the appropriate Federal agency charged with the responsibility of enforcing such law. The head of such agency may disclose such return information to officers and employees of such agency to the extent necessary to enforce such law.

(ii) Taxpayer identity.—If there is return information (other than taxpayer return information) which may constitute evidence of a violation by any taxpayer of any Federal criminal law (not involving tax administration), such taxpayer's identity may also be disclosed under clause (i).

(B) Emergency circumstances.—

(i) Danger of death or physical injury.—Under circumstances involving an imminent danger of death or physical injury to any individual, the Secretary may disclose return information to the extent necessary to apprise appropriate officers or employees of any Federal or State law enforcement agency of such circumstances.

(ii) Flight from Federal prosecution.—Under circumstances involving the imminent flight of any individual from Federal prosecution, the Secretary may disclose return information to the extent necessary to apprise appropriate officers or employees of any Federal law enforcement agency of such circumstances.

(C) Terrorist activities, etc.—

(i) In general.—Except as provided in paragraph (6), the Secretary may disclose in writing return information (other than taxpayer return information) that may be related to a terrorist incident, threat, or activity to the extent necessary to apprise the head of the appropriate Federal law enforcement agency responsible for investigating or responding to such terrorist incident, threat, or activity. The head of the agency may disclose such return information to officers and employees of such agency to the extent necessary to investigate or respond to such terrorist incident, threat, or activity.

(ii) Disclosure to the department of justice.—Returns and taxpayer return information may also be disclosed to the Attorney General under clause (i) to the extent necessary for, and solely for use in preparing, an application under paragraph (7)(D).

(iii) Taxpayer identity.—For purposes of this subparagraph, a taxpayer's identity shall not be treated as taxpayer return information.

(iv) Termination.—No disclosure may be made under this subparagraph after December 31, 2007.

(4) Use of certain disclosed returns and return information in judicial or administrative proceedings.—

(A) Returns and taxpayer return information.—Except as provided in subparagraph (C), any return or taxpayer return information obtained under paragraph (1) or (7)(C) may be disclosed in any judicial or administrative proceeding pertaining to enforcement of a specifically designated Federal criminal statute or related civil forfeiture (not involving tax administration) to which the United States or a Federal agency is a party—

(i) if the court finds that such return or taxpayer return information is probative of a matter in issue relevant in establishing the commission of a crime or the guilt or liability of a party, or

(ii) to the extent required by order of the court pursuant to section 3500 of title 18, United States Code, or rule 16 of the Federal Rules of Criminal Procedure.

(B) Return information (other than taxpayer return information).—Except as provided in subparagraph (C), any return information (other than taxpayer return information) obtained under paragraph (1), (2), (3)(A) or (C), or (7) may be disclosed in any judicial or administrative proceeding pertaining to enforcement of a specifically designated Federal criminal statute or related civil forfeiture (not involving tax administration) to which the United States or a Federal agency is a party.

(C) Confidential informant; impairment of investigations.—No return or return information shall be admitted into evidence under subparagraph (A)(i) or (B) if the Secretary determines and notifies the Attorney General or his delegate or the head of the Federal agency that such admission would identify a confidential informant or seriously impair a civil or criminal tax investigation.

(D) Consideration of confidentiality policy.—In ruling upon the admissibility of returns or return information, and in the issuance of an order under subparagraph (A)(ii), the court shall give due consideration to congressional policy favoring the confidentiality of returns and return information as set forth in this title.

(E) Reversible error.—The admission into evidence of any return or return information contrary to the provisions of this paragraph shall not, as such, constitute reversible error upon appeal of a judgment in the proceeding.

(5) Disclosure to locate fugitives from justice.—

(A) In general.—Except as provided in paragraph (6), the return of an individual or return information with respect to such individual shall, pursuant to and upon the grant of an ex parte order by a Federal district court judge or magistrate under subparagraph (B), be open (but only to the extent necessary as provided in such order) to inspection by, or disclosure to, officers and employees of any Federal agency exclusively for use in locating such individual.

(B) Application for order.—Any person described in paragraph (1)(B) may authorize an application to a Federal district court judge or magistrate for an order referred to in subparagraph (A). Upon such application, such judge or magistrate may grant such order if he determines on the basis of the facts submitted by the applicant that—

(i) a Federal arrest warrant relating to the commission of a Federal felony offense has been issued for an individual who is a fugitive from justice,

(ii) the return of such individual or return information with respect to such individual is sought exclusively for use in locating such individual, and

(iii) there is reasonable cause to believe that such return or return information may be relevant in determining the location of such individual.

(6) Confidential informants; impairment of investigations.—The Secretary shall not disclose any return or return information under paragraph (1), (2), (3)(A) or (C), (5), (7), or (8) if the Secretary determines (and, in the case of a request for disclosure pursuant to a court order described in paragraph (1)(B) or (5)(B), certifies to the court) that such disclosure would identify a confidential informant or seriously impair a civil or criminal tax investigation.

(7) Disclosure upon request of information relating to terrorist activities, etc.—

(A) Disclosure to law enforcement agencies.—

(i) In general.—Except as provided in paragraph (6), upon receipt by the Secretary of a written request which meets the requirements of clause (iii), the Secretary may disclose return information (other than taxpayer return information) to officers and employees of any Federal law enforcement agency who are personally and directly engaged in the response to or investigation of any terrorist incident, threat, or activity.

(ii) Disclosure to State and local law enforcement agencies.—The head of any Federal law enforcement agency may disclose return information obtained under clause (i) to officers and employees of any State or local law enforcement agency but only if such agency is part of a team with the Federal law enforcement agency in such response or investigation and such information is disclosed only to officers and employees who are personally and directly engaged in such response or investigation.

(iii) Requirements.—A request meets the requirements of this clause if—

(I) the request is made by the head of any Federal law enforcement agency (or his delegate) involved in the response to or investigation of any terrorist incident, threat, or activity, and

(II) the request sets forth the specific reason or reasons why such disclosure may be relevant to a terrorist incident, threat, or activity.

(iv) Limitation on use of information.—Information disclosed under this subparagraph shall be solely for the use of the officers and employees to whom such information is disclosed in such response or investigation.

(v) Taxpayer identity.—For purposes of this subparagraph, a taxpayer's identity shall not be treated as taxpayer return information.

(B) Disclosure to intelligence agencies.—

(i) In general.—Except as provided in paragraph (6), upon receipt by the Secretary of a written request which meets the requirements of clause (ii), the Secretary may disclose return information (other than taxpayer return information) to those officers and employees of the Department of Justice, the Department of the Treasury, and other Federal intelligence agencies who are personally and directly engaged in the collection or analysis of intelligence and counterintelligence information or investigation concerning any terrorist incident, threat, or activity. For purposes of the preceding sentence, the information disclosed under the preceding sentence shall be solely for the use of such officers and employees in such investigation, collection, or analysis.

(ii) Requirements.—A request meets the requirements of this subparagraph if the request—

(I) is made by an individual described in clause (iii), and

(II) sets forth the specific reason or reasons why such disclosure may be relevant to a terrorist incident, threat, or activity.

(iii) Requesting individuals.—An individual described in this subparagraph is an individual—

(I) who is an officer or employee of the Department of Justice or the Department of the Treasury who is appointed by the President with the advice and consent of the Senate or who is the Director of the United States Secret Service, and

(II) who is responsible for the collection and analysis of intelligence and counterintelligence information concerning any terrorist incident, threat, or activity.

(iv) Taxpayer identity.—For purposes of this subparagraph, a taxpayer's identity shall not be treated as taxpayer return information.

(C) Disclosure under ex parte orders.—

(i) In general.—Except as provided in paragraph (6), any return or return information with respect to any specified taxable period or periods shall, pursuant to and upon the grant of an ex parte order by a Federal district court judge or magistrate under clause (ii), be open (but only to the extent necessary as provided in such order) to inspection by, or disclosure to, officers and employees of any Federal law enforcement agency or Federal intelligence agency who are personally and directly engaged in any investigation, response to, or analysis of intelligence and counterintelligence information concerning any terrorist incident, threat, or activity. Return or return information opened to inspection or disclosure pursuant to the preceding sentence shall be solely for the use of such officers and employees in the investigation, response, or analysis, and in any judicial, administrative, or grand jury proceedings, pertaining to such terrorist incident, threat, or activity.

(ii) Application for order.—The Attorney General, the Deputy Attorney General, the Associate Attorney General, any Assistant Attorney General, or any United States attorney may authorize an application to a Federal district court judge or magistrate for the order referred to in clause (i). Upon such application, such judge or magistrate may grant such order if he determines on the basis of the facts submitted by the applicant that—

(I) there is reasonable cause to believe, based upon information believed to be reliable, that the return or return information may be relevant to a matter relating to such terrorist incident, threat, or activity, and

(II) the return or return information is sought exclusively for use in a Federal investigation, analysis, or proceeding concerning any terrorist incident, threat, or activity.

(D) Special rule for ex parte disclosure by the IRS.—

(i) In general.—Except as provided in paragraph (6), the Secretary may authorize an application to a Federal district court judge or magistrate for the order referred to in subparagraph (C)(i). Upon such application, such judge or magistrate may grant such order if he determines on the basis of the facts submitted by the applicant that the requirements of subparagraph (C)(ii)(I) are met.

(ii) Limitation on use of information.—Information disclosed under clause (i)—

(I) may be disclosed only to the extent necessary to apprise the head of the appropriate Federal law enforcement agency responsible for investigating or responding to a terrorist incident, threat, or activity, and

(II) shall be solely for use in a Federal investigation, analysis, or proceeding concerning any terrorist incident, threat, or activity.

The head of such Federal agency may disclose such information to officers and employees of such agency to the extent necessary to investigate or respond to such terrorist incident, threat, or activity.

(E) Termination.—No disclosure may be made under this paragraph after December 31, 2007.

(8) Comptroller General.—

(A) Returns available for inspection.—Except as provided in subparagraph (C), upon written request by the Comptroller General of the United States, returns and return information shall be open to inspection by, or disclosure to, officers and employees of the Government Accountability Office for the purpose of, and to the extent necessary in, making—

(i) an audit of the Internal Revenue Service, the Bureau of Alcohol, Tobacco, Firearms, and Explosives, Department of Justice, or the Tax and Trade Bureau, Department of the Treasury, which may be required by section 713 of title 31, United States Code, or

(ii) any audit authorized by subsection (p)(6),

except that no such officer or employee shall, except to the extent authorized by subsection (f) or (p)(6), disclose to any person, other than another officer or employee of such office whose official duties require such disclosure, any return or return information described in section 4424(a) in a form which can be associated with, or otherwise identify, directly or indirectly, a particular taxpayer, nor shall such officer or employee disclose any other return or return information, except as otherwise expressly provided by law, to any person other than such other officer or employee of such office in a form which can be associated with, or otherwise identify, directly or indirectly, a particular taxpayer.

(B) Audits of other agencies.—

(i) In general.—Nothing in this section shall prohibit any return or return information obtained under this title by any Federal agency (other than an agency referred to in subparagraph (A)) or by a Trustee as defined in the District of Columbia Retirement Protection Act of 1977 for use in any program or activity from being open to inspection by, or disclosure to, officers and employees of the Government Accountability Office if such inspection or disclosure is—

(I) for purposes of, and to the extent necessary in, making an audit authorized by law of such program or activity, and

(II) pursuant to a written request by the Comptroller General of the United States to the head of such Federal agency.

(ii) Information from Secretary.—If the Comptroller General of the United States determines that the returns or return information available under clause (i) are not sufficient for purposes of making an audit of any program or activity of a Federal agency (other than an agency referred to in subparagraph (A)), upon written request by the Comptroller General to the Secretary, returns and return information (of the type authorized by subsection (l) or (m) to be made available to the Federal agency for use in such program or activity) shall be open to inspection by, or disclosure to, officers and employees of the Government Accountability Office for the purpose of, and to the extent necessary in, making such audit.

(iii) Requirement of notification upon completion of audit.—Within 90 days after the completion of an audit with respect to which returns or return information were opened to inspection or disclosed under clause (i) or (ii), the Comptroller General of the United States shall notify in writing the Joint Committee on Taxation of such completion. Such notice shall include—

(I) a description of the use of the returns and return information by the Federal agency involved,

(II) such recommendations with respect to the use of returns and return information by such Federal agency as the Comptroller General deems appropriate, and

(III) a statement on the impact of any such recommendations on confidentiality of returns and return information and the administration of this title.

(iv) Certain restrictions made applicable.—The restrictions contained in subparagraph (A) on the disclosure of any returns or return information open to inspection or disclosed under such subparagraph shall also apply to returns and return information open to inspection or disclosed under this subparagraph.

(C) Disapproval by Joint Committee on Taxation.—Returns and return information shall not be open to inspection or disclosed under subparagraph (A) or (B) with respect to an audit—

(i) unless the Comptroller General of the United States notifies in writing the Joint Committee on Taxation of such audit, and

(ii) if the Joint Committee on Taxation disapproves such audit by a vote of at least two-thirds of its members within the 30-day period beginning on the day the Joint Committee on Taxation receives such notice.

(j) Statistical use.—

(1) Department of Commerce.—Upon request in writing by the Secretary of Commerce, the Secretary shall furnish—

(A) such returns, or return information reflected thereon, to officers and employees of the Bureau of the Census, and

(B) such return information reflected on returns of corporations to officers and employees of the Bureau of Economic Analysis, as the Secretary may prescribe by regulation for the purpose of, but only to the extent necessary in, the structuring of censuses and national economic accounts and conducting related statistical activities authorized by law.

(2) Federal Trade Commission.—Upon request in writing by the Chairman of the Federal Trade Commission, the Secretary shall furnish such return information reflected on any return of a corporation with respect to the tax imposed by chapter 1 to officers and employees of the Division of Financial Statistics of the Bureau of Economics of such commission as the Secretary may prescribe by regulation for the purpose of, but only to the extent necessary in, administration by such division of legally authorized economic surveys of corporations.

(3) Department of Treasury.—Returns and return information shall be open to inspection by or disclosure to officers and employees of the Department of the Treasury whose official duties require such inspection or disclosure for the purpose of, but only to the extent necessary in, preparing economic or financial forecasts, projections, analyses, and statistical studies and conducting related activities. Such inspection or disclosure shall be permitted only upon written request which sets forth the specific reason or reasons why such inspection or disclosure is necessary and which is signed by the head of the bureau or office of the Department of the Treasury requesting the inspection or disclosure.

(4) Anonymous form.—No person who receives a return or return information under this subsection shall disclose such return or return information to any person other than the taxpayer to whom it relates except in a form which cannot be associated with, or otherwise identify, directly or indirectly, a particular taxpayer.

(5) Department of Agriculture.—Upon request in writing by the Secretary of Agriculture, the Secretary shall furnish such returns, or return information reflected thereon, as the Secretary may prescribe by regulation to officers and employees of the Department of Agriculture whose official duties require access to such returns or information for the purpose of, but only to the extent necessary in, structuring, preparing, and conducting the census of agriculture pursuant to the Census of Agriculture Act of 1997 (Public Law 105-113).

(6) Congressional Budget Office.—Upon written request by the Director of the Congressional Budget Office, the Secretary shall furnish to officers and employees of the Congressional Budget Office return information for the purpose of, but only to the extent necessary for, long-term models of the social security and medicare programs.

(k) Disclosure of certain returns and return information for tax administration purposes.—

(1) Disclosure of accepted offers-in-compromise.—Return information shall be disclosed to members of the general public to the extent necessary to permit inspection of any accepted offer-in-compromise under section 7122 relating to the liability for a tax imposed by this title.

(2) Disclosure of amount of outstanding lien.—If a notice of lien has been filed pursuant to section 6323(f), the amount of the outstanding obligation secured by such lien may be disclosed to any person who furnishes satisfactory written evidence that he has a right in the property subject to such lien or intends to obtain a right in such property.

(3) Disclosure of return information to correct misstatements of fact.—The Secretary may, but only following approval by the Joint Committee on Taxation, disclose such return information or any other information with respect to any specific taxpayer to the extent necessary for tax administration purposes to correct a misstatement of fact published or disclosed with respect to such taxpayer's return or any transaction of the taxpayer with the Internal Revenue Service.

(4) Disclosure to competent authority under tax convention.—A return or return information may be disclosed to a competent authority of a foreign government which has an income tax or gift and estate tax convention, or other convention or bilateral agreement relating to the exchange of tax information, with the United States but only to the extent provided in, and subject to the terms and conditions of, such convention or bilateral agreement.

(5) State agencies regulating tax return preparers.—Taxpayer identity information with respect to any tax return preparer, and information as to whether or not any penalty has been assessed against such tax return preparer under section 6694, 6695, or 7216, may be furnished to any agency, body, or commission lawfully charged under any State or local law with the licensing, registration, or regulation of tax return preparers. Such information may be furnished only upon written request by the head of such agency, body, or commission designating the officers or employees to whom such information is to be furnished. Information may be furnished and used under this paragraph only for purposes of the licensing, registration, or regulation of tax return preparers.

(6) Disclosure by certain officers and employees for investigative purposes.— An internal revenue officer or employee and an officer or employee of the Office of Treasury Inspector General for Tax Administration may, in connection with his official duties relating to any audit, collection activity, or civil or criminal tax investigation or any other offense under the internal revenue laws, disclose return information to the extent that such disclosure is necessary in obtaining information, which is not otherwise reasonably available, with respect to the correct determination of tax, liability for tax, or the amount to be collected or with respect to the enforcement of any other provision of this title. Such disclosures shall be made only in such situations and under such conditions as the Secretary may prescribe by regulation.

(7) Disclosure of excise tax registration information.—To the extent the Secretary determines that disclosure is necessary to permit the effective administration of subtitle D, the Secretary may disclose—

(A) the name, address, and registration number of each person who is registered under any provision of subtitle D (and, in the case of a registered terminal operator, the address of each terminal operated by such operator), and

(B) the registration status of any person.

(8) Levies on certain government payments.—

(A) Disclosure of return information in levies on financial management service.—In serving a notice of levy, or release of such levy, with respect to any applicable government payment, the Secretary may disclose to officers and employees of the Financial Management Service—

(i) return information, including taxpayer identity information,

(ii) the amount of any unpaid liability under this title (including penalties and interest), and

(iii) the type of tax and tax period to which such unpaid liability relates.

(B) Restriction on use of disclosed information.—Return information disclosed under subparagraph (A) may be used by officers and employees of the Financial Management Service only for the purpose of, and to the extent necessary in, transferring levied funds in satisfaction of the levy, maintaining appropriate agency records in regard to such levy or the release thereof, notifying the taxpayer and the agency certifying such payment that the levy has been honored, or in the defense of any litigation ensuing from the honor of such levy.

(C) Applicable government payment.—For purposes of this paragraph, the term "applicable government payment" means—

(i) any Federal payment (other than a payment for which eligibility is based on the income or assets (or both) of a payee) certified to the Financial Management Service for disbursement, and

(ii) any other payment which is certified to the Financial Management Service for disbursement and which the Secretary designates by published notice.

(9) Disclosure of information to administer section 6311.—The Secretary may disclose returns or return information to financial institutions and others to the extent the Secretary deems necessary for the administration of section 6311. Disclosures of information for purposes other than to accept payments by checks or money orders shall be made only to the extent authorized by written procedures promulgated by the Secretary.

(l) Disclosure of returns and return information for purposes other than tax administration.—

(1) Disclosure of certain returns and return information to Social Security Administration and Railroad Retirement Board.—The Secretary may, upon written request, disclose returns and return information with respect to—

(A) taxes imposed by chapters 2, 21, and 24, to the Social Security Administration for purposes of its administration of the Social Security Act;

(B) a plan to which part I of subchapter D of chapter 1 applies, to the Social Security Administration for purposes of carrying out its responsibility under section 1131 of the Social Security Act, limited, however to return information described in section 6057(d); and

(C) taxes imposed by chapter 22, to the Railroad Retirement Board for purposes of its administration of the Railroad Retirement Act.

(2) Disclosure of returns and return information to the Department of Labor and Pension Benefit Guaranty Corporation.—The Secretary may, upon written request, furnish returns and return information to the proper officers and employees of the Department of Labor and the Pension Benefit Guaranty Corporation for purposes of, but only to the extent necessary in, the administration of titles I and IV of the Employee Retirement Income Security Act of 1974.

(3) Disclosure that applicant for Federal loan has tax delinquent account.—

(A) In general.—Upon written request, the Secretary may disclose to the head of the Federal agency administering any included Federal loan program whether or not an applicant for a loan under such program has a tax delinquent account.

(B) Restriction on disclosure.—Any disclosure under subparagraph (A) shall be made only for the purpose of, and to the extent necessary in, determining the creditworthiness of the applicant for the loan in question.

(C) Included Federal loan program defined.—For purposes of this paragraph, the term "included Federal loan program" means any program under which the United States or a Federal agency makes, guarantees, or insures loans.

(4) Disclosure of returns and return information for use in personnel or claimant representative matters.—The Secretary may disclose returns and return information—

(A) upon written request—

(i) to an employee or former employee of the Department of the Treasury, or to the duly authorized legal representative of such employee or former employee, who is or may be a party to any administrative action or proceeding affecting the personnel rights of such employee or former employee; or

(ii) to any person, or to the duly authorized legal representative of such person, whose rights are or may be affected by an administrative action or proceeding under section 330 of title 31, United States Code,

solely for use in the action or proceeding, or in preparation for the action or proceeding, but only to the extent that the Secretary determines that such returns or return information is or may be relevant and material to the action or proceeding; or

(B) to officers and employees of the Department of the Treasury for use in any action or proceeding described in subparagraph (A), or in preparation for such action or proceeding, to the extent necessary to advance or protect the interests of the United States.

(5) Social Security Administration.—Upon written request by the Commissioner of Social Security, the Secretary may disclose information returns filed pursuant to part III of subchapter A of chapter 61 of this subtitle for the purpose of—

(A) carrying out, in accordance with an agreement entered into pursuant to section 232 of the Social Security Act, an effective return processing program; or

(B) providing information regarding the mortality status of individuals for epidemiological and similar research in accordance with section 1106(d) of the Social Security Act.

(6) Disclosure of return information to Federal, State, and local child support enforcement agencies.—

(A) Return information from Internal Revenue Service.—The Secretary may, upon written request, disclose to the appropriate Federal, State, or local child support enforcement agency—

(i) available return information from the master files of the Internal Revenue Service relating to the social security account number (or numbers, if the individual involved has more than one such number), address, filing status, amounts and nature of income, and the number of dependents reported on any return filed by, or with respect to, any individual with respect to whom child support obligations are sought to be established or enforced pursuant to the provisions of part D of title IV of the Social Security Act and with respect to any individual to whom such support obligations are owing, and

(ii) available return information reflected on any return filed by, or with respect to, any individual described in clause (i) relating to the amount of such individual's gross income (as defined in section 61) or consisting of the names and addresses of payors of such income and the names of any dependents reported on such return, but only if such return information is not reasonably available from any other source.

(B) Disclosure to certain agents.—The following information disclosed to any child support enforcement agency under subparagraph (A) with respect to any individual with respect to whom child support obligations are sought to be established or enforced may be disclosed by such agency to any agent of such agency which is under contract with such agency to carry out the purposes described in subparagraph (C):

(i) The address and social security account number (or numbers) of such individual.

(ii) The amount of any reduction under section 6402(c) (relating to offset of past-due support against overpayments) in any overpayment otherwise payable to such individual.

(C) Restriction on disclosure.—Information may be disclosed under this paragraph only for purposes of, and to the extent necessary in, establishing and collecting child support obligations from, and locating, individuals owing such obligations.

(7) Disclosure of return information to Federal, State, and local agencies administering certain programs under the Social Security Act, the Food Stamp Act of 1977 or title 38, United States Code, or certain housing assistance programs.—

(A) Return information from Social Security Administration.—The Commissioner of Social Security shall, upon written request, disclose return information from returns with respect to net earnings from self-employment (as defined in section 1402), wages (as defined in section 3121(a) or 3401(a)), and payments of retirement income, which have been disclosed to the Social Security Administration as provided by paragraph (1) or (5) of this subsection, to any Federal, State, or local agency administering a program listed in subparagraph (D).

(B) Return information from Internal Revenue Service.—The Secretary shall, upon written request, disclose current return information from returns with respect to unearned income from the Internal Revenue Service files to any Federal, State, or local agency administering a program listed in subparagraph (D).

(C) Restriction on disclosure.—The Commissioner of Social Security and the Secretary shall disclose return information under subparagraphs (A) and (B) only for purposes of, and to the extent necessary in, determining eligibility for, or the correct amount of, benefits under a program listed in subparagraph (D).

(D) Programs to which rule applies.—The programs to which this paragraph applies are:

(i) a State program funded under part A of title IV of the Social Security Act;

(ii) medical assistance provided under a State plan approved under title XIX of the Social Security Act or subsidies provided under section 1860D-14 of such Act;

(iii) supplemental security income benefits provided under title XVI of the Social Security Act, and federally administered supplementary payments of the type described in section 1616(a) of such Act (including payments pursuant to an agreement entered into under section 212(a) of Public Law 93-66);

(iv) any benefits provided under a State plan approved under title I, X, XIV, or XVI of the Social Security Act (as those titles apply to Puerto Rico, Guam, and the Virgin Islands);

(v) unemployment compensation provided under a State law described in section 3304 of this title;

(vi) assistance provided under the Food Stamp Act of 1977;

(vii) State-administered supplementary payments of the type described in section 1616(a) of the Social Security Act (including payments pursuant to an agreement entered into under section 212(a) of Public Law 93-66);

(viii)(I) any needs-based pension provided under chapter 15 of title 38, United States Code, or under any other law administered by the Secretary of Veterans Affairs;

(II) parents' dependency and indemnity compensation provided under section 1315 of title 38, United States Code;

(III) health-care services furnished under section 1710(a)(1)(I), 1710(a)(2), 1710(b), and 1712(a)(2)(B) of such title; and

(IV) compensation paid under chapter 11 of title 38, United States Code, at the 100 percent rate based solely on unemployability and without regard to the fact that the disability or disabilities are not rated as 100 percent disabling under the rating schedule; and

(ix) any housing assistance program administered by the Department of Housing and Urban Development that involves initial and periodic review of an applicant's or participant's income, except that return information may be disclosed under this clause only on written request by the Secretary of Housing and Urban Development and only for use by officers and employees of the Department of Housing and Urban Development with respect to applicants for and participants in such programs.

Only return information from returns with respect to net earnings from self-employment and wages may be disclosed under this paragraph for use with respect to any program described in clause (viii)(IV). Clause (viii) shall not apply after September 30, 2008.

(8) Disclosure of certain return information by Social Security Administration to Federal, State, and local child support enforcement agencies.—

(A) In general.—Upon written request, the Commissioner of Social Security shall disclose directly to officers and employees of a Federal or State or local child support enforcement agency return information from returns with respect to social security account numbers, net earnings from self-employment (as defined in section 1402), wages (as defined in section 3121(a) or 3401(a)), and payments of retirement income which have been disclosed to the Social Security Administration as provided by paragraph (1) or (5) of this subsection.

(B) Restriction on disclosure.—The Commissioner of Social Security shall disclose return information under subparagraph (A) only for purposes of, and to the extent necessary in, establishing and collecting child support obligations from, and locating, individuals owing such obligations. For purposes of the preceding sentence, the term "child support obligations" only includes obligations which are being enforced pursuant to a plan described in section 454 of the Social Security Act which has been approved by the Secretary of Health and Human Services under part D of title IV of such Act.

(C) State or local child support enforcement agency.— For purposes of this paragraph, the term "State or local child support enforcement agency" means any agency of a State or political subdivision thereof operating pursuant to a plan described in subparagraph (B).

(9) Disclosure of alcohol fuel producers to administrators of State alcohol laws.— Notwithstanding any other provision of this section, the Secretary may disclose—

(A) the name and address of any person who is qualified to produce alcohol for fuel use under section 5181, and

(B) the location of any premises to be used by such person in producing alcohol for fuel,

to any State agency, body, or commission, or its legal representative, which is charged under the laws of such State with responsibility for administration of State alcohol laws solely for use in the administration of such laws.

(10) Disclosure of certain information to agencies requesting a reduction under subsection (c), (d), or (e) of section 6402.—

(A) Return information from Internal Revenue Service.—The Secretary may, upon receiving a written request, disclose to officers and employees of any agency seeking a reduction under subsection (c), (d), or (e) of section 6402 and to officers and employees of the Department of the Treasury in connection with such reduction—

(i) taxpayer identity information with respect to the taxpayer against whom such a reduction was made or not made and with respect to any other person filing a joint return with such taxpayer,

(ii) the fact that a reduction has been made or has not been made under such subsection with respect to such taxpayer,

(iii) the amount of such reduction,

(iv) whether such taxpayer filed a joint return, and

(v) the fact that a payment was made (and the amount of the payment) to the spouse of the taxpayer on the basis of a joint return.

(B) Restriction on use of disclosed information.—Any officers and employees of an agency receiving return information under subparagraph (A) shall use such information only for the purposes of, and to the extent necessary in, establishing appropriate agency records, locating any person with respect to whom a reduction under subsection (c), (d), or (e) of section 6402 is sought for purposes of collecting the debt with respect to which the reduction is sought, or in the defense of any litigation or administrative procedure ensuing from a reduction made under subsection (c), (d), or (e) of section 6402.

(11) Disclosure of return information to carry out Federal Employees' Retirement System.—

(A) In general.—The Commissioner of Social Security shall, on written request, disclose to the Office of Personnel Management return information from returns with respect to net earnings from self-employment (as defined in section 1402), wages (as defined in section 3121(a) or 3401(a)), and payments of retirement income, which have been disclosed to the Social Security Administration as provided by paragraph (1) or (5).

(B) Restriction on disclosure.—The Commissioner of Social Security shall disclose return information under subparagraph (A) only for purposes of, and to the extent necessary in, the administration of chapters 83 and 84 of title 5, United States Code.

(12) Disclosure of certain taxpayer identity information for verification of employment status of medicare beneficiary and spouse of medicare beneficiary.—

(A) Return information from Internal Revenue Service.—The Secretary shall, upon written request from the Commissioner of Social Security, disclose to the Commissioner available filing status and taxpayer identity information from the individual master files of the Internal Revenue Service relating to whether any medicare beneficiary identified by the Commissioner was a married individual (as defined in section 7703) for any specified year after 1986, and, if so, the name of the spouse of such individual and such spouse's TIN.

(B) Return information from Social Security Administration.—The Commissioner of Social Security shall, upon written request from the Administrator of the Centers for Medicare & Medicaid Services, disclose to the Administrator the following information:

(i) The name and TIN of each medicare beneficiary who is identified as having received wages (as defined in section 3401(a)), above an amount (if any) specified by the Secretary of Health and Human Services, from a qualified employer in a previous year.

(ii) For each medicare beneficiary who was identified as married under subparagraph (A) and whose spouse is identified as having received wages, above an amount (if any) specified by the Secretary of Health and Human Services, from a qualified employer in a previous year—

(I) the name and TIN of the medicare beneficiary, and

(II) the name and TIN of the spouse.

(iii) With respect to each such qualified employer, the name, address, and TIN of the employer and the number of individuals with respect to whom written statements were furnished under section 6051 by the employer with respect to such previous year.

(C) Disclosure by Centers for Medicare & Medicaid Services.—With respect to the information disclosed under subparagraph (B), the Administrator of the Centers for Medicare & Medicaid Services may disclose—

(i) to the qualified employer referred to in such subparagraph the name and TIN of each individual identified under such subparagraph as having received wages from the employer (hereinafter in this subparagraph referred to as the "employee") for purposes of determining during what period such employee or the employee's spouse may be (or have been) covered under a group health plan of the employer and what benefits are or were covered under the plan (including the name, address, and identifying number of the plan),

(ii) to any group health plan which provides or provided coverage to such an employee or spouse, the name of such employee and the employee's spouse (if the spouse is a medicare beneficiary) and the name and address of the employer, and, for the purpose of presenting a claim to the plan—

(I) the TIN of such employee if benefits were paid under title XVIII of the Social Security Act with respect to the employee during a period in which the plan was a primary plan (as defined in section 1862(b)(2)(A) of the Social Security Act), and

(II) the TIN of such spouse if benefits were paid under such title with respect to the spouse during such period, and

(iii) to any agent of such Administrator the information referred to in subparagraph (B) for purposes of carrying out clauses (i) and (ii) on behalf of such Administrator.

(D) Special rules.—

(i) Restrictions on disclosure.—Information may be disclosed under this paragraph only for purposes of, and to the extent necessary in, determining the extent to which any medicare beneficiary is covered under any group health plan.

(ii) Timely response to requests.—Any request made under subparagraph (A) or (B) shall be complied with as soon as possible but in no event later than 120 days after the date the request was made.

(E) Definitions.—For purposes of this paragraph—

(i) Medicare beneficiary.—The term "medicare beneficiary" means an individual entitled to benefits under part A, or enrolled under part B, of title XVIII of the Social Security Act, but does not include such an individual enrolled in part A under section 1818.

(ii) Group health plan.—The term "group health plan" means any group health plan (as defined in section 5000(b)(1)).

(iii) Qualified employer.—The term "qualified employer" means, for a calendar year, an employer which has furnished written statements under section 6051 with respect to at least 20 individuals for wages paid in the year.

(13) Disclosure of return information to carry out income contingent repayment of student loans.—

(A) In general.—The Secretary may, upon written request from the Secretary of Education, disclose to officers and employees of the Department of Education return information with respect to a taxpayer who has received an applicable student loan and whose loan repayment amounts are based in whole or in part on the taxpayer's income. Such return information shall be limited to—

(i) taxpayer identity information with respect to such taxpayer,

(ii) the filing status of such taxpayer, and

(iii) the adjusted gross income of such taxpayer.

(B) Restriction on use of disclosed information.—Return information disclosed under subparagraph (A) may be used by officers and employees of the Department of Education only for the purposes of, and to the extent necessary in, establishing the appropriate income contingent repayment amount for an applicable student loan.

(C) Applicable student loan.—For purposes of this paragraph, the term "applicable student loan" means—

(i) any loan made under the program authorized under part D of title IV of the Higher Education Act of 1965, and

(ii) any loan made under part B or E of title IV of the Higher Education Act of 1965 which is in default and has been assigned to the Department of Education.

(D) Termination.—This paragraph shall not apply to any request made after December 31, 2007.

(14) Disclosure of return information to United States Customs Service.—The Secretary may, upon written request from the Commissioner of the United States Customs Service, disclose to officers and employees of the Department of the Treasury such return information with respect to taxes imposed by chapters 1 and 6 as the Secretary may prescribe by regulations, solely for the purpose of, and only to the extent necessary in—

(A) ascertaining the correctness of any entry in audits as provided for in section 509 of the Tariff Act of 1930 (19 U.S.C. 1509), or

(B) other actions to recover any loss of revenue, or to collect duties, taxes, and fees, determined to be due and owing pursuant to such audits.

(15) Disclosure of returns filed under section 6050I.—The Secretary may, upon written request, disclose to officers and employees of—

(A) any Federal agency,

(B) any agency of a State or local government, or

(C) any agency of the government of a foreign country, information contained on returns filed under section 6050I. Any such disclosure shall be made on the same basis, and subject to the same conditions, as apply to disclosures of information on reports filed under section 5313 of title 31, United States Code; except that no disclosure under this paragraph shall be made for purposes of the administration of any tax law.

(16) Disclosure of return information for purposes of administering the District of Columbia Retirement Protection Act of 1997—

(A) In general—Upon written request available return information (including such information disclosed to the Social Security Administration under paragraph (1) or (5) of this subsection), relating to the amount of wage income (as defined in section 3121(a) or 3401(a)), the name, address, and identifying number assigned under section 6109, of payors of wage income, taxpayer identity (as defined in subsection 6103(b)(6)), and the occupational status reflected on any return filed by, or with respect to, any individual with respect to whom eligibility for, or the correct amount of, benefits under the District of Columbia Retirement Protection Act of 1997, is sought to be determined, shall be disclosed by the Commissioner of Social Security, or to the extent not available from the Social Security Administration, by the Secretary, to any duly authorized officer or employee of the Department of the Treasury, or a Trustee or any designated officer or employee of a Trustee (as defined in the District of Columbia Retirement Protection Act of 1997), or any actuary engaged by a Trustee under the terms of the District of Columbia Retirement Protection Act of 1997, whose official duties require such disclosure, solely for the purpose of, and to the extent necessary in, determining an individual's eligibility for, or the correct amount of, benefits under the District of Columbia Retirement Protection Act of 1997.

(B) Disclosure for use in judicial or administrative proceedings—Return information disclosed to any person under this paragraph may be disclosed in a judicial or administrative proceeding relating to the determination of an individual's eligibility for, or the correct amount of, benefits under the District of Columbia Retirement Protection Act of 1997.

(17) Disclosure to National Archives and Records Administration.—The Secretary shall, upon written request from the Archivist of the United States, disclose or authorize the disclosure of returns and return information to officers and employees of the National Archives and Records Administration for purposes of, and only to the extent necessary in, the appraisal of records for destruction or retention. No such officer or employee shall, except to the extent authorized by subsection (f), (i)(8), or (p), disclose any return or return information disclosed under the preceding sentence to any person other than to the Secretary, or to another officer or employee of the National Archives and Records Administration whose official duties require such disclosure for purposes of such appraisal.

(18) Disclosure of return information for purposes of carrying out a program for advance payment of credit for health insurance costs of eligible individuals.—The Secretary may disclose to providers of health insurance for any certified individual (as defined in section 7527(c)) return information with respect to such certified individual only to the extent necessary to carry out the program established by section 7527 (relating to advance payment of credit for health insurance costs of eligible individuals).

(19) Disclosure of return information for purposes of providing transitional assistance under medicare discount card program.—

(A) In general.—The Secretary, upon written request from the Secretary of Health and Human Services pursuant to carrying out section 1860D-31 of the Social Security Act, shall disclose to officers, employees, and contractors of the Department of Health and Human Services with respect to a taxpayer for the applicable year—

(i)(I) whether the adjusted gross income, as modified in accordance with specifications of the Secretary of Health and Human Services for purposes of carrying out such section, of such taxpayer and, if applicable, such taxpayer's spouse, for the applicable year, exceeds the amounts specified by the Secretary of Health and Human Services in order to apply the 100 and 135 percent of the poverty lines under such section, (II) whether the return was a joint return, and (III) the applicable year, or

(ii) if applicable, the fact that there is no return filed for such taxpayer for the applicable year.

(B) Definition of applicable year.—For the purposes of this subsection, the term "applicable year" means the most recent taxable year for which information is available in the Internal

Revenue Service's taxpayer data information systems, or, if there is no return filed for such taxpayer for such year, the prior taxable year.

(C) Restriction on use of disclosed information.—Return information disclosed under this paragraph may be used only for the purposes of determining eligibility for and administering transitional assistance under section 1860D-31 of the Social Security Act.

(20) Disclosure of return information to carry out medicare part B premium subsidy adjustment.—

(A) In general.—The Secretary shall, upon written request from the Commissioner of Social Security, disclose to officers, employees, and contractors of the Social Security Administration return information of a taxpayer whose premium (according to the records of the Secretary) may be subject to adjustment under section 1839(i) of the Social Security Act. Such return information shall be limited to—

(i) taxpayer identity information with respect to such taxpayer,

(ii) the filing status of such taxpayer,

(iii) the adjusted gross income of such taxpayer,

(iv) the amounts excluded from such taxpayer's gross income under sections 135 and 911 to the extent such information is available,

(v) the interest received or accrued during the taxable year which is exempt from the tax imposed by chapter 1 to the extent such information is available,

(vi) the amounts excluded from such taxpayer's gross income by sections 931 and 933 to the extent such information is available,

(vii) such other information relating to the liability of the taxpayer as is prescribed by the Secretary by regulation as might indicate in the case of a taxpayer who is an individual described in subsection (i)(4)(B)(iii) of section 1839 of the Social Security Act that the amount of the premium of the taxpayer under such section may be subject to adjustment under subsection (i) of such section and the amount of such adjustment, and

(viii) the taxable year with respect to which the preceding information relates.

(B) Restriction on use of disclosed information.—Return information disclosed under subparagraph (A) may be used by officers, employees, and contractors of the Social Security Administration only for the purposes of, and to the extent necessary in, establishing the appropriate amount of any premium adjustment under such section 1839(i).

(m) Disclosure of taxpayer identity information.—

(1) Tax refunds.—The Secretary may disclose taxpayer identity information to the press and other media for purposes of notifying persons entitled to tax refunds when the Secretary, after reasonable effort and lapse of time, has been unable to locate such persons.

(2) Federal claims.—

(A) In general.—Except as provided in subparagraph (B), the Secretary may, upon written request, disclose the mailing address of a taxpayer for use by officers, employees, or agents of a Federal agency for purposes of locating such taxpayer to collect or compromise a Federal claim against the taxpayer in accordance with sections 3711, 3717, and 3718 of title 31.

(B) Special rule for consumer reporting agency.—In the case of an agent of a Federal agency which is a consumer reporting agency (within the meaning of section 603(f) of the Fair Credit Reporting Act (15 U.S.C. 1681a(f))), the mailing address of a taxpayer may be disclosed to such agent under subparagraph (A) only for the purpose of allowing such agent to prepare a commercial credit report on the taxpayer for use by such Federal agency in accordance with sections 3711, 3717, and 3718 of title 31.

(3) National Institute for Occupational Safety and Health.—Upon written request, the Secretary may disclose the mailing address of taxpayers to officers and employees of the National Institute for Occupational Safety and Health solely for the purpose of locating individuals who are, or may have been, exposed to occupational hazards in order to determine the status of their health or to inform them of the possible need for medical care and treatment.

(4) Individuals who owe an overpayment of Federal Pell grants or who have defaulted on student loans administered by the Department of Education.—

(A) In general.—Upon written request by the Secretary of Education, the Secretary may disclose the mailing address of any taxpayer—

(i) who owes an overpayment of a grant awarded to such taxpayer under subpart 1 of part A of title IV of the Higher Education Act of 1965, or

(ii) who has defaulted on a loan—

(I) made under part B, D, or E of title IV of the Higher Education Act of 1965, or

(II) made pursuant to section 3(a)(1) of the Migration and Refugee Assistance Act of 1962 to a student at an institution of higher education,

for use only by officers, employees, or agents of the Department of Education for purposes of locating such taxpayer for purposes of collecting such overpayment or loan.

(B) Disclosure to educational institutions, etc.—Any mailing address disclosed under subparagraph (A)(i) may be disclosed by the Secretary of Education to—

(i) any lender, or any State or nonprofit guarantee agency, which is participating under part B or D of title IV of the Higher Education Act of 1965, or

(ii) any educational institution with which the Secretary of Education has an agreement under subpart 1 of part A, or part D or E, of title IV of such Act,

for use only by officers, employees, or agents of such lender, guarantee agency, or institution whose duties relate to the collection of student loans for purposes of locating individuals who have defaulted on student loans made under such loan programs for purposes of collecting such loans.

(5) Individuals who have defaulted on student loans administered by the Department of Health and Human Services.—

(A) In general.—Upon written request by the Secretary of Health and Human Services, the Secretary may disclose the mailing address of any taxpayer who has defaulted on a loan made under part C of title VII of the Public Health Service Act or under subpart II of part B of title VIII of such Act, for use only by officers, employees, or agents of the Department of Health and Human Services for purposes of locating such taxpayer for purposes of collecting such loan.

(B) Disclosure to schools and eligible lenders.—Any mailing address disclosed under subparagraph (A) may be disclosed by the Secretary of Health and Human Services to—

(i) any school with which the Secretary of Health and Human Services has an agreement under subpart II of part C of title VII of the Public Health Service Act or subpart II of part B of title VIII of such Act, or

(ii) any eligible lender (within the meaning of section 737(4) of such Act) participating under subpart I of part C of title VII of such Act,

for use only by officers, employees, or agents of such school or eligible lender whose duties relate to the collection of student loans for purposes of locating individuals who have defaulted on student loans made under such subparts for the purposes of collecting such loans.

(6) Blood Donor Locator Service.—

(A) In general.—Upon written request pursuant to section 1141 of the Social Security Act, the Secretary shall disclose the mailing address of taxpayers to officers and employees of the Blood Donor Locator Service in the Department of Health and Human Services.

(B) Restriction on disclosure.—The Secretary shall disclose return information under subparagraph (A) only for purposes of, and to the extent necessary in, assisting under the Blood Donor Locator Service authorized persons (as defined in section 1141(h)(1) of the Social Security Act) in locating blood donors who, as indicated by donated blood or products derived therefrom or by the history of the subsequent use of such blood or blood products, have or may have the virus for acquired immune deficiency syndrome, in order to inform such donors of the possible need for medical care and treatment.

(C) Safeguards.—The Secretary shall destroy all related blood donor records (as defined in section 1141(h)(2) of the Social Security Act) in the possession of the Department of the Treasury upon completion of their use in making the disclosure required under subparagraph (A), so as to make such records undisclosable.

(7) Social security account statement furnished by Social Security Administration.—Upon written request by the Commissioner of Social Security, the Secretary may disclose the mailing address of any taxpayer who is entitled to receive a social security account statement pursuant to section 1143(c) of the Social Security Act, for use only by officers, employees or agents of the Social Security Administration for purposes of mailing such statement to such taxpayer.

(n) Certain other persons.—Pursuant to regulations prescribed by the Secretary, returns and return information may be disclosed to any person, including any person described in section 7513(a), to the extent necessary in connection with the processing, storage, transmission, and reproduction of such returns and return information, the programming, maintenance, repair, testing, and procurement of equipment, and the providing of other services, for purposes of tax administration.

(o) Disclosure of returns and return information with respect to certain taxes.—

(1) Taxes imposed by subtitle E.—Returns and return information with respect to taxes imposed by subtitle E (relating to taxes on alcohol, tobacco, and firearms) shall be open to inspection by or disclosure to officers and employees of a Federal agency whose official duties require such inspection or disclosure.

(2) Taxes imposed by chapter 35.—Returns and return information with respect to taxes imposed by chapter 35 (relating to taxes on wagering) shall, notwithstanding any other provision of this section, be open to inspection by or disclosure only to such person or persons and for such purpose or purposes as are prescribed by section 4424.

(p) Procedure and recordkeeping.—

(1) Manner, time, and place of inspections.—Requests for the inspection or disclosure of a return or return information and such inspection or disclosure shall be made in such manner and at such time and place as shall be prescribed by the Secretary.

(2) Procedure.—

(A) Reproduction of returns.—A reproduction or certified reproduction of a return shall, upon written request, be furnished to any person to whom disclosure or inspection of such return is authorized under this section. A reasonable fee may be prescribed for furnishing such reproduction or certified reproduction.

(B) Disclosure of return information.—Return information disclosed to any person under the provisions of this title may be provided in the form of written documents, reproductions of such documents, films or photoimpressions, or electronically produced tapes, disks, or records, or by any other mode or means which the Secretary determines necessary or appropriate. A reasonable fee may be prescribed for furnishing such return information.

(C) Use of reproductions.—Any reproduction of any return, document, or other matter made in accordance with this paragraph shall have the same legal status as the original, and any such reproduction shall, if properly authenticated, be admissible in evidence in any judicial or administrative proceeding as if it were the original, whether or not the original is in existence.

(3) Records of inspection and disclosure.—

(A) System of recordkeeping.—Except as otherwise provided by this paragraph, the Secretary shall maintain a permanent system of standardized records or accountings of all requests for inspection or disclosure of returns and return information (including the reasons for and dates of such requests) and of returns and return information inspected or disclosed under this section and section 6104(c). Notwithstanding the provisions of section 552a(c) of title 5, United States Code, the Secretary shall not be required to maintain a record or accounting of requests for inspection or disclosure of returns and return information, or of returns and return information inspected or disclosed, under the authority of subsections (c), (e), (f)(5), (h)(1), (3)(A), or (4), (i)(4), or (8)(A)(ii), (k)(1), (2), (6), (8), or (9), (l)(1), (4)(B), (5), (7), (8), (9), (10), (11), (12), (13), (14), (15), (16), (17), or (18), (m), or (n). The records or accountings required to be maintained under this paragraph shall be available for examination by the Joint Committee on Taxation or the Chief of Staff of such joint committee. Such record or accounting shall also be available for examination by such person or persons as may be, but only to the extent, authorized to make such examination under section 552a(c)(3) of title 5, United States Code.

(B) Report by the Secretary.—The Secretary shall, within 90 days after the close of each calendar year, furnish to the Joint Committee on Taxation a report with respect to, or summary of, the records or accountings described in subparagraph (A) in such form and containing such information as such joint committee or the Chief of Staff of such joint committee may designate. Such report or summary shall not, however, include a record or accounting of any request by the President under subsection (g) for, or the disclosure in response to such request of, any return or return information with respect to any individual who, at the time of such request, was an officer or employee of the executive branch of the Federal Government. Such report or summary, or any part thereof, may be disclosed by such joint committee to such persons and for such purposes as the joint committee may, by record vote of a majority of the members of the joint committee, determine.

(C) Public report on disclosures.—The Secretary shall, within 90 days after the close of each calendar year, furnish to the Joint Committee on Taxation for disclosure to the public a report with respect to the records or accountings described in subparagraph (A) which—

(i) provides with respect to each Federal agency, each agency, body, or commission described in subsection (d), (i)(3)(B)(i) or (7)(A)(ii) or (l)(6), and the Government Accountability Office the number of—

(I) requests for disclosure of returns and return information,

(II) instances in which returns and return information were disclosed pursuant to such requests or otherwise,

(III) taxpayers whose returns, or return information with respect to whom, were disclosed pursuant to such requests, and

(ii) describes the general purposes for which such requests were made,

(4) Safeguards.—Any Federal agency described in subsection (h)(2), (h) (5), (i)(1), (2), (3), (5), or (7), (j)(1), (2), or (5), (k)(8), (l)(1), (2), (3), (5), (10), (11), (13), (14), or (17) or (o)(1), the Government Accountability Office, the Congressional Budget Office, or any agency, body, or commission described in subsection (d), (i)(3)(B)(i) or 7(A)(ii), or (l)(6) , (7), (8), (9), (12), (15), or (16), any appropriate State officer (as defined in section 6104(c)), or any other person described in subsection (l)(16), (18), (19), or (20) shall, as a condition for receiving returns or return information—

(A) establish and maintain, to the satisfaction of the Secretary, a permanent system of standardized records with respect to any request, the reason for such request, and the date of such request made by or of it and any disclosure of return or return information made by or to it;

(B) establish and maintain, to the satisfaction of the Secretary, a secure area or place in which such returns or return information shall be stored;

(C) restrict, to the satisfaction of the Secretary, access to the returns or return information only to persons whose duties or responsibilities require access and to whom disclosure may be made under the provisions of this title;

(D) provide such other safeguards which the Secretary determines (and which he prescribes in regulations) to be necessary or appropriate to protect the confidentiality of the returns or return information;

(E) furnish a report to the Secretary, at such time and containing such information as the Secretary may prescribe, which describes the procedures established and utilized by such agency, body, or commission, the Government Accountability Office, or the Congressional Budget Office for ensuring the confidentiality of returns and return information required by this paragraph; and

(F) upon completion of use of such returns or return information—

(i) in the case of an agency, body, or commission described in subsection (d), (i)(3)(B)(i), or (l)(6), (7), (8), (9), or (16), any appropriate State officer (as defined in section 6104(c)), or any other person described in subsection (l)(16), (18), (19), or (20) return to the Secretary such returns or return information (along with any copies made therefrom) or make such returns or return information undisclosable in any manner and furnish a written report to the Secretary describing such manner,

(ii) in the case of an agency described in subsections (h)(2), (h)(5), (i)(1), (2), (3), (5) or (7), (j)(1) or (2), (k)(8), (l)(1), (2), (3), (5), (10), (11), (12), (13), (14), (15), or (17), or (o)(1), the Government Accountability Office, or the Congressional Budget Office, either—

(I) return to the Secretary such returns or return information (along with any copies made therefrom),

(II) otherwise make such returns or return information undisclosable, or

(III) to the extent not so returned or made undisclosable, ensure that the conditions of subparagraphs (A), (B), (C), (D), and (E) of this paragraph continue to be met with respect to such returns or return information, and

(iii) in the case of the Department of Health and Human Services for purposes of subsection (m)(6), destroy all such return information upon completion of its use in providing the notification for which the information was obtained, so as to make such information undisclosable;

except that the conditions of subparagraphs (A), (B), (C), (D), and (E) shall cease to apply with respect to any return or return information if, and to the extent that, such return or return information is disclosed in the course of any judicial or administrative proceeding and made a part of the public record thereof. If the Secretary determines that any such agency, body, or commission, including an agency, an appropriate State officer (as defined in section 6104(c)), or any other person described in subsection (l)(16), (18), (19), or (20), or the Government Accountability Office or the Congressional Budget Office, has failed to, or does not, meet the requirements of this paragraph, he may, after any proceedings for review established under paragraph (7), take such actions as are necessary to ensure such requirements are met, including refusing to disclose returns or return information to such agency, body, or commission, including an agency, an appropriate State officer (as defined in section 6104(c)), or any other person described in subsection (l)(16), (18), (19), or (20), or the Government Accountability Office or the Congressional Budget Office, until he determines that such requirements have been or will be met. In the case of any agency which receives any mailing address under paragraph (2), (4), (6), or (7) of subsection (m) and which discloses any such mailing address to any agent or which receives any information under subsection paragraph (6)(A), (12)(B), or (16) of subsection (l) and which discloses any such information to any agent, or any person including an agent described in subsection (l)(16), this paragraph shall apply to such agency and each such agent or other person (except that, in the case of an agent, or any person including an agent described in subsection (l)(16), any report to the Secretary or other action with respect to the Secretary shall be made or taken through such agency). For purposes of applying this paragraph in any case to which subsection (m)(6) applies, the term "return information" includes related blood donor records (as defined in section 1141(h)(2) of the Social Security Act).

(5) Report on procedures and safeguards.—After the close of each calendar year, the Secretary shall furnish to each committee described in subsection (f)(1) a report which describes the procedures and safeguards established and utilized by such agencies, bodies, or commissions, the Government Accountability Office, and the Congressional Budget Office for ensuring the confidentiality of returns and return information as required by this subsection. Such report shall also describe instances of deficiencies in, and failure to establish or utilize, such procedures.

(6) Audit of procedures and safeguards.—

(A) Audit by Comptroller General.—The Comptroller General may audit the procedures and safeguards established by such agencies, bodies, or commissions and the Congressional Budget Office pursuant to this subsection to determine whether such safeguards and procedures meet the requirements of this subsection and ensure the confidentiality of returns and return information. The Comptroller General shall notify the Secretary before any such audit is conducted.

(B) Records of inspection and reports by the Comptroller General.—The Comptroller General shall—

(i) maintain a permanent system of standardized records and accountings of returns and return information inspected by officers and employees of the Government Accountability Office under subsection (i)(8)(A)(ii) and shall, within 90 days after the close of each calendar year, furnish to the Secretary a report with respect to, or summary of, such records or accountings in such form and containing such information as the Secretary may prescribe, and

(ii) furnish an annual report to each committee described in subsection (f) and to the Secretary setting forth his findings with respect to any audit conducted pursuant to subparagraph (A).

The Secretary may disclose to the Joint Committee any report furnished to him under clause (i).

(7) Administrative review.—The Secretary shall by regulations prescribe procedures which provide for administrative review of any determination under paragraph (4) that any agency, body, or commission described in subsection (d) has failed to meet the requirements of such paragraph.

(8) State law requirements.—

(A) Safeguards.—Notwithstanding any other provision of this section, no return or return information shall be disclosed after December 31, 1978, to any officer or employee of any State which requires a taxpayer to attach to, or include in, any State tax return a copy of any portion of his Federal return, or information reflected on such Federal return, unless such State adopts provisions of law which protect the confidentiality of the copy of the Federal return (or portion thereof) attached to, or the Federal return information reflected on, such State tax return.

(B) Disclosure of returns or return information in State returns.—Nothing in subparagraph (A) shall be construed to prohibit the disclosure by an officer or employee of any State of any copy of any portion of a Federal return or any information on a Federal return which is required to be attached or included in a State return to another officer or employee of such State (or political subdivision of such State) if such disclosure is specifically authorized by State law.

(q) Regulations.—The Secretary is authorized to prescribe such other regulations as are necessary to carry out the provisions of this section.

Gramm-Leach-Bliley Act (1999)

15 U.S.C. §§ 6801-6809, §§ 6821-6827, as amended

Statutes in Context

The Gramm-Leach-Bliley (GLB) Act is more formally known as the Financial Services Modernization Act. Its purpose is to enhance competition in the financial service industry by removing the barriers of the Glass-Steagall Act of 1933. This earlier law prevented different types of financial institutions, such as banks, brokerage houses, and insurers from affiliating with each other. The GLB Act enables the creation of financial conglomerates that provide different kinds of financial services. It also contains regulations concerning the sharing of personal information by financial institutions.

The law permits sharing of personal information within a financial conglomerate as well as the sharing of information with affiliated companies. When financial institutions share information with nonaffiliated companies, they must first provide individuals with the ability to opt out of the disclosure. The GLB also requires that financial institutions provide privacy notices to their customers. It authorizes the FTC and other agencies to establish security standards for nonpublic personal information.

§ 6801. Protection of nonpublic personal information

(a) Privacy obligation policy

It is the policy of the Congress that each financial institution has an affirmative and continuing obligation to respect the privacy of its customers and to protect the security and confidentiality of those customers' nonpublic personal information.

(b) Financial institutions safeguards

In furtherance of the policy in subsection (a) of this section, each agency or authority described in section 6805(a) of this title shall establish appropriate standards for the financial institutions subject to their jurisdiction relating to administrative, technical, and physical safeguards—

(1) to insure the security and confidentiality of customer records and information;

(2) to protect against any anticipated threats or hazards to the security or integrity of such records; and

(3) to protect against unauthorized access to or use of such records or information which could result in substantial harm or inconvenience to any customer.

§ 6802. Obligations with respect to disclosures of personal information

(a) Notice requirements

Except as otherwise provided in this subchapter, a financial institution may not, directly or through any affiliate, disclose to a nonaffiliated third party any nonpublic personal information, unless such financial institution provides or has provided to the consumer a notice that complies with section 6803 of this title.

(b) Opt out

(1) In general

A financial institution may not disclose nonpublic personal information to a nonaffiliated third party unless—

(A) such financial institution clearly and conspicuously discloses to the consumer, in writing or in electronic form or other form permitted by the regulations prescribed under section 6804 of this title, that such information may be disclosed to such third party;

(B) the consumer is given the opportunity, before the time that such information is initially disclosed, to direct that such information not be disclosed to such third party; and

(C) the consumer is given an explanation of how the consumer can exercise that nondisclosure option.

(2) Exception

This subsection shall not prevent a financial institution from providing nonpublic personal information to a nonaffiliated third party to perform services for or functions on behalf of the financial institution, including marketing of the financial institution's own products or services, or financial products or services offered pursuant to joint agreements between two or more financial institutions that comply with the requirements imposed by the regulations prescribed under section 6804 of this title, if the financial institution fully discloses the providing of such information and enters into a contractual agreement with the third party that requires the third party to maintain the confidentiality of such information.

(c) Limits on reuse of information

Except as otherwise provided in this subchapter, a nonaffiliated third party that receives from a financial institution nonpublic personal information under this section shall not, directly or through an affiliate of such receiving third party, disclose such information to any other person that is a nonaffiliated third party of both the financial institution and such receiving third party, unless such disclosure would be lawful if made directly to such other person by the financial institution.

(d) Limitations on the sharing of account number information for marketing purposes

A financial institution shall not disclose, other than to a consumer reporting agency, an account number or similar form of access number or access code for a credit card account, deposit account, or transaction account of a consumer to any nonaffiliated third party for use in telemarketing, direct mail marketing, or other marketing through electronic mail to the consumer.

(e) General exceptions

Subsections (a) and (b) of this section shall not prohibit the disclosure of nonpublic personal information—

(1) as necessary to effect, administer, or enforce a transaction requested or authorized by the consumer, or in connection with—

(A) servicing or processing a financial product or service requested or authorized by the consumer;

(B) maintaining or servicing the consumer's account with the financial institution, or with another entity as part of a private label credit card program or other extension of credit on behalf of such entity; or

(C) a proposed or actual securitization, secondary market sale (including sales of servicing rights), or similar transaction related to a transaction of the consumer;

(2) with the consent or at the direction of the consumer;

(3) (A) to protect the confidentiality or security of the financial institution's records pertaining to the consumer, the service or product, or the transaction therein; (B) to protect against or prevent actual or potential fraud, unauthorized transactions, claims, or other liability; (C) for required institutional risk control, or for resolving customer disputes or inquiries; (D) to persons holding a legal or beneficial interest relating to the consumer; or (E) to persons acting in a fiduciary or representative capacity on behalf of the consumer;

(4) to provide information to insurance rate advisory organizations, guaranty funds or agencies, applicable rating agencies of the financial institution, persons assessing the institution's compliance with industry standards, and the institution's attorneys, accountants, and auditors;

(5) to the extent specifically permitted or required under other provisions of law and in accordance with the Right to Financial Privacy Act of 1978 [12 U.S.C.A. § 3401 et seq.], to law enforcement agencies (including a Federal functional regulator, the Secretary of the Treasury with respect to subchapter II of chapter 53 of Title 31, and chapter 2 of Title I of Public Law 91-508 (12 U.S.C. 1951-1959), a State insurance authority, or the Federal Trade Commission), self-regulatory organizations, or for an investigation on a matter related to public safety;

(6) (A) to a consumer reporting agency in accordance with the Fair Credit Reporting Act [15 U.S.C.A. § 1681 et seq.], or (B) from a consumer report reported by a consumer reporting agency;

(7) in connection with a proposed or actual sale, merger, transfer, or exchange of all or a portion of a business or operating unit if the disclosure of nonpublic personal information concerns solely consumers of such business or unit; or

(8) to comply with Federal, State, or local laws, rules, and other applicable legal requirements; to comply with a properly authorized civil, criminal, or regulatory investigation or subpoena or summons by Federal, State, or local authorities; or to respond to judicial process or government regulatory authorities having jurisdiction over the financial institution for examination, compliance, or other purposes as authorized by law.

§ 6803. Disclosure of institution privacy policy

(a) Disclosure required

At the time of establishing a customer relationship with a consumer and not less than annually during the continuation of such relationship, a financial institution shall provide a clear and conspicuous disclosure to such consumer, in writing or in electronic form or other form permitted by the regulations prescribed under section 6804 of this title, of such financial institution's policies and practices with respect to—

(1) disclosing nonpublic personal information to affiliates and nonaffiliated third parties, consistent with section 6802 of this title, including the categories of information that may be disclosed;

(2) disclosing nonpublic personal information of persons who have ceased to be customers of the financial institution; and

(3) protecting the nonpublic personal information of consumers.

(b) Regulations

Disclosures required by subsection (a) of this section shall be made in accordance with the regulations prescribed under section 6804 of this title.

(c) Information to be included

The disclosure required by subsection (a) of this section shall include—

(1) the policies and practices of the institution with respect to disclosing nonpublic personal information to nonaffiliated third parties, other than agents of the institution, consistent with section 6802 of this title, and including—

(A) the categories of persons to whom the information is or may be disclosed, other than the persons to whom the information may be provided pursuant to section 6802(e) of this title; and

(B) the policies and practices of the institution with respect to disclosing of nonpublic personal information of persons who have ceased to be customers of the financial institution;

(2) the categories of nonpublic personal information that are collected by the financial institution;

(3) the policies that the institution maintains to protect the confidentiality and security of nonpublic personal information in accordance with section 6801 of this title; and

(4) the disclosures required, if any, under section 1681a(d)(2)(A)(iii) of this title.

(d) Exemption for certified public accountants

(1) In general

The disclosure requirements of subsection (a) of this section do not apply to any person, to the extent that the person is—

(A) a certified public accountant;

(B) certified or licensed for such purpose by a State; and

(C) subject to any provision of law, rule, or regulation issued by a legislative or regulatory body of the State, including rules of professional conduct or ethics, that prohibits disclosure of nonpublic personal information without the knowing and expressed consent of the consumer.

(2) Limitation

Nothing in this subsection shall be construed to exempt or otherwise exclude any financial institution that is affiliated or becomes affiliated with a certified public accountant described in paragraph (1) from any provision of this section.

(3) Definitions

For purposes of this subsection, the term "State" means any State or territory of the United States, the District of Columbia, Puerto Rico, Guam, American Samoa, the Trust Territory of the Pacific Islands, the Virgin Islands, or the Northern Mariana Islands.

(e) Model forms

(1) In general

The agencies referred to in section 6804(a)(1) of this title shall jointly develop a model form which may be used, at the option of the financial institution, for the provision of disclosures under this section.

(2) Format

A model form developed under paragraph (1) shall—

(A) be comprehensible to consumers, with a clear format and design;

(B) provide for clear and conspicuous disclosures;

(C) enable consumers easily to identify the sharing practices of a financial institution and to compare privacy practices among financial institutions; and

(D) be succinct, and use an easily readable type font.

(3) Timing

A model form required to be developed by this subsection shall be issued in proposed form for public comment not later than 180 days after October 13, 2006.

(4) Safe harbor

Any financial institution that elects to provide the model form developed by the agencies under this subsection shall be deemed to be in compliance with the disclosures required under this section.

§ 6804. Rulemaking

(a) Regulatory authority

(1) Rulemaking

The Federal banking agencies, the National Credit Union Administration, the Secretary of the Treasury, the Securities and Exchange Commission, and the Federal Trade Commission shall each prescribe, after consultation as appropriate with representatives of State insurance authorities designated by the National Association of Insurance Commissioners, such regulations as may be necessary to carry out the purposes of this subchapter with respect to the financial institutions subject to their jurisdiction under section 6805 of this title.

(2) Coordination, consistency, and comparability

Each of the agencies and authorities required under paragraph (1) to prescribe regulations shall consult and coordinate with the other such agencies and authorities for the purposes of assuring, to the extent possible, that the regulations prescribed by each such agency and authority are consistent and comparable with the regulations prescribed by the other such agencies and authorities.

(3) Procedures and deadline

Such regulations shall be prescribed in accordance with applicable requirements of Title 5 and shall be issued in final form not later than 6 months after November 12, 1999.

(b) Authority to grant exceptions

The regulations prescribed under subsection (a) of this section may include such additional exceptions to subsections (a) through (d) of section 6802 of this title as are deemed consistent with the purposes of this subchapter.

§ 6805. Enforcement

(a) In general

This subchapter and the regulations prescribed thereunder shall be enforced by the Federal functional regulators, the State insurance authorities, and the Federal Trade Commission with respect to financial institutions and other persons subject to their jurisdiction under applicable law, as follows:

(1) Under section 1818 of Title 12, in the case of—

(A) national banks, Federal branches and Federal agencies of foreign banks, and any subsidiaries of such entities (except brokers, dealers, persons providing insurance, investment companies, and investment advisers), by the Office of the Comptroller of the Currency;

(B) member banks of the Federal Reserve System (other than national banks), branches and agencies of foreign banks (other than Federal branches, Federal agencies, and insured State branches of foreign banks), commercial lending companies owned or controlled by foreign banks, organizations operating under section 25 or 25A of the Federal Reserve Act [12 U.S.C.A. § 601 et seq. or 611 et seq.], and bank holding companies and their nonbank subsidiaries or affiliates (except brokers, dealers, persons providing insurance, investment companies, and investment advisers), by the Board of Governors of the Federal Reserve System;

(C) banks insured by the Federal Deposit Insurance Corporation (other than members of the Federal Reserve System), insured State branches of foreign banks, and any subsidiaries of such entities (except brokers, dealers, persons providing insurance, investment companies, and investment advisers), by the Board of Directors of the Federal Deposit Insurance Corporation; and

(D) savings associations the deposits of which are insured by the Federal Deposit Insurance Corporation, and any subsidiaries of such savings associations (except brokers, dealers, persons providing insurance, investment companies, and investment advisers), by the Director of the Office of Thrift Supervision.

(2) Under the Federal Credit Union Act [12 U.S.C.A. § 1751 et seq.], by the Board of the National Credit Union Administration with respect to any federally insured credit union, and any subsidiaries of such an entity.

(3) Under the Securities Exchange Act of 1934 [15 U.S.C.A. § 78a et seq.], by the Securities and Exchange Commission with respect to any broker or dealer.

(4) Under the Investment Company Act of 1940 [15 U.S.C.A. § 80a-1 et seq.], by the Securities and Exchange Commission with respect to investment companies.

(5) Under the Investment Advisers Act of 1940 [15 U.S.C.A. § 80b-1 et seq.], by the Securities and Exchange Commission with respect to investment advisers registered with the Commission under such Act.

(6) Under State insurance law, in the case of any person engaged in providing insurance, by the applicable State insurance authority of the State in which the person is domiciled, subject to section 6701 of this title.

(7) Under the Federal Trade Commission Act [15 U.S.C.A. § 41 et seq.], by the Federal Trade Commission for any other financial institution or other person that is not subject to the jurisdiction of any agency or authority under paragraphs (1) through (6) of this subsection.

(b) Enforcement of section 6801 of this title

(1) In general

Except as provided in paragraph (2), the agencies and authorities described in subsection (a) of this section shall implement the standards prescribed under section 6801(b) of this title in the same manner, to the extent practicable, as standards prescribed pursuant to section 1831p-1(a) of Title 12 are implemented pursuant to such section.

(2) Exception

The agencies and authorities described in paragraphs (3), (4), (5), (6), and (7) of subsection (a) of this section shall implement the standards prescribed under section 6801(b) of this title by rule with respect to the financial institutions and other persons subject to their respective jurisdictions under subsection (a) of this section.

(c) Absence of State action

If a State insurance authority fails to adopt regulations to carry out this subchapter, such State shall not be eligible to override, pursuant to section 1831x(g)(2)(B)(iii) of Title 12, the insurance customer protection regulations prescribed by a Federal banking agency under section 1831x(a) of Title 12.

(d) Definitions

The terms used in subsection (a)(1) of this section that are not defined in this subchapter or otherwise defined in section 1813(s) of Title 12 shall have the same meaning as given in section 3101 of Title 12.

§ 6806. Relation to other provisions

Except for the amendments made of subsections (a) and (b), nothing in this chapter shall be construed to modify, limit, or supersede the operation of the Fair Credit Reporting Act [15 U.S.C.A. § 1681 et seq.], and no inference shall be drawn on the basis of the provisions of this chapter regarding whether information is transaction or experience information under section 603 of such Act [15 U.S.C.A. § 1681a].

§ 6807. Relation to State laws

(a) In general

This subchapter and the amendments made to this subchapter shall not be construed as superseding, altering, or affecting any statute, regulation, order, or interpretation in effect in any State, except to the extent that such statute, regulation, order, or interpretation is inconsistent with the provisions of this subchapter, and then only to the extent of the inconsistency.

(b) Greater protection under State law

For purposes of this section, a State statute, regulation, order, or interpretation is not inconsistent with the provisions of this subchapter if the protection such statute, regulation, order, or interpretation affords any person is greater than the protection provided under this subchapter and the amendments made by this subchapter, as determined by the Federal Trade Commission, after consultation with the agency or authority with jurisdiction under section 6805(a) of this title of either the person that initiated the complaint or that is the subject of the complaint, on its own motion or upon the petition of any interested party.

§ 6808. Study of information sharing among financial affiliates

(a) In general

The Secretary of the Treasury, in conjunction with the Federal functional regulators and the Federal Trade Commission, shall conduct a study of information sharing practices among financial institutions and their affiliates. Such study shall include—

(1) the purposes for the sharing of confidential customer information with affiliates or with nonaffiliated third parties;

(2) the extent and adequacy of security protections for such information;

(3) the potential risks for customer privacy of such sharing of information;

(4) the potential benefits for financial institutions and affiliates of such sharing of information;

(5) the potential benefits for customers of such sharing of information;

(6) the adequacy of existing laws to protect customer privacy;

(7) the adequacy of financial institution privacy policy and privacy rights disclosure under existing law;

(8) the feasibility of different approaches, including opt-out and opt-in, to permit customers to direct that confidential information not be shared with affiliates and nonaffiliated third parties; and

(9) the feasibility of restricting sharing of information for specific uses or of permitting customers to direct the uses for which information may be shared.

(b) Consultation

The Secretary shall consult with representatives of State insurance authorities designated by the National Association of Insurance Commissioners, and also with financial services industry, consumer organizations and privacy groups, and other representatives of the general public, in formulating and conducting the study required by subsection (a) of this section.

(c) Report

On or before January 1, 2002, the Secretary shall submit a report to the Congress containing the findings and conclusions of the study required under subsection (a) of this section, together with such recommendations for legislative or administrative action as may be appropriate.

§ 6809. Definitions

As used in this subchapter:

(1) Federal banking agency

The term "Federal banking agency" has the same meaning as given in section 1813 of Title 12.

(2) Federal functional regulator

The term "Federal functional regulator" means—

(A) the Board of Governors of the Federal Reserve System;

(B) the Office of the Comptroller of the Currency;

(C) the Board of Directors of the Federal Deposit Insurance Corporation;

(D) the Director of the Office of Thrift Supervision;

(E) the National Credit Union Administration Board; and

(F) the Securities and Exchange Commission.

(3) Financial institution

(A) In general

The term "financial institution" means any institution the business of which is engaging in financial activities as described in section 1843(k) of Title 12.

(B) Persons subject to CFTC regulation

Notwithstanding subparagraph (A), the term "financial institution" does not include any person or entity with respect to any financial activity that is subject to the jurisdiction of the Commodity Futures Trading Commission under the Commodity Exchange Act [7 U.S.C.A. § 1 et seq.].

(C) Farm credit institutions

Notwithstanding subparagraph (A), the term "financial institution" does not include the Federal Agricultural Mortgage Corporation or any entity chartered and operating under the Farm Credit Act of 1971 [12 U.S.C.A. § 2001 et seq.].

(D) Other secondary market institutions

Notwithstanding subparagraph (A), the term "financial institution" does not include institutions chartered by Congress specifically to engage in transactions described in section 6802(e)(1)(C) of this title, as long as such institutions do not sell or transfer nonpublic personal information to a nonaffiliated third party.

(4) Nonpublic personal information

(A) The term "nonpublic personal information" means personally identifiable financial information—

(i) provided by a consumer to a financial institution;

(ii) resulting from any transaction with the consumer or any service performed for the consumer; or

(iii) otherwise obtained by the financial institution.

(B) Such term does not include publicly available information, as such term is defined by the regulations prescribed under section 6804 of this title.

(C) Notwithstanding subparagraph (B), such term—

(i) shall include any list, description, or other grouping of consumers (and publicly available information pertaining to them) that is derived using any nonpublic personal information other than publicly available information; but

(ii) shall not include any list, description, or other grouping of consumers (and publicly available information pertaining to them) that is derived without using any nonpublic personal information.

(5) Nonaffiliated third party

The term "nonaffiliated third party" means any entity that is not an affiliate of, or related by common ownership or affiliated by corporate control with, the financial institution, but does not include a joint employee of such institution.

(6) Affiliate

The term "affiliate" means any company that controls, is controlled by, or is under common control with another company.

(7) Necessary to effect, administer, or enforce

The term "as necessary to effect, administer, or enforce the transaction" means—

(A) the disclosure is required, or is a usual, appropriate, or acceptable method, to carry out the transaction or the product or service business of which the transaction is a part, and record or service or maintain the consumer's account in the ordinary course of providing the financial service or financial product, or to administer or service benefits or claims relating to the transaction or the product or service business of which it is a part, and includes—

(i) providing the consumer or the consumer's agent or broker with a confirmation, statement, or other record of the transaction, or information on the status or value of the financial service or financial product; and

(ii) the accrual or recognition of incentives or bonuses associated with the transaction that are provided by the financial institution or any other party;

(B) the disclosure is required, or is one of the lawful or appropriate methods, to enforce the rights of the financial institution or of other persons engaged in carrying out the financial transaction, or providing the product or service;

(C) the disclosure is required, or is a usual, appropriate, or acceptable method, for insurance underwriting at the consumer's request or for reinsurance purposes, or for any of the following purposes as they relate to a consumer's insurance: Account administration, reporting, investigating, or preventing fraud or material misrepresentation, processing premium payments, processing insurance claims, administering insurance benefits (including utilization review activities), participating in research projects, or as otherwise required or specifically permitted by Federal or State law; or

(D) the disclosure is required, or is a usual, appropriate or acceptable method, in connection with—

(i) the authorization, settlement, billing, processing, clearing, transferring, reconciling, or collection of amounts charged, debited, or otherwise paid using a debit, credit or other payment card, check, or account number, or by other payment means;

(ii) the transfer of receivables, accounts or interests therein; or

(iii) the audit of debit, credit or other payment information.

(8) State insurance authority

The term "State insurance authority" means, in the case of any person engaged in providing insurance, the State insurance authority of the State in which the person is domiciled.

(9) Consumer

The term "consumer" means an individual who obtains, from a financial institution, financial products or services which are to be used primarily for personal, family, or household purposes, and also means the legal representative of such an individual.

(10) Joint agreement

The term "joint agreement" means a formal written contract pursuant to which two or more financial institutions jointly offer, endorse, or sponsor a financial product or service, and as may be further defined in the regulations prescribed under section 6804 of this title.

(11) Customer relationship

The term "time of establishing a customer relationship" shall be defined by the regulations prescribed under section 6804 of this title, and shall, in the case of a financial institution engaged in extending credit directly to consumers to finance purchases of goods or services, mean the time of establishing the credit relationship with the consumer.

§ 6821. Privacy protection for customer information of financial institutions

(a) Prohibition on obtaining customer information by false pretenses

It shall be a violation of this subchapter for any person to obtain or attempt to obtain, or cause to be disclosed or attempt to cause to be disclosed to any person, customer information of a financial institution relating to another person—

(1) by making a false, fictitious, or fraudulent statement or representation to an officer, employee, or agent of a financial institution;

(2) by making a false, fictitious, or fraudulent statement or representation to a customer of a financial institution; or

(3) by providing any document to an officer, employee, or agent of a financial institution, knowing that the document is forged, counterfeit, lost, or stolen, was fraudulently obtained, or contains a false, fictitious, or fraudulent statement or representation.

(b) Prohibition on solicitation of a person to obtain customer information from financial institution under false pretenses

It shall be a violation of this subchapter to request a person to obtain customer information of a financial institution, knowing that the person will obtain, or attempt to obtain, the information from the institution in any manner described in subsection (a) of this section.

(c) Nonapplicability to law enforcement agencies

No provision of this section shall be construed so as to prevent any action by a law enforcement agency, or any officer, employee, or agent of such agency, to obtain customer information of a financial institution in connection with the performance of the official duties of the agency.

(d) Nonapplicability to financial institutions in certain cases

No provision of this section shall be construed so as to prevent any financial institution, or any officer, employee, or agent of a financial institution, from obtaining customer information of such financial institution in the course of—

(1) testing the security procedures or systems of such institution for maintaining the confidentiality of customer information;

(2) investigating allegations of misconduct or negligence on the part of any officer, employee, or agent of the financial institution; or

(3) recovering customer information of the financial institution which was obtained or received by another person in any manner described in subsection (a) or (b) of this section.

(e) Nonapplicability to insurance institutions for investigation of insurance fraud

No provision of this section shall be construed so as to prevent any insurance institution, or any officer, employee, or agency of an insurance institution, from obtaining information as part of an insurance investigation into criminal activity, fraud, material misrepresentation, or material nondisclosure that is authorized for such institution under State law, regulation, interpretation, or order.

(f) Nonapplicability to certain types of customer information of financial institutions

No provision of this section shall be construed so as to prevent any person from obtaining customer information of a financial institution that otherwise is available as a public record filed pursuant to the securities laws (as defined in section 78c(a)(47) of this title).

(g) Nonapplicability to collection of child support judgments

No provision of this section shall be construed to prevent any State-licensed private investigator, or any officer, employee, or agent of such private investigator, from obtaining customer information of a financial institution, to the extent reasonably necessary to collect child support from a person adjudged to have been delinquent in his or her obligations by a Federal or State court, and to the extent that such action by a State-licensed private investigator is not unlawful under any other Federal or State law or regulation, and has been authorized by an order or judgment of a court of competent jurisdiction.

§ 6822. Administrative enforcement

(a) Enforcement by Federal Trade Commission

Except as provided in subsection (b) of this section, compliance with this subchapter shall be enforced by the Federal Trade Commission in the same manner and with the same power and authority as the Commission has under the Fair Debt Collection Practices Act [15 U.S.C.A § 1692 et seq.] to enforce compliance with such Act.

(b) Enforcement by other agencies in certain cases

(1) In general

Compliance with this subchapter shall be enforced under—

(A) section 8 of the Federal Deposit Insurance Act [12 U.S.C.A. § 1818], in the case of—

(i) national banks, and Federal branches and Federal agencies of foreign banks, by the Office of the Comptroller of the Currency;

(ii) member banks of the Federal Reserve System (other than national banks), branches and agencies of foreign banks (other than Federal branches, Federal agencies, and insured State branches of foreign banks), commercial lending companies owned or controlled by foreign banks, and organizations operating under section 25 or 25A of the Federal Reserve Act [12 U.S.C.A § 601 et seq. or 611 et seq.], by the Board;

(iii) banks insured by the Federal Deposit Insurance Corporation (other than members of the Federal Reserve System and national nonmember banks) and insured State branches of foreign banks, by the Board of Directors of the Federal Deposit Insurance Corporation; and

(iv) savings associations the deposits of which are insured by the Federal Deposit Insurance Corporation, by the Director of the Office of Thrift Supervision; and

(B) the Federal Credit Union Act [12 U.S.C.A § 1751 et seq.], by the Administrator of the National Credit Union Administration with respect to any Federal credit union.

(2) Violations of this subchapter treated as violations of other laws

For the purpose of the exercise by any agency referred to in paragraph (1) of its powers under any Act referred to in that paragraph, a violation of this subchapter shall be deemed to be a violation of a requirement imposed under that Act. In addition to its powers under any provision of law specifically referred to in paragraph (1), each of the agencies referred to in that paragraph may exercise, for the purpose of enforcing compliance with this subchapter, any other authority conferred on such agency by law.

§ 6823. Criminal penalty

(a) In general

Whoever knowingly and intentionally violates, or knowingly and intentionally attempts to violate, section 6821 of this title shall be fined in accordance with Title 18 or imprisoned for not more than 5 years, or both.

(b) Enhanced penalty for aggravated cases

Whoever violates, or attempts to violate, section 6821 of this title while violating another law of the United States or as part of a pattern of any illegal activity involving more than $100,000 in a 12-month period shall be fined twice the amount provided in subsection (b)(3) or (c)(3) (as the case may be) of section 3571 of Title 18, imprisoned for not more than 10 years, or both.

§ 6824. Relation to State laws

(a) In general

This subchapter shall not be construed as superseding, altering, or affecting the statutes, regulations, orders, or interpretations in effect in any State, except to the extent that such statutes, regulations, orders, or interpretations are inconsistent with the provisions of this subchapter, and then only to the extent of the inconsistency.

(b) Greater protection under State law

For purposes of this section, a State statute, regulation, order, or interpretation is not inconsistent with the provisions of this subchapter if the protection such statute, regulation, order, or interpretation affords any person is greater than the protection provided under this subchapter as determined by the Federal Trade Commission, after consultation with the agency or authority with jurisdiction under section 6822 of this title of either the person that initiated the complaint or that is the subject of the complaint, on its own motion or upon the petition of any interested party.

§ 6825. Agency guidance

In furtherance of the objectives of this subchapter, each Federal banking agency (as defined in section 1813(z) of Title 12), the National Credit Union Administration, and the Securities and Exchange Commission or self-regulatory organizations, as appropriate, shall review regulations and guidelines applicable to financial institutions under their respective jurisdictions and shall prescribe such revisions to such regulations and guidelines as may be necessary to ensure that such financial institutions have policies, procedures, and controls in place to prevent the unauthorized disclosure of customer financial information and to deter and detect activities proscribed under section 6821 of this title.

§ 6826. Reports

(a) Report to the Congress

Before the end of the 18-month period beginning on November 12, 1999, the Comptroller General, in consultation with the Federal Trade Commission, Federal banking agencies, the National Credit Union Administration, the Securities and Exchange Commission, appropriate Federal law enforcement agencies, and appropriate State insurance regulators, shall submit to the Congress a report on the following:

(1) The efficacy and adequacy of the remedies provided in this subchapter in addressing attempts to obtain financial information by fraudulent means or by false pretenses.

(2) Any recommendations for additional legislative or regulatory action to address threats to the privacy of financial information created by attempts to obtain information by fraudulent means or false pretenses.

(b) Annual report by administering agencies

The Federal Trade Commission and the Attorney General shall submit to Congress an annual report on number and disposition of all enforcement actions taken pursuant to this subchapter.

§ 6827. Definitions

For purposes of this subchapter, the following definitions shall apply:

(1) Customer

The term "customer" means, with respect to a financial institution, any person (or authorized representative of a person) to whom the financial institution provides a product or service, including that of acting as a fiduciary.

(2) Customer information of a financial institution

The term "customer information of a financial institution" means any information maintained by or for a financial institution which is derived from the relationship between the financial institution and a customer of the financial institution and is identified with the customer.

(3) Document

The term "document" means any information in any form.

(4) Financial institution

(A) In general

The term "financial institution" means any institution engaged in the business of providing financial services to customers who maintain a credit, deposit, trust, or other financial account or relationship with the institution.

(B) Certain financial institutions specifically included

The term "financial institution" includes any depository institution (as defined in section 461(b)(1)(A) of Title 12), any broker or dealer, any investment adviser or investment company, any insurance company, any loan or finance company, any credit card issuer or operator of a credit card system, and any consumer reporting agency that compiles and maintains files on consumers on a nationwide basis (as defined in section 1681a(p) of this title).

(C) Securities institutions

For purposes of subparagraph (B)—

(i) the terms "broker" and "dealer" have the same meanings as given in section 78c of this title;

(ii) the term "investment adviser" has the same meaning as given in section 202(a)(11) of the Investment Advisers Act of 1940 (15 U.S.C. 80b-2(a)); and

(iii) the term "investment company" has the same meaning as given in section 80a-3 of this title.

(D) Certain persons and entities specifically excluded

The term "financial institution" does not include any person or entity with respect to any financial activity that is subject to the jurisdiction of the Commodity Futures Trading Commission under the Commodity Exchange Act [7 U.S.C.A. § 1 et seq.] and does not include the Federal Agricultural Mortgage Corporation or any entity chartered and operating under the Farm Credit Act of 1971 [12 U.S.C.A. § 2001 et seq.].

(E) Further definition by regulation

The Federal Trade Commission, after consultation with Federal banking agencies and the Securities and Exchange Commission, may prescribe regulations clarifying or describing the types of institutions which shall be treated as financial institutions for purposes of this subchapter.

FTC Act (1914)

15 U.S.C. §§ 41, 45, 46, 57a, 57b, 57b-1, as amended

Statutes in Context

The FTC has acted in numerous cases involving consumer privacy issues. It has done so pursuant to its power to prevent deceptive and unfair trade practices under the FTC Act. This statute also authorizes the FTC to seek civil penalties as well as injunctive remedies.

§ 41. Federal Trade Commission established; membership; vacancies; seal

A commission is created and established, to be known as the Federal Trade Commission (hereinafter referred to as the Commission), which shall be composed of five Commissioners, who shall be appointed by the President, by and with the advice and consent of the Senate. Not more than three of the Commissioners shall be members of the same political party. The first Commissioners appointed shall continue in office for terms of three, four, five, six, and seven years, respectively, from September 26, 1914, the term of each to be designated by the President, but their successors shall be appointed for terms of seven years, except that any person chosen to fill a vacancy shall be appointed only for the unexpired term of the Commissioner whom he shall succeed: *Provided, however*, That upon the expiration of his term of office a Commissioner shall continue to serve until his successor shall have been appointed and shall have qualified. The President shall choose a chairman from the Commission's membership. No Commissioner shall engage in any other business, vocation, or employment. Any Commissioner may be removed by the President for inefficiency, neglect of duty, or malfeasance in office. A vacancy in the Commission shall not impair the right of the remaining Commissioners to exercise all the powers of the Commission.

The Commission shall have an official seal, which shall be judicially noticed.

§ 45. Unfair methods of competition unlawful; prevention by Commission

(a) Declaration of unlawfulness; power to prohibit unfair practices; inapplicability to foreign trade

(1) Unfair methods of competition in or affecting commerce, and unfair or deceptive acts or practices in or affecting commerce, are hereby declared unlawful.

(2) The Commission is hereby empowered and directed to prevent persons, partnerships, or corporations, except banks, savings and loan institutions described in section 57a(f)(3) of this title, Federal credit unions described in section 57a(f)(4) of this title, common carriers subject to the Acts to regulate commerce, air carriers and foreign air carriers subject to part A of subtitle VII of Title 49, and persons, partnerships, or corporations insofar as they are subject to the Packers and Stockyards Act, 1921, as amended [7 U.S.C.A. § 181 et seq.], except as provided in section 406(b) of said Act [7 U.S.C.A. § 227(b)], from using unfair methods of competition in or affecting commerce and unfair or deceptive acts or practices in or affecting commerce.

(3) This subsection shall not apply to unfair methods of competition involving commerce with foreign nations (other than import commerce) unless—

(A) such methods of competition have a direct, substantial, and reasonably foreseeable effect—

(i) on commerce which is not commerce with foreign nations, or on import commerce with foreign nations; or

(ii) on export commerce with foreign nations, of a person engaged in such commerce in the United States; and

(B) such effect gives rise to a claim under the provisions of this subsection, other than this paragraph.

If this subsection applies to such methods of competition only because of the operation of subparagraph (A)(ii), this subsection shall apply to such conduct only for injury to export business in the United States.

(4)(A) For purposes of subsection (a) of this section, the term "unfair or deceptive acts or practices" includes such acts or practices involving foreign commerce that—

(i) cause or are likely to cause reasonably foreseeable injury within the United States; or

(ii) involve material conduct occurring within the United States.

(B) All remedies available to the Commission with respect to unfair and deceptive acts or practices shall be available for acts and practices described in this paragraph, including restitution to domestic or foreign victims.

(b) Proceeding by Commission; modifying and setting aside orders

Whenever the Commission shall have reason to believe that any such person, partnership, or corporation has been or is using any unfair method of competition or unfair or deceptive act or practice in or affecting commerce, and if it shall appear to the Commission that a proceeding by it in respect thereof would be to the interest of the public, it shall issue and serve upon such person, partnership, or corporation a complaint stating its charges in that respect and containing a notice of a hearing upon a day and at a place therein fixed at least thirty days after the service of said complaint. The person, partnership, or corporation so complained of shall have the right to appear at the place and time so fixed and show cause why an order should not be entered by the Commission requiring such person, partnership, or corporation to cease and desist from the violation of the law so charged in said complaint. Any person, partnership, or corporation may make application, and upon good cause shown may be allowed by the Commission to intervene and appear in said proceeding by counsel or in person. The testimony in any such proceeding shall be reduced to writing and filed in the office of the Commission. If upon such hearing the Commission shall be of the opinion that the method of competition or the act or practice in question is prohibited by this subchapter, it shall make a report in writing in which it shall state its findings as to the facts and shall issue and cause to be served on such person, partnership, or corporation an order requiring such person, partnership, or corporation to cease and desist from using such method of competition or such act or practice. Until the expiration of the time allowed for filing a petition for review, if no such petition has been duly filed within such time, or, if a petition for review has been filed within such time then until the record in the proceeding has been filed in a court of appeals of the United States, as hereinafter provided, the Commission may at any time, upon such notice and in such manner as it shall deem proper, modify or set aside, in whole or in part, any report or any order made or issued by it under this section. After the expiration of the time allowed for filing a petition for review, if no such petition has been duly filed within such time, the Commission may at any time, after notice and opportunity for hearing, reopen and alter, modify, or set aside, in whole or in part, any report or order made or issued by it under this section, whenever in the opinion of the Commission conditions of fact or of law have so changed as to require such action or if the public interest shall so require, except that (1) the said person, partnership, or corporation may, within sixty days after service upon him or it of said report or order entered after such a reopening, obtain a review thereof in the appropriate court of appeals of the United States, in the manner provided in subsection (c) of this section; and (2) in the case of an order, the Commission shall reopen any such order to consider whether such order (including any affirmative relief provision contained in such order) should be altered, modified, or set aside, in whole or in part, if the person, partnership, or corporation involved files a request with the Commission which makes a satisfactory showing that changed conditions of law or fact require such order to be altered, modified, or set aside, in whole or in part. The Commission shall determine whether to alter, modify, or set aside any order of the Commission in response to a request made by a person, partnership, or corporation under paragraph (2) not later than 120 days after the date of the filing of such request.

(c) Review of order; rehearing

Any person, partnership, or corporation required by an order of the Commission to cease and desist from using any method of competition or act or practice may obtain a review of such order in the court of appeals of the United States, within any circuit where the method of competition or the act or practice in question was used or where such person, partnership, or corporation resides or carries on business, by filing in the court, within sixty days from the date of the service of such order, a written petition praying that the order of the Commission be set aside. A copy of such petition shall be forthwith transmitted by the clerk of the court to the Commission, and thereupon the Commission shall file in the court the record in the proceeding, as provided in section 2112 of Title 28. Upon such filing of the petition the court shall have jurisdiction of the proceeding and of the question determined therein concurrently with the Commission until the filing of the record and shall have power to make and enter a decree affirming, modifying, or setting aside the order of the Commission, and enforcing the same to the extent that such order is affirmed and to issue such writs as are ancillary to its jurisdiction or are necessary in its judgement to prevent injury to the public or to competitors pendente lite. The findings of the Commission as to the facts, if supported by evidence, shall be conclusive. To the extent that the order of the Commission is affirmed, the court shall thereupon issue its own order commanding obedience to the terms of such order of the Commission. If either party shall apply to the court for leave to adduce additional evidence, and shall show to the satisfaction of the court that such additional evidence is material and that there were reasonable grounds for the failure to adduce such evidence in the proceeding before the Commission, the court may order such additional evidence to be taken before the Commission and to be adduced upon the hearing in such manner and upon such terms and conditions as to the court may seem proper. The Commission may modify its findings as to the facts, or make new findings, by reason of the additional evidence so taken, and it shall file such modified or new findings, which, if supported by evidence, shall be conclusive, and its recommendation, if any, for the modification or setting aside of its original order, with the return of such additional evidence. The judgment and decree of the court shall be final, except that the same shall be subject to review by the Supreme Court upon certiorari, as provided in section 1254 of Title 28.

(d) Jurisdiction of court

Upon the filing of the record with it the jurisdiction of the court of appeals of the United States to affirm, enforce, modify, or set aside orders of the Commission shall be exclusive.

(e) Exemption from liability

No order of the Commission or judgement of court to enforce the same shall in anywise relieve or absolve any person, partnership, or corporation from any liability under the Antitrust Acts.

(f) Service of complaints, orders and other processes; return

Complaints, orders, and other processes of the Commission under this section may be served by anyone duly authorized by the Commission, either (a) by delivering a copy thereof to the person to be served, or to a member of the partnership to be served, or the president, secretary, or other executive officer or a director of the corporation to be served; or (b) by leaving a copy thereof at the residence or the principal office or place of business of such person, partnership, or corporation; or (c) by mailing a copy thereof by registered mail or by certified mail addressed to such person, partnership, or corporation at his or its residence or principal office or place of business. The verified return by the person so serving said complaint, order, or other process setting forth the manner of said service shall be proof of the same, and the return post office receipt for said complaint, order, or other process mailed by registered mail or by certified mail as aforesaid shall be proof of the service of the same.

(g) Finality of order

An order of the Commission to cease and desist shall become final—

(1) Upon the expiration of the time allowed for filing a petition for review, if no such petition has been duly filed within such time; but the Commission may thereafter modify or set aside its order to the extent provided in the last sentence of subsection (b).

(2) Except as to any order provision subject to paragraph (4), upon the sixtieth day after such order is served, if a petition for review has been duly filed; except that any such order may be stayed, in whole or in part and subject to such conditions as may be appropriate, by—

(A) the Commission;

(B) an appropriate court of appeals of the United States, if (i) a petition for review of such order is pending in such court, and (ii) an application for such a stay was previously submitted to the Commission and the Commission, within the 30-day period beginning on the date the application was received by the Commission, either denied the application or did not grant or deny the application; or

(C) the Supreme Court, if an applicable petition for certiorari is pending.

(3) For purposes of subsection (m)(1)(B) of this section and of section 57b(a)(2) of this title, if a petition for review of the order of the Commission has been filed—

(A) upon the expiration of the time allowed for filing a petition for certiorari, if the order of the Commission has been affirmed or the petition for review has been dismissed by the court of appeals and no petition for certiorari has been duly filed;

(B) upon the denial of a petition for certiorari, if the order of the Commission has been affirmed or the petition for review has been dismissed by the court of appeals; or

(C) upon the expiration of 30 days from the date of issuance of a mandate of the Supreme Court directing that the order of the Commission be affirmed or the petition for review be dismissed.

(4) In the case of an order provision requiring a person, partnership, or corporation to divest itself of stock, other share capital, or assets, if a petition for review of such order of the Commission has been filed—

(A) upon the expiration of the time allowed for filing a petition for certiorari, if the order of the Commission has been affirmed or the petition for review has been dismissed by the court of appeals and no petition for certiorari has been duly filed;

(B) upon the denial of a petition for certiorari, if the order of the Commission has been affirmed or the petition for review has been dismissed by the court of appeals; or

(C) upon the expiration of 30 days from the date of issuance of a mandate of the Supreme Court directing that the order of the Commission be affirmed or the petition for review be dismissed.

(h) Modification or setting aside of order by Supreme Court

If the Supreme Court directs that the order of the Commission be modified or set aside, the order of the Commission rendered in accordance with the mandate of the Supreme Court shall become final upon the expiration of thirty days from the time it was rendered, unless within such thirty days either party has instituted proceedings to have such order corrected to accord with the mandate, in which event the order of the Commission shall become final when so corrected.

(i) Modification or setting aside of order by Court of Appeals

If the order of the Commission is modified or set aside by the court of appeals, and if (1) the time allowed for filing a petition for certiorari has expired and no such petition has been duly filed, or (2) the petition for certiorari has been denied, or (3) the decision of the court has been affirmed by the Supreme Court, then the order of the Commission rendered in accordance with the mandate of the court of appeals shall become final on the expiration of thirty days from the time such order of the Commission was rendered, unless within such thirty days either party has instituted proceedings to have such order corrected so that it will accord with the mandate, in which event the order of the Commission shall become final when so corrected.

(j) Rehearing upon order or remand

If the Supreme Court orders a rehearing; or if the case is remanded by the court of appeals to the Commission for a rehearing, and if (1) the time allowed for filing a petition for certiorari has expired, and no such petition has been duly filed, or (2) the petition for certiorari has been denied, or (3) the decision of the court has been affirmed by the Supreme Court, then the order of the Commission rendered upon such rehearing shall become final in the same manner as though no prior order of the Commission had been rendered.

(k) "Mandate" defined

As used in this section the term "mandate", in case a mandate has been recalled prior to the expiration of thirty days from the date of issuance thereof, means the final mandate.

(l) Penalty for violation of order; injunctions and other appropriate equitable relief

Any person, partnership, or corporation who violates an order of the Commission after it has become final, and while such order is in effect, shall forfeit and pay to the United States a civil penalty of not more than $10,000 for each violation, which shall accrue to the United States and may be recovered in a civil action brought by the Attorney General of the United States. Each separate violation of such an order shall be a separate offense, except that in a case of a violation through continuing failure to obey or neglect to obey a final order of the Commission, each day of continuance of such failure or neglect shall be deemed a separate offense. In such actions, the United States district courts are empowered to grant mandatory injunctions and such other and further equitable relief as they deem appropriate in the enforcement of such final orders of the Commission.

(m) Civil actions for recovery of penalties for knowing violations of rules and cease and desist orders respecting unfair or deceptive acts or practices; jurisdiction; maximum amount of penalties; continuing violations; de novo determinations; compromise or settlement procedure

(1)(A) The Commission may commence a civil action to recover a civil penalty in a district court of the United States against any person, partnership, or corporation which violates any rule under this chapter respecting unfair or deceptive acts or practices (other than an interpretive rule or a rule violation of which the Commission has provided is not an unfair or deceptive act or practice in violation of subsection (a)(1) of this section) with actual knowledge or knowledge fairly implied on the basis of objective circumstances that such act is unfair or deceptive and is prohibited by such rule. In such action, such person, partnership, or corporation shall be liable for a civil penalty of not more than $10,000 for each violation.

(B) If the Commission determines in a proceeding under subsection (b) of this section that any act or practice is unfair or deceptive, and issues a final cease and desist order, other than a consent order, with respect to such act or practice, then the Commission may commence a civil action to obtain a civil penalty in a district court of the United States against any person, partnership, or corporation which engages in such act or practice—

(1) after such cease and desist order becomes final (whether or not such person, partnership, or corporation was subject to such cease and desist order), and

(2) with actual knowledge that such act or practice is unfair or deceptive and is unlawful under subsection (a)(1) of this section.

In such action, such person, partnership, or corporation shall be liable for a civil penalty of not more than $10,000 for each violation.

(C) In the case of a violation through continuing failure to comply with a rule or with subsection (a)(1) of this section, each day of continuance of such failure shall be treated as a separate violation, for purposes of subparagraphs (A) and (B). In determining the amount of such a civil penalty, the court shall take into account the degree of culpability, any history of prior such conduct, ability to pay, effect on ability to continue to do business, and such other matters as justice may require.

(2) If the cease and desist order establishing that the act or practice is unfair or deceptive was not issued against the defendant in a civil penalty action under paragraph (1)(B) the issues of fact in such action against such defendant shall be tried de novo. Upon request of any party to such an action against such defendant, the court shall also review the determination of law made by the Commission in the proceeding under subsection (b) of this section that the act or practice which was the subject of such proceeding constituted an unfair or deceptive act or practice in violation of subsection (a) of this section.

(3) The Commission may compromise or settle any action for a civil penalty if such compromise or settlement is accompanied by a public statement of its reasons and is approved by the court.

(n) Standard of proof; public policy consideration

The Commission shall have no authority under this section or section 57a of this title to declare unlawful an act or practice on the grounds that such act or practice is unfair unless the act or practice causes or is likely to cause substantial injury to consumers which is not reasonably avoidable by consumers themselves and not outweighed by countervailing benefits to consumers or to competition. In determining whether an act or practice is unfair, the Commission may consider established public policies as evidence to be considered with all other evidence. Such public policy considerations may not serve as a primary basis for such determination.

§ 46. Additional powers of Commission

The Commission shall also have power—

(a) Investigation of persons, partnerships, or corporations

To gather and compile information concerning, and to investigate from time to time the organization, business, conduct, practices, and management of any person, partnership, or corporation engaged in or whose business affects commerce, excepting banks, savings and loan institutions described in section 57a(f)(3) of this title, Federal credit unions described in section 57a(f)(4) of this title, and common carriers subject to the Act to regulate commerce, and its relation to other persons, partnerships, and corporations.

(b) Reports of persons, partnerships, and corporations

To require, by general or special orders, persons, partnerships, and corporations, engaged in or whose business affects commerce, excepting banks, savings and loan institutions described in section 57a(f)(3) of this title, Federal credit unions described in section 57a(f)(4) of this title, and common carriers subject to the Act to regulate commerce, or any class of them, or any of them, respectively, to file with the Commission in such form as the Commission may prescribe annual or special, or both annual and special, reports or answers in writing to specific questions, furnishing to the Commission such information as it may require as to the organization, business, conduct, practices, management, and relation to other corporations, partnerships, and individuals of the respective persons, partnerships, and corporations filing such reports or answers in writing. Such reports and answers shall be made under oath, or otherwise, as the Commission may prescribe, and shall be filed with the Commission within such reasonable period as the Commission may prescribe, unless additional time be granted in any case by the Commission.

(c) Investigation of compliance with antitrust decrees

Whenever a final decree has been entered against any defendant corporation in any suit brought by the United States to prevent and restrain any violation of the antitrust Acts, to make investigation, upon its own initiative, of the manner in which the decree has been or is being carried out, and upon the application of the Attorney General it shall be its duty to make such investigation. It shall transmit to the Attorney General a report embodying its findings and recommendations as a result of any such investigation, and the report shall be made public in the discretion of the Commission.

(d) Investigations of violations of antitrust statutes

Upon the direction of the President or either House of Congress to investigate and report the facts relating to any alleged violations of the antitrust Acts by any corporation.

(e) Readjustment of business of corporations violating antitrust statutes

Upon the application of the Attorney General to investigate and make recommendations for the readjustment of the business of any corporation alleged to be violating the antitrust Acts in order that the corporation may thereafter maintain its organization, management, and conduct of business in accordance with law.

(f) Publication of information; reports

To make public from time to time such portions of the information obtained by it hereunder as are in the public interest; and to make annual and special reports to the Congress and to submit therewith recommendations for additional legislation; and to provide for the publication of its reports and decisions in such form and manner as may be best adapted for public information and use: *Provided*, That the Commission shall not have any authority to make public any trade secret or any commercial or financial information which is obtained from any person and which is privileged or confidential, except that the Commission may disclose such information (1) to officers and employees of appropriate Federal law enforcement agencies or to any officer or employee of any State law enforcement agency upon the prior certification of an officer of any such Federal or State law enforcement agency that such information will be maintained in confidence and will be used only for official law enforcement purposes, and (2) to any officer or employee of any foreign law enforcement agency under the same circumstances that making material available to foreign law enforcement agencies is permitted under section 57b-2(b) of this title.

(g) Classification of corporations; regulations

From time to time classify corporations and (except as provided in section 57a(a)(2) of this title) to make rules and regulations for the purpose of carrying out the provisions of this subchapter.

(h) Investigations of foreign trade conditions; reports

To investigate, from time to time, trade conditions in and with foreign countries where associations, combinations, or practices of manufacturers, merchants, or traders, or other conditions, may affect the foreign trade of the United States, and to report to Congress thereon, with such recommendations as it deems advisable.

(i) Investigations of foreign antitrust law violations

With respect to the International Antitrust Enforcement Assistance Act of 1994 [15 U.S.C.A. § 6201 et seq.], to conduct investigations of possible violations of foreign antitrust laws (as defined in section 12 of such Act [15 U.S.C.A. § 6211]).

(j) Investigative assistance for foreign law enforcement agencies

(1) In general

Upon a written request from a foreign law enforcement agency to provide assistance in accordance with this subsection, if the requesting agency states that it is investigating, or engaging in enforcement proceedings against, possible violations of laws prohibiting fraudulent or deceptive commercial practices, or other practices substantially similar to practices prohibited by any provision of the laws administered by the Commission, other than Federal antitrust laws (as defined in section 6211(5) of this title, to provide the assistance described in paragraph (2) without requiring that the conduct identified in the request constitute a violation of the laws of the United States.

(2) Type of assistance

In providing assistance to a foreign law enforcement agency under this subsection, the Commission may—

(A) conduct such investigation as the Commission deems necessary to collect information and evidence pertinent to the request for assistance, using all investigative powers authorized by this subchapter; and

(B) when the request is from an agency acting to investigate or pursue the enforcement of civil laws, or when the Attorney General refers a request to the Commission from an agency acting to investigate or pursue the enforcement of criminal laws, seek and accept appointment by a United States district court of Commission attorneys to provide assistance to foreign and international tribunals and to litigants before such tribunals on behalf of a foreign law enforcement agency pursuant to section 1782 of Title 28.

(3) Criteria for determination

In deciding whether to provide such assistance, the Commission shall consider all relevant factors, including—

(A) whether the requesting agency has agreed to provide or will provide reciprocal assistance to the Commission;

(B) whether compliance with the request would prejudice the public interest of the United States; and

(C) whether the requesting agency's investigation or enforcement proceeding concerns acts or practices that cause or are likely to cause injury to a significant number of persons.

(4) International agreements

If a foreign law enforcement agency has set forth a legal basis for requiring execution of an international agreement as a condition for reciprocal assistance, or as a condition for provision of materials or information to the Commission, the Commission, with prior approval and ongoing oversight of the Secretary of State, and with final approval of the agreement by the Secretary of State, may negotiate and conclude an international agreement, in the name of either the United States or the Commission, for the purpose of obtaining such assistance, materials, or information. The Commission may undertake in such an international agreement to—

(A) provide assistance using the powers set forth in this subsection;

(B) disclose materials and information in accordance with subsection (f) of this section and section 57b-2(b) of this title; and

(C) engage in further cooperation, and protect materials and information received from disclosure, as authorized by this subchapter.

(5) Additional authority

The authority provided by this subsection is in addition to, and not in lieu of, any other authority vested in the Commission or any other officer of the United States.

(6) Limitation

The authority granted by this subsection shall not authorize the Commission to take any action or exercise any power with respect to a bank, a savings and loan institution described in section 57a(f)(3) of this title, a Federal credit union described in section 57a(f)(4) of this title, or a common carrier subject to the Act to regulate commerce, except in accordance with the undesignated proviso following the last designated subsection of this section.

(7) Assistance to certain countries

The Commission may not provide investigative assistance under this subsection to a foreign law enforcement agency from a foreign state that the Secretary of State has determined, in accordance with section 2405(j) of the Appendix to Title 50, has repeatedly provided support for acts of international terrorism, unless and until such determination is rescinded pursuant to section 2405(j)(4) of the Appendix to Title 50.

(k) Referral of evidence for criminal proceedings

(1) In general

Whenever the Commission obtains evidence that any person, partnership, or corporation, either domestic or foreign, has engaged in conduct that may constitute a violation of Federal criminal law, to transmit such evidence to the Attorney General, who may institute criminal proceedings under appropriate statutes. Nothing in this paragraph affects any other authority of the Commission to disclose information.

(2) International information

The Commission shall endeavor to ensure, with respect to memoranda of understanding and international agreements it may conclude, that material it has obtained from foreign law enforcement agencies acting to investigate or pursue the enforcement of foreign criminal laws may be used for the purpose of investigation, prosecution, or prevention of violations of United States criminal laws.

(l) Expenditures for cooperative arrangements

To expend appropriated funds for—

(1) operating expenses and other costs of bilateral and multilateral cooperative law enforcement groups conducting activities of interest to the Commission and in which the Commission participates; and

(2) expenses for consultations and meetings hosted by the Commission with foreign government agency officials, members of their delegations, appropriate representatives and staff to exchange views concerning developments relating to the Commission's mission, development and implementation of cooperation agreements, and provision of technical assistance for the development of foreign consumer protection or competition regimes, such expenses to include necessary administrative and logistic expenses and the expenses of Commission staff and foreign invitees in attendance at such consultations and meetings including—

(A) such incidental expenses as meals taken in the course of such attendance;

(B) any travel and transportation to or from such meetings; and

(C) any other related lodging or subsistence.

Provided, That the exception of "banks, savings and loan institutions described in section 57a(f)(3) of this title, Federal credit unions described in section 57a(f)(4) of this title, and common carriers subject to the Act to regulate commerce" from the Commission's powers defined in subsections (a), (b), and (j) of this section, shall not be construed to limit the Commission's authority to gather and compile information, to investigate, or to require reports or answers from, any person, partnership, or corporation to the extent that such action is necessary to the investigation of any person, partnership, or corporation, group of persons, partnerships, or corporations, or industry which is not engaged or is engaged only incidentally in banking, in business as a savings and loan institution, in business as a Federal credit union, or in business as a common carrier subject to the Act to regulate commerce.

The Commission shall establish a plan designed to substantially reduce burdens imposed upon small businesses as a result of requirements established by the Commission under clause (b) relating to the filing of quarterly financial reports. Such plan shall (1) be established after consultation with small businesses and persons who use the information contained in such quarterly financial reports; (2) provide for a reduction of the number of small businesses required to file such quarterly financial reports; and (3) make revisions in the forms used for such quarterly financial reports for the purpose of reducing the complexity of such forms. The Commission, not later than December 31, 1980, shall submit such plan to the Committee on Commerce, Science, and Transportation of the Senate and to the Committee on Energy and Commerce of the House of Representatives. Such plan shall take effect not later than October 31, 1981.

No officer or employee of the Commission or any Commissioner may publish or disclose information to the public, or to any Federal agency, whereby any line-of-business data furnished by a particular establishment or individual can be identified. No one other than designated sworn officers and employees of the Commission may examine the line-of-business reports from individual firms, and information provided in the line-of-business program administered by the Commission shall be used only for statistical purposes. Information for carrying out specific law enforcement responsibilities of the Commission shall be obtained under practices and procedures in effect on May 28, 1980, or as changed by law.

Nothing in this section (other than the provisions of clause (c) and clause (d)) shall apply to the business of insurance, except that the Commission shall have authority to conduct studies and prepare reports relating to the business of insurance. The Commission may exercise such authority only upon receiving a request which is agreed to by a majority of the members of the Committee on Commerce, Science, and Transportation of the Senate or the Committee on Energy and Commerce of the House of Representatives. The authority to conduct any such study shall expire at the end of the Congress during which the request for such study was made.

§ 57a. Unfair or deceptive acts or practices rulemaking proceedings

(a) Authority of Commission to prescribe rules and general statements of policy

(1) Except as provided in subsection (h) of this section, the Commission may prescribe—

(A) interpretive rules and general statements of policy with respect to unfair or deceptive acts or practices in or affecting commerce (within the meaning of section 45(a)(1) of this title), and

(B) rules which define with specificity acts or practices which are unfair or deceptive acts or practices in or affecting commerce (within the meaning of section 45(a)(1) of this title), except that the Commission shall not develop or promulgate any trade rule or regulation with regard to the regulation of the development and utilization of the standards and certification activities pursuant to this section. Rules under this subparagraph may include requirements prescribed for the purpose of preventing such acts or practices.

(2) The Commission shall have no authority under this subchapter, other than its authority under this section, to prescribe any rule with respect to unfair or deceptive acts or practices in or affecting commerce (within the meaning of section 45(a)(1) of this title). The preceding sentence shall not affect any authority of the Commission to prescribe rules (including interpretive rules), and general statements of policy, with respect to unfair methods of competition in or affecting commerce.

(b) Procedures applicable

(1) When prescribing a rule under subsection (a)(1)(B) of this section, the Commission shall proceed in accordance with section 553 of Title 5 (without regard to any reference in such section to sections 556 and 557 of such title), and shall also (A) publish a notice of proposed rulemaking stating with particularity the text of the rule, including any alternatives, which the Commission proposes to promulgate, and the reason for the proposed rule; (B) allow interested persons to submit written data, views, and arguments, and make all such submissions publicly available; (C) provide an opportunity for an informal hearing in accordance with subsection (c) of this section; and (D) promulgate, if appropriate, a final rule based on the matter in the rulemaking record (as defined in subsection (e)(1)(B) of this section), together with a statement of basis and purpose.

(2)(A) Prior to the publication of any notice of proposed rulemaking pursuant to paragraph (1)(A), the Commission shall publish an advance notice of proposed rulemaking in the Federal Register. Such advance notice shall—

(i) contain a brief description of the area of inquiry under consideration, the objectives which the Commission seeks to achieve, and possible regulatory alternatives under consideration by the Commission; and

(ii) invite the response of interested parties with respect to such proposed rulemaking, including any suggestions or alternative methods for achieving such objectives.

(B) The Commission shall submit such advance notice of proposed rulemaking to the Committee on Commerce, Science, and Transportation of the Senate and to the Committee on Energy and Commerce of the House of Representatives. The Commission may use such additional mechanisms as the Commission considers useful to obtain suggestions regarding the content of the area of inquiry before the publication of a general notice of proposed rulemaking under paragraph (1)(A).

(C) The Commission shall, 30 days before the publication of a notice of proposed rulemaking pursuant to paragraph (1)(A), submit such notice to the Committee on Commerce, Science, and Transportation of the Senate and to the Committee on Energy and Commerce of the House of Representatives.

(3) The Commission shall issue a notice of proposed rulemaking pursuant to paragraph (1)(A) only where it has reason to believe that the unfair or deceptive acts or practices which are the subject of the proposed rulemaking are prevalent. The Commission shall make a determination that unfair or deceptive acts or practices are prevalent under this paragraph only if—

(A) it has issued cease and desist orders regarding such acts or practices, or

(B) any other information available to the Commission indicates a widespread pattern of unfair or deceptive acts or practices.

(c) Informal hearing procedure

The Commission shall conduct any informal hearings required by subsection (b)(1)(C) of this section in accordance with the following procedure:

(1)(A) The Commission shall provide for the conduct of proceedings under this subsection by hearing officers who shall perform their functions in accordance with the requirements of this subsection.

(B) The officer who presides over the rulemaking proceedings shall be responsible to a chief presiding officer who shall not be responsible to any other officer or employee of the Commission. The officer who presides over the rulemaking proceeding shall make a recommended decision based upon the findings and conclusions of such officer as to all relevant and material evidence, except that such recommended decision may be made by another officer if the officer who presided over the proceeding is no longer available to the Commission.

(C) Except as required for the disposition of ex parte matters as authorized by law, no presiding officer shall consult any person or party with respect to any fact in issue unless such officer gives notice and opportunity for all parties to participate.

(2) Subject to paragraph (3) of this subsection, an interested person is entitled—

(A) to present his position orally or by documentary submission (or both), and

(B) if the Commission determines that there are disputed issues of material fact it is necessary to resolve, to present such rebuttal submissions and to conduct (or have conducted under paragraph (3)(B)) such cross-examination of persons as the Commission determines (i) to be appropriate, and (ii) to be required for a full and true disclosure with respect to such issues.

(3) The Commission may prescribe such rules and make such rulings concerning proceedings in such hearings as may tend to avoid unnecessary costs or delay. Such rules or rulings may include (A) imposition of reasonable time limits on each interested person's oral presentations, and (B) requirements that any cross-examination to which a person may be entitled under paragraph (2) be conducted by the Commission on behalf of that person in such manner as the Commission determines (i) to be appropriate, and (ii) to be required for a full and true disclosure with respect to disputed issues of material fact.

(4)(A) Except as provided in subparagraph (B), if a group of persons each of whom under paragraphs (2) and (3) would be entitled to conduct (or have conducted) cross-examination and who are determined by the Commission to have the same or similar interests in the proceeding cannot agree upon a single representative of such interests for purposes of cross-examination, the Commission may make rules and rulings (i) limiting the representation of such interest, for such purposes, and (ii) governing the manner in which such cross-examination shall be limited.

(B) When any person who is a member of a group with respect to which the Commission has made a determination under subparagraph (A) is unable to agree upon group representation with the other members of the group, then such person shall not be denied under the authority of subparagraph (A) the opportunity to conduct (or have conducted) cross-examination as to issues affecting his particular interests if (i) he satisfies the Commission that he has made a reasonable and good faith effort to reach agreement upon group representation with the other members of the group and (ii) the Commission determines that there are substantial and relevant issues which are not adequately presented by the group representative.

(5) A verbatim transcript shall be taken of any oral presentation, and cross-examination, in an informal hearing to which this subsection applies. Such transcript shall be available to the public.

(d) Statement of basis and purpose accompanying rule; "Commission" defined; judicial review of amendment or repeal of rule; violation of rule

(1) The Commission's statement of basis and purpose to accompany a rule promulgated under subsection (a)(1)(B) of this section shall include (A) a statement as to the prevalence of the acts or practices treated by the rule; (B) a statement as to the manner and context in which such acts or practices are unfair or deceptive; and (C) a statement as to the economic effect of the rule, taking into account the effect on small business and consumers.

(2)(A) The term "Commission" as used in this subsection and subsections (b) and (c) of this section includes any person authorized to act in behalf of the Commission in any part of the rulemaking proceeding.

(B) A substantive amendment to, or repeal of, a rule promulgated under subsection (a)(1)(B) of this section shall be prescribed, and subject to judicial review, in the same manner as a rule prescribed under such subsection. An exemption under subsection (g) of this section shall not be treated as an amendment or repeal of a rule.

(3) When any rule under subsection (a)(1)(B) of this section takes effect a subsequent violation thereof shall constitute an unfair or deceptive act or practice in violation of section 45(a)(1) of this title, unless the Commission otherwise expressly provides in such rule.

(e) Judicial review; petition; jurisdiction and venue; rulemaking record; additional submissions and presentations; scope of review and relief; review by Supreme Court; additional remedies

(1)(A) Not later than 60 days after a rule is promulgated under subsection (a)(1)(B) of this section by the Commission, any interested person (including a consumer or consumer organization) may file a petition, in the United States Court of Appeals for the District of Columbia circuit or for the circuit in which such person resides or has his principal place of business, for judicial review of such rule. Copies of the petition shall be forthwith transmitted by the clerk of the court to the Commission or other officer designated by it for that purpose. The provisions of section 2112 of Title 28 shall apply to the filing of the rulemaking record of proceedings on which the Commission based its rule and to the transfer of proceedings in the courts of appeals.

(B) For purpose of this section, the term "rulemaking record" means the rule, its statement of basis and purpose, the transcript required by subsection (c)(5) of this section, any written submissions, and any other information which the Commission considers relevant to such rule.

(2) If the petitioner or the Commission applies to the court for leave to make additional oral submissions or written presentations and shows to the satisfaction of the court that such submissions and presentations would be material and that there were reasonable grounds for the submissions and failure to make such submissions and presentations in the proceeding before the Commission, the court may order the Commission to provide additional opportunity to make such submissions and presentations. The Commission may modify or set aside its rule or make a new rule by reason of the additional submissions and presentations and shall file such modified or new rule, and the rule's statement of basis of purpose, with the return of such submissions and presentations. The court shall thereafter review such new or modified rule.

(3) Upon the filing of the petition under paragraph (1) of this subsection, the court shall have jurisdiction to review the rule in accordance with chapter 7 of Title 5 and to grant appropriate relief, including interim relief, as provided in such chapter. The court shall hold unlawful and set aside the rule on any ground specified in subparagraphs (A), (B), (C), or (D) of section 706(2) of Title 5 (taking due account of the rule of prejudicial error), or if—

(A) the court finds that the Commission's action is not supported by substantial evidence in the rulemaking record (as defined in paragraph (1)(B) of this subsection) taken as a whole, or

(B) the court finds that—

(i) a Commission determination under subsection (c) of this section that the petitioner is not entitled to conduct cross-examination or make rebuttal submissions, or

(ii) a Commission rule or ruling under subsection (c) of this section limiting the petitioner's cross-examination or rebuttal submissions,

has precluded disclosure of disputed material facts which was necessary for fair determination by the Commission of the rulemaking proceeding taken as a whole.

The term "evidence", as used in this paragraph, means any matter in the rulemaking record.

(4) The judgment of the court affirming or setting aside, in whole or in part, any such rule shall be final, subject to review by the Supreme Court of the United States upon certiorari or certification, as provided in section 1254 of Title 28.

(5)(A) Remedies under the preceding paragraphs of this subsection are in addition to and not in lieu of any other remedies provided by law.

(B) The United States Courts of Appeal shall have exclusive jurisdiction of any action to obtain judicial review (other than in an enforcement proceeding) of a rule prescribed under subsection (a)(1)(B) of this section, if any district court of the United States would have had jurisdiction of such action but for this subparagraph. Any such action shall be brought in the United States Court of Appeals for the District of Columbia circuit, or for any circuit which includes a judicial district in which the action could have been brought but for this subparagraph.

(C) A determination, rule, or ruling of the Commission described in paragraph (3)(B)(i) or (ii) may be reviewed only in a proceeding under this subsection and only in accordance with paragraph (3)(B). Section 706(2)(E) of Title 5 shall not apply to any rule promulgated under subsection (a)(1)(B) of this section. The contents and adequacy of any statement required by subsection (b)(1)(D) of this section shall not be subject to judicial review in any respect.

(f) Unfair or deceptive acts or practices by banks, savings and loan institutions, or Federal credit unions; promulgation of regulations by Board of Governors of Federal Reserve System, Federal Home Loan Bank Board, and National Credit Union Administration Board; agency enforcement and compliance proceedings; violations; power of other Federal agencies unaffected; reporting requirements

(1) In order to prevent unfair or deceptive acts or practices in or affecting commerce (including acts or practices which are unfair or deceptive to consumers) by banks or savings and loan institutions described in paragraph (3), each agency specified in paragraph (2) or (3) of this subsection shall establish a separate division of consumer affairs which shall receive and take appropriate action upon complaints with respect to such acts or practices by banks or savings and loan institutions described in paragraph (3) subject to its jurisdiction. The Board of Governors of the Federal Reserve System (with respect to banks) and the Federal Home Loan Bank Board (with respect to savings and loan institutions described in paragraph (3)) and the National Credit Union Administration Board (with respect to Federal credit unions described in paragraph (4)) shall prescribe regulations to carry out the purposes of this section, including regulations defining with specificity such unfair or deceptive acts or practices, and containing requirements prescribed for the purpose of preventing such acts or practices. Whenever the Commission prescribes a rule under subsection (a)(1)(B) of this section, then within 60 days after such rule takes effect each such Board shall promulgate substantially similar regulations prohibiting acts or practices of banks or savings and loan institutions described in paragraph (3), or Federal credit unions described in paragraph (4), as the case may be, which are substantially similar to those prohibited by rules of the Commission and which impose substantially similar requirements, unless (A) any such Board finds that such acts or practices of banks or savings and loan institutions described in paragraph (3), or Federal credit unions described in paragraph (4), as the case may be, are not unfair or deceptive, or (B) the Board of Governors of the Federal Reserve System finds that implementation of similar regulations with respect to banks, savings and loan institutions or Federal credit unions would seriously conflict with essential monetary and payments systems policies of such Board, and publishes any such finding, and the reasons therefor, in the Federal Register.

(2) Enforcement. Compliance with regulations prescribed under this subsection shall be enforced under section 1818 of Title 12, in the case of—

(A) national banks and Federal branches and Federal agencies of foreign banks, by the division of consumer affairs established by the Office of the Comptroller of the Currency;

(B) member banks of the Federal Reserve System (other than national banks), branches and agencies of foreign banks (other than Federal branches, Federal agencies, and insured State branches of foreign banks), commercial lending companies owned or controlled by foreign banks, and organizations operating under section 25 or 25(a) of the Federal Reserve Act [12 U.S.C.A. § § 601 et seq., 611 et seq.], by the division of consumer affairs established by the Board of Governors of the Federal Reserve System; and

(C) banks insured by the Federal Deposit Insurance Corporation (other banks referred to in subparagraph (A) or (B)) and insured State branches of foreign banks, by the division of consumer affairs established by the Board of Directors of the Federal Deposit Insurance Corporation.

(3) Compliance with regulations prescribed under this subsection shall be enforced under section 1818 of Title 12 with respect to savings associations as defined in section 1813 of Title 12.

(4) Compliance with regulations prescribed under this subsection shall be enforced with respect to Federal credit unions under sections 1766 and 1786 of title 12.

(5) For the purpose of the exercise by any agency referred to in paragraph (2) of its powers under any Act referred to in that paragraph, a violation of any regulation prescribed under this subsection shall be deemed to be a violation of a requirement imposed under that Act. In addition to its powers under any provision of law specifically referred to in paragraph (2), each of the agencies referred to in that paragraph may exercise, for the purpose of enforcing compliance with any regulation prescribed under this subsection, any other authority conferred on it by law.

(6) The authority of the Board of Governors of the Federal Reserve System to issue regulations under this subsection does not impair the authority of any other agency designated in this subsection to make rules respecting its own procedures in enforcing compliance with regulations prescribed under this subsection.

(7) Each agency exercising authority under this subsection shall transmit to the Congress each year a detailed report on its activities under this paragraph during the preceding calendar year.

The terms used in this paragraph that are not defined in this subchapter or otherwise defined in section 1813(s) of Title 12 shall have the meaning given to them in section 3101 of Title 12.

(g) Exemptions and stays from application of rules; procedures

(1) Any person to whom a rule under subsection (a)(1)(B) of this section applies may petition the Commission for an exemption from such rule.

(2) If, on its own motion or on the basis of a petition under paragraph (1), the Commission finds that the application of a rule prescribed under subsection (a)(1)(B) of this section to any person or class or persons is not necessary to prevent the unfair or deceptive act or practice to which the rule relates, the Commission may exempt such person or class from all or part of such rule. Section 553 of Title 5 shall apply to action under this paragraph.

(3) Neither the pendency of a proceeding under this subsection respecting an exemption from a rule, nor the pendency of judicial proceedings to review the Commission's action or failure to act under this subsection, shall stay the applicability of such rule under subsection (a)(1)(B) of this section.

(h) Restriction on rulemaking authority of Commission respecting children's advertising proceedings pending on May 28, 1980

The Commission shall not have any authority to promulgate any rule in the children's advertising proceeding pending on May 28, 1980, or in any substantially similar proceeding on the basis of a determination by the Commission that such advertising constitutes an unfair act or practice in or affecting commerce.

(i) Meetings with outside parties

(1) For purposes of this subsection, the term "outside party" means any person other than (A) a Commissioner; (B) an officer or employee of the Commission; or (C) any person who has entered into a contract or any other agreement or arrangement with the Commission to provide any goods or services (including consulting services) to the Commission.

(2) Not later than 60 days after May 28, 1980, the Commission shall publish a proposed rule, and not later than 180 days after May 28, 1980, the Commission shall promulgate a final rule, which shall authorize the Commission or any Commissioner to meet with any outside party concerning any rulemaking proceeding of the Commission. Such rule shall provide that—

(A) notice of any such meeting shall be included in any weekly calendar prepared by the Commission; and

(B) a verbatim record or a summary of any such meeting, or of any communication relating to any such meeting, shall be kept, made available to the public, and included in the rulemaking record.

(j) Communications by investigative personnel with staff of Commission concerning matters outside rulemaking record prohibited

Not later than 60 days after May 28, 1980, the Commission shall publish a proposed rule, and not later than 180 days after May 28, 1980, the Commission shall promulgate a final rule, which shall prohibit any officer, employee, or agent of the Commission with any investigative responsibility or other responsibility relating to any rulemaking proceeding within any operating bureau of the Commission, from communicating or causing to be communicated to any Commissioner or to the personal staff of any Commissioner any fact which is relevant to the merits of such proceeding and which is not on the rulemaking record of such proceeding, unless such communication is made available to the public and is included in the rulemaking record. The provisions of this subsection shall not apply to any communication to the extent such communication is required for the disposition of ex parte matters as authorized by law.

§ 57b. Civil actions for violations of rules and cease and desist orders respecting unfair or deceptive acts or practices

(a) Suits by Commission against persons, partnerships, or corporations; jurisdiction; relief for dishonest or fraudulent acts

(1) If any person, partnership, or corporation violates any rule under this subchapter respecting unfair or deceptive acts or practices (other than an interpretive rule, or a rule violation of which the Commission has provided is not an unfair or deceptive act or practice in violation of section 45(a) of this title), then the Commission may commence a civil action against such person, partnership, or corporation for relief under subsection (b) of this section in a United States district court or in any court of competent jurisdiction of a State.

(2) If any person, partnership, or corporation engages in any unfair or deceptive act or practice (within the meaning of section 45(a)(1) of this title) with respect to which the Commission has issued a final cease and desist order which is applicable to such person, partnership, or corporation, then the Commission may commence a civil action against such person, partnership, or corporation in a United States district court or in any court of competent jurisdiction of a State. If the Commission satisfies the court that the act or practice to which the cease and desist order relates is one which a reasonable man would have known under the circumstances was dishonest or fraudulent, the court may grant relief under subsection (b) of this section.

(b) Nature of relief available

The court in an action under subsection (a) of this section shall have jurisdiction to grant such relief as the court finds necessary to redress injury to consumers or other persons, partnerships, and corporations resulting from the rule violation or the unfair or deceptive act or practice, as the case may be. Such relief may include, but shall not be limited to, rescission or reformation of contracts, the refund of money or return of property, the payment of damages, and public notification respecting the rule violation or the unfair or deceptive act or practice, as the case may be; except that nothing in this subsection is intended to authorize the imposition of any exemplary or punitive damages.

(c) Conclusiveness of findings of Commission in cease and desist proceedings; notice of judicial proceedings to injured persons, etc.

(1) If (A) a cease and desist order issued under section 45(b) of this title has become final under section 45(g) of this title with respect to any person's, partnership's, or corporation's rule violation or unfair or deceptive act or practice, and (B) an action under this section is brought with respect to such person's partnership's, or corporation's rule violation or act or practice, then the findings of the Commission as to the material facts in the proceeding under section 45(b) of this title with respect to such person's, partnership's, or corporation's rule violation or act or practice, shall be conclusive unless (i) the terms of such cease and desist order expressly provide that the Commission's findings shall not be conclusive, or (ii) the order became final by reason of section 45(g)(1) of this title, in which case such finding shall be conclusive if supported by evidence.

(2) The court shall cause notice of an action under this section to be given in a manner which is reasonably calculated, under all of the circumstances, to apprise the persons, partnerships, and corporations allegedly injured by the defendant's rule violation or act or practice of the pendency of such action. Such notice may, in the discretion of the court, be given by publication.

(d) Time for bringing of actions

No action may be brought by the Commission under this section more than 3 years after the rule violation to which an action under subsection (a)(1) of this section relates, or the unfair or deceptive act or practice to which an action under subsection (a)(2) of this section relates; except that if a cease and desist order with respect to any person's, partnership's, or corporation's rule violation or unfair or deceptive act or practice has become final and such order was issued in a proceeding under section 45(b) of this title which was commenced not later than 3 years after the rule violation or act or practice occurred, a civil action may be commenced under this section against such person, partnership, or corporation at any time before the expiration of one year after such order becomes final.

(e) Availability of additional Federal or State remedies; other authority of Commission unaffected

Remedies provided in this section are in addition to, and not in lieu of, any other remedy or right of action provided by State or Federal law. Nothing in this section shall be construed to affect any authority of the Commission under any other provision of law.

§ 57b-1. Civil investigative demands

(a) Definitions

For purposes of this section:

(1) The terms "civil investigative demand" and "demand" mean any demand issued by the Commission under subsection (c)(1) of this section.

(2) The term "Commission investigation" means any inquiry conducted by a Commission investigator for the purpose of ascertaining whether any person is or has been engaged in any unfair or deceptive acts or practices in or affecting commerce (within the meaning of section 45(a)(1) of this title) or in any antitrust violations.

(3) The term "Commission investigator" means any attorney or investigator employed by the Commission who is charged with the duty of enforcing or carrying into effect any provisions relating to unfair or deceptive acts or practices in or affecting commerce (within the meaning of section 45(a)(1) of this title) or any provisions relating to antitrust violations.

(4) The term "custodian" means the custodian or any deputy custodian designated under section 57b-2(b)(2)(A) of this title.

(5) The term "documentary material" includes the original or any copy of any book, record, report, memorandum, paper, communication, tabulation, chart, or other document.

(6) The term "person" means any natural person, partnership, corporation, association, or other legal entity, including any person acting under color or authority of State law.

(7) The term "violation" means any act or omission constituting an unfair or deceptive act or practice in or affecting commerce (within the meaning of section 45(a)(1) of this title) or any antitrust violation.

(8) The term "antitrust violation" means—

(A) any unfair method of competition (within the meaning of section 45(a)(1) of this title);

(B) any violation of the Clayton Act [15 U.S.C.A. § 12 et seq.] or of any other Federal statute that prohibits, or makes available to the Commission a civil remedy with respect to, any restraint upon or monopolization of interstate or foreign trade or commerce;

(C) with respect to the International Antitrust Enforcement Assistance Act of 1994 [15 U.S.C.A. § 6201 et seq.], any violation of any of the foreign antitrust laws (as defined in section 12 of such Act [15 U.S.C.A. § 6211]) with respect to which a request is made under section 3 of such Act [15 U.S.C.A. § 6202]; or

(D) any activity in preparation for a merger, acquisition, joint venture, or similar transaction, which if consummated, may result in any such unfair method of competition or in any such violation.

(b) Actions conducted by Commission respecting unfair or deceptive acts or practices in or affecting commerce

For the purpose of investigations performed pursuant to this section with respect to unfair or deceptive acts or practices in or affecting commerce (within the meaning of section 45(a)(1) of this title), all actions of the Commission taken under section 46 and section 49 of this title shall be conducted pursuant to subsection (c) of this section.

(c) Issuance of demand; contents; service; verified return; sworn certificate; answers; taking of oral testimony

(1) Whenever the Commission has reason to believe that any person may be in possession, custody, or control of any documentary material or tangible things, or may have any information, relevant to unfair or deceptive acts or practices in or affecting commerce (within the meaning of section 45(a)(1) of this title), or to antitrust violations, the Commission may, before the institution of any proceedings under this subchapter, issue in writing, and cause to be served upon such person, a civil investigative demand requiring such person to produce such documentary material for inspection and copying or reproduction, to submit such tangible things, to file written reports or answers to questions, to give oral testimony concerning documentary material or other information, or to furnish any combination of such material, answers, or testimony.

(2) Each civil investigative demand shall state the nature of the conduct constituting the alleged violation which is under investigation and the provision of law applicable to such violation.

(3) Each civil investigative demand for the production of documentary material shall—

(A) describe each class of documentary material to be produced under the demand with such definiteness and certainty as to permit such material to be fairly identified;

(B) prescribe a return date or dates which will provide a reasonable period of time within which the material so demanded may be assembled and made available for inspection and copying or reproduction; and

(C) identify the custodian to whom such material shall be made available.

(4) Each civil investigative demand for the submission of tangible things shall—

(A) describe each class of tangible things to be submitted under the demand with such definiteness and certainty as to permit such things to be fairly identified;

(B) prescribe a return date or dates which will provide a reasonable period of time within which the things so demanded may be assembled and submitted; and

(C) identify the custodian to whom such things shall be submitted.

(5) Each civil investigative demand for written reports or answers to questions shall—

(A) propound with definiteness and certainty the reports to be produced or the questions to be answered;

(B) prescribe a date or dates at which time written reports or answers to questions shall be submitted; and

(C) identify the custodian to whom such reports or answers shall be submitted.

(6) Each civil investigative demand for the giving of oral testimony shall—

(A) prescribe a date, time, and place at which oral testimony shall be commenced; and

(B) identify a Commission investigator who shall conduct the investigation and the custodian to whom the transcript of such investigation shall be submitted.

(7)(A) Any civil investigative demand may be served by any Commission investigator at any place within the territorial jurisdiction of any court of the United States.

(B) Any such demand or any enforcement petition filed under this section may be served upon any person who is not found within the territorial jurisdiction of any court of the United States, in such manner as the Federal Rules of Civil Procedure prescribe for service in a foreign nation.

(C) To the extent that the courts of the United States have authority to assert jurisdiction over such person consistent with due process, the United States District Court for the District of Columbia shall have the same jurisdiction to take any action respecting compliance with this section by such person that such district court would have if such person were personally within the jurisdiction of such district court.

(8) Service of any civil investigative demand or any enforcement petition filed under this section may be made upon a partnership, corporation, association, or other legal entity by—

(A) delivering a duly executed copy of such demand or petition to any partner, executive officer, managing agent, or general agent of such partnership, corporation, association, or other legal entity, or to any agent of such partnership, corporation, association, or other legal entity authorized by appointment or by law to receive service of process on behalf of such partnership, corporation, association, or other legal entity;

(B) delivering a duly executed copy of such demand or petition to the principal office or place of business of the partnership, corporation, association, or other legal entity to be served; or

(C) depositing a duly executed copy in the United States mails, by registered or certified mail, return receipt requested, duly addressed to such partnership, corporation, association, or other legal entity at its principal office or place of business.

(9) Service of any civil investigative demand or of any enforcement petition filed under this section may be made upon any natural person by—

(A) delivering a duly executed copy of such demand or petition to the person to be served; or

(B) depositing a duly executed copy in the United States mails by registered or certified mail, return receipt requested, duly addressed to such person at his residence or principal office or place of business.

(10) A verified return by the individual serving any civil investigative demand or any enforcement petition filed under this section setting forth the manner of such service shall be proof of such service. In the case of service by registered or certified mail, such return shall be accompanied by the return post office receipt of delivery of such demand or enforcement petition.

(11) The production of documentary material in response to a civil investigative demand shall be made under a sworn certificate, in such form as the demand designates, by the person, if a natural person, to whom the demand is directed or, if not a natural person, by any person having knowledge of the facts and circumstances relating to such production, to the effect that all of the documentary material required by the demand and in the possession, custody, or control of the person to whom the demand is directed has been produced and made available to the custodian.

(12) The submission of tangible things in response to a civil investigative demand shall be made under a sworn certificate, in such form as the demand designates, by the person to whom the demand is directed or, if not a natural person, by any person having knowledge of the facts and circumstances relating to such production, to the effect that all of the tangible things required by the demand and in the possession, custody, or control of the person to whom the demand is directed have been submitted to the custodian.

(13) Each reporting requirement or question in a civil investigative demand shall be answered separately and fully in writing under oath, unless it is objected to, in which event the reasons for the objection shall be stated in lieu of an answer, and it shall be submitted under a sworn certificate, in such form as the demand designates, by the person, if a natural person, to whom the demand is directed or, if not a natural person, by any person responsible for answering each reporting requirement or question, to the effect that all information required by the demand and in the possession, custody, control, or knowledge of the person to whom the demand is directed has been submitted.

(14)(A) Any Commission investigator before whom oral testimony is to be taken shall put the witness on oath or affirmation and shall personally, or by any individual acting under his direction and in his presence, record the testimony of the witness. The testimony shall be taken stenographically and transcribed. After the testimony is fully transcribed, the Commission investigator before whom the testimony is taken shall promptly transmit a copy of the transcript of the testimony to the custodian.

(B) Any Commission investigator before whom oral testimony is to be taken shall exclude from the place where the testimony is to be taken all other persons except the person giving the testimony, his attorney, the officer before whom the testimony is to be taken, and any stenographer taking such testimony.

(C) The oral testimony of any person taken pursuant to a civil investigative demand shall be taken in the judicial district of the United States in which such person resides, is found, or transacts business, or in such other place as may be agreed upon by the Commission investigator before whom the oral testimony of such person is to be taken and such person.

(D)(i) Any person compelled to appear under a civil investigative demand for oral testimony pursuant to this section may be accompanied, represented, and advised by an attorney. The attorney may advise such person, in confidence, either upon the request of such person or upon the initiative of the attorney, with respect to any question asked of such person.

(ii) Such person or attorney may object on the record to any question, in whole or in part, and shall briefly state for the record the reason for the objection. An objection may properly be made, received, and entered upon the record when it is claimed that such person is entitled to refuse to answer the question on grounds of any constitutional or other legal right or privilege, including the privilege against self-incrimination. Such person shall not otherwise object to or refuse to answer any question, and shall not himself or through his attorney otherwise interrupt the oral examination. If such person refuses to answer any question, the Commission may petition the district court of the United States pursuant to this section for an order compelling such person to answer such question.

(iii) If such person refuses to answer any question on grounds of the privilege against self-incrimination, the testimony of such person may be compelled in accordance with the provisions of section 6004 of Title 18.

(E)(i) After the testimony of any witness is fully transcribed, the Commission investigator shall afford the witness (who may be accompanied by an attorney) a reasonable opportunity to examine the transcript. The transcript shall be read to or by the witness, unless such examination and reading are waived by the witness. Any changes in form or substance which the witness desires to make shall be entered and identified upon the transcript by the Commission investigator with a statement of the reasons given by the witness for making such changes. The transcript shall then be signed by the witness, unless the witness in writing waives the signing, is ill, cannot be found, or refuses to sign.

(ii) If the transcript is not signed by the witness during the 30-day period following the date upon which the witness is first afforded a reasonable opportunity to examine it, the Commission investigator shall sign the transcript and state on the record the fact of the waiver, illness, absence of the witness, or the refusal to sign, together with any reasons given for the failure to sign.

(F) The Commission investigator shall certify on the transcript that the witness was duly sworn by him and that the transcript is a true record of the testimony given by the witness, and the Commission investigator shall promptly deliver the transcript or send it by registered or certified mail to the custodian.

(G) The Commission investigator shall furnish a copy of the transcript (upon payment of reasonable charges for the transcript) to the witness only, except that the Commission may for good cause limit such witness to inspection of the official transcript of his testimony.

(H) Any witness appearing for the taking of oral testimony pursuant to a civil investigative demand shall be entitled to the same fees and mileage which are paid to witnesses in the district courts of the United States.

(d) Procedures for demand material

Materials received as a result of a civil investigative demand shall be subject to the procedures established in section 57b-2 of this title.

(e) Petition for enforcement

Whenever any person fails to comply with any civil investigative demand duly served upon him under this section, or whenever satisfactory copying or reproduction of material requested pursuant to the demand cannot be accomplished and such person refuses to surrender such material, the Commission, through such officers or attorneys as it may designate, may file, in the district court of the United States for any judicial district in which such person resides, is found, or transacts business, and serve upon such person, a petition for an order of such court for the enforcement of this section. All process of any court to which application may be made as provided in this subsection may be served in any judicial district.

(f) Petition for order modifying or setting aside demand

(1) Not later than 20 days after the service of any civil investigative demand upon any person under subsection (c) of this section, or at any time before the return date specified in the demand, whichever period is shorter, or within such period exceeding 20 days after service or in excess of such return date as may be prescribed in writing, subsequent to service, by any Commission investigator named in the demand, such person may file with the Commission a petition for an order by the Commission modifying or setting aside the demand.

(2) The time permitted for compliance with the demand in whole or in part, as deemed proper and ordered by the Commission, shall not run during the pendency of such petition at the Commission, except that such person shall comply with any portions of the demand not sought to be modified or set aside. Such petition shall specify each ground upon which the petitioner relies in seeking such relief, and may be based upon any failure of the demand to comply with the provisions of this section, or upon any constitutional or other legal right or privilege of such person.

(g) Custodial control of documentary material, tangible things, reports, etc.

At any time during which any custodian is in custody or control of any documentary material, tangible things, reports, answers to questions, or transcripts of oral testimony given by any person in compliance with any civil investigative demand, such person may file, in the district court of the United States for the judicial district within which the office of such custodian is situated, and serve upon such custodian, a petition for an order of such court requiring the performance by such custodian of any duty imposed upon him by this section or section 57b-2 of this title.

(h) Jurisdiction of court

Whenever any petition is filed in any district court of the United States under this section, such court shall have jurisdiction to hear and determine the matter so presented, and to enter such order or orders as may be required to carry into effect the provisions of this section. Any final order so entered shall be subject to appeal pursuant to section 1291 of Title 28. Any disobedience of any final order entered under this section by any court shall be punished as a contempt of such court.

(i) Commission authority to issue subpoenas or make demand for information

Notwithstanding any other provision of law, the Commission shall have no authority to issue a subpoena or make a demand for information, under authority of this subchapter or any other provision of law, unless such subpoena or demand for information is signed by a Commissioner acting pursuant to a Commission resolution. The Commission shall not delegate the power conferred by this section to sign subpoenas or demands for information to any other person.

(j) Applicability of this section

The provisions of this section shall not—

(1) apply to any proceeding under section 45(b) of this title, any proceeding under section 11(b) of the Clayton Act (15 U.S.C. 21(b)), or any adjudicative proceeding under any other provision of law; or

(2) apply to or affect the jurisdiction, duties, or powers of any agency of the Federal Government, other than the Commission, regardless of whether such jurisdiction, duties, or powers are derived in whole or in part, by reference to this subchapter.

Electronic Fund Transfer Act, Regulation E (1978)

15 U.S.C. §§ 1693-1693r, as amended

Statutes in Context

This regulation establishes the rights and responsibilities for participants in electronic fund transfer systems. It limits the consumer's liability for unauthorized electronic fund transfers and provides a structure for error resolution procedures when charges are disputed.

§ 1693. Congressional findings and declaration of purpose

(a) Rights and liabilities undefined

The Congress finds that the use of electronic systems to transfer funds provides the potential for substantial benefits to consumers. However, due to the unique characteristics of such systems, the application of existing consumer protection legislation is unclear, leaving the rights and liabilities of consumers, financial institutions, and intermediaries in electronic fund transfers undefined.

(b) Purposes

It is the purpose of this subchapter to provide a basic framework establishing the rights, liabilities, and responsibilities of participants in electronic fund transfer systems. The primary objective of this subchapter, however, is the provision of individual consumer rights.

§ 1693a. Definitions

As used in this subchapter—

(1) the term "accepted card or other means of access" means a card, code, or other means of access to a consumer's account for the purpose of initiating electronic fund transfers when the person to whom such card or other means of access was issued has requested and received or has signed or has used, or authorized another to use, such card or other means of access for the purpose of transferring money between accounts or obtaining money, property, labor, or services;

(2) the term "account" means a demand deposit, savings deposit, or other asset account (other than an occasional or incidental credit balance in an open end credit plan as defined in section 1602(i) of this title), as described in regulations of the Board, established primarily for personal, family, or household purposes, but such term does not include an account held by a financial institution pursuant to a bona fide trust agreement;

(3) the term "Board" means the Board of Governors of the Federal Reserve System;

(4) the term “business day” means any day on which the offices of the consumer’s financial institution involved in an electronic fund transfer are open to the public for carrying on substantially all of its business functions;

(5) the term “consumer” means a natural person;

(6) the term “electronic fund transfer” means any transfer of funds, other than a transaction originated by check, draft, or similar paper instrument, which is initiated through an electronic terminal, telephonic instrument, or computer or magnetic tape so as to order, instruct, or authorize a financial institution to debit or credit an account. Such term includes, but is not limited to, point-of-sale transfers, automated teller machine transactions, direct deposits or withdrawals of funds, and transfers initiated by telephone. Such term does not include—

(A) any check guarantee or authorization service which does not directly result in a debit or credit to a consumer’s account:

(B) any transfer of funds, other than those processed by automated clearinghouse, made by a financial institution on behalf of a consumer by means of a service that transfers funds held at either Federal Reserve banks or other depository institutions and which is not designed primarily to transfer funds on behalf of a consumer;

(C) any transaction the primary purpose of which is the purchase or sale of securities or commodities through a broker-dealer registered with or regulated by the Securities and Exchange Commission;

(D) any automatic transfer from a savings account to a demand deposit account pursuant to an agreement between a consumer and a financial institution for the purpose of covering an overdraft or maintaining an agreed upon minimum balance in the consumer’s demand deposit account; or

(E) any transfer of funds which is initiated by a telephone conversation between a consumer and an officer or employee of a financial institution which is not pursuant to a prearranged plan and under which periodic or recurring transfers are not contemplated;

as determined under regulations of the Board;

(7) the term “electronic terminal” means an electronic device, other than a telephone operated by a consumer, through which a consumer may initiate an electronic fund transfer. Such term includes, but is not limited to, point-of-sale terminals, automated teller machines, and cash dispensing machines;

(8) the term “financial institution” means a State or National bank, a State or Federal savings and loan association, a mutual savings bank, a State or Federal credit union, or any other person who, directly or indirectly, holds an account belonging to a consumer;

(9) the term “preauthorized electronic fund transfer” means an electronic fund transfer authorized in advance to recur at substantially regular intervals;

(10) the term “State” means any State, territory, or possession of the United States, the District of Columbia, the Commonwealth of Puerto Rico, or any political subdivision of any of the foregoing; and

(11) the term "unauthorized electronic fund transfer" means an electronic fund transfer from a consumer's account initiated by a person other than the consumer without actual authority to initiate such transfer and from which the consumer receives no benefit, but the term does not include any electronic fund transfer (A) initiated by a person other than the consumer who was furnished with the card, code, or other means of access to such consumer's account by such consumer, unless the consumer has notified the financial institution involved that transfers by such other person are no longer authorized, (B) initiated with fraudulent intent by the consumer or any person acting in concert with the consumer, or (C) which constitutes an error committed by a financial institution.

§ 1693b. Regulations

(a) Prescription by Board

The Board shall prescribe regulations to carry out the purposes of this subchapter. In prescribing such regulations, the Board shall:

(1) consult with the other agencies referred to in section 1693o of this title and take into account, and allow for, the continuing evolution of electronic banking services and the technology utilized in such services,

(2) prepare an analysis of economic impact which considers the costs and benefits to financial institutions, consumers, and other users of electronic fund transfers, including the extent to which additional documentation, reports, records, or other paper work would be required, and the effects upon competition in the provision of electronic banking services among large and small financial institutions and the availability of such services to different classes of consumers, particularly low income consumers,

(3) to the extent practicable, the Board shall demonstrate that the consumer protections of the proposed regulations outweigh the compliance costs imposed upon consumers and financial institutions, and

(4) any proposed regulations and accompanying analyses shall be sent promptly to Congress by the Board.

(b) Issuance of model clauses

The Board shall issue model clauses for optional use by financial institutions to facilitate compliance with the disclosure requirements of section 1693c of this title and to aid consumers in understanding the rights and responsibilities of participants in electronic fund transfers by utilizing readily understandable language. Such model clauses shall be adopted after notice duly given in the Federal Register and opportunity for public comment in accordance with section 553 of Title 5. With respect to the disclosures required by section 1693c(a)(3) and (4) of this title, the Board shall take account of variations in the services and charges under different electronic fund transfer systems and, as appropriate, shall issue alternative model clauses for disclosure of these differing account terms.

(c) Criteria; modification of requirements

Regulations prescribed hereunder may contain such classifications, differentiations, or other provisions, and may provide for such adjustments and exceptions for any class of electronic fund transfers, as in the judgment of the Board are necessary or proper to effectuate the purposes of this subchapter, to prevent circumvention or evasion thereof, or to facilitate compliance therewith.

The Board shall by regulation modify the requirements imposed by this subchapter on small financial institutions if the Board determines that such modifications are necessary to alleviate any undue compliance burden on small financial institutions and such modifications are consistent with the purpose and objective of this subchapter.

(d) Applicability to service providers other than certain financial institutions

(1) In general

If electronic fund transfer services are made available to consumers by a person other than a financial institution holding a consumer's account, the Board shall by regulation assure that the disclosures, protections, responsibilities, and remedies created by this subchapter are made applicable to such persons and services.

(2) State and local government electronic benefit transfer systems

(A) "Electronic benefit transfer system" defined

In this paragraph, the term "electronic benefit transfer system"—

(i) means a system under which a government agency distributes needs-tested benefits by establishing accounts that may be accessed by recipients electronically, such as through automated teller machines or point-of-sale terminals; and

(ii) does not include employment-related payments, including salaries and pension, retirement, or unemployment benefits established by a Federal, State, or local government agency.

(B) Exemption generally

The disclosures, protections, responsibilities, and remedies established under this subchapter, and any regulation prescribed or order issued by the Board in accordance with this subchapter, shall not apply to any electronic benefit transfer system established under State or local law or administered by a State or local government.

(C) Exception for direct deposit into recipient's account

Subparagraph (B) shall not apply with respect to any electronic funds transfer under an electronic benefit transfer system for a deposit directly into a consumer account held by the recipient of the benefit.

(D) Rule of construction

No provision of this paragraph—

(i) affects or alters the protections otherwise applicable with respect to benefits established by any other provision Federal, State, or local law; or

(ii) otherwise supersedes the application of any State or local law.

(3) Fee disclosures at automated teller machines

(A) In general

The regulations prescribed under paragraph (1) shall require any automated teller machine operator who imposes a fee on any consumer for providing host transfer services to such consumer to provide notice in accordance with subparagraph (B) to the consumer (at the time the service is provided) of—

(i) the fact that a fee is imposed by such operator for providing the service; and

(ii) the amount of any such fee.

(B) Notice requirements

(i) On the machine

The notice required under clause (i) of subparagraph (A) with respect to any fee described in such subparagraph shall be posted in a prominent and conspicuous location on or at the automated teller machine at which the electronic fund transfer is initiated by the consumer.

(ii) On the screen

The notice required under clauses (i) and (ii) of subparagraph (A) with respect to any fee described in such subparagraph shall appear on the screen of the automated teller machine, or on a paper notice issued from such machine, after the transaction is initiated and before the consumer is irrevocably committed to completing the transaction, except that during the period beginning on November 12, 1999, and ending on December 31, 2004, this clause shall not apply to any automated teller machine that lacks the technical capability to disclose the notice on the screen or to issue a paper notice after the transaction is initiated and before the consumer is irrevocably committed to completing the transaction.

(C) Prohibition on fees not properly disclosed and explicitly assumed by consumer

No fee may be imposed by any automated teller machine operator in connection with any electronic fund transfer initiated by a consumer for which a notice is required under subparagraph (A), unless—

(i) the consumer receives such notice in accordance with subparagraph (B); and

(ii) the consumer elects to continue in the manner necessary to effect the transaction after receiving such notice.

(D) Definitions

For purposes of this paragraph, the following definitions shall apply:

(i) Automated teller machine operator

The term "automated teller machine operator" means any person who—

(I) operates an automated teller machine at which consumers initiate electronic fund transfers; and

(II) is not the financial institution that holds the account of such consumer from which the transfer is made.

(ii) Electronic fund transfer

The term "electronic fund transfer" includes a transaction that involves a balance inquiry initiated by a consumer in the same manner as an electronic fund transfer, whether or not the consumer initiates a transfer of funds in the course of the transaction.

(iii) Host transfer services

The term "host transfer services" means any electronic fund transfer made by an automated teller machine operator in connection with a transaction initiated by a consumer at an automated teller machine operated by such operator.

§ 1693c. Terms and conditions of transfers

(a) Disclosures; time; form; contents

The terms and conditions of electronic fund transfers involving a consumer's account shall be disclosed at the time the consumer contracts for an electronic fund transfer service, in accordance with regulations of the Board. Such disclosures shall be in readily understandable language and shall include, to the extent applicable—

(1) the consumer's liability for unauthorized electronic fund transfers and, at the financial institution's option, notice of the advisability of prompt reporting of any loss, theft, or unauthorized use of a card, code, or other means of access;

(2) the telephone number and address of the person or office to be notified in the event the consumer believes than an unauthorized electronic fund transfer has been or may be effected;

(3) the type and nature of electronic fund transfers which the consumer may initiate, including any limitations on the frequency or dollar amount of such transfers, except that the details of such limitations need not be disclosed if their confidentiality is necessary to maintain the security of an electronic fund transfer system, as determined by the Board;

(4) any charges for electronic fund transfers or for the right to make such transfers;

(5) the consumer's right to stop payment of a preauthorized electronic fund transfer and the procedure to initiate such a stop payment order;

(6) the consumer's right to receive documentation of electronic fund transfers under section 1693d of this title;

(7) a summary, in a form prescribed by regulations of the Board, of the error resolution provisions of section 1693f of this title and the consumer's rights thereunder. The financial institution shall thereafter transmit such summary at least once per calendar year;

(8) the financial institution's liability to the consumer under section 1693h of this title;

(9) under what circumstances the financial institution will in the ordinary course of business disclose information concerning the consumer's account to third persons; and

(10) a notice to the consumer that a fee may be imposed by—

(A) an automated teller machine operator (as defined in section 1693b(d)(3)(D)(i) of this title) if the consumer initiates a transfer from an automated teller machine that is not operated by the person issuing the card or other means of access; and

(B) any national, regional, or local network utilized to effect the transaction.

(b) Notification of changes to consumer

A financial institution shall notify a consumer in writing at least twenty-one days prior to the effective date of any change in any term or condition of the consumer's account required to be disclosed under subsection (a) of this section if such change would result in greater cost or liability for such consumer or decreased access to the consumer's account. A financial institution may, however, implement a change in the terms or conditions of an account without prior notice when such change is immediately necessary to maintain or restore the security of an electronic fund transfer system or a consumer's account. Subject to subsection (a)(3) of this section, the Board shall require subsequent notification if such a change is made permanent.

(c) Time for disclosures respecting accounts accessible prior to effective date of this subchapter

For any account of a consumer made accessible to electronic fund transfers prior to the effective date of this subchapter, the information required to be disclosed to the consumer under subsection (a) of this section shall be disclosed not later than the earlier of—

(1) the first periodic statement required by section 1693d(c) of this title after the effective date of this subchapter; or

(2) thirty days after the effective date of this subchapter.

§ 1693d. Documentation of transfers

(a) Availability of written documentation to consumer; contents

For each electronic fund transfer initiated by a consumer from an electronic terminal, the financial institution holding such consumer's account shall, directly or indirectly, at the time the transfer is initiated, make available to the consumer written documentation of such transfer. The documentation shall clearly set forth to the extent applicable—

(1) the amount involved and date the transfer is initiated;

(2) the type of transfer;

(3) the identity of the consumer's account with the financial institution from which or to which funds are transferred;

(4) the identity of any third party to whom or from whom funds are transferred; and

(5) the location or identification of the electronic terminal involved.

(b) Notice of credit to consumer

For a consumer's account which is scheduled to be credited by a preauthorized electronic fund transfer from the same payor at least once in each successive sixty-day period, except where the payor provides positive notice of the transfer to the consumer, the financial institution shall elect to provide promptly either positive notice to the consumer when the credit is made as scheduled, or negative notice to the consumer when the credit is not made as scheduled, in accordance with regulations of the Board. The means of notice elected shall be disclosed to the consumer in accordance with section 1693c of this title.

(c) Periodic statement; contents

A financial institution shall provide each consumer with a periodic statement for each account of such consumer that may be accessed by means of an electronic fund transfer. Except as provided in subsections (d) and (e) of this section, such statement shall be provided at least monthly for each monthly or shorter cycle in which an electronic fund transfer affecting the account has occurred, or every three months, whichever is more frequent. The statement, which may include information regarding transactions other than electronic fund transfers, shall clearly set forth—

(1) with regard to each electronic fund transfer during the period, the information described in subsection (a) of this section, which may be provided on an accompanying document;

(2) the amount of any fee or charge assessed by the financial institution during the period for electronic fund transfers or for account maintenance;

(3) the balances in the consumer's account at the beginning of the period and at the close of the period; and

(4) the address and telephone number to be used by the financial institution for the purpose of receiving any statement inquiry or notice of account error from the consumer. Such address and telephone number shall be preceded by the caption "Direct Inquiries To:" or other similar language indicating that the address and number are to be used for such inquiries or notices.

(d) Consumer passbook accounts

In the case of a consumer's passbook account which may not be accessed by electronic fund transfers other than preauthorized electronic fund transfers crediting the account, a financial institution may, in lieu of complying with the requirements of subsection (c) of this section, upon presentation of the passbook provide the consumer in writing with the amount and date of each such transfer involving the account since the passbook was last presented.

(e) Accounts other than passbook accounts

In the case of a consumer's account, other than a passbook account, which may not be accessed by electronic fund transfers other than preauthorized electronic fund transfers crediting the account, the financial institution may provide a periodic statement on a quarterly basis which otherwise complies with the requirements of subsection (c) of this section.

(f) Documentation as evidence

In any action involving a consumer, any documentation required by this section to be given to the consumer which indicates that an electronic fund transfer was made to another person shall be admissible as evidence of such transfer and shall constitute prima facie proof that such transfer was made.

§ 1693e. Preauthorized transfers

(a) A preauthorized electronic fund transfer from a consumer's account may be authorized by the consumer only in writing, and a copy of such authorization shall be provided to the consumer when made. A consumer may stop payment of a preauthorized electronic fund transfer by notifying the financial institution orally or in writing at any time up to three business days preceding the scheduled date of such transfer. The financial institution may require written confirmation to be provided to it within fourteen days of an oral notification if, when the oral notification is made, the consumer is advised of such requirement and the address to which such confirmation should be sent.

(b) In the case of preauthorized transfers from a consumer's account to the same person which may vary in amount, the financial institution or designated payee shall, prior to each transfer, provide reasonable advance notice to the consumer, in accordance with regulations of the Board, of the amount to be transferred and the scheduled date of the transfer.

§ 1693f. Error resolution

(a) Notification to financial institution of error

If a financial institution, within sixty days after having transmitted to a consumer documentation pursuant to section 1693d(a), (c), or (d) of this title or notification pursuant to section 1693d(b) of this title, receives oral or written notice in which the consumer—

(1) sets forth or otherwise enables the financial institution to identify the name and account number of the consumer;

(2) indicates the consumer's belief that the documentation, or, in the case of notification pursuant to section 1693d(b) of this title, the consumer's account, contains an error and the amount of such error; and

(3) sets forth the reasons for the consumer's belief (where applicable) that an error has occurred,

the financial institution shall investigate the alleged error, determine whether an error has occurred, and report or mail the results of such investigation and determination to the consumer within ten business days. The financial institution may require written confirmation to be provided to it within ten business days of an oral notification of error if, when the oral notification is made, the consumer is advised of such requirement and the address to which such confirmation should be sent. A financial institution which requires written confirmation in accordance with the previous sentence need not provisionally recredit a consumer's account in accordance with subsection (c) of this section, nor shall the financial institution be liable under subsection (e) of this section if the written confirmation is not received within the ten-day period referred to in the previous sentence.

(b) Correction of error; interest

If the financial institution determines that an error did occur, it shall promptly, but in no event more than one business day after such determination, correct the error, subject to section 1693g of this title, including the crediting of interest where applicable.

(c) Provisional recredit of consumer's account

If a financial institution receives notice of an error in the manner and within the time period specified in subsection (a) of this section, it may, in lieu of the requirements of subsections (a) and (b) of this section, within ten business days after receiving such notice provisionally recredit the consumer's account for the amount alleged to be in error, subject to section 1693g of this title, including interest where applicable, pending the conclusion of its investigation and its determination of whether an error has occurred. Such investigation shall be concluded not later than forty-five days after receipt of notice of the error. During the pendency of the investigation, the consumer shall have full use of the funds provisionally recredited.

(d) Absence of error; finding; explanation

If the financial institution determines after its investigation pursuant to subsection (a) or (c) of this section that an error did not occur, it shall deliver or mail to the consumer an explanation of its findings within 3 business days after the conclusion of its investigation, and upon request of the consumer promptly deliver or mail to the consumer reproductions of all documents which the financial institution relied on to conclude that such error did not occur. The financial institution shall include notice of the right to request reproductions with the explanation of its findings.

(e) Treble damages

If in any action under section 1693m of this title, the court finds that—

> **(1)** the financial institution did not provisionally recredit a consumer's account within the ten-day period specified in subsection (c) of this section, and the financial institution (A) did not make a good faith investigation of the alleged error, or (B) did not have a reasonable basis for believing that the consumer's account was not in error; or
>
> **(2)** the financial institution knowingly and willfully concluded that the consumer's account was not in error when such conclusion could not reasonably have been drawn from the evidence available to the financial institution at the time of its investigation,

then the consumer shall be entitled to treble damages determined under section 1693m(a)(1) of this title.

(f) Acts constituting error

For the purpose of this section, an error consists of—

> **(1)** an unauthorized electronic fund transfer;
>
> **(2)** an incorrect electronic fund transfer from or to the consumer's account;
>
> **(3)** the omission from a periodic statement of an electronic fund transfer affecting the consumer's account which should have been included;
>
> **(4)** a computational error by the financial institution;
>
> **(5)** the consumer's receipt of an incorrect amount of money from an electronic terminal;
>
> **(6)** a consumer's request for additional information or clarification concerning an electronic fund transfer or any documentation required by this subchapter; or

(7) any other error described in regulations of the Board.

§ 1693g. Consumer liability

(a) Unauthorized electronic fund transfers; limit

A consumer shall be liable for any unauthorized electronic fund transfer involving the account of such consumer only if the card or other means of access utilized for such transfer was an accepted card or other meanas of access and if the issuer of such card, code, or other means of access has provided a means whereby the user of such card, code, or other means of access can be identified as the person authorized to use it, such as by signature, photograph, or fingerprint or by electronic or mechanical confirmation. In no event, however, shall a consumer's liability for an unauthorized transfer exceed the lesser of—

(1) $50; or

(2) the amount of money or value of property or services obtained in such unauthorized electronic fund transfer prior to the time the financial institution is notified of, or otherwise becomes aware of, circumstances which lead to the reasonable belief that an unauthorized electronic fund transfer involving the consumer's account has been or may be effected. Notice under this paragraph is sufficient when such steps have been taken as may be reasonably required in the ordinary course of business to provide the financial institution with the pertinent information, whether or not any particular officer, employee, or agent of the financial institution does in fact receive such information.

Notwithstanding the foregoing, reimbursement need not be made to the consumer for losses the financial institution establishes would not have occurred but for the failure of the consumer to report within sixty days of transmittal of the statement (or in extenuating circumstances such as extended travel or hospitalization, within a reasonable time under the circumstances) any unauthorized electronic fund transfer or account error which appears on the periodic statement provided to the consumer under section 1693d of this title. In addition, reimbursement need not be made to the consumer for losses which the financial institution establishes would not have occurred but for the failure of the consumer to report any loss or theft of a card or other means of access within two business days after the consumer learns of the loss or theft (or in extenuating circumstances such as extended travel or hospitalization, within a longer period which is reasonable under the circumstances), but the consumer's liability under this subsection in any such case may not exceed a total of $500, or the amount of unauthorized electronic fund transfers which occur following the close of two business days (or such longer period) after the consumer learns of the loss or theft but prior to notice to the financial institution under this subsection, whichever is less.

(b) Burden of proof

In any action which involves a consumer's liability for an unauthorized electronic fund transfer, the burden of proof is upon the financial institution to show that the electronic fund transfer was authorized or, if the electronic fund transfer was unauthorized, then the burden of proof is upon the financial institution to establish that the conditions of liability set forth in subsection (a) of this section have been met, and, if the transfer was initiated after the effective date of section 1693c of this title, that the disclosures required to be made to the consumer under section 1693c(a)(1) and (2) of this title were in fact made in accordance with such section.

(c) Determination of limitation on liability

In the event of a transaction which involves both an unauthorized electronic fund transfer and an extension of credit as defined in section 1602(e) of this title pursuant to an agreement between the consumer and the financial institution to extend such credit to the consumer in the event the consumer's account is overdrawn, the limitation on the consumer's liability for such transaction shall be determined solely in accordance with this section.

(d) Restriction on liability

Nothing in this section imposes liability upon a consumer for an unauthorized electronic fund transfer in excess of his liability for such a transfer under other applicable law or under any agreement with the consumer's financial institution.

(e) Scope of liability

Except as provided in this section, a consumer incurs no liability from an unauthorized electronic fund transfer.

§ 1693h. Liability of financial institutions

(a) Action or failure to act proximately causing damages

Subject to subsections (b) and (c) of this section, a financial institution shall be liable to a consumer for all damages proximately caused by—

(1) the financial institution's failure to make an electronic fund transfer, in accordance with the terms and conditions of an account, in the correct amount or in a timely manner when properly instructed to do so by the consumer, except where—

(A) the consumer's account has insufficient funds;

(B) the funds are subject to legal process or other encumbrance restricting such transfer;

(C) such transfer would exceed an established credit limit;

(D) an electronic terminal has insufficient cash to complete the transaction; or

(E) as otherwise provided in regulations of the Board;

(2) the financial institution's failure to make an electronic fund transfer due to insufficient funds when the financial institution failed to credit, in accordance with the terms and conditions of an account, a deposit of funds to the consumer's account which would have provided sufficient funds to make the transfer, and

(3) the financial institution's failure to stop payment of a preauthorized transfer from a consumer's account when instructed to do so in accordance with the terms and conditions of the account.

(b) Acts of God and technical malfunctions

A financial institution shall not be liable under subsection (a)(1) or (2) of this section if the financial institution shows by a preponderance of the evidence that its action or failure to act resulted from—

(1) an act of God or other circumstance beyond its control, that it exercised reasonable care to prevent such an occurrence, and that it exercised such diligence as the circumstances required; or

(2) a technical malfunction which was known to the consumer at the time he attempted to initiate an electronic fund transfer or, in the case of a preauthorized transfer, at the time such transfer should have occurred.

(c) Intent

In the case of a failure described in subsection (a) of this section which was not intentional and which resulted from a bona fide error, notwithstanding the maintenance of procedures reasonably adapted to avoid any such error, the financial institution shall be liable for actual damages proved.

§ 1693i. Issuance of cards or other means of access

(a) Prohibition; proper issuance

No person may issue to a consumer any card, code, or other means of access to such consumer's account for the purpose of initiating an electronic fund transfer other than—

(1) in response to a request or application therefor; or

(2) as a renewal of, or in substitution for, an accepted card, code, or other means of access, whether issued by the initial issuer or a successor.

(b) Exceptions

Notwithstanding the provisions of subsection (a) of this section, a person may distribute to a consumer on an unsolicited basis a card, code, or other means of access for use in initiating an electronic fund transfer from such consumer's account, if—

(1) such card, code, or other means of access is not validated;

(2) such distribution is accompanied by a complete disclosure, in accordance with section 1693c of this title, of the consumer's rights and liabilities which will apply if such card, code, or other means of access is validated;

(3) such distribution is accompanied by a clear explanation, in accordance with regulations of the Board, that such card, code, or other means of access is not validated and how the consumer may dispose of such code, card, or other means of access if validation is not desired; and

(4) such card, code, or other means of access is validated only in response to a request or application from the consumer, upon verification of the consumer's identity.

(c) Validation

For the purpose of subsection (b) of this section, a card, code, or other means of access is validated when it may be used to initiate an electronic fund transfer.

§ 1693j. Suspension of obligations

If a system malfunction prevents the effectuation of an electronic fund transfer initiated by a consumer to another person, and such other person has agreed to accept payment by such means, the consumer's obligation to the other person shall be suspended until the malfunction is corrected and the electronic fund transfer may be completed, unless such other person has subsequently, by written request, demanded payment by means other than an electronic fund transfer.

§ 1693k. Compulsory use of electronic fund transfers

No person may—

(1) condition the extension of credit to a consumer on such consumer's repayment by means of preauthorized electronic fund transfers; or

(2) require a consumer to establish an account for receipt of electronic fund transfers with a particular financial institution as a condition of employment or receipt of a government benefit.

§ 1693l. Waiver of rights

No writing or other agreement between a consumer and any other person may contain any provision which constitutes a waiver of any right conferred or cause of action created by this subchapter. Nothing in this section prohibits, however, any writing or other agreement which grants to a consumer a more extensive right or remedy or greater protection than contained in this subchapter or a waiver given in settlement of a dispute or action.

§ 1693m. Civil liability

(a) Individual or class action for damages; amount of award

Except as otherwise provided by this section and section 1693h of this title, any person who fails to comply with any provision of this subchapter with respect to any consumer, except for an error resolved in accordance with section 1693f of this title, is liable to such consumer in an amount equal to the sum of—

(1) any actual damage sustained by such consumer as a result of such failure;

(2)(A) in the case of an individual action, an amount not less than $100 nor greater than $1,000; or

(B) in the case of a class action, such amount as the court may allow, except that (i) as to each member of the class no minimum recovery shall be applicable, and (ii) the total recovery under this subparagraph in any class action or series of class actions arising out of the same failure to comply by the same person shall not be more than the lesser of $500,000 or 1 per centum of the net worth of the defendant; and

(3) in the case of any successful action to enforce the foregoing liability, the costs of the action, together with a reasonable attorney's fee as determined by the court.

(b) Factors determining amount of award

In determining the amount of liability in any action under subsection (a) of this section, the court shall consider, among other relevant factors—

(1) in any individual action under subsection (a)(2)(A) of this section, the frequency and persistence of noncompliance, the nature of such noncompliance, and the extent to which the noncompliance was intentional; or

(2) in any class action under subsection (a)(2)(B) of this section, the frequency and persistence of noncompliance, the nature of such noncompliance, the resources of the defendant, the number of persons adversely affected, and the extent to which the noncompliance was intentional.

(c) Unintentional violations; bona fide error

Except as provided in section 1693h of this title, a person may not be held liable in any action brought under this section for a violation of this subchapter if the person shows by a preponderance of evidence that the violation was not intentional and resulted from a bona fide error notwithstanding the maintenance of procedures reasonably adapted to avoid any such error.

(d) Good faith compliance with rule, regulation, or interpretation of Board or approval of duly authorized official or employee of Federal Reserve System

No provision of this section or section 1693n of this title imposing any liability shall apply to—

(1) any act done or omitted in good faith in conformity with any rule, regulation, or interpretation thereof by the Board or in conformity with any interpretation or approval by an official or employee of the Federal Reserve System duly authorized by the Board to issue such interpretations or approvals under such procedures as the Board may prescribe therefor; or

(2) any failure to make disclosure in proper form if a financial institution utilized an appropriate model clause issued by the Board,

notwithstanding that after such act, omission, or failure has occurred, such rule, regulation, approval, or model clause is amended, rescinded, or determined by judicial or other authority to be invalid for any reason.

(e) Notification to consumer prior to action; adjustment of consumer's account

A person has no liability under this section for any failure to comply with any requirement under this subchapter if, prior to the institution of an action under this section, the person notifies the consumer concerned of the failure, complies with the requirements of this subchapter, and makes an appropriate adjustment to the consumer's account and pays actual damages or, where applicable, damages in accordance with section 1693h of this title.

(f) Action in bad faith or for harassment; attorney's fees

On a finding by the court that an unsuccessful action under this section was brought in bad faith or for purposes of harassment, the court shall award to the defendant attorney's fees reasonable in relation to the work expended and costs.

(g) Jurisdiction of courts; time for maintenance of action

Without regard to the amount in controversy, any action under this section may be brought in any United States district court, or in any other court of competent jurisdiction, within one year from the date of the occurrence of the violation.

§ 1693n. Criminal liability

(a) Violations respecting giving of false or inaccurate information, failure to provide information, and failure to comply with provisions of this subchapter

Whoever knowingly and willfully—

> **(1)** gives false or inaccurate information or fails to provide information which he is required to disclose by this subchapter or any regulation issued thereunder; or
>
> **(2)** otherwise fails to comply with any provision of this subchapter;

shall be fined not more than $5,000 or imprisoned not more than one year, or both.

(b) Violations affecting interstate or foreign commerce

Whoever—

> **(1)** knowingly, in a transaction affecting interstate or foreign commerce, uses or attempts or conspires to use any counterfeit, fictitious, altered, forged, lost, stolen, or fraudulently obtained debit instrument to obtain money, goods, services, or anything else of value which within any one-year period has a value aggregating $1,000 or more; or
>
> **(2)** with unlawful or fraudulent intent, transports or attempts or conspires to transport in interstate or foreign commerce a counterfeit, fictitious, altered, forged, lost, stolen, or fraudulently obtained debit instrument knowing the same to be counterfeit, fictitious, altered, forged, lost, stolen, or fraudulently obtained; or
>
> **(3)** with unlawful or fraudulent intent, uses any instrumentality of interstate or foreign commerce to sell or transport a counterfeit, fictitious, altered, forged, lost, stolen, or fraudulently obtained debit instrument knowing the same to be counterfeit, fictitious, altered, forged, lost, stolen, or fraudulently obtained; or
>
> **(4)** knowingly receives, conceals, uses, or transports money, goods, services, or anything else of value (except tickets for interstate or foreign transportation) which (A) within any one-year period has a value aggregating $1,000 or more, (B) has moved in or is part of, or which constitutes interstate or foreign commerce, and (C) has been obtained with a counterfeit, fictitious, altered, forged, lost, stolen, or fraudulently obtained debit instrument; or
>
> **(5)** knowingly receives, conceals, uses, sells, or transports in interstate or foreign commerce one or more tickets for interstate or foreign transportation, which (A) within any one-year period have a value aggregating $500 or more, and (B) have been purchased or obtained with one or more counterfeit, fictitious, altered, forged, lost, stolen, or fraudulently obtained debit instrument; or
>
> **(6)** in a transaction affecting interstate or foreign commerce, furnishes money, property, services, or anything else of value, which within any one-year period has a value aggregating

$1,000 or more, through the use of any counterfeit, fictitious, altered, forged, lost, stolen, or fraudulently obtained debit instrument knowing the same to be counterfeit, fictitious, altered, forged, lost, stolen, or fraudulently obtained—

shall be fined not more than $10,000 or imprisoned not more than ten years, or both.

(c) "Debit instrument" defined

As used in this section, the term "debit instrument" means a card, code, or other device, other than a check, draft, or similar paper instrument, by the use of which a person may initiate an electronic fund transfer.

§ 1693o. Administrative enforcement

(a) Enforcing agencies

Compliance with the requirements imposed under this subchapter shall be enforced under—

(1) section 8 of the Federal Deposit Insurance Act [12 U.S.C.A. § 1818], in the case of—

(A) national banks, and Federal branches and Federal agencies of foreign banks, by the Office of the Comptroller of the Currency;

(B) member banks of the Federal Reserve System (other than national banks), branches and agencies of foreign banks (other than Federal branches, Federal agencies, and insured State branches of foreign banks), commercial lending companies owned or controlled by foreign banks, and organizations operating under section 25 or 25(a) of the Federal Reserve Act [12 U.S.C.A. § § 601 et seq., 611 et seq.], by the Board; and

(C) banks insured by the Federal Deposit Insurance Corporation (other than members of the Federal Reserve System) and insured State branches of foreign banks, by the Board of Directors of the Federal Deposit Insurance Corporation;

(2) section 8 of the Federal Deposit Insurance Act [12 U.S.C.A. § 1818], by the Director of the Office of Thrift Supervision, in the case of a savings association the deposits of which are insured by the Federal Deposit Insurance Corporation;

(3) the Federal Credit Union Act [12 U.S.C.A. § 1751 et seq.], by the Administrator of the National Credit Union Administration with respect to any Federal credit union.

(4) part A of subtitle VII of title 49, by the Secretary of Transportation, with respect to any air carrier or foreign air carrier subject to that part; and

(5) the Securities Exchange Act of 1934 [15 U.S.C.A. § 78a et seq.], by the Securities and Exchange Commission, with respect to any broker or dealer subject to that Act.

The terms used in paragraph (1) that are not defined in this subchapter or otherwise defined in section 3(s) of the Federal Deposit Insurance Act (12 U.S.C. 1813(s)) shall have the meaning given to them in section 1(b) of the International Banking Act of 1978 (12 U.S.C. 3101).

(b) Violations of subchapter deemed violations of pre-existing statutory requirements; additional powers

For the purpose of the exercise by any agency referred to in subsection (a) of this section of its powers under any Act referred to in that subsection, a violation of any requirement imposed under this subchapter shall be deemed to be a violation of a requirement imposed under that Act. In addition to its powers under any provision of law specifically referred to in subsection (a) of this section, each of the agencies referred to in that subsection may exercise, for the purpose of enforcing compliance with any requirement imposed under this subchapter, any other authority conferred on it by law.

(c) Overall enforcement authority of Federal Trade Commission

Except to the extent that enforcement of the requirements imposed under this subchapter is specifically committed to some other Government agency under subsection (a) of this section, the Federal Trade Commission shall enforce such requirements. For the purpose of the exercise by the Federal Trade Commission of its functions and powers under the Federal Trade Commission Act [15 U.S.C.A. § 41 et seq.], a violation of any requirement imposed under this subchapter shall be deemed a violation of a requirement imposed under that Act. All of the functions and powers of the Federal Trade Commission under the Federal Trade Commission Act are available to the Commission to enforce compliance by any person subject to the jurisdiction of the Commission with the requirements imposed under this subchapter, irrespective of whether that person is engaged in commerce or meets any other jurisdictional tests in the Federal Trade Commission Act.

§ 1693p. Reports to Congress

(a) Not later than twelve months after the effective date of this subchapter and at one-year intervals thereafter, the Board shall make reports to the Congress concerning the administration of its functions under this subchapter, including such recommendations as the Board deems necessary and appropriate. In addition, each report of the Board shall include its assessment of the extent to which compliance with this subchapter is being achieved, and a summary of the enforcement actions taken under section 1693o of this title. In such report, the Board shall particularly address the effects of this subchapter on the costs and benefits to financial institutions and consumers, on competition, on the introduction of new technology, on the operations of financial institutions, and on the adequacy of consumer protection.

(b) In the exercise of its functions under this subchapter, the Board may obtain upon request the views of any other Federal agency which, in the judgment of the Board, exercises regulatory or supervisory functions with respect to any class of persons subject to this subchapter.

§ 1693q. Relation to State laws

This subchapter does not annul, alter, or affect the laws of any State relating to electronic fund transfers, except to the extent that those laws are inconsistent with the provisions of this subchapter, and then only to the extent of the inconsistency. A State law is not inconsistent with this subchapter if the protection such law affords any consumer is greater than the protection afforded by this subchapter. The Board shall, upon its own motion or upon the request of any financial institution, State, or other interested party, submitted in accordance with procedures prescribed in regulations of the Board, determine whether a State requirement is inconsistent or affords greater protection. If the Board determines that a State requirement is inconsistent, financial institutions shall incur no liability under the law of that State for a good faith failure to comply with that law, notwithstanding that such determination is subsequently amended, rescinded, or determined by judicial or other authority to be invalid for any reason. This subchapter does not extend the applicability of any such law to any class of persons or transactions to which it would not otherwise apply.

§ 1693r. Exemption for State regulation

The Board shall by regulation exempt from the requirements of this subchapter any class of electronic fund transfers within any State if the Board determines that under the law of that State that class of electronic fund transfers is subject to requirements substantially similar to those imposed by this subchapter, and that there is adequate provision for enforcement.

California's SB1 (2004)

Cal. Fin. Code §§ 4050-4060, as amended

Statutes in Context

California's SB1 provides that, subject to some exceptions, a financial institution must request and receive a consumer's consent (an opt-in requirement) prior to providing "nonpublic personal information" about her to an unaffiliated third party. This requirement is more privacy-protective than the Gramm-Leach-Bliley (GLB) Act, which requires only that the customer be given a chance to opt out. California SB1 also requires, subject to some exceptions, that a financial institution provide a consumer a chance to opt out before her information is shared with an affiliated entity. This requirement is also more privacy-protective than the GLB Act.

§ 4050. Short title

This division shall be known and may be cited as the California Financial Information Privacy Act.

§ 4051. Legislative intent

(a) The Legislature intends for financial institutions to provide their consumers notice and meaningful choice about how consumers' nonpublic personal information is shared or sold by their financial institutions.

(b) It is the intent of the Legislature in enacting the California Financial Information Privacy Act to afford persons greater privacy protections than those provided in Public Law 106-102, the federal Gramm-Leach-Bliley Act, and that this division be interpreted to be consistent with that purpose.

§ 4051.5. Legislative findings and declarations

(a) The Legislature finds and declares all of the following:

(1) The California Constitution protects the privacy of California citizens from unwarranted intrusions into their private and personal lives.

(2) Federal banking legislation, known as the Gramm-Leach-Bliley Act, which breaks down restrictions on affiliation among different types of financial institutions, increases the likelihood that the personal financial information of California residents will be widely shared among, between, and within companies.

(3) The policies intended to protect financial privacy imposed by the Gramm-Leach-Bliley Act are inadequate to meet the privacy concerns of California residents.

(4) Because of the limitations of these federal policies, the Gramm-Leach-Bliley Act explicitly permits states to enact privacy protections that are stronger than those provided in federal law.

(b) It is the intent of the Legislature in enacting this division:

(1) To ensure that Californians have the ability to control the disclosure of what the Gramm-Leach-Bliley Act calls nonpublic personal information.

(2) To achieve that control for California consumers by requiring that financial institutions that want to share information with third parties and unrelated companies seek and acquire the affirmative consent of California consumers prior to sharing the information.

(3) To further achieve that control for California consumers by providing consumers with the ability to prevent the sharing of financial information among affiliated companies through a simple opt-out mechanism via a clear and understandable notice provided to the consumer.

(4) To provide, to the maximum extent possible, consistent with the purposes cited above, a level playing field among types and sizes of businesses consistent with the objective of providing consumers control over their nonpublic personal information, including providing that those financial institutions with limited affiliate relationships may enter into agreements with other financial institutions as provided in this division, and providing that the different business models of differing financial institutions are treated in ways that provide consistent consumer control over information-sharing practices.

(5) To adopt to the maximum extent feasible, consistent with the purposes cited above, definitions consistent with federal law, so that in particular there is no change in the ability of businesses to carry out normal processes of commerce for transactions voluntarily entered into by consumers.

§ 4052. Definitions

For the purposes of this division:

(a) "Nonpublic personal information" means personally identifiable financial information (1) provided by a consumer to a financial institution, (2) resulting from any transaction with the consumer or any service performed for the consumer, or (3) otherwise obtained by the financial institution. Nonpublic personal information does not include publicly available information that the financial institution has a reasonable basis to believe is lawfully made available to the general public from (1) federal, state, or local government records, (2) widely distributed media, or (3) disclosures to the general public that are required to be made by federal, state, or local law. Nonpublic personal information shall include any list, description, or other grouping of consumers, and publicly available information pertaining to them, that is derived using any nonpublic personal information other than publicly available information, but shall not include any list, description, or other grouping of consumers, and publicly available information pertaining to them, that is derived without using any nonpublic personal information.

(b) "Personally identifiable financial information" means information (1) that a consumer provides to a financial institution to obtain a product or service from the financial institution, (2) about a consumer resulting from any transaction involving a product or service between the financial institution and a consumer, or (3) that the financial institution otherwise obtains about a consumer in connection with providing a product or service to that consumer. Any personally identifiable information is financial if it was obtained by a financial institution in connection with providing a financial product or service to a consumer. Personally identifiable financial information includes all of the following:

(1) Information a consumer provides to a financial institution on an application to obtain a loan, credit card, or other financial product or service.

(2) Account balance information, payment history, overdraft history, and credit or debit card purchase information.

(3) The fact that an individual is or has been a consumer of a financial institution or has obtained a financial product or service from a financial institution.

(4) Any information about a financial institution's consumer if it is disclosed in a manner that indicates that the individual is or has been the financial institution's consumer.

(5) Any information that a consumer provides to a financial institution or that a financial institution or its agent otherwise obtains in connection with collecting on a loan or servicing a loan.

(6) Any personally identifiable financial information collected through an Internet cookie or an information collecting device from a Web server.

(7) Information from a consumer report.

(c) "Financial institution" means any institution the business of which is engaging in financial activities as described in Section 1843(k) of Title 12 of the United States Code and doing business in this state. An institution that is not significantly engaged in financial activities is not a financial institution. The term "financial institution" does not include any institution that is primarily engaged in providing hardware, software, or interactive services, provided that it does not act as a debt collector, as defined in 15 U.S.C. Sec. 1692a, or engage in activities for which the institution is required to acquire a charter, license, or registration from a state or federal governmental banking, insurance, or securities agency. The term "financial institution" does not include the Federal Agricultural Mortgage Corporation or any entity chartered and operating under the Farm Credit Act of 1971 (12 U.S.C. Sec. 2001 et seq.), provided that the entity does not sell or transfer nonpublic personal information to an affiliate or a nonaffiliated third party. The term "financial institution" does not include institutions chartered by Congress specifically to engage in a proposed or actual securitization, secondary market sale, including sales of servicing rights, or similar transactions related to a transaction of the consumer, as long as those institutions do not sell or transfer nonpublic personal information to a nonaffiliated third party. The term "financial institution" does not include any provider of professional services, or any wholly owned affiliate thereof, that is prohibited by rules of professional ethics and applicable law from voluntarily disclosing confidential client information without the consent of the client. The term "financial institution" does not include any person licensed as a dealer under Article 1 (commencing with Section 11700) of Chapter 4 of Division 5 of the Vehicle Code that enters into contracts for the installment sale or lease of motor vehicles pursuant to the requirements of Chapter 2B (commencing with Section 2981) or 2D (commencing with Section 2985.7) of Title 14 of Part 4 of Division 3 of the Civil Code and assigns substantially all of those contracts to financial institutions within 30 days.

(d) "Affiliate" means any entity that controls, is controlled by, or is under common control with, another entity, but does not include a joint employee of the entity and the affiliate. A franchisor, including any affiliate thereof, shall be deemed an affiliate of the franchisee for purposes of this division.

(e) "Nonaffiliated third party" means any entity that is not an affiliate of, or related by common ownership or affiliated by corporate control with, the financial institution, but does not include a joint employee of that institution and a third party.

(f) "Consumer" means an individual resident of this state, or that individual's legal representative, who obtains or has obtained from a financial institution a financial product or service to be used primarily for personal, family, or household purposes. For purposes of this division, an individual resident of this state is someone whose last known mailing address, other than an Armed Forces Post Office or Fleet Post Office address, as shown in the records of the financial institution, is located in this state. For purposes of this division, an individual is not a consumer of a financial institution solely because he or she is (1) a participant or beneficiary of an employee benefit plan that a financial institution administers or sponsors, or for which the financial institution acts as a trustee, insurer, or fiduciary, (2) covered under a group or blanket insurance policy or group annuity contract issued by the financial institution, (3) a beneficiary in a workers' compensation plan, (4) a beneficiary of a trust for which the financial institution is a trustee, or (5) a person who has designated the financial institution as trustee for a trust, provided that the financial institution provides all required notices and rights required by this division to the plan sponsor, group or blanket insurance policyholder, or group annuity contract holder.

(g) "Control" means (1) ownership or power to vote 25 percent or more of the outstanding shares of any class of voting security of a company, acting through one or more persons, (2) control in any manner over the election of a majority of the directors, or of individuals exercising similar functions, or (3) the power to exercise, directly or indirectly, a controlling influence over the management or policies of a company. However, for purposes of the application of the definition of control as it relates to credit unions, a credit union has a controlling influence over the management or policies of a credit union service organization (CUSO), as that term is defined by state or federal law or regulation, if the CUSO is at least 67 percent owned by credit unions. For purposes of the application of the definition of control to a financial institution subject to regulation by the United States Securities and Exchange Commission, a person who owns beneficially, either directly or through one or more controlled companies, more than 25 percent of the voting securities of a company is presumed to control the company, and a person who does not own more than 25 percent of the voting securities of a company is presumed not to control the company, and a presumption regarding control may be rebutted by evidence, but in the case of an investment company, the presumption shall continue until the United States Securities and Exchange Commission makes a decision to the contrary according to the procedures described in Section 2(a)(9) of the federal Investment Company Act of 1940.

(h) "Necessary to effect, administer, or enforce" means the following:

(1) The disclosure is required, or is a usual, appropriate, or acceptable method to carry out the transaction or the product or service business of which the transaction is a part, and record or service or maintain the consumer's account in the ordinary course of providing the financial service or financial product, or to administer or service benefits or claims relating to the transaction or the product or service business of which it is a part, and includes the following:

(A) Providing the consumer or the consumer's agent or broker with a confirmation, statement, or other record of the transaction, or information on the status or value of the financial service or financial product.

(B) The accrual or recognition of incentives, discounts, or bonuses associated with the transaction or communications to eligible existing consumers of the financial institution regarding the availability of those incentives, discounts, and bonuses that are provided by the financial institution or another party.

(C) In the case of a financial institution that has issued a credit account bearing the name of a company primarily engaged in retail sales or a name proprietary to a company primarily engaged in retail sales, the financial institution providing the retailer with nonpublic personal information as follows:

(i) Providing the retailer, or licensees or contractors of the retailer that provide products or services in the name of the retailer and under a contract with the retailer, with the names and addresses of the consumers in whose name the account is held and a record of the purchases made using the credit account from a business establishment, including a Web site or catalog, bearing the brand name of the retailer.

(ii) Where the credit account can only be used for transactions with the retailer or affiliates of that retailer that are also primarily engaged in retail sales, providing the retailer, or licensees or contractors of the retailer that provide products or services in the name of the retailer and under a contract with the retailer, with nonpublic personal information concerning the credit account, in connection with the offering or provision of the products or services of the retailer and those licensees or contractors.

(2) The disclosure is required or is one of the lawful or appropriate methods to enforce the rights of the financial institution or of other persons engaged in carrying out the financial transaction or providing the product or service.

(3) The disclosure is required, or is a usual, appropriate, or acceptable method for insurance underwriting or the placement of insurance products by licensed agents and brokers with authorized insurance companies at the consumer's request, for reinsurance, stop loss insurance, or excess loss insurance purposes, or for any of the following purposes as they relate to a consumer's insurance:

(A) Account administration.

(B) Reporting, investigating, or preventing fraud or material misrepresentation.

(C) Processing premium payments.

(D) Processing insurance claims.

(E) Administering insurance benefits, including utilization review activities.

(F) Participating in research projects.

(G) As otherwise required or specifically permitted by federal or state law.

(4) The disclosure is required, or is a usual, appropriate, or acceptable method, in connection with the following:

(A) The authorization, settlement, billing, processing, clearing, transferring, reconciling, or collection of amounts charged, debited, or otherwise paid using a debit, credit or other payment card, check, or account number, or by other payment means.

(B) The transfer of receivables, accounts, or interests therein.

(C) The audit of debit, credit, or other payment information.

(5) The disclosure is required in a transaction covered by the federal Real Estate Settlement Procedures Act (12 U.S.C. Sec. 2601 et seq.) in order to offer settlement services prior to the close of escrow (as those services are defined in 12 U.S.C. Sec. 2602), provided that (A) the nonpublic personal information is disclosed for the sole purpose of offering those settlement services and (B) the nonpublic personal information disclosed is limited to that necessary to enable the financial institution to offer those settlement services in that transaction.

(i) "Financial product or service" means any product or service that a financial holding company could offer by engaging in an activity that is financial in nature or incidental to a financial activity under subsection (k) of Section 1843 of Title 12 of the United States Code (the United States Bank Holding Company Act of 1956). Financial service includes a financial institution's evaluation or brokerage of information that the financial institution collects in connection with a request or an application from a consumer for a financial product or service.

(j) "Clear and conspicuous" means that a notice is reasonably understandable and designed to call attention to the nature and significance of the information contained in the notice.

(k) "Widely distributed media" means media available to the general public and includes a telephone book, a television or radio program, a newspaper, or a Web site that is available to the general public on an unrestricted basis.

§ 4052.5. Prohibition against disclosure of nonpublic personal information

Except as provided in Sections 4053, 4054.6, and 4056, a financial institution shall not sell, share, transfer, or otherwise disclose nonpublic personal information to or with any nonaffiliated third parties without the explicit prior consent of the consumer to whom the nonpublic personal information relates.

§ 4053. Consent requirement to disclose nonpublic personal information; requirements and regulation

(a)(1) A financial institution shall not disclose to, or share a consumer's nonpublic personal information with, any nonaffiliated third party as prohibited by Section 4052.5, unless the financial institution has obtained a consent acknowledgment from the consumer that complies with paragraph (2) that authorizes the financial institution to disclose or share the nonpublic personal information. Nothing in this section shall prohibit or otherwise apply to the disclosure of nonpublic personal information as allowed in Section 4056. A financial institution shall not discriminate against or deny an otherwise qualified consumer a financial product or a financial service because the consumer has not provided consent pursuant to this subdivision and Section 4052.5 to authorize the financial institution to disclose or share nonpublic personal information pertaining to him or her with any nonaffiliated third party. Nothing in this section shall prohibit a financial institution from denying a consumer a financial product or service if the financial institution could not provide the product or service to a consumer without the consent to disclose the consumer's nonpublic personal information required by this subdivision and Section 4052.5, and the consumer has failed to provide consent. A financial institution shall not be liable for failing to offer products and services to a consumer solely because that consumer has failed to provide consent pursuant to this subdivision and Section 4052.5 and the financial institution could not offer the product or service without the consent to disclose the consumer's nonpublic personal information required by this subdivision and Section 4052.5, and the consumer has failed to provide consent. Nothing in this section is intended to prohibit a financial institution from offering incentives or discounts to elicit a specific response to the notice.

(2) A financial institution shall utilize a form, statement, or writing to obtain consent to disclose nonpublic personal information to nonaffiliated third parties as required by Section 4052.5 and this subdivision. The form, statement, or writing shall meet all of the following criteria:

(A) The form, statement, or writing is a separate document, not attached to any other document.

(B) The form, statement, or writing is dated and signed by the consumer.

(C) The form, statement, or writing clearly and conspicuously discloses that by signing, the consumer is consenting to the disclosure to nonaffiliated third parties of nonpublic personal information pertaining to the consumer.

(D) The form, statement, or writing clearly and conspicuously discloses (i) that the consent will remain in effect until revoked or modified by the consumer; (ii) that the consumer may revoke the consent at any time; and (iii) the procedure for the consumer to revoke consent.

(E) The form, statement, or writing clearly and conspicuously informs the consumer that (i) the financial institution will maintain the document or a true and correct copy; (ii) the consumer is entitled to a copy of the document upon request; and (iii) the consumer may want to make a copy of the document for the consumer's records.

(b)(1) A financial institution shall not disclose to, or share a consumer's nonpublic personal information with, an affiliate unless the financial institution has clearly and conspicuously notified the consumer annually in writing pursuant to subdivision (d) that the nonpublic personal information may be disclosed to an affiliate of the financial institution and the consumer has not directed that the nonpublic personal information not be disclosed. A financial institution does not disclose information to, or share information with, its affiliate merely because information is maintained in common information systems or databases, and employees of the financial institution and its affiliate have access to those common information systems or databases, or a consumer accesses a Web site jointly operated or maintained under a common name by or on behalf of the financial institution and its affiliate, provided that where a consumer has exercised his or her right to prohibit disclosure pursuant to this division, nonpublic personal information is not further disclosed or used by an affiliate except as permitted by this division.

(2) Subdivision (a) shall not prohibit the release of nonpublic personal information by a financial institution with whom the consumer has a relationship to a nonaffiliated financial institution for purposes of jointly offering a financial product or financial service pursuant to a written agreement with the financial institution that receives the nonpublic personal information provided that all of the following requirements are met:

(A) The financial product or service offered is a product or service of, and is provided by, at least one of the financial institutions that is a party to the written agreement.

(B) The financial product or service is jointly offered, endorsed, or sponsored, and clearly and conspicuously identifies for the consumer the financial institutions that disclose and receive the disclosed nonpublic personal information.

(C) The written agreement provides that the financial institution that receives that nonpublic personal information is required to maintain the confidentiality of the information and is prohibited from disclosing or using the information other than to carry out the joint offering or servicing of a financial product or financial service that is the subject of the written agreement.

(D) The financial institution that releases the nonpublic personal information has complied with subdivision (d) and the consumer has not directed that the nonpublic personal information not be disclosed.

(E) Notwithstanding this section, until January 1, 2005, a financial institution may disclose nonpublic personal information to a nonaffiliated financial institution pursuant to a preexisting contract with the nonaffiliated financial institution, for purposes of offering a financial product or financial service, if that contract was entered into on or before January 1, 2004. Beginning on January 1, 2005, no nonpublic personal information may be disclosed pursuant to that contract unless all the requirements of this subdivision are met.

(3) Nothing in this subdivision shall prohibit a financial institution from disclosing or sharing nonpublic personal information as otherwise specifically permitted by this division.

(4) A financial institution shall not discriminate against or deny an otherwise qualified consumer a financial product or a financial service because the consumer has directed pursuant to this subdivision that nonpublic personal information pertaining to him or her not be disclosed. A financial institution shall not be required to offer or provide products or services offered through affiliated entities or jointly with nonaffiliated financial institutions pursuant to paragraph (2) where the consumer has directed that nonpublic personal information not be disclosed pursuant to this subdivision and the financial institution could not offer or provide the products or services to the consumer without disclosure of the consumer's nonpublic personal information that the consumer has directed not be disclosed pursuant to this subdivision. A financial institution shall not be liable for failing to offer or provide products or services offered through affiliated entities or jointly with nonaffiliated financial institutions pursuant to paragraph (2) solely because the consumer has directed that nonpublic personal information not be disclosed pursuant to this subdivision and the financial institution could not offer or provide the products or services to the consumer without disclosure of the consumer's nonpublic personal information that the consumer has directed not be disclosed to affiliates pursuant to this subdivision. Nothing in this section is intended to prohibit a financial institution from offering incentives or discounts to elicit a specific response to the notice set forth in this division. Nothing in this section shall prohibit the disclosure of nonpublic personal information allowed by Section 4056.

(5) The financial institution may, at its option, choose instead to comply with the requirements of subdivision (a).

(c) Nothing in this division shall restrict or prohibit the sharing of nonpublic personal information between a financial institution and its wholly owned financial institution subsidiaries; among financial institutions that are each wholly owned by the same financial institution; among financial institutions that are wholly owned by the same holding company; or among the insurance and management entities of a single insurance holding company system consisting of one or more reciprocal insurance exchanges which has a single corporation or its wholly owned subsidiaries providing management services to the reciprocal insurance exchanges, provided that in each case all of the following requirements are met:

(1) The financial institution disclosing the nonpublic personal information and the financial institution receiving it are regulated by the same functional regulator; provided, however, that for purposes of this subdivision, financial institutions regulated by the Office of the Comptroller of the Currency, Office of Thrift Supervision, National Credit Union Administration, or a state regulator of depository institutions shall be deemed to be regulated by the same functional regulator; financial institutions regulated by the Securities and Exchange Commission, the United States Department of Labor, or a state securities regulator shall be deemed to be regulated by the same functional regulator; and insurers admitted in this state to transact insurance and licensed to write insurance policies shall be deemed to be in compliance with this paragraph.

(2) The financial institution disclosing the nonpublic personal information and the financial institution receiving it are both principally engaged in the same line of business. For purposes of this subdivision, "same line of business" shall be one and only one of the following:

(A) Insurance.

(B) Banking.

(C) Securities.

(3) The financial institution disclosing the nonpublic personal information and the financial institution receiving it share a common brand, excluding a brand consisting solely of a graphic element or symbol, within their trademark, service mark, or trade name, which is used to identify the source of the products and services provided.

A wholly owned subsidiary shall include a subsidiary wholly owned directly or wholly owned indirectly in a chain of wholly owned subsidiaries.

Nothing in this subdivision shall permit the disclosure by a financial institution of medical record information, as defined in subdivision (q) of Section 791.02 of the Insurance Code, except in compliance with the requirements of this division, including the requirements set forth in subdivisions (a) and (b).

(d)(1) A financial institution shall be conclusively presumed to have satisfied the notice requirements of subdivision (b) if it uses the form set forth in this subdivision. The form set forth in this subdivision or a form that complies with subparagraphs (A) to (L), inclusive, of this paragraph shall be sent by the financial institution to the consumer so that the consumer may make a decision and provide direction to the financial institution regarding the sharing of his or her nonpublic personal information. If a financial institution does not use the form set forth in this subdivision, the financial institution shall use a form that meets all of the following requirements:

(A) The form uses the same title ("IMPORTANT PRIVACY CHOICES FOR CONSUMERS") and the headers, if applicable, as follows: "Restrict Information Sharing With Companies We Own Or Control (Affiliates)" and "Restrict Information Sharing With Other Companies We Do Business With To Provide Financial Products And Services."

(B) The titles and headers in the form are clearly and conspicuously displayed, and no text in the form is smaller than 10-point type.

(C) The form is a separate document, except as provided by subparagraph (D) of paragraph (2), and Sections 4054 and 4058.7.

(D) The choice or choices pursuant to subdivision (b) and Section 4054.6, if applicable, provided in the form are stated separately and may be selected by checking a box.

(E) The form is designed to call attention to the nature and significance of the information in the document.

(F) The form presents information in clear and concise sentences, paragraphs, and sections.

(G) The form uses short explanatory sentences (an average of 15-20 words) or bullet lists whenever possible.

(H) The form avoids multiple negatives, legal terminology, and highly technical terminology whenever possible.

(I) The form avoids explanations that are imprecise and readily subject to different interpretations.

(J) The form achieves a minimum Flesch reading ease score of 50, as defined in Section 2689.4(a)(7) of Title 10 of the California Code of Regulations, in effect on March 24, 2003, except that the information in the form included to comply with subparagraph (A) shall not be included in the calculation of the Flesch reading ease score, and the information used to describe the choice or choices pursuant to subparagraph (D) shall score no lower than the information describing the comparable choice or choices set forth in the form in this subdivision.

(K) The form provides wide margins, ample line spacing and uses boldface or italics for key words.

(L) The form is not more than one page.

(2)(A) None of the instructional items appearing in brackets in the form set forth in this subdivision shall appear in the form provided to the consumer, as those items are for explanation purposes only. If a financial institution does not disclose or share nonpublic personal information as described in a header of the form, the financial institution may omit the applicable header or headers, and the accompanying information and box, in the form it provides pursuant to this subdivision. The form with those omissions shall be conclusively presumed to satisfy the notice requirements of this subdivision.

Important Privacy Choices for Consumers

You have the right to control whether we share some of your personal information. Please read the following information carefully before you make your choices below.

Your Rights
You have the following rights to restrict the sharing of personal and financial information with our affiliates (companies we own or control) and outside companies that we do business with. Nothing in this form prohibits the sharing of information necessary for us to follow the law, as permitted by law, or to give you the best service on your accounts with us. This includes sending you information about some other products or services.

Your Choices
Restrict Information Sharing With Companies We Own or Control (Affiliates):
Unless you say "No," we may share personal and financial information about you with our affiliated companies.
(_) NO, please do not share personal and financial information with your affiliated companies.

Restrict Information Sharing With Other Companies We Do Business With To Provide Financial Products And Services:
Unless you say "No," we may share personal and financial information about you with outside companies we contract with to provide financial products and services to you.
(_) NO, please do not share personal and financial information with outside companies you contract with to provide financial products and services

. . . .

Time Sensitive Reply
You may make your privacy choice(s) at any time. Your choice(s) marked here will remain unless you state otherwise.
However, if we do not hear from you we may share some of your information with affiliated companies and other companies with whom we have contracts to provide products and services.
Name:
Account or Policy Number(s): [to be filled in by consumer]
Signature:
To exercise your choices do [one of] the following:
(1) Fill out, sign and send back this form to us using the envelope provided (you may want to make a copy for
your records); [#1 is mandatory]
[(2) Call this toll-free number (800) xxx-xxxx or (xxx) xxx-xxxx; [optional]
[(3) Reply electronically by contacting us through the following Internet option: xxxxx.com] [optional]

(B) If a financial institution uses a form other than that set forth in this subdivision, the financial institution may submit that form to its functional regulator for approval, and for forms filed with the Office of Privacy Protection prior to July 1, 2007, that approval shall constitute a rebuttable presumption that the form complies with this section.

(C) A financial institution shall not be in violation of this subdivision solely because it includes in the form one or more brief examples or explanations of the purpose or purposes, or context, within which information will be shared, as long as those examples meet the clarity and readability standards set forth in paragraph (1).

(D) The outside of the envelope in which the form is sent to the consumer shall clearly state in 16-point boldface type "IMPORTANT PRIVACY CHOICES," except that a financial institution sending the form to a consumer in the same envelope as a bill, account statement, or application requested by the consumer does not have to include the wording "IMPORTANT PRIVACY CHOICES" on that envelope. The form shall be sent in any of the following ways:

(i) With a bill, other statement of account, or application requested by the consumer, in which case the information required by Title V of the Gramm-Leach-Bliley Act may also be included in the same envelope.

(ii) As a separate notice or with the information required by Title V of the Gramm-Leach-Bliley Act, and including only information related to privacy.

(iii) With any other mailing, in which case it shall be the first page of the mailing.

(E) If a financial institution uses a form other than that set forth in this subdivision, that form shall be filed with the Office of Privacy Protection within 30 days after it is first used.

(3) The consumer shall be provided a reasonable opportunity prior to disclosure of nonpublic personal information to direct that nonpublic personal information not be disclosed. A consumer may direct at any time that his or her nonpublic personal information not be disclosed. A financial institution shall comply with a consumer's directions concerning the sharing of his or her nonpublic personal information within 45 days of receipt by the financial institution. When a consumer directs that nonpublic personal information not be disclosed, that direction is in effect until otherwise stated by the consumer. A financial institution that has not provided a consumer with annual notice pursuant to subdivision (b) shall provide the consumer with a form that meets the requirements of this subdivision, and shall allow 45 days to lapse from the date of providing the form in person or the postmark or other postal verification of mailing before disclosing nonpublic personal information pertaining to the consumer.

Nothing in this subdivision shall prohibit the disclosure of nonpublic personal information as allowed by subdivision (c) or Section 4056.

(4) A financial institution may elect to comply with the requirements of subdivision (a) with respect to disclosure of nonpublic personal information to an affiliate or with respect to nonpublic personal information disclosed pursuant to paragraph (2) of subdivision (b), or subdivision (c) of Section 4054.6.

(5) If a financial institution does not have a continuing relationship with a consumer other than the initial transaction in which the product or service is provided, no annual disclosure requirement exists pursuant to this section as long as the financial institution provides the consumer with the form required by this section at the time of the initial transaction. As used in this section, "annually" means at least once in any period of 12 consecutive months during which that relationship exists. The financial institution may define the 12-consecutive-month period, but shall apply it to the consumer on a consistent basis. If, for example, a financial institution defines the 12- consecutive-month period as a calendar year and provides the annual notice to the consumer once in each calendar year, it complies with the requirement to send the notice annually.

(6) A financial institution with assets in excess of twenty-five million dollars ($25,000,000) shall include a self-addressed first class business reply return envelope with the notice. A financial institution with assets of up to and including twenty-five million dollars ($25,000,000) shall include a self-addressed return envelope with the notice. In lieu of the first class business reply return envelope required by this paragraph, a financial institution may offer a self-addressed return envelope with the notice and at least two alternative cost-free means for consumers to communicate their privacy choices, such as calling a toll-free number, sending a facsimile to a toll-free telephone number, or using electronic means. A financial institution shall clearly and conspicuously disclose in the form required by this subdivision the information necessary to direct the consumer on how to communicate his or her choices, including the toll-free or facsimile number or Web site address that may be used, if those means of communication are offered by the financial institution.

(7) A financial institution may provide a joint notice from it and one or more of its affiliates or other financial institutions, as identified in the notice, so long as the notice is accurate with respect to the financial institution and the affiliates and other financial institutions.

(e) Nothing in this division shall prohibit a financial institution from marketing its own products and services or the products and services of affiliates or nonaffiliated third parties to customers of the financial institution as long as (1) nonpublic personal information is not disclosed in connection with the delivery of the applicable marketing materials to those customers except as permitted by Section 4056 and (2) in cases in which the applicable nonaffiliated third party may extrapolate nonpublic personal information about the consumer responding to those marketing materials, the applicable nonaffiliated third party has signed a contract with the financial institution under the terms of which (A) the nonaffiliated third party is prohibited from using that information for any purpose other than the purpose for which it was provided, as set forth in the contract, and (B) the financial institution has the right by audit, inspections, or other means to verify the nonaffiliated third party's compliance with that contract.

§ 4053.5. Disclosure of nonpublic personal information by entity that receives information; permitted uses

Except as otherwise provided in this division, an entity that receives nonpublic personal information from a financial institution under this division shall not disclose this information to any other entity, unless the disclosure would be lawful if made directly to the other entity by the financial institution. An entity that receives nonpublic personal information pursuant to any exception set forth in Section 4056 shall not use or disclose the information except in the ordinary course of business to carry out the activity covered by the exception under which the information was received.

§ 4054. Required electronic or written notice to consumers

(a) Nothing in this division shall require a financial institution to provide a written notice to a consumer pursuant to Section 4053 if the financial institution does not disclose nonpublic personal information to any nonaffiliated third party or to any affiliate, except as allowed in this division.

(b) A notice provided to a member of a household pursuant to Section 4053 shall be considered notice to all members of that household unless that household contains another individual who also has a separate account with the financial institution.

(c)(1) The requirement to send a written notice to a consumer may be fulfilled by electronic means if the following requirements are met:

(A) The notice, and the manner in which it is sent, meets all of the requirements for notices that are required by law to be in writing, as set forth in Section 101 of the federal Electronic Signatures in Global and National Commerce Act.

(B) All other requirements applicable to the notice, as set forth in this division, are met, including, but not limited to, requirements concerning content, timing, form, and delivery. An electronic notice sent pursuant to this section is not required to include a return envelope.

(C) The notice is delivered to the consumer in a form the consumer may keep.

(2) A notice that is made available to a consumer, and is not delivered to the consumer, does not satisfy the requirements of paragraph (1).

(3) Any electronic consumer reply to an electronic notice sent pursuant to this division is effective. A person that electronically sends a notice required by this division to a consumer may not by contract, or otherwise, eliminate the effectiveness of the consumer's electronic reply.

(4) This division modifies the provisions of Section 101 of the federal Electronic Signatures in Global and National Commerce Act. However, it does not modify, limit, or supersede the provisions of subsection (c), (d), (e), (f), or (h) of Section 101 of the federal Electronic Signatures in Global and National Commerce Act, nor does it authorize electronic delivery of any notice of the type described in subsection (b) of Section 103 of that federal act.

§ 4054.6. Agreements between financial institutions and affinity partners to issue credit cards or financial products or services; disclosure of information; requirements

(a) When a financial institution and an organization or business entity that is not a financial institution ("affinity partner") have an agreement to issue a credit card in the name of the affinity partner ("affinity card"), the financial institution shall be permitted to disclose to the affinity partner in whose name the card is issued only the following information pertaining to the financial institution's customers who are in receipt of the affinity card: (1) name, address, telephone number, and electronic mail address and (2) record of purchases made using the affinity card in a business establishment, including a Web site, bearing the brand name of the affinity partner.

(b) When a financial institution and an affinity partner have an agreement to issue a financial product or service, other than a credit card, on behalf of the affinity partner ("affinity financial product or service"), the financial institution shall be permitted to disclose to the affinity partner only the following information pertaining to the financial institution's customers who obtained the affinity financial product or service: name, address, telephone number, and electronic mail address.

(c) The disclosures specified in subdivisions (a) and (b) shall be permitted only if the following requirements are met:

(1) The financial institution has provided the consumer a notice meeting the requirements of subdivision (d) of Section 4053, and the consumer has not directed that nonpublic personal information not be disclosed. A response to a notice meeting the requirements of subdivision (d) directing the financial institution to not disclose nonpublic personal information to a nonaffiliated financial institution shall be deemed a direction to the financial institution to not disclose nonpublic personal information to an affinity partner, unless the form containing the notice provides the consumer with a separate choice for disclosure to affinity partners.

(2) The financial institution has a contractual agreement with the affinity partner that requires the affinity partner to maintain the confidentiality of the nonpublic personal information and prohibits affinity partners from using the information for any purposes other than verifying membership, verifying the consumer's contact information, or offering the affinity partner's own products or services to the consumer.

(3) The customer list is not disclosed in any way that reveals or permits extrapolation of any additional nonpublic personal information about any customer on the list.

(4) If the affinity partner sends any message to any electronic mail addresses obtained pursuant to this section, the message shall include at least both of the following:

(A) The identity of the sender of the message.

(B) A cost-free means for the recipient to notify the sender not to electronically mail any further message to the recipient.

(d) Nothing in this section shall prohibit the disclosure of nonpublic personal information pursuant to Section 4056.

(e) This section does not apply to credit cards issued in the name of an entity primarily engaged in retail sales or a name proprietary to a company primarily engaged in retail sales.

§ 4056. Application of division; conditions for release of nonpublic personal information by financial institutions

(a) This division shall not apply to information that is not personally identifiable to a particular person.

(b) Notwithstanding Sections 4052.5, 4053, 4054, and 4054.6, a financial institution may release nonpublic personal information under the following circumstances:

(1) The nonpublic personal information is necessary to effect, administer, or enforce a transaction requested or authorized by the consumer, or in connection with servicing or processing a financial product or service requested or authorized by the consumer, or in connection with maintaining or servicing the consumer's account with the financial institution, or with another entity as part of a private label credit card program or other extension of credit on behalf of that entity, or in connection with a proposed or actual securitization or secondary market sale, including sales of servicing rights, or similar transactions related to a transaction of the consumer.

(2) The nonpublic personal information is released with the consent of or at the direction of the consumer.

(3) The nonpublic personal information is:

(A) Released to protect the confidentiality or security of the financial institution's records pertaining to the consumer, the service or product, or the transaction therein.

(B) Released to protect against or prevent actual or potential fraud, identity theft, unauthorized transactions, claims, or other liability.

(C) Released for required institutional risk control, or for resolving customer disputes or inquiries.

(D) Released to persons holding a legal or beneficial interest relating to the consumer, including for purposes of debt collection.

(E) Released to persons acting in a fiduciary or representative capacity on behalf of the consumer.

(4) The nonpublic personal information is released to provide information to insurance rate advisory organizations, guaranty funds or agencies, applicable rating agencies of the financial institution, persons assessing the institution's compliance with industry standards, and the institution's attorneys, accountants, and auditors.

(5) The nonpublic personal information is released to the extent specifically required or specifically permitted under other provisions of law and in accordance with the Right to Financial Privacy Act of 1978 (12 U.S.C. Sec. 3401 et seq.), to law enforcement agencies, including a federal functional regulator, the Secretary of the Treasury with respect to subchapter II of Chapter 53 of Title 31, and Chapter 2 of Title I of Public Law 91-508 (12 U.S.C. Secs. 1951-1959), the California Department of Insurance or other state insurance regulators, or the Federal Trade Commission, and self-regulatory organizations, or for an investigation on a matter related to public safety.

(6) The nonpublic personal information is released in connection with a proposed or actual sale, merger, transfer, or exchange of all or a portion of a business or operating unit if the disclosure of nonpublic personal information concerns solely consumers of the business or unit.

(7) The nonpublic personal information is released to comply with federal, state, or local laws, rules, and other applicable legal requirements; to comply with a properly authorized civil, criminal, administrative, or regulatory investigation or subpoena or summons by federal, state, or local authorities; or to respond to judicial process or government regulatory authorities having jurisdiction over the financial institution for examination, compliance, or other purposes as authorized by law.

(8) When a financial institution is reporting a known or suspected instance of elder or dependent adult financial abuse or is cooperating with a local adult protective services agency investigation of known or suspected elder or dependent adult financial abuse pursuant to Article 3 (commencing with Section 15630) of Chapter 11 of Part 3 of Division 9 of the Welfare and Institutions Code.

(9) The nonpublic personal information is released to an affiliate or a nonaffiliated third party in order for the affiliate or nonaffiliated third party to perform business or professional services, such as printing, mailing services, data processing or analysis, or customer surveys, on behalf of the financial institution, provided that all of the following requirements are met:

(A) The services to be performed by the affiliate or nonaffiliated third party could lawfully be performed by the financial institution.

(B) There is a written contract between the affiliate or nonaffiliated third party and the financial institution that prohibits the affiliate or nonaffiliated third party, as the case may be, from disclosing or using the nonpublic personal information other than to carry out the purpose for which the financial institution disclosed the information, as set forth in the written contract.

(C) The nonpublic personal information provided to the affiliate or nonaffiliated third party is limited to that which is necessary for the affiliate or nonaffiliated third party to perform the services contracted for on behalf of the financial institution.

(D) The financial institution does not receive any payment from or through the affiliate or nonaffiliated third party in connection with, or as a result of, the release of the nonpublic personal information.

(10) The nonpublic personal information is released to identify or locate missing and abducted children, witnesses, criminals and fugitives, parties to lawsuits, parents delinquent in child support payments, organ and bone marrow donors, pension fund beneficiaries, and missing heirs.

(11) The nonpublic personal information is released to a real estate appraiser licensed or certified by the state for submission to central data repositories such as the California Market Data Cooperative, and the nonpublic personal information is compiled strictly to complete other real estate appraisals and is not used for any other purpose.

(12) The nonpublic personal information is released as required by Title III of the federal United and Strengthening America by Providing Appropriate Tools Required to Intercept and Obstruct Terrorism Act of 2001 (USA Patriot Act; P.L. 107-56).

(13) The nonpublic personal information is released either to a consumer reporting agency pursuant to the Fair Credit Reporting Act (15 U.S.C. Sec. 1681 et seq.) or from a consumer report reported by a consumer reporting agency.

(14) The nonpublic personal information is released in connection with a written agreement between a consumer and a broker-dealer registered under the Securities Exchange Act of 1934 or an investment adviser registered under the Investment Advisers Act of 1940 to provide investment management services, portfolio advisory services, or financial planning, and the nonpublic personal information is released for the sole purpose of providing the products and services covered by that agreement.

(c) Nothing in this division is intended to change existing law relating to access by law enforcement agencies to information held by financial institutions.

§ 4056.5. Persons or entities with license and/or written contractual agreement with another licensed person or entity; disclosure of information; contents of contract

(a) The provisions of this division do not apply to any person or entity that meets the requirements of paragraph (1) or (2) below. However, when nonpublic personal information is being or will be shared by a person or entity meeting the requirements of paragraph (1) or (2) with an affiliate or nonaffiliated third party, this division shall apply.

(1) The person or entity is licensed in one or both of the following categories and is acting within the scope of the respective license or certificate:

(A) As an insurance producer, licensed pursuant to Chapter 5 (commencing with Section 1621), Chapter 6 (commencing with Section 1760), or Chapter 8 (commencing with Section 1831) of Division 1 of the Insurance Code, as a registered investment adviser pursuant to Chapter 3 (commencing with Section 25230) of Part 3 of Division 1 of Title 4 of the Corporations Code, or as an investment adviser pursuant to Section 202(a)(11) of the federal Investment Advisers Act of 1940.

(B) Is licensed to sell securities by the National Association of Securities Dealers (NASD).

(2) The person or entity meets the requirements in paragraph (1) and has a written contractual agreement with another person or entity described in paragraph (1) and the contract clearly and explicitly includes the following:

(A) The rights and obligations between the licensees arising out of the business relationship relating to insurance or securities transactions.

(B) An explicit limitation on the use of nonpublic personal information about a consumer to transactions authorized by the contract and permitted pursuant to this division.

(C) A requirement that transactions specified in the contract fall within the scope of activities permitted by the licenses of the parties.

(b) The restrictions on disclosure and use of nonpublic personal information, and the requirement for notification and disclosure provided in this division, shall not limit the ability of insurance producers and brokers to respond to written or electronic, including telephone, requests from consumers seeking price quotes on insurance products and services or to obtain competitive quotes to renew an existing insurance contract, provided that any nonpublic personal information disclosed pursuant to this subdivision shall not be used or disclosed except in the ordinary course of business in order to obtain those quotes.

(c)(1) The disclosure or sharing of nonpublic personal information from an insurer, as defined in Section 23 of the Insurance Code, or its affiliates to an exclusive agent, defined for purposes of this division as a licensed agent or broker pursuant to Chapter 5 (commencing with Section 1621) of Part 2 of Division 1 of the Insurance Code whose contractual or employment relationship requires that the agent offer only the insurer's policies for sale or financial products or services that meet the requirements of paragraph (2) of subdivision (b) of Section 4053 and are authorized by the insurer, or whose contractual or employment relationship with an insurer gives the insurer the right of first refusal for all policies of insurance by the agent, and who may not share nonpublic personal information with any insurer other than the insurer with whom the agent has a contractual or employment relationship as described above, is not a violation of this division, provided that the agent may not disclose nonpublic personal information to any party except as permitted by this division. An insurer or its affiliates do not disclose or share nonpublic personal information with exclusive agents merely because information is maintained in common information systems or databases, and exclusive agents of the insurer or its affiliates have access to those common information systems or databases, provided that where a consumer has exercised his or her rights to prohibit disclosure pursuant to this division, nonpublic personal information is not further disclosed or used by an exclusive agent except as permitted by this division.

(2) Nothing in this subdivision is intended to affect the sharing of information allowed in subdivision (a) or subdivision (b).

§ 4057. Liability for negligent disclosure of nonpublic personal information; civil penalty and damages; factors to determine amount of penalty

(a) An entity that negligently discloses or shares nonpublic personal information in violation of this division shall be liable, irrespective of the amount of damages suffered by the consumer as a result of that violation, for a civil penalty not to exceed two thousand five hundred dollars ($2,500) per violation. However, if the disclosure or sharing results in the release of nonpublic personal information of more than one individual, the total civil penalty awarded pursuant to this subdivision shall not exceed five hundred thousand dollars ($500,000).

(b) An entity that knowingly and willfully obtains, discloses, shares, or uses nonpublic personal information in violation of this division shall be liable for a civil penalty not to exceed two thousand five hundred dollars ($2,500) per individual violation, irrespective of the amount of damages suffered by the consumer as a result of that violation.

(c) In determining the penalty to be assessed pursuant to a violation of this division, the court shall take into account the following factors:

(1) The total assets and net worth of the violating entity.

(2) The nature and seriousness of the violation.

(3) The persistence of the violation, including any attempts to correct the situation leading to the violation.

(4) The length of time over which the violation occurred.

(5) The number of times the entity has violated this division.

(6) The harm caused to consumers by the violation.

(7) The level of proceeds derived from the violation.

(8) The impact of possible penalties on the overall fiscal solvency of the violating entity.

(d) In the event a violation of this division results in the identity theft of a consumer, as defined by Section 530.5 of the Penal Code, the civil penalties set forth in this section shall be doubled.

(e) The civil penalties provided for in this section shall be exclusively assessed and recovered in a civil action brought in the name of the people of the State of California in any court of competent jurisdiction by any of the following:

(1) The Attorney General.

(2) The functional regulator with jurisdiction over regulation of the financial institution as follows:

(A) In the case of banks, savings associations, credit unions, commercial lending companies, and bank holding companies, by the Department of Financial Institutions or the appropriate federal authority; (B) in the case of any person engaged in the business of insurance, by the Department of Insurance; (C) in the case of any investment broker or dealer, investment company, investment advisor, residential mortgage lender or finance lender, by the Department of Corporations; and (D) in the case of a financial institution not subject to the jurisdiction of any functional regulator listed under subparagraphs (A) to (C), inclusive, above, by the Attorney General.

§ 4058. Authority of department or state agency to regulate financial institutions

Nothing in this division shall be construed as altering or annulling the authority of any department or agency of the state to regulate any financial institution subject to its jurisdiction.

§ 4058.5. Preemption; prospective and retroactive application

This division shall preempt and be exclusive of all local agency ordinances and regulations relating to the use and sharing of nonpublic personal information by financial institutions. This section shall apply both prospectively and retroactively.

§ 4058.7. Combining forms

Nothing in this division shall prevent an insurer, as defined in Section 23 of the Insurance Code, from combining the form required by subdivision (d) of Section 4053 with the form required pursuant to Article 6. 6 (commencing with Section 791) of Chapter 1 of Part 2 of Division 1 of the Insurance Code and state regulations implementing the provisions of that article, provided that the combined form meets the requirements contained in paragraph (1) of subdivision (d) of Section 4053.

§ 4059. Severable provisions

The provisions of this division shall be severable, and if any phrase, clause, sentence, or provision is declared to be invalid or is preempted by federal law or regulation, the validity of the remainder of this division shall not be affected thereby.

§ 4060. Operation of division

This division shall become operative on July 1, 2004.

VII.
BUSINESS RECORDS

Cable Communications Policy Act (1984)

47 U.S.C. §§ 521, 551, 552, as amended

Statutes in Context

The Cable Communications Policy Act (CCPA) regulates cable companies. The excerpts below concern its rules for protection of subscriber privacy. These include requirements providing for written notice to subscribers of the personal information collected. The Act also limits the collection of such information without the prior consent of the cable subscriber.

---

§ 521. Purposes

The purposes of this subchapter are to—

(1) establish a national policy concerning cable communications;

(2) establish franchise procedures and standards which encourage the growth and development of cable systems and which assure that cable systems are responsive to the needs and interests of the local community;

(3) establish guidelines for the exercise of Federal, State, and local authority with respect to the regulation of cable systems;

(4) assure that cable communications provide and are encouraged to provide the widest possible diversity of information sources and services to the public;

(5) establish an orderly process for franchise renewal which protects cable operators against unfair denials of renewal where the operator's past performance and proposal for future performance meet the standards established by this subchapter; and

(6) promote competition in cable communications and minimize unnecessary regulation that would impose an undue economic burden on cable systems.

§ 551. Protection of subscriber privacy

(a) Notice to subscriber regarding personally identifiable information; definitions

(1) At the time of entering into an agreement to provide any cable service or other service to a subscriber and at least once a year thereafter, a cable operator shall provide notice in the form of a separate, written statement to such subscriber which clearly and conspicuously informs the subscriber of—

(A) the nature of personally identifiable information collected or to be collected with respect to the subscriber and the nature of the use of such information;

(B) the nature, frequency, and purpose of any disclosure which may be made of such information, including an identification of the types of persons to whom the disclosure may be made;

(C) the period during which such information will be maintained by the cable operator;

(D) the times and place at which the subscriber may have access to such information in accordance with subsection (d) of this section; and

(E) the limitations provided by this section with respect to the collection and disclosure of information by a cable operator and the right of the subscriber under subsections (f) and (h) of this section to enforce such limitations.

In the case of subscribers who have entered into such an agreement before the effective date of this section, such notice shall be provided within 180 days of such date and at least once a year thereafter.

(2) For purposes of this section, other than subsection (h) of this section—

(A) the term "personally identifiable information" does not include any record of aggregate data which does not identify particular persons;

(B) the term "other service" includes any wire or radio communications service provided using any of the facilities of a cable operator that are used in the provision of cable service; and

(C) the term "cable operator" includes, in addition to persons within the definition of cable operator in section 522 of this title, any person who (i) is owned or controlled by, or under common ownership or control with, a cable operator, and (ii) provides any wire or radio communications service.

(b) Collection of personally identifiable information using cable system

(1) Except as provided in paragraph (2), a cable operator shall not use the cable system to collect personally identifiable information concerning any subscriber without the prior written or electronic consent of the subscriber concerned.

(2) A cable operator may use the cable system to collect such information in order to—

(A) obtain information necessary to render a cable service or other service provided by the cable operator to the subscriber; or

(B) detect unauthorized reception of cable communications.

(c) Disclosure of personally identifiable information

(1) Except as provided in paragraph (2), a cable operator shall not disclose personally identifiable information concerning any subscriber without the prior written or electronic consent of the subscriber concerned and shall take such actions as are necessary to prevent unauthorized access to such information by a person other than the subscriber or cable operator.

(2) A cable operator may disclose such information if the disclosure is—

(A) necessary to render, or conduct a legitimate business activity related to, a cable service or other service provided by the cable operator to the subscriber;

(B) subject to subsection (h) of this section, made pursuant to a court order authorizing such disclosure, if the subscriber is notified of such order by the person to whom the order is directed;

(C) a disclosure of the names and addresses of subscribers to any cable service or other service, if—

(i) the cable operator has provided the subscriber the opportunity to prohibit or limit such disclosure, and

(ii) the disclosure does not reveal, directly or indirectly, the—

(I) extent of any viewing or other use by the subscriber of a cable service or other service provided by the cable operator, or

(II) the nature of any transaction made by the subscriber over the cable system of the cable operator; or

(D) to a government entity as authorized under chapters 119, 121, or 206 of Title 18, except that such disclosure shall not include records revealing cable subscriber selection of video programming from a cable operator.

(d) Subscriber access to information

A cable subscriber shall be provided access to all personally identifiable information regarding that subscriber which is collected and maintained by a cable operator. Such information shall be made available to the subscriber at reasonable times and at a convenient place designated by such cable operator. A cable subscriber shall be provided reasonable opportunity to correct any error in such information.

(e) Destruction of information

A cable operator shall destroy personally identifiable information if the information is no longer necessary for the purpose for which it was collected and there are no pending requests or orders for access to such information under subsection (d) of this section or pursuant to a court order.

(f) Civil action in United States district court; damages; attorney's fees and costs; nonexclusive nature of remedy

(1) Any person aggrieved by any act of a cable operator in violation of this section may bring a civil action in a United States district court.

(2) The court may award—

(A) actual damages but not less than liquidated damages computed at the rate of $100 a day for each day of violation or $1,000, whichever is higher;

(B) punitive damages; and

(C) reasonable attorneys' fees and other litigation costs reasonably incurred.

(3) The remedy provided by this section shall be in addition to any other lawful remedy available to a cable subscriber.

(g) Regulation by States or franchising authorities

Nothing in this subchapter shall be construed to prohibit any State or any franchising authority from enacting or enforcing laws consistent with this section for the protection of subscriber privacy.

(h) Disclosure of information to governmental entity pursuant to court order

Except as provided in subsection (c)(2)(D) of this section, a governmental entity may obtain personally identifiable information concerning a cable subscriber pursuant to a court order only if, in the court proceeding relevant to such court order—

(1) such entity offers clear and convincing evidence that the subject of the information is reasonably suspected of engaging in criminal activity and that the information sought would be material evidence in the case; and

(2) the subject of the information is afforded the opportunity to appear and contest such entity's claim.

§ 552. Consumer protection and customer service

(a) Franchising authority enforcement

A franchising authority may establish and enforce—

(1) customer service requirements of the cable operator; and

(2) construction schedules and other construction-related requirements, including construction-related performance requirements, of the cable operator.

(b) Commission standards

The Commission shall, within 180 days of October 5, 1992, establish standards by which cable operators may fulfill their customer service requirements. Such standards shall include, at a minimum, requirements governing—

(1) cable system office hours and telephone availability;

(2) installations, outages, and service calls; and

(3) communications between the cable operator and the subscriber (including standards governing bills and refunds).

(c) Subscriber notice

A cable operator may provide notice of service and rate changes to subscribers using any reasonable written means at its sole discretion. Notwithstanding section 543(b)(6) of this title or any other provision of this chapter, a cable operator shall not be required to provide prior notice of any rate change that is the result of a regulatory fee, franchise fee, or any other fee, tax, assessment, or charge of any kind imposed by any Federal agency, State, or franchising authority on the transaction between the operator and the subscriber.

(d) Consumer protection laws and customer service agreements

(1) Consumer protection laws

Nothing in this subchapter shall be construed to prohibit any State or any franchising authority from enacting or enforcing any consumer protection law, to the extent not specifically preempted by this subchapter.

(2) Customer service requirement agreements

Nothing in this section shall be construed to preclude a franchising authority and a cable operator from agreeing to customer service requirements that exceed the standards established by the Commission under subsection (b) of this section. Nothing in this subchapter shall be construed to prevent the establishment or enforcement of any municipal law or regulation, or any State law, concerning customer service that imposes customer service requirements that exceed the standards set by the Commission under this section, or that addresses matters not addressed by the standards set by the Commission under this section.

Video Privacy Protection Act (1988)

18 U.S.C. § 2710, as amended

Statutes in Context

The Video Privacy Protection Act (VPPA) prohibits videotape service providers from knowingly disclosing personal information, such as the titles of videocassettes rented or purchased, without the individual's written consent. It creates a private right of action for certain kinds of violations of its requirements. The VPPA also contains several exceptions, including one that permits videotape providers to disclose "the subject matter" of regulated materials "if the disclosure is for the exclusive use of marketing goods and services directly to the consumer." 18 U.S.C. §2710(b)(2)(D)(ii). Videotape service providers can also disclose the names and addresses of their customers if the affected individuals have been given a right to opt out, and if the disclosure does not identify information about the videos that the consumers rent.

§ 2710. Wrongful disclosure of video tape rental or sale records

(a) Definitions.—For purposes of this section—

(1) the term "consumer" means any renter, purchaser, or subscriber of goods or services from a video tape service provider;

(2) the term "ordinary course of business" means only debt collection activities, order fulfillment, request processing, and the transfer of ownership;

(3) the term "personally identifiable information" includes information which identifies a person as having requested or obtained specific video materials or services from a video tape service provider; and

(4) the term "video tape service provider" means any person, engaged in the business, in or affecting interstate or foreign commerce, of rental, sale, or delivery of prerecorded video cassette tapes or similar audio visual materials, or any person or other entity to whom a disclosure is made under subparagraph (D) or (E) of subsection (b)(2), but only with respect to the information contained in the disclosure.

(b) Video tape rental and sale records.—(1) A video tape service provider who knowingly discloses, to any person, personally identifiable information concerning any consumer of such provider shall be liable to the aggrieved person for the relief provided in subsection (d).

(2) A video tape service provider may disclose personally identifiable information concerning any consumer—

(A) to the consumer;

(B) to any person with the informed, written consent of the consumer given at the time the disclosure is sought;

(C) to a law enforcement agency pursuant to a warrant issued under the Federal Rules of Criminal Procedure, an equivalent State warrant, a grand jury subpoena, or a court order;

(D) to any person if the disclosure is solely of the names and addresses of consumers and if—

(i) the video tape service provider has provided the consumer with the opportunity, in a clear and conspicuous manner, to prohibit such disclosure; and

(ii) the disclosure does not identify the title, description, or subject matter of any video tapes or other audio visual material; however, the subject matter of such materials may be disclosed if the disclosure is for the exclusive use of marketing goods and services directly to the consumer;

(E) to any person if the disclosure is incident to the ordinary course of business of the video tape service provider; or

(F) pursuant to a court order, in a civil proceeding upon a showing of compelling need for the information that cannot be accommodated by any other means, if—

(i) the consumer is given reasonable notice, by the person seeking the disclosure, of the court proceeding relevant to the issuance of the court order; and

(ii) the consumer is afforded the opportunity to appear and contest the claim of the person seeking the disclosure.

If an order is granted pursuant to subparagraph (C) or (F), the court shall impose appropriate safeguards against unauthorized disclosure.

(3) Court orders authorizing disclosure under subparagraph (C) shall issue only with prior notice to the consumer and only if the law enforcement agency shows that there is probable cause to believe that the records or other information sought are relevant to a legitimate law enforcement inquiry. In the case of a State government authority, such a court order shall not issue if prohibited by the law of such State. A court issuing an order pursuant to this section, on a motion made promptly by the video tape service provider, may quash or modify such order if the information or records requested are unreasonably voluminous in nature or if compliance with such order otherwise would cause an unreasonable burden on such provider.

(c) Civil action.—(1) Any person aggrieved by any act of a person in violation of this section may bring a civil action in a United States district court.

(2) The court may award—

(A) actual damages but not less than liquidated damages in an amount of $2,500;

(B) punitive damages;

(C) reasonable attorneys' fees and other litigation costs reasonably incurred; and

(D) such other preliminary and equitable relief as the court determines to be appropriate.

(3) No action may be brought under this subsection unless such action is begun within 2 years from the date of the act complained of or the date of discovery.

(4) No liability shall result from lawful disclosure permitted by this section.

(d) Personally identifiable information.—Personally identifiable information obtained in any manner other than as provided in this section shall not be received in evidence in any trial, hearing, arbitration, or other proceeding in or before any court, grand jury, department, officer, agency, regulatory body, legislative committee, or other authority of the United States, a State, or a political subdivision of a State.

(e) Destruction of old records.—A person subject to this section shall destroy personally identifiable information as soon as practicable, but no later than one year from the date the information is no longer necessary for the purpose for which it was collected and there are no pending requests or orders for access to such information under subsection (b)(2) or (c)(2) or pursuant to a court order.

(f) Preemption.—The provisions of this section preempt only the provisions of State or local law that require disclosure prohibited by this section.

Telecommunications Act (1996)

47 U.S.C. § 222, as amended

Statutes in Context

The Telecommunications Act of 1996 amended the previous telecommunications statute, dating largely from 1934, in numerous ways. Its new provisions include rules for protecting the privacy of customer information. The relevant language requires telecommunications carriers to protect the confidentiality of customer information. These provisions establish the important category of "customer proprietary network information," or CPNI, and place restrictions on the use, disclosure of, and access to CPNI.

§ 222. Privacy of customer information

(a) In general

Every telecommunications carrier has a duty to protect the confidentiality of proprietary information of, and relating to, other telecommunication carriers, equipment manufacturers, and customers, including telecommunication carriers reselling telecommunications services provided by a telecommunications carrier.

(b) Confidentiality of carrier information

A telecommunications carrier that receives or obtains proprietary information from another carrier for purposes of providing any telecommunications service shall use such information only for such purpose, and shall not use such information for its own marketing efforts.

(c) Confidentiality of customer proprietary network information

(1) Privacy requirements for telecommunications carriers

Except as required by law or with the approval of the customer, a telecommunications carrier that receives or obtains customer proprietary network information by virtue of its provision of a telecommunications service shall only use, disclose, or permit access to individually identifiable customer proprietary network information in its provision of (A) the telecommunications service from which such information is derived, or (B) services necessary to, or used in, the provision of such telecommunications service, including the publishing of directories.

(2) Disclosure on request by customers

A telecommunications carrier shall disclose customer proprietary network information, upon affirmative written request by the customer, to any person designated by the customer.

(3) Aggregate customer information

A telecommunications carrier that receives or obtains customer proprietary network information by virtue of its provision of a telecommunications service may use, disclose, or permit access to aggregate customer information other than for the purposes described in paragraph (1). A local exchange carrier may use, disclose, or permit access to aggregate customer information other than for purposes described in paragraph (1) only if it provides such aggregate information to other carriers or persons on reasonable and nondiscriminatory terms and conditions upon reasonable request therefor.

(d) Exceptions

Nothing in this section prohibits a telecommunications carrier from using, disclosing, or permitting access to customer proprietary network information obtained from its customers, either directly or indirectly through its agents—

(1) to initiate, render, bill, and collect for telecommunications services;

(2) to protect the rights or property of the carrier, or to protect users of those services and other carriers from fraudulent, abusive, or unlawful use of, or subscription to, such services;

(3) to provide any inbound telemarketing, referral, or administrative services to the customer for the duration of the call, if such call was initiated by the customer and the customer approves of the use of such information to provide such service; and

(4) to provide call location information concerning the user of a commercial mobile service (as such term is defined in section 332(d) of this title)—

(A) to a public safety answering point, emergency medical service provider or emergency dispatch provider, public safety, fire service, or law enforcement official, or hospital emergency or trauma care facility, in order to respond to the user's call for emergency services;

(B) to inform the user's legal guardian or members of the user's immediate family of the user's location in an emergency situation that involves the risk of death or serious physical harm; or

(C) to providers of information or database management services solely for purposes of assisting in the delivery of emergency services in response to an emergency.

(e) Subscriber list information

Notwithstanding subsections (b), (c), and (d) of this section, a telecommunications carrier that provides telephone exchange service shall provide subscriber list information gathered in its capacity as a provider of such service on a timely and unbundled basis, under nondiscriminatory and reasonable rates, terms, and conditions, to any person upon request for the purpose of publishing directories in any format.

(f) Authority to use wireless location information

For purposes of subsection (c)(1) of this section, without the express prior authorization of the customer, a customer shall not be considered to have approved the use or disclosure of or access to—

(1) call location information concerning the user of a commercial mobile service (as such term is defined in section 332(d) of this title), other than in accordance with subsection (d)(4) of this section; or

(2) automatic crash notification information to any person other than for use in the operation of an automatic crash notification system.

(g) Subscriber listed and unlisted information for emergency services

Notwithstanding subsections (b), (c), and (d) of this section, a telecommunications carrier that provides telephone exchange service shall provide information described in subsection (i)(3)(A) of this section (including information pertaining to subscribers whose information is unlisted or unpublished) that is in its possession or control (including information pertaining to subscribers of other carriers) on a timely and unbundled basis, under nondiscriminatory and reasonable rates, terms, and conditions to providers of emergency services, and providers of emergency support services, solely for purposes of delivering or assisting in the delivery of emergency services.

(h) Definitions

As used in this section:

(1) Customer proprietary network information

The term "customer proprietary network information" means—

(A) information that relates to the quantity, technical configuration, type, destination, location, and amount of use of a telecommunications service subscribed to by any customer of a telecommunications carrier, and that is made available to the carrier by the customer solely by virtue of the carrier-customer relationship; and

(B) information contained in the bills pertaining to telephone exchange service or telephone toll service received by a customer of a carrier;

except that such term does not include subscriber list information.

(2) Aggregate information

The term "aggregate customer information" means collective data that relates to a group or category of services or customers, from which individual customer identities and characteristics have been removed.

(3) Subscriber list information

The term "subscriber list information" means any information—

(A) identifying the listed names of subscribers of a carrier and such subscribers' telephone numbers, addresses, or primary advertising classifications (as such classifications are assigned at the time of the establishment of such service), or any combination of such listed names, numbers, addresses, or classifications; and

(B) that the carrier or an affiliate has published, caused to be published, or accepted for publication in any directory format.

(4) Public safety answering point

The term "public safety answering point" means a facility that has been designated to receive emergency calls and route them to emergency service personnel.

(5) Emergency services

The term "emergency services" means 9-1-1 emergency services and emergency notification services.

(6) Emergency notification services

The term "emergency notification services" means services that notify the public of an emergency.

(7) Emergency support services

The term "emergency support services" means information or data base management services used in support of emergency services.

Children's Online Privacy Protection Act (1998)

15 U.S.C. §§ 6501-6506, as amended

Statutes in Context

The Children's Online Privacy Protection Act (COPPA) regulates the collection and use of children's information by Internet websites or online services. As the Act states, it applies to "an operator of a website or online service directed to children, or any operator that has actual knowledge that it is collecting personal information from a child." 15 U.S.C. § 6502(a)(1). COPPA only applies to websites that collect personal information from children under age 13. The Act requires a website that falls under its jurisdiction to post notice of its privacy policies and to obtain consent from parents before collecting or using personal information from children.

§ 6501. Definitions

In this chapter:

(1) Child

The term "child" means an individual under the age of 13.

(2) Operator

The term "operator"—

(A) means any person who operates a website located on the Internet or an online service and who collects or maintains personal information from or about the users of or visitors to such website or online service, or on whose behalf such information is collected or maintained, where such website or online service is operated for commercial purposes, including any person offering products or services for sale through that website or online service, involving commerce—

(i) among the several States or with 1 or more foreign nations;

(ii) in any territory of the United States or in the District of Columbia, or between any such territory and—

(I) another such territory; or

(II) any State or foreign nation; or

(iii) between the District of Columbia and any State, territory, or foreign nation; but

(B) does not include any nonprofit entity that would otherwise be exempt from coverage under section 5 of the Federal Trade Commission Act (15 U.S.C. 45).

(3) Commission

The term "Commission" means the Federal Trade Commission.

(4) Disclosure

The term "disclosure" means, with respect to personal information—

(A) the release of personal information collected from a child in identifiable form by an operator for any purpose, except where such information is provided to a person other than the operator who provides support for the internal operations of the website and does not disclose or use that information for any other purpose; and

(B) making personal information collected from a child by a website or online service directed to children or with actual knowledge that such information was collected from a child, publicly available in identifiable form, by any means including by a public posting, through the Internet, or through—

(i) a home page of a website;

(ii) a pen pal service;

(iii) an electronic mail service;

(iv) a message board; or

(v) a chat room.

(5) Federal agency

The term "Federal agency" means an agency, as that term is defined in section 551(1) of Title 5.

(6) Internet

The term "Internet" means collectively the myriad of computer and telecommunications facilities, including equipment and operating software, which comprise the interconnected world-wide network of networks that employ the Transmission Control Protocol/Internet Protocol, or any predecessor or successor protocols to such protocol, to communicate information of all kinds by wire or radio.

(7) Parent

The term "parent" includes a legal guardian.

(8) Personal information

The term "personal information" means individually identifiable information about an individual collected online, including—

(A) a first and last name;

(B) a home or other physical address including street name and name of a city or town;

(C) an e-mail address;

(D) a telephone number;

(E) a Social Security number;

(F) any other identifier that the Commission determines permits the physical or online contacting of a specific individual; or

(G) information concerning the child or the parents of that child that the website collects online from the child and combines with an identifier described in this paragraph.

(9) Verifiable parental consent

The term "verifiable parental consent" means any reasonable effort (taking into consideration available technology), including a request for authorization for future collection, use, and disclosure described in the notice, to ensure that a parent of a child receives notice of the operator's personal information collection, use, and disclosure practices, and authorizes the collection, use, and disclosure, as applicable, of personal information and the subsequent use of that information before that information is collected from that child.

(10) Website or online service directed to children

(A) In general

The term "website or online service directed to children" means—

(i) a commercial website or online service that is targeted to children; or

(ii) that portion of a commercial website or online service that is targeted to children.

(B) Limitation

A commercial website or online service, or a portion of a commercial website or online service, shall not be deemed directed to children solely for referring or linking to a commercial website or online service directed to children by using information location tools, including a directory, index, reference, pointer, or hypertext link.

(11) Person

The term "person" means any individual, partnership, corporation, trust, estate, cooperative, association, or other entity.

(12) Online contact information

The term "online contact information" means an e-mail address or another substantially similar identifier that permits direct contact with a person online.

§ 6502. Regulation of unfair and deceptive acts and practices in connection with collection and use of personal information from and about children on the internet

(a) Acts prohibited

(1) In general

It is unlawful for an operator of a website or online service directed to children, or any operator that has actual knowledge that it is collecting personal information from a child, to collect personal information from a child in a manner that violates the regulations prescribed under subsection (b) of this section.

(2) Disclosure to parent protected

Notwithstanding paragraph (1), neither an operator of such a website or online service nor the operator's agent shall be held to be liable under any Federal or State law for any disclosure made in good faith and following reasonable procedures in responding to a request for disclosure of personal information under subsection (b)(1)(B)(iii) of this section to the parent of a child.

(b) Regulations

(1) In general

Not later than 1 year after October 21, 1998, the Commission shall promulgate under section 553 of Title 5 regulations that—

(A) require the operator of any website or online service directed to children that collects personal information from children or the operator of a website or online service that has actual knowledge that it is collecting personal information from a child—

(i) to provide notice on the website of what information is collected from children by the operator, how the operator uses such information, and the operator's disclosure practices for such information; and

(ii) to obtain verifiable parental consent for the collection, use, or disclosure of personal information from children;

(B) require the operator to provide, upon request of a parent under this subparagraph whose child has provided personal information to that website or online service, upon proper identification of that parent, to such parent—

(i) a description of the specific types of personal information collected from the child by that operator;

(ii) the opportunity at any time to refuse to permit the operator's further use or maintenance in retrievable form, or future online collection, of personal information from that child; and

(iii) notwithstanding any other provision of law, a means that is reasonable under the circumstances for the parent to obtain any personal information collected from that child;

(C) prohibit conditioning a child's participation in a game, the offering of a prize, or another activity on the child disclosing more personal information than is reasonably necessary to participate in such activity; and

(D) require the operator of such a website or online service to establish and maintain reasonable procedures to protect the confidentiality, security, and integrity of personal information collected from children.

(2) When consent not required

The regulations shall provide that verifiable parental consent under paragraph (1)(A)(ii) is not required in the case of—

(A) online contact information collected from a child that is used only to respond directly on a one-time basis to a specific request from the child and is not used to recontact the child and is not maintained in retrievable form by the operator;

(B) a request for the name or online contact information of a parent or child that is used for the sole purpose of obtaining parental consent or providing notice under this section and where such information is not maintained in retrievable form by the operator if parental consent is not obtained after a reasonable time;

(C) online contact information collected from a child that is used only to respond more than once directly to a specific request from the child and is not used to recontact the child beyond the scope of that request—

(i) if, before any additional response after the initial response to the child, the operator uses reasonable efforts to provide a parent notice of the online contact information collected from the child, the purposes for which it is to be used, and an opportunity for the parent to request that the operator make no further use of the information and that it not be maintained in retrievable form; or

(ii) without notice to the parent in such circumstances as the Commission may determine are appropriate, taking into consideration the benefits to the child of access to information and services, and risks to the security and privacy of the child, in regulations promulgated under this subsection;

(D) the name of the child and online contact information (to the extent reasonably necessary to protect the safety of a child participant on the site)—

(i) used only for the purpose of protecting such safety;

(ii) not used to recontact the child or for any other purpose; and

(iii) not disclosed on the site,

if the operator uses reasonable efforts to provide a parent notice of the name and online contact information collected from the child, the purposes for which it is to be used, and an opportunity for the parent to request that the operator make no further use of the information and that it not be maintained in retrievable form; or

(E) the collection, use, or dissemination of such information by the operator of such a website or online service necessary—

(i) to protect the security or integrity of its website;

(ii) to take precautions against liability;

(iii) to respond to judicial process; or

(iv) to the extent permitted under other provisions of law, to provide information to law enforcement agencies or for an investigation on a matter related to public safety.

(3) Termination of service

The regulations shall permit the operator of a website or an online service to terminate service provided to a child whose parent has refused, under the regulations prescribed under paragraph (1)(B)(ii), to permit the operator's further use or maintenance in retrievable form, or future online collection, of personal information from that child.

(c) Enforcement

Subject to sections 6503 and 6505 of this title, a violation of a regulation prescribed under subsection (a) of this section shall be treated as a violation of a rule defining an unfair or deceptive act or practice prescribed under section 57a(a)(1)(B) of this title.

(d) Inconsistent State law

No State or local government may impose any liability for commercial activities or actions by operators in interstate or foreign commerce in connection with an activity or action described in this chapter that is inconsistent with the treatment of those activities or actions under this section.

§ 6503. Safe harbors

(a) Guidelines

An operator may satisfy the requirements of regulations issued under section 6502(b) of this title by following a set of self-regulatory guidelines, issued by representatives of the marketing or online industries, or by other persons, approved under subsection (b) of this section.

(b) Incentives

(1) Self-regulatory incentives

In prescribing regulations under section 6502 of this title, the Commission shall provide incentives for self-regulation by operators to implement the protections afforded children under the regulatory requirements described in subsection (b) of that section.

(2) Deemed compliance

Such incentives shall include provisions for ensuring that a person will be deemed to be in compliance with the requirements of the regulations under section 6502 of this title if that person complies with guidelines that, after notice and comment, are approved by the Commission upon making a determination that the guidelines meet the requirements of the regulations issued under section 6502 of this title.

(3) Expedited response to requests

The Commission shall act upon requests for safe harbor treatment within 180 days of the filing of the request, and shall set forth in writing its conclusions with regard to such requests.

(c) Appeals

Final action by the Commission on a request for approval of guidelines, or the failure to act within 180 days on a request for approval of guidelines, submitted under subsection (b) of this section may be appealed to a district court of the United States of appropriate jurisdiction as provided for in section 706 of Title 5.

§ 6504. Actions by States

(a) In general

(1) Civil actions

In any case in which the attorney general of a State has reason to believe that an interest of the residents of that State has been or is threatened or adversely affected by the engagement of any person in a practice that violates any regulation of the Commission prescribed under section 6502(b) of this title, the State, as parens patriae, may bring a civil action on behalf of the residents of the State in a district court of the United States of appropriate jurisdiction to—

(A) enjoin that practice;

(B) enforce compliance with the regulation;

(C) obtain damage, restitution, or other compensation on behalf of residents of the State; or

(D) obtain such other relief as the court may consider to be appropriate.

(2) Notice

(A) In general

Before filing an action under paragraph (1), the attorney general of the State involved shall provide to the Commission—

(i) written notice of that action; and

(ii) a copy of the complaint for that action.

(B) Exemption

(i) In general

Subparagraph (A) shall not apply with respect to the filing of an action by an attorney general of a State under this subsection, if the attorney general determines that it is not feasible to provide the notice described in that subparagraph before the filing of the action.

(ii) Notification

In an action described in clause (i), the attorney general of a State shall provide notice and a copy of the complaint to the Commission at the same time as the attorney general files the action.

(b) Intervention

(1) In general

On receiving notice under subsection (a)(2) of this section, the Commission shall have the right to intervene in the action that is the subject of the notice.

(2) Effect of intervention

If the Commission intervenes in an action under subsection (a) of this section, it shall have the right—

(A) to be heard with respect to any matter that arises in that action; and

(B) to file a petition for appeal.

(3) Amicus curiae

Upon application to the court, a person whose self-regulatory guidelines have been approved by the Commission and are relied upon as a defense by any defendant to a proceeding under this section may file amicus curiae in that proceeding.

(c) Construction

For purposes of bringing any civil action under subsection (a) of this section, nothing in this chapter shall be construed to prevent an attorney general of a State from exercising the powers conferred on the attorney general by the laws of that State to—

(1) conduct investigations;

(2) administer oaths or affirmations; or

(3) compel the attendance of witnesses or the production of documentary and other evidence.

(d) Actions by the Commission

In any case in which an action is instituted by or on behalf of the Commission for violation of any regulation prescribed under section 6502 of this title, no State may, during the pendency of that action, institute an action under subsection (a) of this section against any defendant named in the complaint in that action for violation of that regulation.

(e) Venue; service of process

(1) Venue

Any action brought under subsection (a) of this section may be brought in the district court of the United States that meets applicable requirements relating to venue under section 1391 of Title 28.

(2) Service of process

In an action brought under subsection (a), process may be served in any district in which the defendant—

(A) is an inhabitant; or

(B) may be found.

§ 6505. Administration and applicability of act

(a) In general

Except as otherwise provided, this chapter shall be enforced by the Commission under the Federal Trade Commission Act (15 U.S.C. 41 et seq.).

(b) Provisions

Compliance with the requirements imposed under this chapter shall be enforced under—

(1) section 8 of the Federal Deposit Insurance Act (12 U.S.C. 1818), in the case of—

(A) national banks, and Federal branches and Federal agencies of foreign banks, by the Office of the Comptroller of the Currency;

(B) member banks of the Federal Reserve System (other than national banks), branches and agencies of foreign banks (other than Federal branches, Federal agencies, and insured State branches of foreign banks), commercial lending companies owned or controlled by foreign banks, and organizations operating under section 25 or 25(a) of the Federal Reserve Act (12 U.S.C. 601 et seq. and 611 et. seq.), by the Board; and

(C) banks insured by the Federal Deposit Insurance Corporation (other than members of the Federal Reserve System) and insured State branches of foreign banks, by the Board of Directors of the Federal Deposit Insurance Corporation;

(2) section 8 of the Federal Deposit Insurance Act (12 U.S.C. 1818), by the Director of the Office of Thrift Supervision, in the case of a savings association the deposits of which are insured by the Federal Deposit Insurance Corporation;

(3) the Federal Credit Union Act (12 U.S.C. 1751 et seq.) by the National Credit Union Administration Board with respect to any Federal credit union;

(4) part A of subtitle VII of Title 49 by the Secretary of Transportation with respect to any air carrier or foreign air carrier subject to that part;

(5) the Packers and Stockyards Act, 1921 (7 U.S.C. 181 et seq.) (except as provided in section 406 of that Act (7 U.S.C. 226, 227)), by the Secretary of Agriculture with respect to any activities subject to that Act; and

(6) the Farm Credit Act of 1971 (12 U.S.C. 2001 et seq.) by the Farm Credit Administration with respect to any Federal land bank, Federal land bank association, Federal intermediate credit bank, or production credit association.

(c) Exercise of certain powers

For the purpose of the exercise by any agency referred to in subsection (a) of its powers under any Act referred to in that subsection, a violation of any requirement imposed under this chapter shall be deemed to be a violation of a requirement imposed under that Act. In addition to its powers under any provision of law specifically referred to in subsection (a) of this section, each of the agencies referred to in that subsection may exercise, for the purpose of enforcing compliance with any requirement imposed under this chapter, any other authority conferred on it by law.

(d) Actions by Commission

The Commission shall prevent any person from violating a rule of the Commission under section 6502 of this title in the same manner, by the same means, and with the same jurisdiction, powers, and duties as though all applicable terms and provisions of the Federal Trade Commission Act (15 U.S.C. 41 et seq.) were incorporated into and made a part of this chapter. Any entity that violates such rule shall be subject to the penalties and entitled to the privileges and immunities provided in the Federal Trade Commission Act in the same manner, by the same means, and with the same jurisdiction, power, and duties as though all applicable terms and provisions of the Federal Trade Commission Act were incorporated into and made a part of this chapter.

(e) Effect on other laws

Nothing contained in this chapter shall be construed to limit the authority of the Commission under any other provisions of law.

§ 6506. Review

Not later than 5 years after the effective date of the regulations initially issued under section 6502 of this title, the Commission shall—

(1) review the implementation of this chapter, including the effect of the implementation of this chapter on practices relating to the collection and disclosure of information relating to children, children's ability to obtain access to information of their choice online, and on the availability of websites directed to children; and

(2) prepare and submit to Congress a report on the results of the review under paragraph (1).

Telephone Consumer Protection Act (1991)

47 U.S.C. § 227, as amended

Statutes in Context

The Telephone Consumer Protection Act (TCPA) prohibits telemarketers from calling residences and using prerecorded messages without the consent of the called party. It also permits individuals to sue a telemarketer in small claims court for actual loss or up to $500 for each call received after requesting not to be contacted by a company. States may initiate actions against telemarketers engaging in "a pattern" of telephone calls to residents of that state in violation of the Act. 47 U.S.C. §227(f)(1). In 2003, under the authority of the TCPA, the Federal Communications Commission (FCC), in conjunction with the Federal Trade Commission (FTC), established a national Do-Not-Call list.

§ 1039. Fraud and related activity in connection with obtaining confidential phone records information of a covered entity

(a) Criminal violation.—Whoever, in interstate or foreign commerce, knowingly and intentionally obtains, or attempts to obtain, confidential phone records information of a covered entity, by—

(1) making false or fraudulent statements or representations to an employee of a covered entity;

(2) making such false or fraudulent statements or representations to a customer of a covered entity;

(3) providing a document to a covered entity knowing that such document is false or fraudulent; or

(4) accessing customer accounts of a covered entity via the Internet, or by means of conduct that violates section 1030 of this title, without prior authorization from the customer to whom such confidential phone records information relates; shall be fined under this title, imprisoned for not more than 10 years, or both.

(b) Prohibition on sale or transfer of confidential phone records information.—

(1) Except as otherwise permitted by applicable law, whoever, in interstate or foreign commerce, knowingly and intentionally sells or transfers, or attempts to sell or transfer, confidential phone records information of a covered entity, without prior authorization from the customer to whom such confidential phone records information relates, or knowing or having reason to know such information was obtained fraudulently, shall be fined under this title, imprisoned not more than 10 years, or both.

(2) For purposes of this subsection, the exceptions specified in section 222(d) of the Communications Act of 1934 shall apply for the use of confidential phone records information by any covered entity, as defined in subsection (h).

(c) Prohibition on purchase or receipt of confidential phone records information.—

(1) Except as otherwise permitted by applicable law, whoever, in interstate or foreign commerce, knowingly and intentionally purchases or receives, or attempts to purchase or receive, confidential phone records information of a covered entity, without prior authorization from the customer to whom such confidential phone records information relates, or knowing or having reason to know such information was obtained fraudulently, shall be fined under this title, imprisoned not more than 10 years, or both.

(2) For purposes of this subsection, the exceptions specified in section 222(d) of the Communications Act of 1934 shall apply for the use of confidential phone records information by any covered entity, as defined in subsection (h).

(d) Enhanced penalties for aggravated cases.—Whoever violates, or attempts to violate, subsection (a), (b), or (c) while violating another law of the United States or as part of a pattern of any illegal activity involving more than $100,000, or more than 50 customers of a covered entity, in a 12-month period shall, in addition to the penalties provided for in such subsection, be fined twice the amount provided in subsection (b)(3) or (c)(3) (as the case may be) of section 3571 of this title, imprisoned for not more than 5 years, or both.

(e) Enhanced penalties for use of information in furtherance of certain criminal offenses.—

(1) Whoever, violates, or attempts to violate, subsection (a), (b), or (c) knowing that such information may be used in furtherance of, or with the intent to commit, an offense described in section 2261, 2261A, 2262, or any other crime of violence shall, in addition to the penalties provided for in such subsection, be fined under this title and imprisoned not more than 5 years.

(2) Whoever, violates, or attempts to violate, subsection (a), (b), or (c) knowing that such information may be used in furtherance of, or with the intent to commit, an offense under section 111, 115, 1114, 1503, 1512, 1513, or to intimidate, threaten, harass, injure, or kill any Federal, State, or local law enforcement officer shall, in addition to the penalties provided for in such subsection, be fined under this title and imprisoned not more than 5 years.

(f) Extraterritorial jurisdiction.—There is extraterritorial jurisdiction over an offense under this section.

(g) Nonapplicability to law enforcement agencies.—This section does not prohibit any lawfully authorized investigative, protective, or intelligence activity of a law enforcement agency of the United States, a State, or political subdivision of a State, or of an intelligence agency of the United States.

(h) Definitions.—In this section:

(1) Confidential phone records information.—The term "confidential phone records information" means information that—

(A) relates to the quantity, technical configuration, type, destination, location, or amount of use of a service offered by a covered entity, subscribed to by any customer of that covered entity, and kept by or on behalf of that covered entity solely by virtue of the relationship between that covered entity and the customer;

(B) is made available to a covered entity by a customer solely by virtue of the relationship between that covered entity and the customer; or

(C) is contained in any bill, itemization, or account statement provided to a customer by or on behalf of a covered entity solely by virtue of the relationship between that covered entity and the customer.

(2) Covered entity.—The term "covered entity"—

(A) has the same meaning given the term "telecommunications carrier" in section 3 of the Communications Act of 1934 (47 U.S.C. 153); and

(B) includes any provider of IP-enabled voice service.

(3) Customer.—The term "customer" means, with respect to a covered entity, any individual, partnership, association, joint stock company, trust, or corporation, or authorized representative of such customer, to whom the covered entity provides a product or service.

(4) IP-enabled voice service.—The term "IP-enabled voice service" means the provision of real-time voice communications offered to the public, or such class of users as to be effectively available to the public, transmitted through customer premises equipment using TCP/IP protocol, or a successor protocol, (whether part of a bundle of services or separately) with interconnection capability such that the service can originate traffic to, or terminate traffic from, the public switched telephone network, or a successor network.

Controlling the Assault of Non-Solicited Pornography and Marketing (CAN-SPAM) Act (2003)

15 U.S.C. §§ 7701-7713, as amended

Statutes in Context

The Controlling the Assault of Non-Solicited Pornography and Marketing (CAN-SPAM) Act applies to commercial e-mail. It prohibits the knowing sending of commercial messages with the intent to deceive or mislead recipients. The CAN-SPAM Act also requires that a valid opt-out option be made available to e-mail recipients.

§ 7701. Congressional findings and policy

(a) Findings

The Congress finds the following:

(1) Electronic mail has become an extremely important and popular means of communication, relied on by millions of Americans on a daily basis for personal and commercial purposes. Its low cost and global reach make it extremely convenient and efficient, and offer unique opportunities for the development and growth of frictionless commerce.

(2) The convenience and efficiency of electronic mail are threatened by the extremely rapid growth in the volume of unsolicited commercial electronic mail. Unsolicited commercial electronic mail is currently estimated to account for over half of all electronic mail traffic, up from an estimated 7 percent in 2001, and the volume continues to rise. Most of these messages are fraudulent or deceptive in one or more respects.

(3) The receipt of unsolicited commercial electronic mail may result in costs to recipients who cannot refuse to accept such mail and who incur costs for the storage of such mail, or for the time spent accessing, reviewing, and discarding such mail, or for both.

(4) The receipt of a large number of unwanted messages also decreases the convenience of electronic mail and creates a risk that wanted electronic mail messages, both commercial and noncommercial, will be lost, overlooked, or discarded amidst the larger volume of unwanted messages, thus reducing the reliability and usefulness of electronic mail to the recipient.

(5) Some commercial electronic mail contains material that many recipients may consider vulgar or pornographic in nature.

(6) The growth in unsolicited commercial electronic mail imposes significant monetary costs on providers of Internet access services, businesses, and educational and nonprofit institutions that carry and receive such mail, as there is a finite volume of mail that such providers, businesses, and institutions can handle without further investment in infrastructure.

(7) Many senders of unsolicited commercial electronic mail purposefully disguise the source of such mail.

(8) Many senders of unsolicited commercial electronic mail purposefully include misleading information in the messages' subject lines in order to induce the recipients to view the messages.

(9) While some senders of commercial electronic mail messages provide simple and reliable ways for recipients to reject (or "opt-out" of) receipt of commercial electronic mail from such senders in the future, other senders provide no such "opt-out" mechanism, or refuse to honor the requests of recipients not to receive electronic mail from such senders in the future, or both.

(10) Many senders of bulk unsolicited commercial electronic mail use computer programs to gather large numbers of electronic mail addresses on an automated basis from Internet websites or online services where users must post their addresses in order to make full use of the website or service.

(11) Many States have enacted legislation intended to regulate or reduce unsolicited commercial electronic mail, but these statutes impose different standards and requirements. As a result, they do not appear to have been successful in addressing the problems associated with unsolicited commercial electronic mail, in part because, since an electronic mail address does not specify a geographic location, it can be extremely difficult for law-abiding businesses to know with which of these disparate statutes they are required to comply.

(12) The problems associated with the rapid growth and abuse of unsolicited commercial electronic mail cannot be solved by Federal legislation alone. The development and adoption of technological approaches and the pursuit of cooperative efforts with other countries will be necessary as well.

(b) Congressional determination of public policy

On the basis of the findings in subsection (a) of this section, the Congress determines that—

(1) there is a substantial government interest in regulation of commercial electronic mail on a nationwide basis;

(2) senders of commercial electronic mail should not mislead recipients as to the source or content of such mail; and

(3) recipients of commercial electronic mail have a right to decline to receive additional commercial electronic mail from the same source.

§ 7702. Definitions

In this chapter:

(1) Affirmative consent

The term "affirmative consent", when used with respect to a commercial electronic mail message, means that—

(A) the recipient expressly consented to receive the message, either in response to a clear and conspicuous request for such consent or at the recipient's own initiative; and

(B) if the message is from a party other than the party to which the recipient communicated such consent, the recipient was given clear and conspicuous notice at the time the consent was communicated that the recipient's electronic mail address could be transferred to such other party for the purpose of initiating commercial electronic mail messages.

(2) Commercial electronic mail message

(A) In general

The term "commercial electronic mail message" means any electronic mail message the primary purpose of which is the commercial advertisement or promotion of a commercial product or service (including content on an Internet website operated for a commercial purpose).

(B) Transactional or relationship messages

The term "commercial electronic mail message" does not include a transactional or relationship message.

(C) Regulations regarding primary purpose

Not later than 12 months after December 16, 2003, the Commission shall issue regulations pursuant to section 7711 of this title defining the relevant criteria to facilitate the determination of the primary purpose of an electronic mail message.

(D) Reference to company or website

The inclusion of a reference to a commercial entity or a link to the website of a commercial entity in an electronic mail message does not, by itself, cause such message to be treated as a commercial electronic mail message for purposes of this chapter if the contents or circumstances of the message indicate a primary purpose other than commercial advertisement or promotion of a commercial product or service.

(3) Commission

The term "Commission" means the Federal Trade Commission.

(4) Domain name

The term "domain name" means any alphanumeric designation which is registered with or assigned by any domain name registrar, domain name registry, or other domain name registration authority as part of an electronic address on the Internet.

(5) Electronic mail address

The term "electronic mail address" means a destination, commonly expressed as a string of characters, consisting of a unique user name or mailbox (commonly referred to as the "local part") and a reference to an Internet domain (commonly referred to as the "domain part"), whether or not displayed, to which an electronic mail message can be sent or delivered.

(6) Electronic mail message

The term "electronic mail message" means a message sent to a unique electronic mail address.

(7) FTC Act

The term “FTC Act” means the Federal Trade Commission Act (15 U.S.C. 41 et seq.).

(8) Header information

The term “header information” means the source, destination, and routing information attached to an electronic mail message, including the originating domain name and originating electronic mail address, and any other information that appears in the line identifying, or purporting to identify, a person initiating the message.

(9) Initiate

The term “initiate”, when used with respect to a commercial electronic mail message, means to originate or transmit such message or to procure the origination or transmission of such message, but shall not include actions that constitute routine conveyance of such message. For purposes of this paragraph, more than one person may be considered to have initiated a message.

(10) Internet

The term “Internet” has the meaning given that term in the Internet Tax Freedom Act (47 U.S.C. 151 nt).

(11) Internet access service

The term “Internet access service” has the meaning given that term in section 231(e)(4) of Title 47.

(12) Procure

The term “procure”, when used with respect to the initiation of a commercial electronic mail message, means intentionally to pay or provide other consideration to, or induce, another person to initiate such a message on one’s behalf.

(13) Protected computer

The term “protected computer” has the meaning given that term in section 1030(e)(2)(B) of Title 18.

(14) Recipient

The term “recipient”, when used with respect to a commercial electronic mail message, means an authorized user of the electronic mail address to which the message was sent or delivered. If a recipient of a commercial electronic mail message has one or more electronic mail addresses in addition to the address to which the message was sent or delivered, the recipient shall be treated as a separate recipient with respect to each such address. If an electronic mail address is reassigned to a new user, the new user shall not be treated as a recipient of any commercial electronic mail message sent or delivered to that address before it was reassigned.

(15) Routine conveyance

The term “routine conveyance” means the transmission, routing, relaying, handling, or storing, through an automatic technical process, of an electronic mail message for which another person has identified the recipients or provided the recipient addresses.

(16) Sender

(A) In general

Except as provided in subparagraph (B), the term “sender”, when used with respect to a commercial electronic mail message, means a person who initiates such a message and whose product, service, or Internet web site is advertised or promoted by the message.

(B) Separate lines of business or divisions

If an entity operates through separate lines of business or divisions and holds itself out to the recipient throughout the message as that particular line of business or division rather than as the entity of which such line of business or division is a part, then the line of business or the division shall be treated as the sender of such message for purposes of this chapter.

(17) Transactional or relationship message

(A) In general

The term “transactional or relationship message” means an electronic mail message the primary purpose of which is—

(i) to facilitate, complete, or confirm a commercial transaction that the recipient has previously agreed to enter into with the sender;

(ii) to provide warranty information, product recall information, or safety or security information with respect to a commercial product or service used or purchased by the recipient;

(iii) to provide—

(I) notification concerning a change in the terms or features of;

(II) notification of a change in the recipient’s standing or status with respect to; or

(III) at regular periodic intervals, account balance information or other type of account statement with respect to,

a subscription, membership, account, loan, or comparable ongoing commercial relationship involving the ongoing purchase or use by the recipient of products or services offered by the sender;

(iv) to provide information directly related to an employment relationship or related benefit plan in which the recipient is currently involved, participating, or enrolled; or

(v) to deliver goods or services, including product updates or upgrades, that the recipient is entitled to receive under the terms of a transaction that the recipient has previously agreed to enter into with the sender.

(B) Modification of definition

The Commission by regulation pursuant to section 7711 of this title may modify the definition in subparagraph (A) to expand or contract the categories of messages that are treated as transactional or relationship messages for purposes of this chapter to the extent that such modification is necessary to accommodate changes in electronic mail technology or practices and accomplish the purposes of this chapter.

§ 7703. Prohibition against predatory and abusive commercial e-mail

(a) Omitted

(b) United States Sentencing Commission

(1) Directive

Pursuant to its authority under section 994(p) of Title 28 and in accordance with this section, the United States Sentencing Commission shall review and, as appropriate, amend the sentencing guidelines and policy statements to provide appropriate penalties for violations of section 1037 of Title 18, as added by this section, and other offenses that may be facilitated by the sending of large quantities of unsolicited electronic mail.

(2) Requirements

In carrying out this subsection, the Sentencing Commission shall consider providing sentencing enhancements for—

(A) those convicted under section 1037 of Title 18 who—

(i) obtained electronic mail addresses through improper means, including—

(I) harvesting electronic mail addresses of the users of a website, proprietary service, or other online public forum operated by another person, without the authorization of such person; and

(II) randomly generating electronic mail addresses by computer; or

(ii) knew that the commercial electronic mail messages involved in the offense contained or advertised an Internet domain for which the registrant of the domain had provided false registration information; and

(B) those convicted of other offenses, including offenses involving fraud, identity theft, obscenity, child pornography, and the sexual exploitation of children, if such offenses involved the sending of large quantities of electronic mail.

(c) Sense of Congress

It is the sense of Congress that—

(1) Spam has become the method of choice for those who distribute pornography, perpetrate fraudulent schemes, and introduce viruses, worms, and Trojan horses into personal and business computer systems; and

(2) the Department of Justice should use all existing law enforcement tools to investigate and prosecute those who send bulk commercial e-mail to facilitate the commission of Federal crimes, including the tools contained in chapters 47 and 63 of Title 18 (relating to fraud and false statements); chapter 71 of Title 18 (relating to obscenity); chapter 110 of Title 18 (relating to the sexual exploitation of children); and chapter 95 of Title 18 (relating to racketeering), as appropriate.

§ 7704. Other protections for users of commercial electronic mail

(a) Requirements for transmission of messages

(1) Prohibition of false or misleading transmission information

It is unlawful for any person to initiate the transmission, to a protected computer, of a commercial electronic mail message, or a transactional or relationship message, that contains, or is accompanied by, header information that is materially false or materially misleading. For purposes of this paragraph—

(A) header information that is technically accurate but includes an originating electronic mail address, domain name, or Internet Protocol address the access to which for purposes of initiating the message was obtained by means of false or fraudulent pretenses or representations shall be considered materially misleading;

(B) a "from" line (the line identifying or purporting to identify a person initiating the message) that accurately identifies any person who initiated the message shall not be considered materially false or materially misleading; and

(C) header information shall be considered materially misleading if it fails to identify accurately a protected computer used to initiate the message because the person initiating the message knowingly uses another protected computer to relay or retransmit the message for purposes of disguising its origin.

(2) Prohibition of deceptive subject headings

It is unlawful for any person to initiate the transmission to a protected computer of a commercial electronic mail message if such person has actual knowledge, or knowledge fairly implied on the basis of objective circumstances, that a subject heading of the message would be likely to mislead a recipient, acting reasonably under the circumstances, about a material fact regarding the contents or subject matter of the message (consistent with the criteria used in enforcement of section 45 of this title).

(3) Inclusion of return address or comparable mechanism in commercial electronic mail—

(A) In general

It is unlawful for any person to initiate the transmission to a protected computer of a commercial electronic mail message that does not contain a functioning return electronic mail address or other Internet-based mechanism, clearly and conspicuously displayed, that—

(i) a recipient may use to submit, in a manner specified in the message, a reply electronic mail message or other form of Internet-based communication requesting not to receive future commercial electronic mail messages from that sender at the electronic mail address where the message was received; and

(ii) remains capable of receiving such messages or communications for no less than 30 days after the transmission of the original message.

(B) More detailed options possible

The person initiating a commercial electronic mail message may comply with subparagraph (A)(i) by providing the recipient a list or menu from which the recipient may choose the specific types of commercial electronic mail messages the recipient wants to receive or does not want to receive from the sender, if the list or menu includes an option under which the recipient may choose not to receive any commercial electronic mail messages from the sender.

(C) Temporary inability to receive messages or process requests

A return electronic mail address or other mechanism does not fail to satisfy the requirements of subparagraph (A) if it is unexpectedly and temporarily unable to receive messages or process requests due to a technical problem beyond the control of the sender if the problem is corrected within a reasonable time period.

(4) Prohibition of transmission of commercial electronic mail after objection

(A) In general

If a recipient makes a request using a mechanism provided pursuant to paragraph (3) not to receive some or any commercial electronic mail messages from such sender, then it is unlawful—

(i) for the sender to initiate the transmission to the recipient, more than 10 business days after the receipt of such request, of a commercial electronic mail message that falls within the scope of the request;

(ii) for any person acting on behalf of the sender to initiate the transmission to the recipient, more than 10 business days after the receipt of such request, of a commercial electronic mail message with actual knowledge, or knowledge fairly implied on the basis of objective circumstances, that such message falls within the scope of the request;

(iii) for any person acting on behalf of the sender to assist in initiating the transmission to the recipient, through the provision or selection of addresses to which the message will be sent, of a commercial electronic mail message with actual knowledge, or knowledge fairly implied on the basis of objective circumstances, that such message would violate clause (i) or (ii); or

(iv) for the sender, or any other person who knows that the recipient has made such a request, to sell, lease, exchange, or otherwise transfer or release the electronic mail address of the recipient (including through any transaction or other transfer involving mailing lists bearing the electronic mail address of the recipient) for any purpose other than compliance with this chapter or other provision of law.

(B) Subsequent affirmative consent

A prohibition in subparagraph (A) does not apply if there is affirmative consent by the recipient subsequent to the request under subparagraph (A).

(5) Inclusion of identifier, opt-out, and physical address in commercial electronic mail

(A) It is unlawful for any person to initiate the transmission of any commercial electronic mail message to a protected computer unless the message provides—

(i) clear and conspicuous identification that the message is an advertisement or solicitation;

(ii) clear and conspicuous notice of the opportunity under paragraph (3) to decline to receive further commercial electronic mail messages from the sender; and

(iii) a valid physical postal address of the sender.

(B) Subparagraph (A)(i) does not apply to the transmission of a commercial electronic mail message if the recipient has given prior affirmative consent to receipt of the message.

(6) Materially

For purposes of paragraph (1), the term "materially", when used with respect to false or misleading header information, includes the alteration or concealment of header information in a manner that would impair the ability of an Internet access service processing the message on behalf of a recipient, a person alleging a violation of this section, or a law enforcement agency to identify, locate, or respond to a person who initiated the electronic mail message or to investigate the alleged violation, or the ability of a recipient of the message to respond to a person who initiated the electronic message.

(b) Aggravated violations relating to commercial electronic mail

(1) Address harvesting and dictionary attacks—

(A) In general

It is unlawful for any person to initiate the transmission, to a protected computer, of a commercial electronic mail message that is unlawful under subsection (a) of this section, or to assist in the origination of such message through the provision or selection of addresses to which the message will be transmitted, if such person had actual knowledge, or knowledge fairly implied on the basis of objective circumstances, that—

(i) the electronic mail address of the recipient was obtained using an automated means from an Internet website or proprietary online service operated by another person, and such website or online service included, at the time the address was obtained, a notice stating that the operator of such website or online service will not give, sell, or otherwise transfer addresses maintained by such website or online service to any other party for the purposes of initiating, or enabling others to initiate, electronic mail messages; or

(ii) the electronic mail address of the recipient was obtained using an automated means that generates possible electronic mail addresses by combining names, letters, or numbers into numerous permutations.

(B) Disclaimer

Nothing in this paragraph creates an ownership or proprietary interest in such electronic mail addresses.

(2) Automated creation of multiple electronic mail accounts

It is unlawful for any person to use scripts or other automated means to register for multiple electronic mail accounts or online user accounts from which to transmit to a protected computer, or enable another person to transmit to a protected computer, a commercial electronic mail message that is unlawful under subsection (a) of this section.

(3) Relay or retransmission through unauthorized access

It is unlawful for any person knowingly to relay or retransmit a commercial electronic mail message that is unlawful under subsection (a) of this section from a protected computer or computer network that such person has accessed without authorization.

(c) Supplementary rulemaking authority

The Commission shall by regulation, pursuant to section 7711 of this title—

(1) modify the 10-business-day period under subsection (a)(4)(A) or subsection (a)(4)(B) of this section, or both, if the Commission determines that a different period would be more reasonable after taking into account—

(A) the purposes of subsection (a) of this section;

(B) the interests of recipients of commercial electronic mail; and

(C) the burdens imposed on senders of lawful commercial electronic mail; and

(2) specify additional activities or practices to which subsection (b) of this section applies if the Commission determines that those activities or practices are contributing substantially to the proliferation of commercial electronic mail messages that are unlawful under subsection (a) of this section.

(d) Requirement to place warning labels on commercial electronic mail containing sexually oriented material

(1) In general

No person may initiate in or affecting interstate commerce the transmission, to a protected computer, of any commercial electronic mail message that includes sexually oriented material and—

(A) fail to include in subject heading for the electronic mail message the marks or notices prescribed by the Commission under this subsection; or

(B) fail to provide that the matter in the message that is initially viewable to the recipient, when the message is opened by any recipient and absent any further actions by the recipient, includes only—

(i) to the extent required or authorized pursuant to paragraph (2), any such marks or notices;

(ii) the information required to be included in the message pursuant to subsection (a)(5) of this section; and

(iii) instructions on how to access, or a mechanism to access, the sexually oriented material.

(2) Prior affirmative consent

Paragraph (1) does not apply to the transmission of an electronic mail message if the recipient has given prior affirmative consent to receipt of the message.

(3) Prescription of marks and notices

Not later than 120 days after December 16, 2003, the Commission in consultation with the Attorney General shall prescribe clearly identifiable marks or notices to be included in or associated with commercial electronic mail that contains sexually oriented material, in order to inform the recipient of that fact and to facilitate filtering of such electronic mail. The Commission shall publish in the Federal Register and provide notice to the public of the marks or notices prescribed under this paragraph.

(4) Definition

In this subsection, the term "sexually oriented material" means any material that depicts sexually explicit conduct (as that term is defined in section 2256 of Title 18), unless the depiction constitutes a small and insignificant part of the whole, the remainder of which is not primarily devoted to sexual matters.

(5) Penalty

Whoever knowingly violates paragraph (1) shall be fined under Title 18 or imprisoned not more than 5 years, or both.

§ 7705. Businesses knowingly promoted by electronic mail with false or misleading transmission information

(a) In general

It is unlawful for a person to promote, or allow the promotion of, that person's trade or business, or goods, products, property, or services sold, offered for sale, leased or offered for lease, or otherwise made available through that trade or business, in a commercial electronic mail message the transmission of which is in violation of section 7704(a)(1) of this title if that person—

(1) knows, or should have known in the ordinary course of that person's trade or business, that the goods, products, property, or services sold, offered for sale, leased or offered for lease, or otherwise made available through that trade or business were being promoted in such a message;

(2) received or expected to receive an economic benefit from such promotion; and

(3) took no reasonable action—

(A) to prevent the transmission; or

(B) to detect the transmission and report it to the Commission.

(b) Limited enforcement against third parties

(1) In general

Except as provided in paragraph (2), a person (hereinafter referred to as the "third party") that provides goods, products, property, or services to another person that violates subsection (a) of this section shall not be held liable for such violation.

(2) Exception

Liability for a violation of subsection (a) of this section shall be imputed to a third party that provides goods, products, property, or services to another person that violates subsection (a) of this section if that third party—

(A) owns, or has a greater than 50 percent ownership or economic interest in, the trade or business of the person that violated subsection (a) of this section; or

(B)(i) has actual knowledge that goods, products, property, or services are promoted in a commercial electronic mail message the transmission of which is in violation of section 7704(a)(1) of this title; and

(ii) receives, or expects to receive, an economic benefit from such promotion.

(c) Exclusive enforcement by FTC

Subsections (f) and (g) of section 7706 of this title do not apply to violations of this section.

(d) Savings provision

Except as provided in section 7706(f)(8) of this title, nothing in this section may be construed to limit or prevent any action that may be taken under this chapter with respect to any violation of any other section of this chapter.

§ 7706. Enforcement generally

(a) Violation is unfair or deceptive act or practice

Except as provided in subsection (b) of this section, this chapter shall be enforced by the Commission as if the violation of this chapter were an unfair or deceptive act or practice proscribed under section 57a(a)(1)(B) of this title.

(b) Enforcement by certain other agencies

Compliance with this chapter shall be enforced—

(1) under section 1818 of Title 12, in the case of—

(A) national banks, and Federal branches and Federal agencies of foreign banks, by the Office of the Comptroller of the Currency;

(B) member banks of the Federal Reserve System (other than national banks), branches and agencies of foreign banks (other than Federal branches, Federal agencies, and insured State branches of foreign banks), commercial lending companies owned or controlled by foreign banks, organizations operating under section 25 or 25A of the Federal Reserve Act (12 U.S.C. 601 and 611), and bank holding companies, by the Board;

(C) banks insured by the Federal Deposit Insurance Corporation (other than members of the Federal Reserve System) and insured State branches of foreign banks, by the Board of Directors of the Federal Deposit Insurance Corporation; and

(D) savings associations the deposits of which are insured by the Federal Deposit Insurance Corporation, by the Director of the Office of Thrift Supervision;

(2) under the Federal Credit Union Act (12 U.S.C. 1751 et seq.) by the Board of the National Credit Union Administration with respect to any Federally insured credit union;

(3) under the Securities Exchange Act of 1934 (15 U.S.C. 78a et seq.) by the Securities and Exchange Commission with respect to any broker or dealer;

(4) under the Investment Company Act of 1940 (15 U.S.C. 80a-1 et seq.) by the Securities and Exchange Commission with respect to investment companies;

(5) under the Investment Advisers Act of 1940 (15 U.S.C. 80b-1 et seq.) by the Securities and Exchange Commission with respect to investment advisers registered under that Act;

(6) under State insurance law in the case of any person engaged in providing insurance, by the applicable State insurance authority of the State in which the person is domiciled, subject to section 6701 of this title, except that in any State in which the State insurance authority elects not to exercise this power, the enforcement authority pursuant to this chapter shall be exercised by the Commission in accordance with subsection (a) of this section;

(7) under part A of subtitle VII of Title 49 by the Secretary of Transportation with respect to any air carrier or foreign air carrier subject to that part;

(8) under the Packers and Stockyards Act, 1921 (7 U.S.C. 181 et seq.) (except as provided in section 406 of that Act (7 U.S.C. 226, 227)), by the Secretary of Agriculture with respect to any activities subject to that Act;

(9) under the Farm Credit Act of 1971 (12 U.S.C. 2001 et seq.) by the Farm Credit Administration with respect to any Federal land bank, Federal land bank association, Federal intermediate credit bank, or production credit association; and

(10) under the Communications Act of 1934 (47 U.S.C. 151 et seq.) by the Federal Communications Commission with respect to any person subject to the provisions of that Act.

(c) Exercise of certain powers

For the purpose of the exercise by any agency referred to in subsection (b) of this section of its powers under any Act referred to in that subsection, a violation of this chapter is deemed to be a violation of a Federal Trade Commission trade regulation rule. In addition to its powers under any provision of law specifically referred to in subsection (b) of this section, each of the agencies referred to in that subsection may exercise, for the purpose of enforcing compliance with any requirement imposed under this chapter, any other authority conferred on it by law.

(d) Actions by the Commission

The Commission shall prevent any person from violating this chapter in the same manner, by the same means, and with the same jurisdiction, powers, and duties as though all applicable terms and provisions of the Federal Trade Commission Act (15 U.S.C. 41 et seq.) were incorporated into and made a part of this chapter. Any entity that violates any provision of that subtitle is subject to the penalties and entitled to the privileges and immunities provided in the Federal Trade Commission Act in the same manner, by the same means, and with the same jurisdiction, power, and duties as though all applicable terms and provisions of the Federal Trade Commission Act were incorporated into and made a part of that subtitle.

(e) Availability of cease-and-desist orders and injunctive relief without showing of knowledge

Notwithstanding any other provision of this chapter, in any proceeding or action pursuant to subsection (a), (b), (c), or (d) of this section to enforce compliance, through an order to cease and desist or an injunction, with section 7704(a)(1)(C) of this title, section 7704(a)(2) of this title, clause (ii), (iii), or (iv) of section 7704(a)(4)(A) of this title, section 7704(b)(1)(A) of this title, or section 7704(b)(3) of this title, neither the Commission nor the Federal Communications Commission shall be required to allege or prove the state of mind required by such section or subparagraph.

(f) Enforcement by States

(1) Civil action

In any case in which the attorney general of a State, or an official or agency of a State, has reason to believe that an interest of the residents of that State has been or is threatened or adversely affected by any person who violates paragraph (1) or (2) of section 7704(a) of this title, who violates section 7704(d) of this title, or who engages in a pattern or practice that violates paragraph (3), (4), or (5) of section 7704(a) of this title, the attorney general, official, or agency of the State, as parens patriae, may bring a civil action on behalf of the residents of the State in a district court of the United States of appropriate jurisdiction—

(A) to enjoin further violation of section 7704 of this title by the defendant; or

(B) to obtain damages on behalf of residents of the State, in an amount equal to the greater of—

(i) the actual monetary loss suffered by such residents; or

(ii) the amount determined under paragraph (3).

(2) Availability of injunctive relief without showing of knowledge

Notwithstanding any other provision of this chapter, in a civil action under paragraph (1)(A) of this subsection, the attorney general, official, or agency of the State shall not be required to allege or prove the state of mind required by section 7704(a)(1)(C) of this title, section 7704(a)(2) of this title, clause (ii), (iii), or (iv) of section 7704(a)(4)(A) of this title, section 7704(b)(1)(A) of this title, or section 7704(b)(3) of this title.

(3) Statutory damages

(A) In general

For purposes of paragraph (1)(B)(ii), the amount determined under this paragraph is the amount calculated by multiplying the number of violations (with each separately addressed unlawful message received by or addressed to such residents treated as a separate violation) by up to $250.

(B) Limitation

For any violation of section 7704 of this title (other than section 7704(a)(1) of this title), the amount determined under subparagraph (A) may not exceed $2,000,000.

(C) Aggravated damages

The court may increase a damage award to an amount equal to not more than three times the amount otherwise available under this paragraph if—

(i) the court determines that the defendant committed the violation willfully and knowingly; or

(ii) the defendant's unlawful activity included one or more of the aggravating violations set forth in section 7704(b) of this title.

(D) Reduction of damages

In assessing damages under subparagraph (A), the court may consider whether—

(i) the defendant has established and implemented, with due care, commercially reasonable practices and procedures designed to effectively prevent such violations; or

(ii) the violation occurred despite commercially reasonable efforts to maintain compliance the practices and procedures to which reference is made in clause (i).

(4) Attorney fees

In the case of any successful action under paragraph (1), the court, in its discretion, may award the costs of the action and reasonable attorney fees to the State.

(5) Rights of Federal regulators

The State shall serve prior written notice of any action under paragraph (1) upon the Federal Trade Commission or the appropriate Federal regulator determined under subsection (b) of this section and provide the Commission or appropriate Federal regulator with a copy of its complaint, except in any case in which such prior notice is not feasible, in which case the State shall serve such notice immediately upon instituting such action. The Federal Trade Commission or appropriate Federal regulator shall have the right—

(A) to intervene in the action;

(B) upon so intervening, to be heard on all matters arising therein;

(C) to remove the action to the appropriate United States district court; and

(D) to file petitions for appeal.

(6) Construction

For purposes of bringing any civil action under paragraph (1), nothing in this chapter shall be construed to prevent an attorney general of a State from exercising the powers conferred on the attorney general by the laws of that State to—

(A) conduct investigations;

(B) administer oaths or affirmations; or

(C) compel the attendance of witnesses or the production of documentary and other evidence.

(7) Venue; service of process

(A) Venue

Any action brought under paragraph (1) may be brought in the district court of the United States that meets applicable requirements relating to venue under section 1391 of Title 28.

(B) Service of process

In an action brought under paragraph (1), process may be served in any district in which the defendant—

(i) is an inhabitant; or

(ii) maintains a physical place of business.

(8) Limitation on State action while Federal action is pending

If the Commission, or other appropriate Federal agency under subsection (b) of this section, has instituted a civil action or an administrative action for violation of this chapter, no State attorney general, or official or agency of a State, may bring an action under this subsection during the pendency of that action against any defendant named in the complaint of the Commission or the other agency for any violation of this chapter alleged in the complaint.

(9) Requisite scienter for certain civil actions

Except as provided in section 7704(a)(1)(C) of this title, section 7704(a)(2) of this title, clause (ii), (iii), or (iv) of section 7704(a)(4)(A) of this title, section 7704(b)(1)(A) of this title, or section 7704(b)(3) of this title, in a civil action brought by a State attorney general, or an official or agency of a State, to recover monetary damages for a violation of this chapter, the court shall not grant the relief sought unless the attorney general, official, or agency establishes that the defendant acted with actual knowledge, or knowledge fairly implied on the basis of objective circumstances, of the act or omission that constitutes the violation.

(g) Action by provider of Internet access service

(1) Action authorized

A provider of Internet access service adversely affected by a violation of section 7704(a)(1) of this title, 7704(b) of this title, or 7704(d) of this title, or a pattern or practice that violates paragraph (2), (3), (4), or (5) of section 7704(a) of this title, may bring a civil action in any district court of the United States with jurisdiction over the defendant—

(A) to enjoin further violation by the defendant; or

(B) to recover damages in an amount equal to the greater of—

(i) actual monetary loss incurred by the provider of Internet access service as a result of such violation; or

(ii) the amount determined under paragraph (3).

(2) Special definition of "procure"

In any action brought under paragraph (1), this chapter shall be applied as if the definition of the term "procure" in section 7702(12) of this title contained, after "behalf" the words "with actual knowledge, or by consciously avoiding knowing, whether such person is engaging, or will engage, in a pattern or practice that violates this chapter".

(3) Statutory damages

(A) In general

For purposes of paragraph (1)(B)(ii), the amount determined under this paragraph is the amount calculated by multiplying the number of violations (with each separately addressed unlawful message that is transmitted or attempted to be transmitted over the facilities of the provider of Internet access service, or that is transmitted or attempted to be transmitted to an electronic mail address obtained from the provider of Internet access service in violation of section 7704(b)(1)(A)(i) of this title, treated as a separate violation) by—

(i) up to $100, in the case of a violation of section 7704(a)(1) of this title; or

(ii) up to $25, in the case of any other violation of section 7704 of this title.

(B) Limitation

For any violation of section 7704 of this title (other than section 7704(a)(1) of this title), the amount determined under subparagraph (A) may not exceed $1,000,000.

(C) Aggravated damages

The court may increase a damage award to an amount equal to not more than three times the amount otherwise available under this paragraph if—

(i) the court determines that the defendant committed the violation willfully and knowingly; or

(ii) the defendant's unlawful activity included one or more of the aggravated violations set forth in section 7704(b) of this title.

(D) Reduction of damages

In assessing damages under subparagraph (A), the court may consider whether—

(i) the defendant has established and implemented, with due care, commercially reasonable practices and procedures designed to effectively prevent such violations; or

(ii) the violation occurred despite commercially reasonable efforts to maintain compliance with the practices and procedures to which reference is made in clause (i).

(4) Attorney fees

In any action brought pursuant to paragraph (1), the court may, in its discretion, require an undertaking for the payment of the costs of such action, and assess reasonable costs, including reasonable attorneys' fees, against any party.

§ 7707. Effect on other laws

(a) Federal law

(1) Nothing in this chapter shall be construed to impair the enforcement of section 223 or 231 of Title 47, chapter 71 (relating to obscenity) or 110 (relating to sexual exploitation of children) of Title 18, or any other Federal criminal statute.

(2) Nothing in this chapter shall be construed to affect in any way the Commission's authority to bring enforcement actions under FTC Act for materially false or deceptive representations or unfair practices in commercial electronic mail messages.

(b) State law

(1) In general

This chapter supersedes any statute, regulation, or rule of a State or political subdivision of a State that expressly regulates the use of electronic mail to send commercial messages, except to the extent that any such statute, regulation, or rule prohibits falsity or deception in any portion of a commercial electronic mail message or information attached thereto.

(2) State law not specific to electronic mail

This chapter shall not be construed to preempt the applicability of—

(A) State laws that are not specific to electronic mail, including State trespass, contract, or tort law; or

(B) other State laws to the extent that those laws relate to acts of fraud or computer crime.

(c) No effect on policies of providers of Internet access service

Nothing in this chapter shall be construed to have any effect on the lawfulness or unlawfulness, under any other provision of law, of the adoption, implementation, or enforcement by a provider of Internet access service of a policy of declining to transmit, route, relay, handle, or store certain types of electronic mail messages.

§ 7708. Do-Not-E-Mail registry

(a) In general

Not later than 6 months after December 16, 2003, the Commission shall transmit to the Senate Committee on Commerce, Science, and Transportation and the House of Representatives Committee on Energy and Commerce a report that—

(1) sets forth a plan and timetable for establishing a nationwide marketing Do-Not-E-Mail registry;

(2) includes an explanation of any practical, technical, security, privacy, enforceability, or other concerns that the Commission has regarding such a registry; and

(3) includes an explanation of how the registry would be applied with respect to children with e-mail accounts.

(b) Authorization to implement

The Commission may establish and implement the plan, but not earlier than 9 months after December 16, 2003.

§ 7709. Study of effects of commercial electronic mail

(a) In general

Not later than 24 months after December 16, 2003, the Commission, in consultation with the Department of Justice and other appropriate agencies, shall submit a report to the Congress that provides a detailed analysis of the effectiveness and enforcement of the provisions of this chapter and the need (if any) for the Congress to modify such provisions.

(b) Required analysis

The Commission shall include in the report required by subsection (a) of this section—

(1) an analysis of the extent to which technological and marketplace developments, including changes in the nature of the devices through which consumers access their electronic mail messages, may affect the practicality and effectiveness of the provisions of this chapter;

(2) analysis and recommendations concerning how to address commercial electronic mail that originates in or is transmitted through or to facilities or computers in other nations, including initiatives or policy positions that the Federal Government could pursue through international negotiations, fora, organizations, or institutions; and

(3) analysis and recommendations concerning options for protecting consumers, including children, from the receipt and viewing of commercial electronic mail that is obscene or pornographic.

§ 7710. Improving enforcement by providing rewards for information about violations; labeling

The Commission shall transmit to the Senate Committee on Commerce, Science, and Transportation and the House of Representatives Committee on Energy and Commerce—

(1) a report, within 9 months after December 16, 2003, that sets forth a system for rewarding those who supply information about violations of this chapter, including—

(A) procedures for the Commission to grant a reward of not less than 20 percent of the total civil penalty collected for a violation of this chapter to the first person that—

(i) identifies the person in violation of this chapter; and

(ii) supplies information that leads to the successful collection of a civil penalty by the Commission; and

(B) procedures to minimize the burden of submitting a complaint to the Commission concerning violations of this chapter, including procedures to allow the electronic submission of complaints to the Commission; and

(2) a report, within 18 months after December 16, 2003, that sets forth a plan for requiring commercial electronic mail to be identifiable from its subject line, by means of compliance with Internet Engineering Task Force Standards, the use of the characters "ADV" in the subject line, or other comparable identifier, or an explanation of any concerns the Commission has that cause the Commission to recommend against the plan.

§ 7711. Regulations

(a) In general

The Commission may issue regulations to implement the provisions of this Act (not including the amendments made by sections 4 and 12). Any such regulations shall be issued in accordance with section 553 of Title 5.

(b) Limitation

Subsection (a) of this section may not be construed to authorize the Commission to establish a requirement pursuant to section 7704(a)(5)(A) of this title to include any specific words, characters, marks, or labels in a commercial electronic mail message, or to include the identification required by section 7704(a)(5)(A) of this title in any particular part of such a mail message (such as the subject line or body).

§ 7712. Application to wireless

(a) Effect on other law

Nothing in this chapter shall be interpreted to preclude or override the applicability of section 227 of Title 47 or the rules prescribed under section 6102 of this title.

(b) FCC rulemaking

The Federal Communications Commission, in consultation with the Federal Trade Commission, shall promulgate rules within 270 days to protect consumers from unwanted mobile service commercial messages. The Federal Communications Commission, in promulgating the rules, shall, to the extent consistent with subsection (c) of this section—

(1) provide subscribers to commercial mobile services the ability to avoid receiving mobile service commercial messages unless the subscriber has provided express prior authorization to the sender, except as provided in paragraph (3);

(2) allow recipients of mobile service commercial messages to indicate electronically a desire not to receive future mobile service commercial messages from the sender;

(3) take into consideration, in determining whether to subject providers of commercial mobile services to paragraph (1), the relationship that exists between providers of such services and their subscribers, but if the Commission determines that such providers should not be subject to paragraph (1), the rules shall require such providers, in addition to complying with the other provisions of this chapter, to allow subscribers to indicate a desire not to receive future mobile service commercial messages from the provider—

(A) at the time of subscribing to such service; and

(B) in any billing mechanism; and

(4) determine how a sender of mobile service commercial messages may comply with the provisions of this chapter, considering the unique technical aspects, including the functional and character limitations, of devices that receive such messages.

(c) Other factors considered

The Federal Communications Commission shall consider the ability of a sender of a commercial electronic mail message to reasonably determine that the message is a mobile service commercial message.

(d) Mobile service commercial message defined

In this section, the term "mobile service commercial message" means a commercial electronic mail message that is transmitted directly to a wireless device that is utilized by a subscriber of commercial mobile service (as such term is defined in section 332(d) of Title 47) in connection with such service.

§ 7713. Separability

If any provision of this chapter or the application thereof to any person or circumstance is held invalid, the remainder of this chapter and the application of such provision to other persons or circumstances shall not be affected.

Identity Theft Assumption and Deterrence Act (1998)

18 U.S.C. § 1028, as amended

Statutes in Context

The Identity Theft Assumption and Deterrence Act makes it a federal crime to knowingly transfer, without lawful authority, a means of identification of another person with the intent to commit a federal crime or a felony under state or local law.

§ 1028. Fraud and related activity in connection with identification documents, authentication features, and information

(a) Whoever, in a circumstance described in subsection (c) of this section—

(1) knowingly and without lawful authority produces an identification document, authentication feature, or a false identification document;

(2) knowingly transfers an identification document, authentication feature, or a false identification document knowing that such document or feature was stolen or produced without lawful authority;

(3) knowingly possesses with intent to use unlawfully or transfer unlawfully five or more identification documents (other than those issued lawfully for the use of the possessor), authentication features, or false identification documents;

(4) knowingly possesses an identification document (other than one issued lawfully for the use of the possessor), authentication feature, or a false identification document, with the intent such document or feature be used to defraud the United States;

(5) knowingly produces, transfers, or possesses a document-making implement or authentication feature with the intent such document-making implement or authentication feature will be used in the production of a false identification document or another document-making implement or authentication feature which will be so used;

(6) knowingly possesses an identification document or authentication feature that is or appears to be an identification document or authentication feature of the United States or a sponsoring entity of an event designated as a special event of national significance which is stolen or produced without lawful authority knowing that such document or feature was stolen or produced without such authority;

(7) knowingly transfers, possesses, or uses, without lawful authority, a means of identification of another person with the intent to commit, or to aid or abet, or in connection with, any unlawful activity that constitutes a violation of Federal law, or that constitutes a felony under any applicable State or local law; or

(8) knowingly traffics in false or actual authentication features for use in false identification documents, document-making implements, or means of identification;

shall be punished as provided in subsection (b) of this section.

(b) The punishment for an offense under subsection (a) of this section is—

(1) except as provided in paragraphs (3) and (4), a fine under this title or imprisonment for not more than 15 years, or both, if the offense is—

(A) the production or transfer of an identification document, authentication feature, or false identification document that is or appears to be—

(i) an identification document or authentication feature issued by or under the authority of the United States; or

(ii) a birth certificate, or a driver's license or personal identification card;

(B) the production or transfer of more than five identification documents, authentication features, or false identification documents;

(C) an offense under paragraph (5) of such subsection; or

(D) an offense under paragraph (7) of such subsection that involves the transfer, possession, or use of 1 or more means of identification if, as a result of the offense, any individual committing the offense obtains anything of value aggregating $1,000 or more during any 1-year period;

(2) except as provided in paragraphs (3) and (4), a fine under this title or imprisonment for not more than 5 years, or both, if the offense is—

(A) any other production, transfer, or use of a means of identification, an identification document, authentication feature, or a false identification document; or

(B) an offense under paragraph (3) or (7) of such subsection;

(3) a fine under this title or imprisonment for not more than 20 years, or both, if the offense is committed—

(A) to facilitate a drug trafficking crime (as defined in section 929(a)(2));

(B) in connection with a crime of violence (as defined in section 924(c)(3)); or

(C) after a prior conviction under this section becomes final;

(4) a fine under this title or imprisonment for not more than 30 years, or both, if the offense is committed to facilitate an act of domestic terrorism (as defined under section 2331(5) of this title) or an act of international terrorism (as defined in section 2331(1) of this title);

(5) in the case of any offense under subsection (a), forfeiture to the United States of any personal property used or intended to be used to commit the offense; and

(6) a fine under this title or imprisonment for not more than one year, or both, in any other case.

(c) The circumstance referred to in subsection (a) of this section is that—

(1) the identification document, authentication feature, or false identification document is or appears to be issued by or under the authority of the United States or a sponsoring entity of an event designated as a special event of national significance or the document-making implement is designed or suited for making such an identification document, authentication feature, or false identification document;

(2) the offense is an offense under subsection (a) (4) of this section; or

(3) either—

(A) the production, transfer, possession, or use prohibited by this section is in or affects interstate or foreign commerce, including the transfer of a document by electronic means; or

(B) the means of identification, identification document, false identification document, or document-making implement is transported in the mail in the course of the production, transfer, possession, or use prohibited by this section.

(d) In this section and section 1028A—

(1) the term "authentication feature" means any hologram, watermark, certification, symbol, code, image, sequence of numbers or letters, or other feature that either individually or in combination with another feature is used by the issuing authority on an identification document, document-making implement, or means of identification to determine if the document is counterfeit, altered, or otherwise falsified;

(2) the term "document-making implement" means any implement, impression, template, computer file, computer disc, electronic device, or computer hardware or software, that is specifically configured or primarily used for making an identification document, a false identification document, or another document-making implement;

(3) the term "identification document" means a document made or issued by or under the authority of the United States Government, a State, political subdivision of a State, a sponsoring entity of an event designated as a special event of national significance, a foreign government, political subdivision of a foreign government, an international governmental or an international quasi-governmental organization which, when completed with information concerning a particular individual, is of a type intended or commonly accepted for the purpose of identification of individuals;

(4) the term "false identification document" means a document of a type intended or commonly accepted for the purposes of identification of individuals that—

(A) is not issued by or under the authority of a governmental entity or was issued under the authority of a governmental entity but was subsequently altered for purposes of deceit; and

(B) appears to be issued by or under the authority of the United States Government, a State, a political subdivision of a State, a sponsoring entity of an event designated by the President as a special event of national significance, a foreign government, a political subdivision of a foreign government, or an international governmental or quasi-governmental organization;

(5) the term "false authentication feature" means an authentication feature that—

(A) is genuine in origin, but, without the authorization of the issuing authority, has been tampered with or altered for purposes of deceit;

(B) is genuine, but has been distributed, or is intended for distribution, without the authorization of the issuing authority and not in connection with a lawfully made identification document, document-making implement, or means of identification to which such authentication feature is intended to be affixed or embedded by the respective issuing authority; or

(C) appears to be genuine, but is not;

(6) the term “issuing authority”—

(A) means any governmental entity or agency that is authorized to issue identification documents, means of identification, or authentication features; and

(B) includes the United States Government, a State, a political subdivision of a State, a sponsoring entity of an event designated by the President as a special event of national significance, a foreign government, a political subdivision of a foreign government, or an international government or quasi-governmental organization;

(7) the term “means of identification” means any name or number that may be used, alone or in conjunction with any other information, to identify a specific individual, including any—

(A) name, social security number, date of birth, official State or government issued driver’s license or identification number, alien registration number, government passport number, employer or taxpayer identification number;

(B) unique biometric data, such as fingerprint, voice print, retina or iris image, or other unique physical representation;

(C) unique electronic identification number, address, or routing code; or

(D) telecommunication identifying information or access device (as defined in section 1029(e));

(8) the term “personal identification card” means an identification document issued by a State or local government solely for the purpose of identification;

(9) the term “produce” includes alter, authenticate, or assemble;

(10) the term “transfer” includes selecting an identification document, false identification document, or document-making implement and placing or directing the placement of such identification document, false identification document, or document-making implement on an online location where it is available to others;

(11) the term “State” includes any State of the United States, the District of Columbia, the Commonwealth of Puerto Rico, and any other commonwealth, possession, or territory of the United States; and

(12) the term “traffic” means—

(A) to transport, transfer, or otherwise dispose of, to another, as consideration for anything of value; or

(B) to make or obtain control of with intent to so transport, transfer, or otherwise dispose of.

(e) This section does not prohibit any lawfully authorized investigative, protective, or intelligence activity of a law enforcement agency of the United States, a State, or a political subdivision of a State, or of an intelligence agency of the United States, or any activity authorized under chapter 224 of this title.

(f) Attempt and conspiracy.—Any person who attempts or conspires to commit any offense under this section shall be subject to the same penalties as those prescribed for the offense, the commission of which was the object of the attempt or conspiracy.

(g) Forfeiture procedures.—The forfeiture of property under this section, including any seizure and disposition of the property and any related judicial or administrative proceeding, shall be governed by the provisions of section 413 (other than subsection (d) of that section) of the Comprehensive Drug Abuse Prevention and Control Act of 1970 (21 U.S.C. 853).

(h) Forfeiture; disposition.—In the circumstance in which any person is convicted of a violation of subsection (a), the court shall order, in addition to the penalty prescribed, the forfeiture and destruction or other disposition of all illicit authentication features, identification documents, document-making implements, or means of identification.

(i) Rule of construction.—For purpose of subsection (a)(7), a single identification document or false identification document that contains 1 or more means of identification shall be construed to be 1 means of identification.

California Breach Notification Statute—S.B. 1386 (2002)

Cal. Civ. Code §§ 1798.29, 1798.82, 1798.84, as amended

Statutes in Context

The California Breach Notification Statute has exercised a strong influence on other states' data security breach notification laws. It requires data breach notices to be sent when there is evidence of "acquisition" of personal data by a third party. The Act also provides a private right of action for customers of businesses injured by a violation of this law.

§ 1798.29. Agencies owning, licensing, or maintaining, computerized data including personal information; disclosure of security breach; notice requirements

(a) Any agency that owns or licenses computerized data that includes personal information shall disclose any breach of the security of the system following discovery or notification of the breach in the security of the data to any resident of California whose unencrypted personal information was, or is reasonably believed to have been, acquired by an unauthorized person. The disclosure shall be made in the most expedient time possible and without unreasonable delay, consistent with the legitimate needs of law enforcement, as provided in subdivision (c), or any measures necessary to determine the scope of the breach and restore the reasonable integrity of the data system.

(b) Any agency that maintains computerized data that includes personal information that the agency does not own shall notify the owner or licensee of the information of any breach of the security of the data immediately following discovery, if the personal information was, or is reasonably believed to have been, acquired by an unauthorized person.

(c) The notification required by this section may be delayed if a law enforcement agency determines that the notification will impede a criminal investigation. The notification required by this section shall be made after the law enforcement agency determines that it will not compromise the investigation.

(d) For purposes of this section, "breach of the security of the system" means unauthorized acquisition of computerized data that compromises the security, confidentiality, or integrity of personal information maintained by the agency. Good faith acquisition of personal information by an employee or agent of the agency for the purposes of the agency is not a breach of the security of the system, provided that the personal information is not used or subject to further unauthorized disclosure.

(e) For purposes of this section, "personal information" means an individual's first name or first initial and last name in combination with any one or more of the following data elements, when either the name or the data elements are not encrypted:

(1) Social security number.

(2) Driver's license number or California Identification Card number.

(3) Account number, credit or debit card number, in combination with any required security code, access code, or password that would permit access to an individual's financial account.

(f) For purposes of this section, "personal information" does not include publicly available information that is lawfully made available to the general public from federal, state, or local government records.

(g) For purposes of this section, "notice" may be provided by one of the following methods:

(1) Written notice.

(2) Electronic notice, if the notice provided is consistent with the provisions regarding electronic records and signatures set forth in Section 7001 of Title 15 of the United States Code.

(3) Substitute notice, if the agency demonstrates that the cost of providing notice would exceed two hundred fifty thousand dollars ($250,000), or that the affected class of subject persons to be notified exceeds 500,000, or the agency does not have sufficient contact information. Substitute notice shall consist of all of the following:

(A) E-mail notice when the agency has an e-mail address for the subject persons.

(B) Conspicuous posting of the notice on the agency's Web site page, if the agency maintains one.

(C) Notification to major statewide media.

(h) Notwithstanding subdivision (g), an agency that maintains its own notification procedures as part of an information security policy for the treatment of personal information and is otherwise consistent with the timing requirements of this part shall be deemed to be in compliance with the notification requirements of this section if it notifies subject persons in accordance with its policies in the event of a breach of security of the system.

§ 1798.82. Civil actions; violation of title

(a) Any person or business that conducts business in California, and that owns or licenses computerized data that includes personal information, shall disclose any breach of the security of the system following discovery or notification of the breach in the security of the data to any resident of California whose unencrypted personal information was, or is reasonably believed to have been, acquired by an unauthorized person. The disclosure shall be made in the most expedient time possible and without unreasonable delay, consistent with the legitimate needs of law enforcement, as provided in subdivision (c), or any measures necessary to determine the scope of the breach and restore the reasonable integrity of the data system.

(b) Any person or business that maintains computerized data that includes personal information that the person or business does not own shall notify the owner or licensee of the information of any breach of the security of the data immediately following discovery, if the personal information was, or is reasonably believed to have been, acquired by an unauthorized person.

(c) The notification required by this section may be delayed if a law enforcement agency determines that the notification will impede a criminal investigation. The notification required by this section shall be made after the law enforcement agency determines that it will not compromise the investigation.

(d) For purposes of this section, "breach of the security of the system" means unauthorized acquisition of computerized data that compromises the security, confidentiality, or integrity of personal information maintained by the person or business. Good faith acquisition of personal information by an employee or agent of the person or business for the purposes of the person or business is not a breach of the security of the system, provided that the personal information is not used or subject to further unauthorized disclosure.

(e) For purposes of this section, "personal information" means an individual's first name or first initial and last name in combination with any one or more of the following data elements, when either the name or the data elements are not encrypted:

(1) Social security number.

(2) Driver's license number or California Identification Card number.

(3) Account number, credit or debit card number, in combination with any required security code, access code, or password that would permit access to an individual's financial account.

(f) For purposes of this section, "personal information" does not include publicly available information that is lawfully made available to the general public from federal, state, or local government records.

(g) For purposes of this section, "notice" may be provided by one of the following methods:

(1) Written notice.

(2) Electronic notice, if the notice provided is consistent with the provisions regarding electronic records and signatures set forth in Section 7001 of Title 15 of the United States Code.

(3) Substitute notice, if the person or business demonstrates that the cost of providing notice would exceed two hundred fifty thousand dollars ($250,000), or that the affected class of subject persons to be notified exceeds 500,000, or the person or business does not have sufficient contact information. Substitute notice shall consist of all of the following:

(A) E-mail notice when the person or business has an e-mail address for the subject persons.

(B) Conspicuous posting of the notice on the Web site page of the person or business, if the person or business maintains one.

(C) Notification to major statewide media.

(h) Notwithstanding subdivision (g), a person or business that maintains its own notification procedures as part of an information security policy for the treatment of personal information and is otherwise consistent with the timing requirements of this part, shall be deemed to be in compliance with the notification requirements of this section if the person or business notifies subject persons in accordance with its policies in the event of a breach of security of the system.

§ 1798.83. Personal information; disclosure to direct marketers

(a) Except as otherwise provided in subdivision (d), if a business has an established business relationship with a customer and has within the immediately preceding calendar year disclosed personal information that corresponds to any of the categories of personal information set forth in paragraph (6) of subdivision (e) to third parties, and if the business knows or reasonably should know that the third parties used the personal information for the third parties' direct marketing purposes, that business shall, after the receipt of a written or electronic mail request, or, if the business chooses to receive requests by toll-free telephone or facsimile numbers, a telephone or facsimile request from the customer, provide all of the following information to the customer free of charge:

> **(1)** In writing or by electronic mail, a list of the categories set forth in paragraph (6) of subdivision (e) that correspond to the personal information disclosed by the business to third parties for the third parties' direct marketing purposes during the immediately preceding calendar year.
>
> **(2)** In writing or by electronic mail, the names and addresses of all of the third parties that received personal information from the business for the third parties' direct marketing purposes during the preceding calendar year and, if the nature of the third parties' business cannot reasonably be determined from the third parties' name, examples of the products or services marketed, if known to the business, sufficient to give the customer a reasonable indication of the nature of the third parties' business.

(b)(1) A business required to comply with this section shall designate a mailing address, electronic mail address, or, if the business chooses to receive requests by telephone or facsimile, a toll-free telephone or facsimile number, to which customers may deliver requests pursuant to subdivision (a). A business required to comply with this section shall, at its election, do at least one of the following:

> **(A)** Notify all agents and managers who directly supervise employees who regularly have contact with customers of the designated addresses or numbers or the means to obtain those addresses or numbers and instruct those employees that customers who inquire about the business's privacy practices or the business's compliance with this section shall be informed of the designated addresses or numbers or the means to obtain the addresses or numbers.
>
> **(B)** Add to the home page of its Web site a link either to a page titled "Your Privacy Rights" or add the words "Your Privacy Rights" to the home page's link to the business's privacy policy. If the business elects to add the words "Your Privacy Rights" to the link to the business's privacy policy, the words "Your Privacy Rights" shall be in the same style and size as the link to the business's privacy policy. If the business does not display a link to its privacy policy on the home page of its Web site, or does not have a privacy policy, the words "Your Privacy Rights" shall be written in larger type than the surrounding text, or in contrasting type, font, or color to the surrounding text of the same size, or set off from the surrounding text of the same size by symbols or other marks that call attention to the language. The first page of the link shall describe a customer's rights pursuant to this section and shall provide the designated mailing address, e-mail address, as required, or toll-free telephone number or facsimile number, as appropriate. If the business elects to add the words "Your California Privacy Rights" to the home page's link to the business's privacy policy in a manner that complies with this subdivision, and the first page of the link describes a customer's rights pursuant to this section, and provides the designated mailing address, electronic mailing address, as

required, or toll-free telephone or facsimile number, as appropriate, the business need not respond to requests that are not received at one of the designated addresses or numbers.

(C) Make the designated addresses or numbers, or means to obtain the designated addresses or numbers, readily available upon request of a customer at every place of business in California where the business or its agents regularly have contact with customers.

The response to a request pursuant to this section received at one of the designated addresses or numbers shall be provided within 30 days. Requests received by the business at other than one of the designated addresses or numbers shall be provided within a reasonable period, in light of the circumstances related to how the request was received, but not to exceed 150 days from the date received.

(2) A business that is required to comply with this section and Section 6803 of Title 15 of the United States Code may comply with this section by providing the customer the disclosure required by Section 6803 of Title 15 of the United States Code, but only if the disclosure also complies with this section.

(3) A business that is required to comply with this section is not obligated to provide information associated with specific individuals and may provide the information required by this section in standardized format.

(c)(1) A business that is required to comply with this section is not obligated to do so in response to a request from a customer more than once during the course of any calendar year. A business with fewer than 20 full-time or part-time employees is exempt from the requirements of this section.

(2) If a business that is required to comply with this section adopts and discloses to the public, in its privacy policy, a policy of not disclosing personal information of customers to third parties for the third parties' direct marketing purposes unless the customer first affirmatively agrees to that disclosure, or of not disclosing the personal information of customers to third parties for the third parties' direct marketing purposes if the customer has exercised an option that prevents that information from being disclosed to third parties for those purposes, as long as the business maintains and discloses the policies, the business may comply with subdivision (a) by notifying the customer of his or her right to prevent disclosure of personal information, and providing the customer with a cost- free means to exercise that right.

(d) The following are among the disclosures not deemed to be disclosures of personal information by a business for a third party's direct marketing purposes for purposes of this section:

(1) Disclosures between a business and a third party pursuant to contracts or arrangements pertaining to any of the following:

(A) The processing, storage, management, or organization of personal information, or the performance of services on behalf of the business during which personal information is disclosed, if the third party that processes, stores, manages, or organizes the personal information does not use the information for a third party's direct marketing purposes and does not disclose the information to additional third parties for their direct marketing purposes.

(B) Marketing products or services to customers with whom the business has an established business relationship where, as a part of the marketing, the business does not disclose personal information to third parties for the third parties' direct marketing purposes.

(C) Maintaining or servicing accounts, including credit accounts and disclosures pertaining to the denial of applications for credit or the status of applications for credit and processing bills or insurance claims for payment.

(D) Public record information relating to the right, title, or interest in real property or information relating to property characteristics, as defined in Section 408.3 of the Revenue and Taxation Code, obtained from a governmental agency or entity or from a multiple listing service, as defined in Section 1087, and not provided directly by the customer to a business in the course of an established business relationship.

(E) Jointly offering a product or service pursuant to a written agreement with the third party that receives the personal information, provided that all of the following requirements are met:

(i) The product or service offered is a product or service of, and is provided by, at least one of the businesses that is a party to the written agreement.

(ii) The product or service is jointly offered, endorsed, or sponsored by, and clearly and conspicuously identifies for the customer, the businesses that disclose and receive the disclosed personal information.

(iii) The written agreement provides that the third party that receives the personal information is required to maintain the confidentiality of the information and is prohibited from disclosing or using the information other than to carry out the joint offering or servicing of a product or service that is the subject of the written agreement.

(2) Disclosures to or from a consumer reporting agency of a customer's payment history or other information pertaining to transactions or experiences between the business and a customer if that information is to be reported in, or used to generate, a consumer report as defined in subdivision (d) of Section 1681a of Title 15 of the United States Code, and use of that information is limited by the federal Fair Credit Reporting Act (15 U.S.C. Sec. 1681 et seq.).

(3) Disclosures of personal information by a business to a third party financial institution solely for the purpose of the business obtaining payment for a transaction in which the customer paid the business for goods or services with a check, credit card, charge card, or debit card, if the customer seeks the information required by subdivision (a) from the business obtaining payment, whether or not the business obtaining payment knows or reasonably should know that the third party financial institution has used the personal information for its direct marketing purposes.

(4) Disclosures of personal information between a licensed agent and its principal, if the personal information disclosed is necessary to complete, effectuate, administer, or enforce transactions between the principal and the agent, whether or not the licensed agent or principal also uses the personal information for direct marketing purposes, if that personal information is used by each of them solely to market products and services directly to customers with whom both have established business relationships as a result of the principal and agent relationship.

(5) Disclosures of personal information between a financial institution and a business that has a private label credit card, affinity card, retail installment contract, or cobranded card program with the financial institution, if the personal information disclosed is necessary for the financial institution to maintain or service accounts on behalf of the business with which it has a private label credit card, affinity card, retail installment contract, or cobranded card program, or to complete, effectuate, administer, or enforce customer transactions or transactions between the institution and the business, whether or not the institution or the business also uses the personal information for direct marketing purposes, if that personal information is used solely to market products and services directly to customers with whom both the business and the financial institution have established business relationships as a result of the private label credit card, affinity card, retail installment contract, or cobranded card program.

(e) For purposes of this section, the following terms have the following meanings:

(1) "Customer" means an individual who is a resident of California who provides personal information to a business during the creation of, or throughout the duration of, an established business relationship if the business relationship is primarily for personal, family, or household purposes.

(2) "Direct marketing purposes" means the use of personal information to solicit or induce a purchase, rental, lease, or exchange of products, goods, property, or services directly to individuals by means of the mail, telephone, or electronic mail for their personal, family, or household purposes. The sale, rental, exchange, or lease of personal information for consideration to businesses is a direct marketing purpose of the business that sells, rents, exchanges, or obtains consideration for the personal information. "Direct marketing purposes" does not include the use of personal information (A) by bona fide tax exempt charitable or religious organizations to solicit charitable contributions, (B) to raise funds from and communicate with individuals regarding politics and government, (C) by a third party when the third party receives personal information solely as a consequence of having obtained for consideration permanent ownership of accounts that might contain personal information, or (D) by a third party when the third party receives personal information solely as a consequence of a single transaction where, as a part of the transaction, personal information had to be disclosed in order to effectuate the transaction.

(3) "Disclose" means to disclose, release, transfer, disseminate, or otherwise communicate orally, in writing, or by electronic or any other means to any third party.

(4) "Employees who regularly have contact with customers" means employees whose contact with customers is not incidental to their primary employment duties, and whose duties do not predominantly involve ensuring the safety or health of the business's customers. It includes, but is not limited to, employees whose primary employment duties are as cashier, clerk, customer service, sales, or promotion. It does not, by way of example, include employees whose primary employment duties consist of food or beverage preparation or service, maintenance and repair of the business's facilities or equipment, direct involvement in the operation of a motor vehicle, aircraft, watercraft, amusement ride, heavy machinery or similar equipment, security, or participation in a theatrical, literary, musical, artistic, or athletic performance or contest.

(5) "Established business relationship" means a relationship formed by a voluntary, two-way communication between a business and a customer, with or without an exchange of consideration, for the purpose of purchasing, renting, or leasing real or personal property, or any interest therein, or obtaining a product or service from the business, if the relationship is ongoing and has not been expressly terminated by the business or the customer, or if the relationship is not ongoing, but is solely established by the purchase, rental, or lease of real or personal property from a business, or the purchase of a product or service, and no more than 18 months have elapsed from the date of the purchase, rental, or lease.

(6)(A) The categories of personal information required to be disclosed pursuant to paragraph (1) of subdivision (a) are all of the following:

(i) Name and address.

(ii) Electronic mail address.

(iii) Age or date of birth.

(iv) Names of children.

(v) Electronic mail or other addresses of children.

(vi) Number of children.

(vii) The age or gender of children.

(viii) Height.

(ix) Weight.

(x) Race.

(xi) Religion.

(xii) Occupation.

(xiii) Telephone number.

(xiv) Education.

(xv) Political party affiliation.

(xvi) Medical condition.

(xvii) Drugs, therapies, or medical products or equipment used.

(xviii) The kind of product the customer purchased, leased, or rented.

(xix) Real property purchased, leased, or rented.

(xx) The kind of service provided.

(xxi) Social security number.

(xxii) Bank account number.

(xxiii) Credit card number.

(xxiv) Debit card number.

(xxv) Bank or investment account, debit card, or credit card balance.

(xxvi) Payment history.

(xxvii) Information pertaining to the customer's creditworthiness, assets, income, or liabilities.

(B) If a list, description, or grouping of customer names or addresses is derived using any of these categories, and is disclosed to a third party for direct marketing purposes in a manner that permits the third party to identify, determine, or extrapolate any other personal information from which the list was derived, and that personal information when it was disclosed identified, described, or was associated with an individual, the categories set forth in this subdivision that correspond to the personal information used to derive the list, description, or grouping shall be considered personal information for purposes of this section.

(7) "Personal information" as used in this section means any information that when it was disclosed identified, described, or was able to be associated with an individual and includes all of the following:

(A) An individual's name and address.

(B) Electronic mail address.

(C) Age or date of birth.

(D) Names of children.

(E) Electronic mail or other addresses of children.

(F) Number of children.

(G) The age or gender of children.

(H) Height.

(I) Weight.

(J) Race.

(K) Religion.

(L) Occupation.

(M) Telephone number.

(N) Education.

(O) Political party affiliation.

(P) Medical condition.

(Q) Drugs, therapies, or medical products or equipment used.

(R) The kind of product the customer purchased, leased, or rented.

(S) Real property purchased, leased, or rented.

(T) The kind of service provided.

(U) Social security number.

(V) Bank account number.

(W) Credit card number.

(X) Debit card number.

(Y) Bank or investment account, debit card, or credit card balance.

(Z) Payment history.

(AA) Information pertaining to creditworthiness, assets, income, or liabilities.

(8) "Third party" or "third parties" means one or more of the following:

(A) A business that is a separate legal entity from the business that has an established business relationship with a customer.

(B) A business that has access to a database that is shared among businesses, if the business is authorized to use the database for direct marketing purposes, unless the use of the database is exempt from being considered a disclosure for direct marketing purposes pursuant to subdivision (d).

(C) A business not affiliated by a common ownership or common corporate control with the business required to comply with subdivision (a).

(f)(1) Disclosures of personal information for direct marketing purposes between affiliated third parties that share the same brand name are exempt from the requirements of paragraph (1) of subdivision (a) unless the personal information disclosed corresponds to one of the following categories, in which case the customer shall be informed of those categories listed in this subdivision that correspond to the categories of personal information disclosed for direct marketing purposes and the third party recipients of personal information disclosed for direct marketing purposes pursuant to paragraph (2) of subdivision (a):

(A) Number of children.

(B) The age or gender of children.

(C) Electronic mail or other addresses of children.

(D) Height.

(E) Weight.

(F) Race.

(G) Religion.

(H) Telephone number.

(I) Medical condition.

(J) Drugs, therapies, or medical products or equipment used.

(K) Social security number.

(L) Bank account number.

(M) Credit card number.

(N) Debit card number.

(O) Bank or investment account, debit card, or credit card balance.

(2) If a list, description, or grouping of customer names or addresses is derived using any of these categories, and is disclosed to a third party or third parties sharing the same brand name for direct marketing purposes in a manner that permits the third party to identify, determine, or extrapolate the personal information from which the list was derived, and that personal information when it was disclosed identified, described, or was associated with an individual, any other personal information that corresponds to the categories set forth in this subdivision used to derive the list, description, or grouping shall be considered personal information for purposes of this section.

(3) If a business discloses personal information for direct marketing purposes to affiliated third parties that share the same brand name, the business that discloses personal information for direct marketing purposes between affiliated third parties that share the same brand name may comply with the requirements of paragraph (2) of subdivision (a) by providing the overall number of affiliated companies that share the same brand name.

(g) The provisions of this section are severable. If any provision of this section or its application is held invalid, that invalidity shall not affect other provisions or applications that can be given effect without the invalid provision or application.

(h) This section does not apply to a financial institution that is subject to the California Financial Information Privacy Act (Division 1.2 (commencing with Section 4050) of the Financial Code) if the financial institution is in compliance with Sections 4052, 4052.5, 4053, 4053.5, and 4054.6 of the Financial Code, as those sections read when they were chaptered on August 28, 2003, and as subsequently amended by the Legislature or by initiative.

(i) This section shall become operative on January 1, 2005.

§ 1798.84. Waiver and violations of provisions of this title; civil actions and penalties; attorney's fees and costs

(a) Any waiver of a provision of this title is contrary to public policy and is void and unenforceable.

(b) Any customer injured by a violation of this title may institute a civil action to recover damages.

(c) In addition, for a willful, intentional, or reckless violation of Section 1798.83, a customer may recover a civil penalty not to exceed three thousand dollars ($3,000) per violation; otherwise, the customer may recover a civil penalty of up to five hundred dollars ($500) per violation for a violation of Section 1798.83.

(d) Unless the violation is willful, intentional, or reckless, a business that is alleged to have not provided all the information required by subdivision (a) of Section 1798.83, to have provided inaccurate information, failed to provide any of the information required by subdivision (a) of Section 1798.83, or failed to provide information in the time period required by subdivision (b) of Section 1798.83, may assert as a complete defense in any action in law or equity that it thereafter provided regarding the information that was alleged to be untimely, all the information, or accurate information, to all customers who were provided incomplete or inaccurate information, respectively, within 90 days of the date the business knew that it had failed to provide the information, timely information, all the information, or the accurate information, respectively.

(e) Any business that violates, proposes to violate, or has violated this title may be enjoined.

(f) A prevailing plaintiff in any action commenced under Section 1798.83 shall also be entitled to recover his or her reasonable attorney's fees and costs.

(g) The rights and remedies available under this section are cumulative to each other and to any other rights and remedies available under law.

Massachusetts Breach Notification Statute (2007)

201 CMR § 17.00

Statutes in Context

The Massachusetts Breach Notification Statutes mandates "minimum standards to be met in connection with the safeguarding of personal information" about a resident of this state. The statute explicitly applies to both electronic and paper records. It also requires establishment of a "written comprehensive information security program" and sets out elements to be found in such a program. It establishes strong requirements concerning the encryption of personal information.

§17.01 Purpose and Scope

(1) Purpose

This regulation implements the provisions of M.G.L. c. 93H relative to the standards to be met by persons who own, license, store or maintain personal information about a resident of the Commonwealth of Massachusetts. This regulation establishes minimum standards to be met in connection with the safeguarding of personal information contained in both paper and electronic records. Further purposes are to (i) ensure the security and confidentiality of such information in a manner consistent with industry standards, (ii) protect against anticipated threats or hazards to the security or integrity of such information, and (iii) protect against unauthorized access to or use of such information in a manner that creates a substantial risk of identity theft or fraud against such residents.

(2) Scope

The provisions of this regulation apply to all persons that own, license, store or maintain personal information about a resident of the Commonwealth.

§ 17.02: Definitions

The following words as used herein shall, unless the context requires otherwise, have the following meanings:

Breach of security, the unauthorized acquisition or unauthorized use of unencrypted data or, encrypted electronic data and the confidential process or key that is capable of compromising the security, confidentiality, or integrity of personal information, maintained by a person or agency that creates a substantial risk of identity theft or fraud against a resident of the commonwealth. A good faith but unauthorized acquisition of personal information by a person or agency, or employee or agent thereof, for the lawful purposes of such person or agency, is not a breach of security unless the personal information is used in an unauthorized manner or subject to further unauthorized disclosure.

Electronic, relating to technology having electrical, digital, magnetic, wireless, optical, electromagnetic or similar capabilities.

Encrypted, the transformation of data through the use of an algorithmic process, or an alternative method at least as secure, into a form in which meaning cannot be assigned without the use of a confidential process or key, unless further defined by regulation by the Office of Consumer Affairs and Business Regulation.

Person, a natural person, corporation, association, partnership or other legal entity, other than an agency, executive office, department, board, commission, bureau, division or authority of the Commonwealth, or any of its branches, or any political subdivision thereof.

Personal information, a Massachusetts resident's first name and last name or first initial and last name in combination with any one or more of the following data elements that relate to such resident:

> **(a)** Social Security number;
>
> **(b)** driver's license number or state-issued identification card number; or
>
> **(c)** financial account number, or credit or debit card number, with or without any required security code, access code, personal identification number or password, that would permit access to a resident's financial account; provided, however, that "Personal information" shall not include information that is lawfully obtained from publicly available information, or from federal, state or local government records lawfully made available to the general public.

Record or Records, any material upon which written, drawn, spoken, visual, or electromagnetic information or images are recorded or preserved, regardless of physical form or characteristics.

§ 17.03: Duty to Protect and Standards for Protecting Personal Information

(1) Every person that owns, licenses, stores or maintains personal information about a resident of the Commonwealth shall develop, implement, maintain and monitor a comprehensive, written information security program applicable to any records containing such personal information. Such comprehensive information security program shall be reasonably consistent with industry standards, and shall contain administrative, technical, and physical safeguards to ensure the security and confidentiality of such records. Moreover, the safeguards contained in such program must be consistent with the safeguards for protection of personal information and information of a similar character set forth in any state or federal regulations by which the person who owns, licenses, stores or maintains such information may be regulated.

(2) Whether the comprehensive information security program is in compliance with these regulations for the protection of personal information, whether pursuant to section 17.03 or 17.04 hereof, shall be evaluated taking into account:

> **(a)** the size, scope and type of business of the person obligated to safeguard the personal information under such comprehensive information security program;
>
> **(b)** the amount of resources available to such person;

(c) the amount of stored data; and

(d) the need for security and confidentiality of both consumer and employee information.

(3) Without limiting the generality of the foregoing, every comprehensive information security program shall include, but shall not be limited to:

1. Designating one or more employees to maintain the comprehensive information security program;

2. Identifying and assessing reasonably foreseeable internal and external risks to the security, confidentiality, and/or integrity of any electronic, paper or other records containing personal information, and evaluating and improving, where necessary, the effectiveness of the current safeguards for limiting such risks, including but not limited to:

a. ongoing employee (including temporary and contract employee) training;

b. employee compliance with policies and procedures; and

c. means for detecting and preventing security system failures.

3. Developing security policies for employees that take into account whether and how employees should be allowed to keep, access and transport records containing personal information outside of business premises.

4. Imposing disciplinary measures for violations of the comprehensive information security program rules.

5. Preventing terminated employees from accessing records containing personal information by immediately terminating their physical and electronic access to such records, including deactivating their passwords and user names.

6. Taking all reasonable steps to verify that any third-party service provider with access to personal information has the capacity to protect such personal information in the manner provided for in 201 CMR 17.00; and taking all reasonable steps to ensure that such third party service provider is applying to such personal information protective security measures at least as stringent as those required to be applied to personal information under 201 CMR 17.00.

7. Limiting the amount of personal information collected to that reasonably necessary to accomplish the legitimate purpose for which it is collected; limiting the time such information is retained to that reasonably necessary to accomplish such purpose; and limiting access to those persons who are reasonably required to know such information in order to accomplish such purpose or to comply with state or federal record retention requirements.

8. Identifying paper, electronic and other records, computing systems, and storage media, including laptops and portable devices used to store personal information, to determine which records contain personal information, except where the comprehensive information security program provides for the handling of all records as if they all contained personal information.

9. Reasonable restrictions upon physical access to records containing personal information, including a written procedure that sets forth the manner in which physical access to such records is restricted; and storage of such records and data in locked facilities, storage areas or containers.

10. Regular monitoring to ensure that the comprehensive information security program is operating in a manner reasonably calculated to prevent unauthorized access to or unauthorized use of personal information; and upgrading information safeguards as necessary to limit risks.

11. Reviewing the scope of the security measures at least annually or whenever there is a material change in business practices that may reasonably implicate the security or integrity of records containing personal information.

12. Documenting responsive actions taken in connection with any incident involving a breach of security, and mandatory post-incident review of events and actions taken, if any, to make changes in business practices relating to protection of personal information.

§ 17.04: Computer System Security Requirements

Every person that owns, licenses, stores or maintains personal information about a resident of the Commonwealth and electronically stores or transmits such information shall include in its written, comprehensive information security program the establishment and maintenance of a security system covering its computers, including any wireless system, that, at a minimum, shall have the following elements:

(1) Secure user authentication protocols including:

(a) control of user IDs and other identifiers;

(b) a reasonably secure method of assigning and selecting passwords, or use of unique identifier technologies, such as biometrics or token devices;

(c) control of data security passwords to ensure that such passwords are kept in a location and/or format that does not compromise the security of the data they protect;

(d) restricting access to active users and active user accounts only; and

(e) blocking access to user identification after multiple unsuccessful attempts to gain access or the limitation placed on access for the particular system;

(2) Secure access control measures that:

(a) restrict access to records and files containing personal information to those who need such information to perform their job duties; and

(b) assign unique identifications plus passwords, which are not vendor supplied default passwords, to each person with computer access, that are reasonably designed to maintain the integrity of the security of the access controls;

(3) To the extent technically feasible, encryption of all transmitted records and files containing personal information that will travel across public networks, and encryption of all data containing personal information to be transmitted wirelessly.

(4) Reasonable monitoring of systems, for unauthorized use of or access to personal information;

(5) Encryption of all personal information stored on laptops or other portable devices;

(6) For files containing personal information on a system that is connected to the Internet, there must be reasonably up-to-date firewall protection and operating system security patches, reasonably designed to maintain the integrity of the personal information.

(7) Reasonably up-to-date versions of system security agent software which must include malware protection and reasonably up-to-date patches and virus definitions, or a version of such software that can still be supported with up-to-date patches and virus definitions, and is set to receive the most current security updates on a regular basis.

(8) Education and training of employees on the proper use of the computer security system and the importance of personal information security.

§ 17.05: Effective Date

Every person who owns, licenses, stores or maintains personal information about a resident of the Commonwealth shall be in full compliance with 201 CMR 17.00 on or before January 1, 2010.

California Data Security Breach Statute – AB 1950 (2004)

Cal. Civ. Code §§ 1798.81.5, as amended

Statutes in Context

The California Data Security Statute requires "reasonable security procedures and practices" by a firm that owns or licenses personal information about a California resident. These are to be "appropriate to the nature of the information." Moreover, the business is to protect personal information from "unauthorized access, destruction, use, modification, or disclosure. " The statute also requires a business to contractually require reasonable security procedures and practices by a nonaffiliated third party to which it discloses the information.

(a) It is the intent of the Legislature to ensure that personal information about California residents is protected. To that end, the purpose of this section is to encourage businesses that own or license personal information about Californians to provide reasonable security for that information. For the purpose of this section, the phrase "owns or licenses" is intended to include, but is not limited to, personal information that a business retains as part of the business' internal customer account or for the purpose of using that information in transactions with the person to whom the information relates.

(b) A business that owns or licenses personal information about a California resident shall implement and maintain reasonable security procedures and practices appropriate to the nature of the information, to protect the personal information from unauthorized access, destruction, use, modification, or disclosure.

(c) A business that discloses personal information about a California resident pursuant to a contract with a nonaffiliated third party shall require by contract that the third party implement and maintain reasonable security procedures and practices appropriate to the nature of the information, to protect the personal information from unauthorized access, destruction, use, modification, or disclosure.

(d) For purposes of this section, the following terms have the following meanings:

(1) "Personal information" means an individual's first name or first initial and his or her last name in combination with any one or more of the following data elements, when either the name or the data elements are not encrypted or redacted:

(A) Social security number.

(B) Driver's license number or California identification card number.

(C) Account number, credit or debit card number, in combination with any required security code, access code, or password that would permit access to an individual's financial account.

(D) Medical information.

(2) "Medical information" means any individually identifiable information, in electronic or physical form, regarding the individual's medical history or medical treatment or diagnosis by a health care professional.

(3) "Personal information" does not include publicly available information that is lawfully made available to the general public from federal, state, or local government records.

(e) The provisions of this section do not apply to any of the following:

(1) A provider of health care, health care service plan, or contractor regulated by the Confidentiality of Medical Information Act (Part 2.6 (commencing with Section 56) of Division 1).

(2) A financial institution as defined in Section 4052 of the Financial Code and subject to the California Financial Information Privacy Act (Division 1.2 (commencing with Section 4050) of the Financial Code.

(3) A covered entity governed by the medical privacy and security rules issued by the federal Department of Health and Human Services, Parts 160 and 164 of Title 45 of the Code of Federal Regulations, established pursuant to the Health Insurance Portability and Availability Act of 1996 (HIPAA).

(4) An entity that obtains information under an agreement pursuant to Article 3 (commencing with Section 1800) of Chapter 1 of Division 2 of the Vehicle Code and is subject to the confidentiality requirements of the Vehicle Code.

(5) A business that is regulated by state or federal law providing greater protection to personal information than that provided by this section in regard to the subjects addressed by this section. Compliance with that state or federal law shall be deemed compliance with this section with regard to those subjects. This paragraph does not relieve a business from a duty to comply with any other requirements of other state and federal law regarding the protection and privacy of personal information.

VIII.
SCHOOL PRIVACY

Family Educational Rights and Privacy Act (1974)

20 U.S.C. § 1232g, as amended

Statutes in Context

The Family Educational Rights and Privacy Act (FERPA), commonly known as the "Buckley Amendment," generally prohibits schools from releasing student "education records" without the authorization of the student and/or parent. The Act covers virtually all institutional records that are personally identifiable to one or more students. But it applies only to records and information from records, not information per se. Thus, the personal knowledge and observations of school officials that are not part of a record are not covered. Schools must inform students and parents of their rights under FERPA. Schools also generally must provide students and/or parents with access to their education records.

---

§ 1232g. Family educational and privacy rights

(a) Conditions for availability of funds to educational agencies or institutions; inspection and review of education records; specific information to be made available; procedure for access to education records; reasonableness of time for such access; hearings; written explanations by parents; definitions

(1)(A) No funds shall be made available under any applicable program to any educational agency or institution which has a policy of denying, or which effectively prevents, the parents of students who are or have been in attendance at a school of such agency or at such institution, as the case may be, the right to inspect and review the education records of their children. If any material or document in the education record of a student includes information on more than one student, the parents of one of such students shall have the right to inspect and review only such part of such material or document as relates to such student or to be informed of the specific information contained in such part of such material. Each educational agency or institution shall establish appropriate procedures for the granting of a request by parents for access to the education records of their children within a reasonable period of time, but in no case more than forty-five days after the request has been made.

(B) No funds under any applicable program shall be made available to any State educational agency (whether or not that agency is an educational agency or institution under this section) that has a policy of denying, or effectively prevents, the parents of students the right to inspect and review the education records maintained by the State educational agency on their children who are or have been in attendance at any school of an educational agency or institution that is subject to the provisions of this section.

(C) The first sentence of subparagraph (A) shall not operate to make available to students in institutions of postsecondary education the following materials:

(i) financial records of the parents of the student or any information contained therein;

(ii) confidential letters and statements of recommendation, which were placed in the education records prior to January 1, 1975, if such letters or statements are not used for purposes other than those for which they were specifically intended;

(iii) if the student has signed a waiver of the student's right of access under this subsection in accordance with subparagraph (D), confidential recommendations—

(I) respecting admission to any educational agency or institution,

(II) respecting an application for employment, and

(III) respecting the receipt of an honor or honorary recognition.

(D) A student or a person applying for admission may waive his right of access to confidential statements described in clause (iii) of subparagraph (C), except that such waiver shall apply to recommendations only if (i) the student is, upon request, notified of the names of all persons making confidential recommendations and (ii) such recommendations are used solely for the purpose for which they were specifically intended. Such waivers may not be required as a condition for admission to, receipt of financial aid from, or receipt of any other services or benefits from such agency or institution.

(2) No funds shall be made available under any applicable program to any educational agency or institution unless the parents of students who are or have been in attendance at a school of such agency or at such institution are provided an opportunity for a hearing by such agency or institution, in accordance with regulations of the Secretary, to challenge the content of such student's education records, in order to insure that the records are not inaccurate, misleading, or otherwise in violation of the privacy rights of students, and to provide an opportunity for the correction or deletion of any such inaccurate, misleading or otherwise inappropriate data contained therein and to insert into such records a written explanation of the parents respecting the content of such records.

(3) For the purposes of this section the term "educational agency or institution" means any public or private agency or institution which is the recipient of funds under any applicable program.

(4)(A) For the purposes of this section, the term "education records" means, except as may be provided otherwise in subparagraph (B), those records, files, documents, and other materials which—

(i) contain information directly related to a student; and

(ii) are maintained by an educational agency or institution or by a person acting for such agency or institution.

(B) The term "education records" does not include—

(i) records of instructional, supervisory, and administrative personnel and educational personnel ancillary thereto which are in the sole possession of the maker thereof and which are not accessible or revealed to any other person except a substitute;

(ii) records maintained by a law enforcement unit of the educational agency or institution that were created by that law enforcement unit for the purpose of law enforcement;

(iii) in the case of persons who are employed by an educational agency or institution but who are not in attendance at such agency or institution, records made and maintained in the normal course of business which relate exclusively to such person in that person's capacity as an employee and are not available for use for any other purpose; or

(iv) records on a student who is eighteen years of age or older, or is attending an institution of postsecondary education, which are made or maintained by a physician, psychiatrist, psychologist, or other recognized professional or paraprofessional acting in his professional or paraprofessional capacity, or assisting in that capacity, and which are made, maintained, or used only in connection with the provision of treatment to the student, and are not available to anyone other than persons providing such treatment, except that such records can be personally reviewed by a physician or other appropriate professional of the student's choice.

(5)(A) For the purposes of this section the term "directory information" relating to a student includes the following: the student's name, address, telephone listing, date and place of birth, major field of study, participation in officially recognized activities and sports, weight and height of members of athletic teams, dates of attendance, degrees and awards received, and the most recent previous educational agency or institution attended by the student.

(B) Any educational agency or institution making public directory information shall give public notice of the categories of information which it has designated as such information with respect to each student attending the institution or agency and shall allow a reasonable period of time after such notice has been given for a parent to inform the institution or agency that any or all of the information designated should not be released without the parent's prior consent.

(6) For the purposes of this section, the term "student" includes any person with respect to whom an educational agency or institution maintains education records or personally identifiable information, but does not include a person who has not been in attendance at such agency or institution.

(b) Release of education records; parental consent requirement; exceptions; compliance with judicial orders and subpoenas; audit and evaluation of federally-supported education programs; recordkeeping

(1) No funds shall be made available under any applicable program to any educational agency or institution which has a policy or practice of permitting the release of education records (or personally identifiable information contained therein other than directory information, as defined in paragraph (5) of subsection (a) of this section) of students without the written consent of their parents to any individual, agency, or organization, other than to the following—

(A) other school officials, including teachers within the educational institution or local educational agency, who have been determined by such agency or institution to have legitimate educational interests, including the educational interests of the child for whom consent would otherwise be required;

(B) officials of other schools or school systems in which the student seeks or intends to enroll, upon condition that the student's parents be notified of the transfer, receive a copy of the record if desired, and have an opportunity for a hearing to challenge the content of the record;

(C) (i) authorized representatives of (I) the Comptroller General of the United States, (II) the Secretary, or (III) State educational authorities, under the conditions set forth in paragraph (3), or (ii) authorized representatives of the Attorney General for law enforcement purposes under the same conditions as apply to the Secretary under paragraph (3);

(D) in connection with a student's application for, or receipt of, financial aid;

(E) State and local officials or authorities to whom such information is specifically allowed to be reported or disclosed pursuant to State statute adopted—

(i) before November 19, 1974, if the allowed reporting or disclosure concerns the juvenile justice system and such system's ability to effectively serve the student whose records are released, or

(ii) after November 19, 1974, if—

(I) the allowed reporting or disclosure concerns the juvenile justice system and such system's ability to effectively serve, prior to adjudication, the student whose records are released; and

(II) the officials and authorities to whom such information is disclosed certify in writing to the educational agency or institution that the information will not be disclosed to any other party except as provided under State law without the prior written consent of the parent of the student.

(F) organizations conducting studies for, or on behalf of, educational agencies or institutions for the purpose of developing, validating, or administering predictive tests, administering student aid programs, and improving instruction, if such studies are conducted in such a manner as will not permit the personal identification of students and their parents by persons other than representatives of such organizations and such information will be destroyed when no longer needed for the purpose for which it is conducted;

(G) accrediting organizations in order to carry out their accrediting functions;

(H) parents of a dependent student of such parents, as defined in section 152 of Title 26;

(I) subject to regulations of the Secretary, in connection with an emergency, appropriate persons if the knowledge of such information is necessary to protect the health or safety of the student or other persons; and

(J)(i) the entity or persons designated in a Federal grand jury subpoena, in which case the court shall order, for good cause shown, the educational agency or institution (and any officer, director, employee, agent, or attorney for such agency or institution) on which the subpoena is served, to not disclose to any person the existence or contents of the subpoena or any information furnished to the grand jury in response to the subpoena; and

(ii) the entity or persons designated in any other subpoena issued for a law enforcement purpose, in which case the court or other issuing agency may order, for good cause shown, the educational agency or institution (and any officer, director, employee, agent, or attorney for such agency or institution) on which the subpoena is served, to not disclose to any person the existence or contents of the subpoena or any information furnished in response to the subpoena.

Nothing in subparagraph (E) of this paragraph shall prevent a State from further limiting the number or type of State or local officials who will continue to have access thereunder.

(2) No funds shall be made available under any applicable program to any educational agency or institution which has a policy or practice of releasing, or providing access to, any personally identifiable information in education records other than directory information, or as is permitted under paragraph (1) of this subsection, unless—

> **(A)** there is written consent from the student's parents specifying records to be released, the reasons for such release, and to whom, and with a copy of the records to be released to the student's parents and the student if desired by the parents, or
>
> **(B)** except as provided in paragraph (1)(J), such information is furnished in compliance with judicial order, or pursuant to any lawfully issued subpoena, upon condition that parents and the students are notified of all such orders or subpoenas in advance of the compliance therewith by the educational institution or agency.

(3) Nothing contained in this section shall preclude authorized representatives of (A) the Comptroller General of the United States, (B) the Secretary, or (C) State educational authorities from having access to student or other records which may be necessary in connection with the audit and evaluation of Federally-supported education programs, or in connection with the enforcement of the Federal legal requirements which relate to such programs: *Provided,* That except when collection of personally identifiable information is specifically authorized by Federal law, any data collected by such officials shall be protected in a manner which will not permit the personal identification of students and their parents by other than those officials, and such personally identifiable data shall be destroyed when no longer needed for such audit, evaluation, and enforcement of Federal legal requirements.

(4)(A) Each educational agency or institution shall maintain a record, kept with the education records of each student, which will indicate all individuals (other than those specified in paragraph (1)(A) of this subsection), agencies, or organizations which have requested or obtained access to a student's education records maintained by such educational agency or institution, and which will indicate specifically the legitimate interest that each such person, agency, or organization has in obtaining this information. Such record of access shall be available only to parents, to the school official and his assistants who are responsible for the custody of such records, and to persons or organizations authorized in, and under the conditions of, clauses (A) and (C) of paragraph (1) as a means of auditing the operation of the system.

(B) With respect to this subsection, personal information shall only be transferred to a third party on the condition that such party will not permit any other party to have access to such information without the written consent of the parents of the student. If a third party outside the educational agency or institution permits access to information in violation of paragraph (2)(A), or fails to destroy information in violation of paragraph (1)(F), the educational agency or institution shall be prohibited from permitting access to information from education records to that third party for a period of not less than five years.

(5) Nothing in this section shall be construed to prohibit State and local educational officials from having access to student or other records which may be necessary in connection with the audit and evaluation of any federally or State supported education program or in connection with the enforcement of the Federal legal requirements which relate to any such program, subject to the conditions specified in the proviso in paragraph (3).

(6)(A) Nothing in this section shall be construed to prohibit an institution of postsecondary education from disclosing, to an alleged victim of any crime of violence (as that term is defined in section 16 of Title 18), or a nonforcible sex offense, the final results of any disciplinary proceeding conducted by such institution against the alleged perpetrator of such crime or offense with respect to such crime or offense.

(B) Nothing in this section shall be construed to prohibit an institution of postsecondary education from disclosing the final results of any disciplinary proceeding conducted by such institution against a student who is an alleged perpetrator of any crime of violence (as that term is defined in section 16 of Title 18), or a nonforcible sex offense, if the institution determines as a result of that disciplinary proceeding that the student committed a violation of the institution's rules or policies with respect to such crime or offense.

(C) For the purpose of this paragraph, the final results of any disciplinary proceeding—

(i) shall include only the name of the student, the violation committed, and any sanction imposed by the institution on that student; and

(ii) may include the name of any other student, such as a victim or witness, only with the written consent of that other student.

(7)(A) Nothing in this section may be construed to prohibit an educational institution from disclosing information provided to the institution under section 14071 of Title 42 concerning registered sex offenders who are required to register under such section.

(B) The Secretary shall take appropriate steps to notify educational institutions that disclosure of information described in subparagraph (A) is permitted.

(c) Surveys or data-gathering activities; regulations

Not later than 240 days after October 20, 1994, the Secretary shall adopt appropriate regulations or procedures, or identify existing regulations or procedures, which protect the rights of privacy of students and their families in connection with any surveys or data-gathering activities conducted, assisted, or authorized by the Secretary or an administrative head of an education agency. Regulations established under this subsection shall include provisions controlling the use, dissemination, and protection of such data. No survey or data-gathering activities shall be conducted by the Secretary, or an administrative head of an education agency under an applicable program, unless such activities are authorized by law.

(d) Students' rather than parents' permission or consent

For the purposes of this section, whenever a student has attained eighteen years of age, or is attending an institution of postsecondary education, the permission or consent required of and the rights accorded to the parents of the student shall thereafter only be required of and accorded to the student.

(e) Informing parents or students of rights under this section

No funds shall be made available under any applicable program to any educational agency or institution unless such agency or institution effectively informs the parents of students, or the students, if they are eighteen years of age or older, or are attending an institution of postsecondary education, of the rights accorded them by this section.

(f) Enforcement; termination of assistance

The Secretary shall take appropriate actions to enforce this section and to deal with violations of this section, in accordance with this chapter, except that action to terminate assistance may be taken only if the Secretary finds there has been a failure to comply with this section, and he has determined that compliance cannot be secured by voluntary means.

(g) Office and review board; creation; functions

The Secretary shall establish or designate an office and review board within the Department for the purpose of investigating, processing, reviewing, and adjudicating violations of this section and complaints which may be filed concerning alleged violations of this section. Except for the conduct of hearings, none of the functions of the Secretary under this section shall be carried out in any of the regional offices of such Department.

(h) Disciplinary records; disclosure

Nothing in this section shall prohibit an educational agency or institution from—

(1) including appropriate information in the education record of any student concerning disciplinary action taken against such student for conduct that posed a significant risk to the safety or well-being of that student, other students, or other members of the school community; or

(2) disclosing such information to teachers and school officials, including teachers and school officials in other schools, who have legitimate educational interests in the behavior of the student.

(i) Drug and alcohol violation disclosures

(1) In general

Nothing in this Act or the Higher Education Act of 1965 [20 U.S.C.A. § 1001 et seq.] shall be construed to prohibit an institution of higher education from disclosing, to a parent or legal guardian of a student, information regarding any violation of any Federal, State, or local law, or of any rule or policy of the institution, governing the use or possession of alcohol or a controlled substance, regardless of whether that information is contained in the student's education records, if—

(A) the student is under the age of 21; and

(B) the institution determines that the student has committed a disciplinary violation with respect to such use or possession.

(2) State law regarding disclosure

Nothing in paragraph (1) shall be construed to supersede any provision of State law that prohibits an institution of higher education from making the disclosure described in subsection (a) of this section.

(j) Investigation and prosecution of terrorism

(1) In general

Notwithstanding subsections (a) through (i) or any provision of State law, the Attorney General (or any Federal officer or employee, in a position not lower than an Assistant Attorney General, designated by the Attorney General) may submit a written application to a court of competent jurisdiction for an ex parte order requiring an educational agency or institution to permit the Attorney General (or his designee) to—

(A) collect education records in the possession of the educational agency or institution that are relevant to an authorized investigation or prosecution of an offense listed in section 2332b(g)(5)(B) of Title 18, or an act of domestic or international terrorism as defined in section 2331 of that title; and

(B) for official purposes related to the investigation or prosecution of an offense described in paragraph (1)(A), retain, disseminate, and use (including as evidence at trial or in other administrative or judicial proceedings) such records, consistent with such guidelines as the Attorney General, after consultation with the Secretary, shall issue to protect confidentiality.

(2) Application and approval

(A) In general

An application under paragraph (1) shall certify that there are specific and articulable facts giving reason to believe that the education records are likely to contain information described in paragraph (1)(A).

(B) The court shall issue an order described in paragraph (1) if the court finds that the application for the order includes the certification described in subparagraph (A).

(3) Protection of educational agency or institution

An educational agency or institution that, in good faith, produces education records in accordance with an order issued under this subsection shall not be liable to any person for that production.

(4) Record-keeping

Subsection (b)(4) of this section does not apply to education records subject to a court order under this subsection.

No Child Left Behind Act (2001)

20 U.S.C. §§ 1232f-j, 7908, as amended

Statutes in Context

The No Child Left Behind Act places limits on required student surveys that collect information about certain topics or areas. It also requires that local educational agencies, covered by the Act, develop policies concerning privacy and parental access to certain kinds of surveys that collect personal information about students. While these sections of the Act are protective of privacy, a different section of the Act mandates the sharing of student information with Armed Forces recruiters.

§ 1232f. Records

(a) Records kept by recipient; full disclosure; maintenance period

Each recipient of Federal funds under any applicable program through any grant, subgrant, cooperative agreement, loan, or other arrangement shall keep records which fully disclose the amount and disposition by the recipient of those funds, the total cost of the activity for which the funds are used, the share of that cost provided from other sources, and such other records as will facilitate an effective financial or programmatic audit. The recipient shall maintain such records for three years after the completion of the activity for which the funds are used.

(b) Audit examination

The Secretary and the Comptroller General of the United States, or any of their duly authorized representatives, shall have access, for the purpose of audit examination, to any records maintained by a recipient that may be related, or pertinent to, grants, subgrants, cooperative agreements, loans, or other arrangements to which reference is made in subsection (a) of this section, or which may relate to the compliance of the recipient with any requirement of an applicable program.

§ 1232g. Family educational and privacy rights

(a) Conditions for availability of funds to educational agencies or institutions; inspection and review of education records; specific information to be made available; procedure for access to education records; reasonableness of time for such access; hearings; written explanations by parents; definitions

(1)

(A) No funds shall be made available under any applicable program to any educational agency or institution which has a policy of denying, or which effectively prevents, the parents of students who are or have been in attendance at a school of such agency or at such institution, as the case may be, the right to inspect and review the education records of their children. If any material or document in the education record of a student includes information on more than one student, the parents of one of such students shall have the right to inspect and review only such part of such material or document as relates to such student or to be informed of the specific information contained in such part of such material. Each educational agency or institution shall establish appropriate procedures for the granting of a request by parents for access to the education records of their children within a reasonable period of time, but in no case more than forty-five days after the request has been made.

(B) No funds under any applicable program shall be made available to any State educational agency (whether or not that agency is an educational agency or institution under this section) that has a policy of denying, or effectively prevents, the parents of students the right to inspect and review the education records maintained by the State educational agency on their children who are or have been in attendance at any school of an educational agency or institution that is subject to the provisions of this section.

(C) The first sentence of subparagraph (A) shall not operate to make available to students in institutions of postsecondary education the following materials:

(i) financial records of the parents of the student or any information contained therein;

(ii) confidential letters and statements of recommendation, which were placed in the education records prior to January 1, 1975, if such letters or statements are not used for purposes other than those for which they were specifically intended;

(iii) if the student has signed a waiver of the student's right of access under this subsection in accordance with subparagraph (D), confidential recommendations—

(I) respecting admission to any educational agency or institution,

(II) respecting an application for employment, and

(III) respecting the receipt of an honor or honorary recognition.

(D) A student or a person applying for admission may waive his right of access to confidential statements described in clause (iii) of subparagraph (C), except that such waiver shall apply to recommendations only if

(i) the student is, upon request, notified of the names of all persons making confidential recommendations and

(ii) such recommendations are used solely for the purpose for which they were specifically intended. Such waivers may not be required as a condition for admission to, receipt of financial aid from, or receipt of any other services or benefits from such agency or institution.

(2) No funds shall be made available under any applicable program to any educational agency or institution unless the parents of students who are or have been in attendance at a school of such agency or at such institution are provided an opportunity for a hearing by such agency or institution, in accordance with regulations of the Secretary, to challenge the content of such student's education records, in order to insure that the records are not inaccurate, misleading, or otherwise in violation of the privacy rights of students, and to provide an opportunity for the correction or deletion of any such inaccurate, misleading or otherwise inappropriate data contained therein and to insert into such records a written explanation of the parents respecting the content of such records.

(3) For the purposes of this section the term "educational agency or institution" means any public or private agency or institution which is the recipient of funds under any applicable program.

(4)

(A) For the purposes of this section, the term "education records" means, except as may be provided otherwise in subparagraph (B), those records, files, documents, and other materials which—

(i) contain information directly related to a student; and

(ii) are maintained by an educational agency or institution or by a person acting for such agency or institution.

(B) The term "education records" does not include—

(i) records of instructional, supervisory, and administrative personnel and educational personnel ancillary thereto which are in the sole possession of the maker thereof and which are not accessible or revealed to any other person except a substitute;

(ii) records maintained by a law enforcement unit of the educational agency or institution that were created by that law enforcement unit for the purpose of law enforcement;

(iii) in the case of persons who are employed by an educational agency or institution but who are not in attendance at such agency or institution, records made and maintained in the normal course of business which relate exclusively to such person in that person's capacity as an employee and are not available for use for any other purpose; or

(iv) records on a student who is eighteen years of age or older, or is attending an institution of postsecondary education, which are made or maintained by a physician, psychiatrist, psychologist, or other recognized professional or paraprofessional acting in his professional or paraprofessional capacity, or assisting in that capacity, and which are made, maintained, or used only in connection with the provision of treatment to the student, and are not available to anyone other than persons providing such treatment, except that such records can be personally reviewed by a physician or other appropriate professional of the student's choice.

(5)

(A) For the purposes of this section the term "directory information" relating to a student includes the following: the student's name, address, telephone listing, date and place of birth, major field of study, participation in officially recognized activities and sports, weight and height of members of athletic teams, dates of attendance, degrees and awards received, and the most recent previous educational agency or institution attended by the student.

(B) Any educational agency or institution making public directory information shall give public notice of the categories of information which it has designated as such information with respect to each student attending the institution or agency and shall allow a reasonable period of time after such notice has been given for a parent to inform the institution or agency that any or all of the information designated should not be released without the parent's prior consent.

(6) For the purposes of this section, the term "student" includes any person with respect to whom an educational agency or institution maintains education records or personally identifiable information, but does not include a person who has not been in attendance at such agency or institution.

(b) Release of education records; parental consent requirement; exceptions; compliance with judicial orders and subpoenas; audit and evaluation of federally-supported education programs; recordkeeping

(1) No funds shall be made available under any applicable program to any educational agency or institution which has a policy or practice of permitting the release of education records (or personally identifiable information contained therein other than directory information, as defined in paragraph (5) of subsection (a) of this section) of students without the written consent of their parents to any individual, agency, or organization, other than to the following—

(A) other school officials, including teachers within the educational institution or local educational agency, who have been determined by such agency or institution to have legitimate educational interests, including the educational interests of the child for whom consent would otherwise be required;

(B) officials of other schools or school systems in which the student seeks or intends to enroll, upon condition that the student's parents be notified of the transfer, receive a copy of the record if desired, and have an opportunity for a hearing to challenge the content of the record;

(C)

(i) authorized representatives of

(I) the Comptroller General of the United States,

(II) the Secretary, or

(III) State educational authorities, under the conditions set forth in paragraph (3), or

(ii) authorized representatives of the Attorney General for law enforcement purposes under the same conditions as apply to the Secretary under paragraph (3);

(D) in connection with a student's application for, or receipt of, financial aid;

(E) State and local officials or authorities to whom such information is specifically allowed to be reported or disclosed pursuant to State statute adopted—

(i) before November 19, 1974, if the allowed reporting or disclosure concerns the juvenile justice system and such system's ability to effectively serve the student whose records are released, or

(ii) after November 19, 1974, if—

(I) the allowed reporting or disclosure concerns the juvenile justice system and such system's ability to effectively serve, prior to adjudication, the student whose records are released; and

(II) the officials and authorities to whom such information is disclosed certify in writing to the educational agency or institution that the information will not be disclosed to any other party except as provided under State law without the prior written consent of the parent of the student.[1]

(F) organizations conducting studies for, or on behalf of, educational agencies or institutions for the purpose of developing, validating, or administering predictive tests, administering student aid programs, and improving instruction, if such studies are conducted in such a manner as will not permit the personal identification of students and their parents by persons other than representatives of such organizations and such information will be destroyed when no longer needed for the purpose for which it is conducted;

(G) accrediting organizations in order to carry out their accrediting functions;

(H) parents of a dependent student of such parents, as defined in section 152 of title 26;

(I) subject to regulations of the Secretary, in connection with an emergency, appropriate persons if the knowledge of such information is necessary to protect the health or safety of the student or other persons; and

(J)

(i) the entity or persons designated in a Federal grand jury subpoena, in which case the court shall order, for good cause shown, the educational agency or institution (and any officer, director, employee, agent, or attorney for such agency or institution) on which the subpoena is served, to not disclose to any person the existence or contents of the subpoena or any information furnished to the grand jury in response to the subpoena; and

(ii) the entity or persons designated in any other subpoena issued for a law enforcement purpose, in which case the court or other issuing agency may order, for good cause shown, the educational agency or institution (and any officer, director, employee, agent, or attorney for such agency or institution) on which the subpoena is served, to not disclose to any person the existence or contents of the subpoena or any information furnished in response to the subpoena.

Nothing in subparagraph (E) of this paragraph shall prevent a State from further limiting the number or type of State or local officials who will continue to have access thereunder.

(2) No funds shall be made available under any applicable program to any educational agency or institution which has a policy or practice of releasing, or providing access to, any personally identifiable information in education records other than directory information, or as is permitted under paragraph (1) of this subsection, unless—

(A) there is written consent from the student's parents specifying records to be released, the reasons for such release, and to whom, and with a copy of the records to be released to the student's parents and the student if desired by the parents, or

(B) except as provided in paragraph (1)(J), such information is furnished in compliance with judicial order, or pursuant to any lawfully issued subpoena, upon condition that parents and the students are notified of all such orders or subpoenas in advance of the compliance therewith by the educational institution or agency.

(3) Nothing contained in this section shall preclude authorized representatives of

(A) the Comptroller General of the United States,

(B) the Secretary, or

(C) State educational authorities from having access to student or other records which may be necessary in connection with the audit and evaluation of Federally-supported education programs, or in connection with the enforcement of the Federal legal requirements which relate to such programs: Provided, That except when collection of personally identifiable information is specifically authorized by Federal law, any data collected by such officials shall be protected in a manner which will not permit the personal identification of students and their parents by other than those officials, and such personally identifiable data shall be destroyed when no longer needed for such audit, evaluation, and enforcement of Federal legal requirements.

(4)

(A) Each educational agency or institution shall maintain a record, kept with the education records of each student, which will indicate all individuals (other than those specified in paragraph (1)(A) of this subsection), agencies, or organizations which have requested or obtained access to a student's education records maintained by such educational agency or institution, and which will indicate specifically the legitimate interest that each such person, agency, or organization has in obtaining this information. Such record of access shall be available only to parents, to the school official and his assistants who are responsible for the custody of such records, and to persons or organizations authorized in, and under the conditions of, clauses (A) and (C) of paragraph (1) as a means of auditing the operation of the system.

(B) With respect to this subsection, personal information shall only be transferred to a third party on the condition that such party will not permit any other party to have access to such information without the written consent of the parents of the student. If a third party outside the educational agency or institution permits access to information in violation of paragraph (2)(A), or fails to destroy information in violation of paragraph (1)(F), the educational agency or institution shall be prohibited from permitting access to information from education records to that third party for a period of not less than five years.

(5) Nothing in this section shall be construed to prohibit State and local educational officials from having access to student or other records which may be necessary in connection with the audit and evaluation of any federally or State supported education program or in connection with the enforcement of the Federal legal requirements which relate to any such program, subject to the conditions specified in the proviso in paragraph (3).

(6)

(A) Nothing in this section shall be construed to prohibit an institution of postsecondary education from disclosing, to an alleged victim of any crime of violence (as that term is defined in section 16 of title 18), or a nonforcible sex offense, the final results of any disciplinary proceeding conducted by such institution against the alleged perpetrator of such crime or offense with respect to such crime or offense.

(B) Nothing in this section shall be construed to prohibit an institution of postsecondary education from disclosing the final results of any disciplinary proceeding conducted by such institution against a student who is an alleged perpetrator of any crime of violence (as that term is defined in section 16 of title 18), or a nonforcible sex offense, if the institution determines as a result of that disciplinary proceeding that the student committed a violation of the institution's rules or policies with respect to such crime or offense.

(C) For the purpose of this paragraph, the final results of any disciplinary proceeding—

(i) shall include only the name of the student, the violation committed, and any sanction imposed by the institution on that student; and

(ii) may include the name of any other student, such as a victim or witness, only with the written consent of that other student.

(7)

(A) Nothing in this section may be construed to prohibit an educational institution from disclosing information provided to the institution under section 14071 of title 42 concerning registered sex offenders who are required to register under such section.

(B) The Secretary shall take appropriate steps to notify educational institutions that disclosure of information described in subparagraph (A) is permitted.

(c) Surveys or data-gathering activities; regulations

Not later than 240 days after October 20, 1994, the Secretary shall adopt appropriate regulations or procedures, or identify existing regulations or procedures, which protect the rights of privacy of students and their families in connection with any surveys or data-gathering activities conducted, assisted, or authorized by the Secretary or an administrative head of an education agency. Regulations established under this subsection shall include provisions controlling the use, dissemination, and protection of such data. No survey or data-gathering activities shall be conducted by the Secretary, or an administrative head of an education agency under an applicable program, unless such activities are authorized by law.

(d) Students' rather than parents' permission or consent

For the purposes of this section, whenever a student has attained eighteen years of age, or is attending an institution of postsecondary education, the permission or consent required of and the rights accorded to the parents of the student shall thereafter only be required of and accorded to the student.

(e) Informing parents or students of rights under this section

No funds shall be made available under any applicable program to any educational agency or institution unless such agency or institution effectively informs the parents of students, or the students, if they are eighteen years of age or older, or are attending an institution of postsecondary education, of the rights accorded them by this section.

(f) Enforcement; termination of assistance

The Secretary shall take appropriate actions to enforce this section and to deal with violations of this section, in accordance with this chapter, except that action to terminate assistance may be taken only if the Secretary finds there has been a failure to comply with this section, and he has determined that compliance cannot be secured by voluntary means.

(g) Office and review board; creation; functions

The Secretary shall establish or designate an office and review board within the Department for the purpose of investigating, processing, reviewing, and adjudicating violations of this section and complaints which may be filed concerning alleged violations of this section. Except for the conduct of hearings, none of the functions of the Secretary under this section shall be carried out in any of the regional offices of such Department.

(h) Disciplinary records; disclosure

Nothing in this section shall prohibit an educational agency or institution from—

(1) including appropriate information in the education record of any student concerning disciplinary action taken against such student for conduct that posed a significant risk to the safety or well-being of that student, other students, or other members of the school community; or

(2) disclosing such information to teachers and school officials, including teachers and school officials in other schools, who have legitimate educational interests in the behavior of the student.

(i) Drug and alcohol violation disclosures

(1) In general

Nothing in this Act or the Higher Education Act of 1965 [20 U.S.C. 1001 et seq.] shall be construed to prohibit an institution of higher education from disclosing, to a parent or legal guardian of a student, information regarding any violation of any Federal, State, or local law, or of any rule or policy of the institution, governing the use or possession of alcohol or a controlled substance, regardless of whether that information is contained in the student's education records, if—

(A) the student is under the age of 21; and

(B) the institution determines that the student has committed a disciplinary violation with respect to such use or possession.

(2) State law regarding disclosure

Nothing in paragraph (1) shall be construed to supersede any provision of State law that prohibits an institution of higher education from making the disclosure described in subsection (a) of this section.

(j) Investigation and prosecution of terrorism

(1) In general

Notwithstanding subsections (a) through (i) of this section or any provision of State law, the Attorney General (or any Federal officer or employee, in a position not lower than an Assistant Attorney General, designated by the Attorney General) may submit a written application to a court of competent jurisdiction for an ex parte order requiring an educational agency or institution to permit the Attorney General (or his designee) to—

(A) collect education records in the possession of the educational agency or institution that are relevant to an authorized investigation or prosecution of an offense listed in section 2332b (g)(5)(B) of title 18, or an act of domestic or international terrorism as defined in section 2331 of that title; and

(B) for official purposes related to the investigation or prosecution of an offense described in paragraph (1)(A), retain, disseminate, and use (including as evidence at trial or in other administrative or judicial proceedings) such records, consistent with such guidelines as the Attorney General, after consultation with the Secretary, shall issue to protect confidentiality.

(2) Application and approval

(A) In general.— An application under paragraph (1) shall certify that there are specific and articulable facts giving reason to believe that the education records are likely to contain information described in paragraph (1)(A).

(B) The court shall issue an order described in paragraph (1) if the court finds that the application for the order includes the certification described in subparagraph (A).

(3) Protection of educational agency or institution

An educational agency or institution that, in good faith, produces education records in accordance with an order issued under this subsection shall not be liable to any person for that production.

(4) Record-keeping

Subsection (b)(4) of this section does not apply to education records subject to a court order under this subsection.

§ 1232h. Protection of pupil rights

(a) Inspection of instructional materials by parents or guardians

All instructional materials, including teacher's manuals, films, tapes, or other supplementary material which will be used in connection with any survey, analysis, or evaluation as part of any applicable program shall be available for inspection by the parents or guardians of the children.

(b) Limits on survey, analysis, or evaluations

No student shall be required, as part of any applicable program, to submit to a survey, analysis, or evaluation that reveals information concerning—

(1) political affiliations or beliefs of the student or the student's parent;

(2) mental or psychological problems of the student or the student's family;

(3) sex behavior or attitudes;

(4) illegal, anti-social, self-incriminating, or demeaning behavior;

(5) critical appraisals of other individuals with whom respondents have close family relationships;

(6) legally recognized privileged or analogous relationships, such as those of lawyers, physicians, and ministers;

(7) religious practices, affiliations, or beliefs of the student or student's parent; or

(8) income (other than that required by law to determine eligibility for participation in a program or for receiving financial assistance under such program), without the prior consent of the student (if the student is an adult or emancipated minor), or in the case of an unemancipated minor, without the prior written consent of the parent.

(c) Development of local policies concerning student privacy, parental access to information, and administration of certain physical examinations to minors

(1) Development and adoption of local policies

Except as provided in subsections (a) and (b) of this section, a local educational agency that receives funds under any applicable program shall develop and adopt policies, in consultation with parents, regarding the following:

(A)

(i) The right of a parent of a student to inspect, upon the request of the parent, a survey created by a third party before the survey is administered or distributed by a school to a student; and

(ii) any applicable procedures for granting a request by a parent for reasonable access to such survey within a reasonable period of time after the request is received.

(B) Arrangements to protect student privacy that are provided by the agency in the event of the administration or distribution of a survey to a student containing one or more of the following items (including the right of a parent of a student to inspect, upon the request of the parent, any survey containing one or more of such items):

(i) Political affiliations or beliefs of the student or the student's parent.

(ii) Mental or psychological problems of the student or the student's family.

(iii) Sex behavior or attitudes.

(iv) Illegal, anti-social, self-incriminating, or demeaning behavior.

(v) Critical appraisals of other individuals with whom respondents have close family relationships.

(vi) Legally recognized privileged or analogous relationships, such as those of lawyers, physicians, and ministers.

(vii) Religious practices, affiliations, or beliefs of the student or the student's parent.

(viii) Income (other than that required by law to determine eligibility for participation in a program or for receiving financial assistance under such program).

(C)

(i) The right of a parent of a student to inspect, upon the request of the parent, any instructional material used as part of the educational curriculum for the student; and

(ii) any applicable procedures for granting a request by a parent for reasonable access to instructional material within a reasonable period of time after the request is received.

(D) The administration of physical examinations or screenings that the school or agency may administer to a student.

(E) The collection, disclosure, or use of personal information collected from students for the purpose of marketing or for selling that information (or otherwise providing that information to others for that purpose), including arrangements to protect student privacy that are provided by the agency in the event of such collection, disclosure, or use.

(F)

(i) The right of a parent of a student to inspect, upon the request of the parent, any instrument used in the collection of personal information under subparagraph (E) before the instrument is administered or distributed to a student; and

(ii) any applicable procedures for granting a request by a parent for reasonable access to such instrument within a reasonable period of time after the request is received.

(2) Parental notification

(A) Notification of policies

The policies developed by a local educational agency under paragraph (1) shall provide for reasonable notice of the adoption or continued use of such policies directly to the parents of students enrolled in schools served by that agency. At a minimum, the agency shall—

(i) provide such notice at least annually, at the beginning of the school year, and within a reasonable period of time after any substantive change in such policies; and

(ii) offer an opportunity for the parent (and for purposes of an activity described in subparagraph (C)(i), in the case of a student of an appropriate age, the student) to opt the student out of participation in an activity described in subparagraph (C).

(B) Notification of specific events

The local educational agency shall directly notify the parent of a student, at least annually at the beginning of the school year, of the specific or approximate dates during the school year when activities described in subparagraph (C) are scheduled, or expected to be scheduled.

(C) Activities requiring notification

The following activities require notification under this paragraph:

(i) Activities involving the collection, disclosure, or use of personal information collected from students for the purpose of marketing or for selling that information (or otherwise providing that information to others for that purpose).

(ii) The administration of any survey containing one or more items described in clauses (i) through (viii) of paragraph (1)(B).

(iii) Any nonemergency, invasive physical examination or screening that is—

(I) required as a condition of attendance;

(II) administered by the school and scheduled by the school in advance; and

(III) not necessary to protect the immediate health and safety of the student, or of other students.

(3) Existing policies

A local educational agency need not develop and adopt new policies if the State educational agency or local educational agency has in place, on January 8, 2002, policies covering the requirements of paragraph (1). The agency shall provide reasonable notice of such existing policies to parents and guardians of students, in accordance with paragraph (2).

(4) Exceptions

(A) Educational products or services

Paragraph (1)(E) does not apply to the collection, disclosure, or use of personal information collected from students for the exclusive purpose of developing, evaluating, or providing educational products or services for, or to, students or educational institutions, such as the following:

(i) College or other postsecondary education recruitment, or military recruitment.

(ii) Book clubs, magazines, and programs providing access to low-cost literary products.

(iii) Curriculum and instructional materials used by elementary schools and secondary schools.

(iv) Tests and assessments used by elementary schools and secondary schools to provide cognitive, evaluative, diagnostic, clinical, aptitude, or achievement information about students (or to generate other statistically useful data for the purpose of securing such tests and assessments) and the subsequent analysis and public release of the aggregate data from such tests and assessments.

(v) The sale by students of products or services to raise funds for school-related or education-related activities.

(vi) Student recognition programs.

(B) State law exception

The provisions of this subsection—

(i) shall not be construed to preempt applicable provisions of State law that require parental notification; and

(ii) do not apply to any physical examination or screening that is permitted or required by an applicable State law, including physical examinations or screenings that are permitted without parental notification.

(5) General provisions

(A) Rules of construction

(i) This section does not supersede section 1232g of this title.

(ii) Paragraph (1)(D) does not apply to a survey administered to a student in accordance with the Individuals with Disabilities Education Act (20 U.S.C. 1400 et seq.).

(B) Student rights

The rights provided to parents under this section transfer to the student when the student turns 18 years old, or is an emancipated minor (under an applicable State law) at any age.

(C) Information activities

The Secretary shall annually inform each State educational agency and each local educational agency of the educational agency's obligations under this section and section 1232g of this title.

(D) Funding

A State educational agency or local educational agency may use funds provided under part A of title V of the Elementary and Secondary Education Act of 1965 [20 U.S.C. 7201 et seq.] to enhance parental involvement in areas affecting the in-school privacy of students.

(6) Definitions

As used in this subsection:

(A) Instructional material

The term "instructional material" means instructional content that is provided to a student, regardless of its format, including printed or representational materials, audio-visual materials, and materials in electronic or digital formats (such as materials accessible through the Internet). The term does not include academic tests or academic assessments.

(B) Invasive physical examination

The term "invasive physical examination" means any medical examination that involves the exposure of private body parts, or any act during such examination that includes incision, insertion, or injection into the body, but does not include a hearing, vision, or scoliosis screening.

(C) Local educational agency

The term "local educational agency" means an elementary school, secondary school, school district, or local board of education that is the recipient of funds under an applicable program, but does not include a postsecondary institution.

(D) Parent

The term "parent" includes a legal guardian or other person standing in loco parentis (such as a grandparent or stepparent with whom the child lives, or a person who is legally responsible for the welfare of the child).

(E) Personal information

The term "personal information" means individually identifiable information including—

(i) a student or parent's first and last name;

(ii) a home or other physical address (including street name and the name of the city or town);

(iii) a telephone number; or

(iv) a Social Security identification number.

(F) Student

The term "student" means any elementary school or secondary school student.

(G) Survey

The term "survey" includes an evaluation.

(d) Notice

Educational agencies and institutions shall give parents and students effective notice of their rights under this section.

(e) Enforcement

The Secretary shall take such action as the Secretary determines appropriate to enforce this section, except that action to terminate assistance provided under an applicable program shall be taken only if the Secretary determines that—

(1) there has been a failure to comply with such section; and

(2) compliance with such section cannot be secured by voluntary means.

(f) Office and review board

The Secretary shall establish or designate an office and review board within the Department of Education to investigate, process, review, and adjudicate violations of the rights established under this section.

§ 1232i. Limitations on withholding of Federal assistance

(a) Refusal to supply personal data on students or families

Except as provided in section 1232g (b)(1)(D) of this title, the refusal of a State or local educational agency or institution of higher education, community college, school, agency offering a preschool program, or other educational institution to provide personally identifiable data on students or their families, as a part of any applicable program, to any Federal office, agency, department, or other third party, on the grounds that it constitutes a violation of the right to privacy and confidentiality of students or their parents, shall not constitute sufficient grounds for the suspension or termination of Federal assistance. Such a refusal shall also not constitute sufficient grounds for a denial of, a refusal to consider, or a delay in the consideration of, funding for such a recipient in succeeding fiscal years. In the case of any dispute arising under this section, reasonable notice and opportunity for a hearing shall be afforded the applicant.

(b) Noncompliance with nondiscrimination provisions of Federal law

The extension of Federal financial assistance to a local educational agency may not be limited, deferred, or terminated by the Secretary on the ground of noncompliance with title VI of the Civil Rights Act of 1964 [42 U.S.C. 2000d et seq.] or any other nondiscrimination provision of Federal law unless such agency is accorded the right of due process of law, which shall include—

(1) at least 30 days prior written notice of deferral to the agency, setting forth the particular program or programs which the Secretary finds to be operated in noncompliance with a specific provision of Federal law;

(2) the opportunity for a hearing on the record before a duly appointed administrative law judge within a 60-day period (unless such period is extended by mutual consent of the Secretary and such agency) from the commencement of any deferral;

(3) the conclusion of such hearing and the rendering of a decision on the merits by the administrative law judge within a period not to exceed 90 days from the commencement of such hearing, unless the judge finds by a decision that such hearing cannot be concluded or such decision cannot be rendered within such period, in which case such judge may extend such period for not to exceed 60 additional days;

(4) the limitation of any deferral of Federal financial assistance which may be imposed by the Secretary to a period not to exceed 15 days after the rendering of such decision unless there has been an express finding on such record that such agency has failed to comply with any such nondiscrimination provision of Federal law; and

(5) procedures, which shall be established by the Secretary, to ensure the availability of sufficient funds, without regard to any fiscal year limitations, to comply with the decision of such judge.

(c) Failure to comply with imposition of quotas

It shall be unlawful for the Secretary to defer or limit any Federal financial assistance on the basis of any failure to comply with the imposition of quotas (or any other numerical requirements which have the effect of imposing quotas) on the student admission practices of an institution of higher education or community college receiving Federal financial assistance.

§ 1232j. Prohibition on federally sponsored testing

(a) General prohibition

Notwithstanding any other provision of Federal law and except as provided in subsection (b) of this section, no funds provided to the Department of Education or to an applicable program, may be used to pilot test, field test, implement, administer or distribute in any way any federally sponsored national test in reading, mathematics, or any other subject that is not specifically and explicitly provided for in authorizing legislation enacted into law.

(b) Exceptions

Subsection (a) of this section shall not apply to the Third International Mathematics and Science Study or other international comparative assessments developed under the authority of section 9543 (a)(6) of this title and administered to only a representative sample of pupils in the United States and in foreign nations.

§ 7908. Armed Forces recruiter access to students and student recruiting information

(a) Policy

(1) Access to student recruiting information

Notwithstanding section 1232g(a)(5)(B) of this title and except as provided in paragraph (2), each local educational agency receiving assistance under this chapter shall provide, on a request made by military recruiters or an institution of higher education, access to secondary school students names, addresses, and telephone listings.

(2) Consent

A secondary school student or the parent of the student may request that the student's name, address, and telephone listing described in paragraph (1) not be released without prior written parental consent, and the local educational agency or private school shall notify parents of the option to make a request and shall comply with any request.

(3) Same access to students

Each local educational agency receiving assistance under this chapter shall provide military recruiters the same access to secondary school students as is provided generally to post secondary educational institutions or to prospective employers of those students.

(b) Notification

The Secretary, in consultation with the Secretary of Defense, shall, not later than 120 days after January 8, 2002, notify principals, school administrators, and other educators about the requirements of this section.

(c) Exception

The requirements of this section do not apply to a private secondary school that maintains a religious objection to service in the Armed Forces if the objection is verifiable through the corporate or other organizational documents or materials of that school.

(d) Special rule

A local educational agency prohibited by Connecticut State law (either explicitly by statute or through statutory interpretation by the State Supreme Court or State Attorney General) from providing military recruiters with information or access as required by this section shall have until May 31, 2002, to comply with that requirement.

IX.
EMPLOYMENT PRIVACY

Employee Polygraph Protection Act (1988)

29 U.S.C.A. §§ 2001-2009, as amended

Statutes in Context

The Employee Polygraph Protection Act makes it unlawful for private-sector employers to require or request any employee to take or submit to a lie detector test, or to use the results of any lie detector test of any employee or prospective employee. The Act applies only to private-sector employees. It specifically exempts the U.S. government as well as state or local governments from its provisions. There are certain exceptions, however, where employers may use such tests. For example, polygraph tests may be administered in connection with an investigation of economic loss or injury to the employer's business. Moreover, employees who engage in security services, such as armored car services and security alarm services, are exempt from the Act.

---

§ 2001. Definitions

As used in this chapter—

(1) The term "commerce" has the meaning provided by section 203(b) of this title.

(2) The term "employer" includes any person acting directly or indirectly in the interest of an employer in relation to an employee or prospective employee.

(3) The term "lie detector" includes a polygraph, deceptograph, voice stress analyzer, psychological stress evaluator, or any other similar device (whether mechanical or electrical) that is used, or the results of which are used, for the purpose of rendering a diagnostic opinion regarding the honesty or dishonesty of an individual.

(4) The term "polygraph" means an instrument that—

(A) records continuously, visually, permanently, and simultaneously changes in cardiovascular, respiratory, and electrodermal patterns as minimum instrumentation standards; and

(B) is used, or the results of which are used, for the purpose of rendering a diagnostic opinion regarding the honesty or dishonesty of an individual.

(5) The term "Secretary" means the Secretary of Labor.

§ 2002. Prohibitions on lie detector use

Except as provided in sections 2006 and 2007 of this title, it shall be unlawful for any employer engaged in or affecting commerce or in the production of goods for commerce—

(1) Except as provided in sections 2006 and 2007 of this title, it shall be unlawful for any employer engaged in or affecting commerce or in the production of goods for commerce—

(2) directly or indirectly, to require, request, suggest, or cause any employee or prospective employee to take or submit to any lie detector test;

(3) to use, accept, refer to, or inquire concerning the results of any lie detector test of any employee or prospective employee;

(4) to discharge, discipline, discriminate against in any manner, or deny employment or promotion to, or threaten to take any such action against—

> **(A)** any employee or prospective employee who refuses, declines, or fails to take or submit to any lie detector test, or
>
> **(B)** any employee or prospective employee on the basis of the results of any lie detector test; or

(5) to discharge, discipline, discriminate against in any manner, or deny employment or promotion to, or threaten to take any such action against, any employee or prospective employee because—

> **(A)** such employee or prospective employee has filed any complaint or instituted or caused to be instituted any proceeding under or related to this chapter,
>
> **(B)** such employee or prospective employee has testified or is about to testify in any such proceeding, or
>
> **(C)** of the exercise by such employee or prospective employee, on behalf of such employee or another person, of any right afforded by this chapter.

§ 2003. Notice of protection

The Secretary shall prepare, have printed, and distribute a notice setting forth excerpts from, or summaries of, the pertinent provisions of this chapter. Each employer shall post and maintain such notice in conspicuous places on its premises where notices to employees and applicants to employment are customarily posted.

§ 2004. Authority of Secretary

(a) In general

The Secretary shall—

(1) issue such rules and regulations as may be necessary or appropriate to carry out this chapter;

(2) cooperate with regional, State, local, and other agencies, and cooperate with and furnish technical assistance to employers, labor organizations, and employment agencies to aid in effectuating the purposes of this chapter; and

(3) make investigations and inspections and require the keeping of records necessary or appropriate for the administration of this chapter.

(b) Subpoena authority

For the purpose of any hearing or investigation under this chapter, the Secretary shall have the authority contained in sections 49 and 50 of Title 15.

§ 2005. Enforcement provisions

(a) Civil penalties

(1) In general.—Subject to paragraph (2), any employer who violates any provision of this chapter may be assessed a civil penalty of not more than $10,000.

(2) Determination of amount.—In determining the amount of any penalty under paragraph (1), the Secretary shall take into account the previous record of the person in terms of compliance with this chapter and the gravity of the violation.

(3) Collection.—Any civil penalty assessed under this subsection shall be collected in the same manner as is required by subsections (b) through (c) of section 1853 of this title with respect to civil penalties assessed under subsection (a) of such section.

(b) Injunctive actions by Secretary

The Secretary may bring an action under this section to restrain violations of this chapter. The Solicitor of Labor may appear for and represent the Secretary in any litigation brought under this chapter. In any action brought under this section, the district courts of the United States shall have jurisdiction, for cause shown, to issue temporary or permanent restraining orders and injunctions to require compliance with this chapter, including such legal or equitable relief incident thereto as may be appropriate, including, but not limited to, employment, reinstatement, promotion, and the payment of lost wages and benefits.

(c) Private civil actions

(1) Liability.—An employer who violates this chapter shall be liable to the employee or prospective employee affected by such violation. Such employer shall be liable for such legal or equitable relief as may be appropriate, including, but not limited to, employment, reinstatement, promotion, and the payment of lost wages and benefits.

(2) Court.—An action to recover the liability prescribed in paragraph (1) may be maintained against the employer in any Federal or State court of competent jurisdiction by an employee or prospective employee for or on behalf of such employee, prospective employee, and other employees or prospective employees similarly situated. No such action may be commenced more than 3 years after the date of the alleged violation.

(3) Costs.—The court, in its discretion, may allow the prevailing party (other than the United States) reasonable costs, including attorney's fees.

(d) Waiver of rights prohibited

The rights and procedures provided by this chapter may not be waived by contract or otherwise, unless such waiver is part of a written settlement agreed to and signed by the parties to the pending action or complaint under this chapter.

§ 2006. Exemptions

(a) No application to governmental employers

This chapter shall not apply with respect to the United States Government, any State or local government, or any political subdivision of a State or local government.

(b) National defense and security exemption

(1) **National defense**.—Nothing in this chapter shall be construed to prohibit the administration, by the Federal Government, in the performance of any counterintelligence function, of any lie detector test to—

(A) any expert or consultant under contract to the Department of Defense or any employee of any contractor of such Department; or

(B) any expert or consultant under contract with the Department of Energy in connection with the atomic energy defense activities of such Department or any employee of any contractor of such Department in connection with such activities.

(2) **Security**.—Nothing in this chapter shall be construed to prohibit the administration, by the Federal Government, in the performance of any intelligence or counterintelligence function, of any lie detector test to—

(A) **(i)** any individual employed by, assigned to, or detailed to, the National Security Agency, the Defense Intelligence Agency, the National Geospatial-Intelligence Agency, or the Central Intelligence Agency,

(ii) any expert or consultant under contract to any such agency,

(iii) any employee of a contractor to any such agency,

(iv) any individual applying for a position in any such agency, or

(v) any individual assigned to a space where sensitive cryptologic information is produced, processed, or stored for any such agency; or

(B) any expert, or consultant (or employee of such expert or consultant) under contract with any Federal Government department, agency, or program whose duties involve access to information that has been classified at the level of top secret or designated as being within a special access program under section 4.2(a) of Executive Order 12356 (or a successor Executive order).

(c) FBI contractors exemption

Nothing in this chapter shall be construed to prohibit the administration, by the Federal Government, in the performance of any counterintelligence function, of any lie detector test to an employee of a contractor of the Federal Bureau of Investigation of the Department of Justice who is engaged in the performance of any work under the contract with such Bureau.

(d) Limited exemption for ongoing investigations

Subject to sections 2007 and 2009 of this title, this chapter shall not prohibit an employer from requesting an employee to submit to a polygraph test if—

(1) the test is administered in connection with an ongoing investigation involving economic loss or injury to the employer's business, such as theft, embezzlement, misappropriation, or an act of unlawful industrial espionage or sabotage;

(2) the employee had access to the property that is the subject of the investigation;

(3) the employer has a reasonable suspicion that the employee was involved in the incident or activity under investigation; and

(4) the employer executes a statement, provided to the examinee before the test, that—

> **(A)** sets forth with particularity the specific incident or activity being investigated and the basis for testing particular employees,
>
> **(B)** is signed by a person (other than a polygraph examiner) authorized to legally bind the employer,
>
> **(C)** is retained by the employer for at least 3 years, and
>
> **(D)** contains at a minimum—
>
> > **(i)** an identification of the specific economic loss or injury to the business of the employer,
> >
> > **(ii)** a statement indicating that the employee had access to the property that is the subject of the investigation, and
> >
> > **(iii)** a statement describing the basis of the employer's reasonable suspicion that the employee was involved in the incident or activity under investigation.

(e) Exemption for security services

(1) In general

Subject to paragraph (2) and sections 2007 and 2009 of this title, this chapter shall not prohibit the use of polygraph tests on prospective employees by any private employer whose primary business purpose consists of providing armored car personnel, personnel engaged in the design, installation, and maintenance of security alarm systems, or other uniformed or plainclothes security personnel and whose function includes protection of—

(A) facilities, materials, or operations having a significant impact on the health or safety of any State or political subdivision thereof, or the national security of the United States, as determined under rules and regulations issued by the Secretary within 90 days after June 27, 1988, including—

(i) facilities engaged in the production, transmission, or distribution of electric or nuclear power,

(ii) public water supply facilities,

(iii) shipments or storage of radioactive or other toxic waste materials, and

(iv) public transportation, or

(B) currency, negotiable securities, precious commodities or instruments, or proprietary information.

(2) Access

The exemption provided under this subsection shall not apply if the test is administered to a prospective employee who would not be employed to protect facilities, materials, operations, or assets referred to in paragraph (1).

(f) Exemption for drug security, drug theft, or drug diversion investigations

(1) In general

Subject to paragraph (2) and sections 2007 and 2009 of this title, this chapter shall not prohibit the use of a polygraph test by any employer authorized to manufacture, distribute, or dispense a controlled substance listed in schedule I, II, III, or IV of section 812 of Title 21,

(2) Access

The exemption provided under this subsection shall apply—

(A) if the test is administered to a prospective employee who would have direct access to the manufacture, storage, distribution, or sale of any such controlled substance; or

(B) in the case of a test administered to a current employee, if—

(i) the test is administered in connection with an ongoing investigation of criminal or other misconduct involving, or potentially involving, loss or injury to the manufacture, distribution, or dispensing of any such controlled substance by such employer, and

(ii) the employee had access to the person or property that is the subject of the investigation.

§ 2007. Restrictions on use of exemptions

(a) Test as basis for adverse employment action

(1) Under ongoing investigations exemption.—Except as provided in paragraph (2), the exemption under subsection (d) of section 2006 of this title shall not apply if an employee is discharged, disciplined, denied employment or promotion, or otherwise discriminated against in any manner on the basis of the analysis of a polygraph test chart or the refusal to take a polygraph test, without additional supporting evidence. The evidence required by such subsection may serve as additional supporting evidence.

(2) Under other exemptions.—In the case of an exemption described in subsection (e) or (f) of such section, the exemption shall not apply if the results of an analysis of a polygraph test chart are used, or the refusal to take a polygraph test is used, as the sole basis upon which an adverse employment action described in paragraph (1) is taken against an employee or prospective employee.

(b) Rights of examinee

The exemptions provided under subsections (d), (e) and (f) of section 2006 of this title shall not apply unless the requirements described in the following paragraphs are met:

(1) All phases

Throughout all phases of the test—

(A) the examinee shall be permitted to terminate the test at any time;

(B) the examinee is not asked questions in a manner designed to degrade, or needlessly intrude on, such examinee;

(C) the examinee is not asked any question concerning—

(i) religious beliefs or affiliations,

(ii) beliefs or opinions regarding racial matters,

(iii) political beliefs or affiliations,

(iv) any matter relating to sexual behavior; and

(v) beliefs, affiliations, opinions, or lawful activities regarding unions or labor organizations; and

(D) the examiner does not conduct the test if there is sufficient written evidence by a physician that the examinee is suffering from a medical or psychological condition or undergoing treatment that might cause abnormal responses during the actual testing phase.

(2) Pretest phase

During the pretest phase, the prospective examinee—

(A) is provided with reasonable written notice of the date, time, and location of the test, and of such examinee's right to obtain and consult with legal counsel or an employee representative before each phase of the test;

(B) is informed in writing of the nature and characteristics of the tests and of the instruments involved;

(C) is informed, in writing—

(i) whether the testing area contains a two-way mirror, a camera, or any other device through which the test can be observed,

(ii) whether any other device, including any device for recording or monitoring the test, will be used, or

(iii) that the employer or the examinee may (with mutual knowledge) make a recording of the test;

(D) is read and signs a written notice informing such examinee—

(i) that the examinee cannot be required to take the test as a condition of employment,

(ii) that any statement made during the test may constitute additional supporting evidence for the purposes of an adverse employment action described in subsection (a) of this section,

(iii) of the limitations imposed under this section,

(iv) of the legal rights and remedies available to the examinee if the polygraph test is not conducted in accordance with this chapter, and

(v) of the legal rights and remedies of the employer under this chapter (including the rights of the employer under section 2008(c)(2) of this title); and

(E) is provided an opportunity to review all questions to be asked during the test and is informed of the right to terminate the test at any time.

(3) Actual testing phase

During the actual testing phase, the examiner does not ask such examinee any question relevant during the test that was not presented in writing for review to such examinee before the test.

(4) Post-test phase

Before any adverse employment action, the employer shall—

(A) further interview the examinee on the basis of the results of the test; and

(B) provide the examinee with—

(i) a written copy of any opinion or conclusion rendered as a result of the test, and

(ii) a copy of the questions asked during the test along with the corresponding charted responses.

(5) Maximum number and minimum duration of tests.

The examiner shall not conduct and complete more than five polygraph tests on a calendar day on which the test is given, and shall not conduct any such test for less than a 90-minute duration.

(c) Qualifications and requirements of examiners

The exemptions provided under subsections (d), (c) and (f) of section 2006 of this title shall not apply unless the individual who conducts the polygraph test satisfies the requirements under the following paragraphs:

(1) Qualifications

The examiner—

(A) has a valid and current license granted by licensing and regulatory authorities in the State in which the test is to be conducted, if so required by the State; and

(B) maintains a minimum of a $50,000 bond or an equivalent amount of professional liability coverage

(2) Requirements

The examiner—

(A) renders any opinion or conclusion regarding the test—

(i) in writing and solely on the basis of an analysis of polygraph test charts,

(ii) that does not contain information other than admissions, information, case facts, and interpretation of the charts relevant to the purpose and stated objectives of the test, and

(iii) that does not include any recommendation concerning the employment of the examinee; and

(B) maintains all opinions, reports, charts, written questions, lists, and other records relating to the test for a minimum period of 3 years after administration of the test.

§ 2008. Disclosure of information

(a) In general.—A person, other than the examinee, may not disclose information obtained during a polygraph test, except as provided in this section.

(b) Permitted disclosures.—A polygraph examiner may disclose information acquired from a polygraph test only to—

(1) the examinee or any other person specifically designated in writing by the examinee;

(2) the employer that requested the test; or

(3) any court, governmental agency, arbitrator, or mediator, in accordance with due process of law, pursuant to an order from a court of competent jurisdiction.

(c) Disclosure by employer.—An employer (other than an employer described in subsection (a), (b), or (c) of section 2006 of this title) for whom a polygraph test is conducted may disclose information from the test only to—

(1) a person in accordance with subsection (b) of this section; or

(2) a governmental agency, but only insofar as the disclosed information is an admission of criminal conduct.

Americans with Disabilities Act (1990)

42 U.S.C. §§ 12112, 12114, as amended

Statutes in Context

The Americans with Disabilities Act (ADA) prohibits employees from conducting a medical examination or making inquiries "as to whether such applicant is an individual with a disability or as to the nature or severity of such disability." 42 U.S.C. § 12112(d)(2). It exempts drug testing, however, from its definition of medical examination, and also exempts the testing of applicants in safety-sensitive duties that work for entities subject to the jurisdiction of the Department of Transportation.

§ 12112 Discrimination

(d) Medical examinations and inquiries.

(1) In general

The prohibition against discrimination as referred to in subsection (a) shall include medical examinations and inquiries.

(2) Preemployment.

(A) Prohibited examination or inquiry.

Except as provided in paragraph (3), a covered entity shall not conduct a medical examination or make inquiries of a job applicant as to whether such applicant is an individual with a disability or as to the nature or severity of such disability.

§ 12114 Illegal use of drugs and alcohol

(a) Qualified individual with a disability

For purposes of this title, the term "qualified individual with a disability" shall not include any employee or applicant who is currently engaging in the illegal use of drugs, when the covered entity acts on the basis of such use.

(b) Rules of construction

Nothing in subsection (a) shall be construed to exclude as a qualified individual with a disability an individual who—

(1) has successfully completed a supervised drug rehabilitation program and is no longer engaging in the illegal use of drugs, or has otherwise been rehabilitated successfully and is no longer engaging in such use;

(2) is participating in a supervised rehabilitation program and is no longer engaging in such use; or

(3) is erroneously regarded as engaging in such use, but is not engaging in such use;

except that it shall not be a violation of this Act for a covered entity to adopt or administer reasonable policies or procedures, including but not limited to drug testing, designed to ensure that an individual described in paragraph (1) or (2) is no longer engaging in the illegal use of drugs.

(c) Authority of covered entity

A covered entity—

(1) may prohibit the illegal use of drugs and the use of alcohol at the workplace by all employees;

(2) may require that employees shall not be under the influence of alcohol or be engaging in the illegal use of drugs at the workplace;

(3) may require that employees behave in conformance with the requirements established under the Drug-Free Workplace Act of 1988 (41 U.S.C. 701 et seq.);

(4) may hold an employee who engages in the illegal use of drugs or who is an alcoholic to the same qualification standards for employment or job performance and behavior that such entity holds other employees, even if any unsatisfactory performance or behavior is related to the drug use or alcoholism of such employee; and

(5) may, with respect to Federal regulations regarding alcohol and the illegal use of drugs, require that—

(A) employees comply with the standards established in such regulations of the Department of Defense, if the employees of the covered entity are employed in an industry subject to such regulations, including complying with regulations (if any) that apply to employment in sensitive positions in such an industry, in the case of employees of the covered entity who are employed in such positions (as defined in the regulations of the Department of Defense);

(B) employees comply with the standards established in such regulations of the Nuclear Regulatory Commission, if the employees of the covered entity are employed in an industry subject to such regulations, including complying with regulations (if any) that apply to employment in sensitive positions in such an industry, in the case of employees of the covered entity who are employed in such positions (as defined in the regulations of the Nuclear Regulatory Commission); and

(C) employees comply with the standards established in such regulations of the Department of Transportation, if the employees of the covered entity are employed in a transportation industry subject to such regulations, including complying with such regulations (if any) that apply to employment in sensitive positions in such an industry, in the case of employees of the covered entity who are employed in such positions (as defined in the regulations of the Department of Transportation).

(D) Drug testing.

(1) In general

For purposes of this title, a test to determine the illegal use of drugs shall not be considered a medical examination.

(2) Construction.

Nothing in this title shall be construed to encourage, prohibit, or authorize the conducting of drug testing for the illegal use of drugs by job applicants or employees or making employment decisions based on such test results.

(e) Transportation employees

Nothing in this title shall be construed to encourage, prohibit, restrict, or authorize the otherwise lawful exercise by entities subject to the jurisdiction of the Department of Transportation of authority to—

(1) test employees of such entities in, and applicants for, positions involving safety-sensitive duties for the illegal use of drugs and for on-duty impairment by alcohol; and

(2) remove such persons who test positive for illegal use of drugs and on-duty impairment by alcohol pursuant to paragraph (1) from safety-sensitive duties in implementing subsection (c).

X.
INTERNATIONAL PRIVACY

Universal Declaration of Human Rights (1948)

Context

The General Assembly of the United Nations proclaimed the Universal Declaration of Human Rights on December 10, 1948. In its Article 12, the Declaration protects against arbitrary interference with personal privacy.

Preamble

Whereas recognition of the inherent dignity and of the equal and inalienable rights of all members of the human family is the foundation of freedom, justice and peace in the world,

Whereas disregard and contempt for human rights have resulted in barbarous acts which have outraged the conscience of mankind, and the advent of a world in which human beings shall enjoy freedom of speech and belief and freedom from fear and want has been proclaimed as the highest aspiration of the common people,

Whereas it is essential, if man is not to be compelled to have recourse, as a last resort, to rebellion against tyranny and oppression, that human rights should be protected by the rule of law,

Whereas it is essential to promote the development of friendly relations between nations,

Whereas the peoples of the United Nations have in the Charter reaffirmed their faith in fundamental human rights, in the dignity and worth of the human person and in the equal rights of men and women and have determined to promote social progress and better standards of life in larger freedom,

Whereas Member States have pledged themselves to achieve, in co-operation with the United Nations, the promotion of universal respect for and observance of human rights and fundamental freedoms,

Whereas a common understanding of these rights and freedoms is of the greatest importance for the full realization of this pledge,

Now, Therefore THE GENERAL ASSEMBLY proclaims THIS UNIVERSAL DECLARATION OF HUMAN RIGHTS as a common standard of achievement for all peoples and all nations, to the end that every individual and every organ of society, keeping this Declaration constantly in mind, shall strive by teaching and education to promote respect for these rights and freedoms and by progressive measures, national and international, to secure their universal and effective recognition and observance, both among the peoples of Member States themselves and among the peoples of territories under their jurisdiction.

Article 1.

All human beings are born free and equal in dignity and rights. They are endowed with reason and conscience and should act towards one another in a spirit of brotherhood.

Article 2.

Everyone is entitled to all the rights and freedoms set forth in this Declaration, without distinction of any kind, such as race, colour, sex, language, religion, political or other opinion, national or social origin, property, birth or other status. Furthermore, no distinction shall be made on the basis of the political, jurisdictional or international status of the country or territory to which a person belongs, whether it be independent, trust, non-self-governing or under any other limitation of sovereignty.

Article 3.

Everyone has the right to life, liberty and security of person.

* * * *

Article 12.

No one shall be subjected to arbitrary interference with his privacy, family, home or correspondence, nor to attacks upon his honour and reputation. Everyone has the right to the protection of the law against such interference or attacks.

* * * *

OECD Privacy Guidelines (1980)

Guidelines in Context

The Organization for Economic Cooperating and Development (OECD) is a group of leading industrial countries, including the United States, concerned with global economic and democratic development. Its guidelines for privacy protection establish eight key principles for the protection of personal information. Although the OECD privacy guidelines are nonbinding on members of the OECD, they have played a significant role in the development of national law in North America, Europe, and East Asia.

PREFACE

The development of automatic data processing, which enables vast quantities of data to be transmitted within seconds across national frontiers, and indeed across continents, has made it necessary to consider privacy protection in relation to personal data. Privacy protection laws have been introduced, or will be introduced shortly, in approximately one half of OECD Member countries (Austria, Canada, Denmark, France, Germany, Luxembourg, Norway, Sweden and the United States have passed legislation. Belgium, Iceland, the Netherlands, Spain and Switzerland have prepared draft bills) to prevent what are considered to be violations of fundamental human rights, such as the unlawful storage of personal data, the storage of inaccurate personal data, or the abuse or unauthorised disclosure of such data.

On the other hand, there is a danger that disparities in national legislations could hamper the free flow of personal data across frontiers; these flows have greatly increased in recent years and are bound to grow further with the widespread introduction of new computer and communications technology. Restrictions on these flows could cause serious disruption in important sectors of the economy, such as banking and insurance.

For this reason OECD Member countries considered it necessary to develop Guidelines which would help to harmonise national privacy legislation and, while upholding such human rights, would at the same time prevent interruptions in international flows of data. They represent a consensus on basic principles which can be built into existing national legislation, or serve as a basis for legislation in those countries which do not yet have it.

The Guidelines, in the form of a Recommendation by the Council of the OECD, were developed by a group of government experts under the chairmanship of The Hon. Mr. Justice M.D. Kirby, Chairman of the Australian Law Reform Commission. The Recommendation was adopted and became applicable on 23rd September, 1980.

The Guidelines are accompanied by an Explanatory Memorandum intended to provide information on the discussion and reasoning underlining their formulation.

RECOMMENDATION OF THE COUNCIL CONCERNING GUIDELINES GOVERNING THE PROTECTION OF PRIVACY AND TRANSBORDER FLOWS OF PERSONAL DATA (23rd September, 1980)

THE COUNCIL,

Having regard to articles 1(c), 3(a) and 5(b) of the Convention on the Organisation for Economic Co-operation and Development of 14th December, 1960;

RECOGNISING:

- that, although national laws and policies may differ, Member countries have a common interest in protecting privacy and individual liberties, and in reconciling fundamental but competing values such as privacy and the free flow of information;
- that automatic processing and transborder flows of personal data create new forms of relationships among countries and require the development of compatible rules and practices;
- that transborder flows of personal data contribute to economic and social development;
- that domestic legislation concerning privacy protection and transborder flows of personal data may hinder such transborder flows;

Determined to advance the free flow of information between Member countries and to avoid the creation of unjustified obstacles to the development of economic and social relations among Member countries;

RECOMMENDS:

1. That Member countries take into account in their domestic legislation the principles concerning the protection of privacy and individual liberties set forth in the Guidelines contained in the Annex to this Recommendation which is an integral part thereof;

2. That Member countries endeavour to remove or avoid creating, in the name of privacy protection, unjustified obstacles to transborder flows of personal data;

3. That Member countries co-operate in the implementation of the Guidelines set forth in the Annex;

4. That Member countries agree as soon as possible on specific procedures of consultation and co-operation for the application of these Guidelines.

Annex to the Recommendation of the Council of 23rd September 1980

GUIDELINES GOVERNING THE PROTECTION OF PRIVACY AND TRANSBORDER FLOWS OF PERSONAL DATA

PART ONE. GENERAL DEFINITIONS.

1. For the purposes of these Guidelines:

> **a)** "data controller" means a party who, according to domestic law, is competent to decide about the contents and use of personal data regardless of whether or not such data are collected, stored, processed or disseminated by that party or by an agent on its behalf;
>
> **b)** "personal data" means any information relating to an identified or identifiable individual (data subject);
>
> **c)** "transborder flows of personal data" means movements of personal data across national borders.

Scope of Guidelines

2. These Guidelines apply to personal data, whether in the public or private sectors, which, because of the manner in which they are processed, or because of their nature or the context in which they are used, pose a danger to privacy and individual liberties.

3. These Guidelines should not be interpreted as preventing:

> **a)** the application, to different categories of personal data, of different protective measures depending upon their nature and the context in which they are collected, stored, processed or disseminated;
>
> **b)** the exclusion from the application of the Guidelines of personal data which obviously do not contain any risk to privacy and individual liberties; or
>
> **c)** the application of the Guidelines only to automatic processing of personal data.

4. Exceptions to the Principles contained in Parts Two and Three of these Guidelines, including those relating to national sovereignty, national security and public policy ("ordre public"), should be:

> **a)** as few as possible, and
>
> **b)** made known to the public.

5. In the particular case of Federal countries the observance of these Guidelines may be affected by the division of powers in the Federation.

6. These Guidelines should be regarded as minimum standards which are capable of being supplemented by additional measures for the protection of privacy and individual liberties.

PART TWO. BASIC PRINCIPLES OF NATIONAL APPLICATION

Collection Limitation Principle

7. There should be limits to the collection of personal data and any such data should be obtained by lawful and fair means and, where appropriate, with the knowledge or consent of the data subject.

Data Quality Principle

8. Personal data should be relevant to the purposes for which they are to be used, and, to the extent necessary for those purposes, should be accurate, complete and kept up-to-date.

Purpose Specification Principle

9. The purposes for which personal data are collected should be specified not later than at the time of data collection and the subsequent use limited to the fulfillment of those purposes or such others as are not incompatible with those purposes and as are specified on each occasion of change of purpose.

Use Limitation Principle

10. Personal data should not be disclosed, made available or otherwise used for purposes other than those specified in accordance with Paragraph 9 except:

a) with the consent of the data subject; or

b) by the authority of law.

Security Safeguards Principle

11. Personal data should be protected by reasonable security safeguards against such risks as loss or unauthorised access, destruction, use, modification or disclosure of data.

Openness Principle

12. There should be a general policy of openness about developments, practices and policies with respect to personal data. Means should be readily available of establishing the existence and nature of personal data, and the main purposes of their use, as well as the identity and usual residence of the data controller.

Individual Participation Principle

13. An individual should have the right:

a) to obtain from a data controller, or otherwise, confirmation of whether or not the data controller has data relating to him;

b) to have communicated to him, data relating to him

- within a reasonable time;
- at a charge, if any, that is not excessive;
- in a reasonable manner; and

- in a form that is readily intelligible to him;

c) to be given reasons if a request made under subparagraphs(a) and (b) is denied, and to be able to challenge such denial; and

d) to challenge data relating to him and, if the challenge is successful to have the data erased, rectified, completed or amended.

Accountability Principle

14. A data controller should be accountable for complying with measures which give effect to the principles stated above.

PART THREE. BASIC PRINCIPLES OF INTERNATIONAL APPLICATION: FREE FLOW AND LEGITIMATE RESTRICTIONS

15. Member countries should take into consideration the implications for other Member countries of domestic processing and re-export of personal data.

16. Member countries should take all reasonable and appropriate steps to ensure that transborder flows of personal data, including transit through a Member country, are uninterrupted and secure.

17. A Member country should refrain from restricting transborder flows of personal data between itself and another Member country except where the latter does not yet substantially observe these Guidelines or where the re-export of such data would circumvent its domestic privacy legislation. A Member country may also impose restrictions in respect of certain categories of personal data for which its domestic privacy legislation includes specific regulations in view of the nature of those data and for which the other Member country provides no equivalent protection.

18. Member countries should avoid developing laws, policies and practices in the name of the protection of privacy and individual liberties, which would create obstacles to transborder flows of personal data that would exceed requirements for such protection.

PART FOUR. NATIONAL IMPLEMENTATION

19. In implementing domestically the principles set forth in Parts Two and Three, Member countries should establish legal, administrative or other procedures or institutions for the protection of privacy and individual liberties in respect of personal data. Member countries should in particular endeavour to:

a) adopt appropriate domestic legislation;

b) encourage and support self-regulation, whether in the form of codes of conduct or otherwise;

c) provide for reasonable means for individuals to exercise their rights;

d) provide for adequate sanctions and remedies in case of failures to comply with measures which implement the principles set forth in Parts Two and Three; and

e) ensure that there is no unfair discrimination against data subjects.

PART FIVE. INTERNATIONAL CO-OPERATION

20. Member countries should, where requested, make known to other Member countries details of the observance of the principles set forth in these Guidelines. Member countries should also ensure that procedures for transborder flows of personal data and for the protection of privacy and individual liberties are simple and compatible with those of other Member countries which comply with these Guidelines.

21. Member countries should establish procedures to facilitate:

- information exchange related to these Guidelines, and
- mutual assistance in the procedural and investigative matters involved.

22. Member countries should work towards the development of principles, domestic and international, to govern the applicable law in the case of transborder flows of personal data.

Council of Europe Convention on Privacy (1981)

Conventions in Context

The Council of Europe Convention on Privacy establishes important privacy principles for European states that ratify it. Among these is Article 5's principle of "quality of data," which requires information undergoing automatic processing to be obtained fairly and lawfully and to be stored for legitimate purposes and not used in an incompatible fashion.

PREAMBLE

The member States of the Council of Europe, signatory hereto,

Considering that the aim of the Council of Europe is to achieve greater unity between its members, based in particular on respect for the rule of law, as well as human rights and fundamental freedoms;

Considering that it is desirable to extend the safeguards for everyone's rights and fundamental freedoms, and in particular the right to the respect for privacy, taking account of the increasing flow across frontiers of personal data undergoing automatic processing;

Reaffirming at the same time their commitment' to freedom of information regardless of frontiers;

Recognizing that it is necessary to reconcile the fundamental values of the respect for privacy and the free flow of information between peoples,

Have agreed as follows:

CHAPTER I — GENERAL PROVISIONS

Article 1 - Object and purpose

The purpose of this convention is to secure in the territory of each Party for every individual, whatever his nationality or residence, respect for his rights and fundamental freedoms, and in particular his right to privacy, with regard to automatic processing of personal data relating to him ("data protection").

Article 2 - Definitions

For the purposes of this convention:

a. "personal data" means any information relating to an identified or identifiable individual ("data subjected");

b. "automated data file" means any set of data undergoing automatic processing;

c. "automatic processing" includes the following operations if carried out in whole or in part by automated means: storage of data, carrying out of logical and/or arithmetical operations on those data, their alteration, erasure, retrieval or dissemination;

d. "controller of the file" means the natural or legal person, public authority, agency or any other body who is competent according to the national law to decide what should be the purpose of the automated data file, which categories of personal data should be stored and which operations should be applied to them.

***Article 3* - Scope**

1. The Parties undertake to apply this convention to automated personal data files and automatic processing of personal data in the public and private sectors.

2. Any State may, at the time of signature or when depositing its instrument of ratification, acceptance, approval or accession, or at any later time, give notice by a declaration addressed to the Secretary General of the Council of Europe:

> **a.** that it will not apply this convention to certain categories of automated personal data files, a list of which will be deposited. In this list it shall not include, however, categories of automated data files subject under its domestic law to data protection provisions. Consequently, it shall amend this list by a new declaration whenever additional categories of automated personal data files are subjected to data protection provisions under its domestic law;
>
> **b.** that it will also apply this convention to information relating to groups of persons, associations, foundations, companies, corporations and any other bodies consisting directly or indirectly of individuals, whether or not such bodies possess legal personality;
>
> **c.** that it will also apply this convention to personal data files which are not processed automatically.

3. Any State which has extended the scope of this convention by any of the declarations provided for in sub-paragraphs 2.b or c above may give notice in the said declaration that such extensions shall apply only to certain categories of personal data files, a list of which will be deposited.

4. Any Party which has excluded certain categories of automated personal data files by a declaration provided for in sub-paragraph 2.a above may not claim the application of this convention to such categories by a Party which has not excluded them.

5. Likewise, a Party which has not made one or other of the extensions provided for in sub-paragraphs 2.b and c above may not claim the application of this convention on these points with respect to a Party which has made such extensions.

6. The declarations provided for in paragraph 2 above shall take effect from the moment of the entry into force of the convention with regard to the State which has made them-if they have been made at the time of signature or deposit of its instrument of ratification, acceptance, approval or accession, or three months after their receipt by the Secretary General of the Council of Europe if they have been made at any later time. These declarations may be withdrawn, in whole or in part, by a notification addressed to the Secretary General of the Council of Europe. Such withdrawals shall take effect three months after the date of receipt of such notification.

CHAPTER II — BASIC PRINCIPLES FOR DATA PROTECTION

Article 4 - Duties of the Parties

1. Each party shall take the necessary measures in its domestic law to give effect to the basic principles for data protection set out in this chapter.

2. These measures shall be taken at the latest at the time of entry into force of this convention in respect of that Party;

Article 5 - Quality of data

Personal data undergoing automatic processing shall bet

a. obtained and processed fairly and lawfully;

b. stored for specified and legitimate purposes and not used in a way incompatible with those purposes;

c. adequate, relevant and not excessive in relation to the Purposes for which they are stored;

d. accurate and, where necessary, kept up to date;

e. preserved in a form which permits identification of the data subjects for no longer than is required for the purpose for which those data are stored.

Article 6 - Special categories of data

Personal data revealing racial origin, political opinions or religious or other beliefs, as well as personal data concerning health or sexual life, may not be processed automatically unless domestic law provides appropriate safeguards. The same shall apply to personal data relating to criminal convictions.

Article 7 - Data security

Appropriate security measures shall be taken for the protection of personal data stored in automated data files against accidental or unauthorised destruction or accidental loss as well as against unauthorised access, alteration or dissemination.

Article 8 - Additional safeguards for the data subject

Any person shall be enabled:

a. to establish the existence of an automated personal data file, its main purposes, as well as the identity and habitual residence or principal place of business of the controller of the file;

b. to obtain at reasonable intervals and without excessive delay or expense confirmation of whether personal data relating to him are stored in the automated data file as well as communication to him of such data in an intelligible form;

c. to obtain, as the case may be, rectification or erasure of such data if these have been processed contrary to the provisions of domestic law giving effect to the basic principles set out in Articles 5 and 6 of this convention;

d. to have a remedy if a request for confirmation or, as the case may be, communication, rectification or erasure as referred to in paragraphs b and c of this article is not complied with.

Article 9 - **Exceptions and restrictions**

1. No exception to the provisions of Articles 5, 6 and 8 of this convention shall be allowed except within the limits defined in this article.

2. Derogation from the provisions of Articles 5, 6 and 8 of this convention shall be allowed when such derogation is provided for, by the law of the Party and constitutes a necessary measure in a democratic society in the interests of:

> **a.** protecting State security, public safety, the monetary interests of the State or the suppression of criminal offences;
>
> **b.** protecting the data subject or the rights and freedoms of others.

3. Restrictions on the exercise of the rights specified in Article 8, paragraphs b, c, and d, may be provided by law with respect to automated personal data files used for statistics or for scientific research purposes when there is obviously no risk of an infringement of the privacy of the data subjects.

Article 10 - **Sanctions and remedies**

Each Party undertakes to establish appropriate sanctions and remedies for violations of provisions of domestic law giving effect to the basic principles for data protection set out in this chapter.

Article 11 - **Extended protection**

None of the provisions of this chapter shall be interpreted as limiting or otherwise affecting the possibility for a Party to grant data subjects a wider measure of protection than that stipulated in this convention.

CHAPTER III — TRANSBORDER DATA FLOWS

Article 12 - **Transborder flows of personal data and domestic law**

1. The following provisions shall apply to the transfer across national borders, by whatever medium, of personal data undergoing automatic processing or collected with a view to their being automatically processed.

2. A Party shall not, for the sole purpose of the protection of privacy, prohibit or subject to special authorisation transborder flows of personal data going to the territory of another Party.

3. Nevertheless, each party shall be entitled to derogate from the provisions of paragraph 2:

> **a.** insofar as its legislation includes specific regulations for certain categories of personal data or of automated personal data files, because of the nature of those data or those files, except where the regulations of the other Party provide an equivalent protection;
>
> **b.** when the transfer is made from its territory to the territory of a non-Contracting State through the intermediary of the territory of another Party, in order to avoid such transfers

resulting in circumvention of the legislation of the Party referred to at the beginning of this paragraph.

CHAPTER IV — MUTUAL ASSISTANCE

Article 13 - Co-operation between Parties

1. The Parties agree to render each other mutual assistance in order to implement this convention.

2. For that purpose:

a. each Party shall designate one or more authorities, the name and address of each of which it shall communicate to the Secretary General of the Council of Europe;

b. each Party which has designated more than one authority shall specify in its communication referred to in the previous sub-paragraph the competence of each authority.

3. An authority designated by a Party shall at the request of an authority designated by another Party:

a. furnish information on its law and administrative practice in the field of data protection;

b. take, in conformity with its domestic law and for the sole purpose of protection of privacy, all appropriate measures for furnishing factual information relating to specific automatic processing carried out in its territory, with the exception however of the personal data being processed.

Article 14 - Assistance to data subjects resident abroad

1. Each Party shall assist any person resident abroad to exercise the rights conferred by its domestic law giving effect to the principles set out in Article 8 of this convention.

2. When such a person resides in the territory of another Party he shall be given the option of submitting his request through the intermediary of the authority designated by that Party.

3. The request for assistance shall contain all the necessary particulars, relating inter alia to:

a. the name, address and any other relevant particulars identifying the person making the request;

b. the automated personal data file to which the request pertains, or its controller;

c. the purpose of the request.

Article 15 - Safeguards concerning assistance rendered by designated authorities

1. An authority designated by a Party which has received information from an authority designated by another Party either accompanying a request for assistance or in reply to its own request for assistance shall not use that information for purposes other than those specified in the request for assistance.

2. Each Party shall see to it that the persons belonging to or acting on behalf of the designated authority shall be bound by appropriate obligations of secrecy or confidentiality with regard to that information.

3. In no case may a designated authority be allowed to make under Article 14, paragraph 2, a request for assistance on behalf of a data subject resident abroad, of its own accord and without the express consent of the person concerned.

Article 16 - **Refusal of requests for assistance**

A designated authority to which a request for assistance is addressed under Articles 13 or 14 of this convention may not refuse to comply with it unless:

a. the request is not compatible with the powers in the field of data protection of the authorities responsible for replying;

b. the request does not comply with the provisions of this convention;

c. compliance with the request would be incompatible with the sovereignty, security or public policy (ordere - public) of the Party by which it was designated, or with the rights and fundamental freedoms of persons under the jurisdiction of that Party.

Article 17 - **Costs and procedures of assistance**

1. Mutual assistance which the Parties render each other under Article 13 and assistance they render to data subjects abroad under Article 14 shall not give rise to the payment of any costs or fees other than those incurred for experts and interpreters. The latter costs or fees shall be borne by the Party which has designated the authority making the request for assistance.

2. The data subject may not be charged costs or fees in connection with the steps taken on his behalf in the territory of another Party other than those lawfully payable by residents of that Party.

3. Other details concerning the assistance relating in particular to the forms and procedures and the languages to be used, shall be established directly between the parties concerned.

CHAPTER V — CONSULTATIVE COMMITTEE

Article 18 - **Composition of the committee**

1. A Consultative Committee shall be set up after the entry into force of this convention.

2. Each Party shall appoint a representative to the committee and a deputy representative. Any member State of the Council of Europe which is not a Party to the convention shall have the right to be represented on the committee by an observer.

3. The Consultative Committee may, by unanimous decision, invite any non-member State of the Council of Europe which is not a Party to the convention to be represented by an observer at a given meeting.

Article 19 - **Functions of the committee**

The Consultative Committee:

a. may make proposals with a view to facilitating or improving the application of the convention;

b. may make proposals for amendment of this convention in accordance with Article 21;

c. shall formulate its opinion on any proposal for amendment of this convention which is referred to it in accordance with Article 21, paragraph 31

d. may, at the request of a Party, express an opinion on any question concerning the application of this convention.

Article 20 - **Procedure**

1. The Consultative Committee shall be convened by the Secretary General of the Council of Europe. Its first meeting shall be held within twelve months of the entry into force of this convention. It shall subsequently meet at least once every two years and in any case when one third of the representatives of the Parties request its convocation.

2. A majority of representatives of the Parties shall constitute a quorum for a meeting of the Consultative Committee.

3. After each of its meetings, the Consultative Committee shall submit to the Committee of Ministers of the Council of Europe a report on its work and on the functioning of the convention.

4. Subject to the provisions of this convention, the Consultative Committee shall draw up its own Rules of Procedure.

CHAPTER VI — AMENDMENTS

Article 21 - **Amendments**

1. Amendments to this convention may be proposed by a Party, the Committee of Ministers of the Council of Europe or the Consultative Committee.

2. Any proposal for amendment shall be communicated by the Secretary General of the Council of Europe to the member States of the Council of Europe and to every non-member State which has acceded to or has been invited to accede to this convention in accordance with the provisions of Article 23.

3. Moreover, any amendment proposed by a Party or the Committee of Ministers shall be communicated to the Consultative Committee, which shall submit to the Committee of Ministers its opinion on that proposed amendment.

4. The Committee of ministers shall consider the proposed amendment and any opinion submitted by the Consultative Committee and may approve the amendment.

5. The text of any amendment approved by the Committee of Ministers in accordance with paragraph 4 of this article shall be forwarded to the Parties for acceptance.

6. Any amendment approved in accordance with paragraph 4 of this article shall come into force on the thirtieth day after all Parties have informed the Secretary General of their acceptance thereof.

CHAPTER VII — FINAL CLAUSES

Article 22 - Entry into force

1. This convention shall be open for signature by the member States of the Council of Europe. It is subject to ratification, acceptance or approval. Instruments of ratification, acceptance or approval shall be deposited with the Secretary General of the Council of Europe.

2. This convention shall enter into force on the first day of the month following the expiration of a period of three months after the date on which five member States of the Council of Europe have expressed their consent to be bound by the convention in accordance with the provisions of the preceding paragraph.

3. In respect of any member State which subsequently expresses its consent to be bound by it, the convention shall enter into force on the first day of the month following the expiration of a period of three months after the date of the deposit of the instrument of ratification, acceptance or approval.

Article 23 - Accession by non-member States

1. After the entry into force of this convention, the Committee of Ministers of the Council of Europe may invite any State not a member of the Council of Europe to accede to this convention by a decision taken by the majority provided for in Article 20.d of the Statute of the Council of Europe and by the unanimous vote of the representatives of the Contracting States entitled to sit on the committee.

2. in respect of any acceding State, the convention shall enter into force on the first day of the month following the expiration of a period of three months after the date of deposit of the instrument of accession with the Secretary General of the Council of Europe.

Article 24 - Territorial clause

1. Any State may at the time of signature or when depositing its instrument of ratification, acceptance, approval or accession, specify the territory or territories to which this convention shall apply.

2. Any State may at any later date, by a declaration addressed to the Secretary General of the Council of Europe, extend the application of this convention to any other territory specified in the declaration. In respect of such territory the convention shall enter into force on the first day of the month following the expiration of a period of three months after the date of receipt of such declaration by the Secretary General.

3. Any declaration made under the two preceding paragraphs may, in respect of any territory specified in such declaration, be withdrawn by a notification addressed to the Secretary General. The withdrawal shall become effective on the first day of the month following the expiration of a period of six months after the date of receipt of such notification by the Secretary General.

Article 25 - Reservations

No reservation may be made in respect of the provisions of this convention.

Article 26 - **Denunciation**

1. Any Party may at any time denounce this convention by means of a notification addressed to the Secretary General of the Council of Europe.

2. Such denunciation shall become effective on the first day of the month following the expiration of a period of six months after the date of receipt of the notification by the Secretary General.

Article 27 - **Notifications**

The Secretary General of the Council of Europe shall notify the member States of the Council and any State which has acceded to this convention of:

a. any signatures;

b. the deposit of any instrument of ratification, acceptance, approval or accession;

c. any date of entry into force of this convention in accordance with Articles 22, 23 and 241

d. any other act, notification or communication relating to this convention.

In witness whereof the undersigned, being duly authorised thereto, have signed this Convention.

Done at Strasbourg, the 28th day of January 1981, in English and in French, both texts being equally authoritative, in a single copy which shall remain deposited in the archives of the Council of Europe. The Secretary General of the Council of Europe shall transmit certified copies to each member State of the Council of Europe and to any State invited to accede to this Convention.

UN Guidelines for the Regulation of Computerized Personal Files (1990)

Guidelines in Context

The UN Guidelines establish procedures for implementing their "orientations," or principles, to each state. They establish a series of principles for minimum guarantees, which are to be provided for in national legislation.

The procedures for implementing regulations concerning computerized personal data files are left to the initiative of each State subject to the following orientations:

A. PRINCIPLES CONCERNING THE MINIMUM GUARANTEES THAT SHOULD BE PROVIDED IN NATIONAL LEGISLATIONS

1. Principle of lawfulness and fairness

Information about persons should not be collected or processed in unfair or unlawful ways, nor should it be used for ends contrary to the purposes and principles of the Charter of the United Nations.

2. Principle of accuracy

Persons responsible for the compilation of files or those responsible for keeping them have an obligation to conduct regular checks on the accuracy and relevance of the data recorded and to ensure that they are kept as complete as possible in order to avoid errors of omission and that they are kept up to date regularly or when the information contained in a file is used, as long as they are being processed.

3. Principle of the purpose-specification

The purpose which a file is to serve and its utilization in terms of that purpose should be specified, legitimate and, when it is established, receive a certain amount of publicity or be brought to the attention of the person concerned, in order to make it possible subsequently to ensure that:

(a) All the personal data collected and recorded remain relevant and adequate to the purposes so specified;

(b) None of the said personal data is used or disclosed, except with the consent of the person concerned, for purposes incompatible with those specified;

(c) The period for which the personal data are kept does not exceed that which would enable the achievement of the purposes so specified.

4. Principle of interested-person access

Everyone who offers proof of identity has the right to know whether information concerning him is being processed and to obtain it in an intelligible form, without undue delay or expense, and to have appropriate rectifications or erasures made in the case of unlawful, unnecessary or inaccurate entries and, when it is being communicated, to be informed of the addressees. Provision should be made for a remedy, if need be with the supervisory authority specified in principle 8 below. The cost of any rectification shall be borne by the person responsible for the file. It is desirable that the provisions of this principle should apply to everyone, irrespective of nationality or place of residence.

5. Principle of non-discrimination

Subject to cases of exceptions restrictively envisaged under principle 6, data likely to give rise to unlawful or arbitrary discrimination, including information on racial or ethnic origin, colour, sex life, political opinions, religious, philosophical and other beliefs as well as membership of an association or trade union, should not be compiled.

6. Power to make exceptions

Departures from principles 1 to 4 may be authorized only if they are necessary to protect national security, public order, public health or morality, as well as, inter alia, the rights and freedoms of others, especially persons being persecuted (humanitarian clause) provided that such departures are expressly specified in a law or equivalent regulation promulgated in accordance with the internal legal system which expressly states their limits and sets forth appropriate safeguards.

Exceptions to principle 5 relating to the prohibition of discrimination, in addition to being subject to the same safeguards as those prescribed for exceptions to principles I and 4, may be authorized only within the limits prescribed by the International Bill of Human Rights and the other relevant instruments in the field of protection of human rights and the prevention of discrimination.

7. Principle of security

Appropriate measures should be taken to protect the files against both natural dangers, such as accidental loss or destruction and human dangers, such as unauthorized access, fraudulent misuse of data or contamination by computer viruses.

8. Supervision and sanctions

The law of every country shall designate the authority which, in accordance with its domestic legal system, is to be responsible for supervising observance of the principles set forth above. This authority shall offer guarantees of impartiality, independence vis-a-vis persons or agencies responsible for processing and establishing data, and technical competence. In the event of violation of the provisions of the national law implementing the aforementioned principles, criminal or other penalties should be envisaged together with the appropriate individual remedies.

9. Transborder data flows

When the legislation of two or more countries concerned by a transborder data flow offers comparable safeguards for the protection of privacy, information should be able to circulate as freely as inside each of the territories concerned. If there are no reciprocal safeguards, limitations on such circulation may not be imposed unduly and only in so far as the protection of privacy demands.

10. Field of application

The present principles should be made applicable, in the first instance, to all public and private computerized files as well as, by means of optional extension and subject to appropriate adjustments, to manual files. Special provision, also optional, might be made to extend all or part of the principles to files on legal persons particularly when they contain some information on individuals.

B. APPLICATION OF THE GUIDELINES TO PERSONAL DATA FILES KEPT BY GOVERNMENTAL INTERNATIONAL ORGANIZATIONS

The present guidelines should apply to personal data files kept by governmental international organizations, subject to any adjustments required to take account of any differences that might exist between files for internal purposes such as those that concern personnel management and files for external purposes concerning third parties having relations with the organization.

Each organization should designate the authority statutorily competent to supervise the observance of these guidelines.

Humanitarian clause: a derogation from these principles may be specifically provided for when the purpose of the file is the protection of human rights and fundamental freedoms of the individual concerned or humanitarian assistance.

A similar derogation should be provided in national legislation for governmental international organizations whose headquarters agreement does not preclude the implementation of the said national legislation as well as for non-governmental international organizations to which this law is applicable.

EU Data Protection Directive (1995)

Directives in Context

The EU Data Protection Directive establishes common rules for data protection among Member States. It requires EU Member States to enact legislation that is "harmonized" around its standards. A Directive is a form of EU law that is binding for Member States, but only as to the result to be achieved. It allows the national authorities to choose the form and the methods of implementation. The Data Protection Directive imposes obligations on the processors of personal data. It requires the notification of individuals whose data are being collected and gives individuals rights to control the use of data about themselves. The Directive also requires that Member States only transfer personal information to non-Member States that have "adequate" measures of data protection.

Recitals

THE EUROPEAN PARLIAMENT AND THE COUNCIL OF THE EUROPEAN UNION,

Having regard to the Treaty establishing the European Community, and in particular Article 100a thereof,

Having regard to the proposal from the Commission 1 ,

Having regard to the opinion of the Economic and Social Committee 2 ,

Acting in accordance with the procedure referred to in Article 189b of the Treaty 3 ,

1. Whereas the objectives of the Community, as laid down in the Treaty, as amended by the Treaty on European Union, include creating an ever closer union among the peoples of Europe, fostering closer relations between the States belonging to the Community, ensuring economic and social progress by common action to eliminate the barriers which divide Europe, encouraging the constant improvement of the living conditions of its peoples, preserving and strengthening peace and liberty and promoting democracy on the basis of the fundamental rights recognized in the constitution and laws of the Member States and in the European Convention for the Protection of Human Rights and Fundamental Freedoms;

2. Whereas data-processing systems are designed to serve man; whereas they must, whatever the nationality or residence of natural persons, respect their fundamental rights and freedoms, notably the right to privacy, and contribute to economic and social progress, trade expansion and the well-being of individuals;

3. Whereas the establishment and functioning of an internal market in which, in accordance with Article 7a of the Treaty, the free movement of goods, persons, services and capital is ensured require not only that personal data should be able to flow freely from one Member State to another, but also that the fundamental rights of individuals should be safeguarded;

4. Whereas increasingly frequent recourse is being had in the Community to the processing of personal data in the various spheres of economic and social activity; whereas the progress made in information technology is making the processing and exchange of such data considerably easier;

5. Whereas the economic and social integration resulting from the establishment and functioning of the internal market within the meaning of Article 7a of the Treaty will necessarily lead to a substantial increase in cross-border flows of personal data between all those involved in a private or public capacity in economic and social activity in the Member States; whereas the exchange of personal data between undertakings in different Member States is set to increase; whereas the national authorities in the various Member States are being called upon by virtue of Community law to collaborate and exchange personal data so as to be able to perform their duties or carry out tasks on behalf of an authority in another Member State within the context of the area without internal frontiers as constituted by the internal market;

6. Whereas, furthermore, the increase in scientific and technical cooperation and the coordinated introduction of new telecommunications networks in the Community necessitate and facilitate cross-border flows of personal data;

7. Whereas the difference in levels of protection of the rights and freedoms of individuals, notably the right to privacy, with regard to the processing of personal data afforded in the Member States may prevent the transmission of such data from the territory of one Member State to that of another Member State; whereas this difference may therefore constitute an obstacle to the pursuit of a number of economic activities at Community level, distort competition and impede authorities in the discharge of their responsibilities under Community law; whereas this difference in levels of protection is due to the existence of a wide variety of national laws, regulations and administrative provisions;

8. Whereas, in order to remove the obstacles to flows of personal data, the level of protection of the rights and freedoms of individuals with regard to the processing of such data must be equivalent in all Member States; whereas this objective is vital to the internal market but cannot be achieved by the Member States alone, especially in view of the scale of the divergences which currently exist between the relevant laws in the Member States and the need to coordinate the laws of the Member States so as to ensure that the cross-border flow of personal data is regulated in a consistent manner that is in keeping with the objective of the internal market as provided for in Article 7a of the Treaty; whereas Community action to approximate those laws is therefore needed;

9. Whereas, given the equivalent protection resulting from the approximation of national laws, the Member States will no longer be able to inhibit the free movement between them of personal data on grounds relating to protection of the rights and freedoms of individuals, and in particular the right to privacy; whereas Member States will be left a margin for manoeuvre, which may, in the context of implementation of the Directive, also be exercised by the business and social partners; whereas Member States will therefore be able to specify in their national law the general conditions governing the lawfulness of data processing; whereas in doing so the Member States shall strive to improve the protection currently provided by their legislation; whereas, within the limits of this margin for manoeuvre and in accordance with Community law, disparities could arise in the implementation of the Directive, and this could have an effect on the movement of data within a Member State as well as within the Community;

10. Whereas the object of the national laws on the processing of personal data is to protect fundamental rights and freedoms, notably the right to privacy, which is recognized both in Article 8 of the European Convention for the Protection of Human Rights and Fundamental Freedoms and in the general principles of Community law; whereas, for that reason, the approximation of those laws must not result in any lessening of the protection they afford but must, on the contrary, seek to ensure a high level of protection in the Community;

11. Whereas the principles of the protection of the rights and freedoms of individuals, notably the right to privacy, which are contained in this Directive, give substance to and amplify those contained in the Council of Europe Convention of 28 January 1981 for the Protection of Individuals with regard to Automatic Processing of Personal Data;

12. Whereas the protection principles must apply to all processing of personal data by any person whose activities are governed by Community law; whereas there should be excluded the processing of data carried out by a natural person in the exercise of activities which are exclusively personal or domestic, such as correspondence and the holding of records of addresses;

13. Whereas the activities referred to in Titles V and VI of the Treaty on European Union regarding public safety, defence, State security or the activities of the State in the area of criminal laws fall outside the scope of Community law, without prejudice to the obligations incumbent upon Member States under Article 56 (2), Article 57 or Article 100a of the Treaty establishing the European Community; whereas the processing of personal data that is necessary to safeguard the economic well-being of the State does not fall within the scope of this Directive where such processing relates to State security matters;

14. Whereas, given the importance of the developments under way, in the framework of the information society, of the techniques used to capture, transmit, manipulate, record, store or communicate sound and image data relating to natural persons, this Directive should be applicable to processing involving such data;

15. Whereas the processing of such data is covered by this Directive only if it is automated or if the data processed are contained or are intended to be contained in a filing system structured according to specific criteria relating to individuals, so as to permit easy access to the personal data in question;

16. Whereas the processing of sound and image data, such as in cases of video surveillance, does not come within the scope of this Directive if it is carried out for the purposes of public security, defence, national security or in the course of State activities relating to the area of criminal law or of other activities which do not come within the scope of Community law;

17. Whereas, as far as the processing of sound and image data carried out for purposes of journalism or the purposes of literary or artistic expression is concerned, in particular in the audiovisual field, the principles of the Directive are to apply in a restricted manner according to the provisions laid down in Article 9;

18. Whereas, in order to ensure that individuals are not deprived of the protection to which they are entitled under this Directive, any processing of personal data in the Community must be carried out in accordance with the law of one of the Member States; whereas, in this connection, processing carried out under the responsibility of a controller who is established in a Member State should be governed by the law of that State;

19. Whereas establishment on the territory of a Member State implies the effective and real exercise of activity through stable arrangements; whereas the legal form of such an establishment, whether simply 'branch or a subsidiary with a legal personality, is not the determining factor in this respect; whereas, when a single controller is established on the territory of several Member States, particularly by means of subsidiaries, he must ensure, in order to avoid any circumvention of national rules, that each of the establishments fulfils the obligations imposed by the national law applicable to its activities;

20. Whereas the fact that the processing of data is carried out by a person established in a third country must not stand in the way of the protection of individuals provided for in this Directive; whereas in these cases, the processing should be governed by the law of the Member State in which the means used are located, and there should be guarantees to ensure that the rights and obligations provided for in this Directive are respected in practice;

21. Whereas this Directive is without prejudice to the rules of territoriality applicable in criminal matters;

22. Whereas Member States shall more precisely define in the laws they enact or when bringing into force the measures taken under this Directive the general circumstances in which processing is lawful; whereas in particular Article 5, in conjunction with Articles 7 and 8, allows Member States, independently of general rules, to provide for special processing conditions for specific sectors and for the various categories of data covered by Article 8;

23. Whereas Member States are empowered to ensure the implementation of the protection of individuals both by means of a general law on the protection of individuals as regards the processing of personal data and by sectorial laws such as those relating, for example, to statistical institutes;

24. Whereas the legislation concerning the protection of legal persons with regard to the processing data which concerns them is not affected by this Directive;

25. Whereas the principles of protection must be reflected, on the one hand, in the obligations imposed on persons, public authorities, enterprises, agencies or other bodies responsible for processing, in particular regarding data quality, technical security, notification to the supervisory authority, and the circumstances under which processing can be carried out, and, on the other hand, in the right conferred on individuals, the data on whom are the subject of processing, to be informed that processing is taking place, to consult the data, to request corrections and even to object to processing in certain circumstances;

26. Whereas the principles of protection must apply to any information concerning an identified or identifiable person; whereas, to determine whether a person is identifiable, account should be taken of all the means likely reasonably to be used either by the controller or by any other person to identify the said person; whereas the' principles of protection shall not apply to data rendered anonymous in such a way that the data subject is no longer identifiable; whereas codes of conduct within the meaning of Article 27 may be a useful instrument for providing guidance as to the ways in which data may be rendered anonymous and retained in a form in which identification of the data subject is no longer possible;

27. Whereas the protection of individuals must apply as much to automatic processing of data as to manual processing; whereas the scope of this protection must not in effect depend on the techniques used, otherwise this would create a serious risk of circumvention; whereas, nonetheless, as regards manual processing, this Directive covers only filing systems, not unstructured files; whereas, in particular, the content of a filing system must be structured according to specific criteria relating to individuals allowing easy access to the personal data; whereas, in line with the definition in Article 2 (c), the different criteria for determining the constituents of a structured set of personal data, and the different criteria governing access to such a set, may be laid down by each Member State; whereas files or sets of files as well as their cover pages, which are not structured according to specific criteria, shall under no circumstances fall within the scope of this Directive;

28. Whereas any processing of personal data must be lawful and fair to the individuals concerned; whereas, in particular, the data must be adequate, relevant and not excessive in relation to the purposes for which they are processed; whereas such purposes must be explicit and legitimate and must be determined at the time of collection of the data; whereas the purposes of processing further to collection shall not be incompatible with the purposes as they were originally specified;

29. Whereas the further processing of personal data for historical, statistical or scientific purposes is not generally to be considered incompatible with the purposes for which the data have previously been collected provided that Member States furnish suitable safeguards; whereas these safeguards must in particular rule out the use of the data in support of measures or decisions regarding any particular individual;

30. Whereas, in order to be lawful, the processing of personal data must in addition be carried out with the consent of the data subject or be necessary for the conclusion or performance of a contract binding on the data subject, or as a legal requirement, or for the performance of a task carried out in the public interest or in the exercise of official authority, or in the legitimate interests of a natural or legal person, provided that the interests or the rights and freedoms of the data subject are not overriding; whereas, in particular, in order to maintain a balance between the interests involved while guaranteeing effective competition, Member States may determine the circumstances in which personal data may be used or disclosed to a third party in the context of the legitimate ordinary business activities of companies and other bodies; whereas Member States may similarly specify the conditions under which personal data may be disclosed to a third party for the purposes of marketing whether carried out commercially or by a charitable organization or by any other association or foundation, of a political nature for example, subject to the provisions allowing a data subject to object to the processing of data regarding him, at no cost and without having to state his reasons;

31. Whereas the processing of personal data must equally be regarded as lawful where it is carried out in order to protect an interest which is essential for the data subject's life;

32. Whereas it is for national legislation to determine whether the controller performing a task carried out in the public interest or in the exercise of official authority should be a public administration or another natural or legal person governed by public law, or by private law such as a professional association;

33. Whereas data which are capable by their nature of infringing fundamental freedoms or privacy should not be processed unless the data subject gives his explicit consent; whereas, however, derogations from this prohibition must be explicitly provided for in respect of specific needs, in particular where the processing of these data is carried out for certain health-related purposes by persons subject to a legal obligation of professional secrecy or in the course of legitimate activities by certain associations or foundations the purpose of which is to permit the exercise of fundamental freedoms;

34. Whereas Member States must also be authorized, when justified by grounds of important public interest, to derogate from the prohibition on processing sensitive categories of data where important reasons of public interest so justify in areas such as public health and social protection - especially in order to ensure the quality and cost-effectiveness of the procedures used for settling claims for benefits and services in the health insurance system - scientific research and government statistics; whereas it is incumbent on them, however, to provide specific and suitable safeguards so as to protect the fundamental rights and the privacy of individuals;

35. Whereas, moreover, the processing of personal data by official authorities for achieving aims, laid down in constitutional law or international public law, of officially recognized religious associations is carried out on important grounds of public' interest;

36. Whereas where, in the course of electoral activities, the operation of the democratic system requires in certain Member States that political parties compile data on people's political opinion, the processing of such data may be permitted for reasons of important public interest, provided that appropriate safeguards are established;

37. Whereas the processing of personal data for purposes of journalism or for purposes of literary of artistic expression, in particular in the audiovisual field, should qualify for exemption from the requirements of certain provisions of this Directive in so far as this is necessary to reconcile the fundamental rights of individuals with freedom of information and notably the right to receive and impart information, as guaranteed in particular in Article 10 of the European Convention for the Protection of Human Rights and Fundamental Freedoms; whereas Member States should therefore lay down exemptions and derogations necessary for the purpose of balance between fundamental rights as regards general measures on the legitimacy of data processing, measures on the transfer of data to third countries and the power of the supervisory authority; whereas this should not, however, lead Member States to lay down exemptions from the measures to ensure security of processing; whereas at least the supervisory authority responsible for this sector should also be provided with certain ex-post powers, e.g. to publish a regular report or to refer matters to the judicial authorities;

38. Whereas, if the processing of data is to be fair, the data subject must be in a position to learn of the existence of a processing operation and, where data are collected from him, must be given accurate and full information, bearing in mind the circumstances of the collection;

39. Whereas certain processing operations involve data which the controller has not collected directly from the data subject; whereas, furthermore, data can be legitimately disclosed to a third party, even if the disclosure was not anticipated at the time the data were collected from the data subject; whereas, in all these cases, the data subject should be informed when the data are recorded or at the latest when the data are first disclosed to a third party;

40. Whereas, however, it is not necessary to impose this obligation of the data subject already has the information; whereas, moreover, there will be no such obligation if the recording or disclosure are expressly provided for by law or if the provision of information to the data subject proves impossible or would involve disproportionate efforts, which could be the case where processing is for historical, statistical or scientific purposes; whereas, in this regard, the number of data subjects, the age of the data, and any compensatory measures adopted may be taken into consideration;

41. Whereas any person must be able to exercise the right of access to data relating to him which are being processed, in order to verify in particular the accuracy of the data and the lawfulness of the processing; whereas, for .the same reasons, every data subject must also have the right to know the logic involved in the automatic processing of data concerning him, at least in the case of the automated decisions referred to in Article 15 (1); whereas this right must not adversely affect trade secrets or intellectual property and in particular the copyright protecting the software; whereas these considerations must not, however, result in the data subject being refused all information;

42. Whereas Member States may, in the interest of the data subject or so as to protect the rights and freedoms of others, restrict rights of access and information; whereas they may, for example, specify that access to medical data may be obtained only through a health professional;

43. Whereas restrictions on the rights of access and information and on certain obligations of the controller may similarly be imposed by Member States in so far as they are necessary to safeguard, for example, national security, defence, public safety, or important economic or financial interests of a Member State or the Union, as well as criminal investigations and prosecutions and action in respect of breaches of ethics in the regulated professions; whereas the list of exceptions and limitations should include the tasks of monitoring, inspection or regulation necessary in the three last-mentioned areas concerning public security, economic or financial interests and crime prevention; whereas the listing of tasks in these three areas does not affect the legitimacy of exceptions or restrictions for reasons of State security or defence;

44. Whereas Member States may also be led, by virtue of the provisions of Community law, to derogate from the provisions of this Directive concerning the right of access, the obligation to inform individuals, and the quality of data, in order to secure certain of the purposes referred to above;

45. Whereas, in cases where data might lawfully be processed on grounds of public interest, official authority or the legitimate interests of a natural or legal person, any data subject should nevertheless be entitled, on legitimate and compelling grounds relating to his particular situation, to object to the processing of any data relating to himself; whereas Member States may nevertheless lay down national provisions to the contrary;

46. Whereas the protection of the rights and freedoms of data subjects with regard to the processing of personal data requires that appropriate technical and organizational measures be taken, both at the time of the design of the processing system and at the time of the processing itself, particularly in order to maintain security and thereby to prevent any unauthorized processing; whereas it is incumbent on the Member States to ensure that controllers comply with these measures; whereas these measures must ensure an appropriate level of security, taking into account the state of the art and the costs of their implementation in relation to the risks inherent in the processing and the nature of the data to be protected;

47. Whereas where a message containing personal data is transmitted by means of a telecommunications or electronic mail service, the sole purpose of which is the transmission of such messages, the controller in respect of the personal data contained in the message will normally be considered to be the person from whom the message originates, rather than the person offering the transmission services; whereas, nevertheless, those offering such services will normally be considered controllers in respect of the processing of the additional personal data necessary for the operation of the service;

48. Whereas the procedures for notifying the supervisory authority are designed to ensure disclosure of the purposes and main features of any processing operation for the purpose of verification that the operation is in accordance with the national measures taken under this Directive;

49. Whereas, in order to avoid unsuitable administrative formalities, exemptions from the obligation to notify and simplification of the notification required may be provided for by Member States in cases where processing is unlikely adversely to affect the rights and freedoms of data subjects, provided that it is in accordance with a measure taken by a Member State specifying its limits; whereas exemption or simplification may similarly be provided for by Member States where a person appointed by the controller ensures that the processing carried out is not likely adversely to affect the rights and freedoms of data subjects; whereas such a data protection official, whether or not an employee of the controller, must be in a position to exercise his functions in complete independence;

50. Whereas exemption or simplification could be provided for in cases of processing operations whose sole purpose is the keeping of a register intended, according to national law, to provide information to the public and open to consultation by the public or by any person demonstrating a legitimate interest;

51. Whereas, nevertheless, simplification or exemption from the obligation to notify shall not release the controller from any of the other obligations resulting from this Directive;

52. Whereas, in this context, ex post facto verification by the competent authorities must in general be considered a sufficient measure;

53. Whereas, however, certain processing operation are likely to pose specific risks to the rights and freedoms of data subjects by virtue of their nature, their scope or their purposes, such as that of excluding individuals from a right, benefit or a contract, or by virtue of the specific use of new technologies; whereas it is for Member States, if they so wish, to specify such risks in their legislation;

54. Whereas with regard to all the processing undertaken in society, the amount posing such specific risks should be very limited; whereas Member States must provide that the supervisory authority, or the data protection official in cooperation with the authority, check such processing prior to it being carried out; whereas following this prior check, the supervisory authority may, according to its national law, give an opinion or an authorization regarding the processing; whereas such checking may equally take place in the course of the preparation either of a measure of the national parliament or of a measure based on such a legislative measure, which defines the nature of the processing and lays down appropriate safeguards;

55. Whereas, if the controller fails to respect the rights of data subjects, national legislation must provide for a judicial remedy; whereas any damage which a person may suffer as a result of unlawful processing must be compensated for by the controller, who may be exempted from liability if he proves that he is not responsible for the damage, in particular in cases where he establishes fault on the part of the data subject or in case of force majeure; whereas sanctions must be imposed on any person, whether governed by private of public law, who fails to comply with the national measures taken under this Directive;

56. Whereas cross-border flows of personal data are necessary to the expansion of international trade; whereas the protection of individuals, guaranteed in the Community by this Directive does not stand in the way of transfers of personal data to third countries which ensure an adequate level of protection; whereas the adequacy of the level of protection afforded by a third country must be assessed in the light of all the circumstances surrounding the transfer operation or set of transfer operations;

57. Whereas, on the other hand, the transfer of personal data to a third country which does not ensure an adequate level of protection must be prohibited;

58. Whereas provisions should be made for exemptions from this prohibition in certain circumstances where the data subject has given his consent, where the transfer is necessary in relation to a contract or a legal claim, where protection of an important public interest so requires, for example in cases of international transfers of data between tax or customs administrations or between services competent for social security matters, or where the transfer is made from a register established by law and intended for consultation by the public or persons having a legitimate interest; whereas in this case such a transfer should not involve the entirety of the data or entire categories of the data contained in the register and, when the register is intended for consultation by persons having a legitimate interest, the transfer should be made only at the request of those persons or if they are to bc the recipients;

59. Whereas particular measures may be taken to compensate for the lack of protection in a third country in cases where the controller offers appropriate safeguards; whereas, moreover, provision must be made for procedures for negotiations between the Community and such third countries;

60. Whereas, in any event, transfers to third countries may be effected only in full compliance with the provisions adopted by the Member States pursuant to this Directive, and in particular Article 8 thereof;

61. Whereas Member States and the Commission, in their respective spheres of competence, must encourage the trade associations and other representative organizations concerned to draw up codes of conduct so as to facilitate the application of this Directive, taking account of the specific characteristics of the processing carried out in certain sectors, and respecting the national provisions adopted for its implementation;

62. Whereas the establishment in Member States of supervisory authorities, exercising their functions with complete independence, is an' essential component of the protection of individuals with regard to the processing of personal data;

63. Whereas such authorities must have the necessary means to perform their duties, including powers of investigation and intervention, particularly in cases of complaints from individuals, and powers to engage in legal proceedings; whereas such authorities must help to ensure transparency of processing in the Member States within whose jurisdiction they fall;

64. Whereas the authorities in the different Member States will need to assist one another in performing their duties so as to ensure that the rules of protection are properly respected throughout the European Union;

65. Whereas, at Community level, a Working Party on the Protection of Individuals with regard to the Processing of Personal Data must be set up and be completely independent in the performance of its functions; whereas, having regard to its specific nature, it must advise the Commission and, in particular, contribute to the uniform application of the national rules adopted pursuant to this Directive;

66. Whereas, with regard to the transfer of data to third countries, the application of this Directive calls for the conferment of powers of implementation on the Commission and the establishment of a procedure as laid down in Council Decision 87/373/EEC 4;

67. Whereas an agreement on a modus vivendi between the European Parliament, the Council and the Commission concerning the implementing measures for acts adopted in accordance with the procedure laid down in Article 189b of the EC Treaty was reached on 20 December 1994;

68. Whereas the principles set out in this Directive regarding the protection of the rights and freedoms of individuals, notably their right to privacy, with regard to the processing of personal data may be supplemented or clarified, in particular as far as certain sectors are concerned, by specific rules based on those principles;

69. Whereas Member States should be allowed a period of not more than three years from the entry into force of the national measures transposing this Directive in which to apply such new national rules progressively to all processing operations already under way; whereas, in order to facilitate their cost-effective implementation, a further period expiring 12 years after the date on which this Directive is adopted will be allowed to Member States to ensure the conformity of existing manual filing systems with certain of the Directive's provisions; whereas, where data contained in such filing systems are manually processed during this extended transition period, those systems must be brought into conformity with these provisions at the time of such processing;

70. Whereas it is not necessary for the data subject to give his consent again so as to allow the controller to continue to process, after the national provisions taken pursuant to this Directive enter into force, any sensitive data necessary for the performance of a contract concluded on the basis of free and informed consent before the entry into force of these provisions;

71. Whereas this Directive does not stand in the way of a Member State's regulating marketing activities aimed at consumers residing in territory in so far as such regulation does not concern the protection of individuals with regard to the processing of personal data;

72. Whereas this Directive allows the principle of public access to official documents to be taken into account when implementing the principles set out in this Directive,

CHAPTER I — GENERAL PROVISIONS

Article 1 - Object of the Directive

1. In accordance with this Directive, Member States shall protect the fundamental rights and freedoms of natural persons, and in particular their right to privacy with respect to the processing of personal data.

2. Member States shall neither restrict nor prohibit the free flow of personal data between Member States for reasons connected with the protection afforded under paragraph 1.

Article 2 - Definitions

For the purposes of this Directive:

(a) 'personal data 'shall mean any information relating to an identified or identifiable natural person ('data subject'); an identifiable person is one who can be identified, directly or indirectly, in particular by reference to an identification number or to one or more factors specific to his physical, physiological, mental, economic, cultural or social identity;

(b)'processing of personal data'('processing') shall mean any operation or set of operations which is performed upon personal data, whether or not by automatic means, such as collection, recording, organization, storage, adaptation or alteration, retrieval, consultation, use, disclosure by transmission, dissemination or otherwise making available, alignment or combination, blocking, erasure or destruction;

(c) 'personal data filing system' ('filing system') shall mean any structured set of personal data which are accessible according to specific criteria, whether centralized, decentralized or dispersed on a functional or geographical basis;

(d) 'controller' shall mean the natural or legal person, public authority, agency or any other body which alone or jointly with others determines the purposes and means of the processing of personal data; where the purposes and means of processing are determined by national or Community laws or regulations, the controller or the specific criteria for his nomination may be designated by national or Community law;

(e) 'processor' shall mean a natural or legal person, public authority, agency or any other body which processes personal data on behalf of the controller;

(f) 'third party' shall mean any natural or legal person, public authority, agency or any other body other than the data subject, the controller, the processor and the persons who, under the direct authority of the controller or the processor, are authorized to process the data;

(g) 'recipient' shall mean a natural or legal person, public authority, agency or any other body to whom data are disclosed, whether a third party or not; however, authorities which may receive data in the framework of a particular inquiry shall not be regarded as recipients;

(h) 'the data subject's consent' shall mean any freely given specific and informed indication of his wishes by which the data subject signifies his agreement to personal data relating to him being processed.

Article 3 - **Scope**

1. This Directive shall apply to the processing of personal data wholly or partly by automatic means, and to the processing otherwise than by automatic means of personal data which form part of a filing system or are intended to form part of a filing system.

2. This Directive shall not apply to the processing of personal data:

- in the course of an activity which falls outside the scope of Community law, such as those provided for by Titles V and VI of the Treaty on European Union and in any case to processing operations concerning public security, defence, State security (including the economic well-being of the State when the processing operation relates to State security matters) and the activities of the State in areas of criminal law,
- by a natural person in the course of a purely personal or household activity.

Article 4 - **National law applicable**

1. Each Member State shall apply the national provisions it adopts pursuant to this Directive to the processing of personal data where:

(a) the processing is carried out in the context of the activities of an establishment of the controller on the territory of the Member State; when the same controller is established on the territory of several Member States, he must take the necessary measures to ensure that each of these establishments complies with the obligations laid down by the national law applicable;

(b) the controller is not established on the Member State's territory, but in a place where its national law applies by virtue of international public law;

(c) the controller is not established on Community territory and, for purposes of processing personal data makes use of equipment, automated or otherwise, situated on the territory of the said Member State, unless such equipment is used only for purposes of transit through the territory of the Community.

2. In the circumstances referred to in paragraph 1 (c), the controller must designate a representative established in the territory of that Member State, without prejudice to legal actions which could be initiated against the controller himself.

CHAPTER II — GENERAL RULES ON THE LAWFULNESS OF THE PROCESSING OF PERSONAL DATA

Article 5

Member States shall, within the limits of the provisions of this Chapter, determine more precisely the conditions under which the processing of personal data is lawful.

SECTION I - PRINCIPLES RELATING TO DATA QUALITY

Article 6

1. Member States shall provide that personal data must be:

(a) processed fairly and lawfully;

(b) collected for specified, explicit and legitimate purposes and not further processed in a way incompatible with those purposes. Further processing of data for historical, statistical or scientific purposes shall not be considered as incompatible provided that Member States provide appropriate safeguards;

(c) adequate, relevant and not excessive in relation to the purposes for which they are collected and/or further processed;

(d) accurate and, where necessary, kept up to date; every reasonable step must be taken to ensure that data which are inaccurate or incomplete, having regard to the purposes for which they were collected or for which they are further processed, are erased or rectified;

(e) kept in a form which permits identification of data subjects for no longer than is necessary for the purposes for which the data were collected or for which they are further processed. Member States shall lay down appropriate safeguards for personal data stored for longer periods for historical, statistical or scientific use.

2. It shall be for the controller to ensure that paragraph 1 is complied with.

SECTION II - CRITERIA FOR MAKING DATA PROCESSING LEGITIMATE

Article 7

Member States shall provide that personal data may be processed only if:

(a) the data subject has unambiguously given his consent; or

(b) processing is necessary for the performance of a contract to which the data subject is party or in order to take steps at the request of the data subject prior to entering into a contract; or

(c) processing is necessary for compliance with a legal obligation to which the controller is subject; or

(d) processing is necessary in order to protect the vital interests of the data subject; or

(e) processing is necessary for the performance of a task carried out in the public interest or in the exercise of official authority vested in the controller or in a third party to whom the data are disclosed; or

(f) processing is necessary for the purposes of the legitimate interests pursued by the controller or by the third party or parties to whom the data are disclosed, except where such interests are overridden by the interests for fundamental rights and freedoms of the data subject which require protection under Article 1 (1).

SECTION III - SPECIAL CATEGORIES OF PROCESSING

Article 8 - The processing of special categories of data

1. Member States shall prohibit the processing of personal data revealing racial or ethnic origin, political opinions, religious or philosophical beliefs, trade-union membership, and the processing of data concerning health or sex life.

2. Paragraph 1 shall not apply where:

(a) the data subject has given his explicit consent to the processing of those data, except where the laws of the Member State provide that the prohibition referred to in paragraph 1 may not be lifted by the data subject's giving his consent; or

(b) processing is necessary for the purposes of carrying out the obligations and specific rights of the controller in the field of employment law in so far as it is authorized by national law providing for adequate safeguards; or

(c) processing is necessary to protect the vital interests of the data subject or of another person where the data subject is physically or legally incapable of giving his consent; or

(d) processing is carried out in the course of its legitimate activities with appropriate guarantees by a foundation, association or any other non-profit-seeking body with a political, philosophical, religious or trade-union aim and on condition that the processing relates solely to the members of the body or to persons who have regular contact with it in connection with its purposes and that' the data are not disclosed to a third party without the consent of the data subjects; or

(e) the processing relates to data which are manifestly made public by the data subject or is necessary for the establishment, exercise or defence of legal claims.

3. Paragraph 1 shall not apply where processing of the data is required for the purposes of preventive medicine, medical diagnosis, the provision of care or treatment or the management of health-care services, and where those data are processed by a health professional subject under national law or rules established by national competent bodies to the obligation of professional secrecy or by another person also subject to an equivalent obligation of secrecy.

4. Subject to the provision of suitable safeguards, Member States may, for reasons of substantial public interest, lay down exemptions in addition to those laid down in paragraph 2 either by national law or by decision of the supervisory authority.

5. Processing of data relating to offences, criminal convictions or security measures may be carried out only under the control of official authority, or if suitable specific safeguards are provided under national law, subject to derogations which may be granted by the Member State under national provisions providing suitable specific safeguards. However, a complete register of criminal convictions may be kept only under the control of official authority.

Member States may provide that data relating to administrative sanctions or judgements in civil cases shall also be processed under the control of official authority.

6. Derogations from paragraph I provided for in paragraphs 4 and 5 shall be notified to the Commission.

7. Member States shall determine the conditions under which a national identification number or any other identifier of general application may be processed.

Article 9 - **Processing of personal data and freedom of expression**

Member States shall provide for exemptions or derogations from the provisions of this Chapter, Chapter IV and Chapter VI for the processing of personal data carried out solely for journalistic purposes or the purpose of artistic or literary expression only if they are necessary to reconcile the right to privacy with the rules governing freedom of expression.

SECTION IV - INFORMATION TO BE GIVEN TO THE DATA SUBJECT

Article 10 - **Information in cases of collection of data from the data subject**

Member States shall provide that the controller or his representative must provide a data subject from whom data relating to himself are collected with at least the following information, except where he already has it:

(a) the identity of the controller and of his representative, if any;

(b) the purposes of the processing for which the data are intended;

(c) any further information such as

- the recipients or categories of recipients of the data,

- whether replies to the questions are obligatory or voluntary, as well as the possible consequences of failure to reply,

- the existence of the right of access to and the right to rectify the data concerning him in so far as such further information is necessary, having regard to the specific circumstances in which the data are collected, to guarantee fair processing in respect of the data subject.

Article 11 - **Information where the data have not been obtained from the data subject**

1. Where the data have not been obtained from the data subject, Member States shall provide that the controller or his representative must at the time of undertaking the recording of personal data or if a disclosure to a third party is envisaged, no later than the time when the data are first disclosed provide the data subject with at least the following information, except where he already has it:

(a) the identity of the controller and of his representative, if any;

(b) the purposes of the processing;

(c) any further information such as

- the categories of data concerned,

- the recipients or categories of recipients,

- the existence of the right of access to and the right to rectify the data concerning him in so far as such further information is necessary, having regard to the specific circumstances in which the data are processed, to guarantee fair processing in respect of the data subject.

2. Paragraph 1 shall not apply where, in particular for processing for statistical purposes or for the purposes of historical or scientific research, the provision of such information proves impossible or would involve a disproportionate effort or if recording or disclosure is expressly laid down by law. In these cases Member States shall provide appropriate safeguards.

SECTION V - THE DATA SUBJECT'S RIGHT OF ACCESS TO DATA

Article 12 - **Right of access**

Member States shall guarantee every data right to obtain from the controller:

(a) without constraint at reasonable intervals and without excessive delay or expense:

- confirmation as to whether or not data relating to him are being processed and information at least as to the purposes of the processing, the categories of data concerned, and the recipients or categories of recipients to whom the data are disclosed,

- communication to him in an intelligible form of the data undergoing processing and of any available information as to their source,

- knowledge of the logic involved in any automatic processing of data concerning him at least in the case of the automated decisions referred .to in Article 15 (1);

(b) as appropriate the rectification, erasure or blocking of data the processing of which does not comply with the provisions of this Directive, in particular because of the incomplete or inaccurate nature of the data;

(c) notification to third parties to whom the data have been disclosed of any rectification, erasure or blocking carried out in compliance with (b), unless this proves impossible or involves a disproportionate effort.

SECTION VI - EXEMPTIONS AND RESTRICTIONS

Article 13

1. Member States may adopt legislative measures to restrict the scope of the obligations and rights provided for in Articles 6 (1), 10, 11 (1), 12 and 21 when such a restriction constitutes a necessary measures to safeguard:

(a) national security;

(b) defence;

(c) public security;

(d) the prevention, investigation, detection and prosecution of criminal offences, or of breaches of ethics for regulated professions;

(e) an important economic or financial interest of a Member State or of the European Union, including monetary, budgetary and taxation matters;

(f) a monitoring, inspection or regulatory function connected, even occasionally, with the exercise of official authority in cases referred to in (c), (d) and (e);

(g) the protection of the data subject or of the rights and freedoms of others.

2. Subject to adequate legal safeguards, in particular that the data are not used for taking measures or decisions regarding any particular individual, Member States may, where there is clearly no risk of breaching the privacy of the data subject, restrict by a legislative measure the rights provided for in Article 12 when data are processed solely for purposes of scientific research or are kept in personal form for a period which does not exceed the period necessary for the sole purpose of creating statistics.

SECTION VII - THE DATA SUBJECT'S RIGHT TO OBJECT

Article 14 - **The data subject's right to object**

Member States shall grant the data subject the right:

(a) at least in the cases referred to in Article 7 (e) and (f), to object at any time on compelling legitimate grounds relating to his particular situation to the processing of data relating to him, save where otherwise provided by national legislation. Where there is a justified objection, the processing instigated by the controller may no longer involve those data;

(b) to object, on request and free of charge, to the processing of personal data relating to him which the controller anticipates being processed for the purposes of direct marketing, or to be informed before personal data are disclosed for the first time to third parties or used on their behalf for the purposes of direct marketing, and to be expressly offered the right to object free of charge to such disclosures or uses.

Member States shall take the necessary measures to ensure that data subjects are aware of the existence of the right referred to in the first subparagraph of (b).

Article 15 - **Automated individual decisions**

1. Member States shall grant the right to every person not to be subject to a decision which produces legal effects concerning him or significantly affects him and which is based solely on automated processing of data intended to evaluate certain personal aspects relating to him, such as his performance at work, creditworthiness, reliability, conduct, etc.

2. Subject to the other Articles of this Directive, Member States shall provide that a person may be subjected to a decision of the kind referred to in paragraph 1 if that decision:

> **(a)** is taken in the course of the entering into or performance of a contract, provided the request for the entering into or the performance of the contract, lodged by the data subject, has been satisfied or that there are suitable measures to safeguard his legitimate interests, such as arrangements allowing him to put his point of view; or
>
> **(b)** is authorized by a law which also lays down measures to safeguard the data subject's legitimate interests.

SECTION VIII - CONFIDENTIALITY AND SECURITY OF PROCESSING

Article 16 - **Confidentiality of processing**

Any person acting under the authority of the controller or of the processor, including the processor himself, who has access to personal data must not process them except on instructions from the controller, unless he is required to do so by law.

Article 17 - **Security of processing**

1. Member States shall provide that the controller must implement appropriate technical and organizational measures to protect personal data against accidental or unlawful destruction or accidental loss, alteration, unauthorized disclosure or access, in particular where the processing involves the transmission of data over a network, and against all other unlawful forms of processing.

Having regard to the state of the art and the cost of their implementation, such measures shall ensure a level of security appropriate to the risks represented by the processing and the nature of the data to be protected.

2. The Member States shall provide that the controller must, where processing is carried out on his behalf, choose a processor providing sufficient guarantees in respect of the technical security measures and organizational measures governing the processing to be carried out, and must ensure compliance with those measures.

3. The carrying out of processing by way of a processor must be governed by a contract or legal act binding the processor to the controller and stipulating in particular that:

> **1.** the processor shall act only on instructions from the controller,
>
> **2.** the obligations set out in paragraph 1, as defined by the law of the Member State in which the processor is established, shall also be incumbent on the processor.

4. For the purposes of keeping proof, the parts of the contract or the legal act relating to data protection and the requirements relating to the measures referred to in paragraph 1 shall be in writing or in another equivalent form.

SECTION IX - NOTIFICATION

Article 18 - Obligation to notify the supervisory authority

1. Member States shall provide that the controller or his representative, if any, must notify the supervisory authority referred to in Article 28 before carrying out any wholly or partly automatic processing operation or set of such operations intended to serve a single purpose or several related purposes.

2. Member States may provide for the simplification of or exemption from notification only in the following cases and under the following conditions:

- where, for categories of processing operations which are unlikely, taking account of the data to be processed, to affect adversely the rights and freedoms of data subjects, they specify the purposes of the processing, the data or categories of data undergoing processing, the category or categories of data subject, the recipients or categories of recipient to whom the data are to be disclosed and the length of time the data are to be stored, and/or
- where the controller, in compliance with the national law which governs him, appoints a personal data protection official, responsible in particular:
- for ensuring in an independent manner the internal application of the national provisions taken pursuant to this Directive
- for keeping the register of processing operations carried out by the controller, containing the items of information referred to in Article 21 (2), thereby ensuring that the rights and freedoms of the data subjects are unlikely to be adversely affected by the processing operations.

3. Member States may provide that paragraph 1 does not apply to processing whose sole purpose is the keeping of a register which according to laws or regulations is intended to provide information to the public and which is open to consultation either by the public in general or by any person demonstrating a legitimate interest.

4. Member States may provide for an exemption from the obligation to notify or a simplification of the notification in the case of processing operations referred to in Article 8 (2) (d).

5. Member States may stipulate that certain or all non-automatic processing operations involving personal data shall be notified, or provide for these processing operations to be subject to simplified notification.

Article 19 - Contents of notification

1. Member States shall specify the information to be given in the notification. It shall include at least:

(a) the name and address of the controller and of his representative, if any;

(b) the purpose or purposes of the processing;

(c) a description of the category or categories of data subject and of the data or categories of data relating to them;

(d) the recipients or categories of recipient to whom the data might be disclosed;

(e) proposed transfers of data to third countries;

(f) a general description allowing a preliminary assessment to be made of the appropriateness of the measures taken pursuant to Article 17 to ensure security of processing.

2. Member States shall specify the procedures under which any change affecting the information referred to in paragraph I must be notified to the supervisory authority.

Article 20 - **Prior checking**

1. Member States shall determine the processing operations likely to present specific risks to the rights and freedoms of data subjects and shall check that these processing operations are examined prior to the start thereof.

2. Such prior checks shall be carried out by the supervisory authority following receipt of a notification from the controller or by the data protection official, who, in cases of doubt, must consult the supervisory authority.

3. Member States may also carry out such checks in the context of preparation either of a measure of the national parliament or of a measure based on such a legislative measure, which define the nature of the processing and lay down appropriate safeguards.

Article 21 - **Publicizing of processing operations**

1. Member States shall take measures to ensure that processing operations are publicized.

2. Member States shall provide that a register of processing operations notified in accordance with Article 18 shall be kept by the supervisory authority.

The register shall contain at least the information listed in Article 19 (1) (a) to (e).

The register may be inspected by any person.

3. Member States shall provide, in relation to processing operations not subject to notification, that controllers or another body appointed by the Member States make available at least the information referred to in Article 19 (1) (a) to (e) in an appropriate form to any person on request.

Member States may provide that this provision does not apply to processing whose sole purpose is the keeping of a register which according to laws or regulations is intended to provide information to the public and which is open to consultation either by the public in general or by any person who can provide of a legitimate interest.

CHAPTER III — JUDICIAL REMEDIES, LIABILITY AND SANCTIONS

Article 22 - **Remedies**

Without prejudice to any administrative remedy for which provision may be made, inter alia before the supervisory authority referred to in Article 28, prior to referral to the judicial authority, Member States shall provide for the right of every person to a judicial remedy for any breach of the rights guaranteed him by the national law applicable to the processing in Question.

Article 23 - **Liability**

1. Member States shall provide that any person who has suffered damage as a result of an unlawful processing operation or of any act incompatible with the national provisions adopted pursuant to this Directive is entitled to receive compensation from the controller for the damage suffered.

2. The controller may be exempted from this liability, in whole or in part, if he proves that he is not responsible for the event giving rise to the damage.

Article 24 - **Sanctions**

The Member States shall adopt suitable measures to ensure the full implementation of the' provisions of this Directive and shall in particular lay down the sanctions to be imposed in case of infringement of the provisions adopted pursuant to this Directive.

CHAPTER IV — TRANSFER OF PERSONAL DATA TO THIRD COUNTRIES

Article 25 - **Principles**

1. The Member States shall provide that the transfer to a third country of personal data which are undergoing processing or are intended for processing after transfer may take place only if, without prejudice to compliance with the national provisions adopted pursuant to the other provisions of this Directive, the third country in question ensures an adequate level of protection,

2. The adequacy of the level of protection afforded by a third country shall be assessed in the light of all the circumstances surrounding a data transfer operation or set of data transfer operations; particular consideration shall be given to the nature of the data, the purpose and duration of the proposed processing operation or operations, the country of origin and country of final destination, the rules of law, both general and sectoral, in force in the third country in question and the professional rules and security measures which are complied with in that country.

3. The Member States and the Commission shall inform each other of cases where they consider that a third country does not ensure an adequate level of protection within the meaning of paragraph 2.

4. Where the Commission finds, under the procedure provided for in Article 31 (2), that a third country does not ensure an adequate level of protection within the meaning of paragraph 2 of this Article, Member States shall take the measures necessary to prevent any transfer of data of the same type to the third country in question.

5. At the appropriate time, the Commission shall enter into negotiations with a view to remedying the situation resulting from the finding made pursuant to paragraph 4.

6. The Commission may find, in accordance with the procedure referred to in Article 31 (2), that a third country ensures an adequate level of protection within the meaning of paragraph 2 of this Article, by reason of its domestic law or of the international commitments it has entered into, particularly upon conclusion of the negotiations referred to in paragraph 5, for the protection of the private lives and basic freedoms and rights of individuals.

Member States shall take the measures necessary to comply with the Commission's decision.

Article 26 - **Derogations**

1. By way of derogation from Article 25 and save where otherwise provided by domestic law governing particular cases, Member States shall provide that a transfer or a set of transfers of personal data to a third country which does not ensure an adequate level of protection within the meaning of Article 25 (2) may take place on condition that:

> **(a)** the data subject has given his consent unambiguously to the proposed transfer; or
>
> **(b)** the transfer is necessary for the performance of a contract between the data subject and the controller or the implementation of precontractual measures taken in response to the data subject's request; or
>
> **(c)** the transfer is necessary for the conclusion or performance of a contract concluded in the interest of the data subject between the controller and a third party; or
>
> **(d)** the transfer is necessary or legally required on important public interest grounds, or for the establishment, exercise or defence of legal claims; or
>
> **(e)** the transfer is necessary in order to protect the vital interests of the data subject; or
>
> **(f)** the transfer is made from a register which according to laws or regulations is intended to provide information to the public and which is open to consultation either by the public in general or by any person who can demonstrate legitimate interest, to the extent that the conditions laid down in law for consultation" are fulfilled in the particular case.

2. Without prejudice to paragraph 1, a Member State may authorize a transfer or a set of transfers of personal data to a third country which does not ensure an adequate level of protection within the meaning of Article 25 (2), where the controller adduces adequate safeguards with respect to the protection of the privacy and fundamental rights and freedoms of individuals and as regards the exercise of the corresponding rights; such safeguards may in particular result from appropriate contractual clauses.

3. The Member State shall inform the Commission and the other Member States of the authorizations it grants pursuant to paragraph 2.

If a Member State or the Commission objects on justified grounds involving the protection of the privacy and fundamental rights and freedoms of individuals, the Commission shall take appropriate measures in accordance with the procedure laid down in Article 31 (2).

Member States shall take the necessary to comply with the Commission's decision.

4. Where the Commission decides, in accordance with the procedure referred to in Article 31 (2), that certain standard contractual clauses offer sufficient safeguards as required by paragraph 2, Member States shall take the necessary measures to comply with the Commission's decision.

CHAPTER V — CODES OF CONDUCT

Article 27

1. The Member States and the Commission shall encourage the drawing up of codes of conduct intended to contribute to the proper implementation of the national provisions adopted by the Member States pursuant to this Directive, taking account of the specific features of the various sectors.

2. Member States shall make provision for trade associations and other bodies representing other categories of controllers which have drawn up draft national codes or which have the intention of amending or extending existing national codes to be able to submit them to the opinion of the national authority.

Member States shall make provision for this authority to ascertain, among other things, whether the drafts submitted to it are in accordance with the national provisions adopted pursuant to this Directive. If it sees fit, the authority shall seek the views of data subjects or their representatives.

3. Draft Community codes, and amendments or extensions to existing Community codes, may be submitted to the Working Party referred to in Article 29. This Working Party shall determine, among other things, whether the drafts submitted to it are in accordance with the national provisions adopted pursuant to this Directive. If it sees fit, the authority shall seek the views of data subjects or their representatives. The Commission may ensure appropriate publicity for the codes which have been approved by the Working Party.

CHAPTER VI — SUPERVISORY AUTHORITY AND WORKING PARTY ON THE PROTECTION OF INDIVIDUALS WITH REGARD TO THE PROCESSING OF PERSONAL DATA

Article 28 - Supervisory authority

1. Each Member State shall provide that one or more public authorities are responsible for monitoring the application within its territory of the provisions adopted by the Member States pursuant to this Directive.

These authorities shall act with complete independence in exercising the functions entrusted to them.

2. Each Member State shall provide that the supervisory authorities are consulted when drawing up administrative measures or regulations relating to the protection of individuals' rights and freedoms with regard to the processing of personal data.

3. Each authority shall in particular be endowed with:

- investigative powers, such as powers of access to data forming the subject-matter of processing operations and powers to collect all the information necessary for the performance of its supervisory duties,
- effective powers of intervention, such as, for example, that of delivering opinions before processing operations are carried out, in accordance with Article 20, and ensuring appropriate publication of such opinions, of ordering the blocking, erasure or destruction of data, of imposing a temporary or definitive ban on processing, of warning or admonishing the controller, or that of referring the matter to national parliaments or other political Institutions,

- the power to engage in legal proceedings where the national provisions adopted pursuant to this Directive have been violated or to bring these violations to the attention of the judicial authorities.

Decisions by the supervisory authority which give rise to complaints may be appealed against through the courts.

4. Each supervisory authority shall hear claims lodged by any person, or by an association representing that person, concerning the protection of his rights and freedoms in regard to the processing of personal data. The person concerned shall be informed of the outcome of the claim.

Each supervisory authority shall, in particular, hear claims for checks on the lawfulness of data processing lodged by any person when the national provisions adopted pursuant to Article 13 of this Directive apply. The person shall at any rate be informed that a check has taken place.

5. Each supervisory authority shall draw up a report on its activities at regular intervals. The report shall be made public.

6. Each supervisory authority is competent, whatever the national law applicable to the processing in question, to exercise, on the territory of its own Member State, the powers conferred on it in accordance with paragraph 3. Each authority may be requested to exercise its powers by an authority of another Member State.

The supervisory authorities shall cooperate with one another to the extent necessary for the performance of their duties, in particular by exchanging all useful information.

7. Member States shall provide that the members and staff of the supervisory authority, even after their employment has ended, are to be subject to a duty of professional secrecy with regard to confidential information to which they have access.

Article 29 - Working Party on the Protection of Individuals with regard to the Processing of Personal Data

1. A Working Party on the Protection of Individuals with regard to the Processing of Personal Data, hereinafter referred to as 'the Working Party', is hereby set up.

It shall have advisory status and act independently.

2. The Working Party shall be composed of a representative of the supervisory authority or authorities designated by each Member State and of a representative of the authority or authorities established for the Community institutions and bodies, and of a representative of the Commission.

Each member of the Working Party shall be designated by the institution, authority or authorities which he represents. Where a Member State has designated more than one supervisory authority, they shall nominate a joint representative. The same shall apply to the authorities established for Community institutions and bodies.

3. The Working Party shall take decisions by a simple majority of the representatives of the supervisory authorities.

4. The Working Party shall elect its chairman. The chairman's term of office shall be two years. His appointment shall be renewable.

5. The Working Party's secretariat shall be provided by the Commission.

6. The Working Party shall adopt its own rules of procedure.

7. The Working Party shall consider items placed on its agenda by its chairman, either on his own initiative or at the request of a representative of the supervisory authorities or at the Commission's request.

Article 30

1. The Working Party shall:

> **(a)** examine any question covering the application of the national measures adopted under this Directive in order to contribute to the uniform application of such measures;
>
> **(b)** give the Commission an opinion on the level of protection in the Community and in third countries;
>
> **(c)** advise the Commission on any proposed amendment of this Directive, on any additional or specific measures to safeguard the rights and freedoms of natural persons with regard to the processing of personal data and on any other proposed Community measures affecting such rights and freedoms;
>
> **(d)** give an opinion on codes Community level.

2. If the Working Party finds that divergences likely to affect the equivalence of protection for persons with regard to the processing of personal data in the Community are arising between the laws or practices of Member States, it shall inform the Commission accordingly.

3. The Working Party may, on its own initiative, make recommendations on all matters relating to the protection of persons with regard to the processing of personal data in the Community.

4. The Working Party's opinions and recommendations shall be forwarded to the Commission and to the committee referred to in Article 31.

5. The Commission shall inform the Working Party of the action it has taken in response to its opinions and recommendations. It shall do so in a report which shall also be forwarded to the European Parliament and the Council. The report shall be made public.

6. The Working Party shall draw up an annual report on the situation regarding the protection of natural persons with regard to the processing of personal data in the Community and in third countries, which it shall transmit to the Commission, the European Parliament and the Council. The report shall be made public.

CHAPTER VII — COMMUNITY IMPLEMENTING MEASURES

***Article 31* - The Committee**

1. The Commission shall be assisted by a committee composed of the representatives of the Member States and chaired by the representative of the Commission.

2. The representative of the Commission shall submit to the committee a draft of the measures to be taken. The committee shall deliver its opinion on the draft within a time limit which the chairman may lay down according to the urgency of the matter.

The opinion shall be delivered by the majority laid down in Article 148 (2) of the Treaty. The votes of the representatives of the Member States within the committee shall be weighted in the manner set out in that Article. The chairman shall not vote.

The Commission shall adopt measures which shall apply immediately. However, if these measures are not in accordance with the opinion of the committee, they shall be communicated by the Commission to the Council forthwith. In that event:

- the Commission shall defer application of the measures which it has decided for a period of three months from the date of communication,
- the Council, acting by a qualified majority, may take a different decision within the time limit referred to in the first indent.

FINAL PROVISIONS

Article 32

1. Member States shall bring into force the laws, regulations and administrative provisions necessary to comply with this Directive at the latest at the end of a period of three years from the date of its adoption.

When Member States adopt these measures, they shall contain a reference to this Directive or be accompanied by such reference on the occasion of their official publication. The methods of making such reference shall be laid down by the Member States.

2. Member States shall ensure that processing already under way on the date the national provisions adopted pursuant to this Directive enter into force, is brought into conformity with these provisions within three years of this date.

By way of derogation from the preceding subparagraph, Member States may provide that the processing of data already held in manual filing systems on the date of entry into force of the national provisions adopted in implementation of this Directive shall be brought into conformity with Articles 6, 7 and 8 of this Directive within 12 years of the date on which it is adopted. Member States shall, however, grant the data subject the right to obtain, at his request and in particular at the time of exercising his right of access, the rectification, erasure or blocking of data which are incomplete, inaccurate or stored in a way incompatible with the legitimate purposes pursued by the controller.

3. By way of derogation from paragraph 2, Member States may provide, subject to suitable safeguards, that data kept for the sole purpose of historical research need not be brought into conformity with Articles 6, 7 and 8 of this Directive.

4. Member States shall communicate to the Commission the text of the provisions of domestic law which they adopt in the field covered by this Directive.

Article 33

The Commission shall report to the Council and the European Parliament at regular intervals, starting not later than three years after the date referred to in Article 32 (1), on the implementation of this Directive, attaching to its report, if necessary, suitable proposals for amendments. The report shall be made public.

The Commission shall examine, in particular, the application of this Directive to the data processing of sound and image data relating to natural persons and shall submit any appropriate proposals which prove to be necessary, taking account of developments in information technology and in the light of the state of progress in the information society.

Article 34

This Directive is addressed to the Member States.

Done at Luxembourg, 24 October 1995.

Footnotes

(1) OJ No C 277, 5. 11. 1990, p. 3 and OJ No C 311, 27.11.1992, p. 30.
(2) OJ No C 159, 17. 6. 1991, p 38.
(3) Opinion of the European Parliament of 11 March 1992 (OJ No C 94, 13. 4. 1992, p. 198), confirmed on 2 December 1993 (OJ No C 342, 20. 12. 1993, p. 30); Council common position of 20 February 1995 (OJ No C 93, 13. 4. 1995, p. 1) and Decision of the European Parliament of 15 June 1995 (OJ No C 166, 3. 7. 1995).
(4) 0J No L 197, 18. 7. 1987, p. 33

Safe Harbor Arrangement (2000)

Context

The U.S. Department of Commerce and the EU Commission have negotiated a "safe harbor" agreement to help U.S. companies meet the EU Data Protection Directive's "adequacy" requirement for data transfers from EU Member States. The agreement sets out a series of privacy principles. A decision by a U.S. organization to qualify for the safe harbor is entirely voluntary. A company that decides to adhere to these principles must state on the official, dedicated safe harbor Web site that it qualifies for the safe harbor.

COVER LETTER FROM ACTING UNDER SECRETARY ROBERT S. LaRussa TO U.S. ORGANIZATIONS- JULY 21 2000

July 21, 2000

Dear Colleagues:

I am pleased to announce that the U.S. Department of Commerce, in order to foster, promote, and develop international commerce, formally transmitted the Safe Harbor Principles and related documents to the European Commission on July 18, 2000. In addition to being posted on our website (www.ita.doc.gov/ecom), the Safe Harbor Principles and associated documentation will be issued by the Federal Register on Friday, July 21, 2000.

The Principles, which include a set of Frequently Asked Questions (FAQs) that supplement the Safe Harbor Privacy Principles, are intended to serve as authoritative guidance to U.S. companies and other organizations receiving personal data from the European Union. Upon receipt of the Principles, the Commission is expected to issue an "adequacy determination" for the safe harbor arrangement. Organizations receiving personal data transfers from the EU and complying with the Principles will be considered to meet the "adequacy" requirements of the European Union's Directive on Data Protection. The Principles thus establish a predictable basis for such transfers.

Finalizing this arrangement culminates over two years of discussions with the Europeans. The safe harbor is a landmark accord for e-commerce. It bridges the differences between EU and U.S. approaches to privacy protection and will ensure that data flows between the U.S. and the EU are not interrupted. As a result, it should help ensure that e-commerce continues to flourish.

We will provide additional information about scheduling and next steps after the European Commission has issued its "adequacy determination."

Sincerely,
Robert S. LaRussa
Acting Under Secretary for International Trade Administration

SAFE HARBOR PRIVACY PRINCIPLES

ISSUED BY THE U.S. DEPARTMENT OF COMMERCE ON JULY 21, 2000

The European Union's comprehensive privacy legislation, the Directive on Data Protection (the Directive), became effective on October 25, 1998. It requires that transfers of personal data take place only to non-EU countries that provide an "adequate" level of privacy protection. While the United States and the European Union share the goal of enhancing privacy protection for their citizens, the United States takes a different approach to privacyfrom that taken by the European Union. The United States uses a sectoral approach that relies on a mix of legislation, regulation, and self regulation. Given those differences, many U.S. organizations have expressed uncertainty about the impact of the EU-required "adequacy standard" on personal data transfers from the European Union to the United States.

To diminish this uncertainty and provide a more predictable framework for such data transfers, the Department of Commerce is issuing this document and Frequently Asked Questions ("the Principles") under its statutory authority to foster, promote, and develop international commerce. The Principles were developed in consultation with industry and the general public to facilitate trade and commerce between the United States and European Union. They are intended for use solely by U.S. organizations receiving personal data from the European Union for the purpose of qualifying for the safe harbor and the presumption of "adequacy" it creates. Because the Principles were solely designed to serve this specific purpose, their adoption for other purposes may be inappropriate. The Principles cannot be used as a substitute for national provisions implementing the Directive that apply to the processing of personal data in the Member States.

Decisions by organizations to qualify for the safe harbor are entirely voluntary, and organizations may qualify for the safe harbor in different ways. Organizations that decide to adhere to the Principles must comply with the Principles in order to obtain and retain the benefits of the safe harbor and publicly declare that they do so. For example, if an organization joins a self-regulatory privacy program that adheres to the Principles, it qualifies for the safe harbor. Organizations may also qualify by developing their own self- regulatory privacy policies provided that they conform with the Principles. Where in complying with the Principles, an organization relies in whole or in part on self- regulation, its failure to comply with such self-regulation must also be actionable under Section 5 of the Federal Trade Commission Act prohibiting unfair and deceptive acts or another law or regulation prohibiting such acts. (See the annex for the list of U.S. statutory bodies recognized by the EU.) In addition, organizations subject to a statutory, regulatory, administrative or other body of law (or of rules) that effectively protects personal privacy may also qualify for safe harbor benefits. In all instances, safe harbor benefits are assured from the date on which each organization wishing to qualify for the safe harbor self-certifies to the Department of Commerce (or its designee) its adherence to the Principles in accordance with the guidance set forth in the Frequently Asked Question on Self-Certification.

Adherence to these Principles may be limited: (a) to the extent necessary to meet national security, public interest, or law enforcement requirements; (b) by statute, government regulation, or case law that create conflicting obligations or explicit authorizations, provided that, in exercising any such authorization, an organization can demonstrate that its non-compliance with the Principles is limited to the extent necessary to meet the overriding legitimate interests furthered by such authorization; or (c) if the effect of the Directive or Member State law is to allow exceptions or derogations, provided such exceptions or derogations are applied in comparable contexts. Consistent with the goal of enhancing privacy protection, organizations should strive to implement these Principles fully and transparently, including indicating in their privacy policies where exceptions to the Principles permitted by (b) above will apply on a regular basis. For the same reason, where the option is allowable under the Principles and/or U.S. law, organizations are expected to opt for the higher protection where possible.

Organizations may wish for practical or other reasons to apply the Principles to all their data processing operations, but they are only obligated to apply them to data transferred after they enter the safe harbor. To qualify for the safe harbor, organizations are not obligated to apply these Principles to personal information in manually processed filing systems. Organizations wishing to benefit from the safe harbor for receiving information in manually processed filing systems from the EU must apply the Principles to any such information transferred after they enter the safe harbor. An organization that wishes to extend safe harbor benefits to human resources personal information transferred from the EU for use in the context of an employment relationship must indicate this when it self-certifies to the Department of Commerce (or its designee) and conform to the requirements set forth in the Frequently Asked Question on Self-Certification. Organizations will also be able to provide the safeguards necessary under Article 26 of the Directive if they include the Principles in written agreements with parties transferring data from the EU for the substantive privacy provisions, once the other provisions for such model contracts are authorized by the Commission and the Member States.

U.S. law will apply to questions of interpretation and compliance with the Safe Harbor Principles (including the Frequently Asked Questions) and relevant privacy policies by safe harbor organizations, except where organizations have committed to cooperate with European Data Protection Authorities. Unless otherwise stated, all provisions of the Safe Harbor Principles and Frequently Asked Questions apply where they are relevant.

"Personal data" and "personal information" are data about an identified or identifiable individual that are within the scope of the Directive, received by a U.S. organization from the European Union, and recorded in any form.

NOTICE: An organization must inform individuals about the purposes for which it collects and uses information about them, how to contact the organization with any inquiries or complaints, the types of third parties to which it discloses the information, and the choices and means the organization offers individuals for limiting its use and disclosure. This notice must be provided in clear and conspicuous language when individuals are first asked to provide personal information to the organization or as soon thereafter as is practicable, but in any event before the organization uses such information for a purpose other than that for which it was originally collected or processed by the transferring organization or discloses it for the first time to a third party(1).

CHOICE: An organization must offer individuals the opportunity to choose (opt out) whether their personal information is (a) to be disclosed to a third party(1) or (b) to be used for a purpose that is incompatible with the purpose(s) for which it was originally collected or subsequently authorized by the individual. Individuals must be provided with clear and conspicuous, readily available, and affordable mechanisms to exercise choice.

For sensitive information (i.e. personal information specifying medical or health conditions, racial or ethnic origin, political opinions, religious or philosophical beliefs, trade union membership or information specifying the sex life of the individual), they must be given affirmative or explicit (opt in) choice if the information is to be disclosed to a third party or used for a purpose other than those for which it was originally collected or subsequently authorized by the individual through the exercise of opt in choice. In any case, an organization should treat as sensitive any information received from a third party where the third party treats and identifies it as sensitive.

ONWARD TRANSFER: To disclose information to a third party, organizations must apply the Notice and Choice Principles. Where an organization wishes to transfer information to a third party that is acting as an agent, as described in the endnote, it may do so if it first either ascertains that the third party subscribes to the Principles or is subject to the Directive or another adequacy finding or enters into a written agreement with such third party requiring that the third party provide at least the same level of privacy protection as is required by the relevant Principles. If the organization complies with these requirements, it shall not be held responsible (unless the organization agrees otherwise) when a third party to which it transfers such information processes it in a way contrary to any restrictions or representations, unless the organization knew or should have known the third party would process it in such a contrary way and the organization has not taken reasonable steps to prevent or stop such processing.

SECURITY: Organizations creating, maintaining, using or disseminating personal information must take reasonable precautions to protect it from loss, misuse and unauthorized access, disclosure, alteration and destruction.

DATA INTEGRITY: Consistent with the Principles, personal information must be relevant for the purposes for which it is to be used. An organization may not process personal information in a way that is incompatible with the purposes for which it has been collected or subsequently authorized by the individual. To the extent necessary for those purposes, an organization should take reasonable steps to ensure that data is reliable for its intended use, accurate, complete, and current.

ACCESS: Individuals must have access to personal information about them that an organization holds and be able to correct, amend, or delete that information where it is inaccurate, except where the burden or expense of providing access would be disproportionate to the risks to the individual's privacy in the case in question, or where the rights of persons other than the individual would be violated.

ENFORCEMENT: Effective privacy protection must include mechanisms for assuring compliance with the Principles, recourse for individuals to whom the data relate affected by non-compliance with the Principles, and consequences for the organization when the Principles are not followed. At a minimum, such mechanisms must include (a) readily available and affordable independent recourse mechanisms by which each individual's complaints and disputes are investigated and resolved by reference to the Principles and damages awarded where the applicable law or private sector initiatives so provide; (b) follow up procedures for verifying that the attestations and assertions businesses make about their privacy practices are true and that privacy practices have been implemented as presented; and (c) obligations to remedy problems arising out of failure to comply with the Principles by organizations announcing their adherence to them and consequencesfor such organizations. Sanctions must be sufficiently rigorous to ensure compliance by organizations.

1. It is not necessary to provide notice or choice when disclosure is made to a third party that is acting as an agent to perform task(s) on behalf of and under the instructions of the organization. The Onward Transfer Principle, on the other hand, does apply to such disclosures.

LETTER FROM U.S. DEPARTMENT OF COMMERCE TO COMMISSION SERVCES TRANSMITTING THE SAFE HARBOR PRIVACY PRINCIPES AND FAQS ETC.

July 17, 2000

Mr. John Mogg
Director DG Internal Market
European Commission
Office C 107-6/72
Rue de la Loi, 200
1049 Brussels
BELGIUM

Dear Mr. Mogg:

I am pleased to provide you with several documents: 1) the "Safe Harbor Privacy Principles," issued by the U.S. Department of Commerce on July 21, 2000; 2) Frequently Asked Questions (FAQs) that supplement the Safe Harbor Principles; 3) an overview on how organizations' safe harbor commitments will be enforced in the United States; 4) a memorandum on damages available to individuals; 5) the July 14, 2000 letter from the Federal Trade Commission; and 6) the July 14, 2000 letter from the U.S. Department of Transportation.

The Department is providing these documents under its authority to foster, promote, and develop international commerce. Both the Safe Harbor Principles and the FAQs ("the Principles") are intended to serve as authoritative guidance to U.S. companies and other organizations receiving personal data from the European Union and wishing to establish a predictable basis for the continuation of such transfers. The enforcement overview and other supporting documents are intended to explain how U.S. enforcement mechanisms, based either on law and regulation or self-regulation, will satisfy the requirements of the Enforcement Principle and ensure that an organization's commitment to adhere to the Principles will be effectively enforced. The safe harbor documents of course need to be read against the U.S. legal system and its well known features, such as class actions and contingency fees, which allow consumers even with novel claims relatively ready and inexpensive access to the courts and damages where justified.

Organizations can be assured of the benefits of the safe harbor by self-certifying that they adhere to the Principles. The Department of Commerce will arrange for a list to be maintained of all organizations that self-certify their adherence to the Principles. Both the list and the notifications submitted by organizations containing information with regard to their implementation of the Principles will be made publicly available as will any proper and final adverse determination made by a U.S. enforcement body and notified to the Department of Commerce (or its designee) that a safe harbor organization has persistently failed to comply with the Principles. Where in complying with the Principles, an organization relies in whole or in part on self-regulation, its failure to comply with such self-regulation must also be actionable under Section 5 of the Federal Trade Commission Act prohibiting unfair and deceptive acts or another law or regulation prohibiting such acts.

On the basis of these documents, our expectation is that the European Commission will determine that this safe harbor framework provides adequate protection for the purposes of Article 25.1 of the Data Protection Directive and data transfers from the European Union would continue to organizations that participate in the safe harbor. As a result, adherence to the Principles on these terms will reduce the uncertainty about the impact of the "adequacy" standard on personal data transfers to such organizations from EU Member States.

On the basis of our dialogue, we understand that the Commission and Member States will use the flexibility of Article 26 and any discretion regarding enforcement to avoid disrupting data flows to U.S. organizations during the implementation phase of the safe harbor and that the situation will be reviewed in mid 2001. This will give U.S. organizations an opportunity to decide whether to enter the safe harbor and (if necessary) to update their information practices. We will encourage U.S. organizations to enter the safe harbor as soon as possible to enhance privacy protection and because participation in the safe harbor provides greater certainty that data flows will continue without interruption.

During the dialogue, you sought assurances that where the United States enacted privacy legislation providing greater privacy protection than the safe harbor, such protection should be applied to safe harbor data too, in cases where the law applied with respect to U.S. citizens only, but was silent on its applicability with respect to non-U.S. citizens. You noted that the EU Directive on Data Protection applies to all personal information processed in Europe, regardless of the individuals' citizenship or residency. I would like to confirm that we agree that privacy legislation should not apply differently on the basis of nationality, as provided for in paragraph 19(e) of the OECD guidelines and paragraph 70 of the explanatory memorandum and to assure you that if such legislation were proposed in Congress, we would work within the legislative process to avoid any such effects. We will also continue our efforts, in line with our general commitment to regulatory co-operation in the context of the Transatlantic Economic Partnership, to keep you informed of legislative and other developments in the United States in the field of privacy protection of which we are aware, with particular attention to any such developments that may create allowable exceptions to the Principles. Of course, you can raise any concerns about these issues under the review arrangements provided for.

Similarly, on a number of occasions I raised with you the concerns of U.S. industry about the possible effects of the safe harbor as regards jurisdiction and applicable law. I would like to confirm that it is the U.S. intention that participation in the safe harbor does not change the status quo ante for any organization with respect to jurisdiction, applicable law and liability in the European Union. Moreover, our discussions with respect to the safe harbor have not resolved nor prejudged the questions of jurisdiction or applicable law with respect to websites. All existing rules, principles, conventions and treaties relating to international conflicts of law continue to apply and are not prejudiced in any way by the safe harbor arrangement.

Finally, the Department of Commerce will notify the Commission in advance of any proposed FAQs or revisions to existing ones.

Sincerely,
Robert S. LaRussa, Acting

SAFE HARBOR ENFORCEMENT OVERVIEW

July 14, 2000

Safe Harbor Enforcement Overview

Federal and State "Unfair and Deceptive Practices" Authority and Privacy

This memorandum outlines the authority of the Federal Trade Commission (FTC) under Section 5 of the Federal Trade Commission Act (15 U.S.C. §§ 41-58, as amended) to take action against those who fail to protect the privacy of personal information in accordance with their representations and/or commitments to do so. It also addresses the exceptions to that authority and the ability of other federal and state agencies to take action where the FTC does not have authority.(1)

FTC Authority over Unfair or Deceptive Practices

Section 5 of the Federal Trade Commission Act declares "unfair or deceptive acts or practices in or affecting commerce" to be illegal. 15 U.S.C. § 45(a)(1). Section 5 confers on the FTC the plenary power to prevent such acts and practices. 15 U.S.C. § 45(a)(2). Accordingly, the FTC may, upon conducting a formal hearing, issue a "cease and desist" order to stop the offending conduct. 15 U.S.C. § 45(b). If it would be in the public interest to do so, the FTC can also seek a temporary restraining order or temporary or permanent injunction in U.S. district court. 15 U.S.C. § 53(b). In cases where there is a widespread pattern of unfair or deceptive acts or practices, or where it has already issued cease and desist orders on the matter, the FTC may promulgate an administrative rule prescribing the acts or practices involved. 15 U.S.C. § 57a.

Anyone who does not comply with an FTC order is subject to a civil penalty of up to $11,000, with each day of a continuing violation constituting a separate violation.(2) 15 U.S.C. § 45(l). Likewise, anyone who knowingly violates an FTC rule is liable for $11,000 for each violation. 15 U.S.C. § 45(m). Enforcement actions can be brought by either the Department of Justice, or if it declines by the FTC. 15 U.S.C. § 56.

FTC Authority and Privacy

In exercising its Section 5 authority, the FTC takes the position that misrepresenting why information is being collected from consumers or how the information will be used constitutes a deceptive practice.(3) For example, in 1998, the FTC filed a complaint against GeoCities for disclosing information it had collected on its Web site to third parties for purposes of solicitation, and without prior permission, despite its representations to the contrary.(4) The FTC staff has also asserted that the collection of personal information from children, and sale and disclosure of that information, without the parents' consent is likely to be an unfair practice.(5)

In a letter to Director General John Mogg of the European Commission, FTC Chairman Pitofsky noted the limitations on the FTC's authority to protect privacy where there has not been a misrepresentation (or no representation at all) as to how the information collected will be used. FTC Chairman Pitofsky letter to John Mogg (September 23, 1998). However, companies that want to avail themselves of the proposed "safe harbor" will have to certify that they will protect the information they collect in accordance with prescribed guidelines. Consequently, where a company certifies that it will safeguard the privacy of information and then fails to do so, such action would be a misrepresentation and a "deceptive practice" within the meaning of Section 5.

As the FTC's jurisdiction extends to unfair or deceptive acts or practices "in or affecting commerce," the FTC will not have jurisdiction over the collection and use of personal information for noncommercial purposes, charitable fund-raising for example. See Pitofsky letter, p. 3. However, the use of personal information in any commercial transaction will satisfy this jurisdictional predicate. Thus, for example, the sale by an employer of personal information on its employees to a direct marketer would bring the transaction within the purview of Section 5.

Section 5 Exceptions

Section 5 establishes exceptions to the FTC's authority over unfair or deceptive acts or practices with respect to:

* financial institutions, including banks, savings and loans, and credit unions;
* telecommunications and interstate transportation common carriers;
* air carriers; and
* packers and stockyard operators.

See 15 U.S.C. § 45(a)(2). We discuss each exception, and the regulatory authority that takes its place, below.

Financial Institutions (6)

The first exception applies to "banks, savings and loan institutions described in section 18(f)(3) [15 U.S.C. § 57a(f)(3)]" and "Federal credit unions described in section 18(f)(4) [15 U.S.C. § 57a(f)(4)]."(7) These financial institutions are instead subject to regulations issued by the Federal Reserve Board, the Office of Thrift Supervision(8), and the National Credit Union Administration Board, respectively. See 15 U.S.C. § 57a(f). These regulatory agencies are directed to prescribe the regulations necessary to prevent unfair and deceptive practices by these financial institutions(9) and to establish a separate division to handle consumer complaints. 15 U.S.C. § 57a(f)(1). Finally, authority for enforcement derives from section 8 of the Federal Deposit Insurance Act (12 U.S.C. § 1818), for banks and savings and loans, and sections 120 and 206 of the Federal Credit Union Act, for Federal credit unions. 15 U.S.C. §§ 57a(f)(2)-(4).

Although the insurance industry is not specifically included in the list of exceptions in Section 5, the McCarran-Ferguson Act (15 U.S.C. § 1011 et seq.) generally leaves the regulation of the business of insurance to the individual states.(10) Furthermore, pursuant to section 2(b) of the McCarran-Ferguson Act, no federal law will invalidate, impair, or supersede state regulation "unless such Act specifically relates to the business of insurance." 15 U.S.C. § 1012(b). However, the provisions of the FTC Act apply to the insurance industry "to the extent that such business is not regulated by State law." Id. It should also be noted that McCarran-Ferguson defers to the states only with respect to "the business of insurance." Therefore, the FTC retains residual authority over unfair or deceptive practices by insurance companies when they are not engaged in the business of insurance. This could include, for example, when insurers sell personal information about their policy holders to direct marketers of non-insurance products.(11)

Common Carriers

The second Section 5 exception extends to those common carriers that are "subject to the Acts to regulate commerce." 15 U.S.C. § 45(a)(2). In this case, the "Acts to regulate commerce" refer to subtitle IV of Title 49 of the United States Code and to the Communications Act of 1934 (47 U.S.C. § 151 et seq.) (the Communications Act). See 15 U.S.C. § 44.

49 U.S.C. subtitle IV (Interstate Transportation) covers rail carriers, motor carriers, water carriers, brokers, freight forwarders, and pipeline carriers. 49 U.S.C. § 10101 et seq. These various common carriers are subject to regulation by the Surface Transportation Board, an independent agency within the Department of Transportation. 49 U.S.C. §§ 10501, 13501, and 15301. In each instance, the carrier is prohibited from disclosing information about the nature, destination, and other aspects of its cargo that might be used to the shipper's detriment. See 49 U.S.C. §§ 11904, 14908, and 16103. We note that these provisions refer to information regarding the shipper's cargo and thus do not appear to extend to personal information about the shipper that is unrelated to the shipment in question.

As for the Communications Act, it provides for the regulation of "interstate and foreign commerce in communication by wire and radio" by the Federal Communications Commission (FCC). See 47 U.S.C. §§ 151 and 152. In addition to common carrier telecommunications companies, the Communications Act also applies to companies such as television and radio broadcasters and cable service providers which are not common carriers. As such, these latter companies do not qualify for the exception under Section 5 of the FTC Act. Thus, the FTC has jurisdiction to investigate these companies for unfair and deceptive practices, while the FCC has concurrent jurisdiction to enforce its independent authority in this area as described below.

Under the Communications Act, "every telecommunications carrier," including local exchange carriers, has a duty to protect the privacy of customer proprietary information.(12) 47 U.S.C. § 222(a). In addition to this general privacy-protection authority, the Communications Act was amended by the Cable Communications Policy Act of 1984 (the Cable Act), 47 U.S.C. § 521 et seq., to mandate specifically that cable operators protect the privacy of "personally identifiable information" on cable subscribers. 47 U.S.C. § 551.(13) The Cable Act restricts the collection of personal information by cable operators and requires the cable operator to notify the subscriber of the nature of the information collected and how that information will be used. The Cable Act gives subscribers the right of access to the information about them and requires cable operators to destroy that information when it's no longer needed.

The Communications Act empowers the FCC to enforce these two privacy provisions, either at its own initiation or in response to an outside complaint.(14) 47 U.S.C. §§ 205, 403; id. § 208. If the FCC determines that a telecommunications carrier (including a cable operator) has violated the privacy provisions of section 222 or section 551, there are three basic actions it may take. First, after a hearing and determination of violation, the Commission may order the carrier to pay monetary damages.(15) 47 U.S.C. § 209. Alternatively, the FCC may order the carrier to cease and desist from the offending practice or omission. 47 U.S.C. § 205(a). Finally, the Commission may also order an offending carrier to "conform to and observe [any] regulation or practice" that the FCC may prescribe. Id.

Private persons who believe a telecommunications carrier or cable operator has violated the relevant provisions of the Communications Act or the Cable Act may either file a complaint with the FCC or take their claims to a federal district court. 47 U.S.C. § 207. A complainant who prevails in a federal court action against a telecommunications carrier for failure to protect customer proprietary information under the broader section 222 of the Communications Act may be awarded actual damages and attorneys' fees. 47 U.S.C. § 206. A complainant who files suit claiming a privacy violation under the cable-specific section 551 of the Cable Act may, in addition to actual damages and attorneys' fees, also be awarded punitive damages and reasonable litigation costs. 47 U.S.C. § 551(f).

The FCC has adopted detailed rules to implement section 222. See 47 CFR 64.2001-2009. The rules set out specific safeguards to protect against unauthorized access to customer proprietary network information. The regulations require telecommunications carriers to:

- develop and implement software systems that "flag" a customer's notice/approval status when the customer's service record first comes on-screen;

- maintain an electronic "audit trail" to track access to a customer's account, including when a customer's record is opened, by whom, and for what purpose;

- train their personnel on the authorized use of customer proprietary network information, with appropriate disciplinary processes in place;

- establish a supervisory review process to ensure compliance when conducting outbound marketing; and

- certify to the FCC, on an annual basis, how they are complying with these regulations.

Air Carriers

U.S. and foreign air carriers that are subject to Federal Aviation Act of 1958 are also exempt from Section 5 of the FTC Act. See 15 U.S.C. § 45(a)(2). This includes anyone who provides interstate or foreign transportation of goods or passengers, or who transports mail, by aircraft. See 49 U.S.C. § 40102. Air carriers are subject to the authority of the Department of Transportation. In this regard, the Secretary of Transportation is authorized to take action "preventing unfair, deceptive, predatory, or anticompetitive practices in air transportation." 49 U.S.C. § 40101(a)(9). The Secretary of Transportation can investigate whether a U.S. or foreign air carrier, or a ticket agent, has engaged in an unfair or deceptive practice if it is in the public interest. 49 U.S.C. § 41712. After a hearing, the Secretary of Transportation can issue an order to stop the illegal practice. Id. To our knowledge, the Secretary of Transportation has not exercised this authority to address the issue of protecting the privacy of personal information about airline customers.(16)

There are two provisions protecting the privacy of personal information that apply to air carriers in specific contexts. First, the Federal Aviation Act protects the privacy of pilot applicants. See 49 U.S.C. § 44936(f). While allowing air carriers to obtain an applicant's employment records, the Act gives the applicant the right to notice that the records have been requested, to give consent to the request, to correct inaccuracies, and to have the records divulged only to those involved in the hiring decision. Second, DOT regulations require passenger manifest information collected for government use in the event of an aviation disaster to "be kept confidential and released only to the U.S. Department of State, the National Transportation Board (upon the NTSB's request), and the U.S. Department of Transportation." 14 CFR part 243, § 243.9(c) (as added by 63 FR 8258).

Packers and Stockyards

With regard to the Packers and Stockyards Act of 1921 (7 U.S.C. § 181 et seq.), the Act makes it unlawful for "any packer with respect to livestock, meats, meat food products, or livestock products in unmanufactured form, or for any live poultry dealer with respect to live poultry, to engage in or use any unfair, unjustly discriminatory, or deceptive practice or device." 7 U.S.C. § 192(a); see also 7 U.S.C. § 213(a) (prohibiting "any unfair, unjustly discriminatory, or deceptive practice or device" in connection with livestock). The Secretary of Agriculture has the primary responsibility to enforce these provisions, while the FTC retains jurisdiction over retail transactions and those involving the poultry industry. 7 U.S.C. § 227(b)(2).

It is not clear whether the Secretary of Agriculture will interpret the failure by a packer or stockyard operator to protect personal privacy in accordance with stated policy to be a "deceptive" practice under the Packers and Stockyards Act. However, the Section 5 exception applies to persons, partnerships, or corporations only "insofar as they are subject to the Packers and Stockyards Act," Therefore, if personal privacy is not an issue within the purview of the Packers and Stockyards Act, then the exception in Section 5 may very well not apply and packers and stockyard operators would be subject to the authority of the FTC in that regard.

State "Unfair and Deceptive Practices" Authority

According to an analysis prepared by FTC staff, "All fifty states plus the District of Columbia, Guam, Puerto Rico, and the U.S. Virgin Islands have enacted laws more or less like the Federal Trade Commission Act ("FTCA") to prevent unfair or deceptive trade practices." FTC fact sheet, reprinted in Comment, Consumer Protection: The Practical Effectiveness of State Deceptive Trade Practices Legislation, 59 Tul. L. Rev. 427 (1984). In all cases, an enforcement agency has the authority "to conduct investigations through the use of subpoenas or civil investigative demands, obtain assurances of voluntary compliance, to issue cease and desist orders or obtain court injunctions preventing the use of unfair, unconscionable or deceptive trade practices." Id. In 46 jurisdictions, the law allows private actions for actual, double, treble, or punitive damages and, in some cases, recovery of costs and attorney's fees. Id.

Florida's Deceptive and Unfair Trade Practices Act, for example, authorizes the attorney general to investigate and file civil actions against "unfair methods of competition, unfair, unconscionable or deceptive trade practices," including false or misleading advertising, misleading franchise or business opportunities, fraudulent telemarketing, and pyramid schemes. See also N.Y. General Business Law § 349 (prohibiting unfair acts and deceptive practices carried out in the course of business).

A survey conducted this year by the National Association of Attorneys General (NAAG) confirms these findings. Of forty-three states that responded, all have "mini-FTC" statutes or other statutes that provide comparable protection. Also according to the NAAG survey, 39 states indicated they would have the authority to hear complaints by non-residents. With respect to consumer privacy, in particular, 37 out of forty-one states that responded indicated that they would respond to complaints alleging that a company within their jurisdiction was not adhering to its self-declared privacy policy.

1. We do not discuss here all the various Federal statutes that address privacy in specific contexts or state statutes and common law that might apply. Statutes at the federal level that regulate the commercial collection and use of personal information include the Cable Communications Policy Act (47 U.S.C. § 551), the Driver's Privacy Protection Act (18 U.S.C. § 2721), the Electronic Communications Privacy Act (18 U.S.C. § 2701 et seq.), the Electronic Funds Transfer Act (15 U.S.C. §§ 1693, 1693m), the Fair Credit Reporting Act (15 U.S.C. § 1681 et seq.), the Right to Financial Privacy Act (12 U.S.C. § 3401 et seq.), the Telephone Consumer Protection Act (47 U.S.C. § 227), and the Video Privacy Protection Act (18 U.S.C. § 2710), among others. Many states have analogous legislation in these areas. See, e.g., Mass. Gen. Laws ch. 167B, § 16 (prohibiting financial institutions from disclosing customer's financial records to a third party without either the customer's consent or legal process), N.Y. Pub. Health Law § 17 (limiting use and disclosure of medical or mental health records and giving patients the right of access thereto).

2. In such an action, the United States district court can also order injunctive and equitable relief appropriate to enforcing the FTC order. 15 U.S.C. § 45(l)

3. "Deceptive practice" is defined as a representation, omission or practice that is likely to mislead reasonable consumers in a material fashion.

4. See www.ftc.gov/opa/1998/9808/geocitie.htm.

5. See staff letter to Center for Media Education, www.ftc.gov/os/1997/9707/cenmed.htm. In addition, the Children's Online Privacy Protection Act of 1998 confers on the FTC specific legal authority to regulate the collection of personal information from children by website and online service operators. See 15 U.S.C. §§ 6501-6506. In particular, the act requires online operators to give notice and to obtain verifiable parental consent before collecting, using, or disclosing personal information from children. Id., § 6502(b). The act also gives parents a right of access and to refuse permission for the continued use of the information. Id.

6. On November 12, 1999, President Clinton signed the Gramm-Leach-Bliley Act (Pub. L. 106-102, codified at 15 U.S.C. § 6801 et seq.) into law. The Act limits the disclosure by financial institutions of personal information about their customers. The Act requires financial institutions to, inter alia, notify all customers of their privacy policies and practices with respect to the sharing of personal information with affiliates and non-affiliates. The Act authorizes the FTC, the Federal banking authorities and other authorities to promulgate regulations to implement the privacy protections required by the statute. The agencies have issued proposed regulations for this purpose.

7. By its terms, this exception does not apply to the securities sector. Therefore, brokers, dealers and others in the securities industry are subject to the concurrent jurisdiction of the Securities and Exchange Commission and the FTC with respect to unfair or deceptive acts and practices.

8. The exception in Section 5 originally referred to the Federal Home Loan Bank Board which was abolished in August 1989 by the Financial Institutions Reform, Recovery and Enforcement Act of 1989. Its functions were transferred to the Office of Thrift Supervision and to the Resolution Trust Corporation, the Federal Deposit Insurance Corporation, and the Housing Finance Board.

9. While removing financial institutions from the FTC's jurisdiction, Section 5 also stipulates that whenever the FTC issues a rule on unfair or deceptive acts and practices, the financial regulatory Boards should adopt parallel regulations within 60 days. See 15 U.S.C. § 57a(f)(1).

10. "The business of insurance, and every person engaged therein, shall be subject to the laws of the several States which relate to the regulation or taxation of such business." 15 U.S.C. § 1012(a).

11. The FTC has exercised jurisdiction over insurance companies in different contexts. In one case, the FTC took action against a firm for deceptive advertising in a state in which it was not licensed to do business. The FTC's jurisdiction was upheld on the basis that there was no effective state regulation because the firm was effectively beyond the reach of the state. See FTC v. Travelers Health Association, 362 U.S. 293 (1960).

As for the states, seventeen have adopted the model "Insurance Information and Privacy Protection Act" prepared by the National Association of Insurance Commissioners (NAIC). The Act includes provisions for notice, use and disclosure, and access. Also, almost all states have adopted the NAIC's model "Unfair Insurance Practices Act," which specifically targets unfair trade practices in the insurance industry.

12. The term "customer proprietary network information"means information that relates to "the quantity, technical configuration, type, destination, and amount of use of a telecommunications service" by a customer and telephone billing information. 47 U.S.C. § 222(f)(1). However, the term does not include subscriber list information. Id.

13. The legislation does not expressly define "personally identifiable information."

14. This authority encompasses the right to redress for privacy violations under both section 222 of the Communications Act or, with respect to cable subscribers, under section 551 of the Cable Act amendment to the Act. See also 47 U.S.C. § 551(f)(3) (civil action in federal district court is a nonexclusive remedy, offered "in addition to any other lawful remedy available to a cable subscriber.")

15. However, the absence of direct damage to a complainant is not grounds to dismiss a complaint. 47 U.S.C. § 208(a).

16. We understand there are efforts underway within the industry to address the privacy issue. Industry representatives have discussed the proposed safe harbor principles and their possible application to air carriers. The discussion has included a proposal to adopt an industry privacy policy with participating firms expressly subjecting themselves to DOT authority.

DEPARTMENT OF COMMERCE MEMORANDUM ON DAMAGES FOR BREACHES OF PRIVACY, LEGAL AUTHORIZATIONS AND MERGERS AND TAKEOVERS IS U.S. LAW

July 14, 2000

Damages for Breaches of Privacy, Legal Authorizations and Mergers and Takeovers in U.S. Law

This responds to the request by the European Commission for clarification of U.S. law with respect to (a) claims for damages for breaches of privacy, (b) "explicit authorizations" in U.S. law for the use of personal information in a manner inconsistent with the safe harbor principles, and (c) the effect of mergers and takeovers on obligations undertaken pursuant to the safe harbor principles.

A. Damages for Breaches of Privacy

Failure to comply with the safe harbor principles could give rise to a number of private claims depending on the relevant circumstances. In particular, safe harbor organizations could be held liable for misrepresentation for failing to adhere to their stated privacy policies. Private causes of action for damages for breaches of privacy are also available under common law. Many federal and state statutes on privacy also provide for the recovery of damages by private individuals for violations.

The right to recover damages for invasion of personal privacy is well established under U.S. common law.

Use of personal information in a manner inconsistent with the safe harbor principles can give rise to legal liability under a number of different legal theories. For example, both the transferring data controller and the individuals affected could sue the safe harbor organization which fails to honor its safe harbor commitments for misrepresentation. According to the Restatement of the Law, Second, Torts(1):

One who fraudulently makes a misrepresentation of fact, opinion, intention or law for the purpose of inducing another to act or to refrain from action in reliance upon it, is subject to liability to the other in deceit for pecuniary loss caused to him by his justifiable reliance upon the misrepresentation.

Restatement, § 525. A misrepresentation is "fraudulent" if it is made with the knowledge or in the belief that it is false. Id., § 526. As a general rule, the maker of a fraudulent misrepresentation is potentially liable to everyone who he intends or expects to rely on that misrepresentation for any pecuniary loss they might suffer as a result. Id. 531. Furthermore, a party who makes a fraudulent misrepresentation to another could be liable to a third-party if the tortfeasor intends or expects that his misrepresentation would be repeated to and acted upon by the third-party. Id., § 533.

In the context of the safe harbor, the relevant representation is the organization's public declaration that it will adhere to the safe harbor principles. Having made such a commitment, a conscious failure to abide by the principles could be grounds for a cause of action for misrepresentation by those who relied on the misrepresentation. Because the commitment to adhere to the principles is made to the public at large, the individuals who are the subjects of that information as well as the data controller in Europe that transfers personal information to the U.S. organization could all have causes of action against the U.S. organization for misrepresentation.(2) Moreover, the U.S. organization remains liable to them for the "continuing misrepresentation" for as long as they rely on the misrepresentation to their detriment. Restatement, § 535.

Those who rely on a fraudulent misrepresentation have a right to recover damages. According to the Restatement:

The recipient of a fraudulent misrepresentation is entitled to recover as damages in an action of deceit against the maker the pecuniary loss to him of which the misrepresentation is a legal cause.

Restatement, § 549. Allowable damages include actual out-of-pocket loss as well as the lost "benefit of the bargain" in a commercial transaction. Id.; see, e.g., *Boling v. Tennessee State Bank*, 890 S.W.2d 32 (1994) (bank liable to borrowers for $14,825 in compensatory damages for disclosing borrowers' personal information and business plans to bank president who had a conflicting interest).

Whereas fraudulent misrepresentation requires either actual knowledge or at least the belief that the representation is false, liability can also attach for negligent misrepresentation. According to the Restatement, whoever makes a false statement in the course of his business, profession, or employment, or in any pecuniary transaction can be held liable "if he fails to exercise reasonable care or competence in obtaining or communicating the information." Restatement, § 552(1). In contrast with fraudulent misrepresentations, damages for negligent misrepresentation are limited to out-of-pocket loss. Id.., § 552B(1).

In a recent case, for example, the Superior Court of Connecticut held that a failure by an electric utility to disclose its reporting of customer payment information to national credit agencies sustained a cause of action for misrepresentation. *See Brouillard v. United Illuminating Co.*, 1999 Conn. Super. LEXIS 1754. In that case, the plaintiff was denied credit because the defendant reported payments not received within thirty days of the billing date as "late". The plaintiff alleged that he had not been informed of this policy when he opened a residential electric service account with the defendant. The court specifically held that "a claim for negligent misrepresentation may be based on the defendant's failure to speak when he has a duty to do so." This case also shows that "scienter" or fraudulent intent is not a necessary element in a cause of action for negligent misrepresentation. Thus, a U.S. organization which negligently fails to fully disclose how it will use personal information received under the safe harbor could be held liable for misrepresentation.

Insofar as a violation of the safe harbor principles entailed a misuse of personal information, it could also support a claim by the data subject for the common law tort of invasion of privacy. American law has long recognized causes of action relating to invasions of privacy. In a 1905 case,(3) the Georgia Supreme Court found a right to privacy rooted in natural law and common law precepts in holding for a private citizen whose photograph had been used by a life insurance company, without his consent or knowledge, to illustrate a commercial advertisement. Articulating now-familiar themes in American privacy jurisprudence, the court found that the usage of the photograph was "malicious," "false," and tended to "bring plaintiff into ridicule before the world."(4) The foundations of the *Pavesich* decision have prevailed with minor variations to become the bedrock of American law on this topic. State courts have consistently upheld causes of action in the realm of invasion of privacy, and at least 48 states now judicially recognize some such cause of action.(5) Moreover, at least twelve states have constitutional provisions safeguarding their citizens' right to be free from intrusive actions,(6) which in some cases could extend to protect against intrusion by non-governmental entities. See, e.g., Hill v. NCAA, 865 P.2d 633 (Ca. 1994); see also S. Ginder, *Lost and Found in Cyberspace: Informational Privacy in the Age of the Internet*, 34 S.D. L. Rev. 1153 (1997) ("Some state constitutions include privacy protections which surpass privacy protections in the U.S. Constitution. Alaska, Arizona, California, Florida, Hawaii, Illinois, Louisiana, Montana, South Carolina, and Washington have broader privacy protection.")

The Second Restatement of Torts provides an authoritative overview of the law in this area. Reflecting common judicial practice, the Restatement explains that the "right to privacy" encompasses four distinct causes of action in tort under that umbrella. See Restatement, § 652A. First, a cause of action for "intrusion upon seclusion" may lie against a defendant who intentionally intrudes, physically or otherwise, upon the solitude or seclusion of another or his private affairs or concerns.(7) Second, an "appropriation" case may exist when one takes the name or likeness of another for his own use or benefit.(8) Third, the "publication of private facts" is actionable when the matter publicized is of a kind that would be highly offensive to a reasonable person and is not of legitimate concern to the public.(9) Lastly, an action for "false light publicity" is appropriate when the defendant knowingly or recklessly places another before the public in a false light that would be highly offensive to a reasonable person.(10)

In the context of the safe harbor framework, "intrusion upon seclusion" could encompass the unauthorized collection of personal information whereas the unauthorized use of personal information for commercial purposes could give rise to a claim of appropriation. Similarly, the disclosure of personal information that is inaccurate would give rise to a tort of "false light publicity" if the information meets the standard of being highly offensive to a reasonable person. Finally, the invasion of privacy that results from the publication or disclosure of sensitive personal information could give rise to a cause of action for "publication of private facts." (See examples of illustrative cases below.)

On the issue of damages, invasions of privacy give the injured party the right to recover damages for:

(a) the harm to his interest in privacy resulting from the invasion;

(b) his mental distress proved to have been suffered if it is of a kind that normally results from such an invasion; and

(c) special damage of which the invasion is a legal cause.

Restatement, § 652H. Given the general applicability of tort law and the multiplicity of causes of action covering different aspects of privacy interests, monetary damages are likely to be available to those who suffer invasion of their privacy interests as a result of a failure to adhere to the safe harbor principles.

Indeed, state courts are replete with cases alleging invasion of privacy in analogous situations. *Ex Parte AmSouth Bancorporation et al.*, 717 So. 2d 357, for example, involved a class action that alleged the defendant "exploited the trust depositors placed in the Bank, by sharing confidential information regarding Bank depositors and their accounts" to enable a bank affiliate to sell mutual funds and other investments. Damages are often awarded in such cases. In *Vassiliades v. Garfinckel's, Brooks Bros.*, 492 A.2d 580 (D.C. App. 1985), an appellate court reversed a lower court judgement to hold that the use of photographs of the plaintiff "before" and "after" plastic surgery in a presentation in a department store constituted an invasion of privacy through the publication of private facts. In *Candebat v. Flanagan*, 487 So.2d 207 (Miss. 1986), the defendant insurance company used an accident in which plaintiff's wife was seriously injured in an advertising campaign. Plaintiff sued for invasion of privacy. The court held that plaintiff could recover damages for emotional distress and appropriation of identity. Actions for misappropriation can be maintained even if the plaintiff is not personally famous. See, e.g., *Staruski v. Continental Telephone Co.,* 154 Vt. 568 (1990) (defendant derived commercial benefit in using employee's name and photograph in newspaper advertisement). *In Pulla v. Amoco Oil Co.*, 882 F.Supp. 836 (S.D Iowa 1995), an employer intruded on plaintiff employee's seclusion by having another employee investigate his credit card records in order to verify his sick day absences. The court upheld a jury award of $2 in actual damages and $500,000 in punitive damages. Another employer was held liable for publishing a story in the company newspaper about an employee who was terminated for allegedly falsifying his employment records. *See Zinda v. Louisiana-Pacific Corp.,* 140 Wis.2d 277 (Wis.App. 1987). The story invaded the plaintiff's privacy by publication of a private matter because the newspaper circulated in the community. Finally, a college which tested students for HIV after telling them the blood test was for rubella only was held liable for intrusion upon seclusion. See *Doe v. High-Tech Institute, Inc.,* 972 P.2d 1060 (Colo.App. 1998). (For other reported cases, see Restatement, § 652H, Appendix.)

The United States is often criticized for being overly litigious, but this also means that individuals actually can, and do, pursue legal recourse when they believe they have been wronged. Many aspects of the U.S. judicial system make it easy for plaintiffs to bring suit, either individually or as a class. The legal bar, comparatively larger than in most other countries, makes professional representation readily available. Plaintiffs' counsel representing individuals in private claims will typically work on a contingency fee basis, allowing even poor or indigent plaintiffs to seek redress. This brings up an important factor - in the United States, each side typically bears its own lawyers' fees and other costs. This contrasts with the prevailing rule in Europe wherein the losing party has to reimburse the other side for costs. Without debating the relative merits of the two systems, the U.S. rule is less likely to deter legitimate claims by individuals who would not be able to pay the costs on both sides if they should lose.

Individuals can sue for redress even if their claims are relatively small. Most, if not all U.S. jurisdictions, have small claims courts which provide simplified and less costly procedures for disputes below the statutory limits.(11) The potential for punitive damages also offers a financial reward for individuals who might have suffered little direct injury to bring suit against reprehensible misconduct. Finally, individuals who have been injured in the same way can marshal their resources as well as their claims to bring a class-action lawsuit.

A good example of the ability of individuals to bring suit to obtain redress is the pending litigation against Amazon.com for invasion of privacy. Amazon.com, the large online retailer, is the target of a class action, in which the plaintiffs allege that they were not told about, and did not consent to, the collection of personal information about them when they used a software program owned by Amazon called "Alexa." In that case, plaintiffs have alleged violations of the Computer Fraud and Abuse Act in unlawful access to their stored communications and of the Electronic Communications Privacy Act for unlawful interception of their electronic and wire communications. They also claim an invasion of privacy under common law. This stems from a complaint filed by an Internet security expert in December. The suit seeks damages of $1,000 per class member, plus attorneys' fees and profits earned as a result of violations of laws. Given that the number of class members could be in the millions, damages could total billions of dollars. The FTC is also investigating the charges.

Federal and state privacy legislation often provides private causes of action for money damages.

In addition to giving rise to civil liability under tort law, noncompliance with the safe harbor principles could also violate one or another of the hundreds of federal and state privacy laws. Many of these laws, which address both government and private-sector handling of personal information, allow individuals to sue for damages when violations occur. For example:

Electronic Communications Privacy Act of 1986. The ECPA prohibits the unauthorized interception of cellular telephone calls and computer-to-computer transmissions. Violations can result in civil liability of not less than $100 for each day of violation. The protection of the ECPA also extends to unauthorized access or disclosure of stored electronic communications. Violators are liable for damages suffered or forfeiture of profits generated by a violation.

Telecommunications Act of 1996. Under section 702, customer proprietary network information (CPNI) may not be used for any purpose other than to provide telecommunications services. Service subscribers can either submit a complaint to the Federal Communications Commission or file suit in federal district court to recover damages and attorneys' fees.

Consumer Credit Reporting Reform Act of 1996. The 1996 Act amended the Fair Credit Reporting Act of 1970 (FCRA) to require improved notice and right of access for credit reporting subjects. The Reform Act also imposed new restrictions on resellers of consumer credit reports. Consumers can recover damages and attorneys' fees for violations.

State laws also protect personal privacy in a broad range of situations. Areas where the states have taken action include bank records, cable television subscriptions, credit reports, employment records, government records, genetic information and medical records, insurance records, school records, electronic communications, and video rentals.(12)

B. Explicit Legal Authorizations

The safe harbor principles contain an exception where statute, regulation or case law create "conflicting obligations or explicit authorizations, provided that, in exercising any such authorization, an organization can demonstrate that its non-compliance with the principles is limited to the extent necessary to meet the overriding legitimate interests further by such authorization." Clearly, where U.S. law imposes a conflicting obligation, U.S. organizations whether in the safe harbor or not must comply with the law. As for explicit authorizations, while the safe harbor principles are intended to bridge the differences between the U.S. and European regimes for privacy protection, we owe deference to the legislative prerogatives of our elected lawmakers. The limited exception from strict adherence to the safe harbor principles seeks to strike a balance to accommodate the legitimate interests on each side.

The exception is limited to cases where there is an explicit authorization. Therefore, as a threshold matter, the relevant statute, regulation or court decision must affirmatively authorize the particular conduct by safe harbor organizations.(13) In other words, the exception would not apply where the law is silent. In addition, the exception would apply only if the explicit authorization conflicts with adherence to the safe harbor principles. Even then, the exception "is limited to the extent necessary to meet the overriding legitimate interests furthered by such authorization." By way of illustration, where the law simply authorizes a company to provide personal information to government authorities, the exception would not apply. Conversely, where the law specifically authorizes the company to provide personal information to government agencies without the individual's consent, this would constitute an "explicit authorization" to act in a manner that conflicts with the safe harbor principles. Alternatively, specific exceptions from affirmative requirements to provide notice and consent would fall within the exception (since it would be the equivalent of a specific authorization to disclose the information without notice and consent). For example, a statute which authorizes doctors to provide their patients' medical records to health officials without the patients' prior consent might permit an exception from the notice and choice principles. This authorization would not permit a doctor to provide the same medical records to health maintenance organizations or commercial pharmaceutical research laboratories, which would be beyond the scope of the purposes authorized by the law and therefore beyond the scope of the exception.(14) The legal authority in question can be a "stand alone" authorization to do specific things with personal information, but, as the examples below illustrate, it is likely to be an exception to a broader law which proscribes the collection, use, or disclosure of personal information.

Telecommunications Act of 1996

In most cases, the authorized uses are either consistent with the requirements of the Directive and the principles, or would be permitted by one of the other allowed exceptions. For example, section 702 of the Telecommunications Act (codified at 47 U.S.C. § 222) imposes a duty on telecommunications carriers to maintain the confidentiality of personal information that they obtain in the course of providing their services to their customers. This provision specifically allows telecommunications carriers to:

- use customer information to provide telecommunications service, including the publication of subscriber directories;
- provide customer information to others at the written request of the customer; and
- provide customer information in aggregate form.

See 47 U.S.C. § 222(c)(1)-(3). The Act also allows telecommunications carriers an exception to use customer information:

- to initiate, render, bill, and collect for their services;
- to protect against fraudulent, abusive or illegal conduct; and
- to provide telemarketing, referral or administrative services during a call initiated by the customer.(15)

Id., § 222(d)(1)-(3). Finally, telecommunications carriers are required to provide subscriber list information, which can only include the names, addresses, telephone numbers and line of business for commercial customers to publishers of telephone directories. Id., § 222(e).

The exception for "explicit authorizations" might come into play when telecommunications carriers use CPNI to prevent fraud or other unlawful conduct. Even here, such actions could qualify as being in the "public interest" and allowed by the principles for that reason.

Department of Health and Human Services Proposed Rules

The Department of Health and Human Services (HHS) has proposed rules regarding standards for the privacy of individually identifiable health information. See 64 Fed. Reg. 59,918 (Nov. 3, 1999) (to be codified at 45 C.F.R. pts. 160-164). The rules would implement the privacy requirements of the Health Insurance Portability and Accountability Act of 1996, Pub. L. 104-191. The proposed rules generally would prohibit covered entities (i.e. health plans, health care clearinghouses, and health providers that transmit health information in electronic format) from using or disclosing protected health information without individual authorization. See proposed 45 C.F.R. § 164.506. The proposed rules would require disclosure of protected health information for only two purposes: 1) to permit individuals to inspect and copy health information about themselves, see id. at § 164.514; and 2) to enforce the rules, see id. at § 164.522.

The proposed rules would permit use or disclosure of protected health information, without specific authorization by the individual, in limited circumstances. These include for example oversight of the health care system, law enforcement, and emergencies. See id. at § 164.510. The proposed rules set out in detail the limits on these uses and disclosures. Moreover, permitted uses and disclosures of protected health information would be limited to the minimum amount of information necessary. See id. at § 164.506.

The permissive uses explicitly authorized by the proposed regulations are generally consistent with the safe harbor principles or are otherwise allowed by another exception. For example, law enforcement and judicial administration are permitted, as is medical research. Other uses, such as oversight of the health care system, public health function, and government health data systems, serve the public interest. Disclosures to process health care payments and premiums are necessary to the provision of health care. Uses in emergencies, to consult with next-of-kin regarding treatment where the patient's consent "cannot practicably or reasonably be obtained," or to determine the identity or cause of death of the deceased protect the vital interests of the data subject and others. Uses for the management of active duty military and other special classes of individuals aid the proper execution of the military mission or similar exigent situations; and in any event, such uses will have little if any application to consumers in general.

This leaves only the use of personal information by health care facilities to produce patient directories. While such use might not rise to the level of a "vital" interest, the directories do benefit patients and their friends and relations. Also, the scope of this authorized use is inherently limited. Therefore, reliance on the exception in the principles for uses "explicitly authorized" by law for this purpose presents minimal risk to the privacy of patients.

Fair Credit Reporting Act

The European Commission has expressed the concern that the "explicit authorizations" exception would "effectively create an adequacy finding" for the Fair Credit Reporting Act (FCRA). This would not be the case. In the absence of a specific adequacy finding for the FCRA, those U.S. organizations that would otherwise rely on such a finding, would have to promise to adhere to the safe harbor principles in all respects. This means that where FCRA requirements exceed the level of protection embodied in the principles, the U.S. organizations need only to obey the FCRA. Conversely, where the FCRA might fall short, then those organizations would need to bring their information practices into conformity with the principles. The exception would not alter this basic assessment. By its terms, the exception applies only where the relevant law explicitly authorizes conduct that would be inconsistent with the safe harbor principles. The exception would not extend to where FCRA requirements merely do not meet the safe harbor principles.(16)

In other words, we do not intend the exception to mean that whatever is not required is therefore "explicitly authorized." Furthermore, the exception applies only when what is explicitly authorized by U.S. law conflicts with the requirements of the safe harbor principles. The relevant law must meet both of these elements before non-adherence with the principles would be permitted.

Section 604 of the FCRA, for example, explicitly authorizes consumer reporting agencies to issue consumer reports in various enumerated situations. See FCRA, § 604. If in so doing, section 604 authorizes credit reporting agencies to act in conflict with the safe harbor principles, then the credit reporting agencies would need to rely on the exception (unless, of course, some other exception applied). Credit reporting agencies must obey court orders and grand jury subpoenas, and use of credit reports by government licensing, social and child support enforcement agencies serves a public purpose. Id., § 604(a)(1), (3)(D), and (4). Consequently, the credit reporting agency would not need to rely on the "explicit authorization" exception for these purposes. Where it acts in accordance with written instructions by the consumer, the consumer reporting agency would be fully in compliance with the safe harbor principles. Id., § 604(a)(2). Likewise, consumer reports can be procured for employment purposes only with the consumer's written authorization (id., §§ 604(a)(3)(B) and (b)(2)(A)(ii)) and for credit or insurance transactions that are not initiated by the consumer only if the consumer had not opted out from such solicitations (id., § 604(c)(1)(B)). Also, FCRA prohibits credit reporting agencies from providing medical information for employment purposes without the consent of the consumer. Id., § 604(g). Such uses comport with the notice and choice principles. Other purposes authorized by section 604 entail transactions involving the consumer and would be permitted by the principles for that reason. See id., § 604(a)(3)(A) and (F).

The remaining use "authorized" by section 604 relates to secondary credit markets. Id., § 604(a)(3)(E). There is no conflict between use of consumer reports for this purpose and the safe harbor principles per se. It is true that the FCRA does not require credit reporting agencies, for example, to give notice and consent to consumers when they issue reports for this purpose. However, we reiterate the point that the absence of a requirement does not connote an "explicit authorization" to act in a manner other than as required. Similarly, section 608 allows credit reporting agencies to provide some personal information to government agencies. This "authorization" would not justify a credit reporting agency ignoring its commitments to adhere to the safe harbor principles. This contrasts with our other examples where exceptions from affirmative notice and choice requirements operate to explicitly authorize uses of personal information without notice and choice.

Conclusion

A distinct pattern emerges even from our limited review of these statutes:

- The "explicit authorization" in the law generally permits the use or disclosure of personal information without the individual's prior consent; thus, the exception would be limited to the notice and choice principles.

- In most cases, the exceptions authorized by the law are narrowly drawn to apply in specific situations for specific purposes. In all cases, the law otherwise prohibits the unauthorized use or disclosure of personal information that does not fall within these limits.

- In most cases, reflecting their legislative character, the authorized use or disclosure serves a public interest.

- In almost all cases, the authorized uses are either fully consistent with the safe harbor principles or fall into one of the other allowed exceptions.

In conclusion, the exception for "explicit authorizations" in the law will, by its nature, likely be rather limited in scope.

C. Mergers and Takeovers

The Article 29 Working Party expressed concern over situations where an organization within the safe harbor is taken over by, or merged with, a firm which has not made a commitment to follow the safe harbor principles. The Working Party, however, appears to have assumed that the surviving firm would not be bound to apply the safe harbor principles to personal information held by the firm that is taken over, but that is not necessarily the case under U.S. law. The general rule in the United States as to mergers and takeovers is that a company which acquires the outstanding stock of another corporation generally assumes the obligations and liabilities of the acquired firm. See 15 Fletcher Cyclopedia of the Law of Private Corporations § 7117 (1990); see also Model Bus. Corp. Act § 11.06(3) (1979) ("the surviving corporation has all liabilities of each corporation party to the merger"). In other words, the surviving firm in a merger or takeover of a safe harbor organization by this method would be bound by the latter's safe harbor commitments.

Moreover, even if the merger or takeover were effectuated through the acquisition of assets, the liabilities of the acquired enterprise could nevertheless bind the acquiring firm in certain circumstances. 15 Fletcher, § 7122. Even where liabilities did not survive the merger, however, it is worth noting that they also would not survive a merger where the data were transferred from Europe pursuant to a contract — the only viable alternative to the safe harbor for data transfers to the United States. In addition, the safe harbor documents as revised now require any safe harbor organization to notify the Department of Commerce of any takeover and permit data to continue to be transferred to the successor organization only if the successor organization joins the safe harbor. See FAQ 6. Indeed, the United States has now revised the safe harbor framework to require U.S. organizations in this situation to delete information they have received under the safe harbor framework if their safe harbor commitments will not continue or other suitable safeguards are not put in place.

1. Second Restatement of the Law - Torts; American Law Institute (1997).

2. This might be the case, for example, where the individuals relied on the U.S. organization's safe harbor commitments in giving their consent to the data controller to transfer their personal information to the United States.

3. Pavesich v. New England Life Ins. Co., 50 S.E. 68 (Ga. 1905)

4. Id., at 69.

5. An electronic search of the Westlaw database found 2703 reported cases of civil actions in state courts that pertained to "privacy" since 1995. We have previously provided the results of this search to the Commission.

6. See, e.g., Alaska Constitution, Art. 1 Sec. 22; Arizona, Art. 2, Sec. 8; California, Art. 1, Sec. 1; Florida, Art. 1, Sec. 23; Hawaii, Art. 1, Sec. 5; Illinois, Art. 1, Sec. 6; Louisiana, Art. 1, Sec. 5; Montana, Art. 2, Sec. 10; New York, Art. 1, Sec. 12; Pennsylvania, Art. 1, Sec. 1; South Carolina, Art. 1, Sec. 10; and Washington, Art. 1, Sec 7.

7. Id., at Chapter 28, Section 652B.

8. Id., at Chapter 28, Section 652C.

9. Id., at Chapter 28, Section 652D.

10. Id., at Chapter 28, Section 652E.

11. We had previously provided the Commission with information on small-claims actions.

12. A recent electronic search of the Westlaw database yielded 994 reported states cases that related to damages and invasion of privacy.

13. As a point of clarification, the relevant legal authority will not have to specifically reference the safe harbor principles.

14. Similarly, the doctor in this example could not rely on the statutory authority to override the individual's exercise of the opt-out from direct marketing provided by FAQ 12. The scope of any exception for "explicit authorizations" is necessarily limited to the scope of the authorization under relevant law.

15. The scope of this exception is very limited. By its terms, the telecommunications carrier can use CPNI only during a call initiated by the customer. Furthermore, we have been advised by the FCC that the telecommunications carrier may not use CPNI to market services beyond the scope of the customer's inquiry. Finally, since the customer must approve the use of CPNI for this purpose, this provision is not really an "exception" at all.

16. Our discussion here should not be taken as an admission that the FCRA does not provide "adequate" protection. Any assessment of the FCRA must consider the protection provided by the statute in its entirety and not focus only on the exceptions as we do here.

LETTER FROM THE FEDERAL TRADE COMMISSION CONCERNING ITS JURISDICTION OVER CONSUMER PRIVACY ISSUES

July 14, 2000

John Mogg
Director, DG XV
European Commission
Office C 107-6/72
Rue de la Loi, 200
1049 Brussels
BELGIUM

Dear Mr. Mogg:

I understand a number of questions have arisen with regard to my letter to you of March 29, 2000. To clarify our authority on those areas where questions have arisen, I am sending this letter, which, for future ease of reference, adds to and recapitulates some of the text of previous correspondence.

In your visits to our offices and in your correspondence, you have raised several questions about the United States Federal Trade Commission's authority in the online privacy area. I thought it would be useful to summarize my prior responses and to provide additional information about the agency's jurisdiction over consumer privacy issues raised in your most recent letter. Specifically, you ask whether: (1) the FTC has jurisdiction over transfers of employment-related data if done in violation of the U.S. safe harbor principles; (2) the FTC has jurisdiction over non-profit privacy "seal" programs; (3) the FTC Act applies equally to the offline as well as online world; and (4) what happens when the FTC's jurisdiction overlaps with other law enforcement agencies.

FTC Act Application to Privacy

The Federal Trade Commission's legal authority in this area is found in Section 5 of the Federal Trade Commission Act ("FTC Act"), which prohibits "unfair or deceptive acts or practices" in or affecting commerce.(1) A deceptive practice is defined as a representation, omission or practice that is likely to mislead reasonable consumers in a material fashion. A practice is unfair if it causes, or is likely to cause, substantial injury to consumers which is not reasonably avoidable and is not outweighed by countervailing benefits to consumers or competition.(2)

Certain information collection practices are likely to violate the FTC Act. For example, if a web site falsely claims to comply with a stated privacy policy or a set of self-regulatory guidelines, Section 5 of the FTC Act provides a legal basis for challenging such a misrepresentation as deceptive. Indeed, we have successfully enforced the law to establish this principle.(3) In addition, the Commission has taken the position it may challenge particularly egregious privacy practices as unfair under Section 5 if such practices involve children, or the use of highly sensitive information, such as financial records(4) and medical records. The Federal Trade Commission has and will continue to pursue such law enforcement actions through our active monitoring and investigative efforts, and through referrals we receive from self-regulatory organizations and others, including European Union member states.

Backstop Self-Regulation

The FTC will give priority to referrals of non-compliance with self-regulatory guidelines received from organizations such as BBBOnline and TRUSTe.(5) This approach would be consistent with our longstanding relationship with the National Advertising Review Board (NARB) of the Better Business Bureau, which refers advertising complaints to the FTC. The National Advertising Division (NAD) of NARB resolves complaints, through an adjudicative process, concerning national advertising. When a party refuses to comply with an NAD decision, a referral is made to the FTC. FTC staff reviews the challenged advertising on a priority basis to determine if it violates the FTC Act, and often is successful in stopping the challenged conduct or convincing the party to return to the NARB process.

Similarly, the FTC will give priority to referrals of non-compliance with safe harbor principles from EU member states. As with referrals from U.S. self-regulatory organizations, our staff will consider any information bearing upon whether the conduct complained of violates Section 5 of the FTC Act. This commitment can also be found in the safe harbor principles under the Frequently Asked Question (FAQ 11) on enforcement.

GeoCities: The FTC's First Online Privacy Case

The Federal Trade Commission's first Internet privacy case, GeoCities, was based on the Commission's authority under Section 5.(6) In that case, the FTC alleged that GeoCities misrepresented, both to adults and children, how their personal information would be used. The Federal Trade Commission's complaint alleged that GeoCities represented that certain personal identifying information it collected on its Web site was to be used only for internal purposes or to provide consumers with the specific advertising offers and products or services they requested, and that certain additional "optional" information would not be released to anyone without the consumer's permission. In fact, this information was disclosed to third parties who used it to target members for solicitations beyond those agreed to by the member. The complaint also charged that GeoCities engaged in deceptive practices relating to its collection of information from children. According to the FTC's complaint, GeoCities represented that it operated a children's area on its Web site and that the information collected there was maintained by GeoCities. In fact, those areas on the Web site were run by third-parties who collected and maintained the information.

The settlement prohibits GeoCities from misrepresenting the purpose for which it collects or uses personal identifying information from or about consumers, including children. The order requires the company to post on its Web site a clear and prominent Privacy Notice, telling consumers what information is being collected and for what purpose, to whom it will be disclosed, and how consumers can access and remove the information. To ensure parental control, the settlement also requires GeoCities to obtain parental consent before collecting personal identifying information from children 12 and under. Under the order, GeoCities is required to notify its members and provide them with an opportunity to have their information deleted from GeoCities' and any third parties' databases. The settlement specifically requires GeoCities to notify the parents of children 12 and under and to delete their information, unless a parent affirmatively consents to its retention and use. Finally, GeoCities also is required to contact third parties to whom it previously disclosed the information and request that those parties delete that information as well.(7)

ReverseAuction.com

In January 2000, the Commission approved a complaint against, and consent agreement with, ReverseAuction.com, an online auction site that allegedly obtained consumers' personally identifying information from a competitor site (eBay.com) and then sent deceptive, unsolicited e-mail messages to those consumers seeking their business.(8) Our complaint alleged that ReverseAuction violated Section 5 of the FTC Act in obtaining the personally identifiable information, which included eBay users' e-mail addresses and personalized user identification names ("user IDs"), and in sending out the deceptive e-mail messages.

As described in the complaint, before obtaining the information, ReverseAuction registered as an eBay user and agreed to comply with eBay's User Agreement and Privacy Policy. The agreement and policy protect consumers' privacy by prohibiting eBay users from gathering and using personal identifying information for unauthorized purposes, such as sending unsolicited commercial e-mail messages. Thus, our complaint first alleged that ReverseAuction misrepresented that it would comply with eBay's User Agreement and Privacy Policy, a deceptive practice under Section 5. In the alternative, the complaint alleged that ReverseAuction's use of the information to send the unsolicited commercial e-mail, in violation of the User Agreement and Privacy Policy, was an unfair trade practice under Section 5.

Second, the complaint alleged that the e-mail messages to consumers contained a deceptive subject line informing each of them that his or her eBay user ID "will expire soon." Finally, the complaint alleged that the e-mail messages falsely represented that eBay directly or indirectly provided ReverseAuction with eBay users' personally identifiable information, or otherwise participated in dissemination of the unsolicited e-mail.

The settlement obtained by the FTC bars ReverseAuction from committing these violations in the future. It also requires ReverseAuction to provide notice to consumers who, as a result of receiving ReverseAuction's e-mail, registered or will register with ReverseAuction. The notice informs these consumers that their eBay users IDs were not about to expire on eBay, and that eBay did not know of, or authorize, ReverseAuction's dissemination of the unsolicited e-mail. The notice also provides these consumers with the opportunity to cancel registration with

ReverseAuction and have their personal identifying information deleted from ReverseAuction's database. In addition, the order requires ReverseAuction to delete, and refrain from using or disclosing, the personal identifying information of eBay members who received ReverseAuction's e-mail but who have not registered with ReverseAuction. Finally, consistent with prior privacy orders obtained by this agency, the settlement requires ReverseAuction to disclose its own privacy policy on its Internet site, and contains comprehensive record keeping provisions to allow the FTC to monitor compliance.

The ReverseAuction case demonstrates that the FTC is committed to using enforcement to buttress industry self-regulatory efforts in the area of online consumer privacy. Indeed, this case directly challenged conduct that undermined a Privacy Policy and User Agreement protecting consumers' privacy, and that could erode consumer confidence in privacy measures undertaken by online companies. Because this case involved the misappropriation by one company of consumer information protected by another company's privacy policy, it also may have particular relevance to the privacy concerns raised by the transfer of data between companies in different countries.

Notwithstanding the Federal Trade Commission's law enforcement actions in GeoCities, Liberty Financial Cos., and ReverseAuction, the agency's authority in some areas of online privacy is more limited. As noted above, to be reachable under the FTC Act, the collection and use of personal information without consent must constitute either a deceptive or unfair trade practice. Thus, the FTC Act likely would not address the practices of a Web site that collected personally identifiable information from consumers, but neither misrepresented the purpose for which the information was collected, nor used or released the information in a way that was likely to cause substantial injury to consumers. Also, it currently may not be within the FTC's power to broadly require that entities collecting information on the Internet adhere to a privacy policy or to any particular privacy policy.(9) As stated above, however, a company's failure to abide by a stated privacy policy is likely to be a deceptive practice.

Furthermore, the FTC's jurisdiction in this area covers unfair or deceptive acts or practices only if they are "in or affecting commerce." Information collection by commercial entities that are promoting products or services, including collecting and using information for commercial purposes, would presumably meet the "commerce" requirement. On the other hand, many individuals or entities may be collecting information online without any commercial purpose, and thereby may fall outside the Federal Trade Commission's jurisdiction. An example of this limitation involves "chat rooms" if operated by noncommercial entities, e.g., a charitable organization.

Finally, there are a number of full or partial statutory exclusions from the FTC's basic jurisdiction over commercial practices that limit the FTC's ability to provide a comprehensive response to Internet privacy concerns. These include exemptions for many information intensive consumer businesses such as banks, insurance companies and airlines. As you are aware, other federal or state agencies would have jurisdiction over those entities, such as the federal banking agencies or the Department of Transportation.

In cases where it does have jurisdiction, the FTC accepts and, resources permitting, acts on consumer complaints received by mail and telephone in its Consumer Response Center ("CRC") and, more recently, on its Web site.(10) The CRC accepts complaints from all consumers, including those residing in European Union member states. The FTC Act provides the Federal Trade Commission equitable power to obtain injunctive relief against future violations of the FTC Act, as well as redress for injured consumers. We would, however, look to see whether the company has engaged in a pattern of improper conduct, as we do not resolve individual consumer disputes. In the past, the Federal Trade Commission has provided redress for citizens of both the United States and other countries.(11) The FTC will continue to assert its authority, in appropriate cases, to provide redress to citizens of other countries who have been injured by deceptive practices under its jurisdiction.

Employment Data

Your most recent letter sought additional clarification concerning the FTC's jurisdiction in the area of employment data. First, you pose the question whether the FTC could take action under Section 5 against a company that represents it complies with U.S. safe harbor principles but transfers or uses employment-related data in a manner that violates these principles. We want to assure you that we have carefully reviewed the FTC authorizing legislation, related documents, and relevant case law and have concluded that the FTC has the same jurisdiction in the employment-related data situation as it would generally under Section 5 of the FTC Act.(12) That is to say, assuming a case met our existing criteria (unfairness or deception) for a privacy-related enforcement action, we could take action in the employment-related data situation.

We also would like to dispel any view that the FTC's ability to take privacy-related enforcement action is limited to situations where a company has deceived individual consumers. In fact, as the Commission's recent action in the ReverseAuction(13) matter makes clear, the FTC will bring privacy-related enforcement actions in situations involving data transfers between companies, where one company allegedly has acted unlawfully vis a vis another company, leading to possible injury to both consumers and companies. We expect this situation is the one in which the employment issue is most likely to arise, as employment data about Europeans is transferred from European companies to American companies that have pledged to abide by the safe harbor principles.

We do wish to note one circumstance in which FTC action would be circumscribed, however. This would occur in situations in which the matter is already being addressed in a traditional labor law dispute resolution context, most likely a grievance/arbitration claim or an unfair labor practice complaint at the National Labor Relations Board. This would occur, for example, if an employer had made a commitment in a collective bargaining agreement regarding the use of personal data and an employee or union claimed that the employer had breached that agreement. The Commission would likely defer to that proceeding.(14)

Jurisdiction Over "Seal" Programs

Second, you ask whether the FTC would have jurisdiction over "seal" programs administering dispute resolution mechanisms in the United States that misrepresented their role in enforcing the "safe harbor" principles and handling individual complaints, even if such entities were technically "not for profit." In determining whether we have jurisdiction over an entity that holds itself out as a non-profit, the Commission closely analyzes whether the entity, while not seeking a profit for itself, furthers the profit of its members. The Commission has successfully asserted jurisdiction over such entities and as recently as May 24, 1999, the United States Supreme Court, in California Dental Association v. Federal Trade Commission, unanimously affirmed the Commission's jurisdiction over a voluntary nonprofit association of local dental societies in an antitrust matter. The Court held:

The FTC Act is at pains to include not only an entity "organized to carry on business for its own profit," 15 U. S. C. §44, but also one that carries on business for the profit "of its members." . . . . It could, indeed, hardly be supposed that Congress intended such a restricted notion of covered supporting organizations, with the opportunity this would bring with it for avoiding jurisdiction where the purposes of the FTC Act would obviously call for asserting it.

In sum, determining whether to assert jurisdiction over a particular "non-profit" entity administering a seal program would require a factual review of the extent to which the entity provided economic benefit to its for-profit members. If such an entity operated its seal program in a manner that provided an economic benefit to its members, the FTC likely would assert its jurisdiction. As a separate point, the FTC likely would have jurisdiction over a fraudulent seal program that misrepresents its status as a non-profit entity.

Privacy in the Offline World

Third, you note that our prior correspondence has focused on privacy in the online world. While online privacy has been a major concern of the FTC as a critical component to the development of electronic commerce, the FTC Act dates back to 1914 and applies equally in the offline world. Thus, we can pursue offline firms that engage in unfair or deceptive trade practices with regard to consumers' privacy.(15) In fact, in a case brought by the Commission last year, FTC v. TouchTone Information, Inc.,(16) an "information broker" was charged with illegally obtaining and selling consumers' private financial information. The Commission alleged that Touch Tone obtained consumers' information by "pretexting," a term of art coined by the private investigation industry to describe the practice of getting personal information about others under false pretenses, typically on the telephone. The case, filed April 21, 1999, in federal court in Colorado, seeks an injunction and all illegally gained profits.

This law enforcement experience, as well as recent concerns about the merging of offline and online databases, the blurring of distinctions between online and offline merchants, and the fact that a vast amount of personal identifying information is collected and used offline, make clear that significant attention to offline privacy issues is warranted.

Overlapping Jurisdiction

Finally, you pose the question of the interplay of the FTC's jurisdiction with that of other law enforcement agencies, particularly in cases where there is potentially overlapping jurisdiction. We have developed strong working relationships with numerous other law enforcement agencies, including the federal banking agencies and the state attorneys general. We very often coordinate investigations to maximize our resources in instances of overlapping jurisdiction. We also often refer matters to the appropriate federal or state agency for investigation.

I hope this review is helpful. Please let me know if you need any further information.

Sincerely,
Robert Pitofsky

1. 15 U.S.C. § 45. The Fair Credit Reporting Act would also apply to Internet data collection and sales that meet the statutory definitions of "consumer report" and "consumer reporting agency."

2. 15 U.S.C. § 45(n).

3. See GeoCities, Docket No. C-3849 (Final Order Feb. 12, 1999) (available at www.ftc.gov/os/1999/9902/9823015d%26o.htm); Liberty Financial Cos., Docket No. C-3891 (Final Order Aug. 12, 1999) (available at www.ftc.gov/opa/1999/9905/younginvestor.htm). See also Children's Online Privacy Protection Act Rule (COPPA), 16 C.F.R. Part 312 (available at www.ftc.gov/opa/1999/9910/childfinal.htm). The COPPA Rule, which became effective last month, requires operators of Web sites directed to children under 13, or who knowingly collect personal information from children under 13, to implement the fair information practice standards enunciated in the Rule.

4. See FTC v. Touch Tone, Inc., Civil Action No. 99-WM-783 (D.Co.) (filed April 21, 1999) at <www.ftc.gov/opa/1999/9904/touchtone.htm>. Staff Opinion Letter, July 17, 1997, issued in response to a petition filed by the Center for Media Education, at <www.ftc.gov/os/1997/9707/cenmed.htm>.

5. Indeed, the FTC recently filed a complaint in federal district court against a TRUSTe sealholder, Toysmart.com, seeking injunctive and declaratory relief to prevent the sale of confidential, personal customer information collected on the company Web site in violation of its own privacy policy. The FTC learned of this possible law violation directly from TRUSTe. FTC v. Toysmart.com, LLC, Civil Action No. 00-11341-RGS (D.Ma.) (filed July 11, 2000) (available at www.ftc.gov/opa/2000/07/toysmart.htm).

6. GeoCities, Docket No. C-3849 (Final Order Feb. 12, 1999) (available at www.ftc.gov/os/1999/9902/9823015d%26o.htm).

7. The Commission subsequently settled another matter involving the collection of personal information from children online. Liberty Financial Companies, Inc., operated the Young Investor website which was directed to children and teens, and focused on issues relating to money and investing. The Commission alleged that the site falsely represented that personal information collected from children in a survey would be maintained anonymously, and that participants would be sent an e-mail newsletter as well as prizes. In fact, the personal information about the child and the family's finances was maintained in an identifiable manner, and no newsletter or prizes were sent. The consent agreement prohibits such misrepresentations in the future and requires Liberty Financial to post a privacy notice on its children's sites and obtain verifiable parental consent before collecting personal identifying information from children. Liberty Financial Cos., Docket No. C-3891 (Final Order Aug. 12, 1999) (available at www.ftc.gov/opa/1999/9905/younginvestor.htm).

8. See ReverseAuction.com, Inc., Civil Action No. 000032 (D.D.C.) (filed January 6, 2000) (press release and pleadings at www.ftc.gov/opa/2000/01/reverse4.htm).

9. For this reason, the Federal Trade Commission stated in Congressional testimony that additional legislation probably would be required to mandate that all U.S. commercial Web sites directed toward consumers abide by specified fair information practices. "Consumer Privacy on the World Wide Web," Before the Subcommittee on Telecommunications, Trade and Consumer Protection of the House Committee on Commerce United States House of Representatives, July 21, 1998 (the testimony can be found at www.ftc.gov/os/9807/privac98.htm). The FTC deferred calling for such legislation in order to give self-regulatory efforts the opportunity to demonstrate widespread adoption of fair information practices on Web sites. In the Federal Trade Commission's report to Congress on online privacy, "Privacy Online: A Report to Congress," June 1998 (the report can be found at www.ftc.gov/reports/privacy3/toc.htm), the FTC recommended legislation to require that commercial Web sites obtain parental consent before collecting personally identifiable information from children under 13 years old. See footnote 3 supra. Last year, the FTC's report, "Self-Regulation and Privacy Online: A Federal Trade Commission Report to Congress," July 1999 (the report can be found at www.ftc.gov/os/1999/9907/index.htm#13,) found sufficient progress in self-regulation and, accordingly, chose not to recommend legislation at that time.

In May 2000, the Commission issued a third report to Congress, "Privacy Online: Fair Information Practices in the Electronic Marketplace," (the report can be found at www.ftc.gov/os/2000/05/index.htm#22) which discusses the FTC's recent survey of commercial Web sites and their compliance with fair information practices. The report also recommended (by a majority of the

Commission) that Congress enact legislation that would set forth a basic level of privacy protection for consumer-oriented commercial Web sites.

10. See https://www.ftc.gov/ftc/complaint.htm for the Federal Trade Commission's online complaint form.

11. For example, in a recent case involving an Internet pyramid scheme, the Commission obtained refunds for 15,622 consumers totaling approximately $5.5 million. The consumers resided in the United States and 70 foreign countries. See www.ftc.gov/opa/9807/fortunar.htm; www.ftc.gov/opa/9807/ftcrefund01.htm.

12. Except as specifically excluded by the FTC's authorizing statute, the FTC's jurisdiction under the FTC Act over practices "in or affecting commerce" is coextensive with the constitutional power of Congress under the Commerce Clause, United States v. American Building Maintenance Industries, 422 U.S. 271, 277 n. 6 (1975). The FTC's jurisdiction would thus encompass employment-related practices in firms and industries in international commerce.

13. See "Online Auction Site Settles FTC Privacy Charges," FTC News Release (Jan. 6, 2000), available at http://www.ftc.gov/opa/2000/01/reverse4.htm.

14. The determination whether conduct is an "unfair labor practice" or a violation of a collective bargaining agreement is a technical one that is ordinarily reserved to the expert labor tribunals who will hear the complaints, such as arbitrators and the NRLB.

15. As you know from earlier discussions, the Fair Credit Reporting Act also gives the FTC the authority to protect consumers' financial privacy within the purview of the Act and the Commission recently issued a decision pertaining to this issue. See In the Matter of Trans Union, Docket No. 9255 (March 1, 2000) (press release and opinion available at www.ftc.gov/os/2000/03/index.htm#1).

16. Civil Action 99-WM-783 (D.Colo.)(available at http://www.ftc.gov/opa/1999/9904/touchtone.htm) (tentative consent decree pending).

LETTER FROM COMMISSION SERVICES TRANSMITTING THE EUROPEAN COMMISSION'S ADEQUACY FINDING

EUROPEAN COMMISSION
Internal Market DG
Director-General

Brussels, 28.01.00 4074
DG Markt/E-1 D(2000)168

Mr. Robert LaRussa
Under Secretary for International Trade of
the United States Department of Commerce
Washington D.C. 20230
United States of America

Dear Mr. LaRussa,

Thank you for your letter of 17 July with which you enclosed the "Safe Harbor Privacy Principles" and the frequently asked questions and answers (the principles) issued by the

Department of Commerce on 21 July and related material concerning enforcement by public bodies in the United States. I am pleased to inform you that the Commission, exercising the powers conferred on it by Article 25.6 of the Data Protection Directive (95/46/EC), has found that these arrangements would provide adequate protection for the purposes of Article 25.1 of the Directive regarding the transfer of personal data to countries outside the European Union. I enclose a copy of the Commission decision C(2000) 2441 for your information. The Member States are required to comply with decisions of the Commission taken on the basis of Article 25.6.

The Commission decision

The decision provides that data controllers in the EU can transfer personal data processed in accordance with MS law, without providing additional safeguards to ensure their protection, to US-based organisations declaring their adherence to the "safe harbor" principles, provided that they are subject to the statutory powers of a public body empowered to investigate complaints and to obtain relief against unfair or deceptive practices or otherwise effectively ensure compliance with the principles. The effect of this decision is also that any requirements for the prior authorisation of transborder data transfers as provided for under Member State law will be waived, or that approval will be automatically and promptly granted, as regards such transfers to organisations qualifying for the safe harbor. The Directive and Member States' laws implementing it still of course govern the lawfulness of processing in the EU, and Article 25.6 decisions do not affect that in any way. This means that violations of Member State laws by data exporters can result in the blocking of data transfers, notwithstanding the existence of relevant Article 25.6 decisions.

List of Participating US-based Organisations

The Commission welcomes the fact that the Department of Commerce will provide for the maintenance of a list, to be made publicly available and kept up to date on a regular basis, of the US-based organisations which have declared their adherence to the "safe harbor" principles and which notify this to the Department of Commerce or the organisation the Department designates for this purpose. We note also that the Department of Commerce or its designee will make public any proper and final adverse determinations notified to it pertaining to non-compliance with the principles by a "safe harbor" organisation or to other events that might bring to an end an organisation's participation in the "safe harbor", such as a takeover or a merger. This will ensure transparency and clarity about which US-based organisations enjoy "safe harbor" benefits.

Date of entry into effect

Member States are required to ensure that the decision is effective 90 days after its notification to them. After this, US organisations self-certifying their adherence to the "safe harbor" will be assured of "safe harbor" benefits from the date that they notify the Department of Commerce (or its designee) and publicly announce that they have taken the measures necessary to comply with the principles. The Commission and the Member States recognise that US organisations will need some time to consider whether to participate in the "safe harbor" and, if so, to implement privacy policies to put the principles into effect. During the course of our discussions, Member States have demonstrated their willingness to use the flexibility offered by Article 26 of the Directive to avoid interruptions in data flows, so as not to call into question the good faith efforts being made to secure adequate protection for data transferred from the EU. The Commission and the Member States have confirmed their willingness to continue to use this flexibility during the implementation phase of the "safe harbor", so that US organisations have time to decide whether to participate in the "safe harbor" and (if necessary) to update their information processing policies and practices accordingly. If Member States become aware that action needs to be taken which will interrupt data flows to the United States, they will inform the Commission immediately, if possible before such action is taken, and the Department of Commerce will be informed. In this connection, I would draw your attention to the enclosed extract from the minutes of the Article 31 Committee. The situation will be reviewed in the middle of 2001.

In deciding whether to participate in the "safe harbor", organisations should consider that the "safe harbor" represents clear advantages over the existing situation, in terms of speedier transfers, lighter administrative burdens and greater legal certainty. These advantages will benefit the EU transferers of data as well as the US recipients. US organisations may of course join the "safe harbor" at any time, but we consider that the resulting benefits represent strong arguments for their entering the "safe harbor" as quickly as possible.

The proposed review of the implementation phase will take into account the particular needs of the financial services sector. The EU side shares the US goal of identifying a predictable framework for data transfers in and bringing the benefits of the "safe harbor" to the financial services sector, given its economic importance and the high volume of personal data flows in this sector. More time is however needed for further examination of recent developments in US laws governing privacy in the financial sector and of their interaction with the "safe harbor," and specifically for completion in the United States of the Financial Modernization Act regulations. On our side, we shall seek to maintain the momentum developed in the "safe harbor" discussions and, as indicated above, thanks to the flexibility allowed by the Directive itself we do not anticipate problems with interruptions in data flows while good faith efforts continue to address these issues.

Complaint Procedures

It can be expected that claims will arise from time to time that an organisation which has entered the "safe harbor" is not in fact complying with the "safe harbor" principles. As for all cases where complaints concern recipients falling within the scope of a decision taken on the basis of Article 25.6 of the Directive, it will be for the appropriate US bodies to determine whether such claims are founded and if so, to ensure that the organisation takes the measures necessary to come into compliance with the principles as quickly as possible, or is removed from the "safe harbor". Reliance on US enforcement arrangements to ensure a good general level of compliance with the principles is a fundamental aspect of the "adequacy" finding. As indicated by Article 2 of the decision, evidence that any enforcement body in the United States responsible for compliance with the principles is failing to secure compliance may trigger action by the Commission, in consultation with the Member States through the Article 31 Committee, and after informing the Department of Commerce, to reverse, suspend or limit the scope of the decision with respect to such enforcement body. Measures to suspend specific data transfers for reasons connected with compliance problems in the United States can be taken at the national level only in the circumstances and in the manner set out in Article 2, paragraph 1. Moreover, such measures can have only a temporary effect, pending a resolution of the problem by the appropriate enforcement bodies in the United States. These arrangements as a whole reflect our shared twin objectives of avoiding the interruption of transborder data flows and maintaining high data protection standards.

Jurisdiction

During our dialogue, you raised with me the concerns of US industry about the possible effects of the "safe harbor" as regards jurisdiction and applicable law in the European Union. I would like to confirm that it is the Commission's intention that participation in the "safe harbor" does not change the status quo ante for any organisation with respect to jurisdiction, applicable law or liability in the European Union. Moreover, our discussions with respect to the "safe harbor" have not resolved nor prejudged the questions of jurisdiction or applicable law with respect to websites. All existing rules, principles, conventions and treaties relating to international conflicts of law continue to apply and are not prejudiced in any way by the "safe harbor" arrangement.

Use of Contracts - Commission decisions based on Article 26 of the data protection Directive

I should also add that the establishment of the "safe harbor" does not affect the ability of Member States to authorise transfers on the basis of safeguards adduced by the data exporter in accordance with Article 26.2. This means organisations not wishing to qualify for the "safe harbor" could put in place the safeguards necessary for transfers of personal data from the EU to the United States by means of binding written agreements between the transferers and the recipients of data. The Commission may approve model clauses for such agreements under Article 26.4 of the Directive which are binding on the Member States. The Commission and the Member States are of the view that the "safe harbor" principles may be used in such agreements for the substantive provisions on data protection. Such agreements may need to include other provisions on issues such as liability and enforcement, on which decisions have not yet been taken. The Commission has initiated discussions with the Member States in the Article 31 Committee regarding these other provisions, with the aim of adopting a decision under Article 26.4 authorising model agreements which rely on the "safe harbor" principles for the provisions on data processing and other contractual provisions as necessary. Such a decision would mean that transfers covered by contracts in the approved form would be automatically authorised. The Commission is working with the Article 31 Committee to finalise such a decision as soon as possible.

Our dialogue has proved extremely useful in clarifying rules and practices on both sides, identifying much common ground and exchanging information on procedures. The continuation of this dialogue would seem desirable, on a periodic basis and/or when a particular problem makes it necessary. This will allow us to continue to exchange information on relevant developments concerning the implementation of Articles 25 and 26 and developments in the United States, in line with our general commitment to regulatory co-operation in the context of the TransAtlantic Economic Partnership. Thank you for the confirmation in your letter that you believe that privacy legislation should not discriminate on the basis of nationality and your assurance that you will work within the legislative process to avoid any such discrimination resulting from legislation proposed in Congress. We also welcome your offer to continue your efforts to keep us informed about legislative and other developments in the United States in the privacy field of which you may be aware. We shall of course do the same as regards EU legislation and developments in the privacy field. We have accepted the language in the introduction to the principles on explicit authorisations in US law permitting exceptions to be made to the principles in the expectation that these will in practice most frequently reflect a public interest concern and not fall outside the scope of exceptions allowed by the Directive. We would wish the matter to be taken up through the review arrangement in the event that this expectation proved to be incorrect or in the event that discriminatory privacy legislation were adopted in the United States.

As you know, the Commission and the Member States are committed to implementing and enforcing these provisions and any decisions based on them in an even-handed and non-discriminatory manner as between US organisations and those located in other third countries and in the EU and agree that we should monitor whether they have been implemented and enforced in this manner in our continuing dialogue (I enclose an extract from the minutes of the Article 31 Committee on this point, together with a text adopted by the working party established under Article 29 of the Directive.) It is also important to recall that the "safe harbor" reflects a number of features which may be unique to the US constitutional model and legal system and which were taken into account in the US context, but which are not necessarily present outside this context. We continue to prefer legally binding data protection rules, for which the Directive and the OECD guidelines must remain our principal benchmarks and any proposal to regard the "safe harbor" as providing adequate protection outside the US context would have to be examined by the Commission in the light of all the relevant circumstances.

The European Commission and the Member States have committed themselves to conducting an evaluation of the implementation of the decision in 2003 as indicated in Article 3 of the decision, and we hope that the US Government will participate in this review. In any event, the European Commission will inform the US Government before taking any action to modify the decision.

This letter is for your information only and of itself creates no legally binding effects.

(signed)

John F. Mogg

Extract from the minutes of the Article 31 Committee, 22 June 2000

All members of the Committee emphasised that there was no legal basis in the Directive (apart from Article 32 paragraph 2) for a delayed application of the rules or for differentiated treatment as regards a particular group of third country recipients, except in so far as the latter were covered by a decision under Article 25 paragraph 6. This being said, the Committee recalled the different ways in which data transfers were allowable under Article 26 even where protection in the third country in question was not generally adequate. These provisions had ensured that data flows had continued uninterrupted up to now and the Committee expected no change during the implementation phase of the "safe harbor". US organisations will thus have time to decide whether to participate in the "safe harbor" and (if necessary) to update their information processing policies and practices accordingly.

EUROPEAN COMMISSION'S DECISION C(2000) 2441 FINDING THE SAFE HARBOR TO PROVIDE ADEQUATE PROTECTIONS

COMMISSION OF THE EUROPEAN COMMUNITIES

COMMISSION DECISION Of pursuant to Directive 95/46/EC of the European Parliament and of the Council on the adequacy of the protection provided by the Safe Harbor Privacy Principles and related Frequently Asked Questions issued by the US Department of Commerce

(Text with EEA relevance)

THE COMMISSION OF THE EUROPEAN COMMUNITIES,

Having regard to the Treaty establishing the European Community,

Having regard to Directive 95/46/EC of the European Parliament and of the Council of 24 October 1995 on the protection of individuals with regard to the processing of personal data and on the free movement of such data(1), and in particular Article 25(6) thereof,

Whereas:

(1) Pursuant to Directive 95/46/EC Member States are required to provide that the transfer of personal data to a third country may take place only if the third country in question ensures an adequate level of protection and the Member State laws implementing other provisions of the Directive are respected prior to the transfer.

(2) The Commission may find that a third country ensures an adequate level of protection. In that case personal data may be transferred from the Member States without additional guarantees being necessary.

(3) Pursuant to Directive 95/46/EC the level of data protection should be assessed in the light of all the circumstances surrounding a data transfer operation or a set of data transfer operations and in respect of given conditions. The Working Party on Protection of Individuals with regard to the processing of Personal Data established under that Directive(2) has issued guidance on the making of such assessments(3).

(4) Given the different approaches to data protection in third countries, the adequacy assessment should be carried out and any decision based on Article 25(6) of Directive 95/46/EC should be enforced in a way that does not arbitrarily or unjustifiably discriminate against or between third countries where like conditions prevail nor constitute a disguised barrier to trade taking into account the Community's present international commitments.

(5) The adequate level of protection for the transfer of data from the Community to the United States recognised by this Decision, should be attained if organisations comply with the Safe Harbor Privacy Principles for the protection of personal data transferred from a Member State to the United States (hereinafter "the Principles") and the Frequently Asked Questions (hereinafter "the FAQs") providing guidance for the implementation of the Principles issued by the Government of the United States on 21.07.2000. Furthermore the organisations should publicly disclose their privacy policies and be subject to the jurisdiction of the Federal Trade Commission (FTC) under Section 5 of the Federal Trade Commission Act which prohibits unfair or deceptive acts or practices in or affecting commerce, or that of another statutory body that will effectively ensure compliance with the Principles implemented in accordance with the FAQs.

(6) Sectors and/or data processing not subject to the jurisdiction of any of the government bodies in the United States listed in Annex VII to this Decision should fall outside the scope of this Decision.

(7) To ensure the proper application of this Decision, it is necessary that organisations adhering to the Principles and the FAQs can be recognised by interested parties, such as data subjects, data exporters and data protection authorities. To this end the US Department of Commerce or its designee should undertake to maintain and make available to the public a list of organisations self-certifying their adherence to the Principles implemented in accordance with the FAQs and falling within the jurisdiction of at least one of the government bodies listed in Annex VII to this Decision.

(8) In the interests of transparency and in order to safeguard the ability of the competent authorities in the Member States to ensure the protection of individuals as regards the processing of their personal data, it is necessary to specify in this Decision the exceptional circumstances in which the suspension of specific data flows should be justified, notwithstanding the finding of adequate protection.

(9) The "safe harbor" created by the Principles and the FAQs, may need to be reviewed in the light of experience, of developments concerning the protection of privacy in circumstances in which technology is constantly making easier the transfer and processing of personal data and in the light of reports on implementation by enforcement authorities involved.

(10) The Working Party on Protection of Individuals with regard to the processing of Personal Data established under Article 29 of Directive 95/46/EC has delivered Opinions on the level of protection provided by the "safe harbor" Principles in the United States which have been taken into account in the preparation of the present Decision(4).

(11) The measures provided for in this Decision are in accordance with the opinion of the Committee established under Article 31 of Directive 95/46/EC,

HAS ADOPTED THIS DECISION:

Article 1

1. For the purposes of Article 25(2) of Directive 95/46/EC, for all the activities falling within the scope of that Directive, the "Safe Harbor Privacy Principles" (hereinafter "the Principles"), as set out in Annex I to this Decision, implemented in accordance with the guidance provided by the Frequently Asked Questions (hereinafter "the FAQs") issued by the US Department of Commerce on 21.07.2000 as set out in Annex II to this Decision are considered to ensure an adequate level of protection for personal data transferred from the Community to organisations established in the United States, having regard to the following documents issued by the US Department of Commerce:

(a) the safe harbor enforcement overview set out in Annex III,

(b) a memorandum on damages for breaches of privacy and explicit authorisations in US law set out in Annex IV,

(c) a letter from the Federal Trade Commission set out in Annex V,

(d) a letter from the US Department of Transportation set out in Annex VI.

2. In relation to each transfer of data the following conditions shall be met:

(a) the organisation receiving the data has unambiguously and publicly disclosed its commitment to comply with the Principles implemented in accordance with the FAQs, and

(b) the organisation is subject to the statutory powers of a government body in the United States listed in Annex VII to this Decision which is empowered to investigate complaints and to obtain relief against unfair or deceptive practices as well as redress for individuals, irrespective of their country of residence or nationality, in case of non-compliance with the Principles implemented in accordance with the FAQs.

3. The conditions set out in paragraph 2 are considered to be met for each organisation that self-certifies its adherence to the Principles implemented in accordance with the FAQs from the date on which the organisation notifies to the US Department of Commerce (or its designee) the public disclosure of the commitment referred to in paragraph 2(a) and the identity of the government body referred to in paragraph 2(b).

Article 2

This Decision concerns only the adequacy of protection provided in the United States under the Principles implemented in accordance with the FAQs with a view to meeting the requirements of Article 25(1) of Directive 95/46/EC and does not affect the application of other provisions of that Directive that pertain to the processing of personal data within the Member States, in particular Article 4 thereof.

Article 3

1. Without prejudice to their powers to take action to ensure compliance with national provisions adopted pursuant to provisions other than Article 25 of Directive 95/46/EC, the competent authorities in Member States may exercise their existing powers to suspend data flows to an organisation that has self-certified its adherence to the Principles implemented in accordance with the FAQs in order to protect individuals with regard to the processing of their personal data in cases where:

(a) the government body in the United States referred to in Annex VII to this Decision or an independent recourse mechanism within the meaning of letter a) of the Enforcement Principle set out in Annex I to this Decision has determined that the organisation is violating the Principles implemented in accordance with the FAQs; or

(b) there is a substantial likelihood that the Principles are being violated,

there is a reasonable basis for believing that the enforcement mechanism concerned is not taking or will not take adequate and timely steps to settle the case at issue,

the continuing transfer would create an imminent risk of grave harm to data subjects, and

the competent authorities in the Member State have made reasonable efforts under the circumstances to provide the organisation with notice and an opportunity to respond.

The suspension shall cease as soon as compliance with the Principles implemented in accordance with the FAQs is assured and the competent authorities concerned in the Community are notified thereof.

2. Member States shall inform the Commission without delay when measures are adopted on the basis of paragraph 1.

3. The Member States and the Commission shall also inform each other of cases where the action of bodies responsible for ensuring compliance with the Principles implemented in accordance with the FAQs in the United States fails to secure such compliance.

4. If the information collected under paragraphs 1, 2 and 3 provides evidence that any body responsible for ensuring compliance with the Principles implemented in accordance with the FAQs in the United States is not effectively fulfilling its role, the Commission shall inform the US Department of Commerce and, if necessary, present draft measures in accordance with the procedure referred to in Article 31 of Directive 95/46/EC with a view to reversing or suspending the present Decision or limiting its scope.

Article 4

1. This Decision may be adapted at any time in the light of experience with its implementation and/or if the level of protection provided by the Principles and the FAQs is overtaken by the requirements of US legislation.

The Commission shall in any case evaluate the implementation of the present Decision on the basis of available information three years after its notification to the Member States and report any pertinent findings to the Committee established under Article 31 of Directive 95/46/EC, including any evidence that could affect the evaluation that the provisions set out in Article 1 of this

Decision provide adequate protection within the meaning of Article 25 of Directive 95/46/EC and any evidence that the present Decision is being implemented in a discriminatory way.

2. The Commission shall, if necessary, present draft measures in accordance with the procedure referred to in Article 31 of Directive 95/46/EC.

Article 5

Member States shall take all the measures necessary to comply with this Decision at the latest at the end of a period of ninety days from the date of its notification to the Member States.

Article 6

This Decision is addressed to the Member States.

Done at Brussels, For the Commission

Member of the Commission

ANNEX VII

With reference to Article 1(2)(b), the government bodies in the United States empowered to investigate complaints and to obtain relief against unfair or deceptive practices as well as redress for individuals, irrespective of their country of residence or nationality, in case of non-compliance with the Principles implemented in accordance with the FAQs are:

1. The Federal Trade Commission, and

2. The US Department of Transportation.

The Federal Trade Commission acts on the basis of its authority under Section 5 of the Federal Trade Commission Act. The jurisdiction of the Federal Trade Commission under Section 5 is excluded with respect to: banks, saving and loans and credit unions; telecommunications and interstate transportation common carriers, air carriers and packers and stockyard operators. Although the insurance industry is not specifically included in the list of exceptions in Section 5, the McCarran-Ferguson Act(5) leaves the regulation of the business of insurance to the individual states. However, the provisions of the FTC Act apply to the insurance industry to the extent that such business is not regulated by State law. The FTC retains residual authority over unfair or deceptive practices by insurance companies when they are not engaged in the business of insurance.

The US Department of Transportation acts on the basis of its authority under Title 49 United States Code Section 41712. The US Department of Transportation institutes cases based on its own investigations as well as formal and informal complaints received from individuals, travel agents, airlines, US and foreign government agencies.

1 OJ L 281, 23.11.1995, p. 31.

2The web address of the Working Party is: http://www.europa.eu.int/comm/internal_market/en/media/dataprot/wpdocs/index.htm

3 WP12: Transfers of personal data to third countries: Applying Articles 25 and 26 of the EU data protection directive, adopted by the Working Party on 24 July 1998.

4 WP 15: Opinion 1/99 concerning the level of data protection in the United States and the ongoing discussions between the European Commission and the United States.

WP 19: Opinion 2/99 on the Adequacy of the "International Safe Harbor Principles" issued by the US Department of Commerce on 19 April 1999.

WP 21: Opinion 4/99 on the Frequently Asked Questions to be issued by the US Department of Commerce in relation to the proposed "Safe Harbor Principles" on the Adequacy of the "International Safe Harbor Principles".

WP 23: Working document on the current state of play of the ongoing discussions between the European Commission and the United States Government concerning the "International Safe Harbor Principles".

WP 27: Opinion 7/99 on the Level of Data Protection provided by the "Safe Harbor" Principles as published together with the Frequently Asked Questions (FAQs) and other related documents on 15 and 16 November 1999 by the US Department of Commerce.

WP 31: Opinion 3/2000 on the EU/US dialogue concerning the "Safe Harbor" arrangement.

WP 32: Opinion 4/2000 on the level of protection provided by the "Safe Harbor Principles".

515 U.S.C. § 1011 et seq.

The Personal Information Protection and Electronic Documents Act (2000)

Statutes of Canada 2000, chapter 5

Statutes in Context

The Personal Information Protection and Electronic Documents Act (PIPEDA) governs all entities that collect personal information on Canadians. It extends to all "personal information" used in connection with any personal information. PIPEDA requires that the individual grant consent before the collection, use, or disclosure of personal data. The EU Commission found in December 2001 that PIPEDA provided an "adequate" level of privacy protection.

[Assented to April 13th, 2000]

An Act to support and promote electronic commerce by protecting personal information that is collected, used or disclosed in certain circumstances, by providing for the use of electronic means to communicate or record information or transactions and by amending the Canada Evidence Act, the Statutory Instruments Act and the Statute Revision Act

Her Majesty, by and with the advice and consent of the Senate and House of Commons of Canada, enacts as follows:

Short title

1. This Act may be cited as the Personal Information Protection and Electronic Documents Act.

PART 1 **- PROTECTION OF PERSONAL INFORMATION IN THE PRIVATE SECTOR**

Interpretation

Definitions

2. (1) The definitions in this subsection apply in this Part.

"alternative format", with respect to personal information, means a format that allows a person with a sensory disability to read or listen to the personal information.

"commercial activity" means any particular transaction, act or conduct or any regular course of conduct that is of a commercial character, including the selling, bartering or leasing of donor, membership or other fundraising lists.

"Commissioner" means the Privacy Commissioner appointed under section 53 of the Privacy Act.

"Court" means the Federal Court.

"federal work, undertaking or business" means any work, undertaking or business that is within the legislative authority of Parliament. It includes

(a) a work, undertaking or business that is operated or carried on for or in connection with navigation and shipping, whether inland or maritime, including the operation of ships and transportation by ship anywhere in Canada;

(b) a railway, canal, telegraph or other work or undertaking that connects a province with another province, or that extends beyond the limits of a province;

(c) a line of ships that connects a province with another province, or that extends beyond the limits of a province;

(d) a ferry between a province and another province or between a province and a country other than Canada;

(e) aerodromes, aircraft or a line of air transportation;

(f) a radio broadcasting station;

(g) a bank;

(h) a work that, although wholly situated within a province, is before or after its execution declared by Parliament to be for the general advantage of Canada or for the advantage of two or more provinces;

(i) a work, undertaking or business outside the exclusive legislative authority of the legislatures of the provinces; and

(j) a work, undertaking or business to which federal laws, within the meaning of section 2 of the Oceans Act, apply under section 20 of that Act and any regulations made under paragraph 26(1)(k) of that Act.

"organization" includes an association, a partnership, a person and a trade union.

"personal health information", with respect to an individual, whether living or deceased, means

(a) information concerning the physical or mental health of the individual;

(b) information concerning any health service provided to the individual;

(c) information concerning the donation by the individual of any body part or any bodily substance of the individual or information derived from the testing or examination of a body part or bodily substance of the individual;

(d) information that is collected in the course of providing health services to the individual; or

(e) information that is collected incidentally to the provision of health services to the individual.

"personal information" means information about an identifiable individual, but does not include the name, title or business address or telephone number of an employee of an organization.

"record" includes any correspondence, memorandum, book, plan, map, drawing, diagram, pictorial or graphic work, photograph, film, microform, sound recording, videotape, machine-readable record and any other documentary material, regardless of physical form or characteristics, and any copy of any of those things.

Notes in Schedule 1

(2) In this Part, a reference to clause 4.3 or 4.9 of Schedule 1 does not include a reference to the note that accompanies that clause.

2000, c. 5, s. 2; 2002, c. 8, s. 183.

Purpose

3. The purpose of this Part is to establish, in an era in which technology increasingly facilitates the circulation and exchange of information, rules to govern the collection, use and disclosure of personal information in a manner that recognizes the right of privacy of individuals with respect to their personal information and the need of organizations to collect, use or disclose personal information for purposes that a reasonable person would consider appropriate in the circumstances.
Application

Application

4. (1) This Part applies to every organization in respect of personal information that

(a) the organization collects, uses or discloses in the course of commercial activities; or

(b) is about an employee of the organization and that the organization collects, uses or discloses in connection with the operation of a federal work, undertaking or business.

Limit

(2) This Part does not apply to

(a) any government institution to which the Privacy Act applies;

(b) any individual in respect of personal information that the individual collects, uses or discloses for personal or domestic purposes and does not collect, use or disclose for any other purpose; or

(c) any organization in respect of personal information that the organization collects, uses or discloses for journalistic, artistic or literary purposes and does not collect, use or disclose for any other purpose.

Other Acts

***(3)** Every provision of this Part applies despite any provision, enacted after this subsection comes into force, of any other Act of Parliament, unless the other Act expressly declares that that provision operates despite the provision of this Part.

* [Note: Subsection 4(3) in force January 1, 2001, see SI/2000-29.]

Certificate under Canada Evidence Act

4.1 (1) Where a certificate under section 38.13 of the Canada Evidence Act prohibiting the disclosure of personal information of a specific individual is issued before a complaint is filed by that individual under this Part in respect of a request for access to that information, the provisions of this Part respecting that individual's right of access to his or her personal information do not apply to the information that is subject to the certificate.

Certificate following filing of complaint

(2) Notwithstanding any other provision of this Part, where a certificate under section 38.13 of the Canada Evidence Act prohibiting the disclosure of personal information of a specific individual is issued after the filing of a complaint under this Part in relation to a request for access to that information:

(a) all proceedings under this Part in respect of that information, including an investigation, audit, appeal or judicial review, are discontinued;

(b) the Commissioner shall not disclose the information and shall take all necessary precautions to prevent its disclosure; and

(c) the Commissioner shall, within 10 days after the certificate is published in the Canada Gazette, return the information to the organization that provided the information.

Information not to be disclosed

(3) The Commissioner and every person acting on behalf or under the direction of the Commissioner, in carrying out their functions under this Part, shall not disclose information subject to a certificate issued under section 38.13 of the Canada Evidence Act, and shall take every reasonable precaution to avoid the disclosure of that information.

Power to delegate

(4) The Commissioner may not delegate the investigation of any complaint relating to information subject to a certificate issued under section 38.13 of the Canada Evidence Act except to one of a maximum of four officers or employees of the Commissioner specifically designated by the Commissioner for the purpose of conducting that investigation.

2001, c. 41, s. 103.

DIVISION 1 **- PROTECTION OF PERSONAL INFORMATION**

Compliance with obligations

5. (1) Subject to sections 6 to 9, every organization shall comply with the obligations set out in Schedule 1.

Meaning of "should"

(2) The word "should", when used in Schedule 1, indicates a recommendation and does not impose an obligation.

Appropriate purposes

(3) An organization may collect, use or disclose personal information only for purposes that a reasonable person would consider are appropriate in the circumstances.

Effect of designation of individual

6. The designation of an individual under clause 4.1 of Schedule 1 does not relieve the organization of the obligation to comply with the obligations set out in that Schedule.

Collection without knowledge or consent

7. (1) For the purpose of clause 4.3 of Schedule 1, and despite the note that accompanies that clause, an organization may collect personal information without the knowledge or consent of the individual only if

(a) the collection is clearly in the interests of the individual and consent cannot be obtained in a timely way;

(b) it is reasonable to expect that the collection with the knowledge or consent of the individual would compromise the availability or the accuracy of the information and the collection is reasonable for purposes related to investigating a breach of an agreement or a contravention of the laws of Canada or a province;

(c) the collection is solely for journalistic, artistic or literary purposes;

(d) the information is publicly available and is specified by the regulations; or

(e) the collection is made for the purpose of making a disclosure

(i) under subparagraph (3)(c.1)(i) or (d)(ii), or

(ii) that is required by law.

Use without knowledge or consent

(2) For the purpose of clause 4.3 of Schedule 1, and despite the note that accompanies that clause, an organization may, without the knowledge or consent of the individual, use personal information only if

(a) in the course of its activities, the organization becomes aware of information that it has reasonable grounds to believe could be useful in the investigation of a contravention of the laws of Canada, a province or a foreign jurisdiction that has been, is being or is about to be committed, and the information is used for the purpose of investigating that contravention;

(b) it is used for the purpose of acting in respect of an emergency that threatens the life, health or security of an individual;

(c) it is used for statistical, or scholarly study or research, purposes that cannot be achieved without using the information, the information is used in a manner that will ensure its confidentiality, it is impracticable to obtain consent and the organization informs the Commissioner of the use before the information is used;

(c.1) it is publicly available and is specified by the regulations; or

(d) it was collected under paragraph (1)(a), (b) or (e).

Disclosure without knowledge or consent

(3) For the purpose of clause 4.3 of Schedule 1, and despite the note that accompanies that clause, an organization may disclose personal information without the knowledge or consent of the individual only if the disclosure is

(a) made to, in the Province of Quebec, an advocate or notary or, in any other province, a barrister or solicitor who is representing the organization;

(b) for the purpose of collecting a debt owed by the individual to the organization;

(c) required to comply with a subpoena or warrant issued or an order made by a court, person or body with jurisdiction to compel the production of information, or to comply with rules of court relating to the production of records;

(c.1) made to a government institution or part of a government institution that has made a request for the information, identified its lawful authority to obtain the information and indicated that

(i) it suspects that the information relates to national security, the defence of Canada or the conduct of international affairs,

(ii) the disclosure is requested for the purpose of enforcing any law of Canada, a province or a foreign jurisdiction, carrying out an investigation relating to the enforcement of any such law or gathering intelligence for the purpose of enforcing any such law, or

(iii) the disclosure is requested for the purpose of administering any law of Canada or a province;

(c.2) made to the government institution mentioned in section 7 of the Proceeds of Crime (Money Laundering) and Terrorist Financing Act as required by that section;

*__(c.2)__ made to the government institution mentioned in section 7 of the Proceeds of Crime (Money Laundering) Act as required by that section;

(d) made on the initiative of the organization to an investigative body, a government institution or a part of a government institution and the organization

(i) has reasonable grounds to believe that the information relates to a breach of an agreement or a contravention of the laws of Canada, a province or a foreign jurisdiction that has been, is being or is about to be committed, or

(ii) suspects that the information relates to national security, the defence of Canada or the conduct of international affairs;

(e) made to a person who needs the information because of an emergency that threatens the life, health or security of an individual and, if the individual whom the information is about is alive, the organization informs that individual in writing without delay of the disclosure;

(f) for statistical, or scholarly study or research, purposes that cannot be achieved without disclosing the information, it is impracticable to obtain consent and the organization informs the Commissioner of the disclosure before the information is disclosed;

(g) made to an institution whose functions include the conservation of records of historic or archival importance, and the disclosure is made for the purpose of such conservation;

(h) made after the earlier of

(i) one hundred years after the record containing the information was created, and

(ii) twenty years after the death of the individual whom the information is about;

(h.1) of information that is publicly available and is specified by the regulations;

(h.2) made by an investigative body and the disclosure is reasonable for purposes related to investigating a breach of an agreement or a contravention of the laws of Canada or a province; or

(i) required by law.

Use without consent

(4) Despite clause 4.5 of Schedule 1, an organization may use personal information for purposes other than those for which it was collected in any of the circumstances set out in subsection (2).

Disclosure without consent

(5) Despite clause 4.5 of Schedule 1, an organization may disclose personal information for purposes other than those for which it was collected in any of the circumstances set out in paragraphs (3)(a) to (h.2).

2000, c. 5, s. 7, c. 17, s. 97; 2001, c. 41, s. 81; 2004, c. 15, s. 98.

* [Note: Paragraph 7(3)(c.2), as enacted by paragraph 97(1)(a) of chapter 17 of the Statutes of Canada, 2000, will be repealed at a later date.]

Written request

8. (1) A request under clause 4.9 of Schedule 1 must be made in writing.

Assistance

(2) An organization shall assist any individual who informs the organization that they need assistance in preparing a request to the organization.

Time limit

(3) An organization shall respond to a request with due diligence and in any case not later than thirty days after receipt of the request.

Extension of time limit

(4) An organization may extend the time limit

(a) for a maximum of thirty days if

(i) meeting the time limit would unreasonably interfere with the activities of the organization, or

(ii) the time required to undertake any consultations necessary to respond to the request would make the time limit impracticable to meet; or

(b) for the period that is necessary in order to be able to convert the personal information into an alternative format.

In either case, the organization shall, no later than thirty days after the date of the request, send a notice of extension to the individual, advising them of the new time limit, the reasons for extending the time limit and of their right to make a complaint to the Commissioner in respect of the extension.

Deemed refusal

(5) If the organization fails to respond within the time limit, the organization is deemed to have refused the request.

Costs for responding

(6) An organization may respond to an individual's request at a cost to the individual only if

(a) the organization has informed the individual of the approximate cost; and

(b) the individual has advised the organization that the request is not being withdrawn.

Reasons

(7) An organization that responds within the time limit and refuses a request shall inform the individual in writing of the refusal, setting out the reasons and any recourse that they may have under this Part.

Retention of information

(8) Despite clause 4.5 of Schedule 1, an organization that has personal information that is the subject of a request shall retain the information for as long as is necessary to allow the individual to exhaust any recourse under this Part that they may have.

When access prohibited

9. (1) Despite clause 4.9 of Schedule 1, an organization shall not give an individual access to personal information if doing so would likely reveal personal information about a third party. However, if the information about the third party is severable from the record containing the information about the individual, the organization shall sever the information about the third party before giving the individual access.

Limit

(2) Subsection (1) does not apply if the third party consents to the access or the individual needs the information because an individual's life, health or security is threatened.

Information related to paragraphs 7(3)(c), (c.1) or (d)

(2.1) An organization shall comply with subsection (2.2) if an individual requests that the organization

(a) inform the individual about

(i) any disclosure of information to a government institution or a part of a government institution under paragraph 7(3)(c), subparagraph 7(3)(c.1)(i) or (ii) or paragraph 7(3)(c.2) or (d), or

(ii) the existence of any information that the organization has relating to a disclosure referred to in subparagraph (i), to a subpoena, warrant or order referred to in paragraph 7(3)(c) or to a request made by a government institution or a part of a government institution under subparagraph 7(3)(c.1)(i) or (ii); or

(b) give the individual access to the information referred to in subparagraph (a)(ii).

Notification and response

(2.2) An organization to which subsection (2.1) applies

(a) shall, in writing and without delay, notify the institution or part concerned of the request made by the individual; and

(b) shall not respond to the request before the earlier of

(i) the day on which it is notified under subsection (2.3), and

(ii) thirty days after the day on which the institution or part was notified.

Objection

(2.3) Within thirty days after the day on which it is notified under subsection (2.2), the institution or part shall notify the organization whether or not the institution or part objects to the organization complying with the request. The institution or part may object only if the institution or part is of the opinion that compliance with the request could reasonably be expected to be injurious to

(a) national security, the defence of Canada or the conduct of international affairs;

(a.1) the detection, prevention or deterrence of money laundering or the financing of terrorist activities; or

***(a.1)** the detection, prevention or deterrence of money laundering; or

(b) the enforcement of any law of Canada, a province or a foreign jurisdiction, an investigation relating to the enforcement of any such law or the gathering of intelligence for the purpose of enforcing any such law.

Prohibition

(2.4) Despite clause 4.9 of Schedule 1, if an organization is notified under subsection (2.3) that the institution or part objects to the organization complying with the request, the organization

(a) shall refuse the request to the extent that it relates to paragraph (2.1)(a) or to information referred to in subparagraph (2.1)(a)(ii);

(b) shall notify the Commissioner, in writing and without delay, of the refusal; and

(c) shall not disclose to the individual

(i) any information that the organization has relating to a disclosure to a government institution or a part of a government institution under paragraph 7(3)(c), subparagraph 7(3)(c.1)(i) or (ii) or paragraph 7(3)(c.2) or (d) or to a request made by a government institution under either of those subparagraphs,

(ii) that the organization notified an institution or part under paragraph (2.2)(a) or the Commissioner under paragraph (b), or

(iii) that the institution or part objects.

When access may be refused

(3) Despite the note that accompanies clause 4.9 of Schedule 1, an organization is not required to give access to personal information only if

(a) the information is protected by solicitor-client privilege;

(b) to do so would reveal confidential commercial information;

(c) to do so could reasonably be expected to threaten the life or security of another individual;

(c.1) the information was collected under paragraph 7(1)(b);

(d) the information was generated in the course of a formal dispute resolution process; or

(e) the information was created for the purpose of making a disclosure under the Public Servants Disclosure Protection Act or in the course of an investigation into a disclosure under that Act.

However, in the circumstances described in paragraph (b) or (c), if giving access to the information would reveal confidential commercial information or could reasonably be expected to threaten the life or security of another individual, as the case may be, and that information is severable from the record containing any other information for which access is requested, the organization shall give the individual access after severing.

Limit

(4) Subsection (3) does not apply if the individual needs the information because an individual's life, health or security is threatened.

Notice

(5) If an organization decides not to give access to personal information in the circumstances set out in paragraph (3)(c.1), the organization shall, in writing, so notify the Commissioner, and shall include in the notification any information that the Commissioner may specify.

2000, c. 5, s. 9, c. 17, s. 97; 2001, c. 41, s. 82; 2005, c. 46, s. 57; 2006, c. 9, s. 223.

* [Note: Paragraph 9(2.3)(a.1), as enacted by paragraph 97(1)(c) of chapter 17 of the Statutes of Canada, 2000, will be repealed at a later date.]

Sensory disability

10. An organization shall give access to personal information in an alternative format to an individual with a sensory disability who has a right of access to personal information under this Part and who requests that it be transmitted in the alternative format if

(a) a version of the information already exists in that format; or

(b) its conversion into that format is reasonable and necessary in order for the individual to be able to exercise rights under this Part.

***DIVISION 2* – REMEDIES**
Filing of Complaints

Contravention

11. (1) An individual may file with the Commissioner a written complaint against an organization for contravening a provision of Division 1 or for not following a recommendation set out in Schedule 1.

Commissioner may initiate complaint

(2) If the Commissioner is satisfied that there are reasonable grounds to investigate a matter under this Part, the Commissioner may initiate a complaint in respect of the matter.

Time limit

(3) A complaint that results from the refusal to grant a request under section 8 must be filed within six months, or any longer period that the Commissioner allows, after the refusal or after the expiry of the time limit for responding to the request, as the case may be.

Notice

(4) The Commissioner shall give notice of a complaint to the organization against which the complaint was made.

Investigations of Complaints

Powers of Commissioner

12. (1) The Commissioner shall conduct an investigation in respect of a complaint and, for that purpose, may

(a) summon and enforce the appearance of persons before the Commissioner and compel them to give oral or written evidence on oath and to produce any records and things that the Commissioner considers necessary to investigate the complaint, in the same manner and to the same extent as a superior court of record;

(b) administer oaths;

(c) receive and accept any evidence and other information, whether on oath, by affidavit or otherwise, that the Commissioner sees fit, whether or not it is or would be admissible in a court of law;

(d) at any reasonable time, enter any premises, other than a dwelling-house, occupied by an organization on satisfying any security requirements of the organization relating to the premises;

(e) converse in private with any person in any premises entered under paragraph (d) and otherwise carry out in those premises any inquiries that the Commissioner sees fit; and

(f) examine or obtain copies of or extracts from records found in any premises entered under paragraph (d) that contain any matter relevant to the investigation.

Dispute resolution mechanisms

(2) The Commissioner may attempt to resolve complaints by means of dispute resolution mechanisms such as mediation and conciliation.

Delegation

(3) The Commissioner may delegate any of the powers set out in subsection (1) or (2).

Return of records

(4) The Commissioner or the delegate shall return to a person or an organization any record or thing that they produced under this section within ten days after they make a request to the Commissioner or the delegate, but nothing precludes the Commissioner or the delegate from again requiring that the record or thing be produced.

Certificate of delegation

(5) Any person to whom powers set out in subsection (1) are delegated shall be given a certificate of the delegation and the delegate shall produce the certificate, on request, to the person in charge of any premises to be entered under paragraph (1)(d).

Commissioner's Report

Contents

13. (1) The Commissioner shall, within one year after the day on which a complaint is filed or is initiated by the Commissioner, prepare a report that contains

(a) the Commissioner's findings and recommendations;

(b) any settlement that was reached by the parties;

(c) if appropriate, a request that the organization give the Commissioner, within a specified time, notice of any action taken or proposed to be taken to implement the recommendations contained in the report or reasons why no such action has been or is proposed to be taken; and

(d) the recourse, if any, that is available under section 14.

Where no report

(2) The Commissioner is not required to prepare a report if the Commissioner is satisfied that

(a) the complainant ought first to exhaust grievance or review procedures otherwise reasonably available;

(b) the complaint could more appropriately be dealt with, initially or completely, by means of a procedure provided for under the laws of Canada, other than this Part, or the laws of a province;

(c) the length of time that has elapsed between the date when the subject-matter of the complaint arose and the date when the complaint was filed is such that a report would not serve a useful purpose; or

(d) the complaint is trivial, frivolous or vexatious or is made in bad faith.

If a report is not to be prepared, the Commissioner shall inform the complainant and the organization and give reasons.

Report to parties

(3) The report shall be sent to the complainant and the organization without delay.

Hearing by Court

Application

14. (1) A complainant may, after receiving the Commissioner's report, apply to the Court for a hearing in respect of any matter in respect of which the complaint was made, or that is referred to in the Commissioner's report, and that is referred to in clause 4.1.3, 4.2, 4.3.3, 4.4, 4.6, 4.7 or 4.8 of Schedule 1, in clause 4.3, 4.5 or 4.9 of that Schedule as modified or clarified by Division 1, in subsection 5(3) or 8(6) or (7) or in section 10.

Time of application

(2) The application must be made within forty-five days after the report is sent or within any further time that the Court may, either before or after the expiry of those forty-five days, allow.

For greater certainty

(3) For greater certainty, subsections (1) and (2) apply in the same manner to complaints referred to in subsection 11(2) as to complaints referred to in subsection 11(1).

Commissioner may apply or appear

15. The Commissioner may, in respect of a complaint that the Commissioner did not initiate,

(a) apply to the Court, within the time limited by section 14, for a hearing in respect of any matter described in that section, if the Commissioner has the consent of the complainant;

(b) appear before the Court on behalf of any complainant who has applied for a hearing under section 14; or

(c) with leave of the Court, appear as a party to any hearing applied for under section 14.

Remedies

16. The Court may, in addition to any other remedies it may give,

(a) order an organization to correct its practices in order to comply with sections 5 to 10;

(b) order an organization to publish a notice of any action taken or proposed to be taken to correct its practices, whether or not ordered to correct them under paragraph (a); and

(c) award damages to the complainant, including damages for any humiliation that the complainant has suffered.

Summary hearings

17. (1) An application made under section 14 or 15 shall be heard and determined without delay and in a summary way unless the Court considers it inappropriate to do so.

Precautions

(2) In any proceedings arising from an application made under section 14 or 15, the Court shall take every reasonable precaution, including, when appropriate, receiving representations ex parte and conducting hearings in camera, to avoid the disclosure by the Court or any person of any information or other material that the organization would be authorized to refuse to disclose if it were requested under clause 4.9 of Schedule 1.

***DIVISION 3* – AUDITS**

To ensure compliance

18. (1) The Commissioner may, on reasonable notice and at any reasonable time, audit the personal information management practices of an organization if the Commissioner has reasonable grounds to believe that the organization is contravening a provision of Division 1 or is not following a recommendation set out in Schedule 1, and for that purpose may

(a) summon and enforce the appearance of persons before the Commissioner and compel them to give oral or written evidence on oath and to produce any records and things that the Commissioner considers necessary for the audit, in the same manner and to the same extent as a superior court of record;

(b) administer oaths;

(c) receive and accept any evidence and other information, whether on oath, by affidavit or otherwise, that the Commissioner sees fit, whether or not it is or would be admissible in a court of law;

(d) at any reasonable time, enter any premises, other than a dwelling-house, occupied by the organization on satisfying any security requirements of the organization relating to the premises;

(e) converse in private with any person in any premises entered under paragraph (d) and otherwise carry out in those premises any inquiries that the Commissioner sees fit; and

(f) examine or obtain copies of or extracts from records found in any premises entered under paragraph (d) that contain any matter relevant to the audit.

Delegation

(2) The Commissioner may delegate any of the powers set out in subsection (1).

Return of records

(3) The Commissioner or the delegate shall return to a person or an organization any record or thing they produced under this section within ten days after they make a request to the Commissioner or the delegate, but nothing precludes the Commissioner or the delegate from again requiring that the record or thing be produced.

Certificate of delegation

(4) Any person to whom powers set out in subsection (1) are delegated shall be given a certificate of the delegation and the delegate shall produce the certificate, on request, to the person in charge of any premises to be entered under paragraph (1)(d).

Report of findings and recommendations

19. (1) After an audit, the Commissioner shall provide the audited organization with a report that contains the findings of the audit and any recommendations that the Commissioner considers appropriate.

Reports may be included in annual reports

(2) The report may be included in a report made under section 25.

***DIVISION 4* – GENERAL**

Confidentiality

20. (1) Subject to subsections (2) to (5), 13(3) and 19(1), the Commissioner or any person acting on behalf or under the direction of the Commissioner shall not disclose any information that comes to their knowledge as a result of the performance or exercise of any of the Commissioner's duties or powers under this Part.

Public interest

(2) The Commissioner may make public any information relating to the personal information management practices of an organization if the Commissioner considers that it is in the public interest to do so.

Disclosure of necessary information

(3) The Commissioner may disclose, or may authorize any person acting on behalf or under the direction of the Commissioner to disclose, information that in the Commissioner's opinion is necessary to

(a) conduct an investigation or audit under this Part; or

(b) establish the grounds for findings and recommendations contained in any report under this Part.

Disclosure in the course of proceedings

(4) The Commissioner may disclose, or may authorize any person acting on behalf or under the direction of the Commissioner to disclose, information in the course of

(a) a prosecution for an offence under section 28;

(b) a prosecution for an offence under section 132 of the Criminal Code (perjury) in respect of a statement made under this Part;

(c) a hearing before the Court under this Part; or

(d) an appeal from a decision of the Court.

Disclosure of offence authorized

(5) The Commissioner may disclose to the Attorney General of Canada or of a province, as the case may be, information relating to the commission of an offence against any law of Canada or a province on the part of an officer or employee of an organization if, in the Commissioner's opinion, there is evidence of an offence.

Not competent witness

21. The Commissioner or person acting on behalf or under the direction of the Commissioner is not a competent witness in respect of any matter that comes to their knowledge as a result of the performance or exercise of any of the Commissioner's duties or powers under this Part in any proceeding other than

(a) a prosecution for an offence under section 28;

(b) a prosecution for an offence under section 132 of the Criminal Code (perjury) in respect of a statement made under this Part;

(c) a hearing before the Court under this Part; or

(d) an appeal from a decision of the Court.

Protection of Commissioner

22. (1) No criminal or civil proceedings lie against the Commissioner, or against any person acting on behalf or under the direction of the Commissioner, for anything done, reported or said in good faith as a result of the performance or exercise or purported performance or exercise of any duty or power of the Commissioner under this Part.

Libel or slander

(2) For the purposes of any law relating to libel or slander,

(a) anything said, any information supplied or any record or thing produced in good faith in the course of an investigation or audit carried out by or on behalf of the Commissioner under this Part is privileged; and

(b) any report made in good faith by the Commissioner under this Part and any fair and accurate account of the report made in good faith for the purpose of news reporting is privileged.

Consultations with provinces

23. (1) If the Commissioner considers it appropriate to do so, or on the request of an interested person, the Commissioner may, in order to ensure that personal information is protected in as consistent a manner as possible, consult with any person who, under provincial legislation that is substantially similar to this Part, has powers and duties similar to those of the Commissioner.

Agreements

(2) The Commissioner may enter into agreements with any person with whom the Commissioner may consult under subsection (1)

(a) to coordinate the activities of their offices and the office of the Commissioner, including to provide for mechanisms for the handling of any complaint in which they are mutually interested;

(b) to undertake and publish research related to the protection of personal information; and

(c) to develop model contracts for the protection of personal information that is collected, used or disclosed interprovincially or internationally.

Promoting the purposes of the Part

24. The Commissioner shall

(a) develop and conduct information programs to foster public understanding, and recognition of the purposes, of this Part;

(b) undertake and publish research that is related to the protection of personal information, including any such research that is requested by the Minister of Industry;

(c) encourage organizations to develop detailed policies and practices, including organizational codes of practice, to comply with sections 5 to 10; and

(d) promote, by any means that the Commissioner considers appropriate, the purposes of this Part.

Annual report

25. (1) The Commissioner shall, as soon as practicable after the end of each calendar year, submit to Parliament a report concerning the application of this Part, the extent to which the provinces have enacted legislation that is substantially similar to this Part and the application of any such legislation.

Consultation

(2) Before preparing the report, the Commissioner shall consult with those persons in the provinces who, in the Commissioner's opinion, are in a position to assist the Commissioner in reporting respecting personal information that is collected, used or disclosed interprovincially or internationally.

Regulations

26. (1) The Governor in Council may make regulations

(a) specifying, by name or by class, what is a government institution or part of a government institution for the purposes of any provision of this Part;

(a.01) specifying, by name or by class, what is an investigative body for the purposes of paragraph 7(3)(d) or (h.2);

(a.1) specifying information or classes of information for the purpose of paragraph 7(1)(d), (2)(c.1) or (3)(h.1); and

(b) for carrying out the purposes and provisions of this Part.

Orders

(2) The Governor in Council may, by order,

(a) provide that this Part is binding on any agent of Her Majesty in right of Canada to which the Privacy Act does not apply; and

(b) if satisfied that legislation of a province that is substantially similar to this Part applies to an organization, a class of organizations, an activity or a class of activities, exempt the organization, activity or class from the application of this Part in respect of the collection, use or disclosure of personal information that occurs within that province.

Whistleblowing

27. (1) Any person who has reasonable grounds to believe that a person has contravened or intends to contravene a provision of Division 1, may notify the Commissioner of the particulars of the matter and may request that their identity be kept confidential with respect to the notification.

Confidentiality

(2) The Commissioner shall keep confidential the identity of a person who has notified the Commissioner under subsection (1) and to whom an assurance of confidentiality has been provided by the Commissioner.

Prohibition

27.1 (1) No employer shall dismiss, suspend, demote, discipline, harass or otherwise disadvantage an employee, or deny an employee a benefit of employment, by reason that

(a) the employee, acting in good faith and on the basis of reasonable belief, has disclosed to the Commissioner that the employer or any other person has contravened or intends to contravene a provision of Division 1;

(b) the employee, acting in good faith and on the basis of reasonable belief, has refused or stated an intention of refusing to do anything that is a contravention of a provision of Division 1;

(c) the employee, acting in good faith and on the basis of reasonable belief, has done or stated an intention of doing anything that is required to be done in order that a provision of Division 1 not be contravened; or

(d) the employer believes that the employee will do anything referred to in paragraph (a), (b) or (c).

Saving

(2) Nothing in this section impairs any right of an employee either at law or under an employment contract or collective agreement.

Definitions

(3) In this section, "employee" includes an independent contractor and "employer" has a corresponding meaning.

Offence and punishment

28. Every person who knowingly contravenes subsection 8(8) or 27.1(1) or who obstructs the Commissioner or the Commissioner's delegate in the investigation of a complaint or in conducting an audit is guilty of

(a) an offence punishable on summary conviction and liable to a fine not exceeding $10,000; or

(b) an indictable offence and liable to a fine not exceeding $100,000.

Review of Part by parliamentary committee

***29. (1)** The administration of this Part shall, every five years after this Part comes into force, be reviewed by the committee of the House of Commons, or of both Houses of Parliament, that may be designated or established by Parliament for that purpose.

Review and report

(2) The committee shall undertake a review of the provisions and operation of this Part and shall, within a year after the review is undertaken or within any further period that the House of Commons may authorize, submit a report to Parliament that includes a statement of any changes to this Part or its administration that the committee recommends.

* [Note: Part 1 in force January 1, 2001, see SI/2000-29.]

***DIVISION 5* – TRANSITIONAL PROVISIONS**

Application

30. (1) This Part does not apply to any organization in respect of personal information that it collects, uses or discloses within a province whose legislature has the power to regulate the collection, use or disclosure of the information, unless the organization does it in connection with the operation of a federal work, undertaking or business or the organization discloses the information outside the province for consideration.

Application

(1.1) This Part does not apply to any organization in respect of personal health information that it collects, uses or discloses.

Expiry date

> ***(2)** Subsection (1) ceases to have effect three years after the day on which this section comes into force.

Expiry date

> ***(2.1)** Subsection (1.1) ceases to have effect one year after the day on which this section comes into force.

* [Note: Section 30 in force January 1, 2001, see SI/2000-29.]

* [Note: Section 30 in force January 1, 2001, see SI/2000-29.]

PART 2 – **ELECTRONIC DOCUMENTS**

Interpretation

Definitions

31. (1) The definitions in this subsection apply in this Part.

"data" means representations of information or concepts, in any form.

"electronic document" means data that is recorded or stored on any medium in or by a computer system or other similar device and that can be read or perceived by a person or a computer system or other similar device. It includes a display, printout or other output of that data.

"electronic signature" means a signature that consists of one or more letters, characters, numbers or other symbols in digital form incorporated in, attached to or associated with an electronic document.

"federal law" means an Act of Parliament or an instrument, regardless of its name, issued, made or established under an Act of Parliament or a prerogative of the Crown, other than an instrument issued, made or established under the Yukon Act, the Northwest Territories Act or the Nunavut Act.

"responsible authority", in respect of a provision of a federal law, means

> **(a)** if the federal law is an Act of Parliament, the minister responsible for that provision;
>
> **(b)** if the federal law is an instrument issued, made or established under an Act of Parliament or a prerogative of the Crown, the person or body who issued, made or established the instrument; or
>
> **(c)** despite paragraph (a) or (b), the person or body designated by the Governor in Council under subsection (2).

"secure electronic signature" means an electronic signature that results from the application of a technology or process prescribed by regulations made under subsection 48(1).

Designation

(2) The Governor in Council may, by order, for the purposes of this Part, designate any person, including any member of the Queen's Privy Council for Canada, or body to be the responsible authority in respect of a provision of a federal law if the Governor in Council is of the opinion that it is appropriate to do so in the circumstances.

Purpose

32. The purpose of this Part is to provide for the use of electronic alternatives in the manner provided for in this Part where federal laws contemplate the use of paper to record or communicate information or transactions.

Electronic Alternatives

Collection, storage, etc.

33. A minister of the Crown and any department, branch, office, board, agency, commission, corporation or body for the administration of affairs of which a minister of the Crown is accountable to the Parliament of Canada may use electronic means to create, collect, receive, store, transfer, distribute, publish or otherwise deal with documents or information whenever a federal law does not specify the manner of doing so.

Electronic payment

34. A payment that is required to be made to the Government of Canada may be made in electronic form in any manner specified by the Receiver General.

Electronic version of statutory form

35. (1) If a provision of an Act of Parliament establishes a form, the responsible authority in respect of that provision may make regulations respecting an electronic form that is substantially the same as the form established in the provision, and the electronic form may be used for the same purposes as the form established in the provision.

Statutory manner of filing documents

(2) If a non-electronic manner of filing a document is set out in a provision of an Act of Parliament, the responsible authority in respect of that provision may make regulations respecting the filing of an electronic version of the document, and an electronic version of the document filed in accordance with those regulations is to be considered as a document filed in accordance with the provision.

Statutory manner of submitting information

(3) If a non-electronic manner of submitting information is set out in a provision of an Act of Parliament, the responsible authority in respect of that provision may make regulations respecting the manner of submitting the information using electronic means, and information submitted in accordance with those regulations is to be considered as information submitted in accordance with the provision.

Authority to prescribe form, etc.

(4) The authority under a federal law to issue, prescribe or in any other manner establish a form, or to establish the manner of filing a document or submitting information, includes the authority to issue, prescribe or establish an electronic form, or to establish an electronic manner of filing the document or submitting information, as the case may be.

Meaning of "filing"

(5) In this section, "filing" includes all manner of submitting, regardless of how it is designated.

Documents as evidence or proof

36. A provision of a federal law that provides that a certificate or other document signed by a minister or public officer is proof of any matter or thing, or is admissible in evidence, is, subject to the federal law, satisfied by an electronic version of the certificate or other document if the electronic version is signed by the minister or public officer with that person's secure electronic signature.

Retention of documents

37. A requirement under a provision of a federal law to retain a document for a specified period is satisfied, with respect to an electronic document, by the retention of the electronic document if

(a) the electronic document is retained for the specified period in the format in which it was made, sent or received, or in a format that does not change the information contained in the electronic document that was originally made, sent or received;

(b) the information in the electronic document will be readable or perceivable by any person who is entitled to have access to the electronic document or who is authorized to require the production of the electronic document; and

(c) if the electronic document was sent or received, any information that identifies the origin and destination of the electronic document and the date and time when it was sent or received is also retained.

Notarial act

38. A reference in a provision of a federal law to a document recognized as a notarial act in the province of Quebec is deemed to include an electronic version of the document if

(a) the electronic version of the document is recognized as a notarial act under the laws of the province of Quebec; and

(b) the federal law or the provision is listed in Schedule 2 or 3.

Seals

39. A requirement under a provision of a federal law for a person's seal is satisfied by a secure electronic signature that identifies the secure electronic signature as the person's seal if the federal law or the provision is listed in Schedule 2 or 3.

Requirements to provide documents or information

40. A provision of a federal law requiring a person to provide another person with a document or information, other than a provision referred to in any of sections 41 to 47, is satisfied by the provision of the document or information in electronic form if

(a) the federal law or the provision is listed in Schedule 2 or 3;

(b) both persons have agreed to the document or information being provided in electronic form; and

(c) the document or information in electronic form will be under the control of the person to whom it is provided and will be readable or perceivable so as to be usable for subsequent reference.

Writing requirements

41. A requirement under a provision of a federal law for a document to be in writing is satisfied by an electronic document if

(a) the federal law or the provision is listed in Schedule 2 or 3; and

(b) the regulations respecting the application of this section to the provision have been complied with.

Original documents

42. A requirement under a provision of a federal law for a document to be in its original form is satisfied by an electronic document if

(a) the federal law or the provision is listed in Schedule 2 or 3;

(b) the electronic document contains a secure electronic signature that was added when the electronic document was first generated in its final form and that can be used to verify that the electronic document has not been changed since that time; and

(c) the regulations respecting the application of this section to the provision have been complied with.

Signatures

43. Subject to sections 44 to 46, a requirement under a provision of a federal law for a signature is satisfied by an electronic signature if

(a) the federal law or the provision is listed in Schedule 2 or 3; and

(b) the regulations respecting the application of this section to the provision have been complied with.

Statements made under oath

44. A statement required to be made under oath or solemn affirmation under a provision of a federal law may be made in electronic form if

(a) the person who makes the statement signs it with that person's secure electronic signature;

(b) the person before whom the statement was made, and who is authorized to take statements under oath or solemn affirmation, signs it with that person's secure electronic signature;

(c) the federal law or the provision is listed in Schedule 2 or 3; and

(d) the regulations respecting the application of this section to the provision have been complied with.

Statements declaring truth, etc.

45. A statement required to be made under a provision of a federal law declaring or certifying that any information given by a person making the statement is true, accurate or complete may be made in electronic form if

(a) the person signs it with that person's secure electronic signature;

(b) the federal law or the provision is listed in Schedule 2 or 3; and

(c) the regulations respecting the application of this section to the provision have been complied with.

Witnessed signatures

46. A requirement under a provision of a federal law for a signature to be witnessed is satisfied with respect to an electronic document if

(a) each signatory and each witness signs the electronic document with their secure electronic signature;

(b) the federal law or the provision is listed in Schedule 2 or 3; and

(c) the regulations respecting the application of this section to the provision have been complied with.

Copies

47. A requirement under a provision of a federal law for one or more copies of a document to be submitted is satisfied by the submission of an electronic document if

(a) the federal law or the provision is listed in Schedule 2 or 3; and

(b) the regulations respecting the application of this section to the provision have been complied with.

Regulations and Orders

Regulations

48. (1) Subject to subsection (2), the Governor in Council may, on the recommendation of the Treasury Board, make regulations prescribing technologies or processes for the purpose of the definition "secure electronic signature" in subsection 31(1).

Characteristics

(2) The Governor in Council may prescribe a technology or process only if the Governor in Council is satisfied that it can be proved that

(a) the electronic signature resulting from the use by a person of the technology or process is unique to the person;

(b) the use of the technology or process by a person to incorporate, attach or associate the person's electronic signature to an electronic document is under the sole control of the person;

(c) the technology or process can be used to identify the person using the technology or process; and

(d) the electronic signature can be linked with an electronic document in such a way that it can be used to determine whether the electronic document has been changed since the electronic signature was incorporated in, attached to or associated with the electronic document.

Effect of amendment or repeal

(3) An amendment to or repeal of any provision of a regulation made under subsection (1) that has the effect of removing a prescribed technology or process from the regulation does not, by itself, affect the validity of any electronic signature resulting from the use of that technology or process while it was prescribed.

Amendment of schedules

49. For the purposes of sections 38 to 47, the responsible authority in respect of a provision of a federal law may, by order, amend Schedule 2 or 3 by adding or striking out a reference to that federal law or provision.

Regulations

50. (1) For the purposes of sections 41 to 47, the responsible authority in respect of a provision of a federal law may make regulations respecting the application of those sections to the provision.

Contents

(2) Without restricting the generality of subsection (1), the regulations that may be made may include rules respecting any of the following:

(a) the technology or process that must be used to make or send an electronic document;

(b) the format of an electronic document;

(c) the place where an electronic document is to be made or sent;

(d) the time and circumstances when an electronic document is to be considered to be sent or received and the place where it is considered to have been sent or received;

(e) the technology or process to be used to make or verify an electronic signature and the manner in which it is to be used; and

(f) any matter necessary for the purposes of the application of sections 41 to 47.

Minimum rules

(3) Without restricting the generality of subsection (1), if a provision referred to in any of sections 41 to 47 requires a person to provide another person with a document or information, the rules set out in the regulations respecting the application of that section to the provision may be that

(a) both persons have agreed to the document or information being provided in electronic form; and

(b) the document or information in electronic form will be under the control of the person to whom it is provided and will be readable or perceivable so as to be usable for subsequent reference.

Incorporation by reference

(4) Regulations may incorporate by reference the standards or specifications of any government, person or organization, either as they read at a fixed time or as they are amended from time to time.

Effect of striking out listed provision

51. The striking out of a reference to a federal law or provision in Schedule 2 or 3 does not affect the validity of anything done in compliance with any regulation made under section 50 that relates to that federal law or provision while it was listed in that Schedule.

PART 3 **– AMENDMENTS TO THE CANADA EVIDENCE ACT**

52. to 57. [Amendments]

PART 4 **– AMENDMENTS TO THE STATUTORY INSTRUMENTS ACT**

58. and 59. [Amendments]

PART 5 **– AMENDMENTS TO THE STATUTE REVISION ACT**

60. to 71. [Amendments]

PART 6 – COMING INTO FORCE

Coming into force

***72.** Parts 1 to 5 or any provision of those Parts come into force on a day or days to be fixed by order of the Governor in Council made on the recommendation of

> **(a)** in the case of Parts 1 and 2 or any provision of those Parts, the Minister of Industry; and
>
> **(b)** in the case of Parts 3 to 5 or any provision of those Parts, the Minister of Justice.

* [Note: Parts 2, 3 and 4 in force May 1, 2000; Part 1 in force January 1, 2001, see SI/2000-29; Part 5 in force June 1, 2009, see SI/2009-42.]

SCHEDULE 1

(Section 5)

PRINCIPLES SET OUT IN THE NATIONAL STANDARD OF CANADA ENTITLED MODEL CODE FOR THE PROTECTION OF PERSONAL INFORMATION, CAN/CSA-Q830-96

4.1 Principle 1 — Accountability

An organization is responsible for personal information under its control and shall designate an individual or individuals who are accountable for the organization's compliance with the following principles.

4.1.1

Accountability for the organization's compliance with the principles rests with the designated individual(s), even though other individuals within the organization may be responsible for the day-to-day collection and processing of personal information. In addition, other individuals within the organization may be delegated to act on behalf of the designated individual(s).

4.1.2

The identity of the individual(s) designated by the organization to oversee the organization's compliance with the principles shall be made known upon request.

4.1.3

An organization is responsible for personal information in its possession or custody, including information that has been transferred to a third party for processing. The organization shall use contractual or other means to provide a comparable level of protection while the information is being processed by a third party.

4.1.4

Organizations shall implement policies and practices to give effect to the principles, including

> **(a)** implementing procedures to protect personal information;

(b) establishing procedures to receive and respond to complaints and inquiries;

(c) training staff and communicating to staff information about the organization's policies and practices; and

(d) developing information to explain the organization's policies and procedures.

4.2 Principle 2 — Identifying Purposes

The purposes for which personal information is collected shall be identified by the organization at or before the time the information is collected.

4.2.1

The organization shall document the purposes for which personal information is collected in order to comply with the Openness principle (Clause 4.8) and the Individual Access principle (Clause 4.9).

4.2.2

Identifying the purposes for which personal information is collected at or before the time of collection allows organizations to determine the information they need to collect to fulfil these purposes. The Limiting Collection principle (Clause 4.4) requires an organization to collect only that information necessary for the purposes that have been identified.

4.2.3

The identified purposes should be specified at or before the time of collection to the individual from whom the personal information is collected. Depending upon the way in which the information is collected, this can be done orally or in writing. An application form, for example, may give notice of the purposes.

4.2.4

When personal information that has been collected is to be used for a purpose not previously identified, the new purpose shall be identified prior to use. Unless the new purpose is required by law, the consent of the individual is required before information can be used for that purpose. For an elaboration on consent, please refer to the Consent principle (Clause 4.3).

4.2.5

Persons collecting personal information should be able to explain to individuals the purposes for which the information is being collected.

4.2.6

This principle is linked closely to the Limiting Collection principle (Clause 4.4) and the Limiting Use, Disclosure, and Retention principle (Clause 4.5).

4.3 Principle 3 — Consent

The knowledge and consent of the individual are required for the collection, use, or disclosure of personal information, except where inappropriate.

Note: In certain circumstances personal information can be collected, used, or disclosed without the knowledge and consent of the individual. For example, legal, medical, or security reasons may make it impossible or impractical to seek consent. When information is being collected for the detection and prevention of fraud or for law enforcement, seeking the consent of the individual might defeat the purpose of collecting the information. Seeking consent may be impossible or inappropriate when the individual is a minor, seriously ill, or mentally incapacitated. In addition, organizations that do not have a direct relationship with the individual may not always be able to seek consent. For example, seeking consent may be impractical for a charity or a direct-marketing firm that wishes to acquire a mailing list from another organization. In such cases, the organization providing the list would be expected to obtain consent before disclosing personal information.

4.3.1

Consent is required for the collection of personal information and the subsequent use or disclosure of this information. Typically, an organization will seek consent for the use or disclosure of the information at the time of collection. In certain circumstances, consent with respect to use or disclosure may be sought after the information has been collected but before use (for example, when an organization wants to use information for a purpose not previously identified).

4.3.2

The principle requires "knowledge and consent". Organizations shall make a reasonable effort to ensure that the individual is advised of the purposes for which the information will be used. To make the consent meaningful, the purposes must be stated in such a manner that the individual can reasonably understand how the information will be used or disclosed.

4.3.3

An organization shall not, as a condition of the supply of a product or service, require an individual to consent to the collection, use, or disclosure of information beyond that required to fulfil the explicitly specified, and legitimate purposes.

4.3.4

The form of the consent sought by the organization may vary, depending upon the circumstances and the type of information. In determining the form of consent to use, organizations shall take into account the sensitivity of the information. Although some information (for example, medical records and income records) is almost always considered to be sensitive, any information can be sensitive, depending on the context. For example, the names and addresses of subscribers to a newsmagazine would generally not be considered sensitive information. However, the names and addresses of subscribers to some special-interest magazines might be considered sensitive.

4.3.5

In obtaining consent, the reasonable expectations of the individual are also relevant. For example, an individual buying a subscription to a magazine should reasonably expect that the organization, in addition to using the individual's name and address for mailing and billing purposes, would also contact the person to solicit the renewal of the subscription. In this case, the organization can assume that the individual's request constitutes consent for specific purposes. On the other hand, an individual would not reasonably expect that personal information given to a health-care professional would be given to a company selling health-care products, unless consent were obtained. Consent shall not be obtained through deception.

4.3.6

The way in which an organization seeks consent may vary, depending on the circumstances and the type of information collected. An organization should generally seek express consent when the information is likely to be considered sensitive. Implied consent would generally be appropriate when the information is less sensitive. Consent can also be given by an authorized representative (such as a legal guardian or a person having power of attorney).

4.3.7

Individuals can give consent in many ways. For example:

> **(a)** an application form may be used to seek consent, collect information, and inform the individual of the use that will be made of the information. By completing and signing the form, the individual is giving consent to the collection and the specified uses;
>
> **(b)** a checkoff box may be used to allow individuals to request that their names and addresses not be given to other organizations. Individuals who do not check the box are assumed to consent to the transfer of this information to third parties;
>
> **(c)** consent may be given orally when information is collected over the telephone; or
>
> **(d)** consent may be given at the time that individuals use a product or service.

4.3.8

An individual may withdraw consent at any time, subject to legal or contractual restrictions and reasonable notice. The organization shall inform the individual of the implications of such withdrawal.

4.4 Principle 4 — Limiting Collection

The collection of personal information shall be limited to that which is necessary for the purposes identified by the organization. Information shall be collected by fair and lawful means.

4.4.1

Organizations shall not collect personal information indiscriminately. Both the amount and the type of information collected shall be limited to that which is necessary to fulfil the purposes identified. Organizations shall specify the type of information collected as part of their information-handling policies and practices, in accordance with the Openness principle (Clause 4.8).

4.4.2

The requirement that personal information be collected by fair and lawful means is intended to prevent organizations from collecting information by misleading or deceiving individuals about the purpose for which information is being collected. This requirement implies that consent with respect to collection must not be obtained through deception.

4.4.3

This principle is linked closely to the Identifying Purposes principle (Clause 4.2) and the Consent principle (Clause 4.3).

4.5 Principle 5 — Limiting Use, Disclosure, and Retention

Personal information shall not be used or disclosed for purposes other than those for which it was collected, except with the consent of the individual or as required by law. Personal information shall be retained only as long as necessary for the fulfilment of those purposes.

4.5.1

Organizations using personal information for a new purpose shall document this purpose (see Clause 4.2.1).

4.5.2

Organizations should develop guidelines and implement procedures with respect to the retention of personal information. These guidelines should include minimum and maximum retention periods. Personal information that has been used to make a decision about an individual shall be retained long enough to allow the individual access to the information after the decision has been made. An organization may be subject to legislative requirements with respect to retention periods.

4.5.3

Personal information that is no longer required to fulfil the identified purposes should be destroyed, erased, or made anonymous. Organizations shall develop guidelines and implement procedures to govern the destruction of personal information.

4.5.4

This principle is closely linked to the Consent principle (Clause 4.3), the Identifying Purposes principle (Clause 4.2), and the Individual Access principle (Clause 4.9).

4.6 Principle 6 — Accuracy

Personal information shall be as accurate, complete, and up-to-date as is necessary for the purposes for which it is to be used.

4.6.1

The extent to which personal information shall be accurate, complete, and up-to-date will depend upon the use of the information, taking into account the interests of the individual. Information shall be sufficiently accurate, complete, and up-to-date to minimize the possibility that inappropriate information may be used to make a decision about the individual.

4.6.2

An organization shall not routinely update personal information, unless such a process is necessary to fulfil the purposes for which the information was collected.

4.6.3

Personal information that is used on an ongoing basis, including information that is disclosed to third parties, should generally be accurate and up-to-date, unless limits to the requirement for accuracy are clearly set out.

4.7 Principle 7 — Safeguards

Personal information shall be protected by security safeguards appropriate to the sensitivity of the information.

4.7.1

The security safeguards shall protect personal information against loss or theft, as well as unauthorized access, disclosure, copying, use, or modification. Organizations shall protect personal information regardless of the format in which it is held.

4.7.2

The nature of the safeguards will vary depending on the sensitivity of the information that has been collected, the amount, distribution, and format of the information, and the method of storage. More sensitive information should be safeguarded by a higher level of protection. The concept of sensitivity is discussed in Clause 4.3.4.

4.7.3

The methods of protection should include

(a) physical measures, for example, locked filing cabinets and restricted access to offices;

(b) organizational measures, for example, security clearances and limiting access on a "need-to-know" basis; and

(c) technological measures, for example, the use of passwords and encryption.

4.7.4

Organizations shall make their employees aware of the importance of maintaining the confidentiality of personal information.

4.7.5

Care shall be used in the disposal or destruction of personal information, to prevent unauthorized parties from gaining access to the information (see Clause 4.5.3).

4.8 Principle 8 — Openness

An organization shall make readily available to individuals specific information about its policies and practices relating to the management of personal information.

4.8.1

Organizations shall be open about their policies and practices with respect to the management of personal information. Individuals shall be able to acquire information about an organization's policies and practices without unreasonable effort. This information shall be made available in a form that is generally understandable.

4.8.2

The information made available shall include

> **(a)** the name or title, and the address, of the person who is accountable for the organization's policies and practices and to whom complaints or inquiries can be forwarded;
>
> **(b)** the means of gaining access to personal information held by the organization;
>
> **(c)** a description of the type of personal information held by the organization, including a general account of its use;
>
> **(d)** a copy of any brochures or other information that explain the organization's policies, standards, or codes; and
>
> **(e)** what personal information is made available to related organizations (e.g., subsidiaries).

4.8.3

An organization may make information on its policies and practices available in a variety of ways. The method chosen depends on the nature of its business and other considerations. For example, an organization may choose to make brochures available in its place of business, mail information to its customers, provide online access, or establish a toll-free telephone number.

4.9 Principle 9 — Individual Access

Upon request, an individual shall be informed of the existence, use, and disclosure of his or her personal information and shall be given access to that information. An individual shall be able to challenge the accuracy and completeness of the information and have it amended as appropriate.

Note: In certain situations, an organization may not be able to provide access to all the personal information it holds about an individual. Exceptions to the access requirement should be limited and specific. The reasons for denying access should be provided to the individual upon request. Exceptions may include information that is prohibitively costly to provide, information that contains references to other individuals, information that cannot be disclosed for legal, security, or commercial proprietary reasons, and information that is subject to solicitor-client or litigation privilege.

4.9.1

Upon request, an organization shall inform an individual whether or not the organization holds personal information about the individual. Organizations are encouraged to indicate the source of this information. The organization shall allow the individual access to this information. However, the organization may choose to make sensitive medical information available through a medical practitioner. In addition, the organization shall provide an account of the use that has been made or is being made of this information and an account of the third parties to which it has been disclosed.

4.9.2

An individual may be required to provide sufficient information to permit an organization to provide an account of the existence, use, and disclosure of personal information. The information provided shall only be used for this purpose.

4.9.3

In providing an account of third parties to which it has disclosed personal information about an individual, an organization should attempt to be as specific as possible. When it is not possible to provide a list of the organizations to which it has actually disclosed information about an individual, the organization shall provide a list of organizations to which it may have disclosed information about the individual.

4.9.4

An organization shall respond to an individual's request within a reasonable time and at minimal or no cost to the individual. The requested information shall be provided or made available in a form that is generally understandable. For example, if the organization uses abbreviations or codes to record information, an explanation shall be provided.

4.9.5

When an individual successfully demonstrates the inaccuracy or incompleteness of personal information, the organization shall amend the information as required. Depending upon the nature of the information challenged, amendment involves the correction, deletion, or addition of information. Where appropriate, the amended information shall be transmitted to third parties having access to the information in question.

4.9.6

When a challenge is not resolved to the satisfaction of the individual, the substance of the unresolved challenge shall be recorded by the organization. When appropriate, the existence of the unresolved challenge shall be transmitted to third parties having access to the information in question.

4.10 Principle 10 — Challenging Compliance

An individual shall be able to address a challenge concerning compliance with the above principles to the designated individual or individuals accountable for the organization's compliance.

4.10.1

The individual accountable for an organization's compliance is discussed in Clause 4.1.1.

4.10.2

Organizations shall put procedures in place to receive and respond to complaints or inquiries about their policies and practices relating to the handling of personal information. The complaint procedures should be easily accessible and simple to use.

4.10.3

Organizations shall inform individuals who make inquiries or lodge complaints of the existence of relevant complaint procedures. A range of these procedures may exist. For example, some regulatory bodies accept complaints about the personal-information handling practices of the companies they regulate.

4.10.4

An organization shall investigate all complaints. If a complaint is found to be justified, the organization shall take appropriate measures, including, if necessary, amending its policies and practices.

SCHEDULE 2

(Sections 38 to 47, 49 and 51)

Directive on Privacy and Electronic Communications (2002)

Directive 2002/58/EC of the European Parliament and of the Council of July 12, 2002

Directives in Context

Directive 2002/58/EC of the European Parliament and of the Council of July 12, 2002 concerns the processing of personal data and the protection of privacy in the electronic communications sector.

THE EUROPEAN PARLIAMENT AND THE COUNCIL OF THE EUROPEAN UNION,

Having regard to the Treaty establishing the European Community, and in particular Article 95 thereof,

Having regard to the proposal from the Commission,

Having regard to the opinion of the Economic and Social Committee,

Having consulted the Committee of the Regions, Acting in accordance with the procedure laid down in Article 251 of the Treaty,

Whereas:

(1) Directive 95/46/EC of the European Parliament and of the Council of 24 October 1995 on the protection of individuals with regard to the processing of personal data and on the free movement of such data requires Member States to ensure the rights and freedoms of natural persons with regard to the processing of personal data, and in particular their right to privacy, in order to ensure the free flow of personal data in the Community.

(2) This Directive seeks to respect the fundamental rights and observes the principles recognised in particular by the Charter of fundamental rights of the European Union. In particular, this Directive seeks to ensure full respect for the rights set out in Articles 7 and 8 of that Charter.

(3) Confidentiality of communications is guaranteed in accordance with the international instruments relating to human rights, in particular the European Convention for the Protection of Human Rights and Fundamental Freedoms, and the constitutions of the Member States.

(4) Directive 97/66/EC of the European Parliament and of the Council of 15 December 1997 concerning the processing of personal data and the protection of privacy in the telecommunications sector translated the principles set out in Directive 95/46/EC into specific rules for the telecommunications sector. Directive 97/66/EC has to be adapted to developments in the markets and technologies for electronic communications services in order to provide an equal level of protection of personal data and privacy for users of publicly available electronic communications services, regardless of the technologies used. That Directive should therefore be repealed and replaced by this Directive.

(5) New advanced digital technologies are currently being introduced in public communications networks in the Community, which give rise to specific requirements concerning the protection of personal data and privacy of the user. The development of the information society is characterised by the introduction of new electronic communications services. Access to digital mobile networks has become available and affordable for a large public. These digital networks have large capacities and possibilities for processing personal data. The successful cross-border development of these services is partly dependent on the confidence of users that their privacy will not be at risk.

(6) The Internet is overturning traditional market structures by providing a common, global infrastructure for the delivery of a wide range of electronic communications services. Publicly available electronic communications services over the Internet open new possibilities for users but also new risks for their personal data and privacy.

(7) In the case of public communications networks, specific legal, regulatory and technical provisions should be made in order to protect fundamental rights and freedoms of natural persons and legitimate interests of legal persons, in particular with regard to the increasing capacity for automated storage and processing of data relating to subscribers and users.

(8) Legal, regulatory and technical provisions adopted by the Member States concerning the protection of personal data, privacy and the legitimate interest of legal persons, in the electronic communication sector, should be harmonised in order to avoid obstacles to the internal market for electronic communication in accordance with Article 14 of the Treaty. Harmonisation should be limited to requirements necessary to guarantee that the promotion and development of new electronic communications services and networks between Member States are not hindered.

(9) The Member States, providers and users concerned, together with the competent Community bodies, should cooperate in introducing and developing the relevant technologies where this is necessary to apply the guarantees provided for by this Directive and taking particular account of the objectives of minimising the processing of personal data and of using anonymous or pseudonymous data where possible.

(10) In the electronic communications sector, Directive 95/46/EC applies in particular to all matters concerning protection of fundamental rights and freedoms, which are not specifically covered by the provisions of this Directive, including the obligations on the controller and the rights of individuals. Directive 95/46/EC applies to non-public communications services.

(11) Like Directive 95/46/EC, this Directive does not address issues of protection of fundamental rights and freedoms related to activities which are not governed by Community law. Therefore it does not alter the existing balance between the individual's right to privacy and the possibility for Member States to take the measures referred to in Article 15(1) of this Directive, necessary for the protection of public security, defence, State security (including the economic well-being of the State when the activities relate to State security matters) and the enforcement of criminal law. Consequently, this Directive does not affect the ability of Member States to carry out lawful interception of electronic communications, or take other measures, if necessary for any of these purposes and in accordance with the European Convention for the Protection of Human Rights and Fundamental Freedoms as interpreted by the rulings of the European Court of Human Rights. Such measures must be appropriate strictly proportionate to the intended purpose and necessary within a democratic society and should be subject to adequate safeguards in accordance with the European Convention for the Protection of Human Rights and Fundamental Freedoms.

(12) Subscribers to a publicly available electronic communications service may be natural or legal persons. By supplementing Directive 95/46/EC, this Directive is aimed at protecting the fundamental rights of natural persons and particularly their right to privacy, as well as the legitimate interests of legal persons. This Directive does not entail an obligation for Member States to extend the application of Directive 95/46/EC to the protection of the legitimate interests of legal persons, which is ensured within the framework of the applicable Community and national legislation.

(13) The contractual relation between a subscriber and a service provider may entail a periodic or a one-off payment for the service provided or to be provided. Prepaid cards are also considered as a contract.

(14) Location data may refer to the latitude, longitude and altitude of the user's terminal equipment, to the direction of travel, to the level of accuracy of the location information, to the identification of the network cell in which the terminal equipment is located at a certain point in time and to the time the location information was recorded.

(15) A communication may include any naming, numbering or addressing information provided by the sender of a communication or the user of a connection to carry out the communication. Traffic data may include any translation of this information by the network over which the communication is transmitted for the purpose of carrying out the transmission. Traffic data may, inter alia, consist of data referring to the routing, duration, time or volume of a communication, to the protocol used, to the location of the terminal equipment of the sender or recipient, to the network on which the communication originates or terminates, to the beginning, end or duration of a connection. They may also consist of the format in which the communication is conveyed by the network.

(16) Information that is part of a broadcasting service provided over a public communications network is intended for a potentially unlimited audience and does not constitute a communication in the sense of this Directive. However, in cases where the individual subscriber or user receiving such information can be identified, for example with video-on-demand services, the information conveyed is covered within the meaning of a communication for the purposes of this Directive.

(17) For the purposes of this Directive, consent of a user or subscriber, regardless of whether the latter is a natural or a legal person, should have the same meaning as the data subject's consent as defined and further specified in Directive 95/46/EC. Consent may be given by any appropriate method enabling a freely given specific and informed indication of the user's wishes, including by ticking a box when visiting an Internet website.

(18) Value added services may, for example, consist of advice on least expensive tariff packages, route guidance, traffic information, weather forecasts and tourist information.

(19) The application of certain requirements relating to presentation and restriction of calling and connected line identification and to automatic call forwarding to subscriber lines connected to analogue exchanges should not be made mandatory in specific cases where such application would prove to be technically impossible or would require a disproportionate economic effort. It is important for interested parties to be informed of such cases and the Member States should therefore notify them to the Commission.

(20) Service providers should take appropriate measures to safeguard the security of their services, if necessary in conjunction with the provider of the network, and inform subscribers of any special risks of a breach of the security of the network. Such risks may especially occur for electronic communications services over an open network such as the Internet or analogue mobile telephony. It is particularly important for subscribers and users of such services to be fully informed by their service provider of the existing security risks which lie outside the scope of possible remedies by the service provider. Service providers who offer publicly available electronic communications services over the Internet should inform users and subscribers of measures they can take to protect the security of their communications for instance by using specific types of software or encryption technologies. The requirement to inform subscribers of particular security risks does not discharge a service provider from the obligation to take, at its own costs, appropriate and immediate measures to remedy any new, unforeseen security risks and restore the normal security level of the service. The provision of information about security risks to the subscriber should be free of charge except for any nominal costs which the subscriber may incur while receiving or collecting the information, for instance by downloading an electronic mail message. Security is appraised in the light of Article 17 of Directive 95/46/EC.

(21) Measures should be taken to prevent unauthorised access to communications in order to protect the confidentiality of communications, including both the contents and any data related to such communications, by means of public communications networks and publicly available electronic communications services. National legislation in some Member States only prohibits intentional unauthorised access to communications.

(22) The prohibition of storage of communications and the related traffic data by persons other than the users or without their consent is not intended to prohibit any automatic, intermediate and transient storage of this information in so far as this takes place for the sole purpose of carrying out the transmission in the electronic communications network and provided that the information is not stored for any period longer than is necessary for the transmission and for traffic management purposes, and that during the period of storage the confidentiality remains guaranteed. Where this is necessary for making more efficient the onward transmission of any publicly accessible information to other recipients of the service upon their request, this Directive should not prevent such information from being further stored, provided that this information would in any case be accessible to the public without restriction and that any data referring to the individual subscribers or users requesting such information are erased.

(23) Confidentiality of communications should also be ensured in the course of lawful business practice. Where necessary and legally authorised, communications can be recorded for the purpose of providing evidence of a commercial transaction. Directive 95/46/EC applies to such processing. Parties to the communications should be informed prior to the recording about the recording, its purpose and the duration of its storage. The recorded communication should be erased as soon as possible and in any case at the latest by the end of the period during which the transaction can be lawfully challenged.

(24) Terminal equipment of users of electronic communications networks and any information stored on such equipment are part of the private sphere of the users requiring protection under the European Convention for the Protection of Human Rights and Fundamental Freedoms. So-called spyware, web bugs, hidden identifiers and other similar devices can enter the user's terminal without their knowledge in order to gain access to information, to store hidden information or to trace the activities of the user and may seriously intrude upon the privacy of these users. The use of such devices should be allowed only for legitimate purposes, with the knowledge of the users concerned.

(25) However, such devices, for instance so-called 'cookies', can be a legitimate and useful tool, for example, in analysing the effectiveness of website design and advertising, and in verifying the identity of users engaged in on-line transactions. Where such devices, for instance cookies, are intended for a legitimate purpose, such as to facilitate the provision of information society services, their use should be allowed on condition that users are provided with clear and precise information in accordance with Directive 95/46/EC about the purposes of cookies or similar devices so as to ensure that users are made aware of information being placed on the terminal equipment they are using. Users should have the opportunity to refuse to have a cookie or similar device stored on their terminal equipment. This is particularly important where users other than the original user have access to the terminal equipment and thereby to any data containing privacy-sensitive information stored on such equipment. Information and the right to refuse may be offered once for the use of various devices to be installed on the user's terminal equipment during the same connection and also covering any further use that may be made of those devices during subsequent connections. The methods for giving information, offering a right to refuse or requesting consent should be made as user-friendly as possible. Access to specific website content may still be made conditional on the well-informed acceptance of a cookie or similar device, if it is used for a legitimate purpose.

(26) The data relating to subscribers processed within electronic communications networks to establish connections and to transmit information contain information on the private life of natural persons and concern the right to respect for their correspondence or concern the legitimate interests of legal persons. Such data may only be stored to the extent that is necessary for the provision of the service for the purpose of billing and for interconnection payments, and for a limited time. Any further processing of such data which the provider of the publicly available electronic communications services may want to perform, for the marketing of electronic communications services or for the provision of value added services, may only be allowed if the subscriber has agreed to this on the basis of accurate and full information given by the provider of the publicly available electronic communications services about the types of further processing it intends to perform and about the subscriber's right not to give or to withdraw his/her consent to such processing. Traffic data used for marketing communications services or for the provision of value added services should also be erased or made anonymous after the provision of the service. Service providers should always keep subscribers informed of the types of data they are processing and the purposes and duration for which this is done.

(27) The exact moment of the completion of the transmission of a communication, after which traffic data should be erased except for billing purposes, may depend on the type of electronic communications service that is provided. For instance for a voice telephony call the transmission will be completed as soon as either of the users terminates the connection. For electronic mail the transmission is completed as soon as the addressee collects the message, typically from the server of his service provider.

(28) The obligation to erase traffic data or to make such data anonymous when it is no longer needed for the purpose of the transmission of a communication does not conflict with such procedures on the Internet as the caching in the domain name system of IP addresses or the caching of IP addresses to physical address bindings or the use of log-in information to control the right of access to networks or services.

(29) The service provider may process traffic data relating to subscribers and users where necessary in individual cases in order to detect technical failure or errors in the trans- mission of communications. Traffic data necessary for billing purposes may also be processed by the provider in order to detect and stop fraud consisting of unpaid use of the electronic communications service.

(30) Systems for the provision of electronic communications networks and services should be designed to limit the amount of personal data necessary to a strict minimum. Any activities related to the provision of the electronic communications service that go beyond the transmission of a communication and the billing thereof should be based on aggregated, traffic data that cannot be related to subscribers or users. Where such activities cannot be based on aggregated data, they should be considered as value added services for which the consent of the subscriber is required.

(31) Whether the consent to be obtained for the processing of personal data with a view to providing a particular value added service should be that of the user or of the subscriber, will depend on the data to be processed and on the type of service to be provided and on whether it is technically, procedurally and contractually possible to distinguish the individual using an electronic communications service from the legal or natural person having subscribed to it.

(32) Where the provider of an electronic communications service or of a value added service subcontracts the processing of personal data necessary for the provision of these services to another entity, such subcontracting and subsequent data processing should be in full compliance with the requirements regarding controllers and processors of personal data as set out in Directive 95/46/ EC. Where the provision of a value added service requires that traffic or location data are forwarded from an electronic communications service provider to a provider of value added services, the subscribers or users to whom the data are related should also be fully informed of this forwarding before giving their consent for the processing of the data.

(33) The introduction of itemised bills has improved the possibilities for the subscriber to check the accuracy of the fees charged by the service provider but, at the same time, it may jeopardise the privacy of the users of publicly available electronic communications services. Therefore, in order to preserve the privacy of the user, Member States should encourage the development of electronic communication service options such as alternative payment facilities which allow anonymous or strictly private access to publicly available electronic communications services, for example calling cards and facilities for payment by credit card. To the same end, Member States may ask the operators to offer their subscribers a different type of detailed bill in which a certain number of digits of the called number have been deleted.

(34) It is necessary, as regards calling line identification, to protect the right of the calling party to withhold the presentation of the identification of the line from which the call is being made and the right of the called party to reject calls from unidentified lines. There is justification for overriding the elimination of calling line identification presentation in specific cases. Certain subscribers, in particular help lines and similar organisations, have an interest in guaranteeing the anonymity of their callers. It is necessary, as regards connected line identification, to protect the right and the legitimate interest of the called party to withhold the presentation of the identification of the line to which the calling party is actually connected, in particular in the case of forwarded calls. The providers of publicly available electronic communications services should inform their subscribers of the existence of calling and connected line identification in the network and of all services which are offered on the basis of calling and connected line identification as well as the privacy options which are available. This will allow the subscribers to make an informed choice about the privacy facilities they may want to use. The privacy options which are offered on a per-line basis do not necessarily have to be available as an automatic network service but may be obtainable through a simple request to the provider of the publicly available electronic communications service.

(35) In digital mobile networks, location data giving the geographic position of the terminal equipment of the mobile user are processed to enable the transmission of communications. Such data are traffic data covered by Article 6 of this Directive. However, in addition, digital mobile networks may have the capacity to process location data which are more precise than is necessary for the transmission of communications and which are used for the provision of value added services such as services providing individualised traffic information and guidance to drivers. The processing of such data for value added services should only be allowed where subscribers have given their consent. Even in cases where subscribers have given their consent, they should have a simple means to temporarily deny the processing of location data, free of charge.

(36) Member States may restrict the users' and subscribers' rights to privacy with regard to calling line identification where this is necessary to trace nuisance calls and with regard to calling line identification and location data where this is necessary to allow emergency services to carry out their tasks as effectively as possible. For these purposes, Member States may adopt specific provisions to entitle providers of electronic communications services to provide access to calling line identification and location data without the prior consent of the users or subscribers concerned.

(37) Safeguards should be provided for subscribers against the nuisance which may be caused by automatic call forwarding by others. Moreover, in such cases, it must be possible for subscribers to stop the forwarded calls being passed on to their terminals by simple request to the provider of the publicly available electronic communications service.

(38) Directories of subscribers to electronic communications services are widely distributed and public. The right to privacy of natural persons and the legitimate interest of legal persons require that subscribers are able to determine whether their personal data are published in a directory and if so, which. Providers of public directories should inform the subscribers to be included in such directories of the purposes of the directory and of any particular usage which may be made of electronic versions of public directories especially through search functions embedded in the software, such as reverse search functions enabling users of the directory to discover the name and address of the subscriber on the basis of a telephone number only.

(39) The obligation to inform subscribers of the purpose(s) of public directories in which their personal data are to be included should be imposed on the party collecting the data for such inclusion. Where the data may be transmitted to one or more third parties, the subscriber should be informed of this possibility and of the recipient or the categories of possible recipients. Any transmission should be subject to the condition that the data may not be used for other purposes than those for which they were collected. If the party collecting the data from the subscriber or any third party to whom the data have been transmitted wishes to use the data for an additional purpose, the renewed consent of the subscriber is to be obtained either by the initial party collecting the data or by the third party to whom the data have been trans- mitted.

(40) Safeguards should be provided for subscribers against intrusion of their privacy by unsolicited communications for direct marketing purposes in particular by means of automated calling machines, telefaxes, and e-mails, including SMS messages. These forms of unsolicited commercial communications may on the one hand be relatively easy and cheap to send and on the other may impose a burden and/or cost on the recipient. Moreover, in some cases their volume may also cause difficulties for electronic communications networks and terminal equipment. For such forms of unsolicited communications for direct marketing, it is justified to require that prior explicit consent of the recipients is obtained before such communications are addressed to them. The single market requires a harmonised approach to ensure simple, Community-wide rules for businesses and users.

(41) Within the context of an existing customer relationship, it is reasonable to allow the use of electronic contact details for the offering of similar products or services, but only by the same company that has obtained the electronic contact details in accordance with Directive 95/46/EC. When electronic contact details are obtained, the customer should be informed about their further use for direct marketing in a clear and distinct manner, and be given the opportunity to refuse such usage. This opportunity should continue to be offered with each subsequent direct marketing message, free of charge, except for any costs for the transmission of this refusal.

(42) Other forms of direct marketing that are more costly for the sender and impose no financial costs on subscribers and users, such as person-to-person voice telephony calls, may justify the maintenance of a system giving subscribers or users the possibility to indicate that they do not want to receive such calls. Nevertheless, in order not to decrease existing levels of privacy protection, Member States should be entitled to uphold national systems, only allowing such calls to subscribers and users who have given their prior consent.

(43) To facilitate effective enforcement of Community rules on unsolicited messages for direct marketing, it is necessary to prohibit the use of false identities or false return addresses or numbers while sending unsolicited messages for direct marketing purposes.

(44) Certain electronic mail systems allow subscribers to view the sender and subject line of an electronic mail, and also to delete the message, without having to download the rest of the electronic mail's content or any attachments, thereby reducing costs which could arise from downloading unsolicited electronic mails or attachments. These arrangements may continue to be useful in certain cases as an additional tool to the general obligations established in this Directive.

(45) This Directive is without prejudice to the arrangements which Member States make to protect the legitimate interests of legal persons with regard to unsolicited communications for direct marketing purposes. Where Member States establish an opt-out register for such communications to legal persons, mostly business users, the provisions of Article 7 of Directive 2000/31/EC of the European Parliament and of the Council of 8 June 2000 on certain legal aspects of information society services, in particular electronic commerce, in the internal market (Directive on electronic commerce) are fully applicable.

(46) The functionalities for the provision of electronic communications services may be integrated in the network or in any part of the terminal equipment of the user, including the software. The protection of the personal data and the privacy of the user of publicly available electronic communications services should be independent of the configuration of the various components necessary to provide the service and of the distribution of the necessary functionalities between these components. Directive 95/46/EC covers any form of processing of personal data regardless of the technology used. The existence of specific rules for electronic communications services alongside general rules for other components necessary for the provision of such services may not facilitate the protection of personal data and privacy in a technologically neutral way. It may therefore be necessary to adopt measures requiring manufacturers of certain types of equipment used for electronic communications services to construct their product in such a way as to incorporate safeguards to ensure that the personal data and privacy of the user and subscriber are protected. The adoption of such measures in accordance with Directive 1999/5/EC of the European Parliament and of the Council of 9 March 1999 on radio equipment and telecommunications terminal equipment and the mutual recognition of their conformity will ensure that the introduction of technical features of electronic communication equipment including software for data protection purposes is harmonised in order to be compatible with the implementation of the internal market.

(47) Where the rights of the users and subscribers are not respected, national legislation should provide for judicial remedies. Penalties should be imposed on any person, whether governed by private or public law, who fails to comply with the national measures taken under this Directive.

(48) It is useful, in the field of application of this Directive, to draw on the experience of the Working Party on the Protection of Individuals with regard to the Processing of Personal Data composed of representatives of the supervisory authorities of the Member States, set up by Article 29 of Directive 95/46/EC.

(49) To facilitate compliance with the provisions of this Directive, certain specific arrangements are needed for processing of data already under way on the date that national implementing legislation pursuant to this Directive enters into force,

HAVE ADOPTED THIS DIRECTIVE:

Article 1 **- Scope and aim**

1. This Directive harmonises the provisions of the Member States required to ensure an equivalent level of protection of fundamental rights and freedoms, and in particular the right to privacy, with respect to the processing of personal data in the electronic communication sector and to ensure the free movement of such data and of electronic communication equipment and services in the Community.

2. The provisions of this Directive particularise and complement Directive 95/46/EC for the purposes mentioned in paragraph 1. Moreover, they provide for protection of the legitimate interests of subscribers who are legal persons.

3. This Directive shall not apply to activities which fall outside the scope of the Treaty establishing the European Community, such as those covered by Titles V and VI of the Treaty on European Union, and in any case to activities concerning public security, defence, State security (including the economic well-being of the State when the activities relate to State security matters) and the activities of the State in areas of criminal law.

Article 2 **- Definitions**

Save as otherwise provided, the definitions in Directive 95/46/ EC and in Directive 2002/21/EC of the European Parliament and of the Council of 7 March 2002 on a common regulatory framework for electronic communications networks and services (Framework Directive) shall apply.

The following definitions shall also apply:

> **(a)** 'user' means any natural person using a publicly available electronic communications service, for private or business purposes, without necessarily having subscribed to this service;
>
> **(b)** 'traffic data' means any data processed for the purpose of the conveyance of a communication on an electronic communications network or for the billing thereof;
>
> **(c)** 'location data' means any data processed in an electronic communications network, indicating the geographic position of the terminal equipment of a user of a publicly available electronic communications service;
>
> **(d)** 'communication' means any information exchanged or conveyed between a finite number of parties by means of a publicly available electronic communications service. This does not include any information conveyed as part of a broadcasting service to the public over an electronic communications network except to the extent that the information can be related to the identifiable subscriber or user receiving the information;

(e) 'call' means a connection established by means of a publicly available telephone service allowing two-way communication in real time;

(f) 'consent' by a user or subscriber corresponds to the data subject's consent in Directive 95/46/EC;

(g) 'value added service' means any service which requires the processing of traffic data or location data other than traffic data beyond what is necessary for the transmission of a communication or the billing thereof;

(h) 'electronic mail' means any text, voice, sound or image message sent over a public communications network which can be stored in the network or in the recipient's terminal equipment until it is collected by the recipient.

***Article 3* - Services concerned**

1. This Directive shall apply to the processing of personal data in connection with the provision of publicly available electronic communications services in public communications networks in the Community.

2. Articles 8, 10 and 11 shall apply to subscriber lines connected to digital exchanges and, where technically possible and if it does not require a disproportionate economic effort, to subscriber lines connected to analogue exchanges.

3. Cases where it would be technically impossible or require a disproportionate economic effort to fulfill the requirements of Articles 8, 10 and 11 shall be notified to the Commission by the Member States.

***Article 4* - Security**

1. The provider of a publicly available electronic communications service must take appropriate technical and organisational measures to safeguard security of its services, if necessary in conjunction with the provider of the public communications network with respect to network security. Having regard to the state of the art and the cost of their implementation, these measures shall ensure a level of security appropriate to the risk presented.

2. In case of a particular risk of a breach of the security of the network, the provider of a publicly available electronic communications service must inform the subscribers concerning such risk and, where the risk lies outside the scope of the measures to be taken by the service provider, of any possible remedies, including an indication of the likely costs involved.

***Article 5* - Confidentiality of the communications**

1. Member States shall ensure the confidentiality of communications and the related traffic data by means of a public communications network and publicly available electronic communications services, through national legislation. In particular, they shall prohibit listening, tapping, storage or other kinds of interception or surveillance of communications and the related traffic data by persons other than users, without the consent of the users concerned, except when legally authorised to do so in accordance with Article 15(1). This paragraph shall not prevent technical storage which is necessary for the conveyance of a communication without prejudice to the principle of confidentiality.

2. Paragraph 1 shall not affect any legally authorised recording of communications and the related traffic data when carried out in the course of lawful business practice for the purpose of providing evidence of a commercial transaction or of any other business communication.

3. Member States shall ensure that the use of electronic communications networks to store information or to gain access to information stored in the terminal equipment of a subscriber or user is only allowed on condition that the subscriber or user concerned is provided with clear and comprehensive information in accordance with Directive 95/46/EC, inter alia about the purposes of the processing, and is offered the right to refuse such processing by the data controller. This shall not prevent any technical storage or access for the sole purpose of carrying out or facilitating the transmission of a communication over an electronic communications network, or as strictly necessary in order to provide an information society service explicitly requested by the subscriber or user.

***Article 6* - Traffic data**

1. Traffic data relating to subscribers and users processed and stored by the provider of a public communications network or publicly available electronic communications service must be erased or made anonymous when it is no longer needed for the purpose of the transmission of a communication without prejudice to paragraphs 2, 3 and 5 of this Article and Article 15(1).

2. Traffic data necessary for the purposes of subscriber billing and interconnection payments may be processed. Such processing is permissible only up to the end of the period during which the bill may lawfully be challenged or payment pursued.

3. For the purpose of marketing electronic communications services or for the provision of value added services, the provider of a publicly available electronic communications service may process the data referred to in paragraph 1 to the extent and for the duration necessary for such services or marketing, if the subscriber or user to whom the data relate has given his/her consent. Users or subscribers shall be given the possibility to withdraw their consent for the processing of traffic data at any time.

4. The service provider must inform the subscriber or user of the types of traffic data which are processed and of the duration of such processing for the purposes mentioned in paragraph 2 and, prior to obtaining consent, for the purposes mentioned in paragraph 3.

5. Processing of traffic data, in accordance with paragraphs 1, 2, 3 and 4, must be restricted to persons acting under the authority of providers of the public communications networks and publicly available electronic communications services handling billing or traffic management, customer enquiries, fraud detection, marketing electronic communications services or providing a value added service, and must be restricted to what is necessary for the purposes of such activities.

6. Paragraphs 1, 2, 3 and 5 shall apply without prejudice to the possibility for competent bodies to be informed of traffic data in conformity with applicable legislation with a view to settling disputes, in particular interconnection or billing disputes.

***Article 7* - Itemised billing**

1. Subscribers shall have the right to receive non-itemised bills.

2. Member States shall apply national provisions in order to reconcile the rights of subscribers receiving itemised bills with the right to privacy of calling users and called subscribers, for example by ensuring that sufficient alternative privacy enhancing methods of communications or payments are available to such users and subscribers.

***Article 8* - Presentation and restriction of calling and connected line identification**

1. Where presentation of calling line identification is offered, the service provider must offer the calling user the possibility, using a simple means and free of charge, of preventing the presentation of the calling line identification on a per-call basis. The calling subscriber must have this possibility on a per-line basis.

2. Where presentation of calling line identification is offered, the service provider must offer the called subscriber the possibility, using a simple means and free of charge for reasonable use of this function, of preventing the presentation of the calling line identification of incoming calls.

3. Where presentation of calling line identification is offered and where the calling line identification is presented prior to the call being established, the service provider must offer the called subscriber the possibility, using a simple means, of rejecting incoming calls where the presentation of the calling line identification has been prevented by the calling user or subscriber.

4. Where presentation of connected line identification is offered, the service provider must offer the called subscriber the possibility, using a simple means and free of charge, of preventing the presentation of the connected line identification to the calling user.

5. Paragraph 1 shall also apply with regard to calls to third countries originating in the Community. Paragraphs 2, 3 and 4 shall also apply to incoming calls originating in third countries.

6. Member States shall ensure that where presentation of calling and/or connected line identification is offered, the providers of publicly available electronic communications services inform the public thereof and of the possibilities set out in paragraphs 1, 2, 3 and 4.

***Article 9* - Location data other than traffic data.**

1. Where location data other than traffic data, relating to users or subscribers of public communications networks or publicly available electronic communications services, can be processed, such data may only be processed when they are made anonymous, or with the consent of the users or subscribers to the extent and for the duration necessary for the provision of a value added service. The service provider must inform the users or subscribers, prior to obtaining their consent, of the type of location data other than traffic data which will be processed, of the purposes and duration of the processing and whether the data will be transmitted to a third party for the purpose of providing the value added service. Users or subscribers shall be given the possibility to withdraw their consent for the processing of location data other than traffic data at any time.

2. Where consent of the users or subscribers has been obtained for the processing of location data other than traffic data, the user or subscriber must continue to have the possibility, using a simple means and free of charge, of temporarily refusing the processing of such data for each connection to the network or for each transmission of a communication.

3. Processing of location data other than traffic data in accordance with paragraphs 1 and 2 must be restricted to persons acting under the authority of the provider of the public communications network or publicly available communications service or of the third party providing the value added service, and must be restricted to what is necessary for the purposes of providing the value added service.

***Article 10* – Exceptions**

Member States shall ensure that there are transparent procedures governing the way in which a provider of a public communications network and/or a publicly available electronic communications service may override:

> **(a)** the elimination of the presentation of calling line identification, on a temporary basis, upon application of a subscriber requesting the tracing of malicious or nuisance calls. In this case, in accordance with national law, the data containing the identification of the calling subscriber will be stored and be made available by the provider of a public communications network and/or publicly available electronic communications service;
>
> **(b)** the elimination of the presentation of calling line identification and the temporary denial or absence of consent of a subscriber or user for the processing of location data, on a per-line basis for organisations dealing with emergency calls and recognised as such by a Member State, including law enforcement agencies, ambulance services and fire brigades, for the purpose of responding to such calls.

***Article 11* - Automatic call forwarding**

Member States shall ensure that any subscriber has the possibility, using a simple means and free of charge, of stopping automatic call forwarding by a third party to the subscriber's terminal.

***Article 12* - Directories of subscribers**

1. Member States shall ensure that subscribers are informed, free of charge and before they are included in the directory, about the purpose(s) of a printed or electronic directory of subscribers available to the public or obtainable through directory enquiry services, in which their personal data can be included and of any further usage possibilities based on search functions embedded in electronic versions of the directory.

2. Member States shall ensure that subscribers are given the opportunity to determine whether their personal data are included in a public directory, and if so, which, to the extent that such data are relevant for the purpose of the directory as determined by the provider of the directory, and to verify, correct or withdraw such data. Not being included in a public subscriber directory, verifying, correcting or withdrawing personal data from it shall be free of charge.

3. Member States may require that for any purpose of a public directory other than the search of contact details of persons on the basis of their name and, where necessary, a minimum of other identifiers, additional consent be asked of the subscribers.

4. Paragraphs 1 and 2 shall apply to subscribers who are natural persons. Member States shall also ensure, in the frame- work of Community law and applicable national legislation, that the legitimate interests of subscribers other than natural persons with regard to their entry in public directories are sufficiently protected.

***Article 13* - Unsolicited communications**

1. The use of automated calling systems without human intervention (automatic calling machines), facsimile machines (fax) or electronic mail for the purposes of direct marketing may only be allowed in respect of subscribers who have given their prior consent.

2. Notwithstanding paragraph 1, where a natural or legal person obtains from its customers their electronic contact details for electronic mail, in the context of the sale of a product or a service, in accordance with Directive 95/46/EC, the same natural or legal person may use these electronic contact details for direct marketing of its own similar products or services provided that customers clearly and distinctly are given the opportunity to object, free of charge and in an easy manner, to such use of electronic contact details when they are collected and on the occasion of each message in case the customer has not initially refused such use.

3. Member States shall take appropriate measures to ensure that, free of charge, unsolicited communications for purposes of direct marketing, in cases other than those referred to in paragraphs 1 and 2, are not allowed either without the consent of the subscribers concerned or in respect of subscribers who do not wish to receive these communications, the choice between these options to be determined by national legislation.

4. In any event, the practice of sending electronic mail for purposes of direct marketing disguising or concealing the identity of the sender on whose behalf the communication is made, or without a valid address to which the recipient may send a request that such communications cease, shall be prohibited.

5. Paragraphs 1 and 3 shall apply to subscribers who are natural persons. Member States shall also ensure, in the framework of Community law and applicable national legislation, that the legitimate interests of subscribers other than natural persons with regard to unsolicited communications are sufficiently protected.

Article 14 **- Technical features and standardization**

1. In implementing the provisions of this Directive, Member States shall ensure, subject to paragraphs 2 and 3, that no mandatory requirements for specific technical features are imposed on terminal or other electronic communication equipment which could impede the placing of equipment on the market and the free circulation of such equipment in and between Member States.

2. Where provisions of this Directive can be implemented only by requiring specific technical features in electronic communications networks, Member States shall inform the Commission in accordance with the procedure provided for by Directive 98/34/EC of the European Parliament and of the Council of 22 June 1998 laying down a procedure for the provision of information in the field of technical standards and regulations and of rules on information society services.

3. Where required, measures may be adopted to ensure that terminal equipment is constructed in a way that is compatible with the right of users to protect and control the use of their personal data, in accordance with Directive 1999/5/EC and Council Decision 87/95/EEC of 22 December 1986 on standardisation in the field of information technology and communications.

Article 15 **- Application of certain provisions of Directive 95/46/EC**

1. Member States may adopt legislative measures to restrict the scope of the rights and obligations provided for in Article 5, Article 6, Article 8(1), (2), (3) and (4), and Article 9 of this Directive when such restriction constitutes a necessary, appropriate and proportionate measure within a democratic society to safeguard national security (i.e. State security), defence, public security, and the prevention, investigation, detection and prosecution of criminal offences or of unauthorised use of the electronic communication system, as referred to in Article 13(1) of Directive 95/46/EC. To this end, Member States may, inter alia, adopt legislative measures providing for the retention of data for a limited period justified on the grounds laid down in this paragraph. All the measures referred to in this paragraph shall be in accordance with the general principles of Community law, including those referred to in Article 6(1) and (2) of the Treaty on European Union.

2. The provisions of Chapter III on judicial remedies, liability and sanctions of Directive 95/46/EC shall apply with regard to national provisions adopted pursuant to this Directive and with regard to the individual rights derived from this Directive.

3. The Working Party on the Protection of Individuals with regard to the Processing of Personal Data instituted by Article 29 of Directive 95/46/EC shall also carry out the tasks laid down in Article 30 of that Directive with regard to matters covered by this Directive, namely the protection of fundamental rights and freedoms and of legitimate interests in the electronic communications sector.

Article 16 **- Transitional arrangements**

1. Article 12 shall not apply to editions of directories already produced or placed on the market in printed or off-line electronic form before the national provisions adopted pursuant to this Directive enter into force.

2. Where the personal data of subscribers to fixed or mobile public voice telephony services have been included in a public subscriber directory in conformity with the provisions of Directive 95/46/EC and of Article 11 of Directive 97/66/EC before the national provisions adopted in pursuance of this Directive enter into force, the personal data of such subscribers may remain included in this public directory in its printed or electronic versions, including versions with reverse search functions, unless subscribers indicate otherwise, after having received complete information about purposes and options in accordance with Article 12 of this Directive.

Article 17 **– Transposition**

1. Before 31 October 2003 Member States shall bring into force the provisions necessary to comply with this Directive. They shall forthwith inform the Commission thereof. When Member States adopt those provisions, they shall contain a reference to this Directive or be accompanied by such a reference on the occasion of their official publication. The methods of making such reference shall be laid down by the Member States.

2. Member States shall communicate to the Commission the text of the provisions of national law which they adopt in the field governed by this Directive and of any subsequent amendments to those provisions.

Article 18 **– Review**

The Commission shall submit to the European Parliament and the Council, not later than three years after the date referred to in Article 17(1), a report on the application of this Directive and its impact on economic operators and consumers, in particular as regards the provisions on unsolicited communications, taking into account the international environment. For this purpose, the Commission may request information from the Member States, which shall be supplied without undue delay. Where appropriate, the Commission shall submit proposals to amend this Directive, taking account of the results of that report, any changes in the sector and any other proposal it may deem necessary in order to improve the effectiveness of this Directive.

***Article 19* – Repeal**

Directive 97/66/EC is hereby repealed with effect from the date referred to in Article 17(1). References made to the repealed Directive shall be construed as being made to this Directive.

***Article 20* - Entry into force**

This Directive shall enter into force on the day of its publication in the Official Journal of the European Communities.

***Article 21* – Addressees**

This Directive is addressed to the Member States.

Done at Brussels, 12 July 2002.
For the European Parliament
The President P. COX
For the Council
The President T. PEDERSEN

EU Data Retention Directive (2006)

Directives in Context

The European Union (EU) Data Retention Directive (Directive 2006/24/EC) sets standards for Member States to retain certain data which are generated in the use of telecommunications. Article 5 of this Directive sets out the categories of data to be retained; Article 6 requires that this information be kept for periods of not less than six months and not more than two years from the date of the communication.

THE EUROPEAN PARLIAMENT AND THE COUNCIL OF THE EUROPEAN UNION,

Having regard to the Treaty establishing the European Community, and in particular Article 95 thereof,

Having regard to the proposal from the Commission,

Having regard to the Opinion of the European Economic and Social Committee [1],

Acting in accordance with the procedure laid down in Article 251 of the Treaty [2],

Whereas:

(1) Directive 95/46/EC of the European Parliament and of the Council of 24 October 1995 on the protection of individuals with regard to the processing of personal data and on the free movement of such data [3] requires Member States to protect the rights and freedoms of natural persons with regard to the processing of personal data, and in particular their right to privacy, in order to ensure the free flow of personal data in the Community.

(2) Directive 2002/58/EC of the European Parliament and of the Council of 12 July 2002 concerning the processing of personal data and the protection of privacy in the electronic communications sector (Directive on privacy and electronic communications) [4] translates the principles set out in Directive 95/46/EC into specific rules for the electronic communications sector.

(3) Articles 5, 6 and 9 of Directive 2002/58/EC lay down the rules applicable to the processing by network and service providers of traffic and location data generated by using electronic communications services. Such data must be erased or made anonymous when no longer needed for the purpose of the transmission of a communication, except for the data necessary for billing or interconnection payments. Subject to consent, certain data may also be processed for marketing purposes and the provision of value-added services.

(4) Article 15(1) of Directive 2002/58/EC sets out the conditions under which Member States may restrict the scope of the rights and obligations provided for in Article 5, Article 6, Article 8(1), (2), (3) and (4), and Article 9 of that Directive. Any such restrictions must be necessary, appropriate and proportionate within a democratic society for specific public order purposes, i.e. to safeguard national security (i.e. State security), defence, public security or the prevention, investigation, detection and prosecution of criminal offences or of unauthorised use of the electronic communications systems.

(5) Several Member States have adopted legislation providing for the retention of data by service providers for the prevention, investigation, detection, and prosecution of criminal offences. Those national provisions vary considerably.

(6) The legal and technical differences between national provisions concerning the retention of data for the purpose of prevention, investigation, detection and prosecution of criminal offences present obstacles to the internal market for electronic communications, since service providers are faced with different requirements regarding the types of traffic and location data to be retained and the conditions and periods of retention.

(7) The Conclusions of the Justice and Home Affairs Council of 19 December 2002 underline that, because of the significant growth in the possibilities afforded by electronic communications, data relating to the use of electronic communications are particularly important and therefore a valuable tool in the prevention, investigation, detection and prosecution of criminal offences, in particular organised crime.

(8) The Declaration on Combating Terrorism adopted by the European Council on 25 March 2004 instructed the Council to examine measures for establishing rules on the retention of communications traffic data by service providers.

(9) Under Article 8 of the European Convention for the Protection of Human Rights and Fundamental Freedoms (ECHR), everyone has the right to respect for his private life and his correspondence. Public authorities may interfere with the exercise of that right only in accordance with the law and where necessary in a democratic society, inter alia, in the interests of national security or public safety, for the prevention of disorder or crime, or for the protection of the rights and freedoms of others. Because retention of data has proved to be such a necessary and effective investigative tool for law enforcement in several Member States, and in particular concerning serious matters such as organised crime and terrorism, it is necessary to ensure that retained data are made available to law enforcement authorities for a certain period, subject to the conditions provided for in this Directive. The adoption of an instrument on data retention that complies with the requirements of Article 8 of the ECHR is therefore a necessary measure.

(10) On 13 July 2005, the Council reaffirmed in its declaration condemning the terrorist attacks on London the need to adopt common measures on the retention of telecommunications data as soon as possible.

(11) Given the importance of traffic and location data for the investigation, detection, and prosecution of criminal offences, as demonstrated by research and the practical experience of several Member States, there is a need to ensure at European level that data that are generated or processed, in the course of the supply of communications services, by providers of publicly available electronic communications services or of a public communications network are retained for a certain period, subject to the conditions provided for in this Directive.

(12) Article 15(1) of Directive 2002/58/EC continues to apply to data, including data relating to unsuccessful call attempts, the retention of which is not specifically required under this Directive and which therefore fall outside the scope thereof, and to retention for purposes, including judicial purposes, other than those covered by this Directive.

(13) This Directive relates only to data generated or processed as a consequence of a communication or a communication service and does not relate to data that are the content of the information communicated. Data should be retained in such a way as to avoid their being retained more than once. Data generated or processed when supplying the communications services concerned refers to data which are accessible. In particular, as regards the retention of data relating to Internet e-mail and Internet telephony, the obligation to retain data may apply only in respect of data from the providers' or the network providers' own services.

(14) Technologies relating to electronic communications are changing rapidly and the legitimate requirements of the competent authorities may evolve. In order to obtain advice and encourage the sharing of experience of best practice in these matters, the Commission intends to establish a group composed of Member States' law enforcement authorities, associations of the electronic communications industry, representatives of the European Parliament and data protection authorities, including the European Data Protection Supervisor.

(15) Directive 95/46/EC and Directive 2002/58/EC are fully applicable to the data retained in accordance with this Directive. Article 30(1)(c) of Directive 95/46/EC requires the consultation of the Working Party on the Protection of Individuals with regard to the Processing of Personal Data established under Article 29 of that Directive.

(16) The obligations incumbent on service providers concerning measures to ensure data quality, which derive from Article 6 of Directive 95/46/EC, and their obligations concerning measures to ensure confidentiality and security of processing of data, which derive from Articles 16 and 17 of that Directive, apply in full to data being retained within the meaning of this Directive.

(17) It is essential that Member States adopt legislative measures to ensure that data retained under this Directive are provided to the competent national authorities only in accordance with national legislation in full respect of the fundamental rights of the persons concerned.

(18) In this context, Article 24 of Directive 95/46/EC imposes an obligation on Member States to lay down sanctions for infringements of the provisions adopted pursuant to that Directive. Article 15(2) of Directive 2002/58/EC imposes the same requirement in relation to national provisions adopted pursuant to Directive 2002/58/EC. Council Framework Decision 2005/222/JHA of 24 February 2005 on attacks against information systems [5] provides that the intentional illegal access to information systems, including to data retained therein, is to be made punishable as a criminal offence.

(19) The right of any person who has suffered damage as a result of an unlawful processing operation or of any act incompatible with national provisions adopted pursuant to Directive 95/46/EC to receive compensation, which derives from Article 23 of that Directive, applies also in relation to the unlawful processing of any personal data pursuant to this Directive.

(20) The 2001 Council of Europe Convention on Cybercrime and the 1981 Council of Europe Convention for the Protection of Individuals with Regard to Automatic Processing of Personal Data also cover data being retained within the meaning of this Directive.

(21) Since the objectives of this Directive, namely to harmonise the obligations on providers to retain certain data and to ensure that those data are available for the purpose of the investigation, detection and prosecution of serious crime, as defined by each Member State in its national law, cannot be sufficiently achieved by the Member States and can therefore, by reason of the scale and effects of this Directive, be better achieved at Community level, the Community may adopt measures, in accordance with the principle of subsidiarity as set out in Article 5 of the Treaty. In accordance with the principle of proportionality, as set out in that Article, this Directive does not go beyond what is necessary in order to achieve those objectives.

(22) This Directive respects the fundamental rights and observes the principles recognised, in particular, by the Charter of Fundamental Rights of the European Union. In particular, this Directive, together with Directive 2002/58/EC, seeks to ensure full compliance with citizens' fundamental rights to respect for private life and communications and to the protection of their personal data, as enshrined in Articles 7 and 8 of the Charter.

(23) Given that the obligations on providers of electronic communications services should be proportionate, this Directive requires that they retain only such data as are generated or processed in the process of supplying their communications services. To the extent that such data are not generated or processed by those providers, there is no obligation to retain them. This Directive is not intended to harmonise the technology for retaining data, the choice of which is a matter to be resolved at national level.

(24) In accordance with paragraph 34 of the Interinstitutional agreement on better law-making [6], Member States are encouraged to draw up, for themselves and in the interests of the Community, their own tables illustrating, as far as possible, the correlation between this Directive and the transposition measures, and to make them public.

(25) This Directive is without prejudice to the power of Member States to adopt legislative measures concerning the right of access to, and use of, data by national authorities, as designated by them. Issues of access to data retained pursuant to this Directive by national authorities for such activities as are referred to in the first indent of Article 3(2) of Directive 95/46/EC fall outside the scope of Community law. However, they may be subject to national law or action pursuant to Title VI of the Treaty on European Union. Such laws or action must fully respect fundamental rights as they result from the common constitutional traditions of the Member States and as guaranteed by the ECHR. Under Article 8 of the ECHR, as interpreted by the European Court of Human Rights, interference by public authorities with privacy rights must meet the requirements of necessity and proportionality and must therefore serve specified, explicit and legitimate purposes and be exercised in a manner that is adequate, relevant and not excessive in relation to the purpose of the interference,

HAVE ADOPTED THIS DIRECTIVE:

Article 1 - Subject matter and scope

1. This Directive aims to harmonise Member States' provisions concerning the obligations of the providers of publicly available electronic communications services or of public communications networks with respect to the retention of certain data which are generated or processed by them, in order to ensure that the data are available for the purpose of the investigation, detection and prosecution of serious crime, as defined by each Member State in its national law.

2. This Directive shall apply to traffic and location data on both legal entities and natural persons and to the related data necessary to identify the subscriber or registered user. It shall not apply to the content of electronic communications, including information consulted using an electronic communications network.

Article 2 - Definitions

1. For the purpose of this Directive, the definitions in Directive 95/46/EC, in Directive 2002/21/EC of the European Parliament and of the Council of 7 March 2002 on a common regulatory framework for electronic communications networks and services (Framework Directive) [7], and in Directive 2002/58/EC shall apply.

2. For the purpose of this Directive:

(a) "data" means traffic data and location data and the related data necessary to identify the subscriber or user;

(b) "user" means any legal entity or natural person using a publicly available electronic communications service, for private or business purposes, without necessarily having subscribed to that service;

(c) "telephone service" means calls (including voice, voicemail and conference and data calls), supplementary services (including call forwarding and call transfer) and messaging and multi-media services (including short message services, enhanced media services and multi-media services);

(d) "user ID" means a unique identifier allocated to persons when they subscribe to or register with an Internet access service or Internet communications service;

(e) "cell ID" means the identity of the cell from which a mobile telephony call originated or in which it terminated;

(f) "unsuccessful call attempt" means a communication where a telephone call has been successfully connected but not answered or there has been a network management intervention.

***Article 3* - Obligation to retain data**

1. By way of derogation from Articles 5, 6 and 9 of Directive 2002/58/EC, Member States shall adopt measures to ensure that the data specified in Article 5 of this Directive are retained in accordance with the provisions thereof, to the extent that those data are generated or processed by providers of publicly available electronic communications services or of a public communications network within their jurisdiction in the process of supplying the communications services concerned.

2. The obligation to retain data provided for in paragraph 1 shall include the retention of the data specified in Article 5 relating to unsuccessful call attempts where those data are generated or processed, and stored (as regards telephony data) or logged (as regards Internet data), by providers of publicly available electronic communications services or of a public communications network within the jurisdiction of the Member State concerned in the process of supplying the communication services concerned. This Directive shall not require data relating to unconnected calls to be retained.

***Article 4* - Access to data**

Member States shall adopt measures to ensure that data retained in accordance with this Directive are provided only to the competent national authorities in specific cases and in accordance with national law. The procedures to be followed and the conditions to be fulfilled in order to gain access to retained data in accordance with necessity and proportionality requirements shall be defined by each Member State in its national law, subject to the relevant provisions of European Union law or public international law, and in particular the ECHR as interpreted by the European Court of Human Rights.

Article 5 - Categories of data to be retained

1. Member States shall ensure that the following categories of data are retained under this Directive:

(a) data necessary to trace and identify the source of a communication:

(1) concerning fixed network telephony and mobile telephony:

(i) the calling telephone number;

(ii) the name and address of the subscriber or registered user;

(2) concerning Internet access, Internet e-mail and Internet telephony:

(i) the user ID(s) allocated;

(ii) the user ID and telephone number allocated to any communication entering the public telephone network;

(iii) the name and address of the subscriber or registered user to whom an Internet Protocol (IP) address, user ID or telephone number was allocated at the time of the communication;

(b) data necessary to identify the destination of a communication:

(1) concerning fixed network telephony and mobile telephony:

(i) the number(s) dialled (the telephone number(s) called), and, in cases involving supplementary services such as call forwarding or call transfer, the number or numbers to which the call is routed;

(ii) the name(s) and address(es) of the subscriber(s) or registered user(s);

(2) concerning Internet e-mail and Internet telephony:

(i) the user ID or telephone number of the intended recipient(s) of an Internet telephony call;

(ii) the name(s) and address(es) of the subscriber(s) or registered user(s) and user ID of the intended recipient of the communication;

(c) data necessary to identify the date, time and duration of a communication:

(1) concerning fixed network telephony and mobile telephony, the date and time of the start and end of the communication;

(2) concerning Internet access, Internet e-mail and Internet telephony:

(i) the date and time of the log-in and log-off of the Internet access service, based on a certain time zone, together with the IP address, whether dynamic or static, allocated by the Internet access service provider to a communication, and the user ID of the subscriber or registered user;

(ii) the date and time of the log-in and log-off of the Internet e-mail service or Internet telephony service, based on a certain time zone;

(d) data necessary to identify the type of communication:

(1) concerning fixed network telephony and mobile telephony: the telephone service used;

(2) concerning Internet e-mail and Internet telephony: the Internet service used;

(e) data necessary to identify users' communication equipment or what purports to be their equipment:

(1) concerning fixed network telephony, the calling and called telephone numbers;

(2) concerning mobile telephony:

(i) the calling and called telephone numbers;

(ii) the International Mobile Subscriber Identity (IMSI) of the calling party;

(iii) the International Mobile Equipment Identity (IMEI) of the calling party;

(iv) the IMSI of the called party;

(v) the IMEI of the called party;

(vi) in the case of pre-paid anonymous services, the date and time of the initial activation of the service and the location label (Cell ID) from which the service was activated;

(3) concerning Internet access, Internet e-mail and Internet telephony:

(i) the calling telephone number for dial-up access;

(ii) the digital subscriber line (DSL) or other end point of the originator of the communication;

(f) data necessary to identify the location of mobile communication equipment:

(1) the location label (Cell ID) at the start of the communication;

(2) data identifying the geographic location of cells by reference to their location labels (Cell ID) during the period for which communications data are retained.

2. No data revealing the content of the communication may be retained pursuant to this Directive.

Article 6 - **Periods of retention**

Member States shall ensure that the categories of data specified in Article 5 are retained for periods of not less than six months and not more than two years from the date of the communication.

Article 7 - **Data protection and data security**

Without prejudice to the provisions adopted pursuant to Directive 95/46/EC and Directive 2002/58/EC, each Member State shall ensure that providers of publicly available electronic communications services or of a public communications network respect, as a minimum, the following data security principles with respect to data retained in accordance with this Directive:

(a) the retained data shall be of the same quality and subject to the same security and protection as those data on the network;

(b) the data shall be subject to appropriate technical and organisational measures to protect the data against accidental or unlawful destruction, accidental loss or alteration, or unauthorised or unlawful storage, processing, access or disclosure;

(c) the data shall be subject to appropriate technical and organisational measures to ensure that they can be accessed by specially authorised personnel only;

and

(d) the data, except those that have been accessed and preserved, shall be destroyed at the end of the period of retention.

Article 8 - **Storage requirements for retained data**

Member States shall ensure that the data specified in Article 5 are retained in accordance with this Directive in such a way that the data retained and any other necessary information relating to such data can be transmitted upon request to the competent authorities without undue delay.

Article 9 - **Supervisory authority**

1. Each Member State shall designate one or more public authorities to be responsible for monitoring the application within its territory of the provisions adopted by the Member States pursuant to Article 7 regarding the security of the stored data. Those authorities may be the same authorities as those referred to in Article 28 of Directive 95/46/EC.

2. The authorities referred to in paragraph 1 shall act with complete independence in carrying out the monitoring referred to in that paragraph.

Article 10 - **Statistics**

1. Member States shall ensure that the Commission is provided on a yearly basis with statistics on the retention of data generated or processed in connection with the provision of publicly available electronic communications services or a public communications network. Such statistics shall include:

— the cases in which information was provided to the competent authorities in accordance with applicable national law,

— the time elapsed between the date on which the data were retained and the date on which the competent authority requested the transmission of the data,

— the cases where requests for data could not be met.

2. Such statistics shall not contain personal data.

Article 11 - **Amendment of Directive 2002/58/EC**

The following paragraph shall be inserted in Article 15 of Directive 2002/58/EC:

"1a. Paragraph 1 shall not apply to data specifically required by Directive 2006/24/EC of the European Parliament and of the Council of 15 March 2006 on the retention of data generated or processed in connection with the provision of publicly available electronic communications services or of public communications networks [8] to be retained for the purposes referred to in Article 1(1) of that Directive.

Article 12 - **Future measures**

1. A Member State facing particular circumstances that warrant an extension for a limited period of the maximum retention period referred to in Article 6 may take the necessary measures. That Member State shall immediately notify the Commission and inform the other Member States of the measures taken under this Article and shall state the grounds for introducing them.

2. The Commission shall, within a period of six months after the notification referred to in paragraph 1, approve or reject the national measures concerned, after having examined whether they are a means of arbitrary discrimination or a disguised restriction of trade between Member States and whether they constitute an obstacle to the functioning of the internal market. In the absence of a decision by the Commission within that period the national measures shall be deemed to have been approved.

3. Where, pursuant to paragraph 2, the national measures of a Member State derogating from the provisions of this Directive are approved, the Commission may consider whether to propose an amendment to this Directive.

Article 13 - **Remedies, liability and penalties**

1. Each Member State shall take the necessary measures to ensure that the national measures implementing Chapter III of Directive 95/46/EC providing for judicial remedies, liability and sanctions are fully implemented with respect to the processing of data under this Directive.

2. Each Member State shall, in particular, take the necessary measures to ensure that any intentional access to, or transfer of, data retained in accordance with this Directive that is not permitted under national law adopted pursuant to this Directive is punishable by penalties, including administrative or criminal penalties, that are effective, proportionate and dissuasive.

Article 14 - **Evaluation**

1. No later than 15 September 2010, the Commission shall submit to the European Parliament and the Council an evaluation of the application of this Directive and its impact on economic operators and consumers, taking into account further developments in electronic communications technology and the statistics provided to the Commission pursuant to Article 10 with a view to determining whether it is necessary to amend the provisions of this Directive, in particular with regard to the list of data in Article 5 and the periods of retention provided for in Article 6. The results of the evaluation shall be made public.

2. To that end, the Commission shall examine all observations communicated to it by the Member States or by the Working Party established under Article 29 of Directive 95/46/EC.

Article 15 - **Transposition**

1. Member States shall bring into force the laws, regulations and administrative provisions necessary to comply with this Directive by no later than 15 September 2007. They shall forthwith inform the Commission thereof. When Member States adopt those measures, they shall contain a reference to this Directive or shall be accompanied by such reference on the occasion of their official publication. The methods of making such reference shall be laid down by Member States.

2. Member States shall communicate to the Commission the text of the main provisions of national law which they adopt in the field covered by this Directive.

3. Until 15 March 2009, each Member State may postpone application of this Directive to the retention of communications data relating to Internet Access, Internet telephony and Internet e-mail. Any Member State that intends to make use of this paragraph shall, upon adoption of this Directive, notify the Council and the Commission to that effect by way of a declaration. The declaration shall be published in the Official Journal of the European Union.

Article 16 - **Entry into force**

This Directive shall enter into force on the twentieth day following that of its publication in the Official Journal of the European Union.

Article 17 - **Addressees**

This Directive is addressed to the Member States.

Done at Strasbourg, 15 March 2006.

For the European Parliament

The President

J. Borrell Fontelles

For the Council

The President

H. Winkler

[1] Opinion delivered on 19 January 2006 (not yet published in the Official Journal).

[2] Opinion of the European Parliament of 14 December 2005 (not yet published in the Official Journal) and Council Decision of 21 February 2006.

[3] OJ L 281, 23.11.1995, p. 31. Directive as amended by Regulation (EC) No 1882/2003 (OJ L 284, 31.10.2003, p. 1).

[4] OJ L 201, 31.7.2002, p. 37.

[5] OJ L 69, 16.3.2005, p. 67.

[6] OJ C 321, 31.12.2003, p. 1.

[7] OJ L 108, 24.4.2002, p. 33.

[8] OJ L 105, 13.4.2006, p. 54."

Declaration by the Netherlands

pursuant to Article 15(3) of Directive 2006/24/EC

Regarding the Directive of the European Parliament and of the Council on the retention of data processed in connection with the provision of publicly available electronic communications services and amending Directive 2002/58/EC, the Netherlands will be making use of the option of postponing application of the Directive to the retention of communications data relating to Internet access, Internet telephony and Internet e-mail, for a period not exceeding 18 months following the date of entry into force of the Directive.

Declaration by Austria

pursuant to Article 15(3) of Directive 2006/24/EC

Austria declares that it will be postponing application of this Directive to the retention of communications data relating to Internet access, Internet telephony and Internet e-mail, for a period of 18 months following the date specified in Article 15(1).

Declaration by Estonia

pursuant to Article 15(3) of Directive 2006/24/EC

In accordance with Article 15(3) of the Directive of the European Parliament and of the Council on the retention of data generated or processed in connection with the provision of publicly available electronic communications services or of public communications networks and amending Directive 2002/58/EC, Estonia hereby states its intention to make use of use that paragraph and to postpone application of the Directive to retention of communications data relating to Internet access, Internet telephony and Internet e-mail until 36 months after the date of adoption of the Directive.

Declaration by the United Kingdom

pursuant to Article 15(3) of Directive 2006/24/EC

The United Kingdom declares in accordance with Article 15(3) of the Directive on the retention of data generated or processed in connection with the provision of publicly available electronic communications services or of public communications networks and amending Directive 2002/58/EC that it will postpone application of that Directive to the retention of communications data relating to Internet access, Internet telephony and Internet e-mail.

Declaration by the Republic of Cyprus

pursuant to Article 15(3) of Directive 2006/24/EC

The Republic of Cyprus declares that it is postponing application of the Directive in respect of the retention of communications data relating to Internet access, Internet telephony and Internet e-mail until the date fixed in Article 15(3).

Declaration by the Hellenic Republic

pursuant to Article 15(3) of Directive 2006/24/EC

Greece declares that, pursuant to Article 15(3), it will postpone application of this Directive in respect of the retention of communications data relating to Internet access, Internet telephony and Internet e-mail until 18 months after expiry of the period provided for in Article 15(1).

Declaration by the Grand Duchy of Luxembourg

pursuant to Article 15(3) of Directive 2006/24/EC

Pursuant to Article 15(3) of the Directive of the European Parliament and of the Council on the retention of data generated or processed in connection with the provision of publicly available electronic communications services or of public communications networks and amending Directive 2002/58/EC, the Government of the Grand Duchy of Luxembourg declares that it intends to make use of Article 15(3) of the Directive in order to have the option of postponing application of the Directive to the retention of communications data relating to Internet access, Internet telephony and Internet e-mail.

Declaration by Slovenia

pursuant to Article 15(3) of Directive 2006/24/EC

Slovenia is joining the group of Member States which have made a declaration under Article 15(3) of the Directive of the European Parliament and the Council on the retention of data generated or processed in connection with the provision of publicly available electronic communications services or of public communications networks, for the 18 months postponement of the application of the Directive to the retention of communication data relating to Internet, Internet telephony and Internet e-mail.

Declaration by Sweden

pursuant to Article 15(3) of Directive 2006/24/EC

Pursuant to Article 15(3), Sweden wishes to have the option of postponing application of this Directive to the retention of communications data relating to Internet access, Internet telephony and Internet e-mail.

Declaration by the Republic of Lithuania

pursuant to Article 15(3) of Directive 2006/24/EC

Pursuant to Article 15(3) of the draft Directive of the European Parliament and of the Council on the retention of data generated or processed in connection with the provision of publicly available electronic communications services or public communications networks and amending Directive 2002/58/EC (hereafter the "Directive"), the Republic of Lithuania declares that once the Directive has been adopted it will postpone the application thereof to the retention of communications data relating to Internet access, Internet telephony and Internet e-mail for the period provided for in Article 15(3).

Declaration by the Republic of Latvia

pursuant to Article 15(3) of Directive 2006/24/EC

Latvia states in accordance with Article 15(3) of Directive 2006/24/EC of 15 March 2006 on the retention of data generated or processed in connection with the provision of publicly available electronic communications services or of public communications networks and amending Directive 2002/58/EC that it is postponing application of the Directive to the retention of communications data relating to Internet access, Internet telephony and Internet e-mail until 15 March 2009.

Declaration by the Czech Republic

pursuant to Article 15(3) of Directive 2006/24/EC

Pursuant to Article 15(3), the Czech Republic hereby declares that it is postponing application of this Directive to the retention of communications data relating to Internet access, Internet telephony and Internet e-mail until 36 months after the date of adoption thereof.

Declaration by Belgium

pursuant to Article 15(3) of Directive 2006/24/EC

Belgium declares that, taking up the option available under Article 15(3), it will postpone application of this Directive, for a period of 36 months after its adoption, to the retention of communications data relating to Internet access, Internet telephony and Internet e-mail.

Declaration by the Republic of Poland

pursuant to Article 15(3) of Directive 2006/24/EC

Poland hereby declares that it intends to make use of the option provided for under Article 15(3) of the Directive of the European Parliament and of the Council on the retention of data processed in connection with the provision of publicly available electronic communications services and amending Directive 2002/58/EC and postpone application of the Directive to the retention of communications data relating to Internet access, Internet telephony and Internet e-mail for a period of 18 months following the date specified in Article 15(1).

Declaration by Finland

pursuant to Article 15(3) of Directive 2006/24/EC

Finland declares in accordance with Article 15(3) of the Directive on the retention of data generated or processed in connection with the provision of publicly available electronic communications services or of public communications networks and amending Directive 2002/58/EC that it will postpone application of that Directive to the retention of communications data relating to Internet access, Internet telephony and Internet e-mail.

Declaration by Germany

pursuant to Article 15(3) of Directive 2006/24/EC

Germany reserves the right to postpone application of this Directive to the retention of communications data relating to Internet access, Internet telephony and Internet e-mail for a period of 18 months following the date specified in the first sentence of Article 15(1).

APEC Privacy Framework (2004)

Directives in Context

The Asia-Pacific Economic Cooperation (APEC) Privacy Framework consists of more than 20 nations (mostly in Asia) and the United States. The Framework was endorsed by the APEC Ministers in November 2004.

APEC member economies realize the enormous potential of electronic commerce to expand business opportunities, reduce costs, increase efficiency, improve the quality of life, and facilitate the greater participation of small business in global commerce. A framework to enable regional data transfers will benefit consumers, businesses, and governments. Ministers have endorsed the APEC Privacy Framework, recognizing the importance of the development of effective privacy protections that avoid barriers to information flows, ensure continued trade, and economic growth in the APEC region.

Part I. Preamble

1. APEC economies recognize the importance of protecting information privacy and maintaining information flows among economies in the Asia Pacific region and among their trading partners. As APEC Ministers acknowledged in endorsing the 1998 Blueprint for Action on Electronic Commerce, the potential of electronic commerce cannot be realized without government and business cooperation "to develop and implement technologies and policies, which build trust and confidence in safe, secure and reliable communication, information and delivery systems, and which address issues including privacy...". The lack of consumer trust and confidence in the privacy and security of online transactions and information networks is one element that may prevent member economies from gaining all of the benefits of electronic commerce. APEC economies realize that a key part of efforts to improve consumer confidence and ensure the growth of electronic commerce must be cooperation to balance and promote both effective information privacy protection and the free flow of information in the Asia Pacific region.

2. Information and communications technologies, including mobile technologies, that link to the Internet and other information networks have made it possible to collect, store and access information from anywhere in the world. These technologies offer great potential for social and economic benefits for business, individuals and governments, including increased consumer choice, market expansion, productivity, education and product innovation. However, while these technologies make it easier and cheaper to collect, link and use large quantities of information, they also often make these activities undetectable to individuals. Consequently, it can be more difficult for individuals to retain a measure of control over their personal information. As a result, individuals have become concerned about the harmful consequences that may arise from the misuse of their information. Therefore, there is a need to promote and enforce ethical and trustworthy information practices in on- and off-line contexts to bolster the confidence of individuals and businesses.

3. As both business operations and consumer expectations continue to shift due to changes in technology and the nature of information flows, businesses and other organizations require simultaneous input and access to data 24-hours a day in order to meet customer and societal needs, and to provide efficient and cost-effective services. Regulatory systems that unnecessarily restrict this flow or place burdens on it have adverse implications for global business and economies. Therefore, in promoting and enforcing ethical information practices, there is also a need to develop systems for protecting information privacy that account for these new realities in the global environment.

4. APEC economies endorse the principles-based APEC Privacy Framework as an important tool in encouraging the development of appropriate information privacy protections and ensuring the free flow of information in the Asia Pacific region.

5. This Framework, which aims at promoting electronic commerce throughout the Asia Pacific region, is consistent with the core values of the OECD's 1980 Guidelines on the Protection of Privacy and Trans-Border Flows of Personal Data (OECD Guidelines),[2] and reaffirms the value of privacy to individuals and to the information society.

6. The Framework specifically addresses these foundation concepts, as well as issues of particular relevance to APEC member economies. Its distinctive approach is to focus attention on practical and consistent information privacy protection within this context. In so doing, it balances information privacy with business needs and commercial interests, and at the same time, accords due recognition to cultural and other diversities that exist within member economies.

7. The Framework is intended to provide clear guidance and direction to businesses in APEC economies on common privacy issues and the impact of privacy issues upon the way legitimate businesses are conducted. It does so by highlighting the reasonable expectations of the modern consumer that businesses will recognize their privacy interests in a way that is consistent with the Principles outlined in this Framework.

8. Finally, this Framework on information privacy protection was developed in recognition of the importance of:

- Developing appropriate privacy protections for personal information, particularly from the harmful consequences of unwanted intrusions and the misuse of personal information;
- Recognizing the free flow of information as being essential for both developed and developing market economies to sustain economic and social growth;
- Enabling global organizations that collect, access, use or process data in APEC member economies to develop and implement uniform approaches within their organizations for global access to and use of personal information;
- Enabling enforcement agencies to fulfill their mandate to protect information privacy; and,
- Advancing international mechanisms to promote and enforce information privacy and to maintain the continuity of information flows among APEC economies and with their trading partners.

[2] The 1980 OECD Guidelines were drafted at a high level that makes them still relevant today. In many ways, the OECD Guidelines represent the international consensus on what constitutes honest and trustworthy treatment of personal information.

Part II. Scope

The purpose of Part II of the APEC Privacy Framework is to make clear the extent of coverage of the Principles.

Definitions

9. Personal information means any information about an identified or identifiable individual.

9. The Principles have been drafted against a background in which some economies have well-established privacy laws and/or practices while others may be considering the issues. Of those with already settled policies, not all treat personal information in exactly the same way. Some, for example, may draw distinctions between information that is readily searchable and other information. Despite these differences, this Framework has been drafted to promote a consistent approach among the information privacy regimes of APEC economies.

This Framework is intended to apply to information about natural living persons, not legal persons. The APEC Privacy Framework applies to personal information, which is information that can be used to identify an individual. It also includes information that would not meet this criteria alone, but when put together with other information would identify an individual.

10. Personal information controller means a person or organization who controls the collection, holding, processing or use of personal information. It includes a person or organization who instructs another person or organization to collect, hold, process, use, transfer or disclose personal information on his or her behalf, but excludes a person or organization who performs such functions as instructed by another person or organization. It also excludes an individual who collects, holds, processes or uses personal information in connection with the individual's personal, family or household affairs.

10. The APEC Privacy Framework applies to persons or organizations in the public and private sectors who control the collection, holding, processing, use, transfer or disclosure of personal information. Individual economies' definitions of personal information controller may vary. However, APEC economies agree that for the purposes of this Framework, where a person or organization instructs another person or organization to collect, hold, use, process, transfer or disclose personal information on its behalf, the instructing person or organization is the personal information controller and is responsible for ensuring compliance with the Principles.

Individuals will often collect, hold and use personal information for personal, family or household purposes. For example, they often keep address books and phone lists or prepare family newsletters. The Framework is not intended to apply to such personal, family or household activities.

11. Publicly available information means personal information about an individual that the individual knowingly makes or permits to be made available to the public, or is legally obtained and accessed from:

a) government records that are available to the public;

b) journalistic reports; or

c) information required by law to be made available to the public.

11. The APEC Privacy Framework has limited application to publicly available information. Notice and choice requirements, in particular, often are superfluous where the information is already publicly available, and the personal information controller does not collect the information directly from the individual concerned. Publicly available information may be contained in government records that are available to the public, such as registers of people who are entitled to vote, or in news items broadcast or published by the news media.

Application

12. In view of the differences in social, cultural, economic and legal backgrounds of each member economy, there should be flexibility in implementing these Principles.

12. Although it is not essential for electronic commerce that all laws and practices within APEC be identical in all respects, including the coverage of personal information, compatible approaches to information privacy protection among APEC economies will greatly facilitate international commerce. These Principles recognize that fact, but also take into account social, cultural and other differences among economies. They focus on those aspects of privacy protection that are of the most importance to international commerce.

13. Exceptions to these Principles contained in Part III of this Framework, including those relating to national sovereignty, national security, public safety and public policy should be:

a) limited and proportional to meeting the objectives to which the exceptions relate; and,

b) (i) made known to the public; or, (ii)in accordance with law.

13. The Principles contained in Part III of the APEC Privacy Framework should be interpreted as a whole rather than individually, as there is a close relationship among them. For example, the Use Principle is closely related to both the Notice and Choice Principles. Economies implementing the Framework at a domestic level may adopt suitable exceptions that suit their particular domestic circumstances.

Although recognizing the importance of governmental respect for privacy, this Framework is not intended to impede governmental activities authorized by law when taken to protect national security, public safety, national sovereignty or other public policy. Nonetheless, Economies should take into consideration the impact of these activities upon the rights, responsibilities and legitimate interests of individuals and organizations.

Part III. APEC Information Privacy Principles

PRINCIPLES

I. Preventing Harm

14. Recognizing the interests of the individual to legitimate expectations of privacy, personal information protection should be designed to prevent the misuse of such information. Further, acknowledging the risk that harm may result from such misuse of personal information, specific obligations should take account of such risk, and remedial measures should be proportionate to the likelihood and severity of the harm threatened by the collection, use and transfer of personal information.

II. Notice

15. Personal information controllers should provide clear and easily accessible statements about their practices and policies with respect to personal information that should include:

a) the fact that personal information is being collected;

b) the purposes for which personal information is collected;

c) the types of persons or organizations to whom personal information might be disclosed;

COMMENTARY

14. The Preventing Harm Principle recognizes that one of the primary objectives of the APEC Privacy Framework is to prevent misuse of personal information and consequent harm to individuals. Therefore, privacy protections, including self-regulatory efforts, education and awareness campaigns, laws, regulations, and enforcement mechanisms, should be designed to prevent harm to individuals from the wrongful collection and misuse of their personal information. Hence, remedies for privacy infringements should be designed to prevent harms resulting from the wrongful collection or misuse of personal information, and should be proportionate to the likelihood and severity of any harm threatened by the collection or use of personal information.

15-17. The Notice Principle is directed towards ensuring that individuals are able to know what information is collected about them and for what purpose it is to be used. By providing notice, personal information controllers may enable an individual to make a more informed decision about interacting with the organization. One common method of compliance with this Principle is for personal information controllers to post notices on their Web sites. In other situations, placement of notices on intranet sites or in employee handbooks, for example, may be appropriate.

The requirement in this Principle relating to

d) the identity and location of the personal information controller, including information on how to contact them about their practices and handling of personal information;
e) the choices and means the personal information controller offers individuals for limiting the use and disclosure of, and for accessing and correcting, their personal information.

16. All reasonably practicable steps shall be taken to ensure that such notice is provided either before or at the time of collection of personal information. Otherwise, such notice should be provided as soon after as is practicable.

17. It may not be appropriate for personal information controllers to provide notice regarding the collection and use of publicly available information.

when notice should be provided is based on a consensus among APEC member economies. APEC member economies agree that good privacy practice is to inform relevant individuals at the time of, or before, information is collected about them. At the same time, the Principle also recognizes that there are circumstances in which it would not be practicable to give notice at or before the time of collection, such as in some cases where electronic technology automatically collects information when a prospective customer initiates contact, as is often the case with the use of cookies.

Moreover, where personal information is not obtained directly from the individual, but from a third party, it may not be practicable to give notice at or before the time of collection of the information. For example, when an insurance company collects employees' information from an employer in order to provide medical insurance services, it may not be practicable for the insurance company to give notice at or before the time of collection of the employees' personal information.

Additionally, there are situations in which it would not be necessary to provide notice, such as in the collection and use of publicly available information, or of business contact information and other professional information that identifies an individual in his or her professional capacity in a business context. For example, if an individual gives his or her business card to another individual in the context of a business relationship, the individual would not expect that notice would be provided regarding the collection and normal use of that information.

Further, if colleagues who work for the same company as the individual, were to provide the individual's business contact information to potential customers of that company, the individual would not have an expectation that notice would be provided regarding the transfer or the expected use of that information.

III. Collection Limitation

18. The collection of personal information should be limited to information that is relevant to the purposes of collection and any such information should be obtained by lawful and fair means, and where appropriate, with notice to, or consent of, the individual concerned.

18. This Principle limits collection of information by reference to the purposes for which it is collected. The collection of the information should be relevant to such purposes, and proportionality to the fulfillment of such purposes may be a factor in determining what is relevant.

This Principle also provides that collection methods must be lawful and fair. So, for example, obtaining personal information under false pretenses (e.g., where an organization uses telemarketing calls, print advertising, or email to fraudulently misrepresent itself as another company in order to deceive consumers and induce them to disclose their credit card numbers, bank account information or other sensitive personal information) may in many economies be considered unlawful. Therefore, even in those economies where there is no explicit law against these specific methods, they may be considered an unfair means of collection.

The Principle also recognizes that there are circumstances where providing notice to, or obtaining consent of, individuals would be inappropriate. For example, in a situation where there is an outbreak of food poisoning, it would be appropriate for the relevant health authorities to collect the personal information of patrons from restaurants without providing notice to or obtaining the consent of individuals in order to tell them about the potential health risk.

IV. Uses of Personal Information

19. Personal information collected should be used only to fulfill the purposes of collection and other compatible or related purposes except:

a) with the consent of the individual whose personal information is collected;

b) when necessary to provide a service or product requested by the individual; or,

19. The Use Principle limits the use of personal information to fulfilling the purposes of collection and other compatible or related purposes. For the purposes of this Principle, "uses of personal information" includes the transfer or disclosure of personal information.

Application of this Principle requires consideration of the nature of the information, the context of collection and the intended use of the information. The fundamental criterion

c) by the authority of law and other legal instruments, proclamations and pronouncements of legal effect.

in determining whether a purpose is compatible with or related to the stated purposes is whether the extended usage stems from or is in furtherance of such purposes. The use of personal information for "compatible or related purposes" would extend, for example, to matters such as the creation and use of a centralized database to manage personnel in an effective and efficient manner; the processing of employee payrolls by a third party; or, the use of information collected by an organization for the purpose of granting credit for the subsequent purpose of collecting debt owed to that organization.

V. Choice

20. Where appropriate, individuals should be provided with clear, prominent, easily understandable, accessible and affordable mechanisms to exercise choice in relation to the collection, use and disclosure of their personal information. It may not be appropriate for personal information controllers to provide these mechanisms when collecting publicly available information.

20. The general purpose of the Choice Principle is to ensure that individuals are provided with choice in relation to collection, use, transfer and disclosure of their personal information. Whether the choice is conveyed electronically, in writing or by other means, notice of such choice should be clearly worded and displayed clearly and conspicuously. By the same token, the mechanisms for exercising choice should be accessible and affordable to individuals. Ease of access and convenience are factors that should be taken into account.

Where an organization provides information on available mechanisms for exercising choice that is specifically tailored to individuals in an APEC member economy or national group, this may require that the information be conveyed in an "easily understandable" or particular way appropriate to members of that group (e.g., in a particular language). However if the communication is not directed to any particular economy or national group other than the one where the organization is located, this requirement will not apply.

This Principle also recognizes, through the introductory words "where appropriate", that there are certain situations where consent may be clearly implied or where it would not be necessary to provide a mechanism to exercise choice.

As is specified in the Principle, APEC member economies agree that in many situations it would not be necessary or practicable to provide a mechanism to exercise choice when collecting publicly available information. For example, it would not be necessary to provide a mechanism to exercise choice to individuals when collecting their name and address from a public record or a newspaper.

In addition to situations involving publicly available information, APEC member economies also agreed that in specific and limited circumstances it would not be necessary or practicable to provide a mechanism to exercise choice when collecting, using, transferring or disclosing other types of information. For example, when business contact information or other professional information that identifies an individual in his or her professional capacity is being exchanged in a business context it is generally impractical or unnecessary to provide a mechanism to exercise choice, as in these circumstances individuals would expect that their information be used in this way.

Further, in certain situations, it would not be practicable for employers to be subject to requirements to provide a mechanism to exercise choice related to the personal information of their employees when using such information for employment purposes. For example, if an organization has decided to centralize human resources information, that organization should not be required to provide a mechanism to exercise choice to its employees before engaging in such an activity.

VI. Integrity of Personal Information

21. Personal information should be accurate, complete and kept up-to-date to the extent necessary for the purposes of use.

21. This Principle recognizes that a personal information controller is obliged to maintain the accuracy and completeness of records and keep them up to date. Making decisions about individuals based on inaccurate, incomplete or out of date information may not be in the interests of individuals or organizations. This Principle also recognizes that these obligations are only required to the extent necessary for the purposes of use.

VII. Security Safeguards

22. Personal information controllers should protect personal information that they hold with appropriate safeguards against risks, such as loss or unauthorized access to personal information, or unauthorized destruction, use, modification or disclosure of information or other misuses. Such safeguards should be proportional to the likelihood and severity of the harm threatened, the sensitivity of the information and the context in which it is held, and should be subject to periodic review and reassessment.

22. This Principle recognizes that individuals who entrust their information to another are entitled to expect that their information be protected with reasonable security safeguards.

VIII. Access and Correction

23. Individuals should be able to:

a) obtain from the personal information controller confirmation of whether or not the personal information controller holds personal information about them;

b) have communicated to them, after having provided sufficient proof of their identity, personal information about them;

> **i.** within a reasonable time;
>
> **ii.** at a charge, if any, that is not excessive;
>
> **iii.** in a reasonable manner;
>
> **iv.** in a form that is generally understandable; and,

c) challenge the accuracy of information relating to them and, if possible and as appropriate, have the information rectified, completed, amended or deleted.

24. Such access and opportunity for correction should be provided except where:

23-25. The ability to access and correct personal information, while generally regarded as a central aspect of privacy protection, is not an absolute right. This Principle includes specific conditions for what would be considered reasonable in the provision of access, including conditions related to timing, fees, and the manner and form in which access would be provided. What is to be considered reasonable in each of these areas will vary from one situation to another depending on circumstances, such as the nature of the information processing activity. Access will also be conditioned by security requirements that preclude the provision of direct access to information and will require sufficient proof of identity prior to provision of access.

Access must be provided in a reasonable manner and form. A reasonable manner should include the normal methods of interaction between organizations and individuals. For example, if a computer was involved in the transaction or request, and the individual's email address is available, email would be considered "a reasonable manner" to provide information. Organizations that have transacted with an individual may reasonably be expected to answer requests in a form that

(i) the burden or expense of doing so would be unreasonable or disproportionate to the risks to the individual's privacy in the case in question;

ii) the information should not be disclosed due to legal or security reasons or to protect confidential commercial information; or

iii) the information privacy of persons other than the individual would be violated.

25. If a request under (a) or (b) or a challenge under (c) is denied, the individual should be provided with reasons why and be able to challenge such denial.

is similar to what has been used in prior exchanges with said individual or in the form that is used and available within the organization, but should not be understood to require separate language translation or conversion of code into text.

Both the copy of personal information supplied by an organization in response to an access request and any explanation of codes used by the organization should be readily comprehensible. This obligation does not extend to the conversion of computer language (e.g. machine-readable instructions, source codes or object codes) into text. However, where a code represents a particular meaning, the personal information controller shall explain the meaning of that code to the individual. For example, if the personal information held by the organization includes the age range of the individual, and that is represented by a particular code (e.g., "1" means 18-25 years old, "2" means "26-35 years old, etc.), then when providing the individual with such a code, the organization shall explain to the individual what age range that code represents.

Where individual requests access to his or her information, that information should be provided in the language in which it is currently held. Where information is held in a language different to the language of original collection, and if the individual requests the information be provided in that original language, an organization should supply the information in the original language if the individual pays the cost of translation.

The details of the procedures by which the ability to access and correct information is provided may differ depending on the nature of the information and other interests. For this reason, in certain circumstances, it may be impossible, impracticable or unnecessary to change, suppress or delete records.

Consistent with the fundamental nature of access, organizations should always make good faith efforts to provide access. For example, where certain information needs to be protected and can be readily separated from other information subject to an access request, the organization should redact the protected information and make available the other information. However, in some situations, it may be necessary for organizations to deny claims for access and correction, and this Principle sets out the conditions that must be met in order for such denials to be considered acceptable, which include: situations where claims would constitute an unreasonable expense or burden on the personal information controller, such as when claims for access are repetitious or vexatious by nature; cases where providing the information would constitute a violation of laws or would compromise security; or, incidences where it would be necessary in order to protect commercial confidential information that an organization has taken steps to protect from disclosure, where disclosure would benefit a competitor in the marketplace, such as a particular computer or modeling program.

"Confidential commercial information" is information that an organization has taken steps to protect from disclosure, where such disclosure would facilitate a competitor in the market to use or exploit the information against the business interest of the organization causing significant financial loss. The particular computer program or business process an organization uses, such as a modeling program, or the details of that program or business process may be confidential commercial information. Where confidential commercial information can be readily separated from other information subject to an access request, the organization should redact the confidential commercial information and make available the non-confidential information, to the extent that such information constitutes personal information of the individual concerned. Organizations may deny or limit access to the extent that it is not practicable to separate the personal information from the confidential commercial information and where granting access would reveal the organization's own confidential commercial information as defined above, or where it would reveal the confidential commercial information of another organization that is subject to an obligation of confidentiality.

When an organization denies a request for access, for the reasons specified above, such an organization should provide the individual with an explanation as to why it has made that determination and information on how to challenge that denial. An organization would not be expected to provide an explanation, however, in cases where such disclosure would violate a law or judicial order.

IX. Accountability

26. A personal information controller should be accountable for complying with measures that give effect to the Principles stated above. When personal information is to be transferred to another person or organization, whether domestically or internationally, the personal information controller should obtain the consent of the individual or exercise due diligence and take reasonable steps to ensure that the recipient person or organization will protect the information consistently with these Principles.

26. Efficient and cost effective business models often require information transfers between different types of organizations in different locations with varying relationships. When transferring information, personal information controllers should be accountable for ensuring that the recipient will protect the information consistently with these Principles when not obtaining consent. Thus, information controllers should take reasonable steps to ensure the information is protected, in accordance with these Principles, after it is transferred. However, there are certain situations where such due diligence may be impractical or impossible, for example, when there is no on-going relationship between the personal information controller and the third party to whom the information is disclosed. In these types of circumstances, personal information controllers may choose to use other means, such as obtaining consent, to assure that the information is being protected consistently with these Principles. However, in cases where disclosures are required by domestic law, the personal information controller would be relieved of any due diligence or consent obligations.

Part IV. Implementation

27. Part IV provides guidance to Member Economies on implementing the APEC Privacy Framework. Section A focuses on those measures Member Economies should consider in implementing the Framework domestically, while Section B sets out APEC-wide arrangements for the implementation of the Framework's cross-border elements.

A. GUIDANCE FOR DOMESTIC IMPLEMENTATION

I. Maximizing Benefits of Privacy Protections and Information Flows

28. Economies should have regard to the following basic concept in considering the adoption of measures designed for domestic implementation of the APEC Privacy Framework:

29. Recognizing the interests of economies in maximizing the economic and social benefits available to their citizens and businesses, personal information should be collected, held, processed, used, transferred, and disclosed in a manner that protects individual information privacy and allows them to realize the benefits of information flows within and across borders.

30. Consequently, as part of establishing or reviewing their privacy protections, Member Economies, consistent with the APEC Privacy Framework and any existing domestic privacy protections, should take all reasonable and appropriate steps to identify and remove unnecessary barriers to information flows and avoid the creation of any such barriers.

II. Giving Effect to the APEC Privacy Framework

31. There are several options for giving effect to the Framework and securing privacy protections for individuals including legislative, administrative, industry self-regulatory or a combination of these methods under which rights can be exercised under the Framework. In addition, Member Economies should consider taking steps to establish access point(s) or mechanisms to provide information generally about the privacy protections within its jurisdiction. In practice, the Framework is meant to be implemented in a flexible manner that can accommodate various methods of implementation, including through central authorities, multi-agency enforcement bodies, a network of designated industry bodies, or a combination of the above, as Member Economies deem appropriate.

32. As set forth in Paragraph 31, the means of giving effect to the Framework may differ between Member Economies, and it may be appropriate for individual economies to determine that different APEC Privacy Principles may call for different means of implementation. Whatever approach is adopted in a particular circumstance, the overall goal should be to develop compatibility of approaches in privacy protections in the APEC region that is respectful of requirements of individual economies.

33. APEC economies are encouraged to adopt non-discriminatory practices in protecting individuals from privacy protection violations occurring in that Member Economy's jurisdiction.

34. Discussions with domestic law enforcement, security, public health, and other agencies are important to identify ways to strengthen privacy without creating obstacles to national security, public safety, and other public policy missions.

III. Educating and publicising domestic privacy protections

35. For all Member Economies, in particular those Member Economies in earlier stages of development of their domestic approaches to privacy protections, the Framework is intended to provide guidance in developing their approaches.

36. For the Framework to be of practical effect, it must be known and accessible. Accordingly, Member Economies should:

> **a)** publicise the privacy protections it provides to individuals;

b) educate personal information controllers about the Member Economy's privacy protections; and,

c) educate individuals about how they can report violations and how remedies can be pursued.

IV. Cooperation between the Public and Private Sectors

37. Active participation of non-governmental entities will help ensure that the full benefits of the APEC Privacy Framework can be realized. Accordingly, Member Economies should engage in a dialogue with relevant private sector groups, including privacy groups and those representing consumers and industry, to obtain input on privacy protection issues and cooperation in furthering the Framework's objectives. Furthermore, especially in the economies where they have not established privacy protection regimes in their domestic jurisdiction, Member Economies should pay ample attention to whether private sector's opinions are reflected in developing privacy protections. In particular, Member Economies should seek the cooperation of non-governmental entities in public education and encourage their referral of complaints to privacy enforcement agencies, as well as their continuing cooperation in the investigation of those complaints.

V. Providing for appropriate remedies in situations where privacy protections are violated

38. A Member Economy's system of privacy protections should include an appropriate array of remedies for privacy protection violations, which could include redress, the ability to stop a violation from continuing, and other remedies. In determining the range of remedies for privacy protection violations, a number of factors should be taken into account by a Member Economy including:

a) the particular system in that Member Economy for providing privacy protections (e.g., legislative enforcement powers, which may include rights of individuals to pursue legal action, industry self-regulation, or a combination of systems); and

b) the importance of having a range of remedies commensurate with the extent of the actual or potential harm to individuals resulting from such violations.

VI. Mechanism for Reporting Domestic Implementation of the APEC Privacy Framework

39. Member economies should make known to APEC domestic implementation of the Framework through the completion of and periodic updates to the Individual Action Plan (IAP) on Information Privacy.

B. GUIDANCE FOR INTERNATIONAL IMPLEMENTATION

In addressing the international implementation of the APEC Privacy Framework, and consistent with the provisions of Part A, Member Economies should consider the following points relating to the protection of the privacy of personal information:

I. Information sharing among Member Economies

40. Member Economies are encouraged to share and exchange information, surveys and research in respect of matters that have a significant impact on privacy protection.

41. In furthering the objectives of paragraphs 35 and 36, Member Economies are encouraged to educate one another in issues related to privacy protection and to share and exchange information on promotional, educational and training programs for the purpose of raising public awareness and enhancing understanding of the importance of privacy protection and compliance with relevant laws and regulations.

42. Member Economies are encouraged to share experiences on various techniques in investigating violations of privacy protections and regulatory strategies in resolving disputes involving such violations including, for instance, complaints handling and a lternative dispute resolution mechanisms.

43. Member Economies should designate and make known to the other Member Economies the public authorities within their own jurisdictions that will be responsible for facilitating cross-border cooperation and information sharing between economies in connection with privacy protection.

II Cross-border Cooperation in Investigation and Enforcement

44. Developing cooperative arrangements: Taking into consideration existing international arrangements and existing or developing self-regulatory approaches (including those referenced in Part B. III., below), and to the extent permitted by domestic law and policy, Member Economies should consider developing cooperative arrangements and procedures to facilitate cross-border cooperation in the enforcement of privacy laws. Such cooperative arrangements may take the form of bilateral or multilateral arrangements. This paragraph is to be construed with regard to the right of Member Economies to decline or limit cooperation on particular investigations or matters on the ground that compliance with a request for cooperation would be inconsistent with domestic laws, policies or priorities, or on the ground of resource constraints, or based on the absence of a mutual interest in the investigations in question.

45. In civil enforcement of privacy laws, cooperative cross-border arrangements may include the following aspects:

> **a)** mechanisms for promptly, systematically and efficiently notifying designated public authorities in other Member Economies of investigations or privacy enforcement cases that target unlawful conduct or the resulting harm to individuals in those economies;
>
> **b)** mechanisms for effectively sharing information necessary for successful cooperation in cross-border privacy investigation and enforcement cases;
>
> **c)** mechanisms for investigative assistance in privacy enforcement cases;
>
> **d)** mechanisms to prioritize cases for cooperation with public authorities in other economies based on the severity of the unlawful infringements of personal information privacy, the actual or potential harm involved, as well as other relevant considerations;
>
> **e)** steps to maintain the appropriate level of confidentiality in respect of information exchanged under the cooperative arrangements.

III. Cooperative Development of Cross-border Privacy Rules

46. Member Economies will endeavor to support the development and recognition or acceptance of organizations' cross-border privacy rules across the APEC region, recognizing that organizations would still be responsible for complying with the local data protection requirements, as well as with all applicable laws. Such cross-border privacy rules should adhere to the APEC Privacy Principles.

47. To give effect to such cross-border privacy rules, Member Economies will endeavor to work with appropriate stakeholders to develop frameworks or mechanisms for the mutual recognition or acceptance of such cross-border privacy rules between and among the economies.

48. Member Economies should endeavor to ensure that such cross-border privacy rules and recognition or acceptance mechanisms facilitate responsible and accountable cross-border data transfers and effective privacy protections without creating unnecessary barriers to cross-border information flows, including unnecessary administrative and bureaucratic burdens for businesses and consumers.

INDEX